THE IMPERIAL NATION

The Imperial Nation

CITIZENS AND SUBJECTS IN THE BRITISH, FRENCH, SPANISH, AND AMERICAN EMPIRES

Josep M. Fradera

Translated by Ruth MacKay

PRINCETON UNIVERSITY PRESS

PRINCETON & OXFORD

Copyright © 2018 by Princeton University Press

Published by Princeton University Press
41 William Street, Princeton, New Jersey 08540
6 Oxford Street, Woodstock, Oxfordshire OX20 1TR

press.princeton.edu

All Rights Reserved

Library of Congress Control Number: 2018948275
ISBN 978-0-691-16745-9

British Library Cataloging-in-Publication Data is available

Editorial: Amanda Peery
Production Editorial: Kathleen Cioffi
Jacket Design: Amanda Weiss
Jacket Credit: (Top and bottom left) From *Carte d'Europe*, 1769.
             (Bottom right) From *Carte d'Amerique dressée pour l'usage du Roy*, 1780.
Production: Erin Suydam
Publicity: Jodi Price
Copyeditor: Anne Cherry

This book has been composed in Miller

Printed on acid-free paper. ∞

Printed in the United States of America

10 9 8 7 6 5 4 3 2 1

To my son, Pere

CONTENTS

ACKNOWLEDGMENTS

The Imperial Nation: Citizens and Subjects in the British, French, Spanish, and American Empires is an updated and much changed version of *La nación imperial: Derechos, representación y ciudadanía en los imperios de Gran Bretaña, Francia, España y Estados Unidos (1750–1918)*, a two-volume book published in 2015 by Editorial Edhasa, in Barcelona. I had spent two decades researching the history of Spain and its empire, and after 2005, when I published *Colonias para después de un imperio* (*Colonies after Empire*), I decided to try to define and conceptualize the Spanish case, both peninsular and American societies, in line with the broader historiographic debate in international terms. Long ago, I was greatly helped in my intentions by the example of two great historians: John H. Elliot and Stanley J. Stein, and also by the inspiring reading of C. A. Bayly's *Imperial Meridian: The British Empire and the World 1780–1830*, whose book I read before I met him personally. I am also very lucky to share preoccupations and interests with many colleagues and friends. Among them, José María Portillo, Josep M. Delgado Ribas, Bartolomé Clavero, Jesús Millán, Albert Garcia Balañà, and Juan Francisco Fuentes provided help I cannot measure in the long struggle with the main lines of the book. I would like to mention three more here: Jeremy Adelman (Princeton University); Mauricio Tenorio Trillo (University of Chicago), and Alfred McCoy (University of Wisconsin). Also, I want to express thanks for the comments and suggestions of the lucid and generous external readers of the manuscript. Without the friendship and hard work of Ruth MacKay, my translator, it would have been impossible to finish this book. Also, I would like to thank a young historian, Núria Sallés Vilaseca, who checked the possibly overlong bibliography, and the expert copyeditor for Princeton University Press, Anne Cherry. I am very grateful for the support of ICREA (Catalan Institution for Research and Advanced Studies) and of the MINECO-FEDER (HAR 2015–68183-P) has been. Finally, I would like to acknowledge Brigitta van Rheinberg's warm offer to publish with Princeton University Press.

J.M.F.
Barcelona, April 2018

THE IMPERIAL NATION

Introduction

DURING THE REVOLUTIONARY CYCLE between 1780 and 1830, internal crises and continual conflicts seemed to point to the demise of the great European monarchic empires. A century later, however, the empires were still standing. Two of them—the British and the French—governed much of the world, a much larger portion than they had ever dominated or held before. With lesser roles, the Spanish and Portuguese, the United States as Britain's successor, China, and the Ottoman Turks were also still there, and the recently unified Italy and Germany were trying to join the global race for colonies. In *The Imperial Nation*, I attempt to decipher the historical keys of this cycle of destruction and reconstruction of empires.

This book is also about a political transformation at the center of the making and unmaking of European empires. It is about how the idea and practice of "dual constitutions," or specialness (*spécialité* in French)—the existence and workings of different legislative frameworks for the metropolis and for the colonies—constituted the backbone of liberal empires' political development. My purpose is not to present research on ideologies and principles on their own, but rather, to compare and consider, through local crises and experiences, shared ideas about how to rule empires with specific policies and continual corrections. Looking at historical processes from this point of view is, in my opinion, the only conceptual strategy that allows us to properly understand why the successors of the monarchic empires were always empires, but empires of a different sort. They were empires that did not exclude national developments or phenomena, either at home or abroad, places where even the unfree might feel the call to political participation.

In the beginning of the story are the great imperial crises that led to revolutions in the Thirteen Colonies and in France and which entailed demands for political equality for all men, who all possessed rights by birth.[1] The term *man* referred to a free individual in a world of slaves and descendants of slaves. This individual was white because he (it was almost always a he) was European or the descendant of Europeans, usually a property owner or settler, and a member of neither a minority Christian sect nor the Twelve Tribes of Israel. "We, the People" referred to a historically constituted human community with the capacity to proclaim the truth; it did not include those who lived on the margins or even to others within that same community. In this period the ideas of liberty, equality, and representation associated with the universal proclamation of an individual who was born free and should stay free—the ideas that nurtured the Declaration of Independence of the United States (1776) and France's Declaration of the Rights of Man and of the Citizen (1789), as well as its radical offshoot in 1793—spread throughout much of the world. Both in Europe and beyond, the cry for political equality was understood and interpreted literally by many who had not yet been summoned to form part of free humanity, by those who did not qualify to fully join the world the revolutionaries had forged.

This crucial moment was the consequence of deep-seated trends. The prevailing political model among the great empires of the Atlantic world, with the exception of the federal model of the United Provinces, was what H. G. Koenisberger and J. H. Elliott called composite states.[2] The driving force of these monarchic states formed through aggregation lay in simultaneously preserving and modifying the complex balance among former political entities, assembling them in a unified whole despite their diverse parliamentary, legislative, and juridical traditions. This model, here so briefly defined, survived until the late-eighteenth-century revolutions despite endless crises including the War of the Spanish Succession and the Jacobite wars in Scotland. The nature of the state shifted in the 1770s, when the empires became entangled in a great colonial race starting with the War of Jenkins' Ear (1739–48); the race picked up speed in 1757 and did not end until the close of the Napoleonic Wars. Keeping in mind John Brewer's description of the English case, we can see that the state underwent gradual changes and increasingly intruded on civil society.[3] These changes were subtle at first but slowly and surely solidified, allowing centralization and expansion of the embryonic state's capacities and the formation of functionary corps, all with the stated aim of raising and maintaining armies so as to defend the empire on a grander scale. Some of the era's major convulsions, such as American independence, the French crisis of the summer of 1789, and the conflicts in Spanish America and

Brazil, can doubtless be attributed to many causes, but the most notable, aside from the ideological ferment already mentioned, was the extraordinary fiscal pressure by metropolitan states as a result of these conflicts.

It was in this context that resistance to monarchic dictates in the Thirteen Colonies, Spanish and Portuguese America, and the French Antilles were linked to the demands of the state and the notion of certain rights shared by all subjects, even those who lived far away. The construction of the fiscal-military state, the massive cost of war at sea and in the colonies, and new interest in a truly imperial tax system together articulated a set of problems and conflicts that could no longer remain confined within European borders. The resulting consensus in the face of the demands of monarchic-imperial states was based precisely on the rights held by a kingdom's inhabitants, among which was their ability to share to an important degree in the governance of society. This was how discontent was channeled. Responses were often expressed with words and measures from long ago (old theories of natural right, appeals to contracts between ruler and ruled, celebrations of the rights of free-born Englishmen or Spanish-American subjects of the Castilian crown) which were now projected onto a new context in order to finally produce constitutions with imperial reach and universal value. When these formulations of universal citizenship and equality collapsed once the revolutionary cycle ended— the good news having been spread through *urbi et orbe*, with enormous consequences—"special laws" entered the scene to guide the conservative reconstruction of empires. No longer would there be appeals for "to each his own," as with the juridical pluralism and political statutes of the composite monarchies. Rather, these orders defined a dual universe in which inhabitants of the metropolis, who themselves were in the midst of constituting themselves as national communities with rights, and inhabitants of the colonies and faraway possessions would carefully be distinguished from one another in terms of rights and capacities. Thus were the conditions created for inequality under the law.

I suggest that the idea of political rights that made individuals equal, an idea that was profoundly revolutionary and was the foundation of the contemporary world, was discovered almost simultaneously by the metropolis and the colonies. Even a superficial reflection about how that idea first triumphed obliges us to reject the notion, so long celebrated by national European historiographies, of its gestation at home followed by its export to the overseas possessions. The success of the Thirteen Colonies' revolt against Britain is a relevant episode in this history, for they were the first to put egalitarian ideals into practice. The radical phase of the French Revolution, from 1792 to 1794, pushed matters a few steps forward. The Revolution had begun by proclaiming the equality of free individuals, mirroring the American experience, but the complexity of events in the French Antilles led to unexpected developments. Equality among European Frenchmen (except for the tricky situation of Protestants and Jews) unfolded in such a way as to include equality for freemen of color and slaves who either freed themselves or who were emancipated by the Republic.[4]

From that point on, political changes could no longer be limited a priori to circles of reformist aristocrats, late-era champions of the Enlightenment, liberals, or to the solid middle classes who gathered in Europe's leading cities and capitals. Spaniards and Portuguese could confirm this change firsthand during the great upheavals at the start of the nineteenth century when they tried to import the U.S. and French revolutionary experiences, tempered somewhat by subsequent events in revolutionary Paris. The British abroad could also confirm it in India (as C. A. Bayly wrote), in the Caribbean, and in the possessions they had retained in North America (the future Canada).[5] The great transformation that began in 1770 and lasted until the stabilization of a new sort of empire in 1830–40 therefore requires a dual perspective, one that looks simultaneously and equally at what was happening in Europe as well as outside Europe, in the dominions on both sides of the ocean belonging to the monarchies of Britain, France, Spain, and Portugal. While it might appear that the case for equally dense significance in the metropolis and the colonies is merely a rhetorical device for finding similarity in experiences that were very dissimilar both in nature and in importance, I believe that this formulation, valid on both sides of the imperial world, holds up empirically and analytically based on the dynamics of each case and of the whole.

The early chapters of this book introduce these juridical, cultural, and political developments. Wherever European communities grew in the empire—particularly in the Atlantic, given its greater demographic importance and the intensity of linkages with the home countries—institutions and cultural and juridical arguments similar to those in the metropolis had to be established. Furthermore, as those communities were generally located in areas where they were forced to cohabitate with other societies or groups—that is to say, Indians, slaves, descendants of slaves, and freemen of color in America; peoples of other religions and cultures in the rest of the world—ethnocentric biases and hyperbolic claims of European origins attained considerable proportions.

These arguments led to several developments. One of them was colonists' boundless pride in the institutions that governed them; they worked to control these institutions and make them permeable to local needs while also demonstrating exquisite concern not to lag behind the cultural and legal developments of their home countries. Chapter 1 explores various aspects of this obsession to situate themselves alongside their metropolitan compatriots. One example is the scrupulous attention by the British in North America and the Caribbean to the three great pillars of their national political tradition: common law, or natural subjects' "natural allegiance"; representative institutions; and plurality of juridical situations.[6] Another aspect to consider is the emphasis on the personal merits of freemen who were subjects of European kings and the exclusion of other subjects on the basis of legal status or other distinctions. This was the case, for instance, with Spanish Americans' obsessive and widespread insistence on their personal "quality," which in their opinion entitled them to enjoy the same institutions and share the same cultural and religious identity as their metropolitan compatriots, despite the prejudice of the monarchy's agents and administrators, as well as that of recent arrivals from the Iberian Peninsula. In the case of the French Antilles, the crown's relative lack of interest in overseas possessions after Jean-Baptiste Colbert's imperial measures forced the king's American subjects, as well as those residing in Indian enclaves, to develop strategies for resisting distant ministers and the interests of the principal French Atlantic ports. This practice would give rise to a solid juridical tradition (leading to Moreau de Saint-Méry and lasting until the Restoration) of attack on colonial organisms and calls for self-governing entities like those that survived in the metropolis until the 1791 Constitution.

Another factor to consider, which was overlooked earlier but which today is central to these discussions, is that of race. If we attend to the debate regarding such issues as Spanish America's *libres de color* or *castas pardas* (literally "brown castes," referring to blacks and free mulattos), or the concern for establishing racial boundaries in the French Antilles, or the use and abuse of the free/slave metaphor in the British world (including condemnation of English monarchs for having introduced African slavery to begin with), it is easy to understand colonists' desire to be as similar as possible to the metropolis. But, as readers will see, subjects' qualities or color were never used as an argument justifying political solutions. I certainly do not deny the importance of these continual disquisitions on phenotype, which only grew louder in the second half of the nineteenth century, but rather, point out that they took place within the framework of broader political concerns that would continue throughout the crisis of the late monarchic empires of the eighteenth century.

Given this panorama, the great revolutionary wave—which was the political expression of the military and fiscal crisis arising from the imperial wars in the Atlantic and Indian oceans—made colonists feel that they formed part of a political and institutional framework that was not entirely metropolitan, if in fact it ever had been. Quite obviously, the cultural and ideological ferment of those years was not equally intense in all places, within or beyond Europe; there were many distinct circumstances and varieties. Nevertheless, once ideas of integration and equality bloomed, it was only natural that they grew roots and spread throughout the empires, from Santiago de Chile to Québec City, wherever there were communities of European origin capable of forging viable political communities. It was equally inevitable that these communities would desire and need to imitate the metropolis and share in its cultural and juridical traditions. Thus, when the idea of essential political equality among a monarch's subjects knocked at the door, the colonists lost no time in inviting it in.

It is therefore easy to understand how the logic of the processes that began in France and later echoed in the Netherlands, Italy, Spain, and Portugal from 1807 through the 1820s enveloped colonists and metropolitans alike in the same problems and contradictions. These processes were marked by a dialectic aimed at binding the entire monarchic space into one united whole. Compatriots on either side of the imperial divide agreed and disagreed on the issues at stake for Britain, France, Spain, and Portugal, and the various conflicts and their military solutions brought about coalitions and alliances that led to winners and losers. This essential dialectic has begun to be explored only in recent years. The explanation for the delay is simple; for many years, European historiography was dominated by national histories whose attitude toward colonial worlds was one of sublime indifference, stemming more from "racial" notions of the late nineteenth century than from the cultural tone of a century earlier. Efforts over the past few decades to understand empires in both directions and in terms of multiple relationships, an approach that this book seeks to follow, can be seen as making up for lost time. The debates inspired by the theses of John Gallagher and Ronald Robinson regarding informal colonialism and free-trade imperialism, and the collaboration between colonists and administrators with local elites and political structures, were truncated and at times veered toward absurd stances, such as considering if contemporary empires were economic or not. Thus these scholars' intelligent suggestions were stopped in their tracks.[7]

There is no better expression of the idea of a common ground than the logic of the first constitutions that attempted to organize that space.

The U.S. Constitution (the continuation of the empire in North America), the French constitutions of 1793 and 1795, the Spanish Constitution of 1812, and the Portuguese in 1822 all shared the notion of a space where subjects had agreed to transmute their monarch's authority into national sovereignty.[8] As a result, these constitutions embraced and granted full rights to human communities both in the old metropolis and in the new colonies, as we shall see in Chapter 2. This represented a fundamental development in the history of all world societies within the reach of a former king's sovereignty. This universalism was one of the most obvious manifestations behind Lynn Hunt's assertion that "rights questions thus revealed a tendency to cascade."[9] I am calling these universalist constitutions "imperial constitutions" (not "imperialist," for obvious reasons) because they attempted to reach the entire former dynastic monarchic space and even transcend it through proselytism. Imperial constitutions' universal ambition distinguished them in body and soul from those that differentiated between metropolitan and overseas dominions, specifying distinct rights and generally restricting representation to the former. For one thing, their ambitions of integration and proselytism made them fragile and tortured artifacts from the very start, as can be seen in 1787 with Virginia's successful blackmail in Philadelphia to ensure slavery in the South, the exclusion of free peoples of color in France, and Spaniards' suicidal efforts to construct a majority at the Cortes of Cádiz by excluding free people of color from citizenship. In the first case, the exception could be carved out of the well-thought-out framework of the Constitution; in the second and third cases, the solution was to change the entire constitutional architecture.

A second modality of constitution, which I will simply call colonial, can be divided into two large groups. The first comprises those that can be considered a continuation, though perhaps with some reforms, of the order of things, such as the 1791 Constitution of France, which chose to keep colonies on the margins of prevailing metropolitan systems of rights, representation, and institutions. This group also includes the unwritten British constitution, which was equally keen on continuity, as shown by the overwhelming opposition to sharing the Parliament of Westminster with anyone, aside from the strong alliances within the United Kingdom since 1707.[10] In this case, the flexibility of an unwritten constitution allowed for the appropriation of schemes and general dispositions that were characteristic of more unified political entities and therefore contributed to their own modernization (for example, the abolition of slavery throughout the empire while ignoring local assemblies, or the parallel enhancement of the role and power of the Westminster Parliament all over the British possessions).

Chapters 3, 4, 5, 6, and 7 address the outcome of this double crisis of imperial constitutions and the reform of the old constitutions, depending on the case, that formed the basis of the great imperial transformations of the nineteenth century. The perceived risk of proclaimed or implemented equality in a world of expanding colonial relations led to a model that contemporaries called "dual constitutions"; that is, organically constructed systems (though rarely formalized in writing either immediately or in their totality) that included a constitution for the metropolis and none for the colonies; the latter thus were governed through executive orders and decrees in terms of what the French called *spécialité*. This meant that central authority in the colonies was enhanced, for example through the Lord Lieutenant in Dublin and the governors general in Calcutta (and later the viceroy in Delhi after the India Act of 1833), Algiers, and Havana.[11] In general, this remedy avoided the perils that equal or universal rights might entail for imperial stability.

This approach, which had more of a future, was explored in various imperial contexts during the revolutionary period, and it reached its height with the conservative shift of the French Republic after Napoleon's coup of 18 Brumaire. The subsequent Constitution of Year VIII (1799) clearly distinguished national space from that of the empire and the metropolis from the colony, and it put its stamp on a new idea that would have an extraordinary impact: the colonies would be governed by "special laws." This was a move with virtually no constitutional or normative content but with enormous practical consequences, as it instantly allowed for the reestablishment of slavery in the French colonies. This was a unique historical decision that would have been impossible had the metropolis and the French possessions in the Caribbean and the Mascarenes been included within the same legal framework. In hindsight, one must admit that it was successful beyond anyone's wildest expectations. After losing Saint-Domingue/Haiti, the French empire forever maintained a special status for its colonies, or in any case a complex modulation of its unitary and egalitarian designs and recognition of the need to grant an even larger space to exceptional or special measures. As late as the critical years of 1944–46, these were the terms of the debate when the Vichy regime, hardly an admirer of the republican discourse of equality, tried to fit the entire empire within a restrictive, special space.

The success of the Napoleonic solution also can be assessed by the number of imitations it engendered. Spaniards and Portuguese had no doubts as they followed the precedent and launched their inclusive and egalitarian experiments in 1810 and 1820, respectively. Both countries, obviously interested in retaining their empires while ideologically breaking with their monarchic past, chose constitutions that would apply to "all Spaniards" or "all Portuguese" in both hemispheres. As in the French realm, such egalitarian inclusiveness immediately posed the problem of how to manage major conflicts in highly diverse societies. The results were clear to see. Collapse of their respective empires and the challenge of affirming a liberal program in the context of long and bloody civil wars signaled a turn toward colonial constitutions, as Spaniards and Portuguese displaced their colonists from the metropolitan political and institutional structures of the late 1830s and from then on employed the "special" approach to empires founded on liberalism.

The triumph of a formula embracing all a monarch's former subjects in one single system of shared rights within which the "imperial constitutions" were a fundamental piece was the unwelcome outcome of the revolutionary cycle. But the factors that enabled this outcome (threats to territorial or sovereign integrity) would not have pushed matters in that direction had there not been an internal ideological debate that made it all come together. Governance in the monarchic empires did not, in fact, result in unity but rather in universal inequality of rights, privileges, and circumstances. In any case, the odds of a unitary scheme were diminished, both in theory and in practice, in the monarchies that ruled until the revolutionary crises at the turn of the century. Therefore, consensus regarding universal representation of former monarchic subjects was one more reason to maintain territorial unity and the universality of rights. Besides, the old practice of petitions and complaints to the sovereign, to which the crown might respond arbitrarily but rarely outside the established rules governing relations with vassals, was transformed into a new and totalizing idea about representation of national sovereignty. That is, the will for sovereignty was immediately universalized throughout the monarchies' territories. It is therefore not surprising that the big political questions during the revolutionary phase centered on the territorial and social breadth of the right to representation. The dilemmas were many, as can be imagined, starting with how subjects in overseas territories could fit into the representative assemblies then taking shape. Immediately there were tensions regarding the exclusion of peoples from censuses according to their social status (servants and nontaxpayers), financial worth (salaried or without property), gender (an obvious exclusion that was explicitly denounced by the women of the revolutionary Parisian clubs), and racial distinctions (mulattos, blacks, or simply non-Europeans), or because they had been conquered (Indians in the Spanish empire), lived on the margins

(Indians in the Thirteen Colonies), or were formerly enslaved (the *libres de color* in the Spanish empire, with variants in the Portuguese domains).

If there was one thing that defined the passage to modern politics, it was the resolution of this tension between invoked rights and the limits imposed on those rights by those who wished to sustain the social bases of the old world amid a new political order. Given that this tension existed both in metropolitan and overseas dominions, interactions between the two spaces were multiple and diverse. Two examples that we will return to are illustrative. In France, during the transition from constitutional monarchy to republic, the collapse of the notion of active and passive citizen occurred at the same time that free people of color were excluded from citizenship, with extraordinary and grave consequences.[12] Two decades later, the standoff between peninsular Spaniards and Americans during the Cortes of Cádiz led to the exclusion of *castas pardas* and *mestizos de sangley* (descendants of Filipinos and Chinese), provoking an intense debate in the Cortes regarding the scope of a universal citizenship including Spaniards, indigenous peoples, and descendants of Africans. These debates acquired their full significance only in the context of the key factor of modern politics then under construction, that is, the community of citizens that gave the entire system its dynamism. Everywhere, the inclusion of some and the exclusion of others, being part of the community of citizens (and/or electors) or standing outside that community, became a question of political identity, an indication of personhood allowing one to fully participate in the public sphere and take part in formal politics so as to improve the condition of subjects and groups. Membership (or not) lent significance to diverse political statutes and situations throughout complex imperial realities. This was true even in a supposedly unitary space such as the United States, where the overlap between the community of citizens and the expansive inherited empire was perfectly visible, both for those who participated as citizens and those who remained on the margins.

This latent contradiction between the mobilizing potential of the spatial unity of individual/citizen and colonial practices constituting the basis of empire triggered the collapse of unitary experiences during the revolutionary period and put an end to constitutional artifacts that tried to endow those experiences with coherence and meaning. The alleged objective was always the same: it was not advisable to grant constitutional rights to heterogeneous colonial societies. Individuals who hypothetically could be incorporated into the world of citizen-legislator inhabited a sea of unprepared or simply strange people. The metropolitan world was thus reconstructed to impose itself on all imperial space without having to deal with the demands and filters of the notion of unity between the national and imperial spaces, which temporarily would become one whole. It is here that the passage from imperial constitutions to dual constitutions based on specialness was critical. It allowed states, be they monarchic or republican, to move simultaneously in two directions, forging an intense nexus between the community of citizens-electors and colonial interests as a whole while leaving the rest helpless in the face of such restrictive identification. Special formulas allowed many birds to be killed with just one stone. Among the practices of specialness were the primacy of the executive in imperial legislation and decision-making, an end to the annoying presence of colonists in the legislative chambers and councils of central government, and prohibitions against addressing colonial conflicts in formal political terms in the metropolis—meaning both that colonial leaders were reduced to being lobbyists and also that the conflicts widened in scope. As a result, metropolitan power (and its legal repertoire) could be extended on colonial territory to a spectacular degree, and in terms unthinkable at home; colonial leaders now possessed a panoply of repressive devices, pure military might, and criminal law that would have been intolerable to inhabitants of the metropolis.

This was the driving force behind imperial stabilization during the revolutionary era of 1770–1830. However, I do not presume the existence of rigidly separate eras; rather, there were nonlinear processes that overlapped in ways that were not necessarily or exclusively chronological. Faced with arguments of national consensus on an imperial level, the victorious coalitions in the Napoleonic Wars responded by imposing a clearer separation between the metropolitan and overseas worlds. During this stabilization period, the idea of exceptional or special laws depriving imperial government of the rules of consensus and of juridical limits operating in the national space became the norm. This book aims to understand how this "norm" worked. I will stay as far away as possible from teleologies that describe the norm as a "collapse," a "contradiction," or a momentary aberration with regard to liberalism's ideals of political equality. But I also reject the approach of critics who, similarly determined, understand the norm to be evidence of liberalism's inexcusable cynicism. In fact, no one could ever rule simply through ideological definitions. Instead, political and moral debates were worked out amid political crises and events that modeled policies in metropolitan spaces as well as in faraway territories and locations. The focus of this book takes in more than a century of imperial transformations precisely so as to be able to offer as nuanced a description as possible of that relationship among ideologies, policies, and local practice.

Special norms, then, were forged as the outcome of and in order to resolve tensions between the "community of citizens" and imperial governments. The result was the essence of the imperial nation, the political artifact that would become the most dynamic successor of monarchic empires. The formula may appear elementary, but it was extremely complicated to resolve, both in practice and historically. The first such complication was that the two entities, empire and nation, were never either homogenous or worlds apart. With few exceptions, norms regulating suffrage, the key to formal politics in representative regimes, did not linearly follow any definition of what a citizen actually was. French revolutionary discourse postulated a close nexus between one and the other. That is why criticism of the distinction between active and passive citizens in terms of economic status was a basic ingredient of the radical phase in France, which easily can be seen by comparing the constitutions of 1791 and 1793. Thus, the universalization of the figure of "citizen" and the affirmation of the centrality of a culture of citizenship constituted essential moments of the Revolution. Adding to the complication, the irrevocable affirmation of universality, which would appear to echo on the deepest level the very idea of the rights of man and citizen, led straight to the deprivation of political rights based on *domesticité*, a concept that in one word embraced exclusion of servants and a refusal to grant political rights to slaves. Revolutionary moderates considered that excluding servants at home and slaves in the colonies (as well as freemen of color, a serious problem of logic) were two sides of the same operation. It was no surprise, therefore, that both restrictions imploded nearly at the same time, first in the metropolis and immediately afterward in the turbulent Caribbean. Any time the foundational republican ideal was raised, citizenship could not be denied to former slaves and their descendants. In any case, the Second and Third Republics in France would shave the radical edge of that universal vocation through special norms that fragmented both legislative space and the extension of the French *départements* to its overseas possessions. Here we see the juxtaposition of the metropolitan and colonial public spheres, each with its specificities.

A similar overlap occurred with Spain during the great imperial crisis of 1808–10, when the Junta Central promised equality to American colonists with an eye to maintaining national unity. Discussions regarding citizenship for Indians and former slaves brought forth the unexpected fact that there would be more electors in America and the Philippines than in Spain. And in the United States the superimposition was even more intense. In the republican political culture born with independence and lasting through the expansion of suffrage and the slavery debates of the Jacksonian era of the 1830s, colonial situations were reproduced on the level of the nation and national sovereignty. That is, there were special practices in states with republican institutions and in territories awaiting statehood that complied with requisites deriving from the equation between recognizable constituent citizenship and an institutional formula based on representation on all levels (local, national, etc.) Within the nation, strictly speaking, there was a "captive nation" of African slaves that by definition could not be assimilated into the realm of full, nearly universal citizenship that was the ideological (Lockean) origin of republican institutions. But outside that space there was a wide range of impossible assimilations and precarious groups and territories. The entire imperial history of the U.S. republic was conditioned by this superimposition of a community of citizens and a space of effective sovereignty whose exceptional nature lay outside the frontiers of republican forms of government. In all the cases we have mentioned, it was precisely the dynamic relationship between the colonial and metropolitan spaces that created a gravitational space regulated by special formulas, which was the backbone and the heart of the political history of liberal empires.

This gravitational space can be defined only in particular instances. One such instance comprises the norms of knowledge, imitation, and equality in metropolitan and colonial spaces. A theme of this book will be the transmission and emulation of the very idea of rights by metropolitans and colonists, by those who stood within the system and by those on the outside. These were fluid and diffuse categories, of course. Yesterday's citizen could lose his rights tomorrow, or at least see them seriously diminished. A large part of nineteenth-century American and European political history is focused on this perpetual pendular movement in terms of rights, guarantees, political representation, and access to justice. French-Algerian republican colonists knew better than anyone that the status of French citizen and that of *indigène* (which could mean Arab or Berber) were linked, though with intermediate situations (women, servants, emigrants, foreigners, the condemned, beggars, and nomads, to name a few). The importance of French citizenship in North Africa signaled a colonial and imperial resolve to control the majority, a determination that was manifested in many ways, not just through derogatory propaganda and stereotypes but more especially through different possibilities of mobility, access to natural resources, administrative treatment, public and private behavior, and political activities of state subjects depending on where they lived or their specific situation. There, accompanied by no particular act of outward aggression, lay the borderland where repetitive and stereotyped special conditions took shape and were transformed into the arguments of political struggle.

Contemporary practices of transmitting individual or collective experiences of unequal rights are significant in this regard and should be examined more closely. Two such cases have been studied, though not sufficiently. The first is the double-sided experience of regular and voluntary troops during colonial wars. Soldiers exhibited attitudes of superiority toward suppressed populations, but even there the lines of confrontation were not always clear-cut. *Sepoys, zouaves,* and "buffalo soldiers" were a constant and diverse presence in the national and/or colonial armies of the empires. Thousands and thousands of slaves attained rights by joining the Union Army during the Civil War, Spaniards and separatists incorporated Cuban slaves and former slaves into their armies, and Senegalese and Algerians were used during World War I. Obviously, there were differences in terms of recruitment and levies in all these cases, but they exemplify how borders created as a result of "special" categories posed considerable cultural and ideological challenges.

A second example of transmission of experience is emigration. Hundreds of thousands of Europeans left their homes to go overseas, though their political experiences have scarcely been examined. A few examples in the following chapters aim at deepening our understanding in this regard. While Britons who emigrated to the United States throughout the nineteenth century saw their rights and representative capacities grow on local, state, and national levels, suffrage in Britain was notably restricted for most people until the second Reform Act of 1867 and into the twentieth century.[13] The rapid naturalization of European immigrants and the breadth of suffrage in the Republic lay behind aggressive Anglo-British nativist campaigns favoring greater restrictions against Catholics, the Irish, and other more recent emigrants. The struggle around slavery, however, eventually would revitalize political parties and discredit xenophobic nativist movements against Europeans. Meanwhile, English, Irish, and Scottish emigrants in British North America (the future Canada) remained within an old imperial framework but enjoyed greater rights than those who had remained in the British Isles.[14] Later on, the same paradox would emerge in Australia and New Zealand, where the inexistence of landed aristocracies, a mobile agrarian frontier, and the imperial monarchy's need to reach agreements with the local population when resources for imperial defense were seriously challenged created optimal conditions for the emergence of highly representative institutions and broad electoral bodies. Naturally, such gains were detrimental to those who lost control over their own world; empty territories existed only in official terminology, and colonists and transport companies called them empty for obvious reasons. To return to the question: How was this superior equality abroad transmitted, whether or not the emigrant returned home?

The case of Spanish emigrants in the Caribbean in the nineteenth century is similar, though on a different scale. During the second liberal experiment, in 1820–23, Spanish merchants in Havana and their support networks waged a fierce fight against sugar aristocrats, culminating in elections. The merchants' apparent defeat in 1823 and the subsequent pact between the neo-absolutist monarchy of Ferdinand VII and Cuban growers helped stabilize Spanish rule until the definitive consolidation of the liberal state, when the colonies were separated from the constitutional framework. After that, Cuban, Puerto Rican, and Filipino politics traveled down back alleys: lobbying in the capital, "racial balance" in colonial society, immense and constant violence by military authorities in the three insular enclaves. Many Spanish emigrants took advantage of the political vacuum to oppress the local population, but we also know there were others, who shook their head at the shameful political conditions in allegedly full-fledged Spanish provinces, which the more lucid among them considered simply suicidal. Regime change in Spain in 1868 and the separatist movement in Cuba changed the rules of the game, with more space in the Caribbean for rights and representation, though that was not the case in the Philippines. From then on, politics in the colonies was a game of smoke and mirrors; people in Cuba and Puerto Rico demanded that cosmetic metropolitan reforms acquire greater depth and veracity, while Filipinos watched, stunned, as they were excluded from even limited liberal normalization. These transformations took place at the same time as the liberalization of emigration; people began going to new destinations such as Buenos Aires, Rosario, and Montevideo, as well as to French Algeria, where Europeans (many of them Spaniards, but also Italians) were well received for obvious reasons. We know little about the transfer of experiences on either side of the Atlantic between two political systems that were regulated with different rules but populated by peoples who were closely related. Again, the connections and experiences must be analyzed in each of these contexts. But one can easily see that within the gravitational field we referred to earlier, this massive European emigration experience took place in the context of the juxtaposition of a community of citizens in the metropolis and the expansion of liberal empires throughout the world.

In the mid-nineteenth century, special formulas became more stable. There was an apparently irreversible separation between the juridical, political, and constitutional norms of the metropolis and those in the empire, which in general were more restrictive. In Great Britain, the largest empire of the era, that distinction was made more emphatic by the fact that its possessions were spread among territories considered inappropriate for Atlantic representative governmental practices. India, over which control was decided before 1820, was a perfect example of this essential contrast, and the fact was well recognized by Edmund Burke, who complained that much imperial expansion of the time was an inevitable source of corruption. Clearly the case of the British empire is different from the rest in many ways, and this book uses a comparative approach so as to highlight similarities and differences, not to blur them with ahistorical or general categories. After the North American crisis of 1776–83, the Georgian empire commenced a complex restructuring in the Atlantic and in India, the latter being the "swing to the East" that defined the period before the African cycle beginning in the 1880s. Despite the deeply conservative stability of the early nineteenth century, the British empire also exhibited tendencies I have pointed to in its rivals. Internal criticism of parliamentary corruption, starting with the colonial lobbies, and demands for electoral reform would be a constant throughout the century, again and again linking metropolitan and imperial dynamics. Indeed, it was the effort to demonstrate continuity and show the deep-rootedness of the representative tradition that resulted in the preservation of local assemblies that ended up being such a challenge in North America. Furthermore, in British North America it was necessary to entirely rethink the ideological foundations in order to accommodate the majority population of the former Nouvelle France, which was both Francophone and Catholic. No one was unaware that this was merely one facet of the resolution of the eternal conflict with the other Catholic majority, that of Ireland, a critical question when addressing the Irish contribution to the military demands of an empire that was continually expanding. These issues at the dawn of the so-called Second British Empire, along with that of making room for the Indian Raj—both enormous and anomalous, inhabited by cultures and religions of unheard-of proportions and governed by a privileged company with shareholders who often were not even British—were the bases of the narrative of unity and specialness that was so similar to that of its rivals. The British interpreted these variations on an obsolete theme taken from the First Empire as an indication of specialness, though their insularity led them to call it empiricism, failure of an overall plan, or the result of "reluctant imperialism." All this might have formed part of the equation, but it does not explain how things managed to continue for a century and a half. It was all very similar to the situation of the rest, which only makes sense, even setting aside the contrasts in procedure and constitutional and juridical culture between the British, other Europeans, and North Americans.

Once revolutionary turbulence and uncertainty had ended and decolonization had taken place in various phases (1763 and 1802–3 for the French, 1776–83 for the British, 1810–24 for the Spaniards, and 1822 in Portuguese Brazil), the empires we are studying stabilized and commenced to slowly but surely expand both internally and externally. The internal efforts were in the direction of hitherto free societies, either tribes or simply peoples on the margins of seventeenth- and eighteenth-century imperial structures; externally, campaigns aimed at competitors or independent local powers in Asia, Oceania, or Africa. Examples of internal expansion include Spain in the Philippines, starting in the late eighteenth century, and on the northern and southern frontiers of an empire that did not cease growing; French Algeria starting in 1830; dominion over Central Asian tribes and forced sedentariness of entire Indian populations ruled by the East India Company; Dutch expansion in Java after 1825–29; and the removal and destruction of Indian tribes on the North American plains before and after the Civil War. All this is not the topic of this book, though it constituted the canvas on which increasingly dense and irreversible colonial structures—always and everywhere the cornerstones of great imperial constructions—would be displayed. At the same time, imperial powers ventured into the heart of Africa and South America to realize what would be called the second slave era, either doing the job themselves or assigning the dirty work to locals. As for external expansion, it took place throughout the world, leading to wars that would decide how the Pacific and Africa would be carved up through the end of World War I.

It would be a serious error to see this nineteenth-century imperial stabilization through the lens of the proverbial teleology of national histories, which themselves are the heirs of providential Christian narratives of medieval and early modern European expansion. Briefly, according to that account, once all the peoples of America, Asia, and North Africa we have mentioned were dominated by more capable beings who came bearing progress along with exploitation and colonial violence, their assimilation and newly elevated social and political status, previously available only to modern societies, was now guaranteed. If the elevation was slow and could not be realized in the nineteenth century, then the twentieth century awaited. I will not devote much space to this baseless narrative or its corollary—a succession of rights in which exploitation in the past is redeemed by the enjoyment of rights in the present—an argument that is both morally abject and historically false and that also can lead to new eschatalogies (either liberal redemption or its intrinsically evil nature). That is, this argument situates the final results of human actions beyond historical contingency and beyond the ability of individuals or groups (social classes, peoples, nations) to fight for a better future. Social scientists should focus not on these useless redemptive formulas but rather on analysis. In that regard, the notion of imperial stabilization, which clearly did occur, is not incompatible with but rather intrinsic to the complex relationship among constitutional regression, restrictions of rights, and, conversely, the widening of rights for some by virtue of the fact that they were shared in the same political framework. One such example, an instance of inverse specialness, would be the fact that the European population in New Zealand and aboriginal Maoris had universal (male) suffrage before the British population at home. This is a key to understanding both the deep logic of specialness and how difficult it is to know where social groups were in this panorama of rights that were never quite fixed.

Indeed, in the mid-nineteenth century all empires were anxious to define very restrictive boundaries for rights and equality under the law belonging to their colonial subjects, especially those with dark skin. But if they were restrictive in comparison with the metropolis, which marked the accepted threshold, they varied among themselves. In some cases, rights were simply erased. The case of Jamaica and the West Indies is instructive in this sense. With one stroke of the pen in 1865, assemblies previously dominated by planters entirely disappeared (with the exception of the one in Barbados). This act of force, constitutional regression in its purest form, was announced by the Colonial Office as a benefaction for former slaves, though it also deprived mulattos of the voice they had acquired in the assembly, which was hardly a favorable exchange for the recently emancipated. Another example is that of Spain, which underwent grave political setbacks in 1837 with a drastic switch in colonial policy as colonists were expelled from liberal metropolitan institutions. This was a coup against Cuban Creoles, but the subsequent cruelty unleashed during the rule of Leopoldo O'Donnell in the mid-1840s against free people of color and plantation slaves shows that it was far more than that. In fact, the very idea of regression should be studied case by case. Clearly, there were regressions in matters of rights, showing that access to representation and political rights, let alone social rights such as a piece of land, a fair wage, or a just price for products that peasants took to market, was never a straightforward affair, nor was its culmination known when the process began. The case of the U.S. Civil War in terms of republican unity and social and political rights, which I will address in chapter 7, is an excellent example of this recourse to raising social and political status followed by political regression and social decline.

Regulation of special rules was hindered in several ways. First, obviously, was the grim example the imperial powers set throughout the world during the revolutions when, in order to forge a consensus with which to consolidate their political frameworks, they evoked equal rights for subjects of the crown. That evocation was what shaped the structure of imperial constitutions and the complementary idea of universal rights. Later on, the impossibility of maintaining consensus both domestically and in the greater imperial world led to well-known reversals in terms of rights. Sometimes these steps backward came in the form of explicit constitutional regressions, as in the cases mentioned above. But an accounting of rights and representative capacities in imperial spaces must be correlated with what was going on in the metropolis, where reverses concerning rights were both varied and frequent. In Europe, they were generally of two sorts. First there were periodic and frequent suspensions of constitutional law and the imposition of states of siege, elimination of constitutional rights and guarantees, and similarly repressive measures. The nineteenth century (and even more so the twentieth century) was full of these situations, of varying length and gravity. At the same time, twisted arguments along the lines of the *classes dangereux* approach used in Paris in 1840–50 and later proved that rights could not possibly be universalized. The second sort of regression in Europe involved elimination of the revolutionary figure of the universal citizen who had hovered, promisingly though uncertainly, over the great programmatic declarations at the start of the revolutionary cycle and remained present through the Spanish and Portuguese Constitutions of 1812 and 1822 and the French Constitution of 1848. If sovereignty lay with the universal citizen, then establishment of a conservative order was unlikely. A crucial concern of this book is to trace the linkages between metropolitan and imperial transformations of all sorts and how they interacted.

The solution to the dilemma of political equality and social order was to remove the figure of citizen from liberal politics per se, which provoked fear and reminded people of the Great Revolution of 1789. The very idea of citizenship as the foundation of political order vanished beyond the conservative horizon of 1815, while the most basic political rights, the vote and the right to be elected, were from then on regulated by electoral laws that established barriers. It was French, Spanish, British, and U.S. citizens with property, incomes, or other capacities who voted, not the new political subjects with natural rights reinvented by the late-eighteenth-century revolutions. As a result, there was great discussion regarding the characteristics and definitions of the political subject, the national elector. Echoing the very structures of capitalist society, distinctions of wealth and profession immediately took precedence, among other reasons because they were so easily observed in the very heart of the nineteenth-century state, namely the property tax offices. But that economic criterion turned out to be insufficient; so, in addition, the moral qualities of property owners (and later of the middle class, certain professionals, and the so-called worker aristocracy) were measured to see if they were appropriate candidates for full political rights. It is no surprise that one of the great apostles of nineteenth-century reformist liberalism, John Stuart Mill, stated, with typical honesty, that neither "uncivilized" individuals nor British workers were qualified. Similar arguments were used to deprive women of citizenship, the vote, and political identity in general until well into the twentieth century, though Olympe de Gouges, who also had opposed slavery, had claimed these rights already in 1791.

This is the only explanation for the spectacular gap between revolutionary promises (and not just promises, but also profoundly democratic and large-scale experiences) and the effective generalization of universal citizenship in representative political regimes of Europe and America. But these restrictions, along with temporary setbacks or suspensions of rights, were partly motivated by the appearance of the ideal of universal rights and by continual efforts by those on the margins to broaden their rights. Thus, regression at home and regression in imperial spaces were linked at many nexuses that must be investigated. Sometimes these linkages were unexpected, for example when colonial relations meant that the French in Algeria in 1848 and in 1871, the British during the Crimean War, and the Spaniards in Morocco in 1859 or in Cuba in 1868–78 could appropriate plebeian politics from the metropolitan ethnocentric discourse so as to more successfully negotiate political advantages.

If a large majority of Europeans were unqualified to vote or be elected, what about the masses who populated the colonies or who had been displaced by force or "contract" to metropolitan settings? This is a complicated question, and it cannot be fully explored in this book. However, I would like to stress the related issue of constitutional regressions in colonial spaces. Passage from old-regime legislative pluralism to unity of political rights immediately presented empires with knotty problems.

We referred earlier to the dilemma: If social actors such as freemen of color and emancipated slaves in the French and English Antilles, Creoles in the Spanish monarchy, and those emancipated under the Fourteenth Amendment of the U.S. Constitution, who otherwise all would have been excluded, were now integrated, the division of effective and symbolic power would become difficult and unpredictable. Dual constitutions and special formulas brought about a different way of regulating imperial unity. In other words, it brought about a second wave of colonization of the empires. In this light, the Spanish and Portuguese constitutions' exclusion of overseas inhabitants in 1837 and 1838 were large-scale regressions, worthy successors of the first such move, that of Napoleonic France in 1799–1802. So, too, was what happened in 1865 in Jamaica (and the rest of the West Indies except Barbados), where the island's assembly was suspended *sine die*, constituting a full-blown constitutional reversion (according to contemporaries) in an empire that had not previously given in to the temptation of promising equality to its subjects. The British case is important because it indicates the true dimension of the question, beyond the particular constitutional expression of any resolution. Given that the greatest liberal empire of the time was shaken by the same tendencies and problems as the other imperial powers, though without the rhetoric of declarations of rights and equality, emancipated slaves were on the electoral rolls. (This was also the case in the French islands in 1848 and during the Third Republic.) When abolition seemed irresolvable from the metropolitan perspective, the Colonial Office suppressed representation, despite the precedent of the preceding 150 years. This was no anomaly; rather, it fell in line with the practices of all nineteenth-century liberal empires.

Human actions have many motivations and can be surprising and capricious; in contrast, social practices described by historical science with the greatest possible number of examples and variables are never arbitrary. This study was born when I began observing similarities (though not exact repetitions) among special formulas in nineteenth-century empires up to the decolonization of 1947 and beyond. The attempt to provide liberal empires with a political history called for a long journey and many case studies. The synthetic and brief observations in this introduction are general reflections regarding observable patterns in particular cases. It is only there, in the case studies, that the preceding considerations can help us shape a historical analysis.

CHAPTER ONE

The Fall of
Monarchic Empires

SUBJECTS IN MONARCHIC EMPIRES were never completely bereft of rights or some sort of representation, though the latter may have been functionally and territorially limited. This was true even before the great revolutions of 1776, 1789, 1808–10, and 1820–22, which with their example and promise spread new ideas throughout the world about the extension of those rights and the political representation that went along with them.[1] The semantic turn by which a system of accumulative rights in societies governed by notions of legislative pluralism shifted to being a singular right, a foundational political act in a society thought of as being self-regulating, took place via a pact with the monarch or through a sovereign decision that was subsequently historically legitimized. Therefore, the start of the revolutionary cycle signaled the definitive demise of old-regime legislative pluralism and the accompanying notion of composite states or monarchies.[2] Systematic demands for rights and the continuous and always unstable definition of monarchic space and institutions (European politics of the era was characterized by mixed constitutions) were transformed into representation that could be articulated only in a simultaneously emergent national space. Often, these promised rights were said to be universal, though they were difficult, if not impossible, to put into practice. In the end, the claim was that national space should be the "natural" basis for the exercise of sovereignty and representational rights; the space where a self-governing society could provide its own legitimate and appropriate rules. This book addresses those concrete experiences in Spain, France, and Britain, where the monarchy's borders did not coincide with European spaces, and where societies of compatriots abroad felt impelled to participate in political and cultural changes.

This chapter shows how the idea of a free subject endowed with rights and voice was not exported to the colonies, but rather, took shape there in a process parallel to that of the metropolis. Using the examples of the Spanish, France, and British empires, I examine how demands for self-government and representation were sustained in very similar ways and how that can explain the subsequent complex relationship between colonial development and liberalism in the Atlantic empires from 1776 to the 1820s.[3] The crucial point is that the European world and its rules had ceased to be confined by continental borders long before the eighteenth-century winds had spread the good news. Therefore, the transition from subject-citizen with rights to subject-citizen who establishes laws through representation is one that requires examination in the broadest perspective possible.[4]

Emigrants and settlers in conquered territories never thought they would lose the rights they had acquired (and expected to expand) in their home countries. These rights were theirs at birth—"birthright citizenship," as it has been defined by scholars.[5] They had rights because they belonged to a particular society, profession, nation, province, or territory that had been absorbed through a pact, treaty, or conquest, and these entities were arranged in complex hierarchies that sustained an organic idea of society. It is true that the desire to reproduce structures of social and political integration in the colonies was often more intention than reality, and the notion of any mimetic reproduction of European societies would be an absurdity.[6] Nevertheless, subjects who traveled overseas lived in a system of rights and political culture that they understood was identical to what they had known before, and the development of these new societies of compatriots inevitably led to attempts to reproduce the world they had left behind, with which they were in constant communication. Regardless of how much the crown and its embodiment by viceroys or governors were involved in colonization and government, certain common trends emerged from the transactions between royal administration and transplanted European societies, sometimes with greater freedom than in the metropolitan world, thanks to the autonomy that came with distance. Affirmation of royal justice was always key to the formation of a unitary idea shared by societies on opposite sides of the ocean. The gradual taking shape of a common juridical culture led to the establishment of similar representative and organizational institutions, with variations depending on local circumstances.[7] In general, the Iberian pioneers were hesitant about transferring their more or less elective representative institutions overseas.[8] However, this did not mean that institutions of other sorts, including local councils, *cabildos* and *cámaras*, settlers' committees, ecclesiastical synods, and government tribunals (*audiencias*), did not also participate in the creation of a corporate ethos and in the establishment of law, along the lines of other places where limited elective representation had those same capacities.[9]

When we consider this space of disseminated power, representation, and legislation that was typical of the Old Regime, the First British Empire stands out because of its fairly early recognition of colonists' capacity to legislate through elected bodies in the context of an ambiguous definition of spheres between their assemblies and Westminster. To some degree, the triad of the colonial governor, his appointed council, and assemblies resembled the metropolitan political system known as the Westminster System or the Old Representative System.[10] The institutional latticework of plantations and colonies neither in theory nor in practice interfered with Parliament, which was sometimes defined as imperial, particularly during the 1640 revolution, the civil war, and the era of colonial expansion during Cromwell's Protectorate.[11] The eighteenth century saw the paradox of strengthened parliamentary legislative and investigatory powers—what Joanna Innes has called "the machinery of government"—coinciding with more dynamic politics in the Thirteen Colonies and the West Indies and with increasing tension between center and periphery.[12] Here, too, one must try to avoid anachronism and resist being blinded by the transformation in North American politics in the middle of the century, which was not replicated in other parts of the empire, even in those with similar institutional instruments. Tension between center and periphery could be found as well in rival empires organized in different ways. As we will see, what was really distinctive was the conjunction of a lively society across the Atlantic and the simultaneous transformation of the relationship between local politics and the long arm of the empire in each of the colonies. Similar transformations, both in intensity and chronology, could be found in all the Atlantic empires, especially when the needs of war led to the imposition of what has come to be known as the fiscal-military state.[13] Everywhere, at the same time, reinforced military and fiscal power and their bureaucracies brought new tensions to bear on the diverse worlds making up the disjointed beginnings of modern states (or composite monarchies, in this case) that were aggregates of very different pieces.[14] In all of them, colonists resisted tax increases, the loss of their political status, and interference in the autonomy they enjoyed as a result of their distance and the weakness of the crown.[15] This resistance was reflected in the institutions created by modern European empires. In all the cases we are studying, this tension between center and periphery lay at the heart of the revolutions, the falling apart of those composite and aristocratic monarchies, and the subsequent genesis of contemporary empires and nation-states.

Before the Flood

When echoes of the revolution in the streets of Paris reached the wealthy French colonies in the Caribbean, colonists quickly tried to muffle the news and defend their interests vis-à-vis the monarchy. The speed with which they responded is not surprising. For some time they had had their own organizations, the result of long struggles involving political tradition, conflicts with the Ministry of the Navy and the Colonies and other crown entities, organization of a militia, and the imperatives of colonial social and racial structure. Freemen of color could not participate in assemblies (formally recognized just before July 1789) despite in many cases being financially well off, and of course neither could slaves.[16] In contrast to what happened in the metropolis, colonists were not asked to submit *cahiers de doléances* to the Estates General. Indeed, French Minister of Finance Jacques Necker referred to the colonies only tangentially, even though port privileges and colonial demands were constantly on the table during the mid-eighteenth-century economic debate in France.[17] Even the supposed opponents of Jean-Baptiste Colbert's colonial policy, in particular the physiocrats, understood the importance of the relationship.[18] One of them, Pierre Paul Mercier de la Rivière, had been intendant of the Windward Islands (Îles-du-Vent) in 1757–62 and 1763–64. There, especially in Martinique, he had developed a deep understanding of slave plantations.[19] So, his aim to isolate the colonies as far as possible from metropolitan political turmoil was not a question of ignoring them or of lack of interest. Rather, it was the conviction that serious problems would result for the metropolis if those prosperous enclaves were allowed to gain greater freedom and representation. Nonetheless, island assemblies voted on the *cahiers* (which French historian Gaston Letonnelier called *cahiers de remplacement*) in a manner similar to their compatriots, and the same thing happened in other French overseas possessions.[20] The crown had ensured their ability to organize in assemblies, and in the following months there were difficult negotiations over future access to the Estates General and the National Assembly. The following chapter will discuss this process in greater detail, describing the struggle to implement an economic program and the concerted effort to prevent revolutionary governments from daring to alter the social order of slavery in the colonies.

Historians are familiar with this crisis of the French colonial regime but less so with the institutional developments that had defined collective action and experiments coming from above until that point.[21] It is clear that the leading role of the colonial assemblies in the Antilles was the result both of the islands' economic importance and of the transformation of the monarchic empire in the eighteenth century.[22] One must keep in mind that the formation of the French empire was due to very diverse stimuli, starting with the seemingly limitless dissemination of sailors, fishermen, and pirates throughout the Atlantic and along the coasts of Africa.[23] This empire of fishermen and sailors, as Frederick Quinn called it, eventually blended into more conventional forms of settlement, though it never entirely lost its importance.[24] It was well known in the eighteenth century that withdrawal from Newfoundland and the nearby fishing colonies was a severe blow to the French navy, which had recruited sailors there.[25] French Minister of Finance Colbert's plans in 1660–70 to impose some sort of order on this confusing situation had been inspired by reasons of political economy and by a desire to increase state power.[26] The results fell short of his grand strategy, with the possible exception of naval power, the eternal heart of France's colonial expansion, but they did have several consequences. The most notable was the establishment in North America of New France, Voltaire's famous "a few acres of snow" (*quelques arpents de neige*),[27] whose economic justification lay in the fur trade.[28] But despite support from the crown, which was especially interested in maintaining links between Normandy and the Saint Lawrence, the enclave never attracted enough Frenchmen willing to move to that uncertain and cold land. In any case, what developed there was a model of cooperation between colonists and Indians, with the emergence of the *métis*, making further emigration from the mother country unnecessary. This new social group (the *coureurs des bois*) would end up controlling the fur trade as far away as the Great Lakes.[29] French possessions never reached the demographic levels of neighboring New England, which explains their defensive fragility during times of crisis. In 1763, when they were forced to withdraw from part of the colony, the French colonial population barely reached 65,000.[30]

Had the French maintained their local fishing interests and fur trade in the north Atlantic, Colbert's plans to establish outposts on distant seas would not have been viable. Quickly, new options were explored in the Antilles, the Mississippi Delta, the Mascarene Islands, and along the route to

India. In the Caribbean the French established bases in areas theoretically under Spanish sovereignty, while the Mascarenes were ruled by Portugal. By the second half of the seventeenth century, French pirate enclaves devoted to capturing Spanish ships carrying silver and supplies were slowly giving way to small agricultural settlements that later became slave plantations. Throughout the eighteenth century, these colonial building blocks grew, but with great difficulty, the principal impetus coming from the French navy, Colbert's monopoly companies, the slave trade and plantation economy, and the leading port cities.[31]

One indication of the path that would slowly be carved out is the case of the eastern portion of the present-day island of Santo Domingo, which France took from Spain and turned into a land of sugar and coffee plantations.[32] At the same time, naval and colonial minister Étienne-François Choiseul's decision to liquidate the Compagnie des Indes Orientales in 1764 transformed the Mascarenes, which until then had been mere stopping-off points along the way to Pondicherry, on the east coast of India, into plantation territories.[33] This expansion, important both in density and in breadth, would eventually fall victim to tremendous competition from Great Britain. Signposts along that road to collapse included the end of the French Acadie in North America after the Seven Years' War and the Treaty of Paris in 1763, and the additional failure to hold on to the sphere of influence established in southeast India during the capable administrative and military rule of Joseph François Dupleix.[34] The forced withdrawal from these critical territories meant that French plantation interests in the Lesser Antilles and the future Haiti acquired greater standing. It was the end of a long journey whose beginnings lay in the previous century.

What was less predictable was that the French population in the Antilles would be so remarkably proficient at challenging the royal administration and developing their own institutions amid prerevolutionary warfare and discontent, and at creating a political, economic, and juridical culture with which to defend their interests. From the start, these small Creole societies resisted attempts by the monarchy to exert more control; one such attempt came in 1635 (the same year France took Martinique and Guadeloupe) with the establishment of the Compagnie des Indes Occidentales.[35] The Creoles' de facto independence was also helped by the fact that they had closer relations with the Dutch (through their tobacco and sugar markets as well as their processing technology) than with their own mother country. Little by little, these small French societies began to speak up in a manner consistent with that of European countries. The use of contract labor (*engagés*) or deportees was essential for development, just as it was in the Anglo-British colonies in North America and the Caribbean.[36] French settlements grew extremely quickly; Saint-Domingue went from having 47,000 slaves in 1720 to 470,000 on the eve of the Revolution. Guadeloupe went from 17,000 to 86,100 in the same period, and Martinique went from 36,000 to 73,416.[37] Slaves, land, and advanced technology allowed for spectacular agricultural progress, and export crops gave French foreign trade a decidedly Atlantic slant; by the time of the Revolution, they accounted for 60 percent of its value and 50 percent of the tariffs taken in.[38]

France, by then an amphibious state, took careful note of this massive growth of plantation agriculture. It had major military obligations both in Europe and at sea, where it competed with Britain and other seaborne powers.[39] The expense of fighting the War of the Spanish Succession and raising public debt to that end forced the crown to shift its fiscal attention to the colonies, and the weakest but most promising link in this search for revenue were the merchants and planters of the Antilles.[40] From 1713 to 1718, colonists battled with representatives of the crown and the French Atlantic ports to work out a new fiscal framework, known as the Exclusif.[41] Under that plan, colonial products would be exported to French ports, of which Bordeaux was the first, duties were paid, and most of the products would then be reexported.[42] Even under these conditions, competition for tropical agricultural products was keen in northern European markets, even in Great Britain, which of course had its own Caribbean producers.[43] French Antilles colonists were always desirous of engaging in direct trade with their final markets, and as a result conflict and negotiation went hand in hand during this period when Creole "autonomy" was being nurtured; the term is tricky, given that plantation owners, merchants, and royal administrators all shared personal and family ties. The most notable such case, Jean-Baptiste Dubuc du Ferret, was a member of a large landowning family in Martinique who became chief of staff for Choiseul, the eternal minister of the Navy and the Colonies.[44] These endless personal connections, along with continual tariff disputes, formed the backdrop of the development of political, juridical, and institutional viewpoints among the Antilles powers that would survive until the great revolutionary debates in the National Assembly and the Convention.[45]

At least since 1664, colonists in the Antilles who met in local councils (conseils) had agreed to administrative strictures in exchange for protection.[46] This generally meant that judicial posts were reserved for aristocrats and lawyers to the liking of the Ministry of the Navy and the Colonies. Councils were founded in Petit-Goâve and Le Cap (on Saint-Domingue) in 1685 and 1701, respectively, and later on in Port-au-Prince.[47] These recognized and agreed-upon organizational rudiments would become crucial in the early decades of the eighteenth century when it came time to resist fiscal pressure, for example, poll taxes on slaves in Saint-Domingue. In general, royal administrators agreed to landowners' meetings, which we have seen were an old custom, as they allowed rapid consent to certain tax measures. Sometimes, however, the meetings were unauthorized, and therefore somewhat seditious. That was the case during the Gaoulé uprising in Martinique in 1717 and during the tax revolt in the Greater Antilles in 1722–23.[48] Discontent also halted plans by the French controller general of finance, John Law, to establish a new monopoly trading company. In later years, local assemblies, with limited purpose and control from above, gained prominence with the establishment of a rural militia under the command of a marshal (thus called *maréchaussée*), similar to the *gendarmerie* in metropolitan France.[49] Starting in 1733, free blacks and mulattos were recruited to, among other things, prevent attacks on rural properties and catch runaway slaves. As Charles Frostin has pointed out, it was in the context of their growing demands that the great Creole interests learned to use and manipulate the *petits blancs* and free blacks against metropolitan power.[50] Indeed, landowners' decision to withdraw from the *maréchaussée* in Saint-Domingue after the December 1768 conscription riot in Croix-des-Bouquets, on the west side of the island, and their encouragement of the *petits blancs* and freemen of color to participate in the revolt, would have incalculable consequences once the revolution arrived.

These political and social institutions would not have constituted such an important counterbalance to Bourbon royal administration and interests were it not that the colonists had solid doctrinal justifications. Obviously, this development did not come out of nowhere; as we noted earlier, French emigrants came from a country with a long parliamentary history (the *pays d'état*). Brittany, for example, was positively belligerent when it came to defending Bretons' rights.[51] Abroad, as in the metropolis, royal administrators took exception to parliamentary legitimacy during the eighteenth century, though they were unable to defeat it. Ancient parliamentary traditions and the widespread practice of petitioning were greatly strengthened by a new wave of thinking that celebrated assemblies, separation of powers, and the inherent rights of kings' subjects. Charles Louis de Sécondat, better known as the baron de Montesquieu, wrote in favor of such parliamentary continuity, but Jansenists in the administration and champions of natural rights such as Mably and Rousseau articulated a vision leading straight to the idea of a mixed monarchy, one rooted in the historical constitution of laws that the monarchy was obliged to respect.[52]

The balance would thus shift to the side of law. The small but prosperous communities overseas were no strangers to these ideas, and they did what they could to be present in those notebooks of complaints being sent to the Estates General.

But the needs of the colonial world were not the same as those of all the corners of the monarchy. First, there was tension with the great colonial interests at home, particularly the leading ports, whose representatives stalked the hallways of the Ministry of the Navy and the Colonies. Second, starting in the mid-eighteenth century, French Creoles lived atop a powder keg. France may have been a slow starter in the world of sugar plantations, but it made up for lost time in spectacular fashion, so much so that its island products invaded European markets at far more competitive prices than those of its rivals.[53] The case of Saint-Domingue is extraordinary; on the eve of the Revolution it had become the world's greatest sugar colony, with nearly half a million slaves, a number that would continue to grow.[54] Its plantations, or *habitations*, were technologically the most advanced in the world, and this is very important when considering the events that followed.

The rise of the slave plantations, the very heart of the eighteenth-century French empire, led colonists to construct a sophisticated legitimacy of their world. This idea, a distillation of autonomous Creole culture—and based both on the slave economy and on free trade, in that they hoped to do away with the tariffs that confined their world—was developed with the assistance of important jurists, some of whom, such as Médéric Louis Élie Moreau de Saint-Méry, also worked for the royal administration, for revolutionary administrations, and, finally, for Napoleon himself. Another contributor was Émilien Pétit, a magistrate in the Saint-Domingue council. In 1751 he published *Patriotisme américain*, in which he audaciously defended improved relations among rival powers and limitations on their defense spending.[55] Pétit promoted these new ideas about colonies' political status later on, when he was a judicial adviser to Nicolas René Berryer, secretary of state for the navy. His basic idea—to scale back military authority in the islands and encourage local institutions instead—lay at the center of the debate until 1799.[56] The notion of colonial self-government rested on a series of stages in colonial development. Briefly, the first stage was royal authority; next came cession of power to the founders of each of the possessions; and third was a mixed government shared between colonists and monarch. This theory was almost institutionally hegemonic after the Seven Years' War, when Pétit was appointed a member of the High Colonial Council. He elaborated on it in his *Droit public ou Gouvernement des colonies françaises*, published in

1771, the immediate antecedent to the 1787 reform by which the monarchy finally agreed to turn territorial chambers into representative assemblies chosen by colonists, entities inspired by both the Spanish *audiencias* and the assemblies in the British West Indies. In Pétit's view, this form of self-government was essential for ensuring both proper colonial representation and the development of specific legislation for overseas possessions.

Demands for laws of their own and the right to legislative pluralism inspired the work of two leading French colonial figures of the second half of the eighteenth century: Hilliard d'Auberteuil and Moreau de Saint-Méry, who both represented what was called the *résistance parlementaire*.[57] The former was most conspicuously responsible for the hard racial edge of institutional development, exemplified in his attempt to impose a complete racial hierarchy throughout the French Caribbean.[58] With royal permission, d'Auberteuil in 1776–77 published *Considérations sur l'état présent de la colonie française de Saint-Domingue*, a fierce criticism of both metropolitan impositions and Creole social norms. It was so fierce, in fact, that it was immediately withdrawn from circulation. Nonetheless, the idiosyncratic writer succeeded Pétit on a legislative committee established by Secretary of State for the Navy Antoine de Sartine in 1778.[59] After the American Revolution and a new war with England, it was most necessary to listen very carefully to the powerful Creole elites. Moreau de Saint-Méry's contributions to the debate mark the high point of the public vocation in France before the French Revolution. His book, *Lois et Constitutions des colonies françaises de l'Amérique sous le vent*, published in the key year 1787, when colonists' right to form representative assemblies had finally been recognized, is an impressive display of erudition with one basic political purpose: to demonstrate the impossibility of applying metropolitan legislation in the Caribbean possessions.[60]

His analysis, based on arguments that Abbé Raynal had already used in his *Histoire des deux Indes* (1770), formed the basis of Creole opposition to *despotisme ministériel* during the first phase of the Revolution.[61] Earlier, these arguments had underlain claims for legislative power and representation.[62] By the 1780s it was clear that the fight for Creole autonomy was taking place on two fronts: claims for self-government and demands that the crown cease its interference. If the former reflected a long struggle to limit the crown's reach on the islands, the latter was essential for blocking intrusive maneuvers by pressure groups representing French ports and also for mitigating certain aspects of slavery in the Antilles. The dispute with metropolitan interests lasted throughout the period during which monopoly and tariff reforms were implemented, ending with what was called the *exclusif mitigée*. As for demands that the crown stop interfering, this can be seen most clearly with disputes regarding reforms of the Code Noir (1685), that is, repression and punishment of African slaves and their descendants.[63] Palliative measures adopted during the slavery debate in France were seen as a *casus belli* by the planters, who felt besieged.[64] Therein lies the full meaning of Creole demands for autonomy, though the demands were not limited to questions of race and slavery.

What truly made colonists uneasy was their declining numbers vis-à-vis African slaves and their descendants. Slavery and color were two different things, but, as John Garrigus has shown, they blended to create a previously unheard of level of racial anxiety that would last well into the nineteenth century.[65] The principal problem was that of free mulattos' ability to compete with whites in government and economic life, given that the French colonial system did not prevent them from owning land or slaves. They had been upwardly mobile since the end of the seventeenth century and had established themselves in a wide range of areas, including sugar, indigo, and forestry. Some of the *livres de couleur* families, such as the Raymonds, Begasses, Trichets, Hérards, and Boisronds, would later acquire great influence and wealth.[66] Julien Raymond, for example, spent some of his time in Paris and had a good reputation at the royal court as the political situation began changing. The matter of the status of freemen of color was probably exaggerated before and after 1789, which is understandable only if we take into account the growing importance of racial divisions in Saint-Domingue and, gradually, in Martinique and Guadeloupe. The paradox was that while the Creoles, crucial allies in a society with so many unfree people, continued moving up the social and economic ladder, starting in 1767 they were excluded from public office.[67] Colonists' boycott of the *maréchaussée* can be understood here as part of the growing tension between two social groups with essentially identical social characteristics but separated by a line that would have far-reaching consequences. In the two decades before the Revolution, lines of race, color, and origin were defined more clearly and with greater consequence both by local magistrates and by the crown, which was sensitive to the arguments of colonists and their propagandists, among them treatise writers. As white planters demanded representation, so too did wealthy mulattos.[68] Echoes of racial prejudice made their way swiftly through the Antilles and reached the home country along with speculation regarding the stratification of colonial societies (so beloved by Moreau de Saint-Méry) and the spread of derogatory myths about Africans (their rites, medicines, and poisons).[69] One of the more extreme examples was Pierre-Victor Malouet, a leader in the antiemancipation fight during the Revolution and the Napoleonic restoration, who in 1788 published a nasty racist tirade, *Mémoire sur l'esclavage des nègres*.[70] Indeed, the paradox was glaring: the debate about the evils of slavery that would bring about the establishment of the abolitionist Société des Amis des Noirs shortly before the Revolution were taking place just as colonial society and large portions of France were becoming increasingly concerned with race and color.[71]

In the end, the crucial role of the sugar plantations pushed island leaders toward what would be called colonial autonomy (the other side of *despotisme ministériel*), that is, concentrating decision-making in the crown's administrative entities and drawing up a program of colonial particularity that could be properly respected only with governmental institutions run by themselves. All this was outlined in their *cahiers de doléances*, which they sent to Paris even though no one had asked them to.

Light amid the Darkness

French colonies obtained formal recognition that they could establish representative organisms only in 1787, but this right was consubstantial with the First British Empire practically since the start of Atlantic expansion. As with France, the early assemblies of shareholders in the colonial companies gave rise to institutional arrangements that would prove very stable. The famous triad of the colonial governor, his co-opted council, and the colonists' assembly replicated, on a smaller scale, the political system at home. The Old Representative System was the most solid antecedent of responsible governments during the Victorian era; liberal and at the same time moderately democratic. And given that this system, in its mature phase, was the model that advocates of autonomy in rival French and Spanish colonies aspired to, its prestige and relevance only increased. The lively assemblies in the Thirteen Colonies, which during the two decades before 1776 fought efforts by London to control them and impose laws, made the experience of colonial self-government all the more alluring. But this interpretation of the political history of monarchic empires is not only true, it is also highly conventional, and therefore I would like to suggest some variations, both for this case in particular and in comparative terms.

Corporative organizations emerged in the British possessions in the same manner as the chartered companies in the metropolis. Generally speaking, companies allowed merchants or aristocrats seeking their fortune to have access to the government in the colonies, giving rise to an embryonic political and military government.[72] Thus, the formal expansion of English and British interests in the New World did not require an extension of state institutions or administrative apparatus, which would be the logical counterpoint to the companies' corporative institutions in later years.[73] Historians have called this laissez-faire attitude "salutary neglect," using an expression coined by Edmund Burke, an elegant formulation of the first era's flexibility and the later era's rigidity during the wars between empires.[74] Despite the physical distance, conflicts over sovereignty with rival nations were frequent even in the early stages.[75] When companies were threatened, they automatically assumed that their metropolis would come to their defense. But nothing was that simple. Building European societies on other continents on a scale larger than a factory or a processing plant required new settlers and ways of defending those settlers from other Europeans and from indigenous peoples. The politics of *terra nullius* may have led settlers to believe they owned their new lands, but rarely was that a reflection of reality. In short, new settlements could be secured through only two means: reproduction of the home country's rural family household or construction of a colonial society based on servitude, either imported or local.[76] In the British case, both means were used within the same institutional solution, which developed modestly in the West Indies, New England, and around Chesapeake Bay.

In the early phases, agents of the crown were conspicuously absent. It was only when settlements entered into crisis or when territories had reached a certain administrative breadth that the crown made its presence felt overseas, as when the Commonwealth made shows of force in Barbados and Virginia.[77] Practically speaking, this center-periphery tension led to the appearance nearly everywhere of colonial governors, advised by councils whose members were loyal supporters. During Cromwell's campaign against Spain in the Caribbean, known as the Western Design, the balance of power shifted temporarily in favor of the imperial center, which for the first time was equipped with an aggressive colonial policy and motivated by religious fervor.[78] During the interregnum, the contractual relationship between companies and crown gave way to a legislative empire, and this was the case no matter what the degree to which inherent metropolitan limitations allowed colonists practical autonomy in their territories.[79] In fact, all the North American and Caribbean colonies grew, to some degree, independently of the mercantile or religious origins of their founding companies.[80] In the end, the assemblies were the only manner of fiscally sustaining the colonies and ensuring a militia system.[81] In this regard, the long and independent trajectory of the East India Company beyond the Cape of Good Hope shows how different it was to organize colonies for compatriots who wished to govern territories than it was to administer commerce in the interstices of stable societies, politically constituted in terms similar to those in Europe. In the long term, however, the East India Company would end up taking ideas of justice and sovereignty to its Asian entrepôts, as C. A. Bayly wrote.[82] Naturally, the organization of power in each one of the colonies was quite different, extending from elections by freemen in Connecticut and Rhode Island to elections agreed upon by the Massachusetts assembly and governor, to appointments of crown-approved governors and councils in the more aristocratic colonies such as Maryland.[83]

The origin of the colonial assemblies of North America and the Caribbean, aside from their very specific British aspects, was quite similar to the experience of other Atlantic empires. As elsewhere, the establishment and strengthening of more or less elected or negotiated representative bodies grew from less ambitious motivations. Absent any secure royal authority, it was the stockholders' meetings, sometimes still on European soil, that examined company activities.[84] In practice, formal procedures were pretty much all the same, regardless if they were settlement or merchant companies, or had been inspired by religious dissidence. Other factors contributing to assemblies' institutionalization were that the General Court, to which stockholders could appeal, was seriously insufficient, and that the overhaul of the judicial apparatus, theoretically put in place by the 1701 Settlement Act, was taking place very slowly. In order to resolve these difficulties, assemblies appeared in the major colonies throughout the seventeenth century, including Barbados, Massachusetts, and Virginia.[85] The inspiration for these efforts in part lay in parliamentary debates at home, a reflection of Westminster's new role, but these events cannot be conflated with what happened one hundred years later in North America.[86] The only serious effort to grant the North American colonists a viable structure came in 1684 with the experiment of the Dominion of New England, which was a stupendous failure.[87] Aside from that, the extension of assemblies—in Jamaica, which was taken from Spain in 1655 and got an assembly in 1664 that became stable only in the early eighteenth century, and in Georgia, whose assembly dates from 1730—came up against two major obstacles. The first was that nobility still carried weight; two examples are Anthony Ashley Cooper, 1st Earl of Shaftesbury (and patron of John Locke, a relationship of considerable ideological import), who was a Lord Proprietor of Carolina; and the Duke of York, of the colony that bears his name, acquired from the Dutch.[88] The second obstacle, in which Locke himself was also involved, was the matter of who should be represented in the assemblies—all freeholders and freemen, or only property holders of certain standing. Generally the first option won out, though with income and acreage holdings taken into account. In combination with the end of restrictions in New England, which had accorded rights only to members of the local Reformed (Calvinist) church, this meant that electoral suffrage was quite broad. Jews and Catholics were still excluded, except in Maryland, the only colony founded by Catholics.[89]

The institutional situation in the West Indies was more or less the same. The practice of establishing assemblies emerged simultaneously in Bermuda and Virginia. As J. H. Elliott has shown, authorization of assemblies and colonists' involvement was the only avenue for resolving governmental and fiscal problems.[90] Jamaica, which Cromwell captured from Spain as part of his expansionist Western Design, is illustrative in this respect. The assembly was established in the 1660s, and its early years were taken up with a long-running tax battle with the Privy Council (established in 1675 as the Lords of Trade and Plantations).[91] The exasperated monarchic government threatened more than once to impose Poynings' Law, a 1494 statute limiting the Irish Parliament from meeting without English approval.[92] The dispute lasted four decades, ending only in 1728–29, when the island's assembly agreed to make fixed payments to the crown. It was an exceptional agreement, according to Jack Greene, and it allowed Jamaica to develop a political system quite similar to those of other colonies.[93]

A few decades later, when the situation in North America had reached crisis proportions, the First British Empire's institutional machinery was well in place. In theory, the governor (who also was captain general) had full powers in accordance with imperial policy and was in charge of the colonial government. In practice, however, his capacities were limited by his distance from the imperial capital, the lack of a competent administration, and the organizational abilities of the locals, which forced him to continuously exercise a negative authority—in other words, he had to do whatever he could to avoid irritating the king's unhappy subjects. As a result, the assemblies essentially held almost all the power.[94] To start with, they could legislate, though again, only in theory; the governor's advisory council could amend their legislation, given that eventually the crown would have to assent. In the Caribbean, these were pure formalities until slavery became the main dispute; nobody questioned the elected chamber's jurisdiction.[95] But given the delicate balance of powers between locals and crown, it was never clear who had the last word on elections. As a result, appointments largely depended on pressure in London by local landed powers.

Figures such as the sugar plantation owner William Beckford, a member of William Pitt the Elder's circle, were key in this regard.[96] The assemblies also had high-profile agents in London, such as Benjamin Franklin of Pennsylvania, who handled finances, petitions, and demands from the colonies for two decades.[97] For many, this system was the only remedy for the defects of their virtual representation (in absentia) in the lower house of Parliament, to which they would never otherwise have access.[98]

As in the French and Iberian possessions, notables not only dominated the assemblies and local posts but also enjoyed the hegemony that came with a broad social consensus, from which thousands and thousands of slaves, servants, freemen of color, convicts, women, and vagabonds were excluded. In this context, works by the well-known writers Edward Long and Bryan Edwards played a role similar to that of the juridical and descriptive treatises in the French Antilles, discussed above.[99] Long was a committed slaveowner in Jamaica and highly knowledgeable about the world of sugar plantations.[100] He also was a tireless polemicist and an excellent historian with deep stores of knowledge to put behind his cause (his grandfather had been a member of its first assembly). He could envision Jamaica separate from the British empire but not separate from the world of slave plantations, from the "world of orders," as he put it.[101] A close follower of Locke, he believed that the Jamaican assembly, not the royal government, was "the right and inheritance of the people," and as a radical Whig he lay all the faults of despotic, aristocratic government at the feet of the crown.[102] He ceaselessly hurled insults at governors and councilors for having usurped the assembly's powers. Drawing on his endless knowledge of Jamaican and Caribbean society, he forcefully defended the notion of colonial particularity, the distinct and separate natures of English and Jamaican society. His *History of Jamaica* (1774), a direct defense of slavery and denigration of slaves, and among the first to introduce a veiled "racial" argument,[103] would become a basic sourcebook for generations of Jamaican landowners. His warnings and disdain for those "invested with power at discretion" vanished when it came to the absolute power in the hands of slave owners.[104] Meanwhile, in the metropolis, the antislavery movement gained ground in nonconformist and radical circles.

Bryan Edwards's *The History Civil and Commercial of the British West Indies* can be seen as a continuation of the work of his friend Long.[105] Published in 1793 in two volumes, it reflected the major changes the empire had undergone, among them the North American crisis and the ardent antislavery debate in England. Edwards was more moderate than Long in his approach, representing Caribbean Whiggism.[106] He was an advocate of a clear distinction between internal and external legislation, and in the case of the latter he argued in favor of colonial assemblies' autonomy and freedom from meddling by Westminster.[107] Unlike his counterparts in North America, Edwards believed that constitutional conflicts, and the social realities that lay beneath them, should be resolved through a new imperial pact. His racial attitudes were similar to Long's, but the possibility of an imperial agreement led him to accept the beginnings of what would be called the amelioration of the lives of slaves, an obvious act of interference by the metropolis.[108] Despite Long's and Edwards's admiration for English constitutional traditions, this was a delicate moment, given that, despite their similarities, metropolitan and Antillean societies were moving in very different directions. The growing importance of the House of Commons in eighteenth-century England was an outcome of popular politics within and outside of Parliament, despite limitations imposed by the franchise and electoral districting.[109] That transformation showed, as it had in some of the North American colonies, that a society dominated by free individuals had expectations and hopes and that a new middle class was on the rise. In the West Indies, in contrast, planters imposed sharper divisions between property owners in the assemblies and the growing number of people who served their interests.

The fault line of imperial stability would end up being the connection between North America and Britain. As Michael Braddick has so clearly demonstrated, the First British Empire never satisfactorily resolved the tension between local civility (which may be defined as material interests plus the English patriarchal culture) and the needs of the fiscal-military imperial state.[110] When competition among rival empires and conflicts on North American soil intensified in the second half of the eighteenth century, the contradiction became irreconcilable except in those places where colonial realities became too much for British colonists, requiring more protection from the Leviathan. In his in-depth study of the First Empire in North America, Jack Greene showed how opposition between slavery and free labor infiltrated areas where the development of slavery favored economic growth: in Chesapeake Bay, the Carolinas, and Georgia.[111] This division of labor, which Douglass North pointed to as one of the basic factors in the development of the Thirteen Colonies and the republic, provided North America with an extraordinary dynamism, which often collided with British interests.[112] Conflicts accumulated in the backcountry, areas of potential colonial expansion, regarding taxes imposed on commodities through the Navigation Acts, and there was competition with the Antilles and the Mediterranean and disagreements with the East India Company.

While the disputes added up, Parliament and the local assemblies remained unable to find ways of reforming their hierarchical relationship.[113]

Instead, that divided world would be the birthplace of the greatest transformation of the first empire's political traditions. The starting point was the presence in the colonies of freeborn Englishmen with inherent rights. This was the legacy that defined the empire of compatriots and that had lent form to institutions. This was the world that embraced British indentured servants while excluding them (along with African slaves), the world that Samuel Johnson would observe in his famous passage on Virginians where he sarcastically mentioned the contrast between words of liberty and the presence of the excluded. This Greco-Roman tension, so to speak, this tradition of freedom for equals, would undergo a radical transformation with the ideas of Locke and William Blackstone, who perfectly captured Americans' need to affirm possession of their continent, liberate themselves from the crown, and develop specific manifestations of freedom.[114] Those ideas became objectified around a dual ideological stance: the right to English common law no matter where the imperial subject happened to be, and the right to representative assemblies in their own territories. Neither formed part of the unwritten constitution of the monarchy. This balance between royal power and its legislative expression (through Westminster) was subject to dueling interpretations: either the imperial center's legislative supremacy was emphasized or the colonists' nonrenounceable autonomy was proclaimed. For decades, what Benjamin Franklin called the middle doctrine prevailed, which permitted a delicate balance between the two.[115] During the bitter debates over the Stamp Act, he wisely noted that Americans' freedoms had been established and solidified before Parliament's legislative reach had been expanded.[116] Of all the issues at stake, imperial defense and subsequent taxation were the most tangled and the least liable to be resolved through compromise. At its heart, this was a debate about obedience and sovereignty.

Despite rising tensions between the two sides, the notion of belonging to an empire that entailed mutual obligations weakened only very slowly. For decades, governors of the West Indies and the continental colonies continued governing, albeit with difficulties, in the framework of the inherited institutional system and mutual obligations that were more or less precisely enumerated. And yet, the system reached a crisis point in the mid-eighteenth century. Like its rivals, the British empire could not absorb the rising contradiction between its military and financial obligations and colonists' resistance to being held responsible for the part that was allegedly theirs.[117] And, again, as for its rivals, military engagement (during the War of Jenkins' Ear and, especially, the Seven Years' War, or French and Indian War) would prove fatal. The reasons were obvious; as John Brewer has explained, the fiscal-military state developed in response to the demands of war, intensifying pressure on disposable income.[118]

In this atmosphere of escalation, constitutional culture and the balance between local representation and state demands underwent momentous transformations. The periphery's desire that the center ease the pressure gave way to what we might call a desire to recover the previous century's practical autonomy. Indeed, the crown's weakness and the English revolutionary crisis permitted colonists to remain distant from metropolitan demands, with the possible exception of Cromwell's Western Design, already mentioned, and efforts to shore up New England's institutional framework, both of which failed in the medium run. After 1760, nothing was the same. The emergence of the Parliament of Westminster as the legislative force and director of all British politics was the key factor in the change, both in Britain and in relations with Ireland and the overseas colonies.[119] With the crown's more intrusive stance, the relative positions of colonial governors, their advisers, and their patronage were put into question both in North America and in the West Indies, and in the latter case the plantation owners, who dominated the assemblies, had to calculate very carefully indeed, for reasons that have already been made clear. But in North America consensus began to crumble, leaving a stark division between Tories, who wished to remain loyal to the throne at all cost, and the patriots. The schism at first did not affect general collective identification with the empire's ideological underpinnings: British identity, exclusion of native and enslaved people and their descendants, Protestantism, common law, and property-based broad suffrage.

These circumstances led to alterations in colonists' lives, especially where white British communities were the strongest. Measures taken in North America are well known: limitations on certain sectors of the export market, with Chesapeake tobacco being the most obvious; restrictions on illegal trade with other countries' Caribbean possessions; and increasing interest in the stability of the domestic frontier and, as a result, expansion beyond the Appalachians, with the 1763 Royal Proclamation Line placing large swaths of territory under military jurisdiction.[120] All this disturbed relations with the center, though none of it justified independence, and in any case the Caribbean possessions were equally affected. The measures imposed by Northern Secretary George Grenville (later prime minister) to repay the war debt were what pushed North American separatist leanings in new and highly dynamic directions.[121]

Colonial politics by then had become a torment for London. The increasingly aggressive assemblies had acquired more powers, and instead of acting to help governors divide fiscal responsibility and militia duties, they had managed to situate themselves right at the center of American and Caribbean political life. Even so, the hypertrophy did not necessarily make rupture or institutional change inevitable, though it certainly provided some of the necessary conditions.[122] Adding to their legislative capacity and influence, assemblies now were key political players, making governors highly uneasy.[123] In the face of their undisputed political centrality, imperial authorities generally applied the principle of nonrepugnancy when deciding if laws were coherent with those of England.[124]

The growing political importance of elected chambers was not simply the result of daily institutional or jurisprudential activities, but rather, the other way around; conflicts, at times irrelevant in and of themselves, ended up having an institutional impact. In those conditions, power and authority by definition were negotiated, given that the empire had no coercive powers. When it came down to it, the Thirteen Colonies and the West Indies followed different paths during negotiations to settle the Seven Years' War debt. On the American continent, the exceptional measures proved to be a calvary for governors; in the Caribbean, however, local leaders accepted the measures in the framework of their habitual negotiating.[125] One must keep in mind that the cost of maintaining an army on the continent went from 660,000 pounds sterling in 1749–55 to 5,489,000 pounds in 1756–63, an increase not found anywhere else.[126] Grenville's solutions for paying military expenses, most significantly the Stamp Act, were what catalyzed the constitutional conflict. On the one hand, the center invoked the right of the king-in-parliament to impose imperial legislation, while in the colonies it was clear that no taxation could be imposed without subjects' consent.[127] Treatise writers and political leaders tried to suggest that representation was virtual, but the argument generally was dismissed. Confidence was on the verge of collapse.

It is worth asking why the West Indies remained loyal while North America did not. They avoided direct involvement in the Seven Years' War, which they also did not have to pay for, and they were spared the propaganda war unleashed on the North American continent.[128] But the cost for the empire in money and lives was very high in the West Indies too (of the 89,000 British imperial soldiers sent there from 1793 to 1801, half died). Nevertheless, the war made it clear to the British (as well as to the French and Spanish) that plantation owners' loyalty depended on the empire's satisfying their most urgent needs, most especially getting products to market and protecting a society based on a large number of slaves. During the various wars, the British empire expanded considerably, attacking rival territories such as Havana (1762–63), Guadeloupe, Martinique, St. Lucia (all in 1794), and Saint-Domingue, the latter a preventive move in the face of a failed slave revolt.[129] So the loss of North American territory to some degree was compensated elsewhere by 1783,[130] the same year the British took the Spanish island of Trinidad, important not only because of its plantations but also because it was so close to the mainland, making it a center for contraband. Above all, the West Indies remained loyal because they needed protection from their enormous slave population, a point urgently driven home with the second slave war in Jamaica in 1795.[131] In all British possessions combined, 428,000 of the half million inhabitants were slaves. In 1830, the high-water mark for colonial slavery, there were 702,000 slaves and just 75,000 whites. In Jamaica, the largest of Britain's colonies, the slave population reached 100,000 in 1739; 180,000 in 1768; 210,000 in 1785; and 325,000 in 1810. During this entire period, the white population never grew past 30,000. Meanwhile, in Barbados, there were 42,000 slaves in 1710; 63,000 in 1770; and 83,000 in 1833, shortly before emancipation. During those same years, the white population was 13,000, 16,000, and 15,000, respectively.[132] Obviously, a siege mentality prevailed among the whites, who lived in permanent fear that events would follow the path of Haiti during the Revolution. But the West Indies were not entirely free of jurisdictional disputes with imperial powers; indeed, in 1766 Jamaica had a serious confrontation with Governor William Henry Lyttleton, who previously had served in South Carolina.[133] But the need for physical and economic protection, and assistance through measures such as the Molasses Act of 1733 and the Sugar Act of 1764, which were aimed at the competition (especially the French), help explain why the imperial consensus was not challenged during this revolutionary cycle.[134]

Some years ago, C. A. Bayly described in striking terms the horizons of a free Englishman born abroad, even somewhere where there was no English community of importance, in spaces that did not belong to the first empire—for example, Mughal India.[135] There, too, East India Company employees felt protected by their status as English or British, and as the company developed as a military-fiscal machine it reproduced many characteristics of the British model, including the ability to organize diplomacy and warfare. But as Bayly pointed out, the East India Company was never just another jurisdiction in India. As a surrogate power of the crown, it acquired a strong sense of sovereignty and the need to impose law on its employees and on the relationship between them and local powers, including the Royal British Navy. With each expansion of power, especially fiscal power, the company's sense of its own position and obligations was strengthened. So, in 1717, when Emperor Farrukhsiyar gave the East India Company trading powers and tax exemptions in Bengal, the company assumed that these new capacities included sovereignty.[136] Thus, the political and legal culture of the first empire was the antecedent of the extraordinary expansion of that idea of sovereignty as the East India Company became an autochthonous power starting in 1757.

So the Last Shall Be First, and the First Last

The empire created by Castile in the sixteenth and seventeenth centuries might seem the least likely candidate to grant representative rights to subjects scattered throughout crown dominions. But that would be a hasty conclusion. Spain had founded settlements in the Canary Islands and America more than a hundred years before its future rivals. Spain's presence in the New World was a clear outgrowth of its late-medieval social and political organization. Norms and patterns were exported across the ocean by successive waves of conquerors, settlers, functionaries, and churchmen. It was a world organized on the basis of law and rights of individuals and collectives; the law came from the crown of Castile, to which the Indies constitutionally belonged. One of the most fundamental of Castilian legal formulas was the establishment of a municipal council, or *cabildo*, whose existence was directly derived from the relationship between the monarch and his or her subjects.[137] The Indies and the Canaries (and, later on, the Philippines) were Castilian territories, but unlike the kingdoms of Navarre or Galicia, or the three kingdoms making up the Crown of Aragon, they did not possess representative institutions (Cortes). Castilian cities were the leading force in the Cortes until Charles V defeated the *comunero* rebels in 1520, a victory too early to fully explain the imposition of royal authority in the Indies in later periods.[138] But the defeat of the Castilian cities did not impede organizational models from being developed in the Indies; indeed, the law of the kingdom of Castile was extended to municipalities in conquered territories, and royal administration and institutions were quickly put in place.[139] Given that colonization by Castile was essentially a private affair, both militarily and financially, with the crown as shareholder and sovereign at the same time, it was essential that the monarch's delegated power be institutionalized.[140] It was equally vital that royal embodiment in the political figure of the viceroy and the judiciary be set up, as owners of all lands under the jurisdiction of Castile, no matter how far away, had the right to be heard by royal courts.[141] Thus, the various components of government in the Indies and the juridical structure underlying it took shape in a manner that was not always linear but was never arbitrary, following the ideological and cultural vectors of the peninsula: royal justice and law, a particular relationship (called the Real Patronato) between church and crown, and the rights of the king's Castilian subjects. Finally, two additional legal questions would emerge from the conquest: the rights of conquered peoples, the Indians; and particular rights held by settlers as a result of pacts with the monarchy, most notably the institution of the *encomienda*, which gave them jurisdictional rights over people. All this implied the construction of a political society that prolonged Castilian law and sovereignty, but with dramatic differences. They were kingdoms, and they were also colonies in the genuine meaning of the word.[142]

The empire was the product of private conquest and royal authority enacted through law, favors (*mercedes* and *gracias*) enumerated in the conditions (*capitulaciones*) of conquest, and the presence of royal administration on conquered territory. To quote legal historian José María Ots Capdequí, "America had to be reconquered nearly immediately after it was discovered. It was chiefly the bureaucratic bodies—the judges, prosecutors, courts, court reporters, notaries, and royal finance officials—who truly were behind this, shall we call it, second conquest, which was more political than military."[143] Until the late-eighteenth-century reforms and, on a different level, the Cortes of Cádiz in 1810–14, the imperial political and institutional framework really did not change. Jurisdiction lay at the center of the bureaucratic and tax capacities of a distant royal power. The crown moved quickly to populate that enormous and distant space with institutions and jurisdictions, in order to prevent any possible "feudalization" by *encomenderos* who had been given Indians in order to Christianize them.[144] This entailed affirmation of royal sovereignty, given that in societies with legislative pluralism, whoever has sovereignty can limit other jurisdictions. In this regard, the most important step was the development of legislation specific to the Indies, a list of laws and edicts whose purpose was not to replace Castilian legislation but rather to become part of it as a necessary component to account for the differences between the New World and the Old World. The *Recopilación de leyes de los reynos de las Indias* in 1680, for example, clearly stated this purpose and furthermore stated that Castilian law should follow the outlines established in the Laws of Toro (1505).[145] From there, casuistically based legislation would develop in parallel fashion on both sides of the Atlantic with one shared purpose.

With these distinctions, the Spanish American world was constituted on paper as an empire organized on the basis of law, with the *audiencias* occupying a central place. This is paradoxical, following as it did a period of tremendously vicious warfare during which indigenous peoples and their rulers were slaughtered. It was a paper empire in which jurists and magistrates were pillars holding up the entire institutional order. It also was marked by extraordinary juridical imagination, culminating in Juan de Solórzano Pereira's immense *Política indiana* (1648) and in the *Recopilación*.[146] The militia had less authority than the judiciary until the mid-eighteenth-century Bourbon militarization, when we begin noticing that the incipient and typical institutions of the fiscal-military state existed side by side with old practices and norms.[147] Conflicts between Spaniards and subject peoples were handled through legalistic quibbling and meticulous ceremony.[148]

The ubiquity of law and courts coexisted with the monarchy's undisguised concern that local interests might achieve other forms of representation. The crown asserted its authority in the colonies while at the same time curbing corporative representation on the peninsula. Law supplanted the politics of legislation of the king in the Cortes through normative institutions, a practice that had faded in Castile —in contrast to the intricate regulations prevailing in the Crown of Aragon, until they were abolished by military force after the War of the Spanish Succession.[149] As a result, the king reduced his political consideration for the Indies kingdoms, an institutional facade supposedly still operating in Europe. That posture was reaffirmed by the position of the king's Council of the Indies, which legislated (that is, governed) those territories; the council was always close to the king and far, far away from its American subjects. So, if the monarchy was a coherent political entity articulated around the notion of royal mystique and an organic juridical culture, political space was necessarily fragmented, giving the various territories originally belonging to it a certain degree of autonomy.[150] The distribution of power confirmed the unity of the whole. In short, in America and the Philippines, law (understood to mean political decision-making and the distribution of power) made up for distance, an inevitable consequence of the enormous breadth of this empire with roots in the late Middle Ages. In comparison with the constitutional crises involving Aragon, Catalonia, Naples, and Portugal, Castile's distance from America was crucial, more so than Britain's distance in 1640, 1659, or 1688.

In this context, it is easy to understand why the monarchy and its jurists were reluctant to grant representative capacities to American territories similar to those enjoyed (sometimes) by Spain's European territories. Nevertheless, on more than one occasion the crown considered establishing a Cortes in America. In 1611, for example, Viceroy Montesclaros wrote the Council of the Indies from Peru arguing against having a Cortes there, so someone must have proposed it.[151] In 1635, the viceroy of New Spain, for obvious fiscal reasons, was authorized to open bids for four offices of *procurador*, or member of the Cortes of Castile; candidates could be from New Spain, Guatemala, New Galicia, Santo Domingo, or the Philippines.[152] More than one hundred years later the idea came up again when tensions between Creoles and *peninsulares* were on the rise. The contrast between these realities and the colonial nature of the American world clearly affected American identity, though self-identification as Americans would have to wait. Spaniards in the New World both were and were not living in the same world as Spaniards at home; they were equal and different at the same time. Unlike empires of compatriots, the Spanish world in America could not function as a mimesis of the original, be it socially or politically or culturally. In Castile and the other kingdoms of the Hispanic Monarchy, there was no trace of other peoples who were suppressed from the thirteenth to the fifteenth centuries, and those who remained were reduced to excluded minorities on the verge of extinction. In any case, the notion of a united, diverse, exclusionary society vanished with the War of Granada (1568–71) and the well-known expulsions of the Jews in 1381 and 1492 and of the Moorish minority in 1609.[153] The Indies, in contrast to Spain, were not and could not be homogeneous. In the New World, ideological wars could not lead to expulsion and extermination; they had to remain on another plane so as not to undermine the social foundations of the colony.[154] The church would end up occupying a key position alongside the *audiencias* and judges in the construction of this new society of "castes," not in the old sense of the word but in a new sense indicating that obligations and spaces now were to be decided by a person's origin. There would be "two republics" in this society: one of Spanish rulers, the other of everyone else, including Indians, African slaves, and their descendants.[155] Indians, often called "small souls," would always be in the majority. Paternalism by the crown therefore was a necessary condition for a society that was simultaneously colonial and organically unitary.

This is the proper context for considering Spanish colonial rulers' voice and that of their descendants in the most vast empire of its time, and the most truly colonial Atlantic empire. In this regard, the deliberative site above all others was the Real Acuerdo, the plenary of each *audiencia* where the viceroy and magistrates with political, legislative, and jurisdictional capacities voted. It was a space of reconciliation for the administration of justice and government and for metropolitan and local interests (including those of Indians, who had their own path of access). Authority there was the expression of territorial power and the very substance of organization in America. There, viceroys and captains general met with magistrates, lawyers, judges, and prosecutors to work out legal matters both transcendental and particular, along with the ever-important protocol involved in the networks of obligations and rights. Political practice in the Indies was such that *audiencias* had the last word over viceroys and lesser authorities and even issued final performance reports at the end of their tenure. They furthermore managed deliberative and jurisdictional relations with *cabildos*, towns, and the *república de indios*.[156]

In the absence of the viceroy, the political-juridical *audiencias* would assume full powers—an indication of their independence—and at times they appointed judges (*oidores*) to manage key matters such as probate. In such cases, judges clearly governed, and there were no theoretical restrictions. Delegation along these lines could also be more permanent, in specialized areas of jurisprudence. Among the most important of these were cases for the treasury (*hacienda*), the essential and most stable nucleus of power in the Indies; another example was that of "protectors" and "courts" for Indians, one of the facets of government that triggered the most jurisdictional disputes because it affected the crown, the *audiencias*, and the church. While the Amerindian population was being decimated, the crown, in tune with the larger doctrinal debate regarding the condition of the Indians, tried to figure out mechanisms for defending them. The job of "defender of the Indians" was given to Bartolomé de las Casas in 1516, who was succeeded by Juan de Zumárraga in 1529. The doctrinal debate lost steam, but the job remained, partly because its presence helped channel demands by lawyers handling suits between *encomenderos* (the "lords of the Indians") and Spaniards in general.[157] That was the case when Francisco de Toledo, viceroy of Peru and the great architect of imperial policy, in 1574 approved regulations for the General Defender of Indians in his territory.[158] In New Spain matters were always quite different, starting from the early days when Viceroy Antonio de Mendoza tried to establish a specialized jurisdiction and lasting until the 1590s during the tenure of Luis de Velasco, who definitively formalized a special court with specific attributions (excluding criminal law, which remained in the hands of the *audiencias*).[159]

Monarchic and imperial power in America was formed along these intricate but logical institutional gridlines. Local power was constructed similarly, and administered by *audiencias* and *cabildos* reserved for Spanish

Americans. Native Americans, whose political structures had been de-capitated, were governed by figures such as *señores principales* or *señores de Indios*, especially regarding tax and labor obligations.[160] Transactions between officers of the *audiencias* and local institutions were extremely important. Sale of offices—the formalization of access to the highest decision-making posts for Indian affairs—was especially crucial, as was the replication of this transaction to the Council of the Indies when high functionaries of the *audiencias* were promoted to the council.[161] Sale of offices was a fund-raising move of desperation that had been used over and over since the times of Charles V in the early sixteenth century. But the practice truly took off during the reign of his son, Philip II, and expanded from there to affect political life in Castile and America through the end of the seventeenth century. The practice was similar to that of other European monarchies plagued by the same problems of war and finance.[162] Sale of of-fices regulated professional life and meant candidates needed to have fam-ily support or protectors. In theory, jurisdictional posts were exempt from sale so as to keep the royal judiciary out of inevitable venality disputes. But here, too, rules could be bent, and we find the very seventeenth-century solution of not exactly selling the office but rather the "position," that is, ac-cess to the office, which implied risk for the candidate's family, who would be left without the post if he were to be disqualified or die. Aside from these complications, the crown began to actively sell posts starting in 1687, a mo-ment of serious financial difficulties. The value of the top-level political and juridical posts in the Indies ran from 2,000 to 20,000 pesos, depending on their level and location, from Lima to the Philippines. If colonists wanted the posts, they also had to pay for a trip to Madrid, where they would have to remain until they got what they were seeking.

This was the context in which Creoles and locals (a necessary distinc-tion) sought positions on councils and courts, and it was the subject of a classic study by Mark Burkholder and D. S. Chandler.[163] Starting with the case of Miguel Núñez de Sanabria, a resident of Lima who, thanks to a special dispensation in 1687, was appointed judge (*alcalde del crimen*) in the criminal court there, the writers traced how judicial offices began being sold on a massive level.[164] The practice became permanent espe-cially after 1693, when "sons of the fatherland" received permission to buy posts in their own districts.[165] After the War of the Spanish Succession, Americans' access to posts increased as the crown weakened and the debt rose. That is why in the 1720s the Council of the Indies began considering whether to limit Americans' access to public posts, which the council be-lieved had only encouraged corruption and ineptitude.[166] In subsequent decades, the debate would subtly edge toward discussions of candidates' alleged ethnicity—that is, if they were *peninsulares* or *radicados* (the word *Creole* had various formulations, but none was used by Creoles themselves, so as not to damage their prestige)—and this was the context in which the idea of imperial administration exclusively in the hands of peninsulars began taking shape. From the vantage point of the center, reducing local presence meant increasing Spain's influence in America, recolonizing America, or, to use the language used in the previous discussion of other empires, constricting effective autonomy. From this perspective, propertied Spanish Americans were as liable to be partial as were magistrates who married the daughters of rich and powerful local families. The influence of the "sons of the fatherland" diminished in the second half of the eighteenth century, but the presence of the *radicados*, disguised in one way or another, remained to the end of the empire.

In the end, the key question was the degree of influence that "people of quality" could have on their respective local corporative bodies and supralocal governmental instances such as the *audiencias*. The crown struggled in vain to control access to these bodies by restricting *cabildo* memberships to descendants of conquerors and the first generation of settlers.[167] Nevertheless, fiscal needs and matters of public order meant these restrictions often were not followed, undermining the crown's ability to limit access; this was the case, for example, with open town meetings (*cabildos abiertos*), an old Castilian tradition that allowed everyone to attend meetings on certain occasions. As Anthony MacFarlane showed for New Spain and Sergio Serulnikov showed for Charcas, when the empire began showing signs of exhaustion, the open town meetings became deliberative and identity-forming protagonists.[168]

City councils and courts of law were where Americans began using their voice and weighing their interests. As in the other empires, the top authorities, in this case viceroys and captains general, struggled mightily to impose their authority and the imperial priorities that were their mandate. But, lacking military force and trapped in the legislative and jurisdictional web of monarchic affairs at a time when the monarchy was extremely weak, top authorities rarely actually had much authority in the face of the array of social powers in the hands of locals and Indians. Venality in theory greased the wheels of empire, but in fact it was attracting interests of the opposite sort. And the close relations between local powers and the church, whose charitable works and establishments functioned as colonial banks, made things even more difficult. Years ago John Leddy Phelan lucidly described this situation as a combination of flexibility and authority, the prevailing formula until the Bourbon Reforms of the later eighteenth century, which were aimed precisely at destroying the model.[169] Sale of offices and the exclusion of Americans as a means of holding on to administrative control would be joined by a new administrative model, fueled by economic and demographic growth, that introduced fiscal measures similar to those of Spain's rivals and encouraged forms of government that broke with the old secular balance.[170] This was a badly designed administrative revolution in the hands of politicians who were hardly exemplary when it came to handling public funds and interested above all in short-term gains.[171]

And the reforms were incomplete. A new class of officials, the intendants, undercut viceroys' authority over militia and administration without actually dismantling the old power system or destroying strong local roots.[172] In many cases, the reforms were not even implemented in time, setting off new conflicts in societies that were highly complex (owing to their truly colonial nature).[173] Here the problem was less the absence of formal representation than the quality and trustworthiness of transactions between Spanish officials and vested interests in America.[174] One example was tax collection, in which Indian tributaries suffered increases in their obligations.[175] Another example was the nightmare of the *castas pardas* (free people of color, in British terminology), who made a return appearance at the end of the Spanish empire when one would have thought that the long-ago religious arguments for pure blood had expired.[176] Though, in the seventeenth and eighteenth centuries, it was church and family who watched over and controlled *limpieza de sangre*, the state's involvement throughout society and the economy complicated matters.[177] Subject to new census rules based on ethnic distinctions and militias based on ethnicity, the population mobilized around notions of identity, and once that Pandora's box was open, there was no going back.[178] The degree to which deep unrest by free blacks, mulattos, and Indians starting in the 1780s and 1790s ignited Creole resentment against the empire's institutions is a matter of debate to this day.[179]

A World in Ruins

Between the Seven Years' War (1756–63) and the Napoleonic Wars (1803–15), every European monarchic empire collapsed. During that long period, warfare, invasions, and popular uprisings seemed to merge into one general conflict whose aim was to resolve imperial hegemony as well as settle relations between states and privileged colonial groups. Given this instability, it proved impossible to promote a new fiscal-military state capable of interfering in the societies it governed without also accepting involvement by newly emergent social sectors. Through revolutions and reforms, these emergent social interests blazed trails and imposed means of representation and political participation, meanwhile keeping alive many features of the old-regime way of ruling (the cult of monarchy, aristocratic titles, heavy symbolism, and court ceremonies). That process, full of twists and turns, culminated at the end of the nineteenth century. Among the transformations of that era was a total reconfiguration of the relationship between the state and new social groups that appeared during the revolutionary period. Though monarchies and aristocracy marked a continuity with the old order, relations between political and social powers had most certainly shifted in a new direction.

The greatest paradox was that the mid-eighteenth-century objective of freeing the state from the aristocracy and subjecting populations to administrative controls and intrusion for military and financial purposes came to fruition only with the consolidation of the liberal state. In other words, the old monarchic and aristocratic power structure could not resist its own program. It found itself having to make pacts with bourgeois capitalists, accept new forms of national legitimacy, and move away from the old arguments of privilege and blood. By the mid-nineteenth century, the process was complete. The system of power and honor sometimes referred to as the Old Regime, which lasted until 1914, functioned according to arguments that had little in common with the previous century.

As interstate competition in the eighteenth century hastened the arrival of the fiscal-military state, the conflicts that would end up ruining the empires took place both at the center and on the periphery.[180] Interactions and conflicts between the metropolis and the colonies were constant, and, naturally, had unpredictable results. The war of 1756–63 showed that monarchical states could not manage at all without getting into colonial pockets.[181] Reforms by the British (most notably the Stamp Act), the French (tariffs), and the Iberians (the Bourbon Reforms in Spain and the Pombaline Reforms in Portugal) were all aimed at collecting more money from overseas communities or through commerce between the metropolis and the colonies.[182] Colonial financial contributions were indispensable for imperial defense, whose costs to maintain were increasing at a spectacular rate. Otherwise, royal subjects in the metropolis would have to pay a greater share, and as a result the chances of internal crisis would also have risen. But there were other consequences of the wars that were just as important as how to share military costs. One was the drawing of new borders and the exchange of territories that undercut colonists' vision of their world as well as their idea about the protection they were owed in compensation for living in contact with very different populations. Such cases in America included negotiations over the Viceroyalty of Río de la Plata, French Louisiana, and Nouvelle France during and after the Seven Years' War. Beyond America we have the liquidation of French interests in southern India as well as the invasion of Manila (responding to the invasions of Havana and Trinidad) and its subsequent return by the British, bringing about a total transfiguration of the old colonial order there. The Royal Proclamation of 1763 in North America marked the start of the Thirteen Colonies' disassociation from the imperial colonial perspective, with obvious results. With that in mind, we can form two conclusions, which will be explored throughout the following chapters. First, war was the factor that changed the nature of the state. The changes were perceived and experienced both by Europeans at home and by their compatriots in the colonies; they all understood what was happening to the Leviathan. Second, just as societies established themselves on the periphery amid all the conflict, imperial states were transformed despite the conflicts (in Spain, the hunger riots in 1766; in London, the Gordon Riots in 1780; the uprisings all over Paris in 1789). The cycle of revolutions that began in Philadelphia in 1776 and found its way through Paris, Madrid, and Lisbon points to the boundaries of this world that now lay in ruins. At the same time, these events, along with wars on other continents, were defining a new sort of state and a new sort of empire.

The revolutionary cycle showed that structures of power that had appeared in the eighteenth century, breaking up the old equilibrium among the various parts of composite monarchies, led to a new state model, and also to war and revolution. The new fiscal-military state, with ambitions to rule the world, diminished or threatened intermediate institutions that previously had moderated the exercise of royal authority. Tax-collecting and economic policies aimed at stimulating trade on terms favorable to the state were a notorious source of conflict. The crisis of 1776–83 made it clear to contemporaries that colonial societies had grown up, had political rights, and were not going to give in to force. Their revolution was based on ideas of freedom, as opposed to the will of the monarch, which could only be interpreted as the complete overthrow of the authoritarian imperative of the fiscal-military state at the service of the crown. The new community of interests (the old, reformed nation or the newly invented one) would take its place, filling in for the loyalty that had held the monarchical empires together. And the British experience would be repeated again and again—by France, the Netherlands, Spain, and Portugal.

CHAPTER TWO

The Collapse of Imperial Constitutions

THE ATLANTIC REVOLUTIONS—North America in 1775, France in 1789, Spain in 1810, Portugal in 1820—signaled the end of monarchic empires and the start of a new political cycle. Monarchic loyalty—the heavy weight of jurisdictional power of magistrates and legislative pluralism, with its mix of paternalism, privilege, and repression—gave way to a world in which the whole of historically constituted rights and virtual representation (if it existed) allowed for representation (singular, not plural) in assemblies that demanded that legislation and its execution be joined. In other words, legislative bodies wished to impose their sovereignty.[1] A subject with rights yielded to a citizen-elector who exercised the right of political representation alongside compatriots without, obviously, losing his status as a subject of the state. No one could escape that great transformation, which lasted until 1830, that great upheaval that shook America from north to south and whose echoes reached African coasts, India, Southeast Asia, and the Spanish Philippines.[2] Not even Britain, the most victorious of empires and the axis of the anti-Napoleonic coalitions, could avoid adapting to the spirit of the times or avoid the need for major internal reforms.

During the revolutionary cycle, there were two options for imperial continuity; two possible heirs or alternatives to the old monarchic culture of loyalty (which had never disappeared), patronage, and co-optation around which both the metropolis and its offshoots revolved. The first of the two options was the constitution of an empire of compatriots who were bound by some uncertain notion of equal rights; this was the possibility first tried out in countries that led the revolutionary changes.

Everywhere revolutionaries called on the populations of empires for their cooperation, solidarity, and unity. The second option involved transforming old-regime statutes and institutions created through accumulation—generally casuistically, though not arbitrarily, being that they were born of the same juridical culture—into truly colonial constitutions, that is, ones that distinguished more openly between spheres of rights and representation in the metropolis and in other worlds that, while under metropolitan sovereignty, did not form part of it. Both possibilities—the novelty of an empire of compatriots and likewise a reformist continuity—failed in the Atlantic world. The latter possibility did not fail, however, in empires that were far away or on the periphery of the liberal and revolutionary transformations that defined the Atlantic core, and the imperial nation would launch its brilliant international career from the ashes of that dual failure, which shone a light for contemporaries in the late eighteenth century. This chapter examines the process leading from the crisis of monarchic empires to the collapse of national empires, which provided the necessary conditions for the emergence of what we define as the imperial nation: the combination of a community of metropolitan citizens at home plus special formulas for colonial spaces abroad or at home.

All these distinctions between monarchic empires, imperial constitutions, reforms leading to colonial constitutions, constitutional regressions, and, finally, imperial nations is not simply wordplay, which is the worst sort of indulgence for a historian. On the contrary, appropiate concepts and definitions are crucial in order to shed light on nineteenth-century revolutionary transformations. At the outset, we shall examine why "imperial constitutions"—written and arbitrated for all territories belonging until then to monarchic empires—collapsed amid the political crisis that shattered the Atlantic world and beyond for some decades. It should be clear by now that the idea of "imperial constitutions" does not refer to strictly juridical-political artifacts but to implicit pacts that made those constitutions possible for the sake of the revolutionary notion of equality, and/or to preserve consensus regarding unity of the old political spaces. The brief nature of this political and constitutional moment in no way makes it less significant, either in the Atlantic world or beyond.

The Family of Imperial Constitutions

The logic of imperial constitutions dominated politics for two decades in the Atlantic and its prolongations toward Africa, India, and the Philippines. The family in question comprised constitutions with four

characteristics. The first was an explicit intent to embrace the entire monarchic sphere passed down from the Old Regime—"unité de la République ou la mort," in the exasperated words of the most radical phase of the
French Revolution.[3] Second, this would be done under one constitution
and one single system of rights. Third, even when constitutions were designed so as to consolidate political and representative space, some social
groups were still excluded. And fourth, this more or less explicit exclusion
usually included slaves and African descendants, Chinese descendants in
the Spanish Philippines, and non-Catholics in the Iberian world—which
led to inevitable tensions within a framework of revolutionary rights that
guaranteed equality before the king or the republic. These were the seeds
that doomed this genre of constitutions.[4] From this point of view, constitutions that we might call imperial constitute a small and rather short-
lived family, indeed. But though they were few in number, their influence
was immense, as numbers mattered less than the transcendence of the
cases and their impact worldwide. They were one of the principal instruments for the circulation of revolutionary ideas at the turn of the century.

During the revolutionary period, imperial constitutions coexisted with
other sorts of constitutions that were decidedly colonial (and/or colonialist),
at times top-down transformations of old-regime systems of government.
How to distinguish one from the other? With the simplicity that justifies
such elementary taxonomies, the most basic distinction was that while imperial constitutions tried to impose one single legislative framework on all
the king's or republic's free subjects wherever they were, the colonial versions by definition were plural systems of laws and practices, distinguishing
what was valid for free individuals in the metropolis and abroad and what
was valid for those who lived in the colonies and overseas. [5]

If we wish to place these constitutional models back where historical
processes cast them in the first place, in 1780–1830, we can see that approval of written constitutions was the only known way of preserving the
unity of the old monarchic empires. In this sense, multiplicity of rights and
representative capacities suddenly turned into the idea of the general will
of a new political subject who emerged out of the crisis, a subject those
rights emanated not from the logic of (old) constitutions but rather from
the subject's very existence, from the variations and nuances of natural
law.[6] As stated in the definition of the word *égalité* in the *Encyclopédie* by
the great scholar Louis de Jaurcourt, natural equality is "that which exists
among all men by the very essence of their nature."[7] This transmutation
of old rights into the "natural" logic of the freeborn individual, who was
the subject of the U.S. Declaration of Independence as well as the French

Declaration of the Rights of Man and of the Citizen, lay at the heart of the universal claims of the first constitutions, their rise and their fall; the "triumph and death of natural law," to quote Florence Gauthier.[8] If individual rights did not rest on historical foundations, then the only other acceptable limitations were the frontiers of the old monarchic empire, where decisions would be made regarding representation of this individual now freed of his chains.[9] In any case, in this world born of monarchic empires, still a far cry from the fragmentation of the modern nation, the community of citizens was simply the sum total of those who lived within borders drawn by kings of the past. The nation existed where a community of countrymen had once been formed. Sometimes these cultural limits went beyond the obvious because the community included some who in principle did not respond to that cultural archetype. The explosion of the Atlantic slave trade in the eighteenth century, beyond providing clear benefits for labor markets and plantation economies, resulted from the fact that it clearly marked who was in and who was out of that world of rights legitimized by belonging, custom, and law. And slaves and their descendants were not the only ones excluded from representation and rights; there were foreigners, gypsies, migrants, and members of minority religions. Even taking these considerations into account, one paradox of the crisis was that the inherited nation-empire was not marked off by the coasts, mountain ranges, or rivers of Europe, but rather, pertained to towns on the other side of the ocean, mostly though not entirely in the New World. For that reason, when French and North American revolutionaries saw borders (in the latter case, the British empire across the ocean), they saw blurred borders demanding that their ideas be spread to the other side. The limits of the empires of freedom, the bulwark against European despotism, were inclusive in the interior and also expansionist toward places as remote as they were undefined. Here the republican ideal can be understood as the constant reproduction of the revolutionary model of equal rights for all. If political brothers were scattered among the continents, it was this universalist logic that gave birth to nation-empires of which imperial constitutions were the most polished ideological expression.[10] For the same reason, their failure led to the rise of nations with colonies, as well as new nations where colonies once stood, which together were one identical expression of the ideal of equality. The breakup of the Spanish empire is the best example of this, with no hope for continuity between the attempt to proffer a constitutionally guaranteed common framework and the continual problem of a system of rights (and exclusions), both in the nineteenth-century empire and in the new American republics.[11]

No constitution, of course, is the result of one single ideology or a mere synthesis, for better or for worse, of prevailing ideas. All were grounded on common underpinnings of patrician, aristocratic, and paternalistic householder values that crossed divides between countries, regimes, and religions all over the world. In this sense, all the constitutions approved in the years we are studying marked fragile transitions between juridical-constitutional systems and the stimuli and limits imposed by complex realities. Clear evidence of this assertion lies with the imperial constitutions themselves, at least in their intention to cross metropolitan boundaries and social parameters. How many were there? The family had the following members: North America in 1783, France in 1793 (not applied) and 1795, Spain in 1812 (and to some degree the Napoleonic Bayonne Statute of 1808), Portugal in 1822, and the *charte octroyée* of Portugal in 1826, which did not affect the crown's former American territories but did include those in Africa and Asia. Seven in all; a modest family whose importance lay in the expansion of the ideas of rights and political representation and/or republican (sometimes) and democratic ideals.

Filling out the picture by looking not just at the light but also at the shadows, how many colonial constitutions were there, almost simultaneously? France in 1791 and 1799 (Year VIII); Holland in 1798, never formally approved (modeled on the French version of 1795[12] and entirely off-limits to the colonies [Article 231] for fear of a slave revolt in Curaçao);[13] and all the rest that followed the ideological matrix of Napoleon's Year VIII constitution—the first to explicitly separate metropolis from colony—such as those of Spain and Portugal in 1837 and 1838, respectively, which closed the cycle.[14] All these significantly altered the dynamics that had governed the progress of the constitutional family discussed earlier. Britain after U.S. independence should be placed within these coordinates, given that the ideas of representation, sovereign nation, and specialness can be found throughout the development of the Second British Empire. The United States, so densely unitary in 1783 and so inclined to make exceptions later on, also would end up combining domestic federal development with the rules of specialness for those assimilated within its sovereignty but excluded from the community of rights defined and upheld by the Constitution.

The Universality of Natural Law

The most famous and enduring of written constitutions, that of the United States in 1783, is a full-fledged declaration of universalism and empire. It postulates a new world order based on pluralism and uniqueness. A new political body was being established that was the continuation of the monarchic empire in the New World, whose only territorial limits were those imposed by its own institutions. This continuity is often not taken sufficiently into account or is considered only from the vantage point of intellectual foundations (Locke's *Second Treatise of Government*, of course, but also Blackstone's institutional tradition).[15] The ubiquitous Thomas Jefferson unequivocally and quite rightly defined this continuity as the "empire of liberty," an empire that would unremittingly reproduce republican liberty and institutions as far away as Panama, if needed.[16] The new republic's fears led it to secure its future throughout a continent it considered its own, expanding across the Appalachians, defeating the remaining Tory pockets in the South, and buying large swaths of land from France and Spain. The best example of this imposition of a general idea onto territory governed by Spanish and French law was the 1803 Louisiana Purchase, signed by Jefferson (once again), who was serving his first presidential term, and Napoleon's emissaries. This was the fulfillment of the ideal of the universal republic, organized along federal lines but unitary in its exemplary institutional balance and in its proselytizing republican ethos, which made it impossible to think of territorial acquisitions as colonies.

The early Republic was very cautious about the universality of the message of freedom and equality that the Declaration of Independence proclaimed to be a self-evident truth. The framers of the Constitution discussed some of these early doubts extensively, especially those having to do with slaves and Indians. Many such exclusionary feelings were made explicit in the first Naturalization Act of March 1790, which preserved American citizenship for "free white people" of "good character." Slaves were practically invisible in the written Constitution, the tip of the constitutional iceberg. Slavery was outlawed in the North and legalized in the South, and the Northwest Ordinance of 1787 provided that new states would be free of slavery, an agreement that prevailed until 1820, though in fact it was applied in territorial terms to allow slavery in the new Southern states.[17] In theory, only territories in which slavery already existed could be incorporated as states under the same conditions as those places that had continued colonial slavery—a fiction that allowed slavery's continual expansion until the California crisis of 1848.[18]

The Three-Fifths Compromise of the Constitutional Convention, by which two-fifths of the slaves (referred to as "numbers" or "fugitives") simply were not counted, was a means of determining membership in the House of Representatives. The sphere of equality thus included the categorization of slaves as a "foreign nation" that could be eliminated, as

Jefferson had said, and this stance was later adopted also by Abraham Lincoln and the antislavery Free-Soilers who defended republican unity against the South.[19] Citizenship belonged to free persons of economic means, which included women and free people of color. These groups were excluded from electoral rolls in the decades following independence. On the eve of the Civil War, only Massachusetts (where slavery was illegal and black people were scarce) continued including blacks in the electoral rolls.

Indians, meanwhile, were divided into two large groups. Those who lived in territories now belonging to states and who were taxpayers would be included in the electoral rolls and would have citizenship. But those tribes considered as foreign nations (falling under the jurisdiction of international law after Chief Justice John Marshall's 1831 decision in *Cherokee Nation v. Georgia*, which was unevenly implemented) would, paradoxically, be subject to the federal government. Republican unity thus prolonged the logic of the prior inclusion/expulsion paradigm. As a result, signing treaties with the Indians was reserved for Congress. The Republic continued the long tradition of treaties with Indian nations that had been instituted by the British, though without the humanitarian gloss of the latter, culminating with the 1763 royal proclamation that attempted to separate colonized territories from those in the hands of the natives. Thus, the U.S. Constitution is an example of how universalist and unitary foundations of an imperial constitution were transformed *mutatis mutandis* into a genuine colonial constitution, with special formulas allowing for local circumstances but without modifying the basic text. The institutional development of the nation easily absorbed slavery in some states and two categories of treatment (exclusion or inclusion) of Indians. From the European perspective, such a situation was unheard of; in Europe, imperial constitutions gave way to genuinely colonial texts whose articles regulated the bases of colonial specialness.

Unlike the United States—or, even more so, Spain, Portugal, and France—Britain never adapted to the demands of that model and therefore cannot be included in the imperial family proper. There are two reasons for this: first, the imperial crisis of 1776–83 mostly took place on the periphery and did not endanger the stability of metropolitan institutions. This was not the case in North America, which broke away, nor in France, Spain, and Portugal, where the crises were first metropolitan and then reached the overseas territories. Second, the British empire was the overall winner of the period between the Seven Years' War and the Napoleonic Wars.[20] Nevertheless, the gravity of American independence made Britain seriously question its own strategy, with solutions that are best understood in light of what happened in the other cases. The conditions underlying imperial constitutions—the desire to preserve inherited political space, ceding rights in the framework of a unitary ethos—affected winners and losers alike in the revolutionary cycle. Here the taxonomies that we mentioned earlier matter less than determining what was in play in quite distinct contexts.

Imperial recovery took place in three directions. First was the reinforcement of basic political and military structures, particularly the colonial governorship (both a political and a military post)—the proconsular authority that dominated imperial history until the twentieth century.[21] The second direction of simultaneously strategic importance and adamant denial in this hypothetical march toward an imperial constitution was the reaffirmation of Westminster as a legislative chamber for the entire empire. This jurisdiction expanded with the integration of the Irish Protestant minority in 1802, the Catholic Relief Act of 1829, and later, after the 1832 Reform Act permanently eliminated the lobbies serving the interests of the Caribbean and East India Company planters.[22] The consolidation of the United Kingdom and the end of virtual representation for loyal colonists went hand in hand. The third direction toward what I have called imperial recovery comprised a series of measures aimed at mitigating the decline of the idea of shared empire. In this context I will mention three important contributing factors. The first was the 1778 Taxation of Colonies Act, by which Parliament, anxious to mollify North Americans during the war, waived its right to tax colonies and territories. This measure, which was of utmost importance in the subsequent definition of the Second British Empire, though the course would be "corrected" decades later, when imperial defense costs were transferred to the possessions. The second contributing factor, or process, was the transformation of abolitionism, when what had been almost exclusively an activity of the Protestant churches became state doctrine—a transformation that, according to Christopher Brown, was the only way to rehabilitate the empire amid revolution.[23] Abolitionism also constituted a frontal attack on the established interests in the West Indies and Mauritius. And the third factor leading to the formation of the imperial constitution was the application of the theory of imperial trusteeship, which was articulated by Edmund Burke during the crises of North America and the East India Company and brought about the impeachment of its governor general, Warren Hastings.[24] This theory, though applied irregularly and always subject to local conditions, established the rules that good government must respect in territories without representative institutions; it was seen as the moral foundation for an imperial politics that could instill confidence in subjects, be they European or not, and create ties of affection among all lands under the crown's sovereignty.

The inclusive logic of imperial constitutions weighed heavily in the three remaining cases: France, Spain, and Portugal. The events leading to the first of the French constitutions (September 3, 1791), entailed the untangling of many dilemmas. Among these were the dissonances between Anglophiles, who wished to retain a supposed constitution of the kingdom, and *les américains*, who wanted to reestablish the body politic entirely[25]; between the exaltation of the citizen (who barely appears in the U.S. Constitution) and the insidious distinctions between active and passive citizens; and the political puzzle of what to do with the colonies. As we saw earlier, the rich French Caribbean colonies, Saint-Domingue in particular, had for some time been demanding autonomy along English lines, with assemblies, but their autonomy also would protect slavery.[26] Article 1 of the Constitution of 1791 provided that colonies would be separate from the metropolis and that a decision on representation would come at a later date. This exclusion reappeared more rigorously in Title VII, Article 8, which stated two very important things: "Les colonies et possessions françaises dans l'Asie, l'Afrique et l'Amérique, quoiqu'elles fassent partie de l'Empire français, ne sont pas comprises dans la présente Constitution [French colonies and possessions in Asia, Africa, and America, regardless of whether they form part of the French empire, are not included in this Constitution]." Easy to say, but impossible to enforce. From the very start, Saint-Domingue colonists, standing in the visitors' gallery at the National Assembly, demanded they be included. They wanted to be wherever decisions about their future were going to be made and were determined that those decisions not alter the foundation of their productive system, which was slavery. This was the moment, after all, when serious discussions were under way concerning the limits of the colonial arrangement between the crown and the merchants, shippers, and port authorities. For the Antilles and the Mascarenes, the most important tasks were to impede freemen of color from rising up the social ladder and to halt the circulation of abolitionist propaganda from the Société des Amis des Noirs; for the metropolis, however, the main task was to keep the colonists down. The collapse of the monarchy and the Spanish-English invasion of the French Antilles brought about a crisis on the plantations, the militarization of freemen of color, and, thanks to a complete vacuum of power, self-emancipation of the slaves in the summer of 1791. From then on everything would change, both there and everywhere else in the New World.

The period between the French constitutions of June 24, 1793 (Year I), and August 22, 1795 (Year III)—the former under the republican Convention and the latter under the Directory—encapsulates the political transformation of French colonial space.[27] These were both genuinely imperial constitutions, in that they did not differentiate metropolitan from colonial space; although the former, never applied, was radical-democratic and the latter, known as the Thermidorian Reaction, was liberal.[28] The former established the basis for universal suffrage (including freed slaves), while the latter above all proclaimed the rights of property, law, and order. Both were equally invested in the indivisible unity of the republic beyond metropolitan borders. The 1793 Constitution, suspended after a month with the state of exception and then the Terror, which we will return to in the following chapter, did not specify how it would be applied. On the contrary, Article 1 declared that the French Republic was *une et indivisible*, a statement that would become part of future French constitutions, though many introduced surreptitious distinctions among territories that undermined the very meaning of the phrase. But in 1793 there was no mention at all of territorial differences except insofar as the naturalization of foreigners in France was concerned (Article 4). In short, rights, norms, and institutions were one and the same for all in the nation of citizens.

Article 18 of the Declaration of the Rights of Man and of the Citizen, from the 1793 constitution, reads as follows: "Tout homme peut engager ses services, son temps; mais il ne peut se vendre, ni être vendu; sa personne n'est pas une propriété aliénable. La loi ne reconnaît point de domesticité; il ne peut exister qu'un engagement de soins et de reconnaissance, entre l'homme qui travaille et celui qui l'emploie." [29] This can, of course, be read as an affirmation of the universality of citizenship on metropolitan soil and the end of lordship over domestic servants,[30] and it marks the first positive affirmation of universal male suffrage (for those over twenty-one) and eligibility for public posts. It can be seen also as an expression of the desire to integrate freed slaves within the nation, to "constitutionalize general freedom." Slavery was always the other side of the citizenship coin, both in ancient times and during the Revolution, and especially in societies where it was of prime importance.[31] Enthusiasm for inclusiveness did not require such sublime pretensions. Indeed, the message of unity seemed the only way of protecting national sovereignty from foreign invasion while at the same time ensuring slaves' loyalty to the Republic—even those who, under the leadership of Toussaint Louverture, had agreed to serve under the Spanish flag. The liberator's famous *volte-face* took place in May 1794, permitting reorganization of whites loyal to the Convention, freemen of color, and freed slaves under the authority of the Republic. In other words, the written constitution, in hibernation because of the Terror, would not be applied; the unwritten constitution would rely on the social consensus that pointed to a break with the old monarchic-colonial constitutional formulas of 1791.[32] It extended alliances beyond metropolitan soil with freed slaves and *gens de couleur libres* despite colonists' reticence, while at the same time casting rebellious peasants, royalists, and Girondins outside the legal framework.[33]

The Directory's political fallback text maintained the old unitary logic. Beyond general considerations, however, its emphasis on property and security and its warnings against factionalism and democracy, all a reaction against recent events, are noteworthy. It is in this context that one must interpret the fact that it defined citizenship in terms of tax payments and merits; "citizen" was still an operative term, though it would soon decline to the status of "elector" and "notable."[34] The most outstanding point concerned territorial division, which appears in Title I. Unlike the Montagnard Constitution of 1793, the Directory's text was a bit devious in separating metropolitan territories from the *colonies françaises* when enumerating the various divisions. It proposed eighty-nine departments for the metropolis and from eleven to thirteen (four to six for Saint-Domingue) and seven for the remaining colonies of the Caribbean, Africa, and Asia. This territorial articulation is anything but irrelevant. Take, for example, the definition of French citizenship according to whether or not someone was born there or was a foreigner who had resided seven consecutive years "in France." The "colonial" departments were part of the republican space but apparently were not part of France. Was this a contradiction or an anomaly? In her study of the 1795 Constitution, Miranda Frances Spieler argued convincingly that overseas possessions were never departmentalized or made institutionally equivalent to metropolitan territories.[35] From this perspective, the subtle discrimination in the constitution reveals the clearly "colonialist" intentions of the Directory and of rapporteur François-Antoine de Boissy d'Anglas.

It is not in a literal reading of the text but in its application that one obtains a more precise understanding of the different treatment of colonies and metropolis. The situation prior to Napoleon's seizure of power was fluid. In September 1796 there were elections, including for legislatures in the colonies controlled by French revolutionaries. The old French empire was fragmented among territories rent by revolution (Saint-Domingue, Guadeloupe, French Guyana), controlled by antirevolutionary, proslavery forces (the Mascarene Islands), and those that had fallen into British hands with the help of the planters' fifth column (Martinique).[36] Saint-Domingue was a particularly spectacular laboratory, where the republican experiment and the viability of the imperial constitution were put to the test.[37] The neo-Jacobin period of 1797–98 was the high point for accord between political developments in the Antilles and political unification projects in the metropolis. Political events included Toussaint's complicated rise to power as military and political ruler; unification projects included the law of January 1, 1798 (Nivôse, Year VI), the most audacious attempt to institutionalize overseas French territories after the republican coup d'état of September 4 the previous year.[38] This law was extraordinarily important, and it was the swan song of French political unitary development from the proclamation of the Directory to the rise of Napoleon. When that assemblage was sunk, with the coups of June 18 (30 Prairial) and November 9, 1799 (18 Brumaire), the roads to revolution were blocked for a very long time. Toussaint's constitution of July 7, 1801, represented continuity of a process that had been interrupted in the metropolis, namely, of the French revolutionary process as specialness, which already was the rule in French constitutional order. Toussaint's capture, deportation, and death in France signaled the end of the unitary project that had first come to life with the alliances—with their military underpinnings—established by the French revolutionary *commissaires* who arrived on the island in September 1792.[39] The reinstatement of slavery in the French colonies, a historical anomaly, underlined the return of effective colonialist politics, as one can clearly see in the Constitution of Year VIII, whose Title VII, Article 91, laid out the essence of the dual constitutional system: "The form of government of the French colonies is determined by special laws."

The Improbable Citizen

The language of natural law served perfectly as monarchic sovereignty gave way to the unity of national sovereignty. In this new space of equals, the subject who would exercise sovereignty had to be defined: this would be the modern citizen-subject (because a citizen is always, by definition, a subject), who would replace the subject endowed with the rights discussed in chapter 1. The problem was that no one knew exactly which characteristics that sovereign subject, who was free to associate with others and to alter the nature of the old constitution of the kingdom so persistently affirmed by jurists, should actually possess. The first liberal constitutions in the Iberian countries—Spain's in 1812 and Portugal's in 1822—are illustrative in this sense.

The North American and French political and constitutional examples and the entire panorama we have thus far described were the precursors of Spain and Portugal. Contrary to what is generally affirmed, Spain's 1812 Constitution was not the first to provide parliamentary seats for those abroad; nor was it the first to include political rights for non-Europeans. As we have seen, that honor belonged to the French Convention, whose measures were upheld later in the Council of Five Hundred (1795–99), which admitted mulattos, freemen of color, and recently freed slaves. Spaniards knew about this illustrious precedent, the seed of great historical changes that would affect their own Caribbean colonies. Therefore, while the first Spanish liberal constitution was in large part inspired by the 1791 representative monarchic constitution of France (except for the Declaration of the Rights of Man and of the Citizen, which received scant recognition in Spain), the foundations of its imperial vision lay in modifications of the openly republican versions of 1793 and 1795. Spain, just like its predecessors and enemies, was forced into an inclusive solution, given the crisis of the Napoleonic invasion and the danger that its enormous American and Asian empire might collapse. Thus, circumstances and constitutional ideals walked hand in hand for the time being.

The 1812 Constitution of Cádiz, written in that city while it was under British authority, is a perfect example of the imperial model while we are examining its application. (The French and their Spanish and American collaborators, the royal family included, approved another imperial constitution with similar intentions.[40]) The Cádiz text did not apply only to peninsular Spaniards, to use the terminology of the times, but to all those who lived in the monarchy's territories, wherever they might be.[41] And that included even those who lived the farthest away, in the Philippines.[42] The constitution's imperial reach was the subject of written commentaries at the time; the best-known, which circulated after the events themselves, was by Álvaro Flórez Estrada, an Asturian revolutionary, who wrote that Spain did not possess colonies but rather territories of equal standing to those in Europe. In his estimation, the delegates in Cádiz had simply restored original equality among all.[43] His argument led him to the momentous observation that overseas territories were not colonies at all because they were inhabited by equals. Such a statement should not deceive us; he himself made clear, with his very European and very white arguments, that other inhabitants were not all the same and that there were important differences between Americans of European origin and their counterparts in Europe. Enjoyment of rights by Indians and descendants of Africans (the *castas pardas*) was controversial and depended on a later decision (in 1811). The dissension (*disensiones*) that Flórez Estrada referred to in his title was between European Spaniards and American Spaniards, a conflict between equals.[44] As a framework of rights and representation, the constitution was designed in genuinely ethnocentric terms, though political convenience and contingencies may have impelled delegates to invite those not initially considered worthy of participation.

Flórez Estrada's discussions of Indians and *castas pardas*, with his sprinkled allusions to the uncultured, are most revealing,[45] and the constitutional process in Cádiz took a complicated turn as the delegates defined the limits of citizenship and decided who would be in and who out. Indians, who were the majority, were given citizenship and representation with no restrictions whatsoever because the rights of nation and the Catholic community made that an imperative.[46] The exclusion of slaves was unquestioned, but the matter of the *castas pardas* turned out to be the most difficult issue for the constituent Cortes.[47] Metropolitans' position was not simply one of complete ethnocentrism, but rather, the result of a complex cost-benefit analysis. The inherent rights of *citizenship* (a term that is absent from future Spanish constitutions) were exercised in the framework of social relations proper to the late eighteenth century. Given that, and taking into account the widely shared ethnocentrism among European elites on both sides of the Atlantic, it is hard to imagine that Indians and free people of color were ever envisioned as being truly active elements, rivals, or competitors in the political society that would be governed by new rules. In the Spanish case, the long interplay between social dynamics and state regulations could not be erased in one stroke.[48] Peninsular and American Spaniards needed to include those groups in electoral rolls, just as the largely locally autonomous mobilization against the Napoleonic invasion made it necessary to grant the vote to adult males, something that would have powerful and long-lasting consequences. But it was entirely unthinkable that future representatives would be anything but educated, European Catholics with not a trace of suspicion in their bloodline. Article 22 of the Constitution opened the door of citizenship in strictly old-regime terms, allowing it to the excluded on the basis of merit or service, which led to a wide range of conflicts and petitioning, especially among officers of the colored militias.[49]

It is worth reflecting on the tilt toward universalism in the proclamation of equality in Cádiz, which preceded approval of the constitution. The constitution arose as a weapon against invaders, a way of preserving the unity of the monarchic body politic. It was further limited by the fact that the Napoleonic constitution of Bayonne (the Bayonne Statute), which was quickly imposed in that city on a group of leading Spaniards, including the monarch, had already been approved in the presence of a worthy American contingent.[50] Therefore the monarchy was understood to be a unified whole beyond dynasties and beyond the political identity of the peninsular kingdoms (including America, as part of Castile). But the historicist inspiration of the statesmen Gaspar Melchor de Jovellanos and Antonio de Capmany, the Junta Suprema Central (which assumed governmental capacities during the invasion), and associates of Lord Holland (a learned Whig, friend of Jovellanos, and protector of Spanish exiles in London), which aimed at a positive reading of the "ancient constitution of the kingdom," was one thing; getting rid of history and old laws was another matter entirely. The approved text represented a break with the past, in the sense that it would be materially and ideologically impossible to implement a historicist operation aimed at recovering constitutional traditions from the Hispanic Monarchy. That rupture meant that historical reasons were pushed aside in favor of a reading based on national sovereignty as the only source of legislation. The Spanish moment was thus a repetition of the debate that divided the French from 1789 to 1791. The need to incorporate Americans and Filipinos into the revolutionary process and offer them an inclusive common framework had a great deal to do with peninsular liberals' ability to overcome other political agendas in the Cortes and the constitutional commission.[51] In the view of the hegemonic group, America did not require separate treatment, and neither did the various peninsular territories and corporations. The only acceptable cultural connotation was Catholicism, which was assumed to be shared by everyone and which bestowed identity on subjects and the entire nation on both sides of the Atlantic.

All these factors combined to make the 1812 Constitution a unitary, peninsular, overseas artifact—in other words, imperial. The majority liberal faction in the constituent Cortes imposed a text that created its very object—the Spanish nation as a complete transmutation of the inherited empire. In the absence of historical reasons, constituent delegates were well aware of the social and territorial heterogeneity of the monarchy, and they needed to define a greater force in order to push the process onward and help construct the new liberal (the term was first used then) society. This force had to be the Cortes, the power par excellence consecrated by the Constitution; the only power not subject to the oversight of judges, the only power that stood above all society's fissures. Neither "federalism" nor respect for political bodies of the past lay anywhere on the first liberal generation's horizon. The objective of solidifying the liberal process was understandable, given the circumstances and the geographic dimensions in play, but it made for very difficult resolutions. If the Cortes was to be the legislative *deus ex machina,* then a solid parliamentary majority identified with the founding process had to be built. That was the argument that led to the definitive restriction of citizenship and exclusion of the *castas pardas.* And that, in turn, altered the rules of equality to the benefit of some and definitively undid the consensus with American liberals to include freemen of color in the census (the Hispanic version of North America's Three-Fifths Compromise). This was how the bases of the truly imperial constitution were undermined.

The *juntas* that arose with the collapse of the state and its betrayal by the Spanish monarchy never seriously considered representation for Americans and Filipinos. Neither the Junta Gubernativa del Reino, constituted in April 1808, nor the Junta Suprema Central, which appeared on September 25, 1808, nor the Seville Junta showed the slightest intention of incorporating those who lived overseas into the entities in charge of the anti-Napoleonic resistance. As in France, circumstances on the ground ended up dynamiting the reform (and salvation) strategy for the monarchy, a strategy that relied on continuity and on maintaining a clear hierarchy between metropolis and overseas territories. Juntas were established in America once word reached the New World of events in Spain; Napoleon quickly approved the constitution in Bayonne, offering a novel way of resolving relations between the metropolis and the empire; and Gabriel Yermo, a wealthy advocate of the Spanish party, staged a coup d'état in Mexico City in August 1808, creating a vacuum of power there.[52] As a result, the idea of reform in absentia for Americans was transformed into direct legislative participation as the Cortes unleashed a plethora of laws, decrees, and orders going far beyond any mere proposal for a constitution. This shift was visible first in the summons to Americans to attend the Junta Central on January 22, 1809, and later with the promise of strict representational equality in the Cortes on October 15, 1810, after peninsulars attempted to defraud the Americans by occupying more seats than corresponded to their numbers.[53] With the dissolution of the Junta Central and the formation of a regency early in 1810 whose objective was solely to convoke the Cortes and oversee a new constitution, calls and promises for egalitarianism continued, though with a variety of efforts to ensure metropolitan control over the monarchy's provisional organs.[54] This phase, once the 1812 Constitution was in place, was to prove critical after open conflict broke out between "peninsular Spaniards" and "American Spaniards."

The constitution approved in March 1812 included peninsulars, Americans, and Filipinos in the same imperial architecture, in accordance with the emphatic declaration in Title I, Article 1: "The Spanish nation is the sum of all Spaniards of both hemispheres." From there, the Constitution never faltered. But the crisis of Cádiz had its origins in this dual imperial and egalitarian nature. The pivotal factor was Spanish delegates' strategy of imposing reforms on Spain and the empire from the Cortes, something not provided for by the Constitution and which reflected mistrust on the part of an executive at the future mercy of a monarch openly averse to liberalism.[55] This was the underlying reason for the exaggerated conception of the Cortes as the engine of a new order. Therefore, it was essential above all to ensure a majority for peninsular Spaniards in the Cortes, using extensive indirect universal male suffrage, and also to ensure that there were no intermediate powers (as with U.S. federalism, which Spanish delegates obsessively accused Spanish-American delegates of wanting to imitate) that could get in the way of reform legislation on European or American soil. This was the political perspective that put "racial" discourse by peninsular delegates into play as they excluded free blacks and mulattoes from the electoral rolls. The objective was to eliminate immediately any possibility of an American majority in the chambers, a constant nightmare given the demographic uncertainty of the empire. The political framework had changed, but the old imperial culture of ethnic distinctions remained in place.

The decision to exclude descendants of Africans from citizenship was a polarizing one. The Constitution stated that *castas pardas* and freemen of color were free Spanish subjects, with the important specification that freed slaves (*libertos*) would also be subjects, "starting from when they obtain freedom *en las Españas*." Such an altruistic intention would not survive Chapter IV, Article 18: "Those Spaniards who on both sides can trace their origins to Spanish dominions in either hemisphere and who reside in any town in those dominions are citizens."[56] All free individuals with African ancestors would be excluded. The motivation for this bizarre decision (note, again, that the exclusion of slaves did not require an explanation) was to keep around one-third of the American population off the electoral rolls. By going down this twisted path, a peninsular majority in the legislature could be guaranteed. But the move set off an unprecedented crisis in the constitutent Cortes and in later political entities assigned to apply the criterion, both during the wars against Napoleon and during the Liberal Triennium (1820–23). The shifting justifications offered by the politician most responsible for the measure, Agustín de

Argüelles Álvarez, show two things: that people with African blood in their veins, whatever the proportion, were excluded as the result of political calculations; and also that the decision resonated with old ideas about the superiority of European Spaniards over Americans, regardless of the Americans' origins. Distinctions were hard to sort out, as with the actions of the Cortes, which tried to eliminate certain restrictions on free people of color in America while taking into account the Spanish belief that the Indies was a place where bloodlines and social standing mixed in a highly suspicious and undesirable fashion. This was a fallback to an eighteenth-century understanding of imperial societies, and it only intensified under the representative government's obligation to distribute parliamentary representation by counting votes, that is, by counting electors. In the end, the crisis of the *castas pardas* and opposition to the exercise of legislative capacities by peripheral state administration ("federalism") were the issues that most undermined the consensus that should have ensured the imperial constitution's viability.

The Strange Life of the Imperial Constitutions

The Portuguese Constitution of September 23, 1822, followed the path trod by Spain. For most Portuguese liberals—especially for Manuel Fernandes Tomás, a delegate from the province of Beira and president of the constitutional commission—the Spanish case was exemplary. Starting from the Napoleonic Wars and continuing after March 1820, when the 1812 Constitution was proclaimed anew, Spain was a reference point, to such a degree that some radical liberals even considered unifying the two countries under the umbrella of the Constitution of Cádiz.[57] They translated the Spanish text and adopted its tone and orientation for their own constitution, which was approved March 1, 1821, starting with the definition of the new nation in Section II, Article 16: "The Portuguese nation is the sum of all Portuguese of both hemispheres."[58] The constitution also affirms the nation's independence with regard to the ruling dynasty and proclaims Catholicism to be the state religion. On the other hand, there are clear differences regarding the relationship between the monarch and the Cortes; King João VI was in Rio de Janeiro under British protection (having fled Napoleon's troops in 1807), an entirely different sort of threat for the liberals meeting in Lisbon.[59] Even after the constituent process, the Spanish constitution remained an influence on the final document approved by the Lisbon Cortes a year and a half later. The definition of the Portuguese nation, for example (Title II, Article 20), is identical and includes a list of all its provinces in Europe, America, Africa, and Asia. Reference to the Catholic church (Title II, Article 25) is also the same, though foreigners are given more leeway to practice their faith. This relative concession reflects the greater variety of the Portuguese empire (Islam in East Africa, Hinduism in Goa, Buddhism and Confucianism in Macau) and its strategic alliance with the British. Article 21 contains a broader definition of a citizen, incorporating freed slaves and omitting any exclusionary formula comparable to that of Spain.[60] Limits on the exercise of political rights, curiously enough, concern participation in elections (the text mentions "passive citizens," a contradiction in terms) and the right to stand for office. Here we have discrimination against certain social groups, but not groupings of free individuals classified by ethnicity. In other words, they were not trying to affect the census (upward, as in the United States in 1783, or downward, as in Spain in 1812) as part of a struggle between peoples of European origin. Rather, the intent was to avoid complications with the presence of large numbers of freemen of color in the political process. In the case of Portugal, Title III, Article 34, Section VII, is particularly noteworthy, establishing that "freed slaves born in foreign lands" may not be elected, affecting both freed slaves in Brazil and in the African possessions, that is, non-Creole slaves.[61] This provision seems more cautionary, given the enormous slave population in Brazil and Africa, than an actual weapon against Europeans there.[62] That was why the measure drew less attention than that of neighboring Spain in the midst of its political struggles.

The constitution of July 20, 1826, which was granted by Pedro I, emperor of Brazil after the abdication of his father, João VI (who, in turn, named Princess Maria da Glória as queen of Portugal), prolonged aspects of the previous constitution. It is an important document in the history of Portugal, as it would be retained, with some changes, throughout most of the nineteenth century. Ironically, it was the emperor of the emancipated American kingdom who granted the political statute to the old metropolis. Nevertheless, the relationship between the two political entities was purely dynastic, with no negative effects on their respective political independence. Once again, the constitution was articulated on an imperial plane. The Kingdom of Portugal was defined as "the political association of all Portuguese citizens" in Europe, Africa, and Asia, specifying territories just as the 1822 Constitution had done. Portuguese citizens were those born in Portugal who were not Brazilian citizens, a nuance that indicates the disproportionate presence of Brazilians in the African colonies. But in accordance with the discrete exclusions in the section concerning elections, not everyone had the same rights. Indeed, the constitution demanded that in order to vote in primary elections (in which Portuguese citizens chose electors who in turn would elect deputies), one had to have a yearly income of 100,000 reis; in addition, those barred from electoral colleges were also excluded from all other elections, including for municipalities. These provisions were important because they further reduced the number of people who could be electors: one needed an annual income of 200,000 reis in personal property and one could not have been convicted of a crime or be a freed slave. The latter group was mostly excluded already by economic criteria. Similar provisions appeared in subsequent nineteenth-century constitutions. All free individuals were Portuguese citizens (slavery continued in the Portuguese African colonies until the 1850s), though not everyone had the same rights and capacities.[63]

None of the constitutions belonging to the imperial family survived the tests to which they were subjected. Moreover, every one of these strange political artifacts contained devices and gambits that later on would guide constitutional frameworks suitable to the colonial foundations of those societies. Such an affirmation may strike some as odd, given the longevity of the U.S. Constitution. But from the proper angle, one can see that imperial constitutions arose in order to ensure continuity of rights by all free individuals living in the old monarchies or in spaces freed by anticolonial revolutions, which was not at all incompatible with the dawn of imperial projects such as those of the United States and Brazil. These entailed an idea of shared rights and also allowed them to seize spaces that, because of external threats or crises of loyalty, had somehow become disconnected. Such moves were branded with the basic principle that "all men are born free and equal," forcing them to resolve the equation of individual liberty and representation/rights that rose in opposition to the inherent inequality of monarchies, to produce a new entity, the modern nation. Imperial constitutions therefore were the perfect superimposition of, on the one hand, the nation as a community of citizens and, on the other, its imperial projection on the entire political body, which was an aggregate of very diverse parts. The defense of national sovereignty in extreme conditions (the attack on the French Republic from the Rhine, the British invasion of Martinique and Saint-Domingue with Spanish help, the 1807–08 invasion of the Iberian Peninsula and South American independence) did the rest.

Imperial constitutions belonged to a period with an expiration date. In general, it was a matter of substituting one text for another and, more important, signing pacts that would become the foundation of nineteenth-century national and imperial projects. This transition characterized the cases of France, Spain, and, with some variations, Portugal. As we will see in the next chapter, Napoleon's coup of 18 Brumaire opened the way for radical readjustment of the model by Sièyes, Talleyrand, and the other high officials of the royal Ministry of the Navy and the Colonies who slowly returned to their old posts. The Constitution of Year VIII (1799) made it obvious which path would be followed. Title VII, Article 91, clearly stated: "Le régime des colonies françaises est déterminé par des lois spéciales." No one knew at that point which "special laws" the First Consul referred to. But they must have known that these were not the same laws as those governing the metropolis, the France of Europe, where the indivisible unity of republic and empire was proclaimed. The reinstatement of slavery with the law of May 20, 1802, clarified matters. But subsequent developments in French colonialism would show that it was not just slavery that motivated the philanthropy of those living "to the north of this hemisphere," in the prophetic words of Boissy d'Anglas as he defended the Constitution of 1795. In 1837 Spain approved a new constitution, the second after Cádiz, containing a new article that came verbatim from Napoleon's. A year later, Portugal, following more or less in its neighbor's path, introduced the same clause in Title X, Article 137, of the liberal constitution.

Imperial constitutions were over. Bit by bit and one by one, they were replaced with properly colonial constitutions that either regulated political exception in the framework of empires or, as in the case of the United States, developed flexible formulas that were similar to specialness but that adapted more closely to the unwritten constitution governing daily life in colonial enclaves. Yet a difficult problem remained: how to remove an idea from the minds of people living throughout four continents—the idea that had given rise to that now extinguished family of constitutions— that men are born free and equal.

CHAPTER THREE

The Genealogy of Napoleon's "Special Laws" for the Colonies

THE FRENCH CONSTITUTION OF 1799 (Year VIII) is a fundamental document in the history of nineteenth-century European colonialism. It was the first to express explicitly (though Napoleon said he preferred short and obscure constitutions[1]) the basic tenets of postrevolutionary colonial politics in Europe and in countries founded by Europeans, such as the Kingdom of Brazil and the United States.[2] Very concisely, it stated that colonies were to be governed through "special laws" outside the normal metropolitan constitutional, political, and juridical framework. The very idea of *spécialité* made sense only after a long battle for equality both within metropolitan France and in its overseas colonies. Contemporaries called this separation between two spaces a "dual constitution." This was an artifact that obviously contrasted with "imperial constitutions," in its attempt to embrace all the king's former subjects within one common system of rights and representation. In that sense, it entailed undoing advances achieved by the French constitutions of 1793 and 1795, both rooted in republican unity, with all their limitations. The reinstatement of slavery in the French Antilles and the Mascarene Islands on 30 Floreal, Year X (1802) (local authorities in the Mascarene Islands as well as in Martinique, before it surrendered to the British, had successfully resisted the Convention's attempts to abolish slavery there) and in Guadeloupe in May 1803 clarified the real consequences of that move.[3] Metropolitan political life would no longer be the mirror in which colonists saw themselves, and colonial administrators both in the mother country and overseas now had free rein. It is no exaggeration to say that special laws brought about the reconstruction of the old monarchic empire and the extension of its territorial ambitions. But the outcome would not be a copy of the original or of the unwieldy unitary and universalist idea we discussed earlier.

This chapter explores the genesis, starting in 1799, of France's turn to *lois spéciales*, which would be imitated by Spain and Portugal in their constitutions of 1837 and 1838, respectively.[4] The chapters that follow will show how later colonial developments—and not just in France—gave meaning to and fulfilled statements of intentions that were made at the end of one era and that signaled the start of another, still uncertain, era.

The Metropolitan Genesis of the Idea of Spécialité

The French Revolution ensured that colonialism and slavery (different questions, though with much overlap) would be long-standing issues with far-reaching impact. From 1797 to 1799, known as the neo-Jacobin period, the conservatives had the upper hand, until the coup of 18 Brumaire (November 9–10, 1799). Napoleon's move was well received by the French, who were tired of constant warfare and weak governments. The Directory, which had opted for a central electoral system, was notoriously weak[5]; so much so that the regime, while trying to stabilize the revolution, had to forcibly exclude its adversaries, as it was defeated in each and every one of the elections it held.[6] The first of its coups, on September 4, 1797, was against the royalists, who had clearly won the elections; the second, in May 1798, was ambiguously against the neo-Jacobins, who had been victorious one month earlier.[7] The royalists already had been harshly repressed since the Paris revolt of October 5, 1795, when the Directory consolidated its power. That crisis was averted by General Paul Barras, who engineered the 1797 coup (and came up with the slogan *L'ordre, la paix, la liberté*), along with a young Corsican general who was his protégé, known afterward as General Vendémiaire.[8] Napoleon Bonaparte would get involved in another coup against the royalists when they won the 1797 elections (and organized several uprisings[9]), though he gave the dirty work to Pierre François Augereau, a military officer whom he trusted. As events sped by, political actors quickly learned to use force when elections did not turn out as they had hoped. The regular army would be vitally helpful to them in the West and South of France, where dissidence at times merged with endemic banditry.[10]

These metropolitan dynamics were not unrelated to developments in the colonies as a result of the 1799 Constitution, a collaborative effort by the First Consul himself and Emmanuel-Joseph Sièyes that put an end to a long period of duality in French revolutionary politics.[11] Indeed, one of the particularities of the Revolution was that it operated on two fronts nearly from the start. The first front concerned institutionalization of revolutionary principles and was in evidence in the constitutions of 1791, 1793, and 1795, with their declarations of rights; the first constitution was monarchic-liberal, the second was Montagnard, and the third was republican, approved after the fall of Robespierre and the radical phase of Year II. At the heart of the extraordinary dynamism of French constitutional alterations lay the great political debates on the definition and extension of citizenship and popular sovereignty, the dilemmas between monarchy and republic and between unity and "federalism," the wisdom of spreading the revolution through war, and, finally, the question of whether or not to abolish slavery in the colonies.

The second front concerned another institutional project that would emerge after the dramatic circumstances of Louis XVI's attempted flight. At that point, coinciding with the threat of a German invasion over the Rhine, the National Assembly decided to create a second power structure that could assume legal responsibilities and implement repressive measures that had not been foreseen in laws or in the Declaration of the Rights of Man and of the Citizen.[12] The Convention commenced feverish legislative activity aimed at distinguishing citizens with rights from those outside the law and organizing the committees of public safety. It also established a system of central delegates known as *représentants en mission, délegués,* or *comissaires civiles,* whose job it was to take "all necessary measures to ensure public order and guarantee state security."[13] This parallel arm of the state was crucial for enacting revolutionary power during the constituent and legislative Assembly, the Convention, and the Directory. These commissars had broad civil and military powers (including promotions[14] and vigilance) which were vital for organizing military campaigns and implementing repression, both in France and in the colonies.[15] They could take extraordinary political and administrative measures to ensure those ends, since in large part they were filling the vacuum left behind after the dismantling of royal provincial authority. When the country was divided up into departments, these commissars often took charge of more than one demarcation, joining together in councils to oversee several departments when they deemed it necessary.

So this dual organizational system was not invented by the Montagnards; it preceded the radicalization of the Revolution. Measures were taken against the *émigrés* (the first to be declared *hors-la-loi*) as early as

1791 and then, more forcefully, after the summer of 1792. The crucial factor pushing matters in this direction was the war, which at that point was being fought in the Rhine Valley and the Low Countries. At the same time, popular participation in elections was growing fitfully despite theoretical expansion of the electorate with the law of August 12, 1792.[16] It was in this contradictory panorama that the Legislative Assembly decided to create the protean commissars who would take over political and military duties at the front. These exceptional institutional officials could autonomously direct military campaigns without the jurisdictional limitations of ordinary administration, which tended to be more conservative than those of society at large.[17] In the words of one historian, "Étant tout à la fois l'oeil de Paris et son bras séculier, ainsi que des représentants du 'souverain,' ils disposent des pouvoirs illimités et peuvent intervenir sur tous les domaines."[18] In any case, though ordinary legislation affected the entire administration, commissars obeyed orders only from the Convention. Forming part of the inner circle of the revolutionary power structure and generally being appointed (always provisionally, and then often dismissed for exceeding their authority) by Convention committees, they wielded power over local authorities.[19] The dramatic pace of events and the increase of domestic and foreign threats starting in April 1793 turned these delegates into decision-making agents who commanded (though not on their own) the revolutionary army and took repressive measures against the Revolution's many enemies.[20] Yet their autonomy did not mean they worked outside the law or ignored orders from the Convention; the centralized power structure that was extended through these commissars would be used after Thermidor to purge Robespierrists from popular societies and to free prisoners.[21]

Commissars' extraordinary activities were not confined to metropolitan France. On the contrary, they exercised authority in the colonial possessions as well. It was no coincidence that news of the slave uprising in Saint-Domingue moved Jacques-Pierre Brissot, one of the founders (with Étienne Clavière) of the Société des Amis des Noirs in February 1788,[22] to declare war on the counterrevolutionary forces and make a humanitarian peace offering to everyone else.[23] With war going on both within and outside the country, institutionalization of the 1791 monarchic constitution advanced very slowly, and radicalization of the revolutionary process meant having to resort to increasingly extraordinary measures during the Directory.

Emancipation was the best-known instance of these extraordinary measures. Commissars Léger-Félicité Sonthonax and Étienne Polverel, who would become key figures in the alliance between the Parisian sans-culottes and Caribbean slaves, tried to channel the spontaneous revolts that broke out on plantations in the northern part of Saint-Domingue.[24] From the start, their job was of a mostly military nature, given the circumstances, both domestically and against the British invaders and their Spanish allies.[25] The commissars' arrival on the island in September 1792 was aimed at ensuring the rights of freemen of color, guaranteed by the law of April 4, 1791. They would do this by commanding freemen's militias, thus offsetting colonists' likely collaboration with rival powers.[26] The commissars used their position at the head of the loyal militias to send escaped slaves back to their workplace. This was the start of the difficult task of figuring out how to protect a plantation economy without a servile labor force, a dilemma that Toussaint Louverture and his successors in republican Haiti would have to confront later. Faced with the destruction of Le Cap in June 1793, the impossibility of reestablishing any sort of productive capacity, plus the opposition of Governor Galbaud, the commissars opted on August 29, 1793, to proclaim emancipation, a radical measure that would be constitutionalized by the Convention on February 4, 1794.[27] The work of commissar Victor Hugues in Guadaloupe is also well known; he first announced the slaves' freedom and then participated in their reenslavement under the aegis of Napoleon, as Guadaloupe was unable to follow Saint-Domingue's path of autonomy and independence.[28] All these measures, (all faits accomplis), destroyed the 1791 constitutional framework and the agreement between colonists and the proslavery Committee on Colonies established in March 1790 (where Antoine Barnave, on March 8, 1790, called for a differentiation between metropolitan and colonial law) to keep the colonies outside the metropolitan revolutionary process and far away from universal citizenship and equality.

In this context, Year II (October 6, 1793, to September 21, 1794) was exceptional.[29] It is also important for the French understanding of the relationship between formal institutional power and effective power on the ground. The proclamation of the republic in the summer of 1792 and the execution of Louis XVI took place during full-fledged war against a long list of enemies, with the bitter defeat of the Convention armies in Neerwinden, the betrayal by General Dumouriez, and the first British blockade of French ports. That all led up to the first *levée en masse*, of 300,000 soldiers in March 1793, and heightened repression throughout the country. At the same time, the peasantry of western France, along with royalist and church allies, joined in an uprising (*La Chouannerie*), a war among Frenchmen that placed entire provinces outside the law.[30] Warfare within this fractured society was not confined to the area between

Bordeaux and Normandy nor just to the countryside (as evidenced by de-
nunciations against commissar Jean-Baptiste Carrier's brutal repression
in Nantes) but extended toward the south as well.[31] And, in addition to
the conflict between the Revolution and royalists, there was resistance
from cities dominated by the Girondins.[32] There were times when local
power passed into the hands of the so-called federalists but ended up with
monarchists, who were better able to resist militarily. Among the most
noteworthy such events of this period were Fouché de Nantes and Jean-
Marie Collot d'Herbois's bloody crushing of their adversaries in Lyon, the
massacre after the capture of Marseille, and the recapture by Bonaparte
(then a protégé of Augustin Robespierre) of Toulon from the British and
their counterrevolutionary allies.[33] Indeed, the war in the Vendée, with
more than 200,000 fatalities, was not much different from future colonial
wars. In the words of David Bell, the violence and brutality against Ven-
deans' lives and way of life "set a new European standard in atrocities,"
particularly if we consider the reaction in the context of a revolutionary
world's vision, in which violent struggle is understood to be an ideological
force transcending the borders of the old monarchic empires.[34] It would
be an anachronism to consider the various parties in struggle as simple
compatriots: this was before the birth of the modern nation per se, their
language had been imposed on them, and their culture was the result of
tenacious and well-known inculcation.[35] The violence in Western France
overlapped immediately with true colonial campaigns in Saint-Domingue
and Egypt;[36] indeed, Lazare Carnot, the future minister of war and the interior after 18 Brumaire, referred to the Caribbean conflict as the "colonial
Vendée," an indication that the comparison is more than apt.[37] Prejudice
was aimed simultaneously at both domestic counterrevolutionaries and
slaves and at freemen of color abroad. Black and mulatto soldiers from
the Antilles were sent to fight in the Vendée in June 1793 but could not be
trusted to fight in the colonies themselves.[38]

The important point here is that the accumulation of conflicts, one
on top of another, led to the suspension of the recently approved republican constitution in July 1793, a measure that Robespierre defended in the
name of the survival of the Revolution. This is crucial, because it shows
how the constitutional void was being filled by a series of measures that
led to the Terror and all its repressive legislation, including the sinister
decree of March 10, 1793, declaring that anyone suspected of counterrevolutionary activities was an outlaw.[39] Later, an extraordinary criminal court
was established, serving essentially as political police, with the relentless Antoine Quentin Fouquier-Tinville as chief prosecutor. Convention

delegates and their two most important committees, Public Safety and General Security, had been used throughout France and the colonies on previous occasions, but now they were increasingly and significantly present.[40] Throughout these events and the period of the Convention and the Directory, Abbé Sièyes (a theorist of natural law), Barras (ideologue of the 1797 coup d'état), Jean-Jacques Régis de Cambacérès (future Second Consul and the Convention member who, along with Philippe-Antoine Merlin de Douai, introduced and defended the decree of September 19, 1793, persecuting suspects), and Napoleon (Barras's right arm in the military) consolidated their political experience.[41] During these years of extraordinary political activity, proconsuls were granted both civil and military powers, leaving very little room for the judiciary and opening the door to flexible interpretations of the law in response to local circumstances. In any case, this was not a predesigned state of exception, nor were the measures outside of or exceeding laws emanating from the center. Rather, the situation grew out of a particular historical experience: the transformation of defensive patriotism into politics justified by "necessity" and by a combination of reasons of state and an exercise of power unmediated by representation or legal guarantees.[42] Jurisdictional and hierarchical disputes appeared everywhere as a result of events that seemed to elude the control of revolutionaries and their adversaries alike, from the Girondins to the royalists to the European monarchic governments in the counterrevolutionary coalition.[43]

It was one thing if the revolutionary process did not correspond to its ideological designs but quite something else if there were no cultural tools to give consensus and meaning to solutions. As the Revolution fought its multiple enemies, the key moment was the suspension of the 1793 Constitution, which had been written and approved in just one month precisely to compensate for the total collapse of monarchic sovereignty. It was the first modern republican constitution of Europe and the most truly unitary and universalist of all the revolutionary constitutions. But the legal vacuum and continual threats led revolutionaries to install a "revolutionary government"—"la forme des institutions dans un moment de vacance constitutionelle," in the words of historian Patrice Gueniffey—and committees in each town or city quarter.[44] The repression was most clearly seen in the legislation of March and April of 1793 that created the Committee of Public Safety and declared all enemies of the revolution to be *hors-la-loi*.[45] This marked the beginning of a conception of citizenship (and its concomitant degradation, with the loss of rights) that would separate French radicalism from the foundations of nineteenth-century liberal regimes.

These decisions also ended up giving commissars enormous latitude, though their work was not simply blindly destructive. The great repressive wave that began in the summer of 1792, picked up speed after the assassination of Jean-Paul Marat, and was embodied in the Terror laws passed by the Convention and its two principal committees had one clear objective: to avoid indiscriminate bloodshed by the people. But elimination of one's adversaries cannot be rash: it must be legally justified, politically directed, and, furthermore, instructive.[46] These are not ideas that come out of nowhere; rather, they emerge from a very radical interpretation of the meaning of natural law. As Dan Edelstein has written, "only natural law provided the higher legal authority with which to challenge the Constitution's legitimacy."[47] The king's treason stood in contrast to the virtues of the people and their leaders, who did not require laws in order to act justly. Natural law made that unnecessary. This is an old idea, as Edelstein points out, part of the physiocratic notion of an *ordre naturel* and of course also related to Sièyes's position in 1789 that natural laws preceded the social contract and the nation itself.[48] Any violation of natural law situated the individual beyond citizenship. Thus, the destruction of the individual, either physical or civic (after all, the latter might be reversed) was not only understandable but also desirable and not subject to appeal. The revolution thus realized the logic of massive reprisals. Maximilien Robespierre himself, in his speech on Christmas Day, 1793, clearly distinguished the actions of a constitutional government and a revolutionary government. This dynamic of total political struggle would continue for a considerable time.[49]

The fall of the "Incorruptible" and the Montagnards in July 1794 put an end to identification of the general will with principles allowing the elimination of each and every one of the Revolution's enemies, both on the right and on the left. The key factor in the restoration of a republic based on the rule of law was the Constitution of 1795, written by the leading jurist Boissy d'Anglas, which embraced the two pillars of a representative regime: elections and judicial independence. Despite the Directory's good intentions and hard work, however, it failed on both counts, in part because it did not have a constitutional mechanism with which to resolve disputes between the executive and the legislative branches.[50] Candidacies for elections were more freely formalized than before, and new electoral practices were a preview of political contests of the future.[51] But despite these novelties, the Thermidor regime could not eliminate exceptional violence.[52] Émigrés who returned to France after an amnesty, and the Church (starting in 1795, churches were reopening, leading to the

1802 Concordat), were none too willing to negotiate.[53] The end of the endemic street violence in Paris must not blind us to the fact that conflict and reprisals continued in most of the rest of France in addition to the French Antilles. Royalists, Jacobins, right-wing radicals (the *égorgeurs*), and left-wing radicals (Babeuf's aborted conspiracy of May 1796, supported by many Jacobins[54]) continued fighting to impose their agendas, either by restoring the monarchy or by returning to the radicalism of the Convention.[55] This conflict between electoral practices and factionalism, spurred on by the simultaneous presence of Jacobins and monarchists, led to a series of coups d'état, the last of which would be led by Napoleon in the colonies in 1799, and reaffirmed in 1802.

A Crisis of Republican Unity

A new vision for the French empire began solidifying in this period, which was characterized by tension between law and judiciary and by low participation in irrelevant elections, states of siege, the army's crackdowns on bandits and rebellious peasants, and chronic factionalism. Latent repression in the metropolis spread over into the colonies in the efforts to restore order and to manage the flow of traffic for future expansion. This reborn imperial vocation had two aims: first, the reestablishment of labor on the plantations, which depended on agents, commissars, and revolutionary army officers; and second, the recovery of positions in British India after French interests there collapsed, leading to the loss of Joseph François Dupleix's brilliant achievements as governor general in the mid-eighteenth century.[56] One of the strongest voices in favor of renewing overseas expansion was Talleyrand, whose knowledge of European and worldwide imperial politics was second to none. He had been pushed aside during the Montagnard years, but in the aftermath he delivered a speech at the recently established National Institute (later the Collège de France) outlining the need to recover the state's former foreign objectives.[57] In his *Essai sur les avantages à retirer de Colonies Nouvelles dans les circonstances présentes*, delivered on July 27, 1797, the great thinker advocated taking the colonial initiative, though not at any price and not necessarily in America, where, he doubted, there was any space remaining for the ambitions of his country or of any other European country. He also had doubts about whether the reconstructed and pacified French Antilles would be a good base of support. He showed no hesitation, however, in identifying Africa as the proper place to go, and he would find innumerable supporters for that position during the Napoleonic era and beyond. Among the enthusiasts of renewed expansionism and the commencement of a new imperial cycle were many former officers of the Ministry of the Navy and the Colonies who had recovered their posts during the counterrevolutionary years of the Directory and after Napoleon's coup d'état; these included Moreau de Saint-Méry, François Barbé-Marbois, Pierre-Alexandre-Laurent Forfait, and Jean-Baptiste Guillemin de Vaivre, who all returned to their old jobs in colonial administration and the Council of State.[58] Many moved up the ladder after the 1797 elections, which were won by the so-called Clichy party, whose watchword was the reestablishment of political and social peace at any cost. One example of the new circle was Pierre-Victor Malouet, who had become an English agent after fleeing to London in 1792 and had worked up an Anglo-French plan to get the sugar islands back into the fold. In so doing he surely had a well-placed ally in Joséphine de Tascher de la Pagerie, the daughter of Martinique planters and wife of the First Consul.

The years 1797–98 constituted a key period in the construction of the new French colonial politics. They also were a time of tense ideological struggle and a sense that conflict was inevitable, once the rise of Napoleon and the antirevolutionary forces was replicated in Saint-Domingue with the increasing authority of Toussaint, who embodied both a reply to and a denial of the metropolis.[59] At the same time, the First Consul and other high-ranking officials repeatedly spoke in favor of reinstituting slavery where it had been abolished; this would be the cornerstone of the new colonial policy.[60] As the leadership was being reshuffled, the protagonists of the prior cycle—mulattos and free blacks in the French Caribbean and revolutionaries at home—were still politically influential, a presage of the definitive separation of Saint-Domingue in 1802. For example, the law of 12 Nivôse in Year VI (1798) was both an unmitigated reaffirmation of inclusive politics and at the same time an ambitious attempt to resolve the situation left over from the revolutionary years.[61] The law was the Revolution's clearest response to "the constitutional organization of the colonies," the endpoint of a process that had already reached its end in practice. It was for that reason that General Étienne Laveaux, the highest military authority in Saint-Domingue and an open advocate of inclusive politics, defined it as a "system of absolute unity;"[62] and a historian of our time has said it augured "republican isonomy," or equality before the law.[63] The law can be seen as the immediate antecedent of the great reform (or regression) of 1799–1802, the period following Napoleon's coup of 18 Brumaire. The 1798 law, for instance, spelled out the tasks of the seven envoys to the islands, who would enforce compliance with the Constitution (Title I, Articles 7 and 8), and defined the criteria by which the plantation economy would be protected now that slavery had been eliminated, first from below and later legislatively. Slavery and its world were the subject of much attention. Title III, Articles 14 and 15, were key, as they guaranteed citizenship to freed slaves whose age was uncertain or was confirmed by four witnesses, and also to those not born on French soil; that is, it extended citizenship to black Africans in the Antilles.[64] This elevation to citizenship must be understood within the context of the proposed reconstruction of the plantations (now without slaves), a project supported both by the revolutionaries in Paris and the blacks and mulattos in charge of the Saint-Domingue army.[65] Only then can one understand the harsh measures against vagabonds, a sign of the absolute lack of confidence in freed slaves and fears that a "new Guinea" of independent peasants might be established, an expression that would become widespread.[66] "Patriotic" landowners received institutional support, and a series of allegedly nonconstitutional norms were abolished, among them the Code Noir of 1685 (Title IV, Article 3), which was impossible to apply in these circumstances.[67] At the same time, departments were institutionalized (the north and south of Saint-Domingue were divided between Samaná and l'Inganne), subject to the Constitution and explicitly referenced (Article 23) in the section on the judiciary.[68]

But the law represented more than all this: it was an explicit attempt to impose the department system on overseas possessions, to turn slaves who had fought in the revolutionary armies into citizens, and to establish the bases for all *cultivateurs* to become citizens. Together, these three measures were the epitome of republican unity. They represented an attempt to fill the "vacant units" (in Spieler's words) that metropolitan constitutional development had created in the colonies.[69] Former slaves in Guadaloupe voted in the 1799 elections and elected (white) representatives, and those in Saint-Domingue took over political and military power. At the same time, Minister of the Navy Eustache Bruix, a Saint-Domingue native, tried to enforce separation of blacks and mulattos in the French army, which both groups resisted, understanding correctly that it was a first step toward depriving them of citizenship. Those responsible for implementing the new policies were very much opposed to losing their nearly unlimited military powers and to the idea of recently freed slaves as full-fledged voting citizens. Nearly all were firm supporters of restoring order on the plantations, and order meant something dangerously close to slavery, abolished just a few years earlier. The paradox is that the military officers who rose with Toussaint had been freemen of color before

emancipation and were just as appreciative of the importance of reestablishing military and productive order, though at the price of diminishing
freed slaves' autonomy.[70]

For those who had staged the republican coup of September 4, 1797,
the law of 12 Nivôse, Year VI, was the swan song. Behind the legislation
aimed at providing the inhabitants of the Antilles and the metropolis with
juridical equality, one can see the hand of Commissar Léger-Félicité Sonthonax; he and Étienne Polverel were among the authors of the compromise between the freed slaves of Saint-Domingue and the newborn French
Republic.[71] But its practical implementation was the remit of Laveaux,
who was responsible for giving Toussaint the maximum political and military authority on the island.[72] Laveaux, who had arrived in 1792 with
Sonthonax and Polverel, was the military ruler of Saint-Domingue from
June 1794 to the summer of 1796, the most difficult period for French sovereignty, during which the British and their Spanish allies invaded and
ended up capturing Martinique.[73] Sonthonax later oversaw French policy
there, when the Directory sent him from May 1796 to August of the following year, at which point Toussaint forced him to become a deputy in
the Directory and leave the island. From his departure until 1799, Laveaux
was president of the Conseil des Anciens, a legislative entity established by
the Constitution of Year III. Ultimately he was expelled from Guadeloupe
after being accused of favoring an agreement with Toussaint.[74]

Napoleon broke his promise to respect the law of general liberty
(16 Pluviôse of Year II) when he traitorously and wickedly announced the
new Constitution of Year VIII (1799), the first truly colonial and neoimperial document of its kind since the Revolution.[75] This was a return to
the recent past of the 1791 Constitution, which had still excluded colonies from the legislative framework of the parliamentary monarchy, and
it made slavery constitutional once again. Or perhaps it could be seen as a
return to a more distant past, that of the Old Regime, which had accepted
slavery as a private right to be protected. But, in fact, it was a return to a
fictitious past in the hope that France could transcend time and elude the
Revolution's mandate of equality. Before that 1799 swerve, Minister of Justice Cambacérès and Colonial Minister Forfait had drawn up a proposal
to minimize the 16 Pluviôse decree.[76] Similarly, there were several plans
afoot to launch a military invasion of Saint-Domingue, headed by General
Leclerc, and reimpose slavery. In other words, everything was in place to
make the 1799 Constitution a founding document.[77] The place of colonial possessions in the new nation, in the imperial nation, had never been
formulated so transparently. It was to be an exceptional place, a special

place. But the exception was barely defined. It would take shape, and it would be prolonged and consolidated, on the ground, through the actions of metropolitan authorities who now no longer felt constrained by notions of republican unity.[78]

The Constitution of Year VIII brazenly granted the executive the autonomy it needed to separate the overseas empire from the community of citizens. The new, unquestioned authorities accepted few of the proposals put forward by the judicial committee of which Sièyes was one of the most prominent members.[79] The outcome would be entirely to the liking of the First Consul. Gone were the declarations of rights, and though there were two legislative chambers (the Tribunal and the Corps Législatif), and the consultative, nonelected Conseil d'État, all initiatives in that regard were to be entirely transferred to the executive. The First Consul, protected by Article 41 ("le premier consul promulgue les lois . . ."), would take care of everything.[80] The future reserved for the colonists was precisely and concisely laid out in Title VII, Article 91: "Le régime des colonies françaises est déterminé par des lois spéciales."[81] This "less is more" stipulation, stating that the colonial regime would now be determined by special laws outside the metropolitan constitutional framework, would be hugely successful far beyond Waterloo. Its triumphant ascendancy is easy to explain. It was not simply a provision but rather the total restoration of old practices that had separated colonies and metropolis conceptually during the monarchy. The difference was that now it would have another meaning, given the assumption of the unitary ideal of the Republic as the basis of the nation: it would embody the exception within the framework of a Republic that was *une et indivisible*, words that constituted the mainstay of the political system (Title I, Article 1) even though the Constitution admonished that the mandate of unity extended only to *territoire européen*.[82] So this was not the restoration of old-regime legislative pluralism; rather, it was the elevation of constitutional exceptionalism, the beginning of a long and triumphant history of "dual constitutions," as they were known by jurists. Success would be unstoppable, but one must gaze beyond the French example to appreciate that fact fully. The French were first (along with the French-controlled Batavian Republic, with its slave-owning colonies in the Antilles), but they would be followed by the Spanish and then the Portuguese.[83] Most surprising of all was that the constitution prepared by Toussaint in 1801 proclaimed in its first article, "Saint-Domingue, dans toute son étendue . . . forme le territoire d'une seule colonie, qui fait partie de l'Émpire français, mais qui est soumise à des lois particulières."[84] Here was the triumph of special laws, now implanted in a new colonial order that was worlds apart from the intentions of those who had fought for constitutional changes in the metropolis. The reinstatement of slavery on July 16, 1802, in the places where it had not been effectively abolished, and in May 1803 in Guadeloupe, would make everything clear.[85]

Words are never innocent, and certainly not in the mouth of a victorious general. Contemporaries, particularly those living in the most turbulent French possessions, had no doubt as to the significance of *spécialité*. But just in case anyone was unsure, there was a second, equally crucial decision: the shameful restoration of slavery on May 20, 1802 (30 Floréal of Year X). Slavery would be immediately restored in places where slavery had not been abolished on the ground, and later in other places, such as Guadeloupe, where the July 1802 decree was not proclaimed until May of the following year.[86] Here again, the law of 30 Floreal was deliberately synthetic.[87] This historically unique and bitter step backward was inevitable once Napoleon personally ordered Forfait in late 1799 to hold assemblies of white colonists to get a sense of what the situation in the Antilles was.[88] After that, everyone knew which way the wind was blowing. In the colonial ministry, a former legislator and now a high functionary, François Granet, was also working on a plan to reintroduce slavery. Article 1 of the law of 30 Floréal stated that in colonies returned to France under the Treaty of Amiens, "l'esclavage sera maintenu conformément aux lois et règlements antérieures à 1789 [slavery will be maintained according to the laws and regulations in place prior to 1789]," which included (Article 2) those in the Indian Ocean. Florence Gauthier has incisively asked what exactly was being reestablished—the 1685 Code Noir or the eighteenth-century reforms?—and replied that it was the reprise of "la législation des théoriciens ségrégationnistes qui avaient élevé une barrière entre liberté et esclavage par le préjugé de couleur [legislation by champions of segregation who had raised a barrier between liberty and slavery on the basis of color]."[89]

And what was to happen to the rest of the French empire, shattered by war and internal conflicts? The answer would have to wait. Napoleon knew that the best time to restore order was just after signing the Amiens treaty. But there were great differences among the various parts of the empire —which included the prefectural system, crony monarchies led by his own brothers, the Confederation of the Rhine, and the Duchy of Warsaw— many of them deeply affected by the revolutionary cycle.[90] In order for the reestablishment of slavery to work, the enlightened practice of slave trafficking was permitted in accordance with laws dating from before 1789.[91] The First Consul was supported in these decisions by the entourage he had assembled three years earlier, including Denis Décres of the Ministry of the Navy and the Colonies, and Honoré Joseph Antonin Ganteaume of the Council of State.[92] On July 2, 1802 (13 Messidor of Year X), they decreed that all free blacks and mulattos who entered French European territory would be imprisoned.[93] It was the end of one era and the start of another, which would last until 1848, when slavery would finally, definitively be abolished in the French colonies and when transoceanic citizenship once again became a reality.

CHAPTER FOUR

The British Empire beyond the American Crisis

THE NORTH AMERICAN CRISIS would be the most serious ever undergone by the British empire until Indian independence in 1947. It was so catastrophic and provoked such divisions within British society that many of the policy decisions of the following decades would be taken with the aim of mitigating its consequences.[1] But while certain government practices and choices were made in the shadow of that bitter defeat, Great Britain in no way renounced its imperial vocation. Indeed, having spectacularly strengthened its state apparatus along with military might and fiscal power, it soon became the world's leading power, and London became the world's commercial and financial capital.[2] At the same time, the French Revolution and the gradual rise of the Napoleonic regime—a major rival in the race to world power—spurred Britain to reorganize its imperial weight and extend its hegemony well beyond the limits of the territories it had dominated before the American Revolution.[3]

The transformation of British dominions after the loss of the Thirteen Colonies has been written about, both well and widely.[4] Territorial and institutional changes brought about a reorganization of British rule over its North American and South Asian enclaves.[5] Briefly, North America and the Caribbean were stabilized (and the latter was extended after the seizure of Trinidad, Tobago, Saint Lucia, and Martinique after 1794); the East India Company marked off a huge hegemonic space in India, Ceylon, and Southeast Asia; and further possessions were established in the Mediterranean, the Cape of Good Hope (1806, formerly Dutch) and Mauritius (1810, formerly French). In short, an empire built on a majority of British settlers and slaves gave way to one in which colonists ruled a population representing a variety of religions (Catholicism, Hinduism, and Islam) and "races" (a concept not yet relevant).[6] In addition, huge commercial areas in Latin America and Southern Europe were "informally" dominated by the British, whose capital and products were decisive in facilitating further penetration.[7] The opium monopoly and tea trade to the rest of the world ensured British merchants' presence throughout South and Southeast Asia.[8]

At the heart of this recovery and extension of influence was a sharp but not always visible ideological battle in the domestic sphere between champions of the old system of commercial protectionism (e.g., sugar growers in the Caribbean, large landowners and rent seekers, the East India Company) and the new industrialists, urban radicals, and influential intellectuals who opposed monopolies and excessive taxation, which they saw as a form of wealth redistribution to privileged groups.[9] The moral battle over the slave trade was a sign that things would soon change.[10] Also at stake was the transformation of the British state itself, which, without the administrative and fiscal reforms of William Pitt the Younger leading up to the 1832 reforms, would not have had the necessary fiscal base or flexibility necessary to survive the North American crisis and the Napoleonic blockade.[11] Once the war with France was over, the British empire entered a new phase marked by the abolition of slavery; emigration facilitated by social reformers, which brought about heightened tension with native peoples of North America, Oceania, and southern Africa, as well as with British commercial monopolies; and consolidation for a few more decades of the East India Company's rule in Asia and southern Africa.[12] This new phase illustrates how difficult it is for contradictory new times to absorb old political traditions. Imperial connections were reinforced without abandoning notions of rights and representation, which, thanks to the revolutions and various failed imperial constitutions, had by then spread around the world.

In this chapter I explore how the grand ideas of the previous chapters—representation and sovereignty, voice and loyalty, the instruments of imperial governments—were revised in light of the British empire's crisis in the 1770s and the subsequent transformations outlined above.[13] Britain was able to retain certain inherited features of the old colonial regime and alter them from above, unencumbered by revolutionary rupture. The principal engine of institutional change for the empire was a function of Britain's peculiar position on the international stage; paradoxically, its incipient liberal and parliamentary system would also become the central nervous system (and bank) for a conservative alliance or coalition formed to isolate radical French governments—starting in the summer of 1792, leading to the first blockade of French ports, and ending with Waterloo.[14] This meant that Britain favored continuity and had a certain fondness for the eighteenth-century institutional system as it proceeded to snuff out any revolutionary threats; and thus, the new imperial position tended to progressively incorporate corrections to the model that had prevailed during the crises of the First Empire.[15]

Two issues combined to steer matters forward. First, there was a need to ensure the unity of empire through consensus and at the same time maintain the empire's power mechanisms.[16] Second, Britain had to put a stop to the centrifugal tendencies that emerged after the American War of Independence and the partial British withdrawal from Irish politics in 1782, after Henry Grattan's celebrated declaration of parliamentary independence.[17] In the latter instance, government institutions in Dublin adopted a tone that anticipated policies in the crown's white settlements (Canada, New Zealand, and Australia) a century later, an interregnum before the Acts of Union in 1801.[18] The relationship between these two issues worked to impede the constitutional project that was the king-in-parliament from legislating about or for the imperial ensemble.

As Jack Greene has written, the North American crisis showed that the British empire could be weak; its power was not limitless.[19] The most obvious manifestation of the breadth of the late-eighteenth-century crisis was the nearly total disappearance of the already blurred frontier between local and imperial matters as the North American troubles went hand in hand with debates over the Quebec Act (Acte de Québec) of 1774 and the Irish rebellion of 1782. These three conflicts, which all centered on the exercise of authority in a decentralized empire, helped solidify the configuration that David Milobar has called a constitutional center and periphery.[20] On one side of the barricade stood those who favored strengthening and protecting the liberties of overseas crown subjects and who thus favored the inertias of the old colonial system that for years had been sufficiently flexible to accommodate those demands.[21] Quite diverse segments of the British imperial world were united on these points, including nonconformists and Low Church Anglicans in the metropolis, the radicals of London and other cities, and a broad political and cultural sector, based on country traditions,[22] who opposed strong government and any power associated with large commercial interests and the persuasive (or, to some, corrupting) capacity of privileged companies, among which the East India Company was the most emblematic. On the opposite side, facing off against this democratic and continuist conglomerate, was an alliance created through necessity and conviction, which the aforementioned historian called the constitutional center. The fundamental element uniting its followers was their desire to exalt the power of king and Parliament, the mainstay holding up the entire eighteenth-century political system, English in origin but British and imperial in its development.[23] This tendency rested on a belief that protecting a timeless and unchanged constitution, the sum of practices resulting from customs in the context of a jumble of local assemblies and rights, would be utter and inconceivable defeatism, especially in times of revolution and imperial competition. Given Great Britain's grave circumstances, the discourse of continuity made no sense without strengthening the state, the solid nucleus of constitutional practice.[24] Military defeat at the hands of the Americans accelerated adoption of policies and institutional solutions for which the constitutional center had been fighting since the Seven Years' War. The empire that resulted was, however, in the words of Peter Marshall, "a different kind of empire, which directly challenged earlier ideals. It was an empire of which the territorial base had greatly expanded, in itself a source of deep concern."[25] The new imperial politics would make it necessary to reconcile liberty and order, which certainly had not been easy up to that point. New solutions were needed; those of the past had been overused and had failed.[26]

In this panorama of a newly strengthened empire with more powerful bureaucratic and military instruments, the invocation of liberty was no mere rhetorical concession. On the contrary, it was the guarantee of a just and lasting order, the ethos that distinguished the British empire from its rivals. Rome's decline, as Edward Gibbon and Adam Ferguson had shown their contemporaries, had been caused by degenerate government over other peoples and by the abandonment of Rome's own institutions in favor of authoritarianism and corruption.[27] The great orator Edmund Burke warned early and often of the well-known risks of governmental excess in North America (in the 1760s he skillfully represented New York's interests before Parliament), India, and Ireland.[28] But the great liberal was also a firm supporter of the supremacy of Westminster, which was the guarantee of morality in the empire and the only possible restraint against despotism by imperial agents.[29] From this perspective, it is easy to understand how proponents of stronger imperial and military power might also praise the virtues of liberty, shifting smoothly into the officially modulated version of abolitionist proposals. From 1780 to 1830, morality, liberty, and authority would be joined together in new and problematic ways.

The big question for champions of liberty, which they could not answer, was how and with which instruments one could govern territories acquired through conquest rather than through settlement—in other words, territories inhabited by peoples with cultural, legal, and political conceptions different than one's own. With that in mind, the experiments and reforms carried out in places with heterogeneous situations and societies should be reexamined. Imperial power in Ireland, northern India, British North America, and even in Asian and African enclaves now reflected substantial variations from standard procedure during the First British Empire. Paradoxically, the instruments wielded by rulers did not change much; they continued to be scarce and unrefined. Without wishing to underestimate the administrative changes and proconsular practices introduced in America and India, the key issue was not so much colonial military capacity as it was defining a new command structure in local contexts where some form of consensus was necessary.[30] Starting with the experiences in Ireland and Canada, what John Benyon has called "the most important of British paramountcies" were developed, a chain of possessions and power complexes that would ensure the viability of an empire expanding on four continents.[31] This is the background for proper consideration of the four variables of imperial reconstitution: more executive power, limits on colonial representation, an agreement not to extract taxes from the colonies, and colonial subjects' distance from Westminster.

Affirmation of imperial sovereignty in the framework of new adjustments between center and periphery altered the ideological scenery on both sides. The metropolis loosened its grip on the idea of rights inherent to the English by virtue of their birth, which had been the ideological basis of the colonists' political autonomy during the North American crisis. Two influential writers summarized this perspective toward the end of the era, in the 1830s and 1840s, with particular attention to the complex paths between metropolis and colonies. The first of the two, George Cornewall Lewis, the most systematic of the English essayists on these and other subjects, was a friend and correspondent of John Stuart Mill.[32] He undertook the task of demolishing the previous century's ideas and replacing them with a purely historical position on the nature of government,[33] outlining his ideas in *An Essay on the Government of Dependencies* after being invited by the colonial secretary, Lord Glenelg, to join a commission studying the political status of Malta.[34] He wrote his book in 1836–38 while in Malta, in the company of the greatest jurist of the time, John Austin.[35] The work was a full-scale celebration of the supremacy of imperial government, justified through the idea of the indivisibility of sovereignty. The argument ends with an emphatic defense of the very essence of empire: "The entire territory subject to a supreme government possessing several dependencies (that is to say, a territory formed of a dominant country together with its dependencies), is sometimes styled an *empire*; as when we speak of the British empire. Agreeably with this acceptation of the word empire, the supreme government of a nation, considered with references to its dependencies, is called the *imperial government*, and the imperial Parliament is considered the *imperial parliament*, as distinguished from the provincial parliament or dependency."[36] Shortly afterward, Herman Merivale, a contemporary of Lewis, gave a series of lectures, among the most deeply analytical explorations of these questions.[37] Leaving the tricky question of government and parliamentary authority to the very end, he said of past policies that "their tendency, on the whole, was to construct subordinate commonwealths, not merely united to the mother-state for purposes of commerce and external relations, but of which the domestic institutions were to be controlled and modelled by the superior power at home."[38] He deferred to Lewis, the leading writer in this area, in defining "paternal jurisdiction."[39] Both men similarly emphasized the center's sovereignty over all imperial matters, a position that represented the death knell for eighteenth-century theories of inalienable rights and also reflected the diversity of the empire, which was preventing any single governmental formula from emerging.[40] There is no more useless concept for defining these developments than empiricism; solutions for governing an expanding empire based on constitutional and juridical traditions, experience, and reflection do not add up to empirical adaptability.[41]

American Colonial Laboratories: Canada and the West Indies

The areas that best illustrate changes in how the empire was governed after the American Revolution were the remaining North American territories and the West Indies; these were preserved despite the Americans' expansionist desires and were made explicit with the Louisiana Purchase in 1803, the U.S. invasion of Canada in 1812–13, and the Monroe Doctrine in 1823 (even with its defensive undertones).[42] In both Canada and the Caribbean, the imperial political complex was reinforced, though in different ways. In brief, while British North American stabilization after the Acadian exodus during the Seven Years' War meant that some forms of political collaboration were now open to Francophones and Catholics, in the Caribbean the British took measures that affected the very essence of the sugar plantation complex.[43] In both places there was an atmosphere of respect for the balance between central authority and the institutional system of the first empire, which was far more decentralized,[44] and this atmosphere of respect for balance involved recognizing the complexity and heterogeneity of the societies making up a world empire.[45]

The creation of British North America as a stable political entity meant that a series of complex questions had to be addressed.[46] The first was to find the key to stability, given the ethnic and cultural divisions that up to now had been relatively absent in the empire of compatriots; in Canada one had to deal with Catholic Francophones and with Indian nations. Less important on a demographic or social plane was the question of slaves who had found refuge there along with their loyalist owners, though the slaves would become free with general abolition.[47] The Royal Proclamation of October 1763 drew a dividing line between the colonial backcountries and the Indian nations that fixed the limits of royal authority at the same time.[48] Aside from the monarchy's evident humanitarian intentions, there were also the expansionist ambitions of New York, Pennsylvania, and Virginia to deal with. The Quebec Act (including important secret instructions) constituted the true foundation of the new possession before the American deluge.[49] At the stroke of a pen, relations between Catholics and the empire were altered once French civil law and Catholicism were accepted.[50] Government supremacy was key for the establishment of frontiers separating crown lands (those able to be colonized) from those reserved for future allies in the Indian nations.[51] It is important to keep in mind that the decision to draw the line between the two societies was made during Pontiac's War, which itself signaled a revival among the native inhabitants of the Ohio Valley, Great Lakes region, and Illinois Country.

Adjustments to the line drawn in 1763 could not strengthen the imperial position without first resolving tensions with the *canadiens*, some 100,000 people constituting the majority of the future province of Québec.[52] If, at first, terms for their integration in the empire were harsh—they were denied a representative assembly, French civil law was eliminated, the seigneurial regime was dismantled along with the Catholic tithe, and the fur and pelt trade with the vast territory known as *pays d'en haut* was limited—such discrimination could not last long. (In contrast, Upper Canada—today's Ontario—was later developed by the imperial government as a refuge for Tories fleeing from the other side of the border, sometimes with their slaves). *Seigneuries* (the "clergy reserves") were confiscated and given to Anglican parishes in the region.[53] The need for rectification in Québec was clear. French law was reintroduced, Catholicism was respected, and the loyalty oath to the crown was deemed acceptable for joining the Legislative Council that advised the governor (though for a long time the French, despite their numbers, remained a minority in that body).[54] But these measures brought about new problems, the major one being tenacious resistance from the Anglophone Protestant minority. Merchants and other emigrants from the British Isles demanded special protection, as did military stragglers who had gone north for refuge after losing to the Americans. There also were Iroquois who had allied themselves with the British and were unsure about their future along the vast border being negotiated between the new republic and the old empire.[55]

These divisions among inhabitants help explain the political division of the country into four provinces in 1784 and six in 1791: Upper and Lower Canada (the old province of Québec), Newfoundland, New Brunswick, Cape Breton, and Nova Scotia, the latter two the result of the first conquest of Nouvelle France and the Acadians' departure.[56] Given the variety of situations and the insufficiency of all prior efforts, it was a major undertaking to stabilize the two Québécois provinces, especially as the defeated continued arriving until and after the War of 1812.[57] Despite their proven loyalty, these refugees were coming to a place where there was a delicate balance between elected assemblies and monarchic governing authorities, since legislative assemblies were reestablished in 1791–92, constituting a counterpoint to governors appointed by London.[58] The principal task was to manage the enormous amounts of land reserved for the crown and make them competitive with U.S. lands, which were administered by companies, and attractive to British immigrants. This was one of the major challenges for the imperial administration throughout the nineteenth century. An even greater challenge was to find the constitutional balance in the other large province, which was both Francophone and Catholic, with its Anglophone colonists, immigrants, and administrators. The milestone in this regard was the 1791 Constitutional Act, which (along with Pitt's India Act of 1784) was the basis of the new empire after defeat at the hands of the republican forces of the United States and was a device for governmental stability.[59] Suddenly *ius sanguinis* was replaced with *ius solis*, so that *canadiens* could enjoy rights and political representation wherever the French population was a clear majority. From then on, Catholics could take their seats with a simple oath, a marked difference from other places, such as Ireland and Trinidad, that also had assemblies and massive Catholic populations. These measures and the Roman Catholic Relief Act (also of 1791), whatever their obvious limitations with regard to civil equality, indicated the path that would be taken in 1802 and 1829 in Ireland (yet another milestone for the empire, where alliances during the North American crisis had created a very delicate situation).[60] The aim

of controlling these developments from above constituted both an opportunity and a potential Achilles' heel; the opportunity and the risk both
lay with governors' ability to form alliances with contentious factions. In
order to consolidate their position, governors strengthened the authority
of the nonelected Council so as to avoid long political battles with elected
assemblies, and at the same time used patronage to build an aristocracy
associated with the crown, thus reproducing on a smaller scale the mechanisms of Great Britain itself before the 1832 reforms.[61] In the medium run,
the most important thing was to tighten the nexus between government in
London and the local executive and military forces that guaranteed survival against the aggressive republicans to the south. In Grenville's words,
the aim was to preserve the "due mixture of the Monarchical and aristocratic parts of the British Constitution."[62] Given that with the 1778 Declar-
atory Act the British government had committed itself to not raising taxes
in the colonies, this implied a major transfer of resources from the center
to distant possessions.

From the start, seeds for future crises had been sown. The idea was
to integrate the Francophone majority into the empire's constitutional
paternalist system while at the same time building fortifications around
what was meant to be a British constitution in the conservative sense. This
meant that the government and its nonelected chamber were not answer-
able to any parliamentary majority, either Anglophone or Francophone,
and also that the government had a free hand to expand its power through
the church, the army, and patronage.[63] In these circumstances, it was no
surprise that there was tension between the lower house of French Lower
Canada and the British executive. It made no difference that in the 1820s,
with constant conflicts between the governor general, George Ramsey, 9th
Earl of Dalhousie, and the speakers of the chamber (including, on several
occasions, the Catholic leader of the *patriotes*, Louis-Joseph Papineau),
the two houses had been merged as a way of getting around the Catholic
majority in one of them.[64] Tax disputes, the impossibility of accommo-
dating the old French seigneurial land tenure system within an empire
trapped by incessant financial pressures, and the rebellions in Lower and
Upper Canada of 1837–38 marked the critical decade before the Canadian
civil war. The flexibility of the late eighteenth century appeared to have
reached its limit.

The ninety-two demands raised in Westminster in 1834 by the
patriotes—who preferred that name to *canadiens*, to show they were the
leading opposition to the imperial blood compact—indicated the level of
unhappiness.[65] The demands were rejected out of hand despite support

from important figures in Parliament. The rebellions illustrated the limits of British North America's place in the general political framework of the empire.[66] When calls for greater equality and positive integration were ignored even though the British had appeared to welcome such initiatives, Papineau and a sector of Québécois society opted for republican insurrection, which benefited from French and Belgian turmoil in 1830.[67] By criticizing the narrowness of the imperial framework, rather than focusing on ethnic divisions, they also managed to channel the discontent of many Irish and Britons who were not happy with government paternalism. The continual flow of emigrants from the metropolis, many of them fleeing terrible rural crises in Ireland and elsewhere, raised social tensions in a possession where the crown and, to the west, the Hudson's Bay Company acted as grand landlords over what were known as "vacant lands."[68] In the end, radicalized Anglophones and suffering Francophones were defeated by the imperial army, and many were executed or deported to Tasmania. Papineau and William Lyon Mackenzie, the principal leaders, went into exile in the United States. In the aftermath of the revolt by the *patriotes*, on February 10, 1838, the constitution of Lower Canada was suspended.[69] Their defeat enabled the Catholic Church to speak for Francophones and allowed the British administration to find a more generous and lasting solution.

The reform that one may intuit here had a name. For many years the Durham Report, or "Report on the Affairs of British North America," had been regarded as the masterpiece of imperial reformism and the cornerstone of modern Canada. The 1839 report by John Lambton, 1st Earl of Durham, advocated two things: institutional unification and, taking advantage of British immigration, massive Anglicization.[70] The latter was a controversial issue, so much so that the report's author lost his reputation as a result of his involvement. As for the unification, the 1841 Act of Union, which merged the two Canadian provinces, was a response to the pessimist stance of those in charge of imperial policy, particularly Lord Grey of Howick (Durham's brother-in-law, who had appointed him governor) and James Stephen in the Colonial Office. What was new was not so much Durham's ideas but the broad reorientation of the empire regarding its large possessions.[71] This entailed an effort to introduce some sort of "simple and ingenious device" (in Durham's words) so as to divide powers of "responsible government" and thereby loosen up relations between elective assemblies (the key to popular politics) and the colonial executive.[72] The intention was to shape an empire based on multiple obligations while winning over domestic public opinion, which was opposed to any more spending. The only way of limiting the costs of empire in a restrictive liberal-representative system was to win commitments from overseas parliamentary majorities to pay their share of territorial defense. Through this opening the Canadian crisis would find resolution in the twenty years prior to formal recognition of self-government in 1867.[73]

In the West Indies, meanwhile, old forms of First Empire representation were maintained as that empire was crumbling. In addition, West Indies assemblies were exported to some of the Ceded Islands (acquired from France during the late-eighteenth-century wars), most especially Trinidad, although a period of transition between the inherited forms of governance and the British one was tolerated.[74] It was only much later, during the Jamaican crisis of 1865, that the old model of imperial government would be reexamined. At the heart of that system, prolonged amid the great revolutionary experiments, lay assemblies of planters who constituted the counterweight to imperial power and its local personifications in governors and their councils. Preserving that balance would have been reasonable while the Thirteen Colonies were breaking away, but the revolutionary cycle had introduced factors that seriously undermined it. One of those factors was crucial: the social institution of slavery had become discredited.[75] As we saw earlier, the existence of a large slave population was a decisive issue until the end of the eighteenth century; in Jamaica there was a strong and consistent Whig culture of racial self-government, as advocated by Edward Long. A few decades later, in an empire undergoing transformation, that apparently solid Caribbean tradition began looking like a conspicuous anachronism. The very existence of servile labor had been questioned in the metropolis since the 1780s. New moral opposition to slavery, encouraged from below by Protestant sects and radicals and encouraged from above for other reasons, would lead to the first abolition of the slave trade in 1807 and the so-called amelioration policies after the Napoleonic Wars. These politics were a clear challenge to the planters who overwhelmingly dominated insular assemblies.

On alert after the North American crisis, Britain tried to protect the West Indies from turmoil. First, governors chose not to impose taxes to help pay for the enormous military efforts in the Caribbean (especially during the invasion of the Spanish part of Santo Domingo) during the revolutionary wars. Precautions were even greater in the former Dutch colonies that became British Guyana; Trinidad, taken from Spain in 1797; and the Ceded Islands, which changed hands several times during the conflicts. In all these places the old forms of government and representative bodies inherited from the former occupying powers were tolerated. The idea was to slowly shift the balance of power rather than force sudden changes.

But despite the good intentions, matters proved problematic. In Grenada, one of the Ceded Islands, conflict between the British and Catholic French populations was endemic, sometimes caused by overly harsh practices by authorities. That was the case with General Melville, the Scottish governor of the island, who wished not only to irritate the French but to force them to withdraw from the local assembly and sign a declaration against the Catholic doctrine of transubstantiation, which was not unusual in courts of law but was very much so in representative assemblies. After the French returned to their seats three years later, it was the British who walked out, unhappy at now being the minority. But the British ultimately imposed their conditions—exactly what they were unable to do at that very moment in British North America. Things were even more complicated in the possessions captured from the French, such as Martinique and Guadaloupe, where decisions were motivated by the unpleasantries in dealings with non-Britons in Canada. The outcome was a strange and unique mix of authority in the hands of the governor(s) (the highest military authority, despite the council of advisers, thereby resolving the old French problem of imbalance between governor and intendent), religious tolerance (after some misguided experiments like Melville's in Grenada), respect for prevailing civil law, and a land policy firmly in the hands of the imperial government.[76] A similar solution was found in Trinidad, which was of enormous strategic importance for launching commercial attacks against the Spanish-controlled mainland. At first the British tried a Canadian-style solution, "the provisional continuation of our [Spaniards'] laws and religion"; in other words, Catholicism and the Laws of the Indies. They even respected the tradition of the *cabildo*, or representative council, where the same three groups gathered as before: Spaniards, French, and freemen of color. But when these groups demanded an assembly like that of Jamaica or Barbados, the answer—after more than a decade of indecision (1797–1808)—was no. Both the conflict and the report on the conflict by Governor Thomas Picton are interesting; he made clear his scant confidence in the locals, particularly the bad example that would be set by allowing participation by freemen of color, whom he called "irreclaimable Republicans."[77] In the end, fear of the plantations and the repression of slaves in 1805 led to the suspension of the assembly just five years later, and power returned to the highest authorities.[78] It was a preview of what would happen in Jamaica and the rest of the Caribbean (except Barbados) a half century later.

The example of Trinidad was soon applied in other colonies in the stormy Caribbean. First was Guyana, taken from the Dutch in 1796; the British were keen on not letting it fall into French hands. Several small colonies captured during the war with France were reorganized in similar fashion, quickly adapting to the demands of the revolutionary commotion and the collapse of their respective metropoles. The British followed a well-respected line of action, consisting of accepting a place's institutional inheritance but making it far more manageable through reforms that strengthened high authorities' capacities. Around 1830 this approach would become known as "crown colonies," one of the models most frequently used in the following century.[79] This was a variation of direct government with no representative filters or counterweight other than rights established by law; most important, it was a model that depended on the axis between governors and the Colonial Office in London. And given that it was the metropolitan government that decided what the internal "constitution" should be, and that it had absolutely no intention of replicating the First Empire's triad of governor-council-assembly, the British had an enormous amount of flexibility from one place to another. This exercise of "pure sovereignty," to quote Lewis, allowed them to drape themselves in the garments of English political tradition (such as organizing legislative councils starting in 1831) or to veer toward complete assimilation through legislative assemblies (though without responsible government, unlike in British North America, which had important communities of European British origin) and acceptance of the imperfect coexistence of diverse religions and juridical regimes.[80] The formula, whose genesis lay in America, especially in the Caribbean, later spread to Gibraltar, Malta, Mauritius, the Seychelles, Ceylon, Singapore, and Hong Kong—the entire new geography of the British empire after the Napoleonic Wars.[81]

The most important lesson of the defeat against the Thirteen Colonies was that imperial authority had to be strong and flexible at the same time. It was a useful lesson for the possessions that had been incorporated at the turn of the eighteenth to the nineteenth century, but it was especially useful for the old colonies in the Caribbean. Indeed, planters' questionable loyalty was the essence of the problem in islands with the most solid veteran British populations. They may have remained loyal during the American War of Independence, but their loyalty had its limits and was aimed at protecting the institution that sustained their entire social system.[82] That institution was being threatened at home with the rise of abolitionism, be it morally motivated or politically expedient in the metropolis. In the sugar islands, which were the crown's oldest possessions (along with Ireland), the government was basically in the hands of the assemblies, as a result of institutional developments over the preceding century and the withdrawal of the British from internal affairs after American independence. British abolitionist James Stephen, who was well informed about the Antilles, wrote to William Wilberforce that a rift could be forged in the old colonies by following the example of Trinidad, that is, with greater domestic government intervention.[83] The first manifestation in this regard was an obligatory census of the slave population organized by abolitionists, a measure that was particularly necessary in 1815, given that the French, whose large islands had been returned to them, were not necessarily going to respect the prohibition on trafficking.[84] The census led to a stark confrontation between the British government and the planters, who dominated the assemblies and had a strong lobby in Westminster. In 1820 they fell into line on that issue, though the census did not end up having the consequences sought by abolitionists; they had seen it as an instrument with which to ameliorate the slaves' plight, but Tory governments and the assemblies managed to resist those initiatives.[85] More than economics, it was the long abolitionist crusade that was the first and the inexorable factor in the crisis of slavery.[86]

This was the key to what would happen in subsequent decades: efforts at home to reform slavery would be effectively resisted by local assemblies that had a remarkable ability to halt initiatives from the center.[87] The reforms ended up being reduced to partial measures, such as prohibiting corporal punishment, protecting slaves' religious practices (an important issue for the dissenters, who were active among the slaves and the key to Baptist churches' success), or the right to claim manumission along the lines of what happened in Spain.[88] Assemblies pretended to cooperate, but slave uprisings in Barbados and Demerara (part of Guyana) in 1816 and 1823, respectively, showed that progress had been slow, and the same thing happened in Jamaica in late 1831 and early 1832 on the eve of definitive abolition.[89] The entire institutional structure was in question, given that the assemblies obviously were not cooperating and little could be expected from Westminster until the 1832 reforms. When the Jamaican assembly approved the Consolidated Slave Acts (1816, 1826, and 1829), for example, the disinterest in the measures' implementation was obvious to everyone. As David Murray explained, London's authoritarian stance was especially evident with the rise of James Stephen and Henry Taylor, who made an effort to learn what was going on in the islands; they were in direct contact with the Colonial Office and the governors and also used informal channels of communication with churches, abolitionists, and cities.[90] When amelioration reached its limits, there were timid efforts to reform the Antillean governments. The 2nd Earl Grey and Viscount Goderich in the Colonial Office, for example, wrote a proposal to reform the government of both the old and the new colonies. But in the midst of these efforts, major political reforms eliminated the Antilles lobby (along with the East India Company), and in January 1833, Earl Grey, Stephen, and Taylor began drawing up a proposal for general emancipation that suited the desires of both Parliament and the empire.[91] As a result, France, Spain, and Denmark, which all still had Caribbean possessions with slavery, were left vulnerable.

An Imperial Parliament

North American reforms and the end of slavery in the Antilles and Mauritius clearly showed that the metropolis had the ability to swap old colonial structures for new ones. In saying this, I am not advocating the revival of the old imperial historiography—"teaching patriotism by example," in the apt phrase of C. A. Bayly—that was put out of its misery decades ago.[92] On the contrary, my aim is not only to reestablish global consideration of imperial dynamics between colonial societies and the metropolis but also to think in complex ways about each of these two poles, which were equally capable of generating power systems. This is true for Europe as well as for non-European empires such as Brazil and the United States, which were exceptions but certainly not unique. Societies on both sides of the colony/ metropolis divide were transformed in parallel fashion according to the characteristics of developed nineteenth-century societies: industry and agricultural capitalism, urbanization and massive forced or voluntary emigration, representative institutions, the definition of a new political subject (citizen and/or elector), and, of course, the ambition to assert themselves over less developed societies in their own space of sovereignty or beyond.

Parliament itself is an important factor here. The 1832 reforms put an end to the era of virtual representation inherited from the eighteenth century along with well-known forms of corruption through lobbies.[93] As became obvious with the Irish dynamic, no one could be surprised at how the lower house used subrogation to divide up the various British societies, a tradition dating from the start of the century. Until the reforms, that explicit division of power replicated the peculiar way in which West Indian and Indian interests were represented, meaning, respectively, by slaveholding planters from Jamaica and Barbados or by the East India Company, a shareholder company with power over millions of subjects in South Asia.[94] The manner in which slavery reforms were discussed pointed the way for the elimination of planters' virtual, albeit effective, representation at Westminster.[95] This was an era marked by so-called colonial reforms and claims of self-government by "white" (countrymen and the assimilated) colonies, all with intricate contradictions between the continuation of the old imperial expansion and calls for so-called free-trade imperialism.[96] Without the centrality of parliamentary life, neither the development of increasingly influential public opinion nor the formation of parliamentary majorities—both typical of the British empire since 1832—would have taken shape. While it is true that since the end of the 1700s, government's growing role had introduced an essential variation into the constitutional dynamic of king-in-parliament as being central to the system, it is no less true that with the affirmation and purges of Parliament during the great reform campaigns, the end of the Corn Laws, improvements in industrial working conditions, and the abolition of slavery, the old-style parliamentary game was gone. In the center of it all lay the imperial Parliament, the mightiest and most praised of parliaments until the election of an Indian to its ranks in 1892.[97]

The demise of colonial lobbies in the lower house was a critical step in this process without which the new definition of Parliament as a truly imperial chamber would have been impossible. But elimination of virtual representation meant figuring out how parliamentary representation could be imperial or, on the contrary, if open representation by colonists should be allowed. There were many who thought it possible and desirable to integrate and stabilize a range of political entities around the idea of collective representation that would be imperial in composition; this was similar to the formulas of the 1706–1707 and 1800–1801 Acts of Union for Scotland and Ireland, respectively.[98] In this sense, parliamentary precedents were well defined. The concern, and the possible solution, had taken shape during the North American crisis, when certain political and intellectual sectors accepted the hypothesis of an imperial parliament congruent with an expanding empire.[99] For a while it was the position of James Otis and Benjamin Franklin, who represented Massachussetts and Pennsylvania, respectively, at Parliament (Franklin appears to have been the author of the famous slogan linking taxation and representation) and also of Francis Maseres, who wrote an articulate defense in a 1770 pamphlet.[100] The idea of parliamentary integration was also discussed in Great Britain; Adam Smith was a proponent, and it seems he conferred privately with Franklin on the matter.[101] The Scotsman was so convinced, in fact, he came up with the wild idea that, since there were more subjects on the other side of the Atlantic than in Britain, the elected assembly should move there.[102] Jeremy Bentham was another defender of the imperial parliament. Pitt thought integration should take place in both chambers, an idea that was later dropped.[103] When British Prime Minister

Lord North's commissioners raised the idea, the Americans decided it was too late, and once it was discarded, the alternative was clear: similar representational forms that would be subordinate where compatriots and the assimilated had the majority. The case of British North America showed how adaptation would take place, and the example was followed later in Australia, New Zealand, and the Cape Colony.

Until then, as was noted earlier, Ireland was the only place with both colonial and imperial connotations where parliamentary integration had taken place. First it was integrated into the Westminster orbit; then, in 1829, impediments to (majority) Catholic political rights were lifted, and in 1832 the Irish minority entered Parliament.[104] Once Wellington fell from power, reforms were implemented, the Irish minority was integrated, and the possibility of adapting similar solutions elsewhere began being considered, just as the Irish case had closely followed that of Canada. The radical Joseph Hume, who had dealings with the Canadians, calculated the number of members of Parliament corresponding to India, the West Indies, and even the islands in the English Channel.[105] But nothing was to come of that, and the Irish reforms closed off inclusive options forever. Two observations are essential for understanding the end of this story. First, Irish integration was vital for military reasons and for internal security, as the Irish Volunteers had shown during American Revolution and the revolts and the crushing of Wolfe Tone's United Irishmen and the Act of Union of 1801 had clearly confirmed.[106] After that, Irish Protestants would occupy key positions in the British army, both at home and in the colonies, reproducing the prominent position of the Scots in the administration and military forces of the East India Company. And second, the reforms in the end reduced the number of seats so as to eliminate the rotten boroughs providing virtual representation for the West Indies and the nabobs of the East India Company.[107] The (painful) prospect of reforming slavery and chipping away at the great company's privileges and financial shortages—demands raised by increasingly mobilized segments of industrial British cities and radical London intellectuals—meant the rotten boroughs had to go.[108] And thus, either passively or actively, the centrality and imperial supremacy of the Parliament of Westminster was reinforced.

Neither Representation nor Assimilation

No place better exemplified the imperial authority that emerged from the wars with France than British India. This was an interesting paradox: a charter company to which the crown had granted exclusive commercial rights in Asia in 1602 had led the grand effort of establishing an Asian empire on the world map.[109] The company's mission was to defend shareholders' commercial interests, but in the context of rivalry with the Dutch and the French, along with the eighteenth-century crisis of the Mughal empire, it also was obliged to conduct diplomatic and military affairs, essentially exercising sovereignty.[110] British-French conflict, and conflicts between each of them with local powers, became highly fluid starting in 1707, with the near collapse of the Timurid empire. Until the end of the seventeenth century, small European armies had been unable to defeat the Mughal cavalry, but by the mid-eighteenth century the victories were many and swift. The change was due not only to better military technology but also to the French and British companies' greater commitment to territorial and diplomatic expansion. With the Anglo-French war of 1739, things took a new turn with fierce struggles to dominate major ports and their hinterlands, and the European companies began recruiting Indian sepoys for their military operations. Before capturing Bengal, the British took Madras in 1746 and extended their control over Arcot, Bombay, Pondicherry, and Chandanagore.

After defeating the French in 1756, some months later Robert Clive defeated the army of Siraj ud-Daulah, the last ruler (nabob) of Bengal.[111] British forces immediately set out from Calcutta to conquer Mysore, where Hyder Ali's Muslim dynasty had managed to synchronize a European-style military revolution with major internal transformations. Military expansion toward the Malabar coast and Hyder Ali's patent alliance with the French only increased the risk for the British. Tipu Sultan (Hyder Ali's eldest son), with his unequivocal relations with the Jacobin Club in the capital, became the bête noire of the British, who did everything they could to remove him.[112] Between the capture and destruction of Seringapatam in 1799 and the definitive defeat of the Maratha Confederacy in 1818, British military power became hegemonic in the subcontinent, going "from conquest to conquest," in the words of David Washbrook.[113]

Expansion transformed the East India Company and definitively altered the balance of power in India and all of Asia. The heart of this transformation lay in the company's heightened ability to administer the tribute system (*diwan*) that the Mughals had established in Bengal and the adjacent provinces of Bihar, Orissa, and Oudh, which were soon annexed.[114] "To rule is to tax," in the astute words of Dutch historian Peter Boomgaard, and so the incursion of company officials into the complicated realities of the Bengali interior forced the British to begin building a genuine state.[115] It was a hybrid power, in which Mughal functionaries continued using their old tribute system and many of their old tax collectors. This taxa-tion system, in Marshall's words, "tried to extract a large proportion of the resources of the mass of the population and [its] workings had a crucial effect on the distribution of local power throughout the province."[116] The ultimate objective was to finance direct trade between Bengal and Great Britain and thus save the earlier expense of importing massive amounts of money, which had not been to the liking of the company's London head-quarters.[117] British supremacy depended on collaboration with the high military command and high functionaries of the Mughal empire. These overlapping sovereignties are a key point if we are to understand Britain's rapid expansion and consolidation in India, which took place with Indian soldiers and money, with the aid of native dignitaries and rulers, in an exercise of power that was both shared and unequal.[118]

And yet, the complexities of tax collection were such that East India Company director Warren Hastings was forced to introduce a new, more professionalized corps of collectors, who would dominate Indian history until the demise of the company in 1857.[119] At the same time, efforts were made to better understand India's past, its administration of justice, and the basis for its "ancient constitution."[120] This was not entirely altruis-tic, being that the aim was to reproduce and then adapt old forms into a new state machinery that would be neither indigenous nor European. Hastings himself, who had promoted governance of the conquered prov-inces according to local practices, faced a parliamentary impeachment in London.[121] He was accused of abuse, corruption, and arbitrariness (in Hastings's own words, the feared collusion of Western venality and Eastern corruption); the investigation ran from 1787 to 1795, when the House of Lords finally acquitted him.[122] Burke, in the Commons, was es-pecially vociferous, with the alarming news reaching London about events in the company's dominions and his moral concerns about the empire.[123] In humanitarian circles both within and outside the political system, the misery of the Indian peasantry was obviously linked to respect for the con-stitution of the society over which Britain exercised dominion. Respect in that sense led straight to Burke's "trusteeship," the degree of power that could legitimately be exercised over societies without qualified represen-tation.[124] Anything else ran the risk of authoritarianism and corruption.

The British government for a long time had been keen on controlling the company, not necessarily for humanitarian reasons but because it was unsure as to the costs and consequences that territorial dominion might entail. The first parliamentary inquest, in 1767, was prompted by that concern and was aimed at clarifying the company's objectives as well as establishing its own contribution to its state-guaranteed protection, which ended up being 400,000 pounds a year. These inquiries led to Lord North's Regulating Act of 1773, the first serious attempt to control this strange monster that had come to life in the early seventeenth century. There were warnings that the East India Company might collapse, which British public opinion perceived as the result of excess, bad government, and outright theft. The company was forced to reform its army of native and British troops, in exchange for which it received the worldwide monopoly of the Chinese tea trade—the same Tea Act that was one of the causes of the Boston Tea Party. But these measures could not stabilize the East India Company, and as a result, dual authority was instituted that would last until the company was finally dissolved after the Indian Rebellion of 1857. Savings at any cost, as well as stability, were sought with the implementation of direct control and the appointment of Lord Cornwallis as governor general and commander in chief of all India.[125] Pitt then combined imperial authority with executive administrative authority. The Board of Control appointed by Parliament was charged with keeping up with everything going on in the subcontinent and had access to the correspondence between the director, in Calcutta, and the Court of Directors in London.[126] It was in these years that plans were drawn up to take Java and the other possessions of the Dutch East India Company, part of the Anglo-French rivalry. The end of the commercial monopoly in Asia in 1813 (aside from tea, which ended in 1833) shows the deep overlap between imperial politics in general and governance of company possessions. From then on, government in India was no longer a matter only for the East India Company.

The most important outcome of the imperial experience in India was the tribute system known as the Permanent Settlement of Bengal.[127] The tersely worded agreement centered on the *zamindars*, who were both landowners and tax collectors. These were occasionally hereditary posts, and thus the British saw them through the lens of their own land-tenure system as Asian equivalents of figures at home. Cornwallis and John Shore, his successor as governor general in Calcutta, proposed converting them into the mainstay of rural Bengal, giving them sufficient stability, including rents, so that they could bring about improvements in agriculture and property administration.[128] In practice, of course, things were more complicated, including deciding to whom exactly peasants should pay their rents in the dynamic and complex world of late-seventeenth-century Bengali agriculture.

In any case, the nature of the system left little room for maneuver, and the limits of Cornwallis's proposal meant that British administrators had

to act in two directions at once. First they encouraged British functionaries to look at other fiscal solutions, with monopolies turning out to be
the best solution. Among these fiscal monopolies, salt and opium became
critical pieces of a gigantic extraction machine, with opium the key to
maintaining the tea trade and further penetrating the Qing empire and
Southeast Asia.[129] The second set of actions entailed altering land revenue
systems in the other British presidencies (Bengal, Madras, and Bombay)
and territories coming under British control. The resultant Ryotwari System (literally, peasant system), developed by Sir Thomas Munro, governor of Madras since 1819, was based less on the organizational capacity
of large land holdings than on peasant communities.[130] British collectors
were both crucial and intrusive, and the formula would be exported to
Java by the young Thomas Raffles, with lasting consequences, even after
the Dutch returned.[131] The indirect outcome of all this back-and-forth was
to force the East India Company to establish more extensive and efficient
administration. During the 1820s and 1830s, the man in charge of doing
this was none other than James Mill, author of a canonical history of India
and father of John Stuart (also an EIC bureaucrat). Wielding David Ricardo's theory of land rents, Mill and his fellow Benthamites opposed the
Bengali solution, which they believed only strengthened the landed aristocracy whose metropolitan counterparts they loathed and whose interests
they hoped would crumble in the face of reforms on the subcontinent.[132]

Agricultural tribute systems were of great interest to British colonial administrators and their intellectual mentors in the metropolis.[133]
Later on, historians would also find them interesting, to the point that
it seemed not much remained to be said.[134] The question, however, was
not the tribute itself but how it was inserted into the productive, social,
and political structures of each place, as Robert Travers and Jon Wilson
both show in recent books.[135] The essential thing is to understand how
the East India Company became the true heir of the Timurid empire and
its successor states. It levied taxes, fashioned elite collaborators, and administered justice—that is, it defined a sovereign space. It did all this with
no representational restrictions along the lines of the form of government
prevalent in the nineteenth-century British empire. But there was one
difference: India could never be, and never was, a colony.[136] C. A. Bayly
defined this sort of proconsular dominion as "military despotism."[137]
Richard Wellesley consolidated dominion in the military arena by finally
defeating the Maratha Confederacy when he was governor general, and
dominion continued in place under reformist directors such as Dalhousie
and Lord William Bentinck until the 1857 Indian Rebellion, when the

company was nationalized. By then, new priorities were in place and British public opinion was far more articulated and demanding. In the end, the extension of guarantees of equality in India or throughout the rest of the "empire of strangers" would have coincided oddly with new measures regarding property taxes, land revenue, and other fiscal devices. All of which, of course, added up to the making of the imperial nation.

CHAPTER FIVE

Theory and Practice of French *Spécialité*

UNTIL THE 1848 REVOLUTION and the Second Republic, the French had rejected the possibility of imperial citizenship as an expression of political unity. From the vantage point of the republican developments of 1793–95, this path can properly be called a constitutional regression. In its place they established colonial governmental institutions that for many years separated metropolitan political developments from those in the shrunken empire after the Napoleonic Wars. Spain and Portugal followed the same path, with one difference: the reestablishment of absolutism in Iberia after French troops withdrew meant that discussions regarding the political status of colonists were postponed until the liberal revolutions of 1835–40.[1] This chapter will discuss the French imperial experience in the mid-nineteenth century.

The key date for the French in terms of straightening out questions regarding the status of colonies and colonists was 1830, when French politics took a liberal turn after the Bourbon restoration and the start of colonization in Algeria. Before then, French overseas possessions had regressed into slavery, both in the Caribbean and the Mascarenes, though the latter had never been affected by revolutionary-era abolitionism, and in any case Great Britain took Mauritius in 1810.[2] The great revolutionary transformations simply disappeared: slaves who had been free were once again in chains (with the exception of Saint-Domingue/Haiti, which was no longer French and had approved its own constitution in 1816–17 but would be subject to harsh economic sanctions by France), slave traffickers were back in business, and any notion of institutional unity between metropolis and colonies was considered a revolutionary aberration.[3] Only after 1830, once the mildly liberal Orléans monarch took the throne, was the political situation of the Antilles and the minority *gens de couleur* taken up again and palliated, though slavery would continue existing for nearly twenty more years.[4] Louis Philippe inherited from the Bourbons the beginnings of a colonial presence in North Africa, a longtime French aspiration, and with the Algerian occupation, the French began distinguishing new and old colonies.[5] The distinction between new and old exposed an infinite number of complications that would end up defining the key notion of *spécialité* (specialness); it also came up against widely accepted ideas throughout the empire regarding republican unity. The old colonies were those in the Caribbean, the four original parishes of Senegal (Saint Louis, Gorée, Dakar, and Rufisque), Réunion, and the *comptoirs* in India (Pondicherry, Chandanagore, Yanaon, Karaikal, and Mahé).[6] The new colonies were Algeria and subsequent acquisitions in Africa, Asia, and Oceania.

The different treatments meted out to new and old that first appeared in the 1820s became clearer during the reign of Louis Philippe and even more so after 1848, when the idea of colonial citizenship was back on the agenda.[7] Once the institutional organization of the colonies promoted by the old monarchic empire had been swept aside by the 1789 Revolution, and the one proposed by subsequent governments had been crossed out by Napoleon's pen in Year VIII (as discussed in chapter 3), it became obvious during the Bourbon restoration that new forms had to be solidified.[8] This reorganization included ordinances in 1825, 1827, and 1828 for Réunion, the French Antilles, and Guyana in line with Napoleon's old goal of creating a new colonial status, or special laws.[9] Nothing much altered with the regime change of 1830. The new constitution affirmed that colonies would be *régies par des lois particulières*, that is, without intervention by the legislature nor subject to elections.[10] The constitution of April 24, 1833, provided that all free people living in the old colonies would have political rights and representation in colonial councils established according to highly restrictive census criteria.[11] This would be known as *assimilation modérée*, a notion that would survive, with variations, into the twentieth century.[12] The government's primordial intention was to keep most of the population on the margins while promoting certain social groups, particularly free whites and mulattos, whose integration was essential if colonial relations were to become more flexible. In practice, the only free mulattos considered suitable for political rights were in the Antilles and Senegal.[13] Algeria, obviously, had other problems, as a result of which the French established a specific framework while the territory was still subject to harsh military occupation.[14] It was divided into three large zones in 1845, when very few French emigrants were moving there.[15] One of the zones was under military control, the second was under a mixed regime, and the third (along the coast, the most populated) would have civil administration similar to that of the metropolis. Thus, through executive rather than legislative means, a form of rule was institutionalized that granted the army enormous political power.[16]

The political changes of 1848 altered all this, and the reasons are evident, both in the old and the new colonies, for the revolutions affected the very foundation that made that distinction possible to begin with.[17] The first major experiment was the definitive abolition of slavery in the Antilles and Réunion, going back to the days of 1794–95 and the bright example of the British ten years earlier.[18] Former slaves would once again be citizens, as they had been during the brief but intense years of the Convention and the Directory. The new republican program that emerged from the Assembly also "departmentalized" the colonies and admitted colonial representatives into the legislature. Matters had somewhat returned to the revolutionary path of republicanism.[19] But the Algerian situation was more delicate. The Parisian revolution had turned slaves into French citizens, but citizenship was not confined to the Antilles and Senegal; it also (surprisingly) affected the territory under civil administration along the Algerian coast, a French department since 1847. A colony by royal decree, with absolutely no republican precedent, was suddenly inhabited by French citizens with full rights.[20] And if that were not enough, the establishment of three French departments in North Africa in December of 1848 pointed to the precise separation of two dynamics—a classical colonial society and a *petite France* with citizens in the interior—and this situation would have repercussions throughout the empire. Formally incongruent but solidly ethnocentric, the French divided part of the possession in two: one had departments, citizens, and legislative representatives, while the other had inhabitants with no rights living under military occupation. It was, in the words of a later French jurist, a *monstruosité juridique*.[21]

This dualism within a dualism would turn out to be explosive. The special laws led to incompatibilities that the Second Republic had no particular interest in resolving. The republican constitution of November 1848 made that clear: "La République française est démocratique, une et indivisible," it declared, adding in Article 109, "le territoire de l'Algérie et des colonies françaises est déclaré territoire français, et sera régi par des lois particulières jusqu'à ce qu'une loi spéciale les place sous le régime de cette Constitution."[22] This unrealized intention survived throughout the Second Republic and the regime of Louis Napoleon, which lasted until 1871.[23]

Vieilles Colonies, New Citizens

The second republican experiment of 1848 started off by looking backward to the great transformations that had begun in 1789. One of its first reforms was the abolition of slavery, on April 27 of that year.[24] This was, above all, an act of republican affirmation, a statement that what had been interrupted would now continue.[25] Slavery was understood to be a flagrant violation of republican principles, an inspiring perspective but one that twisted reality. The abolition decree by Minister of the Navy and the Colonies, François Arago, and his undersecretary, Victor Schoelcher, an abolitionist from Alsace, was an act of republican purification, the "grande réparation," in the words of Alexandre Ledru-Rollin.[26] In fact, what was being decreed was that the maxim that French soil freed the unfree who walked on that ground would now be extended to the colonies.[27] This affected even Algeria, where a different form of slavery was well established within an institutional system that the French, paradoxically, had promised to respect when the bey surrendered. In the other African possession, Senegal, which had almost 10,000 slaves in 1845, the measure was also problematic, as we will see. Martin Klein called what happened in Saint-Louis and Gorée "abolition and retreat": formal abolition at the moment of republican enthusiasm and retreat almost immediately afterward.[28] Altogether, 262,564 slaves were freed throughout the French colonies as a result of the republic's sovereign decision.[29] This second (and final) abolition was something that could not wait.[30] The French past and the British example worked together to enable a reform that was put together in just six weeks. This was not an impossible task from a technical angle; the republican government had a huge amount of documentation from the Convention and the various informational and abolitionist commissions from the 1830s and 1840s. Moreover, it had plenty of information and opinions about the British experiment a few years earlier, which served as an incentive not just for the Guizot and Thiers governments but also for the slaves themselves, as was made clear with the 1848 uprising in Martinique, at the time the largest French slave population (72,859), which made emancipation practically obligatory.[31] The built-up pressure of the back-and-forth history of France brought about some alleviation—for example, the Mackau Law of 1845 gave slaves the right to purchase themselves—but the impact and number were limited.[32] So it was no surprise that the slaves on the two largest islands, Martinique and Guadeloupe, rose up on May 20–23, 1848, forcing the governors to proclaim emancipation two weeks before the decree actually reached the Antilles. This was what triggered the complementary measure of giving French citizenship to the slaves, led to the collapse of slavery in the rest of the French colonies, and also set off uprisings in Dutch and Danish possessions, forcing them to unveil their own abolition plans. Spain managed to maintain control over Cuba and Puerto Rico, an anomaly explained in part by the repression of 1845–46, when authorities with one stroke had stymied British abolitionists and the slaves themselves by brutally putting down the Conspiracy of La Escalera.[33]

Emancipation by the French led straight to assimilation plans designed to ensure republican consensus and eliminate the stigma of 1802, when slavery had so ignobly been reinstated. Assimilation meant three things: the granting of universal masculine French citizenship to recently freed slaves, representation in the National Assembly, and elimination of the colonial councils established in 1833, which were overly engaged in fiscal questions and insufficiently representative. Instead, commissars capable of undertaking serious reforms would be sent out.[34] But once again, measures in the metropolis were not easily transferred to the colonies. For one thing, the first legislative elections were not held in the colonies, as they overlapped with the general emancipation. By law, the colonies won their political representation: three representatives for Martinique and Guadaloupe, three for Réunion, and one each for Guyana and Senegal. When elections were subsequently called, the deputies elected in the Antilles were blacks and mulattos who identified with general emancipation along the lines of the ideas of Victor Schoelcher, who was responsible for the most important humanitarian efforts during the republican era.[35]

It was quite clear that nothing would be the same again, even taking into account social practices left over from slavery. As a result, a fierce struggle ensued between those who represented the old plantation model and those defending the revolutionary tradition. One example was the election of Cyril Bissette, a well-known mulatto abolitionist who famously had been expelled from the Antilles in 1824 and then, in a spectacular political circus, became a key figure in the planters' campaign under the slogan *Order and work*.[36] Slowly, local forces gained control of the reformist campaign and even managed to replace the first commissars, Alexandre Gatine and the mulattto François-Auguste Perrinon, who had championed emancipation, with others more clearly identified with property and control over emancipated workers.[37] In this republican but highly volatile context, authorities had no compunction about using violence; one such instance was the fierce repression on the small island of Marie-Galante. As Armand Nicolas pointed out, the image of chaos projected by the plantocracy throughout France was counterbalanced with that of the newly appointed governor, Armand-Joseph Bruat, who was surprised when he landed in Martinique to find peace and quiet in the fields.[38]

And yet, political pressure from landowners, merchants, and shipowners in the major ports gradually pushed assimilation measures in increasingly colonial directions. The French Antilles, where the notion of colonial citizenship was the most developed, suffered from the fact that other parts of the empire, notably Algeria, Senegal, and Réunion, were lagging behind. Once again, a pyramid emerged that reflected not the equality promoted by early commissars but rather an emphasis on productivity, including highly concentrated land ownership, and that made it impossible for an independent peasant class to emerge. Commissars were replaced by governors, one of whom (Martinique's) became governor general.[39] Once slavery was abolished and slave owners dispossessed of their political and social authority, the republican state found itself in the uncomfortable position of intermediary in the organization of a labor market. After a brief period during which abolitionists tried to integrate freed slaves into republican life, the French governments, well aware of the risks, moved quickly to pass special legislation. That was the objective of the Colonial Commission (established in November 1849 and lasting until August 1851), once Schoelcher's proposals for assimilation were pushed aside.[40] Colonists had an important presence on the commission and were prepared to use their influence as much as possible in the direction of limiting freed slaves' autonomy.[41] The commission's labors indicated the path to be taken: the free labor force would be reincorporated in the fields, and at the same time massive numbers of Chinese and African laborers were imported. Furthermore, encouraging foreign migrant labor was the perfect way to devalue former slaves in the labor market.

The numbers show the importance of this migration, which would be equally notable in the Caribbean possessions of the British, Dutch, and Spanish. From 1853 to 1885, a total of 79,700 contract workers (*engagés*) entered the French islands; if we include Guyana, the total reached 90,000.[42] The influx was even greater in Réunion, where 49,000 Indians from the subcontinent and 35,000 workers from elsewhere arrived.[43] Many died under the harsh conditions.[44] For those in power, the point was to maximize centralization and create a truly colonial government, as

Nelly Schmidt has correctly pointed out.[45] The law of February 13, 1852, was a fundamental building block, authorizing local authorities to apply often incoherent punishments, though there were differences in how it played out, depending on former slaves' ability to move away from sugar plantations and establish themselves as small independent peasants, their permanent aspiration.[46] The recomposition of local and central power was what allowed old vested interests to survive abolition. If the republic was inaugurated with the Martinique uprising, the Second Empire ended two decades later with the Lubin affair, a scandal concerning a young black man punished for responding to attacks from a group of white men.[47] In between, there was a silent revolution under way: the mulatto bourgeoisie was rising, preparing to dominate the power structure in the islands during the Third Republic. Colonial citizenship was tangible and true only where social groups emerged with the ability to act and defend themselves.

Before that, the transformation of the old colonies was uneven. In Guadeloupe, for example, sugar plantations coexisted with the expansion of small growers who depended less on sugar as they rediscovered more basic crops. Often, both before and after 1848, landowners complained about the competition. The contrast between these two productive models had important ecosystemic effects, as well, because small landowners, former slaves, worked land unoccupied by the plantations, usually in hilly terrain.[48] The last census of slaves showed 72,000; in 1851 the number of *cultivateurs* linked to plantations had fallen to around 20,000.[49] This steady exodus of former slaves was compensated by the foreign contract laborers as well as by stiffer control over those who remained and by efforts to draw women and children into plantation work. The results were not that clear. The state was fully involved in discipline and recruitment of the plantation labor force, but the population of independent peasants on the margins continued to grow, once again raising the specter of Africanization, *une petite* Guinée.[50]

The situation was quite different in the French possessions in India and Africa. To use Africa as an illustration, in the four Senegalese parishes and the interior portion claimed by France, emancipation was practically a farce, as authorities managed to ignore the article of the Constitution declaring that French soil bestowed immediate freedom.[51] The problem was how to manage expansion toward the interior, which would not be resolved until Louis Faidherbe became governor.[52] One way of dealing with the problem was to place minors under the control of a tutorial council, which just meant handing them over to their former (or new) owners under conditions resembling slavery. At the same time, freed slaves in the old parishes, of whom there were very few, were forced to join the French army, which solved two problems at once, enabling expansion toward the Waalo kingdom in the interior. So, if the French could not own slaves, Faidherbe—a competent administrator with long experience in the Antilles and Algeria—proposed greater and more flexible distinctions among "citizens," "subjects," and "nationals."[53] Expansion into Waalo resolved the post-1848 predicament of freeing the slaves in the old parishes while retaining slavery as an indigenous institution in the rest of the territory.[54] It was a subtle difference that lasted well into the twentieth century in French and British colonies.[55] Slavery also was abolished in Algeria, with two provisos. Given that it was an "Ottoman" institution and quite different than elsewhere, control over slaves was scarce and unreliable, and they were often confused with domestic servants of uncertain status. Second, true freed slaves could not follow the same path as their brethren in the old colonies. In Algeria, French citizenship was only for those born in the metropolis, those who had emigrated to North Africa.[56]

Algeria: An "Arab Kingdom" for Citizens and Subjects Alike

The coup d'état of December 2, 1851, by Louis-Napoleon Bonaparte sent matters back to where they had been before the republic. Slavery would not be reinstated, though it continued its ambiguous existence. Citizenship for former slaves was subject to the whims of metropolitan politics and the situation in the colonies themselves. The 1852 constitution made official the former bifurcation between old and new colonies and was part of the political regression of Napoleonic restoration, all supposedly in the spirit of 1789. The regression was of two sorts: voting rights were limited in the hexagon (*découpage*), and legislative activity was focused on the *sénatus-consulte*, a peculiar sort of legislation that the emperor made all his own.[57] Title IV, Article 27, of the constitution of 1852 declared that that would be the manner of dealing with "la Constitution des colonies et de l'Algèrie."[58] After the uncertainty and insufficiencies of colonial politics during the Second Republic, Napoleon III was motivated to promote specialness. To quote François Miclo, "l'histoire des institutions colonials se confond pratiquement avec l'histoire de la spécialité à partir du milieu du XIXe siècle."[59]

A *sénatus-consulte* in 1854 cleared the way for the emperor's undisputed authority by eliminating the colonies' already pathetic political representation in the legislature. While the old Antilles colonies would receive legislation from the Senate and through the principle of *spécialité*, Algeria and the rest (including Senegal) would be governed directly through decrees,[60] and so, specialness and discretion proceeded as ever. Even when the state affirmed that slavery could not be reinstated in the Caribbean, assimilation was effectively short-circuited (though, as we saw, it had already run into trouble during the republic).[61] Diminished legislation was balanced with more authority by colonial governors and their advisers.

Legislation from above, without having to pass through the filter of elected representatives, was especially important in Algeria. Indeed, one of the characteristics of the Second Empire was the shift from the Antilles to Algeria as the great colonial testing ground.[62] The republic had governed North Africa by decree, but Napoleon III did it through the *sénatus-consulte*, which had both normative and propagandistic weight. Algeria's status as a new colony was derived above all from the military nature of the undertaking, part of the emperor's interest in Africa in particular and conquest in general. This "guerre interminable," to quote Marc Michel, would last well into the twentieth century.[63] Conquest of territory nominally under the rule of the Algiers bey, a distant servant of the Ottomans, required endless numbers of military skirmishes over three decades. In 1830 some 37,000 soldiers were sent over, but they were not enough to secure surrender of the population, despite the military's promises to respect local customs and religion. Ten years later, the invasion turned into a horrendous defeat, which was blamed on Marshal Bertrand Clauzel. The relentless war coincided with the *ex novo* construction of a large colonial regime based on orders, decrees, and government decisions that were barely sketched out in writing. Even before any formal decision had been made, Algeria was set apart from the legislative dynamic, weak as it was, that attempted to govern the old colonies. Algeria was what Charles-André Julien called "le régime des décrets," a very nineteenth-century colony where liberals legislated without any actual liberal legislation.[64]

But this act of outright seizure stripped of any even tenuous legitimization was not simply about legislation. "Tribal" resistance led by Emir Abdelkader worked to prolong both uncertainty and military engagement; only in 1836, after Thomas Robert Bugeaud arrived in Algiers, was colonial power secured.[65] He reorganized the French forces, founded the Foreign Legion, and began recruiting local soldiers (the *zouaves* or *spahis*), taking his cue from the East India Company. The essence of the new military program was brutal punishment of the enemy and all collaborators.[66] This was the *guerre du ravageur*, to use a graphic expression that synthesizes the idea of an occupation army that destroys all resistance.[67] In Tocqueville's cold logic, colonization could work only with "l'aide d'une procédure sommaire et d'un tribunal expéditif."[68] It worked; at the end of 1843,

Abdelkader's insurgent troops were forced over the border, an imprecise line, to seek protection from the sultan of Morocco. The combination of fierce repression and military presence, plus political-administrative specialness, became the essence of the Algerian regime and was the model followed elsewhere.[69] In the 1850s, after the resistance had been isolated in the mountains and the desert oases and the French had dominated the fertile plains of Mitidija, Oran, and Constantine, the only areas outside their control were those of the Berbers, whose distinctiveness from the Arabs at this point began to be defined and which would be of great importance in French colonial politics later on. Once they too were finally subjected, the Berbers allied with the French while the Arabic population, less attached to private property and apparently marked by the stigma of polygamy, would remain permanent adversaries.

The political project for the colony was substantially modified only after Napoleon III decided to follow the glorious African path trod by his dynasty's founder. Earlier, Bugeaud and his successors had secured two fundamental things. First was the creation of the image of the soldier-farmer, the unlikely heir to the Roman empire in North Africa. The image was not successful at first in attracting people from the metropolis, but migration grew during the Second Republic, and by 1851 there were some 100,000 immigrants. Second, once occupation was consolidated, institutionalization was the next step. In 1845 Algeria was divided into two parts, to be administered by either civil or military authorities, and a third, mixed space was later added. The civilian zone was along the coast, the area with the highest number of Europeans, and it was there that the Second Republic later established three Algerian departments, which pleased European inhabitants and the regime's democratic spirit but which also necessarily created a situation that remained volatile until the colony's end. Thus, French North Africa was an anomaly that made sense only in the context of the French specialness and constitutional duality that had not been designed with that end. The municipalities and departments in one of the three parts of the territory had the usual essential figures of French administration: a prefect with a council and a city council. The difference was that the people who had lived along the coast until 1830 would now simply be inert shadows.

These administrative changes lay at the heart of colonists' identification with the French republican project that promised citizenship to colonists and excluded everyone else.[70] Colonists also were antimilitarist, as they understood the army to be the protector of the subject population. It is important to remember that France would not grant any colony the status of a department until 1946, with the failed attempt to reconstruct the empire disguised as the French Union. During the Second Republic, emigrants and deported prisoners were shipped to the Algerian departments to colonize the territory and bring about that strange experiment of an Algeria that was both French and North African. Meanwhile, in the rest of North Africa where France had sovereignty, two different administrative spaces were formed. One comprised the mixed communes, where the so-called Armée d'Afrique exercised limited control and where integration was a problem; the other was entirely under the control of the army, whose powers grew after the anti-French uprisings of 1844–49 and the ferocious fight against Abdelkader and his followers.

The military zone led to the formation of areas known as *bureaux arabes*.[71] These were conceived by General Christophe de Lamoricière, a Saint-Simonist, and would be solidified during Bugeaud's presence in later years. The function of the *bureaux* was to control the indigenous population in limited areas. For reasons that will become clear, they became very important during the Second Empire because they were controversially close to the local population, and entirely within Napoleon III's vision of the "Arab kingdom." They also divided the army, as the officer class was more willing to identify with what Patricia Lorcin has called "benevolent paternalism," the administrative version of arabophilia, than was the high command.[72] The latter were aristocrats in origin and values, while officers were more easily seduced by the siren song of riches from land seizures and other colonization projects. Given the tensions regarding the different modalities of administration, the *bureaux* turned into the archetype or principal vehicles of military colonization, angering colonists and their representatives in Algeria and the home country. This was a paradox; on the one hand, relocation efforts (*cantonnement*) by the military produced "vacant" lands (occupied the previous day by Algerians) that could now be colonized.[73] This land quickly moved into colonists' hands, sometimes in violation of the wishes of the military, the emperor himself, and his Arabophiles, who wanted to protect sedentary tribes' communal properties.[74] The army's ambiguity on this point was increasingly subject to criticism by proponents of a civilian regime at the service of good French colonists, many of them sincere republicans. Since the times of Bugeaud, the Armée d'Afrique was crucial in opening the space of colonization, subjecting the Arab-Berber population, and maintaining a delicate balance between Algerians and European colonists until 1879, when civilian rule was implemented throughout the colony.

These balances and contradictions gave shape to the culmination of specialness in the colony: Napoleon III's notion of turning the territory into an Arab kingdom: a North African political entity in Napoleon's image and under the sovereignty of an obviously republican nation.[75] The emperor's objectives here— which had been proposed already during the reign of Louis Philippe of Orléans and which Napoleon had fondly nurtured since the start of his empire as a way of crowning his cousin Jérôme—existed in a peculiar context.[76] He had nothing much in common with the colonists, owing them little for his rise, and he was suspicious of their distrust in him. He listened closely to the advice of the Arabophiles who surrounded him, along with the military, especially Patrice de Mac-Mahon and those closest to the *bureaux arabes*.[77]

Of particular interest in this group close to the emperor were the writers Frédéric Lacroix and Ismayl Urbain. Neither was born in France; Lacroix was born in Mauritius and had been a republican prefect in Algiers in 1848, which gave him a broad network of informers and collaborators, both civilian and military. Urbain was born in Guyana, the illegitimate son of a Marseille merchant and a slave woman. His true name was Thomas Appoline, but in 1835 while in Egypt he converted to Islam and, in accordance with his new religious identity, changed his name.[78] He also was a social reformer; the followers of Saint-Simon would remain an intellectual presence in French colonialism up through the days of Ferdinand de Lesseps and the Suez Canal.[79] After Urbain arrived in Algeria in late 1837 he married an Arab woman from Constantine and decided to devote his life to reconciliation between Europe and Islam. During the years of the emperor's *grand tournant* toward the idea of an Arab kingdom, Urbain published his most important works, including *L'Algérie pour les Algériens* (1860) and *L'Algérie française: Indigènes et immigrants* (1862).[80] The high point of his career was his work with the Arab kingdom project when he accompanied Napoleon on the latter's second visit to Algeria, in 1865.[81] Urbain's writings reflected a vision of Algeria far distant from the one he knew. He opposed the ceaseless spoliation of Arab and Berber lands, French domination of the administration and town councils, and marginalization of indigenous peoples at all levels of the educational system. He knew firsthand what he was talking about, particularly regarding the land. John Ruedy described well the methods by which land was taken away from those who lived there.[82] First came the land supposedly belonging to the Turkish bey, and then that of religious charities (*habous*, in the most common French transliteration).[83] These land transfers damaged important foundations of Algerian society but met the needs of early immigrants, most of them poor peasants from western France. But the real attack on arable land had not yet begun; the next stage was seizures of land belonging to those who had fled or who had resisted the French. As Ruedy said, it was an "exceedingly slow process."[84] In an effort to make things more fluid, colonists could gain access to abandoned or underused lands whose collective ownership was unclear. In other words, it was an arbitrary process. Starting in 1851, when the new rules began, and for the next twelve years, 134,489 hectares passed over to colonial hands, with the imperial state acting as the principal beneficiary and administrator of "vacant" land.[85] The army, using the *cantonnement* system, was the executor: it evicted, occupied, subjected, and then created a property market ensuring the eventual settlement of the entire territory.[86] By the time measures were taken to halt the most outrageous land transfers in the 1860s, during efforts to create the Arab kingdom, colonization companies were well established and controlled great amounts of territory. For example, the Société Genevoise received 20,000 hectares from the state.[87] In any case, good intentions were stopped short by the 1864 Algerian uprising, and reforms were postponed during subsequent years of political instability. The confiscation never halted, as shown by the upheavals of 1871 and 1879.[88]

The key piece of imperial colonization was the *sénatus-consulte* of 1865, establishing rules for French citizenship for Muslims. This put an end to the irony of a colony of French citizens with full rights dominating a population of French "subjects," a contradiction found in *tristes tropiques* around the globe. The emperor wished to avoid two radically distinct situations in the colony and to accomplish this with a bifurcation that, for reasons linked to republican history, allowed citizenship in the old Antilles colonies and even in the old parishes of Senegal. But Napoleon III, with his dynasty's typical nonchalance, ended up complicating an already complicated and poisonous situation. Algeria's status as French territory was evident by virtue of the three departments populated by French "citizens" who were as much citizens as those living in the mother country. But being that Algeria was under a special regime, the rules were not homogeneous, nor did they need to be. The great jurist Émile Larcher defined this constitutional confusion as follows: "Si l'Algérie était une colonie, la législation algérienne ne serait qu'une partie de la législation coloniale. Mais en France, on considère l'Algérie moins comme une colonie que comme un prolongement du territoire métropolitain. Tout au moins l'Algérie a-t-elle, parmi les possessions françaises, une situation toute spéciale: elle a une législation propre, distincte du droit commun et ne pouvait rentrer dans la législation coloniale."[89] The existence of a civil status reserved only for European (not just French) colonists made it necessary to more strictly define what the rest of the colony's inhabitants (Muslims, Jews, foreigners) were or could be. The result of the tension between origin, religion, and political status was clear from 1859 to the reforms of 1865, but it was only during the Third Republic that the various conditions were more completely formulated.

The barely used concept of citizenship in constitutions and constitutional practice during much of the nineteenth century became the barometer for defining the place of colonized peoples. With the exception of the 1848 constitution, which returned to the revolutionary tradition, French constitutional practice was firmly embedded in "nationality," which was less binding, less risky than citizenship. So, a citizen was a French national who had political rights established by electoral laws. Other nationals, such as young people, women, vagabonds, debtors, and felons, were excluded. But these reserves were so numerous that the very idea of citizenship lost its original meaning and began to be used only in legal documents with narrow relevance.[90] In this calculatingly ambiguous framework, the definition of the Algerian people's status became less confined, as it had less to do with metropolitan reality, that poison pill for the Napoleonic imagination. Many writers had no compunction in calling the situation medieval, with the French as the lords and the Algerians as the serfs. Things reached the point that a French subject had to become naturalized if he wished to acquire French nationality in the colony and under French sovereignty. In short, the Algerians became nationals without nationality, a strange antechamber to citizenship and absolutely beyond the pale of conventional law. As the jurist Jacques Aumont-Thiéville wrote in the early twentieth century, "Les indigènes musulmans sont donc français; mais ils ne sont pas des *citoyens* français; ce sont des *sujets* français. La distinction entre le sujet et le citoyen qui n'a, dans notre droit métropolitain, qu'une influence minime, prend ici au contraire une exceptionelle importance."[91]

A paradoxical situation would be constructed atop this deliberate logic, and it would last as long as the empire lasted. The Second Empire invented confessional citizenship for Algerians linked to an individual's religion, an interesting feature for an empire designed with republican hues.[92] This new approach was based on old ones, of course, particularly the granting of French citizenship to the plantation colonies—to freemen of color in 1833 and freed slaves in 1848. But that case, though a precedent, was citizenship as social reparation; in North Africa, things happened differently. There were contradictions between General Bourmont's proclamation when he entered Algiers that he would respect the religion and customs of the new French subjects, the declaration in 1834 that Algeria was French territory, and the creation two decades later of departments with legal distinctions between those who lived there and those who did not.[93] While the formula used in the Caribbean was one of ambiguous co-optation, in North Africa the formula was a disruptive hierarchy that only intensified the relentless erosion of material conditions. Since 1854, the areas where punishments fitting for a *régime du sabre* were carried out grew larger than those dominated by customary Muslim law, considered valid only as long as it did not interfere with the new lords.[94]

Amid all this, the *sénatus-consulte* of 1865 allowed French citizenship for Muslims, Arabs, and Berbers. Its gestation well reflects the state of affairs in the colony: it was an appeal from an Algerian Jew to the appeals court in Paris that brought about the surprising ruling that nothing could impede a Frenchman in French territory from requesting French nationality. The ruling established how one could acquire nationality, along with the civil and political rights associated with living in a certain place; Pandora's box had been opened.[95] The imperial *sénatus-consulte* tried to fix this problem by saying that while it was true that indigenous Muslims were French even though they were subject to special laws, they could request the enjoyment of laws enjoyed by all Frenchmen and thus be subject to the laws of France. Indeed they could request; satisfaction was another matter altogether.

It is not difficult to see the reasoning behind the Napoleonic plan of 1865.[96] The emperor was determined to turn the colony into an Arab kingdom and thus had to come up with some sort of balancing concession for Algerian Jews and Muslims.[97] The concession was to be a peculiar one, individual and by the graciousness of French authorities, to be used at their discretion. In other words, nobody's automatic rights to anything were being recognized.[98] This was a "confessional" citizenship (or nonconfessional, in the case of Muslims);[99] the subject was to renounce his religion and customs, which apparently were entirely incompatible with his new civil status. In practice, giving up one's religion and customs meant being outside one's own community. To further complicate matters, the Crémieux Decree of 1870 tried to avoid these pitfalls and the element of graciousness by granting automatic citizenship to all Algerian Jews, who thus could avoid having to abjure their faith and their culture, unlike Muslims.[100] The Jews thus were transformed into a Trojan horse amid Muslim believers who constituted the overwhelming majority. At the same time, nonassimilated Muslims slipped down the ladder and became *indigènes*, a status then taking shape that would be the definitive mark of a punitive regime of exclusion extending throughout all French possessions in Africa, Asia, and Oceania.[101]

The Code de l'Indigénat (1881) was the result of a half century of *spécialité* and brutal rule in Algeria; it also was an excellent device with which to later define the absence of rights by indigenous peoples throughout the French empire, which quickly expanded under the Third Republic.[102]

It was the interplay between colony and metropolis that ended up configuring the hierarchies, inclusions, and exclusions of the imperial nation in the mid-nineteenth century. Starting at the top, we have full-fledged citizens with recognized rights, surrounded by people who did not have and would never have those rights. Next along the ladder were citizens without departments, that is, with no representation in the old colonies until the establishment of the Third Republic. And finally, we have the various situations in Algeria, including citizens with departments; subjects who might be promoted and others who might not, depending on what they wanted or where they lived; and the *indigènes*, subject to a penal system of social and political exclusion that would become the norm in Algeria and the other possessions.[103] This constellation of options was regulated according to local particularities, which leads us to believe that the practice of specialness, from Napoleon Bonaparte to his nephew and then into the Third Republic, had succeeded beyond the First Consul's most extravagant dreams.

CHAPTER SIX

Spain and Its Colonies

THE SURVIVAL OF THE OLDEST

DURING THE NAPOLEONIC WARS and the following decade, the great Spanish empire collapsed like a house of cards. Until the 1820s it had managed to resist internal turmoil and threats from outside. But Creole dissidence in America and the fragility of the second liberal experiment in 1820–23 triggered the final disintegration of that enormous world in America and Asia.[1] Ferdinand VII's absolutist monarchy fought back, but the newly independent republics' hostility was relentless.[2] Then a new project emerged from the ruins. It was smaller, to be sure, but not to be dismissed; this neoimperial phenomenon in Cuba, Puerto Rico, and the Philippines, as well as in a few enclaves in North Africa and the Gulf of Guinea, would survive until 1898.[3] Thus Spain, a country that had had difficulty following the path of other European nations with colonial as-pirations, in the mid-nineteenth century joined the club with ambitions to enlarge its dominions and influence. The Pacific expedition of 1862–66, combining emigration, the guano business in the Chincha Islands, and at-tacks on the older colonies, along with the Hispano-Moroccan War (1859–60), together demonstrated its vocation.[4] But the Cuban insurrection in October 1868 entirely upset those possibilities, and Spain was forced to face the sad fact that it had to defend what it had instead of dreaming of hypothetical expansion.

The notion of inexorable decline overseen by ignorant friars and in-competent, cruel, and corrupt bureaucrats existed only because of the historiographic myth fabricated in 1898 amid competition among impe-rial countries.[5] For the United States, with its well-planned military occu-pation of the three Spanish possessions that year, denigration of the old imperial whale was a vital strategic move.[6] Although Spain's overseas presence in the nineteenth century had been severely hampered by the crisis in the early decades, its subsequent development during the century did not differ much from that of other European colonial powers, consisting of slave labor or forced-contract labor in the colonies, the liberal break with the old absolutist monarchies, and mediocre economic growth with very modest consumption.[7] Nevertheless, if we put aside Anglo-British normative comparative models, which only distort matters, it is undeniable that Spain regained rule over its insular colonies and, starting in the mid-nineteenth century, waged a campaign of systematic aggression against North Africa in a late but hostile penetration into the interior of the Gulf of Guinea and the Western Sahara.[8] In short, the Spanish case was not the exception but the rule as it transformed the old empire into a liberal capitalist society with the aim of participating in divvying up the world.[9] Both by tradition and by right, Spain behaved as an imperial nation, in a manner similar to that of the other experiences analyzed in this book.

Until the collapse of 1821–24, the Spanish empire had continued growing. It grew out from the Kingdom of Quito, the Viceroyalty of Peru, and New Granada, in the territory inhabited by the Guaranis between Portuguese Brazil and the Spanish world—from the Viceroyalty of Río de la Plata and Chile toward Patagonia; in northern New Spain, through Chichimeca country and along the Santa Fe trail to California; and along the Venezuelan coast, through the Visayan Islands and Mindanao in the Philippines. This attempt to fully and irreversibly absorb peoples who had never before been incorporated was a colonial effort that had begun centuries earlier.[10] It was a job handed down by the old empire to the independent republics, which conscientiously continued the task during the following century. Until the very end, the empire devoted men and immense resources, most notably silver, to stretch its borders as far as it possibly could.[11]

Liberalism and "Special Overseas Laws"

During discussions in 1836 to draw up a constitution to take the place of the 1812 Constitution of Cádiz, a group of capable liberal politicians led by Ramón Gil de Cuadra, who was close to the minister of finance, Juan Álvarez Mendizábal, decided to resolve once and for all the problem of making the American territories fit in with the rest.[12] Gil de la Cuadra knew America and its leaders well, as he had been minister of the interior during the 1821–22 liberal Cortes, when the issue was raised. While the liberal generation of Cádiz had felt trapped by the Junta Central's and the regency's promises of equality between those whom they called "peninsular Spaniards" and "American Spaniards," the generation who took over after the definitive crisis of the absolutist monarchy and the transitional regime of the Royal Statute (Estatuto Real) of 1834 had learned all too well the lessons of secession. Therefore it was considered advisable to reestablish a hierarchy between the metropolis and the dominions of the Antilles and the Philippines. The solution consisted in gaining time, along the lines of the French Constitution of 1799, which had been approved the same month that Napoleon Bonaparte became First Consul, putting an end to the revolutionary process and leaving the colonies at the mercy of future decisions.[13] Before approving the new constitution that would replace that of 1812, therefore, the Cortes approved a royal decree suspending the constitutional text being debated in the three colonies. As a result, they prevented representatives elected in Cuba, Puerto Rico, and the Philippines from taking their seats. Next, they protected the *facultades omnímodas* granted to the captain general in each of the colonies by the decree of May 28, 1825.[14] The new decree eliminated the separation between political and military authority established by the Cortes in April 1820, a clearly liberal mandate, and bestowed enormous powers on the captains general, a situation that would endure until 1898.

It would be a mistake to see these important decisions as part of some fatal destiny or to think that such disproportionate measures had attracted the attention of other European empires. The new liberal cycle in Spain aimed to establish the foundation for a national project designed in Cádiz and to unite the destinies of metropolis and colonies through a pact between liberals on both sides of the divide. There were several ideological factors in the first age of liberalism, however, that hindered that goal. Among them was the rupture with the Creole world during the constitutional experiments of 1810–14 and 1820–23, a significant warning.[15] In addition, many *ayacuchos* (military men who had participated in the continental wars) joined groups that would lead to the establishment of the two major monarchic parties. Finally, the third and definitive cycle of liberal change in Spain grew out of a very decentralized movement and included violent episodes in major Spanish cities, probably the most violent of which was the burning of convents, monasteries, and the largest textile factory in Barcelona in the summer of 1835. In this climate of tension and violence, the revolutionary uprising of General Manuel Lorenzo in Santiago de Cuba in September 1836 set off all the alarms.[16] This was the complete opposite of a separatist or Creole rising, given that its goal was to implement in Cuba the 1812 Constitution, which had just been put back into effect in Spain; Lorenzo wished to integrate, not separate. But his call to action had not been approved by Tacón, the authoritarian captain general of Havana, who received clear orders to put an end to Lorenzo's autonomous movement. As in Cádiz, writing a new constitution was the obvious way to guide political change from the periphery and halt powerful local liberals who threatened plans for limited, top-down changes.

The Cuban situation was crucial; the island was in the midst of an economic transformation, with slave plantations being the most important element, though the British embargo prevented new slaves from being brought over from Africa. The island's extraordinary wealth—the so-called overseas surplus, a continual flow of riches from Cuba to the Spanish state—was no small matter to the minister of finance and future prime minister, Juan Álvarez Mendizábal.[17] In the city and province of Santiago de Cuba, a less concentrated productive structure allowed for an alliance between liberal military men, Creole smallholders, and merchants from the peninsular periphery (because commercial networks provided for the movement not only of products but also of ideas and political plans).[18] Political stability and protection were essential for the large plantation owners, *la sacarocracia*, to use the collective term coined by Cuban historian Manuel Moreno Fraginals for the sugar lords.[19] For that reason, when liberal changes arrived, these men formalized plans for self-government in the context of the Spanish monarchy—the third time this had occurred in the century; there had been similar attempts during prior liberal eras, though the third time would lack the revolutionary connotations of 1808 and 1822. The intellectual father of the project, Francisco de Arango y Parreño, was a man whose interests and family were intimately linked to the great sugar plantations. When Arango joined the Council of the Indies in 1817 he managed to win two concessions that the sugar growers had wanted for years: liberalization of commerce, and elimination of the Royal Tobacco Factory in Havana, an arm of the state in the colony and, logically enough, the institution that defended small tobacco producers (the *vegueros*) who sold their crops to the state. In 1830 the monarchy had promoted Arango to a phantasmagorical Council and Chamber of the Indies. Cubans were accustomed to defending their positions before the monarchy's central institutions, taking advantage of their weaknesses, and so, during the civil wars in Spain between absolutists and liberals, Cubans realized that the institutional moment had arrived for defending their class interests before the metropolitan government and even for giving in to British pressure to abolish the slave trade.[20] Under the circumstances, a government of their own in Cuba was the best alternative.

The paradox was that Arango's model was none other than the old British institutional formula of assemblies and councils around the governor of the West Indies. These assemblies, which served as representational spaces during the first colonization and the seventeenth-century civil war, were mini-Westminsters and, as soon as slavery became important, had always been dominated by planters. Arango called on the Spanish monarchy for a similar formula with an eye on what might happen in Britain once the slave trade was abolished, as forces inside and outside Parliament went on the offensive in 1833 to abolish slavery entirely. The year was important, because at that moment, with Spanish absolutism breathing its last gasps, the administration was trying to organize provinces along the lines of French prefectures. The man at the center of that effort was Javier de Burgos, who had planned and implemented the undertaking in 1822 in response to orders from the Cortes.[21] The late absolutist regime's orders now to the wily Granadan marked a golden opportunity for Cubans to transform the whole island into a *diputación*, the starting point for self-government. Arango's project thus artfully and covertly formed part of the state's plans to establish a new administrative apparatus throughout the kingdom, including in the three colonies. But even at that transitional moment, Cubans' wishes were not respected, and their project to constitute a representative space was rejected as an unacceptable challenge to the island's authorities, who remained the only center of authority and state representation, an arrangement that the metropolis would aim to protect in the coming years.[22]

The confluence of these initiatives led to the creation of a treasury department (Subdelegación de Fomento) for Cuba on October 23, 1833, one month before the same administrative office was implemented in the rest of Spain. Arango undoubtedly was behind the operation, which could not have been to the liking of Captain General Tacón or the metropolitan government.[23] The next step, a pamphlet titled "Indicaciones sobre el gobierno civil de Cuba," revealed the intentions of the Cuban and his friends.[24] The institutionalization of government on the island in the hope that one day it might fall into Cuban hands was a declaration of intentions that fooled no one, and for that reason the text was written very carefully, apparently limiting itself to matters of economic development, which was well received by the state. But by chapter 5, referring to towns and cities, the proposal became clearer. The captain general had too many jurisdictions, the pamphlet stated, and relieving him of civil authority and townships would undermine neither his authority nor the prestige of the old viceroyalty. Wouldn't it be a good idea to help the island's rulers divide up jurisdictions and thus attain a more effective administration?

As could be expected, Arango's efforts failed. While the *habanero* tried convincing Spanish authorities of the virtues of his plan, the metropolitan government did what it could to protect its own authority in matters of politics, taxation, and the economy.[25] Putting an end to any doubt, two royal decrees, dated March 21 and May 26, 1834, renewed the extraordinary powers of the captains general in the three island colonies.[26] The decrees were issued after Ferdinand VII's death and one month after Javier de Burgos's resignation. Having reached an impasse, Tacón, a war veteran who had been present at the final battle against the armies of Bolívar and San Martín, arrived in Cuba. He came with precise instructions to impose and strengthen his authority throughout the administration, with the exception of the office of intendent Claudio Martínez de Pinillos, who was both efficient and corrupt in carrying out orders from the metropolis and always happy to assist plantation owners.[27] Tacón's relentless rise was the counterpoint to Cuban landowners' losses. A variety of sources recount that it was the captain general himself who told Arango that his proposals for a civil government were out of order. He further pressured the metropolitan government to reaffirm his powers through a royal order of February 18, 1835, and he took drastic steps to ensure that this reaffirmation would have teeth. It did, indeed: he exiled the writer and political opponent José Antonio Saco, and he reinforced the powers of the Executive Military Commission, an entity that openly challenged the island's highest court, the Real Audiencia de Puerto Príncipe, which appealed the invasive maneuver to the Council of the Indies but lost.[28]

From 1834 to 1868, there was a new and determined tone to the construction of authority. The colonies were excluded from the constitutional framework that began being discussed in early 1837 and was promulgated on June 18 of that year. After Ferdinand VII's death, before the constitution, the politicians in charge of the ship of state began taking measures to reduce the role of the overseas dominions in metropolian and colonial institutions. The regression can clearly be seen in discussions over what sort of representation the Cubans, Puerto Ricans, and Filipinos would have under the Royal Statute. At that point, the Council of Government agreed to postpone any decision and delay overseas elections for as long as possible. Even so, it could not avoid elections for representatives. Amid uncertainty, liberal Cubans drew up their political program, expressing their desire to participate in the changes taking place on the peninsula. The best summary of those desires was by José Antonio Saco in his "Letter from a patriot, or the cries of Cubans to their representatives." It was published anonymously after Tacón expelled Saco from the island. Although the Cortes had limited powers under the Royal Statute, the text included each and every one of the political, institutional, and judicial demands put forward by the islanders since the start of the century. They were loyal to the monarchy but they wanted administrative, judicial, and fiscal reforms; limitations to the captain general's jurisdictions; and the establishment of a provincial junta with the capacity to veto legislation promulgated by Madrid. This program was to be delivered to Cuban representatives at the Cortes so they could defend it, but its possibilities were limited and the captains general of San Juan, Manila, and Havana did what they could to abort all hopes for change. Tacón in particular made it clear that he would not relinquish a single one of his responsibilities, including the capacity to preside over meetings of the elections junta that chose the island's representatives to the Cortes from among the small group of people included on the electoral rolls. Despite these limitations, those chosen— Juan Montalvo and Arango y Parreño for Havana, and Sebastián Kindelán for Santiago de Cuba—fit the prototype of the Cuban liberal so detested by Captain GeneralTacón.[29] Puerto Rico chose two representatives and the Philippines one, though it had many more inhabitants.

The return of the Constitution of Cádiz after a series of liberal military uprisings in various Spanish cities in 1836 further damaged relations between the captain general, the intendant for finance, and the Cubans. All attempts at calculated ambiguity were forgotten. The focus of this tension throughout the entire Spanish colonial world was on Havana, though repercussions would be felt in Spain, Europe, and even the United States, because, among other places, the Creole propaganda machine was operating in Bordeaux and in Key West, Florida.[30] The political debate between Spaniards and Americans, in which some *peninsulares* shared the latters' criticism of authorities' harsh tactics, moved onto new terrain as Tacón's wish to preserve the status quo gained the support of the great Spanish merchant interests.[31] Their goal was to prevent new elections in Cuba, which they feared would stir up politics in the metropolis as well. The revolutionary uprisings of August 1836 in Spain entirely changed things: the cabinet of Francisco Javier de Istúriz, a member of one of two monarchic parties, fell, making the prior elections irrelevant. The Constitution of Cádiz was dusted off, the progressive José María Calatrava took over the cabinet (with Mendizábal as minister of finance), and tensions with the Cubans were resolved.[32] Here we must return to Santiago de Cuba; when news from Spain reached the island, General Manuel Lorenzo proclaimed the constitution in Santiago without waiting for the captain general in Havana to do so. His initiative, and the support he enjoyed in certain sectors of the city, alarmed the authorities, especially sugar plantation owners and merchants, allowing Tacón to take harsh action against Lorenzo and his followers. In any case, the metropolitan government vetoed the proclamation of the constitution in the colonies and thus backed up Tacón's efforts to resore order. The use of troops and the blockade of the port of Santiago did the rest.

The last chapter would be approval of a new constitution to replace the 1812 Constitution of Cádiz that had included "peninsular Spaniards and American Spaniards from both hemispheres" in the great national project. Instead, there would be a genuine constitution to reestablish the empire. The Cortes debate extended through the first half of 1837 and finally ended with the text being passed in June. Progressives' proposals for the overseas provinces were discussed in February and March and basically came down to two things: no political representation for Cuba, Puerto Rico, or the Philippines; and a separate legislative mechanism for them, to be arranged under the future constitution. The common denominator was obvious: the colonies would be removed from the new constitutional framework.[33] The solution that the constitutional commission put forward defined the future of colonial policy; unspecified "special laws," inspired by the French example, would regulate the future of the three overseas enclaves. In other words, the problem of the colonies' "specificity" and their "heterogeneity," in the terms used by contemporaries, was resolved. The heterogeneity referred to by legislators was obvious: of the 700,000 inhabitants in the Cuban census of 1827, only 300,000 could be considered truly Spanish, as the rest were slaves or had black blood flowing in their veins.[34] In Puerto Rico, there were 159,864 inhabitants elegible to vote, from a total of 332,002 included in the 1834 electoral rolls. As for the Philippines, with more than 3 million inhabitants, European Spaniards added up to just 6,000.

The issue, however, was not the numbers but the risk that the presence in the Cortes of people from the colonies might destabilize imperial policy in general. The recent experience of the decolonization wars on the continent, which was the great orator Agustín Argüelles's argument for Americans' lack of loyalty, from the very first lay heavy in an atmosphere with few transactional leanings. As a result, the commission opted to exclude colonials from political representation and promise special laws whose definition was a complete mystery. Argüelles, Mendizábal himself, and Vicente Sancho, of the progressive party, insisted that political representation in the overseas possessions was impossible.[35] The minister of finance was belligerent, no doubt influenced by the fact that his ministry had to use money from the Cuban treasury to pay for the costly and cruel civil war on the peninsula. A few representatives in the Cortes were opposed, saying, for example, that there was no contradiction between promulgating special legislation for the overseas provinces and having those provinces send representatives to the Cortes, but the majority prevailed.

Aside from the singularly bitter experience of the wars of independence on the American continent and the undeniable fiscal repercussions, the insistence on the colonies' "specificity" and "peculiarity" (again the terms used by contemporaries) was very much of its time. Representative liberalism was clearly an exotic plant in the context of mid-century European empires, and a campaign for equal representation by *peninsulares* and *ultramarinos* would go nowhere fast. In the debates, Vicente Sancho, with piercing clarity, summed up the solution proposed by the majority of deputies from both parties:[36] "[I]n my analysis of the 1812 Constitution, I said that it contained different laws for the overseas provinces than for the Peninsula. I made the following things clear: first, that the definition of Spaniards in the 1812 Constitution is actually two definitions, one for the overseas provinces and one for the Peninsula . . . and in talking about the overseas provinces I limit myself to the Antilles, that is, the islands of Cuba and Puerto Rico. At that time I said that the word "free" [*libres*], which is found in the articles defining Spaniards, was there precisely because of the Antilles, where there are slaves, and one can see the consequences established by that difference."[37] For the sake of clarity he added, "what are these constitutions that are drawn up to ensure the rights of men? They come down to two words that make any good man's heart beat stronger: liberty and equality. All possible constitutions are that and only that. But in those countries, these words, which sound so pleasant to our ears, are words of death and extermination."[38]

All this insistence on heterogeneity led to outright plagiarism of Napoleonic legislation. The constitutional commission's final resolution untied the political and legal knot in relations between Spaniards and Cubans, and at the same time it set the agenda for overseas policy for a long time. As with all foundational documents, the commission's was short and clear; it expelled overseas representatives from the Cortes and promised to approve the ill-defined special laws at some unspecified future date.[39] Put simply, it closed the liberal cycle that had opened up with the constitutional debates of Cádiz during the Napoleonic Wars and excluded people in the American and Asian colonies from the constitution's benefits— the very benefits that had been made available to them in 1810. Those in favor of responding to the colonies harshly could not muster the same support for the options of expulsion and the passage of special laws. A few deputies, including Domingo María Vila, Fermín Caballero, and González Alonso, tenaciously opposed the majority decision.[40] Their efforts were in vain, and the expulsion of colonial representatives—those from Puerto Rico until 1869, those from Cuba until ten years later, and those from the Philippines until the end of the colony—was approved by an overwhelming majority, though the measure neither promised nor denied anything in particular. The final version became the first additional disposition of the 1837 constitution: "The overseas provinces shall be governed by special laws." Short but enormously important; and if there were any remaining doubts, two days later the Cortes approved a measure of clarification. This distilled commandment would appear again in the Spanish constitutions of 1845, 1869 (with two important alterations), and 1876, in other words, until the end of Spain's presence in America and Asia, and it would be prolonged in the African enclaves in the twentieth century.

The formula was taken from Article 91 of the Napoleonic Constitution of December 1799, which provided for military government in the plantation colonies during the state of exception and the reestablishment of slavery in 1802. In both the French and the Spanish cases, the concretization of *spécialité* locked in a long constitutional vacuum in their respective colonies. Some called the solution a "double constitution," meaning one constitution for the metropolis and the virtual absence of a constitution, an exceptional regime, in the colonies. The nation of citizens thus was adjusted in accordance with the never-ending colonial logic. The cycle of revolutions in the Atlantic world had led to this abrupt break, which would last until decolonization.

Special Laws and Supreme Rule

The basic outlines of government created in 1837 lasted with only superficial changes until the end of Spanish colonialism itself. In fact, they lasted much longer, because this precedent would reappear with U.S. exceptional jurisprudence in Puerto Rico and the Philippines, known as the "insular cases," a way of defining the constitutional excentricity of those countries. Acquired by force, the possessions would not be "states" of the union, nor "territories" waiting for admission, nor "colonies" openly recognized as such.[41] But the three situations were not identical. Cuba's "independence," achieved during the second anticolonial war, would effectively be governed by the Platt Amendment of December 1901, a sword of Damocles until 1934.[42] This measure (similar to one in the Army Appropriations Acts of 1867 and 1916), established the right to domestic intervention and limited the young republic's international relations. Juridical interference allowed for a second U.S. intervention in 1906–9, just before the so-called race war of 1912. The latter was an uprising by black and mulatto soldiers and officers who belonged to the Partido Independiente de Color, unhappy with policies that discriminated in favor of European immigrants, most of them Spanish.[43] In response, President José Miguel Gómez was forced to reassure Washington that law and order would be preserved, an important issue given the Afro-Cuban movement's deep colonial roots.[44] As historian Alejandro de la Fuente has shown, the United States was very hesitant to forcefully incorporate a colony of Cuba's importance with such serious domestic racial tensions.[45] It is important to keep in mind that the constitutional vacuum in the two Caribbean enclaves was reminiscent of their position in the late Spanish empire.[46] The Philippines was the first great experiment in this sense, setting aside the precedents of Hawaii and Guam (the rest of the Marianas having been sold to Germany, which kept them until World War I), which had clear strategic objectives but placed fewer demands on the population.

Earlier, during the time of special laws and the elimination of formal political representation, the constitutional void in the Spanish overseas world was compensated for by greater political and military powers in the hands of the three captaincies general. This construction did not exist in a vacuum. On the contrary, it was based on a very concrete social structure: continuity of the Antilles slave plantations and, elsewhere, enormous numbers of blacks, free mulattos, and Chinese contract laborers under the colonial state's control in the "collections" of northern Luzon Island.[47] In the Antilles, Spaniards insisted on the impossibility of maintaining liberal institutions, taking into consideration the "hetereogeneity" of the population, an argument easily extrapolated to its Asian possession. There, exclusion of the wealthy Creole, Filipino, and Chinese-Filipino mestizo minority, known as *mestizos de sangley*, allowed for extension of territorial dominion with no modifications whatsoever to the authoritarian nature of political-military rule.[48] It goes without saying that the nature of this constitutional vacuum and of this form of government was not remarked on in European imperial government offices, under the system that C. A. Bayly pointedly called "proconsular despotism."[49]

During the events and debates of 1837, Cubans discovered the value of referring to the assemblies of the first and second British empires.[50] The reference had an illustrious precursor in Arango, the best informed among Cubans. Through him, they called for an assembly that would protect them and protect slavery, along the lines of the West Indies assemblies. They also wished to reduce the captain general's jurisdiction to that of a colonial governor, that is, an interlocutor and guarantor of public order and an intermediary with the metropolitan government. The outstanding Cuban writer of this era, José Antonio Saco, developed these ideas in his *Paralelo entre la isla de Cuba y las colonias inglesas*.[51] From the first page, he posed a possible political space that might enjoy autonomy from Spain. His model clearly was the British constitutional tradition, updated (without slaves) through the Canadian constitutional crisis and the Durham Report of 1837. The experience of the northern corners of the great empire had shown that relations between colony and metropolis were not necessarily doomed. Even Saco admitted that his book and his political positions might be regarded as pro-British, an inclination he immediately denied harboring. Quite obviously, Cuban interest in local representative institutions of the old empire and their transformations during the nineteenth century in no way questioned the continuity of mass slavery in the Spanish Antilles. Slavery and the clandestine slave trade meant the Cuban operation was all smoke and mirrors. In any case, as had happened so often before, Spanish authorities did not give an inch. Chastised and bitter after the continental wars and convinced of the benefits of what they called "racial balance" in the Antilles, they had no interest at all in allowing Cuban landowners to convert their social power into representative power.

With the acceptance of the idea of special laws, though no one knew what they were nor when they would appear, Cubans and their allies in Madrid obtained the fall of Captain General Miguel Tacón, their greatest enemy. It was a pyrrhic victory, and an expensive one. The newly "empowered" Cubans also found support among a group of Spanish politicians including Alejandro Oliván and Rafael Benavides, and the Catalans Jaume Badia and Domingo Vila, both closely connected to the important export sector in the port of Matanzas. For some of those who knew the island well, consensus with moneyed Cuban landowners was preferable to having to rely exclusively on military might or on the fear of an impending slave revolt. The arrival in Havana of Joaquín Ezpeleta Enrile and his successors did not signal any effective change in political-military rule, and that was true also in Puerto Rico and the Philippines. Little by little, then, a powerful colonial structure with few limitations was being built. Metropolitan authority might be hateful for its oppressive and despotic treatment of the islanders, but it was indispensable for controlling plantation slaves. What we can term a liberal dictatorship was the deliberate construction of a constitutional and political vacuum in the wake of three periods of political representation in the empire: 1810–14, 1820–23, and 1834–36. This vacuum would be filled by what was called *poder omnímodo* (absolute power), with no institutional counterbalances from the old colonial order or bothersome legislative representatives from overseas.

Once this process of imperial reaffirmation was complete, things moved in entirely unpredictable ways in the 1840s. First, the establishment of military authority in each of the colonies ended up depending not only on Spanish ministries and speeches in the Cortes but also on events, and especially on what Spanish administrators called "racial balance," a deliberate administration of relations among phenotypically distinguishable groups in each one of Spain's possessions.[52] The first place where circumstances led to large-scale implementation of authority in this regard was the farthest away of the possessions, the Philippines, in 1840–41. This was a different scenario than Caribbean plantations and their slave system, though there were sugar plantations (without slaves) in the province of Pampanga.[53] Once it was clear that representation would be impossible in places with profound racial divisions, the principle could be extended throughout the archipelago; slavery in the sultanates of Mindanao and Sulú, a sizeable Chinese-mestizo population, and an important though not exclusive Tagalog population in Luzon made for a diversity begging to be administered.[54] This was the first place where a deliberately violent form of political rule was used to delimit each group's spatial limits.[55] In this regard, Spanish authorities, who remembered the dramatic events of the 1810s and 1820s in Manila, were permanently suspicious of communitarian confraternities; in particular, news of the activities of the San José de Tayabas confraternity set off alarm bells.[56] The organization's founder, Apolinario de la Cruz, known to his followers as Brother Pule, was originally a peasant but had received some Catholic schooling.[57] He worked mainly in the poor neighborhoods of *intramuros* Manila, but at some point returned to his hometown, Lucban, in the former province of Tayabas, an area with a long tradition of rural insurgency.[58] There the confraternity grew quickly as a religious and mutual aid organization and, surprisingly, de la Cruz enjoyed the help and protection of Domingo de Rojas, an important banker and liberal activist.[59] But the worst piece of news for Spanish authorities was that the confraternity would not admit Spanish members. So Captain General Marcelino Oráa, a classic liberal military officer and veteran of the peninsular civil wars, decided to get involved. After a siege lasting several days in the mountains around San Cristobal, Apolinario de la Cruz's peasant followers, whose weapons did not include firearms, were defeated. Hundreds of casualties were left lying on the ground, and the Spanish authorities, not content with the victory, executed de la Cruz and other leaders without bothering with a trial or legal formalities.

The crushing of the confraternity was not an isolated incident, but, rather, one of a series of similar events. Several things were going on: there was a clear connection between political violence in the metropolis and overseas, the new rules of the game included manipulation of racial distinctions in the colonies, and the three captaincies general saw their powers grow as they were transformed into the absolute center of colonial life. Sinibaldo de Más, the great sinologist, intellectual, and world traveler from Barcelona, a man familiar with Portuguese Asia, China, and the opium trade, was a firsthand observer of the events of Tayabas and wrote his subsequent encyclopedic study of the islands convinced that they should be independent.[60]

But the most serious lesson in colonial politics took place, as could be expected, in Cuba, the richest of Spain's colonies, with the Conspiracy of La Escalera, a series of slave protests and revolts starting in January 1844.[61] Domingo del Monte, a Cuban landowner, philanthropist, and intellectual, had communicated with someone in Boston regarding his concerns about slave discontent, mentioning especially that slaves had established contact with David Turnbull, His Majesty's representative on the mixed commission to end the Havana slave trade. This unsurprising information was passed on to U.S. authorities (among them Daniel Webster, then secretary of state) and thence to Spain. Fears of a massive slave uprising, always with the specter of Haiti looming, seemed to be realized in 1843 with several small rebellions in the Matanzas mills. The recently appointed captain general, Leopoldo O'Donnell, decided to take action and kill two birds with one stone. He orchestrated a massive campaign of repression and, with no legal procedures, arrested and tortured hundreds and executed seventy-eight people, setting off a spiral of bloody violence that terrified good Cuban society and diminished their appetite for opposing Madrid.[62] The wave of repression affected free mixed-bloods as well and led to the demobilization of militias that had been established in the late eighteenth century. Among the victims of La Escalera was the mulatto poet Plácido (Gabriel de la Concepción Valdés), well known in cultural circles in Matanzas and Havana and a protégé of del Monte, who himself was accused of generic crimes that could not be proved.

Puerto Rico was subjected to a similar reign of terror. Juan Prim arrived there as captain general when the conservative government in Madrid decided to remove him from Spain (after his brief exile in Paris), to keep him away from political conspiracies.[63] Soon after arriving in San Juan, he wrote to his mother about the nature of his job, using language that left no room for doubt: "There are many advantages to being captain general; one is in charge of everything and appears like a viceroy,"

he wrote, adding, "whoever wins in Spain [referring to interparty con-
flicts], this [Puerto Rico] will always remain the same, at least during my
reign."[64] In a few words, he had said it all. Over the following months,
deploying repressive measures and racial hatred, he dismantled what was
left of the island's old regime and confirmed the captaincy general as a
center of despotic power.[65] Opportunity presented itself with the persecution of the bandit José Ignacio Ávila, known as El Águila (the eagle). When
the highly popular figure escaped from jail after having enjoyed a certain
amount of tolerance by judicial authorities, Prim had the excuse he needed
to affirm his position and intimidate his adversaries, turning his attention back to slavery.[66] Throughout the Caribbean, rumors about what was
happening in Paris starting in February 1848 had made for tense times,
and when news of the July Revolution finally reached the island, Prim decided to take the initiative. His subsequent harsh and punitive orders (in
a decree called a *bando*) aimed at slaves and free blacks, which he lumped
together as the "African race," took authorities in Madrid by surprise and
shocked the island's population.[67] Among other things, the bando ordered
the death penalty for any slave or free black who used a weapon against a
white person; allowed any slave owner to carry out executions in case of
insurrection; and permitted the death penalty in cases of summary judgment in the space of just twenty-four hours. The general was interested in
being promoted, and he knew who might make that possible.

Unexpectedly, it was a slave revolt on the little Danish island of Sante-
Croix that finally allowed the impulsive captain general to take action in
July. It was the right moment to apply what he called "healthy terror,"
the inspiration for his orders, which in the future would be called the
Bando against the African Race.[68] Prim went to the neighboring island
with troops, and a few hours later the British consul in San Juan told his
government that forty slaves had been executed. Two weeks later he took
similar measures in Puerto Rico itself. Rumors of an uprising on the sugar
plantations of Ponce had inspired his drastic intervention, involving two
executions and multiple whippings that nearly killed the victims. Soon
afterward he reenacted the scene in Vega Baja, the site of absolutely no
uprisings at all, executing one person and whipping many, as he had done
before.[69] Madrid was so alarmed by the news that Prim was relieved of
his post. He would be replaced by an ultraconservative Catholic, Juan de
la Pezuela, who arrived with clear orders to heal the wounds and calm the
British, who were concerned about Spain's tolerance for the clandestine
slave traffic. Pezuela repealed the bando and shifted his attention to controlling former slaves through the use of internal passports.[70]

The dramatic occurrences of the 1840s made clear to contemporaries what sort of situation they had built in the preceding years. It showed that the liberal revolution overseas had been successfully closed off, thanks to expansion of military control (essentially the same state of exception applied in the metropolis at critical moments), the shrinking of consultative and judicial institutions dating from the old empire, and the absence of the new instruments of liberal regimes such as representation, the press, and the freedom to establish political parties. Cuban politics were pushed to systemic extremes, where they would remain until the two anticolonial wars of 1868–78 and 1895–98. The colonial framework on the islands and the African enclaves was undone by the Cuban model. That said, it is important to emphasize yet again that these events were not indicative of Spanish exceptionalism or of an inability to incorporate elements of liberal government into its colonial spaces. In 1848, France opened up a path to citizenship and representation for its Caribbean colonies, after having established exceptional formulas from 1802 until then that liquidated revolutionary notions of representation, but it is advisable not to mistake the nature of this mellowing in colonial politics, which was the result of France needing to tighten the screws in Algeria, where the occuption of 1830 had become extraordinarily complicated. It is also wise to keep in mind the West Indies in 1865, where incidents in Jamaica quite similar to the Cuban repression of 1843 allowed British imperial authorities to liquidate the old planter assemblies, take measures against former slaves, and frighten educated mulattos who aspired to move up the social ladder.[71] Only in Barbados, where planters had absolute control, were the venerable forms of self-government allowed to continue. Barbados was a model of total exclusion that survived the catastrophe in the rest of the West Indies and facilitated the seamless transition of slave labor to contract labor, which actually was not much different.

Liberal Nation and Empire

The praetorial model I have described was consolidated in theory and in practice in each of the insular enclaves. With societies intimidated and divided by slave labor and huge social differences, the all-powerful captains general and special laws excluding people from political representation in the colonies and lawmaking in the metropolis could construct colonial politics as one united whole. The framework lasted until U.S. troops arrived in 1898. The Americans took note of the legal limbo of the insular cases and prolonged that status for years in Puerto Rico and the Philippines.[72]

Once colonial order had been reinforced and internal competitors moved aside, Spanish governments could breathe a sigh of relief and limit themselves to brushing off attempts to annex Cuba to the slave states of the U.S. South.[73] The precedent can be found a decade earlier, in 1835, when a group of planters left Louisiana with their slaves in search of new land, went to present-day Texas, and then rebelled against Mexico rather than free their slaves.[74] The model of the Texas republic inspired the fervent Cuban champions of slavery who wished to hitch their future as well to the star of the great neighboring republic.[75]

In the last such attempt, the Spanish general Narciso López, a native of Venezuela and veteran of the wars of independence, landed in Cárdenas (province of Matanzas) in May 1850 with a small army of mercenaries organized in New Orleans with the protection of Louisiana Governor John A. Quitman.[76] Spain captured López and executed him by firing squad in September of the following year. Once nostalgic operations such as these had played themselves out, the 1860s were marked by the outward construction of the imperial nation after its long retreat in the wake of 1824.

Compared to its great imperial past, domination over three insular colonies did not seem like much to Spanish rulers, who were keen to join the European neoimperial dynamic in any way possible, no matter how modestly.[77] It was essential to assimilate the national strivings that in other places, including Russia, Ireland, and central and southern Europe, were channeled toward secret revolutionary urban bourgeois militias. This civil liberal energy, at times republican, could, in the end, be absorbed only by regular armies. The first case, which would become the model for this sort of military mobilization with deep nationalist and imperialist roots in civil society was the Crimean War, the most obvious example of the unification of the national project and imperial ambition.[78] Furthermore, the unpopularity of the Russian empire among liberal thinkers, including radicals (witness Karl Marx's obsessive suspicions that secret Russian diplomacy lay behind all repression worldwide), was a golden opportunity for British imperial nationalism. From 1853 to 1856, the Romanov empire fought in the Crimean peninsula against the great European nations and the Ottoman empire, which may have been the sick man of Europe, but Great Britain, France, and Sardinia considered it necessary in order to maintain continental strategic balance.[79] On the other side, the tsarist empire had aspirations of controlling the Dardanelles and conquering Ottoman territories along the European coast so as to better keep an eye on grain shipments from the fertile fields of Ukraine.[80] Crimea was an important lesson for liberal European nations, especially for Great Britain, with economics and politics walking hand in hand and popular enthusiasm fully recovered after the unpleasantries in India a few years earlier.

Spain, too, learned the lessons of international politics, as the following four incidents will illustrate. The first was a modest, limited war in North Africa.[81] The only sites involved were Ceuta, Melilla, the Alhucema and Chafarina Islands off the Moroccan coast, and the fishing grounds off Sidi Ifni (which had importance until the 1930s). There were no territorial gains in the interior of Africa in subsequent decades. The idea of taking Tangiers, a long cherished dream given its location by the Strait of Gibraltar, was quashed, apparently because of British opposition. Despite its limited expansion, the war had immense impact on the popular imagination. The huge circulation of pamphlets, books, lithographs, and propaganda indicate the maturity of liberal public opinion around questions so typical of the era: circumstantial Orientalism, ancestral Catholicism, and the new liberal nationalism.[82] In addition, the conflict had two aspects hitherto missing from political mobilization in Spain. The first was the undeniable racialization of popular politics, to use Albert García Balañà's expression.[83] The enemy was described as African, Muslim, and nonwhite, and was presented that way in images. Previously I have used the idea of double patriotism as an essential element of regional cultural revivalism in Spain, for example the campaign to recover languages such as Catalan.[84] It is obvious that mobilization against a common enemy easily defined in denigratory terms paved the way for popular mobilization that embraced regional energy and general Spanish nationalism, with no one stopping to question the fraud that lay behind the war of aggression.[85] And second, mobilization of volunteers proved to be a brilliant ingredient in the invention of the liberal nation atop the reborn empire. The war in Morocco confirmed and hugely extended in the metropolis something that had first emerged during the wars of independence in South America and in Cuban politics: the enormous resources for the imperial nation under construction that came from the recruitment of urban workers and artisans and from the formation of militias. If any figure embodied the ambiguous identification between the construction of the liberal state and the creation of a popular local base, it was Juan Prim, a military officer with years of experience in the world of popular militias. He bombed Barcelona in 1843 during the most critical moment of the struggle between the two great liberal factions; he carried out relentless racial revenge in Puerto Rico; as we saw, he was an accredited international observer in the Crimean War; and he commanded troops during the African war and the Mexican expedition in 1862. At the end of it all, he became one of the leaders of the progressive liberal party.[86] Furthermore, Prim would be the leading protagonist of the political changes of 1868 that led to the expulsion of Isabel II and the crowning of a Savoy as the Spanish monarch, an experiment that did not hold up well and quickly led to the brief Republic of 1873–74.[87] He became prime minister and was assassinated, by a person or persons who were never caught, on December 27, 1870. It was said he was negotiating the sale of Cuba to the United States.

The second and third international instances were Spain's logistical and naval support for French ambitions in Southeast Asia (including its incursion into present-day Vietnam in 1858–62) and the occupation of Santo Domingo in 1858–61 and 1865. Spain's involvement in the French protectorate of Annam was legitimized, as so often, by pointing to persecution of missionaries in terms that nonetheless could not help but reveal France's true intentions. Less commented on was the fact that European expansion in Southeast Asia benefited from motivation and infrastructure drawn from the longtime opium trade and the massive consumption of the drug in China and among Chinese contract laborers.[88] Annexation of the Mekong Delta was the antecedent to the far more costly conquest of what is today Vietnam, Cambodia, and Laos. The road was being paved for France's eventual construction during the Third Republic of the Indochinese Union, a conglomerate of diverse situations for which Paul Doumer built an administrative and constitutional structure at the turn of the century.[89] For Spain, the Vietnamese expedition was a way of showing friendship with Napoleon III, which was essential if Spain wanted to continue its project in North Africa, given the geostrategic importance of French Algeria (and the presence of thousands of Spanish emigrants in Oran, the westernmost department of the colony) and France's influence in Morocco itself.[90] The occupation of Santo Domingo, meanwhile, was the result of two things: a request by a political faction on the island in the 1840s that Spain annex it; and the U.S. Civil War, which put an end to threats by the South toward Cuba.[91]

The fourth time Spain flexed its colonial muscle was during military operations hyperbolically known as the war in the Pacific. In fact, this added up to three different moves, all aimed at showing Europe and the United States what Spain's role might be: a military expedition; hostility toward the former continental colonies, with which diplomatic relations had not yet been established; and a scientific expedition of some importance, the first one since the eighteenth century.[92] Technical changes in navigation and the transmission of news had entirely changed the world by the 1850s and 1860s, allowing participation by countries not on the old list of competitors.[93] A less speculative factor in the 1850s also provoked interest in the oceans: the possible use of guano nitrates for large-scale agriculture and for the manufacture of gunpowder for both military and civilian purposes. Rising demand pushed the United States, Great Britain, Germany, and other northern European countries to send envoys to Pacific islands that had huge untouched reserves of nitrates (though pre-Columbian inhabitants had been well aware of them). The United States was first; in August 1856 it passed a law claiming rightful possession of the islands as long as they were not "within the lawful jurisdiction of any other government." U.S. individuals claimed some one hundred small islands with no known sovereignty. Germany later on focused its interests on Nuaru, in Micronesia, with around twenty square kilometers, taking it over in 1888 and holding on to it until 1914, when it was passed over to the British Phosphate Commission, a profitable joint trusteeship among British, Australian, and New Zealand investors.[94] The largest guano islands had a different fate; the Chincha Islands, just off the Peruvian coast, began exporting natural nitrates only in the mid-1840s to the United States and Europe. Spain occupied the Chinchas in 1864–66, during a conflict with Chile and Peru (supported by Ecuador and Bolivia, which the old metropolis still did not recognize).[95] The little war of aggression included bombing Valparaíso from offshore on March 31, 1866, not exactly a glorious moment in Spanish history. The war ended without Spain winning anything, but it served the purpose of forcing Spain to recognize the countries involved and to sign commercial and friendly treaties with them. Spain also withdrew at the same time from Santo Domingo and Mexico, where it had intervened in response to requests by local factions, part of the old country's dream of expanding and protecting its position in America and the Caribbean.[96] It failed in Santo Domingo, a preview of the inevitable end of slavery in the Spanish Antilles.[97]

Neither Autonomy nor Reforms

The first major revolt in Cuba came in early 1868 in Santiago de Cuba Province, while Spain was undergoing a dynastic change and had a brief republic from February 1873 to December 1874. The uprising, which also affected Puerto Rico, lasted for a decade. And so, right when the system of the three colonies, which had been reorganized in the 1840s, finally appeared to be on firm ground, the Spanish empire was drawn into an anticolonial struggle in the Caribbean and deep, often hidden discontent in the Philippines. The conflicts would last until the wars of 1895–98, with obvious results: the

United States intervened in Cuba and Puerto Rico in July 1898 and occupied the Philippines in August 1899, the logical corollary of what had happened in the Antilles.[98] The Treaty of Paris between Spain and the United
States at the end of 1899 opened the way to formal occupation of all three
(with the addition of the German occupation of the Caroline Islands, north
of New Guinea[99]), along with hefty indemnities to the defeated colonial
power and operations to crush resistance and to establish governments
overseen by the U.S. military, which was there for the long term.

The final thirty years of the last Spanish empire were characterized by
three interlocking processes that together lay at the heart of the conflict
between overseas and metropolitan interests and ultimately led to collapse. The first was the definitive abolition of slavery, which in Puerto Rico
came in 1873 and in Cuba in 1886—the last act of abolition in America
aside from Brazil.[100] Clearly, the end of the infamous institution, which
for years had been attacked and challenged in Europe and America, did
not put an end to the racialization of social relations and hierarchies,
which continued under U.S. or republican rule. Second, Spain had tried to
implement political reforms overseas that recalled the French distinction
between new and old colonies. While in the Antilles—at least in a peaceful
Puerto Rico—the idea was to backtrack to 1837 and reintegrate colonists
within metropolitan institutions, that possibility was never even considered for the Philippines.[101] Hypothetical reparations were out of the question for the farthest of Spain's possessions, causing resentment among
leaders and elites there who began taking note of nation-state constructions elsewhere in Asia. And third, based both on the internal situation in
each of the Spanish colonies and on changes in the French *vielles colonies*
and the British white settlements, there was increasing desire—even
demand—for institutions of their own, for modalities of self-government
that, as historians Ucelay-Da Cal and Núñez Seixas have shown, were
being demanded simultaneously overseas and in Spain itself.[102]

Military rule and the absence of any sort of political representation had
already shown signs of exhaustion before the critical year of 1868, with
the start of the first Cuban war of secession and the political changes in
Spain. The foreign operations of the Liberal Union (O'Donnell's political
party) in Africa and America provided no returns whatsoever, but they did
produce considerable debt. The Spanish government, aware of the complaints these adventures inspired and of the need to limit administrative
and defensive expenses overseas, and confident that it had the ability to
control things from above, in 1866 hinted at reforms to come. It is likely
that this was inspired in part by petitions for institutional reform signed

by thousands of Cubans and presented to Captain General Francisco Serrano, one of the strongmen behind Spain's regime change. Attending to those long-ignored demands opened up a schism in the metropolis's heretofore irconclad position in favor of isolating the colonies from the winds of change blowing through Spain. But, responding to the demands, an investigatory panel (*junta de información*) was convoked for October of that year and charged with reforming the statute governing the three insular colonies.[103] The final proposal was signed by the young Antonio Cánovas del Castillo, at that point minister of overseas possessions—a new position created in the image of (and with the same name as) the French model.[104] It began by saying that progress in the Antilles, where slavery still existed, depended on a different statute from that of the Philippines or Fernando Poo (Bioko), off the coast of Africa.[105] Given who the members of the junta were—ministry personnel, administrators recently arrived from the colonies, municipal representatives, and a few members chosen directly by the administration—there was not much room for hope.[106] It is true that a few reformists from the islands attended the meetings in Madrid, but they were on their own during the group's discussions. After no progress whatsoever, the next change of government (from O'Donnell to Pánfilo de Narváez, who was completely intransigent) and the subsequent leadership change in the overseas ministry spelled the end of the experiment. Neither slavery nor political regime was a candidate for reform.

At the point where the Spanish government had shown it had no initiative, the uprising in Santiago de Cuba Province changed everything all at once. The insurrection began in October 1868 on the eastern half of the island, where there were relatively fewer slaves and more free peasants working in small and medium-size sugar and coffee fields.[107] The revolt's main leader, Carlos Manuel de Céspedes, was a representative of those small landowners, many of whom were deep in debt. At first it was not clear if the movement favored independence and emancipation; rather, the issues were taxes, land reform, and resentment over the color line that governed Cuban society as a whole after fifty years of slave plantations and the importation of 780,000 slaves.[108] News of the political changes in Spain one month earlier, with Queen Isabel II losing her throne, placed Cuban demands on new territory. Armed rural protests far from the world of the great liberal reformers in Havana suddenly turned into a direct confrontation with the entire Spanish regime. Spain's response, in the hands of the despotic Captain General Francisco Lersundi, was to rely on the Spanish army and a group of volunteers recruited and paid for among loyal Spaniards (the so-called *integristas*) to establish strict control over cities and territories. The volunteers, who numbered some 30,000, played a key role in the repression of cities and sugar mills, permitting authorities to concentrate most of the regular army at the front.[109] They were joined by reinforcements from the peninsula, dressed out with symbolic regional paraphernalia reminiscent of the war in Africa ten years earlier. An army comprising 180,000 soldiers joined up with the enormous social and economic power of the Spaniards on the island, a mix of merchants, employees, and emigrants up and down the social ladder.[110] From 1868 to 1894, before the second and definitive war began, more than 400,000 Spanish emigrants went to Cuba, a country with just 1.5 million inhabitants.

The war, which quickly became a civil war, lasted an entire decade, with strong regional, social, and racial aspects. Spaniards and Cubans immediately were divided. Not all Cubans supported the struggle against Spain in favor of secession, and Spaniards themselves were split. Once the provisional government that emerged from the September uprising took charge, it replaced Lersundi with Domingo Dulce in Havana and offered to reform the colonial political statute, an offer unacceptable to *integristas*, who favored the status quo and wanted to crush the subversives. The government's offer to Cubans and Puerto Ricans, made through Dulce, was obviously to give them back their political representation in metropolitan institutions once the rebel army, led by Antonio Maceo and Calixto García, laid down their arms. The rebels' refusal, along with serious problems of law and order in Havana and other cities on the island, led to a new collapse after the brief opening. Dulce then switched strategies altogether and commenced arresting, executing, and deporting his opponents, waging a military campaign of "reconcentration" that especially hurt the civilian population; this was the way of waging warfare against an irregular army that the Spanish military had already practiced during its short occupation of Santo Domingo.[111] The tactics would be brought out again in 1896 and 1897 in terrible episodes that can only be compared to the Boer Wars of South Africa or the German campaigns in Namibia in the early twentieth century.[112] Naturally, General Arthur MacArthur also used them in 1900–1902 to halt resistance by Filipino insurgents who had overcome the Spanish in Luzon and Visayas.[113] In the latter case, the death toll was entirely imperial: 4,000 U.S. soldiers and 20,000 Filipinos, along with some 200,000 deaths attributed to hunger and disease.[114]

The war in Cuba ended because the two armies were exhausted and unable to win. With the end of liberal reforms and the fall of the First Republic in Spain in early 1874, the status quo returned, both on the peninsula and in the colonies. The end of hostilities in 1878 did not bring

about the end of slavery, however, though obviously its days were numbered and the process of abolition was under way.[115] Emancipation had
been implemented in Puerto Rico in 1873, during the Ten Years' War (the
first phase of the Cuban War for Independence).[116] But the smaller island
was quite different than Cuba, which was the key to Spain's continued
presence in America.[117] Even so, the transition to free labor affected both
posseessions, drawing a fine line between changes in the productive model
and rural discontent.[118] Additionally, lower yields and the loss of rhythm
for small and medium-size slave plantations was obvious once the slave
trade ceased in the early 1860s due to pressure from the British (though
there were dispersed arrivals until 1873).[119] The total numbers of slaves,
including urban and rural, and men and women, are instructive: 286,942
in 1827; 436,495 in 1841; 374,806 in 1855; 371,366 in 1856; 287,620 in 1871;
and 200,000 in 1877.[120] The arrival of some 125,000 Chinese contract
workers turned out to be an insufficient and problematic way of feeding
the plantation owners' voracious appetite for more labor.[121]

The appointment of General Arsenio Martínez Campos in 1876 as head
of the Spanish army in Cuba, with authority over the captain general, was
unprecedented. Martínez Campos deployed some 100,000 soldiers, a
spectacular number, and demonstrated a surprising ability to wage war in
Clausewitzian terms, as a continuation of politics by other means. He held
on to the rear guard by allowing newspapers to be published and legaliz-
ing political and social organizations, including organizations of skilled
tobacco workers and other laborers.[122] His approach and credibility in
the year and a half he was in Cuba played an important role in the drawing up of a secret agreement with the moderate sector of the republican
army. On the insurgent side, two leading military officers, Máximo Gómez
and Antonio Maceo, would not sign, considering it surrender.[123] On the
Spanish side, the controversial General Manuel de Salamanca and the
conservative politician Romero Robledo also considered the agreement
dishonorable. Nevertheless, the Spanish government, led by Cánovas del
Castillo, along with José Elduayen Gorriti as overseas minister, accepted
and defended it.[124] The agreement would lead to the Pact of Zanjón in
February 1878.[125] Its essence, to no one's surprise, sent long-neglected
colonial matters back to the political drawing board. Some key concessions had been made earlier in the pacified Puerto Rico of 1869–70; they
included representation in Spanish institutions, according to a decree of
March 1, 1878; establishment of political parties on the island; broader
suffrage (though still male and income-based); and greater freedom of the
press and association, which had been out of the question before Martínez

Campos's arrival. When he became captain general after the war, he proceeded to administratively reorganize the island and establish a system for municipal elections (regulated on June 21, 1878), essentially extending (with some restrictions) the provincial and municipal laws of Spain. Above all it was important to ensure that a party system could function and that there be a party made up mostly of Spaniards who were firmly in favor of a closer relationship with the metropolis. It would be called the Unconditional Spanish Party of Puerto Rico (or the Party of the Constitutional Union of Cuba), always loyal to Spain regardless of who was in office. In addition, a Liberal party was formed to defend the interests of the Creoles, who opposed the political statues dating from 1837 and were critical of Spain's tax and tariff policies.[126]

The general understanding in Spanish historiography is that the Pact of Zanjón between Spanish authorities and Cuban insurgents was principally aimed at reintegrating Spanish political institutions. But it is also possible to see the conflict and its apparent solution more broadly. Spanish military authorities, and, to a lesser extent, the government and politicians in both Cuba and Spain, understanding that a military victory was impossible without enormous human and economic costs, offered insurgents the opportunity to be present in the Spanish Cortes and to reorganize Cuban political and administrative structures. The problem was that, starting in the 1880s, Cuba faced far larger problems, which these solutions, no matter how generous, could not resolve. To begin with, as with Puerto Rico and the coffee industry, the internationalization of the Cuban sugar and tobacco industries had made the island an important commercial partner with the United States and Great Britain.[127] Meanwhile, the presence of many Cuban workers in Florida cigar factories and workshops had drawn the two countries even closer.[128] The slow pace of abolition in Cuba complicated things further. In 1870, reformist minister Segismundo Moret ordered what was called "freedom of the wombs," that is, freedom for all children born of slave mothers, in addition to freedom for those over sixty years old and for 10,000 already emancipated slaves who had nonetheless been forced to work. But pressure from powerful merchants and landowners, along with the Santiago de Cuba war and the collapse of the First Republic in Spain, served to extend slavery a decade longer. At the same time, production was being concentrated into work units called *centrales*, which combined labor by slaves and by free smallholders (*cólonos*), who sold their sugar cane.[129] Formal abolition came on February 13, 1880, but in fact, the *patronato* system (comparable to the apprenticeship system in the West Indies) meant that for 100,000 slaves the end would come only five years later.[130] Ada Ferrer's research on the Ten Years' War (1868–78) and then its sequel in the so-called *guerra chiquita* (1879–1880), waged by those who did not accept the terms of the Pact of Zanjón, has shown how war, flight, and self-liberation came about at the same time and parallel with the officially ordered process, ending in the inevitable abolition in 1886 and the liberation of the last 25,000 slaves.[131] Similarly, Rebecca Scott has described eloquently how individual and collective self-liberation was on the rise during the decade preceding definitive abolition.[132]

Slavery gave birth to profound racial and social divisions that lasted throughout the twentieth century, and former slaves' access to rights enjoyed by the rest of the island's inhabitants would continue encountering obstacles, subtle though they may have been. Many former slaves had participated fully in all three anticolonial wars, in which insurgents proclaimed the equality of all Cubans.[133] In the few years between Zanjón and the last war, from 1882 to 1895, Cuban elites sought a more favorable place for themselves in the Spanish political system.[134] The best-thought-out approach was self-government (*autonomía*) for Cuba, which drew its inspiration in part from peninsular debates during the federal republic of 1873–74 and ideological developments in some Spanish regions in the 1880s, most notably Catalonia. If republicans looked to the United States or Switzerland for their examples, the more moderate proposals by monarchic liberals drew sustenance from the Victorian British empire's dominions, especially with the establishment of the Canadian Confederation (*Confédération canadienne*) on July 1, 1867. At that point, the Cuban Liberal Party demanded autonomy through its alliance with the Spanish liberals, led by Práxedes Mariano Mateo Sagasta. In the end, a large majority of the Spanish Cortes rejected the proposal on June 21, 1886.[135] In 1893, when there were renewed fears about crisis in Cuba, Antonio Maura, minister of overseas possessions in Sagasta's new cabinet, proposed a series of Cuban institutions with broad jurisdictions, though not broad enough to threaten the authority of the captaincy general and without using the word *autonomy*. For the second time the proposal was rejected by the Cortes, thanks to strong opposition by the conservatives, brutally articulated by their leader, Cánovas del Castillo.[136] Later proposals drawn up during the definitive war of independence were nothing more than useless exercises in propaganda. The fluid social frontiers in the postslavery world, massive immigration, limited political space in the relationship between colony and metropolis, and the highly consolidated economic links with the U.S. market were all factors that allowed President McKinley to intervene.

The same happened in the Philippines, a vitally strategic location for the United States, as can be seen by its armed intervention and cruel repression against those who fought the late Spanish empire.[137]

In 1898, the paths of two imperial nations intersected, and size, geography, and economics made the outcome entirely predictable. Spain's fin-de-siècle crisis and U.S. imperial optimism eloquently show that in both cases, nation and empire were one.

CHAPTER SEVEN

The Long Road to 1898

AMONG HIS MANY DUTIES, Thomas Jefferson would occupy himself by drawing maps of the expansion of the Thirteen Colonies; a map of 1784, for instance, features made-up classical names like Polypotamia and Metropotamia.[1] It would be a mistake to see the Virginian's speculations—acts of supreme power, like Adam naming the animals—as merely a hobby, even if neither the boundaries nor the names survived. After all, he was one of the outstanding builders of the imperial nation, of the republican empire par excellence, with ambitions to reach Panama and the southern seas.[2] And he knew what he was doing. For it was in the northern, Atlantic world, more than anywhere else, that a national community and imperial ambition would be freely and resolutely built, joined to the myth of the free republic, the "chosen country," in Jefferson's evocative words.[3] So it is reasonable to think of the development of the United States of America as the construction of a new sort of political entity and at the same time as a continuation of the British empire in the New World.[4] This super-imposition helps to describe the complex overlapping as well as illustrate the potential of the imperial nation, even if its center of gravity had shifted outside Europe. The aim of this chapter is to highlight the ways in which the formation of the United States was comparable to the processes de-scribed elsewhere in this book concerning the other empires.

Imperial Constitution

The independence of the Thirteen Colonies marked the start of both the refoundation of the British empire and the foundation of the imperial re-public of the United States of North America. The former colonists, afraid of rival monarchical-aristocratic empires, had no choice but to protect their sovereign space as completely as possible, from the narrow strip of land along the East Coast to the rest of the continent, to be "sole lords and proprietors of a vast tract of the continent," as George Washington said in 1787.[5] Thus, appropriation of "America," of the entire continent, was the new nation's only possible direction.[6] Furthermore, the newborn political entity was a community of citizens that invoked sovereignty over both people and space.[7]

The political and institutional construction of the nation-state was designed in detail to address these aims and to ensure the free reproduction *ad infinitum* of a community of equal, free, and virtuous citizens, while also guaranteeing the continuity of the social foundations inherited from colonial society.[8] Expulsion of entire social groups from the republican order, and their necessary subjugation, was by no means accidental; it was a precise concretization of "the American mind," to quote Jefferson.[9] The first laws regarding the formation of the new states reflected the Founding Fathers' ideas about social and political order: this was to be a republic of citizens, originating in Europe and ruling over an expanse of clearly colonial situations that were comparable to those in the monarchical empires that threatened from the north and the south, endangering the new republic's very survival. Exclusion constituted the practical negation of the universal rights proclaimed in the Declaration of Independence.[10] But this was inevitable, considering the justifications for separation from Great Britain, discomfort around the slavery question (ever since Pennsylvania in 1780 passed the first law of gradual abolition), and pacification of the Indians—the factors leading up to the Royal Proclamation of 1763 at the end of the Seven Years' War.[11] The legacy of the colonial era and the subsequent division of the country around these questions were clear to see.[12]

The fragile political entity was thus born of social and ethnic patterns acceptable to the colonists who rose up against George III. The first example of this pattern came at the dawn of the republic, with the 1790 naturalization law.[13] One of the law's requirements was that citizenship be available only to individuals who were "free white persons" having "good moral character," a requirement that excluded British loyalists.[14] Provisions were also made for the naturalization of citizens' children born abroad. In pointing to those eligible for naturalization, the law obviously also pointed to those who were ineligible. This was a provisional (and preventive) law; from 1783 to 1808, some 170,000 African slaves entered the United States.[15] Excluded were the unfree, the free descendants of slaves, American Indians, and indentured servants, of whom there were untold numbers in eighteenth-century North America.[16] However, in the decade following independence, indentured servitude showed a striking decline, leaving color as the operative distinction. These early measures later were confirmed with new naturalization laws in 1795, 1798, and 1802, which added as a requirement the amount of time a potential naturalized citizen must have resided in the country before requesting status.[17] From the start, then, a dichotomy was established between "We, the People" and "Others," to use Benjamin Ringer's expression, and the dichotomy was reinforced every ten years with every new census.[18]

This purging of citizenship led to further complexities for the new liberal-representative states. The essential question was to define the relationship around the establishment of a political community and the decision around who could be full members of that community.[19] Two related institutions are relevant here: the franchise and the local (and supralocal) militias, both key pieces of early republican organization from below. Political organization was deliberately decentralized ("We are all federalists," Jefferson said in his first presidential address) and in a constant state of war, be it with British North America, France, the Spanish empire to the south, or internal enemies.[20] And the latter, including fugitive slaves and Indians, were easily lured by outside enemies from the old metropolis to the British and French Caribbean and Haiti, where the phantom of abolition endured amid slavery.[21]

Despite efforts to provide homogeneity to the new nation and give positive meaning to "We, the People," the social and political order clearly was unequal from the very start, as intended.[22] Most (former) colonists wished to keep slavery or were willing to tolerate its continuity in those states that relied on it as a key part of their social fabric.[23] A literal reading of the text that gave shape to the national project reveals how closely it was tied to the existing social reality, despite all its Greco-Roman abstractions. A long list of important inclusions and exclusions limited universal citizenship—most obviously that of Africans, which Quakers turned into a cause in the early days after independence.[24] But slaves were not the only ones; American Indians "not taxed"—the vast majority—also were there. The Constitution thus defined both those who formed part of "the people" as well as those who did not, those who had absolutely no access to mechanisms of integration.

The Constitution referred to slaves explicitly in three of its articles and implicitly in five more.[25] The most explicit references were those on fugitive slaves (Section 2, Article 4), requiring states to return them to their legitimate owners (a provision that should be considered alongside the Fugitive Slave Act of 1793). Elsewhere there is an explicit statement that the slave trade cannot be prohibited, though in fact it would be abolished twenty years after the Constitution was ratified, once the Founding Fathers were gone.[26] And third, slaves are explicitly considered in numerical terms concerning political representation and fiscal responsibility.

These numerical terms are of particular relevance because they influenced constitutional architecture and opened the way for the republic's dual development. The chief point of contention in Philadelphia concerned, precisely, slaves' presence on electoral rolls and their future fiscal role. Quite clearly, there was disagreement among the delegates. The compromise, the Three-Fifths Agreement, favored slave states, in that it included a portion of the slaves as electors.[27] The agreement inspired the Marquis de Mirabeau to rhetorically propose in the French National Assembly that oxen and horses be represented there since representatives from Saint-Domingue could include slaves in order to increase their seats. The agreement proved critical in allowing Jefferson to defeat Alexander Hamilton for president and in removing federalists from power, after months of heated debate.[28] Jefferson's two terms were a godsend for southern slaveowners and allowed the states to increase their powers vis-à-vis the federal government. His successor, republican James Madison, was accused of doing the same.[29] And the Louisiana Purchase in 1803 led to the expansion of slavery and to a redefinition of the borders with the Indian nations.[30] Robin Einhorn has shown how the numbers had a decisive impact on the early republic's fiscal state, and also that the solution emerged out of quite diverse fiscal cultures.[31] While the federal government was responsible for taxation on foreign trade and a few scarcely developed monopolies, states and municipalities obtained direct, transfer, and property taxes.[32] It is no surprise, then, that the central state was, from the start, weak and lacking in resources. The debates between federalists and antifederalists focused on the very heart of the question of where power would lie.[33] The unsteady solution they arrived at lasted a few decades and guaranteed that the former colonies would have near sovereignty in defining their internal social order. Any notion of abolition from above, along the lines of what the British had done, was therefore completely utopian.[34] When abolition did take hold in the North after the Revolution, its progress was state by state, and in some cases with great parsimony, for example, in New York. Furthermore, and of great significance, northern states imposed two conditions for the admission of territories as proper states.[35] In conformity with the country's foundations, the essential norm was the existence of a republican government sustained by a sufficient number of inhabitants. Furthermore, nonslave states dictated that backcountry territories could not attain statehood if they maintained slavery. It is logical, therefore, that Article 6 of the 1787 ordinance, which invoked this requirement, be emphasized as the appropriate legal framework for development based on European immigration into areas formerly populated by Iroquois, French, and *métis* of the old *pays d'en haut*.[36] But at the same time, the Southwest Ordinance of May 26, 1790, did allow the extension of slavery into Tennessee, Kentucky, Mississippi, Oklahoma, Arkansas, and Missouri.[37] There was a clear line of colonial development in the new republic, parallel to the formalization of the centrality of the community of citizens. At the center of this political engine sat the independent property owner, as imagined by the early republicans, who would evolve later into the homesteader and Free-Soiler.[38] The division between free states and slave states, which was stabilized with the Missouri Compromise of 1820, was the first and most decisive split in the country, and until the full onset of the mid-century crisis, the republic comprised two national projects.[39]

Slaves and their descendants, as we have noted, were not the only human beings eliminated from the imagined community of equal citizens. The exact identity of "Indians not taxed," referred to in the Constitution (Article 1, Section 2), is a matter of speculation, but it is quite clear that the category meant nothing good for the continent's original inhabitants. It allowed their presence on electoral rolls as long as they paid taxes and adopted a socially acceptable and sedentary lifestyle. But though the provisions were included in some treaties, they were never put into practice; nor was the mandate to establish states with majority Indian populations (in the 1778 agreement with Delaware, for example).[40] The same was true of Indians separated from their own societies, who were bound by a decision handed down by James Kent, of the New York Court of Errors (the appellate court), deeming them ineligible for citizenship because they had been born under the jurisdiction of their tribes.[41] So this was a case of naturalization, governed by the norms already discussed. The same would happen to free and independent descendants of slaves—even those who had gained their freedom by fighting against the British, though many white colonists had opposed their presence in the army.[42] In this case, however, there were no arguments of intermediate jurisdictions, as with the Indians. Blocking manumission and the movement of free blacks was a shaky ideological operation amid the British debate getting under way at that point, especially after Lord Mansfield's ruling in *Somerset v. Stewart* (1772), which marked the beginning of the end for silence on the subject of slavery.[43] As arguments against slavery gained weight in Britain and in North America, its defenders were obliged to shift to racial arguments, always backed up with references to states' rights.[44] To complicate matters further, many inhabitants of the new states were free blacks, the offspring of Africans who had arrived in the Thirteen Colonies more than a century earlier.[45] Born free or freed by their owners, these people were, in theory, eligible for citizenship. As a result, the first electoral rolls were relatively inclusive, which is obvious if we consider that from then on they were repeatedly subject to exclusions. But exclusions proved problematic. When the new state of Missouri in 1820 tried to eliminate an entire social group, many jurists and much of the public were opposed, arguing that individual or partial exclusions resulting from state laws (affecting, for example, the poor, minors, or nonfreeholders) could not be extended to the whole.[46] It was impossible to defend wholesale exclusions of "native," rights-holding populations from the republican polity, from property rights, or from the rights and obligations of citizenship. But, at the same time, free blacks could not simply be admitted in the old or the new South, where slavery still constituted the basis of prosperity. They were free but they could not be citizens, an anomalous state of limbo along the republican horizon. So, at the same time as the new country's fundamental political tenets were being worked out—expansion of the franchise, bipartisanism (which disappeared only in 1820–24), democratization, positive "factionalism" (in Madison's terms), and identification between owner and elector—the electoral rolls were purged.[47]

Thus, the early republican decades simultaneously involved, on the one hand, broadening suffrage and loosening property requirements in many state electoral laws and, on the other, constructing the profile of citizens eligible for political participation.[48] This profile was increasingly recognizable: European men of a certain age and with families. Georgia, South Carolina, and Virginia explicitly excluded free blacks even if they met all the other criteria. Being that many considered citizenship a privilege granted by the state where one lived—the "stake-in-society" theory—they developed the idea that citizens were representatives for women, minors, the propertyless, and the nonwhite.[49] Toward the end of the colonial era the colonies' assemblies, recognizing the notion of indirect representation, were based on broad electoral rolls but never approached universal suffrage. Reforms had been undertaken in six colonies: Pennsylvania, New Hampshire, Vermont, New Jersey, Georgia, and Maryland; in others (such as New York and North Carolina) the rolls were somewhat restricted, and in Massachusetts even more restricted. So, broader political participation was a good project for the new republican regime. It got under way immediately in Pennsylvania, where nearly universal suffrage was established in 1776, pushed along by the Continental Congress, which considered it the best way to vanquish those who had doubts about the Revolution.[50] Vermont then eliminated all property and wealth requirements, though it did insist on voters swearing allegiance to the Revolution and belonging to the local church.[51] Georgia, under pressure from Savannah artisans, followed suit. But New York and Connecticut upheld their limitations. The logical counterbalance to opening up the franchise was to impose property and religious eligibility rules for public officials. All states allowed Jews and Catholics to vote.[52]

Broadening the franchise (only in Vermont was it universal for men) allowed states to include a majority of patriots and to exclude Tories who would not swear allegiance to the new institutions. It also allowed for the integration of those who had fought against the British and their native allies during the War of Independence and again in 1812.[53] At the same time, inclusion of property conditions (such as the famous fifty acres of the Northwest Ordinance) was a way of stabilizing the republic of property owners while draping it in nationalism.[54] Later on, property requirements would lose importance, in part because state and local qualifications were not especially demanding. But wealth requirements would survive over the following decades; only by paying a certain amount of taxes could one be included on the rolls.[55] Republican political life was characterized by a struggle to define its democratic reach, though the struggle would be resolved on the level of state reforms, which was where Federalists and Republicans of the North and South waged battle.[56] While the community of citizens imposed its norms (the underlying conflict between patrician and popular political control), the status of "others" would repeatedly be reconsidered so as to benefit a more homogeneous ideal citizen. In other words, incorporating poor whites into the franchise was a way of guaranteeing that they would serve in militias whenever slaves threatened to rebel.[57]

The problem of Indian nations living in contact with or on the margins of the former Thirteen Colonies remained. Those on the margins initially did not need any more precise definition; they were considered to be outside republican life and subject to treaties with foreign nations under the direct administration of the federal government. Furthermore, as the treaties were between unequal parties, they did not necessarily have to be respected and could be ignored altogether if that seemed desirable.[58] Balance among peoples, a notion characteristic of the last decades of British rule, was now thought to be an "old way of reasoning" that must be eliminated.[59] Treaties were just another tool (wielded by his secretary of war, Henry Knox) in the civilization toolbox Jefferson had put together at the turn of the century. Andrew Jackson, responsible for the war against the Seminole and Creek, made this quite clear in a letter to President Monroe in 1817: "I have long viewed treaties with the Indians an absurdity not to be reconciled to the principles of our government . . . If Indians are the subjects of the United States, inhabiting its territory and acknowledging its sovereignty, then is it not absurd for the sovereign to negotiate by treaty with the subjects?"[60] The future president's position had some basis in colonists' decisions in previous decades.[61] The European colonial community's position had defined itself through a series of systematic ruptures with the above-mentioned balance as it concerned Indians.[62] During the Seven Years' War, frontier vigilantes (the most famous such group was known as the Paxton Boys) attacked Indians in general, not just those who were clear allies of British efforts to eliminate the French presence.[63] The Pennsylvania backcountry's elusive frontier, to use Eric Hinderaker's expression, became the perfect place because it "made racial boundaries theoretically absolute."[64] Persecution continued after the war, when the victorious United States was still unable to impose its own regional geopolitical perspective after the withdrawal of the British to the north and the Fallen Timbers massacre of August 1794.[65] Neither the Treaty of Paris of 1783 nor that of Ghent in 1814, which put an end to the War of 1812, was respected by the militias or by the Continental Army, which continued fighting to destroy the Iroquois in the Ohio Valley and the Creek, Choctaw, Chickasaw, and Cherokee to the southeast.[66] The Paxton Boys' style was picked up by the militias under Jackson's command and would also follow Spain's shameful cession of Florida to the United States in 1819 under the Adams-Onís Treaty (also known as the Transcontinental Treaty or the Florida Purchase), which turned out to be key for the establishment of the subsequent Cotton Belt.[67] A lot had happened since the Creek people went to Havana in 1760 to ask the king of Spain for help in their fight against the British.[68]

The republic's general development was clearly stated in its texts, which were then applied to particular situations over the first twenty years. Europe's empire in North America, now the United States, had reclaimed the continent and had learned to construct a community of citizens atop a vast array of colonial situations. This is sounding familiar. One must not compare what cannot be compared, and circumstances may have been different, yet at the same time, once the cycle of revolutions had passed, the problems of making and unmaking empires were similar.[69]

Republican Spécialité: The Louisiana
Purchase and Indian Country

European empires, or empires with European roots, faced the challenge of stabilizing and expanding after the deep crises of the mid-eighteenth century and the Napoleonic Wars. While monarchical empires of the past could tolerate fragmented judicial and social development in their possessions—given the absence of any aspiration on their part for equalization or cultural unification of their subjects (beyond the unification entailed in the extension of royal power)—such heterogeneity was more complicated for representative states in the absence of moral ties among inhabitants and among the various parts. As Gordon Wood noted (though without reaching the opportune conclusion), "Monarchy imagined its society in traditional and prenational terms, as a mosaic of quasicorporate communities, and thus had little trouble in embracing African slavery and Indians as subjects. But republicanism created citizens, and since citizens were all equal to one another, it was difficult for the Revolutionaries to include Blacks and Indians as citizens in the new republican states they were trying to create."[70] And yet they had to find a political formula enabling them to accommodate parts of their world where the weight of the past and anthropological differences among inhabitants were significant. The most marked contradiction was the one throughout the Atlantic between the community of citizens (whether they were called citizens, subjects, or electors) and the nonfree. The contradiction could not be ameliorated simply by denying the unitary reach of the classical liberal ethos. Rather, it was resolved through affirmation of a parallel, subordinate solution, the one the French had called *spécialité* and which, with linguistic and practical variations, would end up being the rule in many places. In the decades after U.S. independence, the Louisiana Purchase and the creation of Indian Country in Oklahoma are relevant examples of the construction of a political and legislative exception amid the unstoppable occupation of the continent and the reproduction *ad infinitum* of the community of virtuous citizens.

The first of these two examples mainly concerns expansion. The Founding Fathers were not at all hesitant in referring to their imperial vocation. In George Washington's words, his was an "imperial nation," while Jefferson wrote many times about the empire's features and uncertain limits.[71] "Empire" was no drawback in the minds of republicans who admired, though not without some doubts, the Roman example of expansive citizenship.[72] Indeed, they saw themselves as the Romans' most conspicuous heirs, assuming the mantle handed down by the Florentines and the seventeenth-century English.[73] Their problem was not this glorious past but rather, the other side of Roman citizenship—slavery—and how to adapt to the colonial rules of all expansive empires. The word *colonial* could not be easily imported into the American republican lexicon without damaging Roman patricians' lofty self-image. And yet, slavery and colonial notions of unfree labor played as important a role in the New World as did Livy's ideas of citizenship. There is no better example of this than the expansion beyond the border left behind by the British in 1763, which brought the destruction of the societies living in Ohio, the world of the Miami, Wyandot, Potawatomi, Delaware, and Iroquois, along with their French and British partners.[74] This was the key to second-generation freeholder expansion, what Jefferson brought about in a territory beyond his control, thus contributing to an uncertain republican unity. If the lands formerly occupied by Indians and now by colonists from Europe or from the former colonies (of the 400,000 who arrived between 1811 and 1820, most settled in the Ohio Valley) did not become states, they could easily be left open for foreign imperial interference.[75] It is only by using considerable imagination that we can envision the social, cultural, and linguistic variation of a world that vanished in two generations' time, giving way to the relentless pressure of colonial structures that reproduced themselves again and again.[76]

In this regard, the Louisiana Purchase was the most important event in the early republican period.[77] It put an end to a long series of conflicts with the Spanish empire over river and maritime trade and pointed the way to national consolidation.[78] The combination of a national community based on representative institutions, plus the development of a truly colonial space, with its montage of specialness, unmistakingly corresponds to what we understand to be the imperial nation. Acquisition of the enormous tract of land from the French, who preferred consolidating their position in the Caribbean, marked the end of European empires in North America, with the exception of the future British North America. This was the end of Nouvelle France and the definitive retreat of Spain, despite the existence of neutral ground between the Purchase and Spain's precarious holdings between the Sabine and Arroyo Hondo rivers.

The Louisiana Purchase included two types of social space: first, the territory between the Appalachians and the Mississippi, between New Orleans and St. Louis, which the United States would take from native peoples; second, slave territory in lands fought over with the Seminole after the Adams-Onís Treaty of 1819 with Spain (which had recovered Florida in 1783).[79] Without occupation of the land between Florida and

Louisiana, formerly administered by Spain (France got it back only one year before the purchase), the Cotton Belt would have been unthinkable, and so too would the sugar plantations, on former tobacco and indigo lands, which took advantage of the French Caribbean sugar crisis. The Louisiana Purchase made way for entirely new colonial operations with New Orleans and the Mississippi Delta, which throughout the eighteenth century had been the gateway between the Caribbean and North America. New Orleans called for something more than simple subjugation to republican power, given the existence of an entire juridical culture established during French and Spanish rule over the city, the port, the hinterland, and the parishes, and the diverse population made up of French Acadian emigrants, Spaniards, Canary Islanders, and many descendants of slaves, most of them from the French Caribbean. In the words of one historian of law, there was a "clash of legal traditions."[80] The degree to which this was a truly different place can be shown by the fact that Aaron Burr had a plan to create a new republic there, with New Orleans as its capital.[81]

The Louisiana Purchase also compensated for northern expansion into the Ohio Valley and Great Lakes region. The new southern dynamic, what Adam Rothman called a "domestication" of slavery, accelerated the expansion of sugar and cotton.[82] It contributed enormously to the most important aspect of U.S. spécialité, along with federalism, which was the division of the country into two social and cultural entities. The South offered an agrarian-commercial model with slaves that the republican administration wished to perpetuate and even expand.[83] Meanwhile, the North continued its march westward, led by independent farmers. These two forms of expansion constituted the basis of both nation and empire, and the division would be enshrined after the new republican pact of 1820.[84] The essential "colonialness" of the Louisiana Purchase lies not simply in the incorporation of a huge stretch of land but also in the degraded social and juridical conditions of a large number of people who lived there. Peter Kastor put it this way: "Despite all the noise of discontent and signs of instability, Louisiana is most striking for the *absence* of resistance to American authority, separatist appeal, and ethnic political polarization among white residents. Louisiana is equally striking for the *presence* of accommodation and the desperate struggle of white Louisianans to insert themselves into the social, commercial, and political networks. In less than a generation, Louisiana went from a place that seemed on the brink of separatism or racial revolt to one of the most loyal states in the union with one of America's most repressive slave regimes."[85] The rapid assimilation of the local elites was the flip side of the degradation of free blacks and an expression of the peculiar position of New Orleans and its hinterland in national and imperial space. Examples include the city's resistance against the British in 1812 (on which Jackson hung his military prestige) and during the Civil War, leading to its capture on May 1, 1862.[86] Between those two points, New Orleans was the basis for an idea of a sort of borderland embracing the Caribbean and New Spain, under U.S. hegemony and with slaves, an equation that seduced Cuban slavers fed up with British abolition and had some bearing on the crisis that gave rise to the slave republic of Texas.[87]

The destiny of New Orleans's elites was closely connected to that of the black and mulatto majority. The former repeatedly said they wished to join southern slave society and maintain the flow of slaves, either from Africa or from within the United States itself, though this was impossible after 1804. As Walter Johnson recently explained, the possibility of new slave imports never entirely died there.[88] Hopes in that regard were put forward, again and again, in line with the "Remonstrance of the People of Louisiana Against the Political System Adopted by Congress for Them," a communication submitted to the Senate one year after the Louisiana Purchase, when the status of the new territory was being debated.[89] Louisiana's quick ratification of its state constitution—which allowed it to benefit from the traffic of human beings between new and old colonies— and the first elections of 1812 sealed Louisiana's integration. The problem was that slavery in Mississippi and New Orleans had risen in a distant imperial context that was more porous than that of the early nineteenth century. Champions of southern federalism warned of the dangers: the inhabitants of lower Louisiana were not at all prepared to be useful citizens, and therefore the 1804 integration plan altered the timeline for how long the territory would take to adapt to the republic; it also included a governmental scheme leading to full and inexorable integration. The scheme established the basic institutions of a state: a governor appointed by Washington (William C. C. Clairbone was the first), a thirteen-member Legislative Council, and a three-justice Superior Court.[90] The powerful Spanish-like city council remained, and orders were given to repress any internal dissent (the possibility Burr had mentioned) and, most important, to control former and current slaves in this "atmosphere of massive re-enslavement."[91] To that end, a city guard was established in 1809 and given broad repressive powers. Local elites, anxious to take charge of the process themselves, were wary of the plan in general. As an alternative to this very unrepublican exceptional power, which had virtually no electoral base, locals requested a sort of colonial autonomy, and the first element would be to ensure the steady arrival of slaves, despite rising condemnation of the practice in other states. In other words, they demanded rapid integration into the republican political order and also wished to preserve the old political and legal structure handed down by the French and Spanish, with enough leeway to be able to lead the expansion of slavery there.[92]

Any sort of legislative adaptation would require unusual and diverse solutions. One example was to postpone the introduction of English common law, including trial juries, until the state constitution was approved in 1812. Another was the prolonged and awkward conglomeration of legislation on slavery and race relations for what George Dargo called "America's first imperial possessions."[93] Three pieces of legislation were of particular importance here: the 1805 Land Act, the Black Code the following year, and the Louisiana Civil Code of 1808 (formally titled, "A Digest of the Civil Laws Now in Force in the Territory of Orleans, with Alterations and Amendments Adapted to its Present Form of Government"). The general idea was that the future state constitution would unify older measures and laws and define the position of slaves and former slaves differently than the old laws of Louis XIV and seventeenth-century Spanish and French codes had done. It may have been ambiguous, but the old French Code Noir at least granted free blacks litigation rights similar to those of Europeans, and it also upheld their economic and property rights.[94] Equally ambiguous was the application of the Spanish manumission formula by the slaves themselves (called *coartación*), which was eliminated for slaves younger than thirty, adding the stipulation that the owner had to consent.[95] The new administration, as well as the arrival of colonists from elsewhere in the United States, shifted the balance; new laws emphasized owners' total control over slaves and free blacks, whose numbers were increasing tremendously in New Orleans—which made strict control over the marriage market another important matter.[96] The last of the necessary pieces was to remove free blacks from the electoral rolls, often by preventing them from benefiting from the naturalization law. This had been passed in 1790 with an eye to future nonwhite immigrants, but now it was being used against those who lived in a territory that had been incorporated into the republic. In Rebecca Scott's words, "In the decades that preceded the Civil War, Louisiana's legislators systematically tightened the constraints of African descent, slave and free, rural and urban."[97]

The result was that "Americanized" Louisiana in 1830 looked a lot more like its neighboring territories than it had twenty years earlier. But that was still not enough, and in 1842 the state prohibited the entry of free blacks, which reduced the census of free people both in absolute and proportional terms.[98] This endless tinkering with the rules of the game followed a familiar logic: "The rules prescribing the police and conduct to be observed with respect to slaves in this territory, their enfranchisement and the punishment of their crimes and offenses are fixed by special laws of the Legislatures."[99] The endpoint in this transformation was the 1808 Louisiana Civil Code, or Digest, which remained in effect until 1825, a compilation of all relevant U.S., French, and Spanish legislation.[100] In it we can see which local and state concerns dominated until the Civil War; this was indeed a truly special situation, and it was characteristic of the colonial basis of the Atlantic empires. It is no coincidence that it was prepared by a team of three jurists with French and English training—Louis Moreau de Lislet, Jean Noël Destrehan, and James Brown—who would later collaborate in 1811–12 in drawing up the state constitution. Slavery and race were not the only complications, but they were the essential matters, along with regulation of marriage and inheritance. But the case of a sugar plantation owner who used Spain's *Leyes de los reynos de las Indias* to protest against seizure of his property exemplifies the legal hurdles involved in marrying juridical cultures, so much so that in 1820, Moreau de Lislet (with help from Henry Carleton) translated the Digest into English to help the courts straighten matters out.[101]

This was not the only case in which republican imperial sovereignty was consolidated with inherited structures from the colonial era that required unexpected legislative solutions. Another case from the early republican era was the construction of "Indian Country," starting in the 1830s. Though the story is well known, it is worth thinking about the foundations of that internal colonized space where the Indians of the Southeast were transported. And it is important to avoid any confusion in terminology. Historically, Indian Country referred to those parts of the continent inhabited by Indians; it was the Constitution and, later, the laws governing the new states that changed the meaning of the term. The new nation's constitutional identity rested on a key distinction: the United States did not possess colonies. Rather, it comprised states and territories; and strictly speaking, only states, given that republican unity meant that only territories with republican institutions and sufficient electors could become states. The process by which sovereignty was established was clear: a group of colonists inhabited *terra nullius* (the Lockean term was always used to describe initial settlement) and then, once potential electors were there in sufficient numbers, they could solicit membership in the Republic according to the above-mentioned norms.[102] Thus the nation-state's and the imperial nation's terms of construction were defined, as sovereign space went considerably beyond that of states constituted according to the statehood norm.[103] On paper it was perfectly clear. The specialness, the unwritten constitution, was defined later on, as with the other cases described in this book. Three examples are relevant: the appearance of Indian reservations after the Civil War and the Indian Wars, which removed Indians from citizenship until 1924; the decades-long delay in recognizing certain territories as states, such as Alaska, Arizona, and New Mexico, so that they spent years in a limbo that can only be considered a sort of colonial specialness; and the acquisition and claimed sovereignty over territories that were neither one nor the other, such as Hawaii and the "insular cases" of the three islands taken from Spain in 1898.[104]

Before norms were developed, the establishment of Indian Country was the most obvious case in which the criteria for republican unity were left aside. That vast territory where Indians from both sides of the Appalachians had been moved could not even be maintained as a territory while it awaited admission as a state. Oklahoma would become a state only in 1907, after waiting twenty years—ever since the 1889 amendment to the Indian Appropriations Act and recognition the following year of its territorial status made way for the entrance of white colonists on lands "ceded" by the Indians.

Let us return to the transformation of the interior after the Seven Years' War and to political relations with Indians living on the borders of the Thirteen Colonies. To the surprise of Philip Schuyler, Henry Knox, and military authorities, the Indians were not prepared to abandon their lands or dissolve themselves into a European society that showed no willingness to ease their integration. The colonists, quite simply, wanted the Indians' land.[105] As described by Richard White and James Merrell, two of the great revisionists in early frontier studies, the transformation of those societies as sovereignty was altered did not stop with the Revolution and the early republic.[106] On the contrary, the era between the Seven Years' War and independence gave new dynamism to relations between Indians and Europeans, albeit with contradictions among the former. Political alliances and cultural changes divided their societies into those who wished to use everything at their disposal to effect social and political change and those who favored returning to the old ways, be they real or invented. That was why religious leaders such as Tecumseh and Neolin played such an important role in the eastern Indians' last phase of autonomy.[107] But physical space, rather than cultural matters, was the pivot for the most significant changes. Virginia tobacco farmers, the rice growers of the Carolinas, and the sugar and cotton plantation owners in the Southeast defined the Thirteen Colonies' expansive horizon.[108] Harassment, aggressive militia activity whose origins lay in the fight against the British, and the desire to displace Indians from the Appalachians and the Ohio and Mississippi valleys proved to be an unstoppable combination that led straight to Indian Removal in 1830–33.[109]

Georgia and South Carolina's aggressive stance in this regard lends credence to the hypothesis that tribes that continued occupying lands coveted by those two states, despite moving around during the wars, were subject to especially harsh removal procedures. Three decades after the Jeffersonian model of civilization was first applied through commerce, litigation between whites and Indians over removal became permanent and grew continuously. From 1823 to 1830, two crucial Supreme Court cases addressed the endless purge with rulings declaring that eminent domain, be it individual or collective preemption, was a lawful act. In *Johnson v. McIntosh* (1823), the court declared the republican government to be the only legitimate purchaser of lands occupied by Indians. This juridically constructed monopoly meant that Indians' historic rights over their lands and natural resources were of lesser quality than those of the United States and therefore must be ceded to the latter; and furthermore, following the same tortured logic, that individual or collective appropriations to date were retroactively legal. Indeed, Jefferson himself, who had always been interested in relations with the Indians, could not help noting in a draft of his *Notes on the State of Virginia*, "It is true that these purchases were sometimes made with the price in one hand and the sword in the other."[110]

In an impressive leap forward, *Cherokee Nation v. Georgia* (1831) and its partner, *Worcester v. Georgia* (1832), fixed the codification of Indian relations. Paradoxically, the rulings defined Indian nations as both "sovereign nations" and "wards" of the U.S. government. As entities covered by international law, Indian nations could enter into treaties with Washington. Once a bilateral relationship was established, these treaties formed part of U.S. law and could be revised by the United States, the ultimate owner of American land. Thus, Indian sovereignty was a contradiction in terms. They were "domestic dependent nations," societies subject to wardship.[111] Chief Justice John Marshall's written decision aimed not only to affirm authority over Indians but also to reach matters of state construction. By situating sovereignty in the republican political center, it established the principle of wardship over others. In other words, Marshall reaffirmed the ambivalent "trust doctrine."[112] In this particular case, the decision affirmed the authority of the federal state to regulate Indian relations while denying Indians' right to sue states in the U.S. Supreme Court, and states were to respect treaties between Indian nations and the federal government—a doubtful prospect, though without it the Indians could do little.[113] President Jackson, hero of the war against the Seminole and the British, immediately announced that he would not interfere in Georgia's highly complicated efforts to expel its Indians.

This ambiguous juridical fiction reinforced state plenary powers and preemption, and both would be crucial throughout the nineteenth and twentieth centuries. As Charles Wilkinson has written, jurisprudence then (which has never been overturned) avoided the tricky question of Indian sovereignty, which was reduced to little more than local self-government subject to the guardianship and supervision of republican authorities, something akin to a protectorate or colonial trusteeship under U.S. sovereignty, even before occupation.[114] From the turn of the century to Jackson's presidency, successive republican administrations wavered between relocating the Indians or counting on the eventual erosion of their lifestyle and their inevitable decadence. Jefferson and Monroe, who favored the latter option, left open the possibility of concentrating Indians somewhere so as to free up the lands and forests where they previously had lived. Monroe's paternalism on this point was exemplary; in one of his last statements before leaving the presidency in 1825, he referred to the need to move southern tribes out, but, he added, the move should be "voluntary."[115] A year earlier, Monroe himself had referred to displacements as "revolting to humanity, and utterly unjustifiable."[116]

This, then, was the sinister and ambiguous jurisprudential context in which the 1830 Indian Removal Act was approved, and subsequent events surprised no one.[117] For example, the Chickasaw, based in the present-day states of Alabama and Mississippi, waged legendary resistance against efforts to remove them, led by their equally legendary negotiator, Chief Levi Colbert. Given the unity and determination of the tribe, government delegate Thomas L. McKenney offered them a chance to visit the lands they were to receive in exchange. Twelve Chicasaws went to this promised land, where they met with members of the Choctaw and Creek. After a full year traveling through Missouri, Arkansas, and Oklahoma, they remained unpersuaded. The Indian Removal Act sealed their destiny, and their protests to Jackson led nowhere. They were expelled in 1837, forced to accept what was given to them.[118] There in Indian Country, Chickasaw leader Holmes Colbert wrote a constitution for his people that reaffirmed them as a nation in exile, Israel in Egypt.

The case of the Cherokee was slightly different. Their long struggle against Georgia and South Carolina as a result of the U.S. Supreme Court rulings raised the dilemma of gradual tribal erosion or immediate expulsion. Ever since the eighteenth century, the proud and capable Cherokee had engaged in negotiations with their European, British, and Creole neighbors, a process through which the Indians had assimilated and adapted their social and economic patterns.[119] One institution they adopted from the outside world—slavery —would have especially grave consequences, but it was not the only one. The changes they were undergoing were deep and relentless, in part due to the presence of many mixed-bloods and an influential network of Presbyterian missions. Their undeniable acculturation inspired ambiguous admiration.[120] In the early 1820s, the silversmith Sequoyah (also called George Guess) wrote a Cherokee syllabary so his language could be written, which led to the appearance of newspapers. Conversion to Protestantism was also substantial. But the most notorious element of the change came with the drastic reform of Cherokee customs (including education and political organization) so as to stop criticism by their white neighbors. The effort was in vain, however, for the arrival of Andrew Jackson to the presidency in 1829, along with a hunger for land coinciding with high cotton prices, put an end to the tribe's struggles with Georgia. Jackson eased the way for construction of the state of Tennessee on lands claimed by the Indians, whose absolute refusal to be moved merely made matters worse.[121]

Jackson's arrival in the White House enabled access to the federal administration by those who favored massive expulsion of those "relics of a departed age" as a way of putting an end to endless litigation.[122] The measure was ratified in 1830 not just for the Cherokee but for all Indians living on lands that the Louisiana Purchase had isolated between Mississippi and the old colonies that contributed labor and capital.[123] Desperate, the Cherokee decided to respond with every tool they had, including legal ones.[124] They approved a bilingual constitution clearly inspired by that of the United States, and they took it to Washington to be recognized, a surprising act whose only precedent was the document presented by the Delaware to the Continental Congress. While the Cherokee awaited a reply from Congress or the Supreme Court that would never arrive, they were riven by internal conflicts. Finally, the Treaty of New Echota in 1838 obliged them to leave their lands and undertake the long journey of deportation, during which many died of cold and hunger.[125] Their destination was Indian Country, that ominous artifact of political definition by default, a vast repository for the tribes of the Ohio Valley and Mississippi, a geographic space whose shape was uncertain and whose political and administrative definition was confused.[126] It was neither state nor territory; it was something special. Indeed, it was compared to Van Diemen's

Land (Tasmania). Later, after the Indian Appropriations Act was ratified in 1851, this arrangement would lead to temporary reservations, which were solidified between 1871 and 1889.[127]

The Great Divide

The nation-state took shape after the Civil War, before which it hardly could have been defined in conventional terms.[128] Southern elites' urgent need to develop a true southern nationalism in the 1840s makes it very difficult to define the years before 1865 in terms of a nation or united nation-state.[129] In this new context, the old "captive nation" of slaves and their descendants was called on to join the republican community supposedly created through the three new constitutional amendments.[130] But ten years later, once Reconstruction was over, the hopes and expectations both of African Americans who had fought in the Union Army and of the forces that had envisioned integration as being indispensable for overcoming Confederate resistance had lost much of their strength. The subsequent model developed along the classic lines of imperial nations. Two aspects were quite obvious. First came the remodeling of the community of citizens, with the exclusion of nearly everyone of African descent. This segregationist solution, which later would be exported to other segments of society, found support in a surprising version of colonial specialness: "home rule." The second aspect was the genocide of the Indians, the establishment of the reservations, and the theft of their natural resources. This was the final liquidation, in juridical, moral, and material terms, of the old "middle ground" between whites and Indians that might have brought about transformation and relative survival.

African Americans and Native Americans occupied a similar space in the post-1865 republic. The war against the Confederacy had affirmed the unity of the country and of the community of citizens that would forever be its center of gravity. Though slavery had not been the principal target of the North, nonetheless it was a hateful institution that must be eliminated; and yet, emancipated slaves had an uncertain future. Lincoln believed for some time that Jefferson's idea of "extrication" of the "captive nation" was desirable, though the expense made it impossible.[131] It was not at all clear that former slaves were prepared to form part of the new republican society, which was very demanding regarding new members. The free-soil ideology typical of many republicans who assumed leadership positions after 1865 called for citizens who were independent yeomen farmers, working lands that had been given to them. This was the vision affirmed in the 1862 Homestead Act, when more than 1.5 million emigrants from the East Coast or from Europe acquired new land.[132] Former slaves' work habits were too questionable to be acceptable in this refined, ethnocentric scheme of things, though Reconstruction agricultural policies would attempt in 1866 to incorporate them as independent peasants. Even worse was the semisedentary social organization and collective ownership of the Great Plains Indians. It was highly problematic, to say the least, that these people or Asian immigrants in California be integrated as national subjects.[133] Segregation, exclusion, and massive regulation of immigration were thus essential parts of the formation of the community of republican citizens.[134]

Charles Sumner, one of the great ideologues of Radical Reconstruction, as it is known, had warned of the possibility of "slavery under an alias," or disguised slavery.[135] Indeed, the institution of slavery as such died in 1865, but the social relations that replaced it were ambiguous. The Thirteenth, Fourteenth, and Fifteenth amendments were introduced precisely to rule out an exclusionary regime.[136] The same was true of the Civil Rights Act of April 1866, designed to prevent the reestablishment of unfree labor and to compel effective citizenship for the emancipated. But Lincoln's successor, Andrew Johnson, vetoed the bill.[137] With southern whites unconvinced as to the goodness of these aims, the federal government had no political or administrative ability to impose them. However, it could insist that southern states adapt their constitutions to the newly approved amendments, by which the U.S. Constitution would be shown to trump states' rights and put an end to the ideology of duality, in Ringer's words, characteristic of the years leading up to the Dred Scott decision.[138] But ratification of the Fifteenth Amendment, on February 3, 1870, showed that things were not necessarily moving in that direction; former states of the Confederacy immediately countered by approving the Black Code.[139]

Exclusion of blacks from the electoral rolls took place differently in the North and the South. By March 1867, when the Reconstruction Act was approved, only six northern states allowed them to vote.[140] The rest were considering what to do; their indecision reflected scant federal control and persistent lobbying by freedmen and some Republicans (such as Richard Henry Dana Jr.), making for a marked contrast with the South.[141] The latter states, in order to be reaccepted into the republic as purified, had to present tangible proof that their electoral rolls had been opened up. But this process was slow and littered with obstacles. The rise of white supremacists, along with northern doubts about the federal government's ability to extend control over the South, meant that bit by bit the egalitarian ambitions of the Fifteenth Amendment were watered down.[142] Andrew Johnson's intransigence regarding the Black Code, along with his veto of Reconstruction and rights legislation, pointed the way to a predictable erosion of the gains made as a result of the war. Grant's subsequent presidency and the imposition of Reconstruction corrected matters concerning both agrarian policy and the broadening of the electoral rolls. In just one decade, the young republic had experienced the two extremes of possible solutions to the problems brought about by the end of slavery.[143]

The great inversion of equality began with the 1876 presidential elections. Once Democrats had the majority of the popular vote, Reconstruction and the Republican vision of the three constitutional amendments were bound to undergo serious revision, both from above and from below. Beyond the so-called Bourbon constitutions, which were rushed through in an effort to halt the egalitarian measures of victors and African Americans, a populist movement arose to ensure that those objectives would be implemented on the local level.[144] Associations and organizations from the Jim Crow era devoted themselves to subordinating former slaves and their descendants at work, in politics, and throughout society.[145] Written and unwritten laws and white supremacists' use of religious or biological justifications (the "one-drop rule") worked to legitimize exclusion. The legal doctrine of "separate but equal," confirmed in *Plessy v. Ferguson*, appeared to formally respect the Fourteenth Amendment but in fact upheld segregation.[146] Toward the end of the century, eleven former states of the Confederacy had entirely removed blacks from the electoral rolls, while others simply made it very difficult for them to vote, and the states found support for their measures in the U.S. Supreme Court, which eroded the impact of the Enforcement Acts of 1870 and 1871 and undermined congressional powers with the ominous "equal but separate" provision in 1877.[147] The North, meanwhile, showed indifference regarding the fate of southern blacks.[148] To quote Ira Berlin, "Contention over the meaning of freedom divided Northerners even as opposition to secession united them."[149]

The other side of social, religious, and cultural exclusion was the failure of Reconstruction agrarian policy.[150] A plan promoted by Congressman Thaddeus Stevens of Pennsylvania to expropriate the holdings of large landowners and redistribute the land was immediately canceled.[151] Public-sector intervention in the economy was decisive on two fronts: the settlement of homesteaders in the Midwest and agrarian policies in the postbellum South. Concessions such as the famous forty acres and a mule to freed slaves, which were not to the liking of General Sherman, were designed to ensure the existence of an independent peasantry, but the federal government's refusal to engage in large-scale confiscations limited the reach of such efforts.[152] The federal agency known as the Freedmen's Bureau implemented programs which, though small, were important in a political context that had little patience for government intervention in the economic realm.[153] But the bureau was shut down in 1872, and the new peasants faced serious hurdles concerning access to land, the high price of credit, and unequal treatment in the courts.[154] At the same time, a return to plantation labor was unthinkable. The solution was sharecropping, which was what most former slaves turned to,[155] but this meant that they had to give up half of their harvest of cotton, the land was so poor that farmers could not save, and their standard of living was well below that of wage-earners.[156] Once the Freedmen's Bureau was closed and northern officials went back to the North, things got even worse. As could be expected, many southern blacks emigrated north and west in the late nineteenth century.[157]

In 1885, on the eve of major legislative changes, Commissoner of Indian Affairs John Atkins wrote, "The idea of maintaining permanently an *imperium in imperio* such as now exists, must, in some respects, be abandoned."[158] The changes he referred to concerned Indian Country, the territory to which Indians had been expelled since the 1830s. This was no ordinary territory, quite obviously, though it was also true that other territories' road to statehood had been repeatedly delayed. Its exceptional nature and juridical ambiguity, the result of what Charles Wilkinson called "barriers to unitary doctrine," condemned it to extinction. The only possible ending was for it to go away gradually, regardless of the trauma inflicted on its inhabitants.[159] The issue was not the Indians' geographic location but rather the elimination of a sui generis buffer state at a time when settler capitalism and capitalism as such was expanding throughout the Midwest.[160] The challenge was to turn Indians into farmers, as otherwise they would starve to death, which in fact was happening, both in Indian Country and along the Pacific coast, where new forms of confinements were beginning to be put into place. The 1868 Treaty of Fort Laramie led to an ersatz creation somewhere between the old Indian Country and the reservation of the future; this was the Great Sioux Reservation, including part of the territories of South Dakota and Nebraska. But the reservation "solution" really only began its relentless rise in the decades following the Civil War. The Great Sioux Reservation was divided up into five units in 1889, two years after the passage of legislation establishing procedures for land access. To quote Paul Stuart, "United States Indian policy changed greatly between the end of the Civil War and the passage of the Burke Act in 1906. Although policy-makers experimented with the establishment of a reservation policy in the decade before the Civil War, the old objectives of removal and concentration still dominated most official plans for dealing with the 'Indian problem' in 1865. During the next forty years, Congress and the Indian Office established the reservation system for American Indians and subsequently created a mechanism of destroying it."[161] If the aim was to avoid contact between whites and Indians, internal colonization led to the inevitable reduction of space occupied by the latter.[162]

The Civil War was a key transition point from one vision to another. During the war, the Great Indian Nations' alliance with the Confederacy provoked considerable tension and discomfort, especially given that some tribes owned slaves. The war also gave the Great Plains nations a certain degree of freedom, leading to open warfare against the Union, which regarded the Indians as a Trojan horse at the service of the South. Abraham Lincoln himself resolved to take action against this fifth column and ordered harsh measures, including the execution of thirty-eight Indian chiefs in Mankato (Minnesota) in 1862. The so-called Indian Wars, or Sioux Wars, that began during the Civil War and continued against seminomadic peoples on the Great Plains were simply a continuation. Nor were military campaigns geographically limited to the Plains, as evidenced by the Comanche war in the Southwest, which ended in 1875. The effective end of treaties and the enormous violence of these conflicts made clear that things had changed. Grant's peace policy signaled a transition to a new sort of relationship with Indians that entailed a more military, more colonial approach. Sherman's "master plan" of all-out warfare, which relied on the railroad, reprisals, and massive deportations, was crucial. Both he and his right-hand man, Philip Sheridan, were firm believers in scorched-earth policies, which led to the tribes' eventual extinction due to exhaustion, hunger, and illness. Reservations were the next step.

Land and natural resources were once again the basic issues.[163] In the postwar republican world, the Indians' lifestyle and organization were increasingly seen as impossible as well as irredeemable.[164] The new order granting limitless federal reach was affirmed in 1869, when Congress eliminated obligations to compensate Indians (Lakota and Sioux, in this case) for lands allotted to colonists, based on the Indians' alleged inability to use the land properly. That was the context for the Dawes Severalty Act of 1887, or General Allotment Act. Here Henry Dawes showed how to divide up lands into reservations for the Indians, with the "excess" moving onto the open market. The law was designed as a means for placing Indians in certain areas, but the practical result was to reassign some 60 percent of their lands to homesteaders, and was widely seen as an enormous success. Consensus on this point is illustrated by the fact that the measure lasted as long as it did, despite alterations that did nothing to undermine its basic content; modifications were made in 1891, with the Curtis Act in 1898, and with the Burke Act of 1906. The Curtis Act took provisions first implemented in the Great Plains and extended them to the "Five Civilized Tribes" (Cherokee, Chickasaw, Choctaw, Creek, and Seminole), whose treaties until then had protected them. This, then, was the end of the long history of territorial exception. Oklahoma's path to statehood was now open, a process that cost Native Americans nearly 100 million acres.[165] The basic point of the Allotment Act was, in Stuart Banner's words, "the ideal of assimilation . . . which envisioned carving up the Indian reservations into fee simple plots owned by individuals and families, in the same way whites owned their land."[166] This was met with great enthusiasm by everyone invested in reducing Indians' autonomy and space: railroad owners and lumber companies, along with those interested in acquiring land or in any way related to the establishment of towns in the Midwest and the West, where the population was growing every day.

Dawes himself was a U.S. senator from Massachusetts, serving from 1874 to 1892, when he was succeeded by Henry Cabot Lodge, the future champion of expansion in 1898. Like Lincoln, Dawes had been a Whig and had fought the Radical Republicans and Andrew Johnson's reconciliation policy with southern growers. Dawes collaborated with Sumner on Indian policy, and in 1881 was appointed to the Committee on Indian Affairs, despite the fact that there were few if any Indians left in his home state. He had been a decided proponent of Indian assimilation and had opposed the treaties, which led him to directly confront Secretary of Interior Carl Schurz, a reformer of strong convictions. Once on the committee, Dawes put together a strong coalition to defend Indian policy. After President Grover Cleveland created the Dawes Commission (1893–1914), Dawes, as its first chairman, continued his labors and was put in charge of relations with the relocated Five Civilized Tribes, where he advocated dismantling tribal governments, eliminating communal property, and identifying and registering tribe members through the famous Dawes Rolls.

He and his allies concentrated on the transfer of Indian lands, which would be subdivided into parcels for colonists, preferably of European origin; these landowners would serve as examples to the Indians, who would now work as peasants. But not everyone agreed with the plan, starting with the Indians themselves, who had signed treaties with the U.S. government in which the latter promised to defend their lands. Thanks to pressure from the Radical Republicans, who did not share the commisson's individualist vision, the Five Tribes' lands in Oklahoma, along with those of the Osage and a few other nations, were temporarily placed out of the reach of the commission and the Dawes Act.[167] Resistance to expropriation meant the survival of Indian Country for another decade, but it was doomed. The Curtis Act of 1898 put an end to the fight once and for all. In any case, the new inhabitants of Oklahoma, whose borders more or less coincided with the old Indian Country, were unwilling to respect controls dictated by Washington regarding land sales and taxes. By 1911, one-third of the Indians had received plots of land but, at the same time, of the 60 million acres that had been subdivided, 38 million went to reservations and 22 million to whites. Those in the hands of Indians, whether individually or in reservations, were not entirely removed from the market, as the classic cycle of debt and expropriation remained the rule. From 1902 until 1910, some 775,000 acres belonging to Indians were sold to pay off debts. In 1934, some 100,000 Indians were classified as landless, living in miserable conditions in cities or in rural areas.[168] All that was left to them were the reservations, where they were strictly controlled within tight geographic spaces.[169]

Welcome to the Club

In the preceding pages I have tried to show that the construction of the United States was comparable to that of the other nineteenth-century imperial nations I have examined. These nations were constructed, along with empires, through a process of reclaiming or taking sovereign spaces where they established the community of citizens that constituted their foundation.[170] If this interpretation is correct, then the events of 1898, when Spain lost its last possessions in the Caribbean and the Pacific, can be seen as one more step in a long journey to empire based on social and political definitions held by elites well before American independence.[171] After 1776, the establishment of a "republic of property-owners," a republic of citizen-electors, became essential. The process grew, both as slavery ceased being an option and Indians and blacks were excluded from political and civil life, and it continued with the plunder of Mexico in 1836 and 1848 and the creation of a colonial complex with Hawaii, Guam, the three Spanish colonies, and Panama from 1894 to 1904.

The difference between the years before and after 1865 is that in the latter part of the century, insistence on republican unity would be much greater, and this shift would also entail a more colonial tone, more *spécial-ité*, toward whatever was left on the margins. After the Civil War, definitive affirmation of federal plenary powers ensured both the construction of colonialism at home and the expansion of the empire abroad. The imperial nation took shape as a result of the interaction between domestic issues and the construction of a border empire.[172]

Enormous ideological efforts were made in the postbellum period to define the new citizen in such a way that freed slaves were included. As we have seen, the limits of those efforts were quite clear after a decade. A barrier went up between chosen citizens and those other subjects of the state, who could not immediately, or perhaps ever, attain a foothold on the pedestal. Electoral exclusion went hand in hand with segregation, yet this was not simply yet another form of exclusion. It was resisted and occasionally halted both from below and in the courts and would be broken only with the country's international involvements in the twentieth century, notably the world wars. In the wake of the South's defeat, freed slaves and Indians both underwent fatal developments, but even that turmoil was not enough to ensure the gigantic challenge of incorporating border areas into this expansive republic. Once the Republic of Texas came to an end, Mexicans were forcibly integrated and would become citizens "at the proper time"; huge portions of Mexico were usurped in 1848, with the people living on those lands thrust into an unstable situation, side by side with Indians. A second immigration door had opened up, with the Pacific now being added to the East Coast.[173] As a result, a new wave of white nativism began growing again after 1880.[174] The railway and cheaper maritime transportation meant that for the first time the country was colonized from coast to coast. Extinction of the buffalo and beaver doomed small settlements surviving in the interstices of expansion and urbanization.[175] Something similar occurred in the Canadian Federation with the destruction of the world of the *métis*, though they desperately resisted, under the leadership of Louis Riel. In some cases, railroad companies themselves acted as immigration operators, picking up laborers in Ireland or China and handing out plots of American land to them. The end result was spectacular; during the eight years after the end of the war, 3 million people entered the country, during which time the United States attracted foreign capital, mostly British, and doubled its railroad network.[176] The swift expansion would not halt until World War I, though there were moments of crisis in 1873, 1878, and 1887–93. Between 1881 and 1930, 27.6 million people entered the United States, and a new social and racial hierarchy began taking shape, helped along by federal and state laws limiting immigration of certain people.[177] The census every ten years and laws banning interracial marriage once again (or still) acted as the foundation for the construction of republican society, with its inclusions and exclusions.[178] Ethnocentrism was not the key to internal development of the country; on the contrary, development, based on a recognizable past, imposed the norms and means of control to ensure a social dynamic based on settler capitalism and the simultaneous expansion of state powers.

Internal growth and external expansion were bound to meet. The path had been paved well before the United States, in competition for global domination, became yet another empire in the 1890s. But, unlike Germany—the other new power at this point—the U.S. had an imperial framework that by then had gestated for many years. The first indication of a change in this sense was the "Open Door" policy, a total redefinition of the idea of sovereignty from the 1810s. This new approach was not aimed just at China; it had been tested in Japan in 1854 and in Korea in 1871. Here we are following Walter LaFeber's extension of the chronology back to the imperial vision of the post–Civil War generation when William Seward was secretary of state.[179] Seward, following in the steps of John Quincy Adams, and a great admirer of the British empire, was well aware of what he was doing.[180] The diplomatic complications of the Civil War, especially keeping the Confederacy isolated from its most important clients (mainly Britain), provided a lesson for the later nineteenth century on how to use power relations as the Monroe Doctrine withered.[181] Their ideological vision included not just operations to extend markets beyond the continent but also to expand into national space.[182] This was exemplified with the purchase of Alaska ("Seward's Icebox") in 1867, one more way of limiting Britain (along with the crisis of the Hudson's Bay Company, the world's largest landlord) to the north, the south, and in the Caribbean and Mexico. In this sense, imperial construction was the capacity to coherently articulate different colonial situations in the framework of political solutions derived from prior experience.[183] The year 1898, therefore, was a moment of both continuity and rupture.

This imperial arc was marked by specialness, by formulas that nobody wanted—given that they involved voluntary constitutional restrictions— but that everybody nonetheless used. In the past such situations were frequent; they involved the coexistence of juridical cultures in one space, discretion and military authority in Indian Country, a juridical limbo on the reservations, and the transformation of colonial ideas of hierarchy into limits on citizenship in "national" space. These entirely uncapricious superimpositions constitute the marrow of the imperial nation. Notions of white supremacy turned every context into a racial context, far beyond the slave South. The global solution of white, Anglo-Saxon, Christian imperialism in the versions designed by William McKinley, William Howard Taft, and Theodore Roosevelt allowed wounds from the Civil War to heal and created a new military and moral unity for the United States. The Alaska Purchase of 1867, the territory's incorporation in 1912, and the long wait before it became a state in 1959 reflect the constitutional complexity of acquiring new territories. In the Caribbean, the complexity was exacerbated by internal questions. The possibility of intervening in Cuba (where Carlos Manuel de Céspedes proclaimed independence from Spain in 1868) or in Santo Domingo or Haiti threatened to reopen racial conflicts in those countries. The establishment of military bases in the Pacific and southern Africa during the presidencies of James Garfield and Chester Arthur shows how U.S. territorial ambitions in this sense were being reduced.

The creation of insular possessions in the Caribbean and the Pacific reflects the strategy of *spécialité* beyond the nation-state. There was notable ignorance about the constitutional and political status of the political entities to which sovereignty was now extended. At the same time, the casuistry of specialness through jurisprudence continued, using "insular cases" over which Congress had "plenary powers" to define jurisprudence according to the written and unwritten rules of U.S. constitutional culture. As Emlin McClain clarified in 1906, "The constitutional restrictions thus resting on the exercise of federal power with reference to territories will be the restrictions of an unwritten, not those of a written constitution. . . . It will necessarily follow that the limitations of this unwritten constitution cannot be enforced by judicial action, but must depend on their enforcement upon the same influences which enforced the rules of the unwritten constitution of Great Britain."[184] In a complementary fashion, this ambiguity made it possible to affirm that the United States, which had been created through a revolution against the British empire, could never acquire or administer formal colonies. Clearly, the elements of its archipelago of outposts were not "formal" colonies.

Opportunities to define the country's foreign policy in imperial terms were easy to come by: Hawaii and Samoa; Puerto Rico, Philippines, Guam, the Marianas, and the conditional occupation of Cuba after war with Spain; the invasions of Santo Domingo and Haiti; and the purchase of the Virgin Islands from Denmark.[185] And, of course, there was the construction of the Panama Canal. Despite the relative ease of these operations (except in the case of the Philippines), temporary occupations turned out to be a major challenge on several fronts: the relationship between internal space and imperial construction, the use of special formulas, and constitutional regression in some of the societies just mentioned, in many cases exceeded the parameters of the times.[186]

The struggle in Samoa against the Germans and the altered position regarding Hawaii were the first steps of the U.S. imperial campaign in the Pacific. The opening shot came with Seward's treaty with the Hawaiians, at which point the islands moved into a capitalist dynamic, especially after the California Gold Rush. During the Cleveland administration, with Thomas Bayard as secretary of state, the islands' strategic and commercial role would be more precisely defined; they would be an "outpost of American commerce and the stepping-stone of the growing trade of the Pacific," according to the president.[187] For decades, merchants, whalers, shippers, and missionaries visited Hawaii. There also was an important sugar-export business on the islands, and many different countries were interested in tax benefits for easier access to the elastic U.S. market (over the protests of Louisiana sugar growers). But no matter the disguise, there was more than enough evidence of the similarity to other imperial powers. The task was to grant permanent protection to interests that might be threatened by other countries, as in the case of the Germans in Samoa who fought to impose their presence in the exclusive colonial club recognized by history. During this period, Pacific Islanders treated Europeans as absolute equals. But that would not survive sugar expansion, foreign acquisition of land, and the arrival of a new Asian workforce. Ironically, the Samoan crisis ended up strengthening U.S. projection in the Pacific by reinforcing U.S. relations with the Hawaiian monarchy, leading to the establishment of the protectorate in 1889–90. Since the 1820s, there had been an unusual balancing act in Hawaii among the ruling dynasty, the local aristocracy, and U.S. and European colonial powers. The result was a sort of ersatz constitutional monarchy. In 1810 the founder of the dynasty, Kamehameha I, had reached a pact with the aristocracy that established a sort of bicameral system that protected the islands from outside pressures from whalers, merchants, and missionaries. The Hawaiian example makes one think of the Cherokee during this same time, and, of missionary William Richards, a New Englander who came to Hawaii with the Constitution in one hand and a Bible in the other, just as his Presbyterian brethren had done with the Cherokee. In 1840, during the reign of Kamehameha III, Hawaii's first constitution was approved, including a Bill of Rights; it would be revised in 1852 and 1864, the latter version lasting until 1887. At that time, as a result of a bilateral treaty signed in 1875, the islands depended on rice and sugar exports to the United States. But a group opposed to growing dependence on the United States won the elections. Secretary of State James G. Blaine promised protection for sugar growers and ensured a military presence in Pearl Harbor. Then economic instability stirred up conflicts among the growers (many of whom were from the United States), a shrinking local population, and Asian immigrant workers, leading to a coup d'état against Kalakaua in 1887 and his forced abdication. As in the Caribbean, new trade tariffs had an enormous and damaging impact on the islands. In 1893, Kalakaua's successor, Queen Liliuokalani, revoked the constitution that had been imposed in 1887, angering planters and bringing about intervention by the U.S. military; she was overthrown in what was obviously a full-force constitutional setback. A republican government was established in 1894 by an American, Sanford Ballard Dole, allegedly to prevent the Hawaiian monarchy from seeking help from Britain. President Cleveland decided against annexation and instead proclaimed the brief republican government, which would be followed by an unsuccessful attempt to restore the monarchy and by protests against foreign intervention. The Newlands Resolution, passed by Congress in July 1898, annexed the republic to the United States, and Hawaii would become a state in 1959, along with Alaska.

Shifting our focus now to the Caribbean, the story is similar. Four events were crucial: intervention in Venezuela, conquest of the Spanish colonies in the Antilles, the creation of Panama, and the later occupations of Santo Domingo and Haiti.[188] The annexations of the former Spanish possessions were the most constitutionally complicated. As with the Louisiana Purchase, the republican administration had to shape territory with a European population and fragments of constitutional politics. Puerto Rico and Cuba had been reintroduced into the framework of the Spanish constitution after Spain's fortunes took a turn with the Ten Years' War and slavery was abolished in 1873 and 1886. That was not true for the Philippines, where elimination of constitutional possibilities in 1837 remained the case until the Americans' arrival. The rhetoric of backwardness was aimed at showing how impossible it would be to implement true constitutional remedies. Cuba was the exception, owing to its internal complexity, its history of insurrection, and the weight of racial democracy that the war and the Cuban Revolutionary Party had imposed, and there the solution was a sort of guardianship without effective territorial dominion. Elsewhere, as in Hawaii, denigration was the rule, followed by special jurisprudential formulas for "insular cases." Much of that jurisprudence was the work of the Bureau of Insular Affairs, part of the Department of War under the leadership of Col. Clarence Edwards, who had been chosen because of his experience in the Philippines. Some of his decisions recall solutions implemented a quarter century earlier in the Great Plains. The logic behind denigration was to eliminate any doubts regarding authority. Paul Kramer offered a brilliant description of the Filipino case, where U.S. and Spanish interests were intertwined from 1837 to 1869, when the Philippines were separated from the constitutional processes under way in the Caribbean: "Opponents of *ex proprio vigore* launched a doctrine of incorporation that would become the dominant politico-legal framework for the United States' colonial empire: its goal was to insulate the United States politically from its new colonies while protecting continental North American territories from otherwise unlimited 'plenary' congressional powers."[189] The Treaty of Paris, signed on December 10, 1898, therefore was very clear that rights for the inhabitants of the acquired enclaves would be a question of *tabula rasa*.[190] According to Article 9 of the treaty, "Civil rights and the political status of natural inhabitants of the territories herewith ceded to the United States shall be determined by Congress." José Trías Monge, an authority on Puerto Rican constitutionalism, has correctly referred to that island's political status after 1898 as a "constitutional regression," with which it lost citizenship and universal suffrage, representation in the Spanish legislature, and self-government (which had been granted to the island at the last minute). Puerto Ricans had not exactly gone from heaven to hell, but neither had they passed from Catholic barbarism to Protestant republican civilization. The origins of this new constitutional obscurity can be found in the "insular cases" and "organic laws" for their territories.

The war of 1898, the growing demand for territory, and the relentless denigration of their adversaries had made the United States opt for risky legal solutions whose remote antecedents lay in the 1803 Louisiana Purchase. This "murky zone between formal statehood and official independence," to quote Joseph E. Fallon, was home to a rich and heterclite assemblage of societies under the paternalist rule of the United States.[191] They would be the beneficiaries of a range of successive and simultaneous colonial statutes: commonwealth, free association, unincorporated and organized territory, and unincorporated and unorganized territory.

CHAPTER EIGHT

The Imperial Nation

IN THE MID-NINETEENTH CENTURY, European nations with important colonial possessions succeeded in creating systems that regulated and distinguished the rights of inhabitants in their nation-states par excellence from those in their sovereign territories. The extension of political and social rights in the metropolis depended on the correlation of two main factors. The first concerned political rules in a framework of representation and rights, the harsh confrontation with old-regime practices (nonelected bodies; resistance from the nobility and the clergy, which themselves were undergoing reform), and the political system's ability to absorb demands emerging from social transformations.[1] The second factor lies in the ethos of each of these "national" worlds that was pushing them toward stability: a republican consensus or effective constitutional monarchical reformism (not exempt from debate and crisis); shifts in notions of citizenship, which were crucial for mass political identity since the great turn-of-the-century transformations but of lesser importance to national politics as a whole; and the shared destiny of the nation (and its empire) in the face of a hostile exterior, given that, starting in the eighteenth century, war was the principal means for consolidating the collective and the development of rights linked to national belonging.[2]

The revolutions proclaimed that the nation as a community of the politically free was situated, or should be situated, at the center of collective life and that it was populated by rights-holding citizens—an ambiguous concept that nonetheless had been linked from the start of the modern age to the enduring antecedent of subjecthood.[3] This message was updated during the European revolutions of 1848. In the long cycle from 1787–89 until the mid-nineteenth century, when the idea was again loudly preached, nations and empires had to coexist. The idea of citizenship

expressed both involuntary belonging (by birth, residence, or naturalization) and a bundle of rights that this new subject could exercise within the
political framework of nations or empires, or sometimes both.[4] Therefore
the slow and painful development of a community of politically free individuals, which had formed the ideological aspiration of the revolutions of
1780–1830, became the center of gravity of political debate. The dynamic
around the rights that citizenship appeared to embody (though the reality
fell short) gave meaning to nineteenth-century politics, to its inclusions
and exclusions, being that the value of an idea does not depend entirely
on its legal or textual regulation. The concept above all others was that of
"nation," the result of loyalties from below and consensus from above; this
was the essential referent of a new age, due to its potential for transforming politics and language. That immense performative potential forced
states and their highest courts to adapt themselves again and again to the
construction of a new political space and to the cultural and psychological
referents that lent solidity to the group. Republican consensus, monarchical loyalty, and the invocation of universal citizenship or its implementation through successive electoral reforms were roads that all led to a similar destination: the fusion of state and nation such that they were blended
into something usually referred to as the nation-state. The outcome of
this always problematic identification was the possibility of alternative nationalisms, of more than one national project in one sovereign space. This
was particularly true in the colonies, where the power of a metropolitan
national community might be accompanied by alternative reactive or sub-
national (though not necessarily divisive) projects along imprecise ethnic
boundaries in the remote corners of the empire.[5]

One of the results of the Atlantic revolutionary cycle was that the border regulating access to "citizenship" associated with a national community was blurred.[6] This community, like the nation itself, could be only
one, though it could be read in various manners according to location or
status.[7] Also, voting and representation depended less on the idea of "citizenship" than on that of subjecthood, be it French or any other (the basis
of rights was expressed already in the third article of Toussaint Louverture's constitution of 1801), which would become the norm throughout
most of the world in the nineteenth and twentieth centuries.[8] Therefore,
appeals to national sovereignty incited and legitimated participation by
social groups that felt they were being addressed by sovereignty, regardless
of the inclusions and exclusions authorized by electoral rolls and old state
borders.[9] *Aux armes, citoyens*! was the battle cry, far beyond the French
borders and well into its overseas empire, though it would be nearly one

hundred years before many of those citizens, because of their sex, age, or social status, could join the select club of electors and those who could be elected; in other words, before they could become full citizens. A crucial component of national construction lay in covering this distance, a process that ran in parallel to that of bestowing cultural characteristics (preferably historical ones) on the ideal of community.[10] The revolutions in the great monarchical empires of the Atlantic also blurred the border of rights and, therefore, that of the ideal nation. The indivisibility of the nation and its citizenship—that is, its national sovereignty—meant that rights' extent had to be specified with rules whose definition marked the contemporary ideological horizon.[11] The first of these rules distinguished between active and passive citizenship or concerned sex, social status, and race (as with the Dred Scott decision by the U.S. Supreme Court, to which we will return).[12] Electoral rolls were critical in the establishment of these distinctions and in establishing who would be a full citizen and who would not.[13] For that reason, increases in the number of eligible voters is seen as an indicator, insufficient though it may be (both then and now) of a population's integration into its political system.

The limits of the national political structure and the societies over which it exercised sovereignty were also fuzzy. The nation-state rarely took shape for purely metropolitan purposes; rather, it attempted to embrace in its entirety the old monarchical space. The French revolutionary crisis, whose epicenter lay in the broken alliance between the Parisian sans-culottes and the freed slaves of the Antilles, is the best example of the shadowy limits of a nation that proclaimed itself both metropolitan and imperial. Another example is the fact that the echoes and practices of imperial constitutions had reached Goa and Pondicherry, the Guyanas and Manila. It is no surprise, therefore, that the idea of a France beyond European borders reappeared in the French Antilles in 1848, when revolutionary and universal citizenship was instated for the second time. A similar conflict regarding the definition of the nation can be seen with the expulsion of slaves' descendants from electoral rolls in the United States both before and after the Civil War. After the war, universal male citizenship was defined as something acquired at birth, "as opposed to the consensual assumptions that guided the political handiwork of 1776 and 1787."[14] The idea of citizenship as a code of civil and political rights is the reason why the empire occasionally guaranteed rights to those living beyond metropolitan borders, as we said in chapter 2. That was the issue with the case known as the Don Pacifico affair between Great Britain and Greece in 1847–50 involving a Jew of Portuguese descent born in Gibraltar whose shop in Athens was attacked.[15] Here the state, for reasons of prestige, defended its subject-citizens wherever they might be. The notion of hypothetical imperial citizenship—*civis romanus sum*, as Lord Palmerston, quoting Cicero, proudly proclaimed on that occasion—had little to do with metropolis and colonies under the same flag regulating inclusion and exclusion as they wished. In the particularly varied British dominions, and later in Spanish Cuba and Puerto Rico, "sole citizenship" had different meanings depending on where one was. In short, this variety was the outcome of imperial reconstruction through special laws in the decades after the revolutions and the Napoleonic Wars. In this chapter we shall see how these norms were intertwined with national developments and how metropolis and empire overlapped.

The apparent paradox of the imperial nation—a concept that accounts for some of the problems we are addressing but which cannot replace empirical descriptions of each case—emerges from the intersection between political development at home and responses beyond the borders. It is clear that here we are not referring to simply a nation with an empire, a mere aggregation of concepts that might be studied separately. Rather, the matter is more complex. In short, the nation was transformed by the empire, and the empire was transformed by the nation. To quote Krishan Kumar, "Empires can be nations writ large; nation-states empires under another name."[16] It is only in that context that experiences such as French national construction in the three Algerian departments, starting in 1848, or the creation of white settlements by the British after the Canadian experiment of 1867, or the failure of the creation of a Spanish nation in Cuba after 1882 make any sense at all. When the nation placed itself at the center of national life in those sites where the great revolutions of 1780–1830 took place, the impact would irreversibly transform the nature of the state and its dominion over distant territories as it co-opted some and excluded others. Special laws regulated and defined personal status and access in a space where distinctions that were operative in the metropolis and those of the colonies were conflated. Rules of exclusion and inclusion, whose descriptions in specific cases occupy the central portion of this book, are inconceivable apart from the particular *spécialité* adopted for each place and situation. Their specific, historically determined combination incorporated territorial government, social logic, and ethnic or racial color. The administration of distant possessions often provided an element of cohesion for national construction. The extent of political and social changes in the metropolis modified relations between metropolitan politics and colonial societies. If the finales of the revolutionary crises of the early nineteenth century were generally resolved (though not always) with widespread regression of rights in colonial spaces outside Europe, the consolidation of liberal politics within the metropolis added to imbalances typical of the imperial nation. This was, in essence, the sum of the metropolitan nation plus the world of the empire, with relations between the two poles regulated by special laws. And if anything began defining the rules of play at mid-century it was the continual transfer of political and cultural experiences in both directions, as social mobility, emigration, large administrative and military movements, and the traffic of written texts and culture never ceased.[17] The formalization of these rules of play and the intensification of exchange drew the metropolitan space closer to imperial developments.[18] This chapter will examine this process from two separate angles.

Of the cases included in this book, only the British empire, victor in the struggle for control of Europe and its area of influence, followed the path of solid reform. Its ambiguous efforts can be seen in various ways. First were those reforms applied in the recently constituted British North America, largely Francophone and Catholic until the mid-nineteenth century.[19] Consolidation of a place inhabited by such a vast array of peoples— American Indians, French, *métis*, Britons, and slaves from the former Thirteen Colonies—entailed modifying practices well established in the North American colonial world. It naturally involved altering the Protestant, Anglo-British foundation of the First Empire and accepting an emergent pluralism. As if that were not enough, pressure from Protestants south of the Canadian border and a promise not to burden colonists with new taxes—an agreement reached during the North American crisis— made political imagination even more necessary. Second, there was the problem of the slave trade, which had been prohibited, the first step in the eventual abolition of slavery. The most important point here, as indicated by C. L. Brown, was the co-optation of humanitarian arguments by the British imperial establishment, backed by its enormous military power. This had a powerful impact on imperial consensus, restoring the moral force that had deeply eroded in the American Civil War.[20] These reforms consolidated the common denominator of "Britishness" from the previous century, adding a strong dose of paternalism toward the less fortunate.[21] In this regard, the U.S. and British cases were not equivalent; the federal government could not impose on the states the abolition of the slave trade or the eventual abolition of slavery; neither could become part of the debate in the United States. On the contrary, the republican foundations of the country allowed far greater integration of popular will than in any European state, including Restoration France, which would become clear during the second antiimperial war against Great Britain, the War of 1812.[22] The third front of interventionist paternalism opened with the Bengal crisis, which led to the impeachment of Warren Hastings, governor of the East India Company in Calcutta.[23] This especially affected judicial practices and respect for local landowners and their allegedly ancient laws, as was the case with the White Mughals and men such as Edmund Burke who, from an epic cultural distance, were scandalized by the company's bad government.[24] The foundations of the mid-century imperial nation were defined where internal reforms and interventionist paternalism in the empire met; this blend has been aptly called "social imperialism."[25]

British developments cannot be extrapolated from other Atlantic cases. On the European continent, the end of the Napoleonic Wars led to very conservative monarchic restorations; in the Spanish case it can only be called reactionary. In France as well as Spain and Portugal, constitutional concerns would resurface only in the 1830s, first with France and then in the Iberian countries.[26] This was when the "dual constitutions," which permitted political rights that were invalid overseas, were consolidated for the long run. France worked out a Solomonic solution by dividing its empire into two large groups, the new and the old colonies, which were governed by ad hoc ordinances, a system complicated in 1848 with the addition of Algeria, a little North African France comprising three departments for French emigrants, that is, "citizens" with full rights. Spain and Portugal went down a different path, both drastically removing their colonies from any constitutional framework while promising, with familiar Napoleonic trickery, "special laws" that would never actually appear. Instead of laws to make up for their expulsion from constitutional consideration, the colonies would enjoy autocratic power delivered from the metropolis, the antecedent of the twentieth-century liberal dictatorship, along with the old juridical traditions, regulations, and ordinances passed to snuff out any challenges.[27] These various solutions—based on juridical traditions though altered after the events of the 1830s in accordance with the nature and position of the various colonial worlds—all had this in common: colonial spaces, no matter how important (and some of them were, indeed, important), were not able to replicate the system of political rights and guarantees for nationals that was the rule in the metropolis. This is the context in which the new nation took shape, the context in which alternative national projects in Cuba and Puerto Rico appeared, as we have seen, already in the 1840s and 1850s, before the modest shift of the 1868 regime change.[28]

By "imperial nation" I mean something beyond what we think about when we use the term *nation-state*, an aggregation that often dissolves the complexity of its two parts.[29] Sovereignty in an empire includes both those in the metropolis and those abroad.[30] The imperial state thus refers to large complexes created by metropolitan societies where national politics governs through the development of the community of subjects-citizens-electors with rights, and also to spaces under their sovereignty where special rules modify from above and from below the content or social extension of metropolitan norms.[31] The imperial nation, then, is the sum of the national complex plus the empire governed through rules. The emergence and consolidation of this historical artifact, which is crucial for understanding the development of liberal-representative empires until 1947, was not an outcome but rather a given. First, it was the response to a revolutionary crisis that lasted well into the nineteenth century and whose most basic elements were broken promises and the subsequent resistance by colonial societies, especially those with European roots. Second, it was the result of the continual traffic of information about the different rights afforded in colony and metropolis.[32]Third, emulation, eventually leading to decolonization, was unstoppable. These contradictions, inherent in worlds that were interconnected but governed by different rules, became most obvious during times of crisis and open conflict. And last, but not least, an understanding of how the empire became part of the nation, and vice versa, is possible only through relevant examples and comparisons.

Distant Compatriots

The idea of granting political status to compatriots abroad indicates the profound contradiction of nineteenth-century imperial formation. This status generally rested on national belonging more than on citizenship. Aside from the two great republican experiences, and never as something universal, it merely defined individuals versus foreigners subject to the same national sovereignty or versus inhabitants of foreign nations. This limited version of citizenship did not involve a high degree of rights.[33] It was constricted and regulated by laws that were both highly variable and erratic, depending on the context and particular situation. If there was one thing that defined the empires we are examining it was the complexity involved in administering very diverse situations that were nonetheless all influenced by one and the same revolutionary cycle, which had deeply changed the rules of play during the eighteenth-century monarchic empires. At the center of it all lay the hypothesis of citizenship linked to belonging and loyalty, and this hypothesis was impossible to eliminate. Not one of the great imperial stabilization efforts after the Napoleonic Wars could wipe out the idea of a shared community on both sides of the colony/metropolis great divide.

In Restoration France, the very notion of universal masculine citizenship disappeared as if by magic. In this case, the metropolis was made equal to, or degraded to, the situation put into place in the colonies by the former First Consul with the 1799 Constitution, which separated rights in the imperial possessions from those on French soil. It was clear that the idea of a patriotic *citoyen* in the plantation colonies was highly problematic, and experience in this regard in Haiti in 1804 would greatly influence subsequent generations, as would other republican experiments in the Caribbean such as in the captaincy of Caracas and the Viceroyalty of New Granada.[34] The "universal citizen" of the Montagnard Constitution of 1793 disappeared in the metropolis until 1848, and then remained onstage throughout the Second Empire and the Third Republic.[35] But "citizen" as defined by the Revolution was muffled by the electoral rolls. Meanwhile, in the Antilles, Guyana, Senegal, and Réunion, planters pushed to continue excluding the colonies from the metropolitan political framework, thus quashing republican efforts. The citizens of yesterday were transformed not only into subjects but also into slaves. With the fall of Louis Philippe of Orléans in 1848, however, republicans emphatically and as one demanded universal masculine citizenship in the metropolis, emancipation of the slaves (though there were some doubts in this regard), and reintegration of former slaves into the French republican space. The old colonies were part of France, part of the national community that was the aspiration of republicans. From May to December 1848, from Martinique to Réunion, 250,000 slaves were freed, reviving the failed notion of universal citizenship that would affirm a nation beyond the republic's European territory, as had happened in 1793–98. As I showed in chapter 5, that would not be the case. The old colonies were not departmentalized. Instead, the crucial factor in nineteenth-century French colonial history would be the creation of three departments in the recently conquered Algeria, and there the figure of citizen acquired a very different meaning. The idea was not to join metropolitan territory to an extra-European reality (geographically close as it may have been) but rather to construct a figure that would separate an entire social group from the rest of the population and deprive them of rights. Republican unity and universality in Algeria became the flip side of the exclusion of the colonial subject. The cruel war of conquest there, as elsewhere, was predicated on shrinking oft-proclaimed republican universality. Colonists' brand of republicanism, their active political participation in Third Republic institutions, and their racial outlook were all translated into a firm refusal, couched in religious terms, to meaningfully broaden the rights of Arabs and Berbers.[36] In order to fill the legislative gap produced by this exclusion, metropolitan authorities imposed a fierce collection of laws and penalties ending with the Code de l'Indigénat approved by the Third Republic in 1881.[37] This sinister form of repression was perfect for both subjecting and punishing Algerians through collective means and confiscations that would have been impossible in the metropolis, while at the same time exalting the status of French citizens established in the colony.[38] This illustrious approach would be extended through time and space, setting the tone for French colonial life in new colonies in Africa, Asia, and the Pacific.[39] The code was abolished in Algeria in 1919, and electoral rolls were reformed and broadened for local elections in compensation for Algeria's sacrifice on the borders and in factories during World War I; but the code was reinstated just one year later, in part the result of pressure by distinguished French citizens *outre-mer* (overseas).[40] As Peter Dunwoodie put it, "The *question indigène*, as posed by the French in colonial Algeria, thus actually begs the question, because it was articulated within what was initially perceived as a monologue of domination, promoting only a self-valorizing French model."[41] Clearly, an empire based on violence and repression cannot last; it can survive only through variable consensus and assimilation.[42] In the case of Algeria, that entailed attempts to broaden electoral rolls for local and *douar* elections, include prominent figures in the *délégation financière* (a colonial chamber with limited capacities, opened in 1898), exclude *évolués* (educated, assimilated mixed-bloods) from the rigors of the Code de l'Indigénat, and make 37,000 Jews (with the Crémieux Decree, October 24, 1870) and, later, Italians and Spaniards into citizens in the departments of Constantine and Oran. There is, no doubt, coherence in this opposition between the republican ideal at home and the departmental Algeria, between slaves' aspirations and the subsequent diminished citizenship they received. Again, the demarcation of rights and representative capacity took shape in the framework of the imperial nation, where every person's and every social group's status everywhere, including in the metropolis, was marked.

The same process took place in the great rival empire, the empire that won. Once Britain stabilized its position in America, a series of reforms were implemented to integrate some of George IV's subjects into the Second British Empire. These reforms were not conceived of with the entire empire in mind but only for the free colonists of British origin in

North America. Canada would be the laboratory. Starting with the 1774 Quebec Act and its extensions in 1783 and 1791, the British government aimed to integrate two groups of European origin, French and British, under crown sovereignty.[43] The key was to guarantee both groups access to political participation without compromising the governability of this British bastion with an aggressive and expansionist republic just over the border. As we saw in chapter 4, the experiment in the province of Québec affected relations between the British, on the one hand, and Catholics in the metropolis and in Ireland, on the other, and, as a result, also with Protestant dissenters, the nucleus of liberal Victorian reform, which set off a series of reforms that would end with the Irish Home Rule campaigns after the great famine "drew a line between political emancipation and citizenship."[44] The expansion of active citizenship (which in Britain lacked the resonance of the term in France) took place through a succession of measures regulating the right to vote and to participate in local and national politics, a method defined then (and sometimes still) as constitutional nationalism. The reform of the empire (British North America and Ireland) was, in this regard, the obligatory antecedent of the great 1832 reform of central institutions, which in turn enabled further imperial measures, such as the elimination of the nabob lobbies of the East India Company and the West Indies planters. To that degree, the radical Benthamites' belief that imperial reforms were what allowed domestic reforms was correct. But the great and often postponed reform in the end merely emphasized that "the English political system was in flux between 1830 and 1867, and the nature of the organization of the Parliament, and who should qualify for the vote, were at the center of change."[45] Thus, the succession of electoral reforms expanded political participation and the centrality of the community of citizens without breaking the essential structure or backbone of the monarchic-Anglican-aristocratic complex.[46] In other words, gradually the very meaning of the idea of citizen-elector was modified so as to situate it at the heart of political debate. But the expansion of political participation and of national consensus was not a product only for the domestic market.[47] Expansion at home cannot be understood apart from broader national agreements about the justification and necessity of the empire for expansive political entities. Developments such as the white settlements preceded it, and similar events would follow, though not all British subjects were called on to benefit and participate in an undertaking that should not be seen in a linear fashion. At times liberal consensus in the metropolis led to retrenchment in the imperial sphere (an "aggressive strategy of containment," in the words of Jack Snyder.[48]) Extreme examples are those of the Little Englanders, who considered empire an unnecessary expense, or reformists such as John Bright, who thought that excessive imperial unity would only bring about heightened tensions.[49] This split was obvious in later debates regarding the fiscal cost of world empire.[50] But liberalism's position changed in the 1880s with events in Egypt beginning in 1882 and in southern Africa, the first time that the entire empire mobilized to defend its integrity.[51] Charles Masterman's book *Heart of Empire* (1901) perfectly exemplified the disjuncture of the times.[52] The exclusion of peoples throughout vast expanses of the empire for reasons of governability or suspected cultural or racial inferiority also reinforced consensus among the elect.[53]

An empire should be understood as a collection of interconnected situations in which the metropolis serves as the transmitter of ideas and information. The great reform experiments of 1790–1832 were the antecedent of a general transformation in relations between the political community and imperial administration throughout those interconnected spaces. British North America in the first half of the nineteenth century made way for the subsequent structures of the dominion and the Canadian Federation in 1867. At the turn of the century, nearly half of all emigrants were choosing the white dominions as their destination.[54] Massive British immigration (800,000 people from 1860 to 1900) brought about further reinforcement of British nationalism there.[55] As in New South Wales and the rest of the Australian colonies (which took in 1 million immigrants during the same period), the influx of Britons transformed colonies into responsible governments, states of their respective federations.[56] British communities in these colonies did everything they could to reproduce their societies of origin, and British identity was part of that effort, though with variations.[57] Elements of this effort included the cult of the monarchy, the system of education, marriage markets, the established church, customs, and the notion of participating in a culture—the "democratic imaginary," to use Patrick Joyce's phrase—that formed the basis of political participation.[58] This was the apparently normative path, the one that best joined the imperial ethos and the extension of the national community both within and outside of British frontiers.[59] It was the example that the crown colonies, those with less importance and subject to greater imperial control, were supposed to follow.[60]

I am not interested in following traditional British historiography's teleological account of an empire subject to constant and random reform, with no apparent direction. That is not the issue. Our challenge is to understand how the consolidation and expansion of the second British empire during the Victorian era took place in such close association with the development of the national community in its interior.[61] In other words, we must try to understand how national development forced changes in traditional means of government along the lines of what was happening in the metropolis itself.[62] The process of imperial "nationalization" could be defined as the articulation of a new relationship among the military and bureaucratic elites (including judges) who had governed the empire so as to accommodate the desires and consensus of those who stood to gain from mid-nineteenth-century electoral reforms, such as the middle class and the upper-level working class. It would be deceptively easy to regard this new imperial governance as the result of political reforms at home that had an impact in the territories. On the contrary, there was constant interaction, and the interaction generated paradoxes. For example, Britons in North America and Oceania—de facto minorities in their new countries—often enjoyed greater political and social rights than did their compatriots at home.[63] The absence of previous limitations on their rights, along with the need to enhance a kind of aristocracy of rights, helped strengthen their position vis-à-vis the colonial administration. The necessity for consensus altered the relationship between the two sides, and reforms gave new life and breadth to the community of equal citizens that constituted its foundation. That is the issue. And that is where imperial history and national history overlap in ways that have yet to be sufficiently explored. This dynamic also shaped the Creole revolts of the late eighteenth century and the dawning of the modern nation, and a century later, the modern nation had become the code regulating how individuals belonged to a group and what their rights were.

Having gotten this far, two problems must be dealt with: on the one hand, expressions of national and imperial cohesion such as the cult of the monarchy and preservation of "English values" amid a world of "inferiors," the military might that accompanied the whole process, and the exaltation of the capacity of self-government, among others,[64] and, on the other hand, the ramifications for the losers, from Ireland to the "inferior races" throughout the empire.[65] The affirmative and the exclusionary were both regulated by special laws and would influence each other, since internal cohesion was essential if the empire's inherent violence and the threats it faced were to be properly managed.[66] The new nation of citizens after the 1867 electoral reforms would have to address these challenges, deal with social reforms at home, define the new place of India in the empire, and stabilize the white settlements.

Citizenship in Limbo

The articulation of a national community at the center of the metropolitan imperial world and its asymmetrical relationships with distant communities immediately created a world apart, the world of those who do not participate. With its deep roots in the eighteenth century, namely state religion, loyalty to monarch, and hatred of internal and external enemies, nineteenth-century national projects would be far more rigorous in matters of exclusion.[67] The list of the excluded is a long one, and it applies to some degree to the metropolis as well. First came compatriots who were not allowed to participate in decision-making in the metropolis, the heart of full citizenship as defined during the French Revolution (the *citoyen actif*). Bases for exclusion varied throughout the nineteenth century, but nearly everywhere, nonparticipants were identified as workers, those of little means, the youth of working age, vagabonds, itinerants (such as the Roma), felons, ex-prisoners and, of course, women, as well as nonnationals who lived in metropolitan society. As the jurist Danièle Lochack very perceptively noted, citizenship by nature was a highly elusive category because it defined, as we have seen, belonging and rights.[68] That is why the construction of a national community was so critical. It anticipated and socialized individuals—regardless of whether they were full citizens—with a strong sense of horizontal belonging and identity, of integration in a national community that was by nature transversal and projected toward a particular vision of the future. In this regard, the national community had an impressive force even for those who exercised political power within it, but also for those who aspired to join. This inclusivity with an eye on the future helps explain the power behind alternative nationalisms that were radically unconnected from and even antagonistic to state institutions. In those cases, what unified them were moral or cultural considerations leading to broad social coalitions.[69]

If social life in the metropolis allowed for broad integration through shared experiences—empire, with its wars, armies, and more or less diffuse ethnocentrism; education; public debate—exclusion of the majority was the norm in colonial worlds. But even there, the idea of a citizenship broader than that of the mid-nineteenth century had been planted with the revolutions. The most obvious resolution of the contradiction between receptive political communities and the exclusion of freemen along with slaves and servants was the shock of the first wave of abolition in much of the French, English, and Spanish worlds. From there, the list of the excluded only grew longer throughout the nineteenth century; in addition to franchise restrictions (which on occasions were no harsher than those in the metropolis itself), there were exclusions on the basis of social status or alleged racial or cultural inferiority. These people, for centuries the "wretched of the earth" in colonies and territories of deportation and punishment, were never homogeneous.[70] They included those who had the capacity to participate even though they belonged to social groups denied participation in the civic community. Some were economically independent, with levels of wealth and education comparable or superior to those of citizens in the metropolis. The origins of this phenomenon were evident already during the revolutionary years, when local landowners and the popular classes, including descendants of slaves, took part in electoral campaigns as voters and candidates; examples include emancipated slaves elected to the French National Assembly and the election of (Dionisio) Inca Yupanqui to the Cortes of Cádiz, the first audible rumbles of the avalanche of changes that would prove inevitable. In the following decades, growing electoral rolls in the British colonies and universal citizenship in France in 1848 raised the issue once again. Conversely, it is important to keep in mind how important the formation of national communities in the empire would prove to be for its governance. Algeria, Réunion, Australia, New Zealand, and Canada were greatly strengthened, as far as integration and imperial patriotism went, through massive exclusion—sometimes of the majority but certainly of those who had rights of possession, no matter how the idea of useful labor might be summoned up and twisted to legitimize theft.[71] National formation and the sense of belonging worked together as elements of cohesion and affirmation of possession from which others were excluded.[72] Here too, the concept of imperial nation captures these interrelations, which bestowed such solidity and consensus on the territorial expansion of liberal empires.

There is no better example of the difficulty of defining group space than the position of former slaves in territories where abolition had made it necessary to figure out what to do with these newly free but very different individuals. In successive waves—between 1833 and 1838 in the British empire, in 1848 in the French empire, during the years following radical republican experiments in the United States, and in the 1870s in Brazil and the Spanish colonies—former slaves became landless peasants deprived of all rights and entirely (or nearly entirely) excluded from the political realm. Slaves had no recognized civil status, and former slaves' status was uncertain. That had not always been the case, however, and it would not remain the case. Citizenship of former slaves in Saint-Domingue, the antecedent of the Republic of Haiti, which provided such vital assistance to

Simón Bolívar and his allies in the secessionist wars against Spain, was remembered by subsequent generations.[73] Even so, abolition was repeatedly postponed, depending on the circumstances in each place. Strict electoral laws worked to delay any real recognition of the problem, which nevertheless reappeared with the declaration of universal citizenship in 1848 France and via electoral reforms elsewhere. I address these matters not only for their intrinsic importance but because the contradiction anywhere between slavery and rights was a substantial and relevant component of the "special" politics that would end up transforming monarchic empires into empires befitting liberal countries.

There were, generally speaking, two great casuistic questions behind emancipation. Only twice—in Great Britain in 1833 and in France in 1848 (setting aside the self-emancipation of Saint-Domingue)—was the freedom of slaves a matter decided by the metropolis in line with early nineteenth-century liberal thought. In both those cases, change was the result of a series of circumstances that led people to believe that latent or open conflict in the Antilles was linked to the need for certain political changes at home.[74] In Great Britain, domestic political reform destroyed the East India Company and planters' lobbies at Westminster, while an elected Irish minority was created with the Roman Catholic Relief Act of 1830. Abolitionism and open rebellion in Jamaica in 1831 were the essential backdrop to emancipation there.[75] After slavery was reestablished by Napoleon at the start of the century, the new Second Republic set the stage for its definitive abolition, and this was *casus belli* for good republicans. But another matter altogether was what to do with former slaves, as we saw in chapter 5; with the law in their hands, they could now become universal citizens (if they were males). The fight over the rights of freed slaves was a crucial part of the politics of specialness that all French governments, be they monarchic, republican, or neo-Napoleonic, formulated in terms of the distinction between new and old colonies. For Spain and the United States, abolition was accompanied by wars that revealed serious national and imperial crises. This was also the case to some degree with Brazil during the war with Paraguay (1864–70), in which Brazilian imperial soldiers occupied the latter country until 1876.[76] This was clearly a national war demanding enormous mobilization of troops, many of whom were descendants of slaves from Río de la Plata or actual Brazilian slaves; the war claimed up to 300,000 casualties, which energized the country's republican movement.[77] As we have seen, in vaguely liberal contexts, military mobilization signified national interests and was always more or less translated into terms of rights or the opening up of political possibilities to excluded social groups.

The events of 1865 in Jamaica are a good example of the linkage between the freeing of the slaves and the nature of liberal politics in the metropolis. On October 11 of that year, a group of former slaves in Morant Bay, in southeast Jamaica, attacked the local prison and took weapons.[78] In a battle with the militia, they killed eighteen soldiers and wounded more than thirty. Seven of the armed rebels also died. From there, the survivors moved on to lands owned by rich planters and attacked blacks and mulattos who worked for them.[79] In the following days, the multitude grew in size, spreading from the parish of St. Thomas to the nearby towns of St. David and Portland. They acted in small groups and were well led by Paul Bogle, a freeman born of a free mother, a smallholder and a member of the Baptist church. A police officer said he had heard him swear on the Bible and speaking to his followers in a language the officer could not understand. In response to all this, Governor Edward John Eyre, who had come from Australia with a reputation for having treated the Aborigines well, declared a state of siege and proceeded to put down the revolt by military means. The result was a massacre: eighty-five rebels were killed, and many more were wounded. The subsequent repression was equally violent: 354 rebels were convicted after summary judgment, 600 were whipped, and around 1,000 homes were destroyed. The governor then ordered the arrest of George William Gordon, a mulatto whom he accused of being the instigator. Gordon was the son of a white planter and a slave and a member of the same church where Bogle had been deacon; he was also one of the fiercest critics in the Jamaican assembly, representing the most radical sector of the "town party," and moreover, he was editor of the *Jamaica Watchman and People's Free Press*, a newspaper.[80] People like Gordon had tried for years to channel the complaints of the poor Jamaican peasantry, former slaves who had survived the so-called period of apprenticeship. Their objective was to reach the Colonial Office without having to go through the assembly, which had always been controlled by planters. After a trial riddled with irregularities, Gordon was shot.

What might have been just one more crisis of hunger and repression in the world of slavery turned out to be a ticking bomb for Britain, with important repercussions regarding special laws. Eyre may have thought he'd won, but the metropolis did not share that opinion. When the news reached Britain in early November, public opinion was divided: some argued that the energetic governor had simply restored order, but others maintained he had abused his authority, disrespected the rule of law, and displayed an appalling lack of political tact.[81] Surprisingly, the Colonial Office appears to have accepted at first the version presented in the governor's report, but incredulity quickly disturbed the calm imperial waters. Churches and religious abolitionists who met at Exeter Hall in London were the first to protest.[82] Soon afterward a group of liberal reformists who called themselves the Jamaica Committee campaigned to put the governor on trial in order to determine what had actually happened. The empire had set a grand example by abolishing slavery and could not turn its back on the emancipated. As Catherine Hall has shown, the strong connections between the two worlds would not allow it, and neither would the terms of the debate in the metropolis.[83]

British society was deeply divided as more was learned about the events, and there were some who questioned the very nature of the empire.[84] The Colonial Office rectified its initial reaction and decided to investigate, establishing a special commission to that end. A very somber picture began to emerge. Eyre was dismissed, and a judicial inquest was opened into actions by officers and soldiers. The chief of the Colonial Office, Edward Cardwell, made it quite clear that imposition of martial law had been unjustified and that the governor's behavior had been imprudent and disproportionate. At the same time, public opinion also was in a state of excitement, with tensions heightened as a result of the ongoing cruelties of the Crimean War and the recent events in India leading to the nationalization of the East India Company, not to mention the division of opinions regarding the U.S. Civil War.[85] Imperial disturbances had become a domestic concern.

The debate regarding Jamaica further divided British politicians and intellectuals regarding the significance of the empire. There were distinguished figures on both sides of Eyre's case. Chief among his defenders was Thomas Carlyle, a fierce critic of English industrialism and the "steam-engine intellectuals" at its service. His essay lambasting the Exeter Hall nonconformists and those whom he called "Nigger Philanthropists" was titled "Shooting Niagara: And After?"; it was a frenzied compendium of racist arguments. And that was not his first attempt; his 1849 "Occasional Discourse on the Negro Question," an article published in *Fraser's Magazine for Town and Country*, was revived as a pamphlet in 1853 with "Negro" replaced by "Nigger." His proposal therein for a sort of medieval indentured servitude for freed slaves led his former student, John Stuart Mill, to publicly distance himself. But Carlyle's position on Jamaica was supported by notables such as John Ruskin, Charles Dickens, Alfred Tennyson, Anthony Trollope, Charles Kingsley, and by Carlyle's sometime secretary, the Irishman James Anthony Froude, who much later had great success with *Oceana, or England and her Colonies* (1886), an absurd apology for Victorian empire. The other side of the debate, led by Mill, also featured some of the leading lights of politics and culture: Charles Darwin, Thomas Huxley, Thomas F. Buxton, Herbert Spencer, and the group of reformist liberals led by John Bright. They, of course, were joined by the Exeter Hall religious groups.

If for many the empire was a (literal) matter of property to be protected against internal and external threats, for others guardianship over other worlds could only be based on a strong moral imperative. By the time news from Jamaica reached Britain, debates had been going on for some time regarding the economic and human costs of empire. Those who lost their lives defending it were mostly those who could not benefit from the 1867 electoral reforms, which did not extend to workers, peasants, or the landless. In the aftermath of Jamaica, Mill, with his characteristic honesty, told an audience of workers that though he was running for office they still could not vote because they were not ready to be raised to full citizenship.[86] His argument did not exclude the idea of improvement for women and workers in the short run and in the national context, in contrast to the empire, where others could not benefit from that reformist élan.[87] Morality and respect for law in the empire were simply an extension of the supposedly collective morality in the national sphere.[88] Both at home and abroad, education was the indispensable lever for lifting the multitudes so that they might restrain their passions as the educated classes did. Individual arguments thus became collective ones, as Mill tried to show regarding the impossibility of self-government in India.[89] But the West Indies were not exactly the same, as the question there was not dominion over other peoples or societies generally viewed as inferior who could rise only if they were under guardianship. Rather, they posed a genuine moral and social problem for Britons of good conscience, because from the very start (that is, since the elimination of the original inhabitants) society there had been constituted by Europeans. They were new societies comprising conationals and transplanted Africans and Asians, something that the antislavery movement, especially the evangelicals, had pointed out an infinite number of times.[90] The American Civil War, that hellish mix of colonial and national interests, had brought these questions home to places where cotton, sugar, slavery, and rights were essentially local questions. The misery of former slaves in the empire's slums, as they were frequently called, revealed the limits of the empire's moral capital: the end of the slave trade, the politics of amelioration, and emancipation from above in 1833.

But the passionate debate that followed the Morant Bay rebellion was not limited to the social status of emancipated slaves. Rather, it led straight to a recipe for political specialness that by now is easy to recognize. Elected assemblies in all the islands (except Barbados, where planters had complete control) were eliminated, ensuring enviable stability. But it also marked recognition by the metropolitan government that improvements could not be imposed through that particular traditional political instrument referred to by contemporaries as constitutional regression. This is a concept that few historians swayed by the linear vision of British imperial development have attended to. Given the impossibility of satisfying the hopes of a divided mass of citizens, the solution was to create a new space without rights, a vacuum.

Everywhere that colonial slavery had been a central institution, the rights of freed slaves was on the agenda. The distressing end of the post-slavery experiment in the United States is an example of the tensions within an imperial nation. In contrast to the countries that emerged after Spain's imperial crisis, which abolished slavery quickly in the 1820s, the former Thirteen Colonies maintained it, with no hope for a solution during the first republican stage. Three areas quickly emerged: the Chesapeake and its backcountry, where slavery was expanding; the Middle Colonies and the North, where slavery was dying a slow death; and the new states in the North and West that could not be admitted with slavery. Even more than the example of Brazil, the U.S. experience of slavery in an independent nation is very relevant to our study of the formation of special laws. Nation and empire were projected over the same territory, as we saw in the preceding chapter, though they did not exactly coincide. Colonial slavery was immediately nationalized after the 1787 Northwest Ordinance prohibited slavery in the new territory and, later on, during the disputes in the wake of the 1820 Missouri Compromise.[91] These special laws, implemented in territories where sovereignty was invoked, defined a space for slavery and a space for the community of citizens. In the South, the nation—with its multitude of human beings who would never win their freedom—necessarily had to cohabit with the empire.[92] That is why, from Thomas Jefferson to Abraham Lincoln himself, the manifest destiny of that social group was not inclusion in the community of citizens but rather removal, either to Africa or to Panama. By the same token, a space had to be carved outside the nation for American Indians who were not taxpayers or who lived outside the supposed boundaries of the republic, which represented the vast majority; thus, a series of six statutes culminating in the 1834 Indian Intercourse Act (also known as the Indian Nonintercourse Act) defined what would become known as Indian Country, the precursor of the reservation system.[93] This extraordinary case permits us to observe two simultaneous processes: the development of slavery and the exclusion of the Indians, on the one hand; and, on the other, the formation of two nations under just one state.[94]

From the beginning, the young republic divided its territory in this manner. The split between South and North came about thanks to the extraordinarily dynamic slave plantation system, which was fueled by the English cloth industry's ceaseless demand for cotton and a growing consumer base that wanted tobacco.[95] Later agreements such as the Missouri Compromise, the establishment of what became known as the Mason-Dixon line, the Kansas-Nebraska Act of 1854 (which opened the door to slavery throughout the union), and, finally, the Dred Scott decision of March 1857 sealed the division of the republic.[96] Within that order of things, the power of the states was greater than that of the federal government and marked continuity with a key element of the constitution of social power under British dominion expressed in the early ideas of confederation.[97] This was the most significant meaning of federalism.[98] Judicial rulings, the regulation of matrimony, and obligations associated with active citizenship such as participation in the militia together all imposed white homogeneity on the mid-century electoral census in the context of the great constitutional ambiguity that allowed the states to regulate the presence (or, more often, the absence) of nonwhites on the rolls.[99] In the 1840s and 1850s, the growing importance of northern nativism would be brought to bear on the construction of a nation/community of citizens, pushing the slavery debate aside.[100] Following Eric Foner's argument, this would be the last hurrah for European-origin colonists, future homesteaders whose movement would have no place within slavery, which was expanding under the banner of "popular sovereignty" and whose constitutional place was being demanded by the (electoral) majority.[101] In this situation, war was an extension of politics by other means. As is well known, the Civil War was not initially about ending slavery or a reflection of the weakness of the abolition movement, but rather, represented a conflict over unity and the imposition of northern industrialization over southern agriculture.[102]

After the war, the great experiment in "national" construction in the framework of U.S. imperial formation took place with the extension of universal citizenship (and all its historical significance) to Confederate states and former slaves. During the first postbellum decade, military occupation of the South (a way of continuing Sherman's "total war") at first meant that proposals by radical republicans and representatives of the freed slaves had considerable viability. The amendments to the Constitution were introduced in Congress along with such measures as the April 1866 Civil Rights Act in order to heal the divisions that had led to war.[103] In this context of enormous fluidity, former slaves joined the electoral rolls while southern states quickly passed the infamous segregationist Black Codes.[104] Questionable and hastily assembled white majorities representing the needs of large landowners attempted to exclude potential black voters and maintain control over the black labor force, which had been mobilized during and after the war.[105] The hopes of former slaves were further dashed by divisions in the North, where few states enacted measures of equality. Blacks could vote in just five states (all of them in New England) before the war; by the time the last of the Reconstruction Acts were approved, the number was six.[106] While southern states had to purify themselves before reentering the Union, no similar demand was placed on northern states, where segregation remained unpunished. One year after the war ended, just six Confederate states had rejoined; the others (Virginia, Georgia, Mississippi, and Texas) resisted until they were forced to submit.[107] Finally, a series of rulings by the U.S. Supreme Court in 1883 made clear that civil rights lay beyond congressional jurisdiction.[108] Several decades later the results were clear: voting rights were nullified in eleven states, and African American representation in Congress was obliterated. It was in the resulting space between the corrective constitutional amendments and electoral and political practice on the ground that we find special rules imposed that defined the limits of nation and empire; the nation-empire border that Stephen A. Douglas—who died before the war—and Charles Sumner saw disappear in the face of southern white supremacy, of which Jim Crow was the clearest manifestation.[109]

It is ironic that the fierce struggle for republican unity opened the door to a new cycle of specialness. Even before the hopes of former slaves were extinguished, pressure was renewed against the relocated inhabitants of Indian Country and the Great Plains.[110] In a classic dynamic of settler capitalism, homesteaders were unwilling to continue paying taxes for a war to protect them or to relinquish any land or political space to those who did not share their appreciation for property and freedom.[111] For them, genocide and confinement were better options. The powerful "civic nationalism" that triumphed at the center of U.S. imperial expansion, to quote Gary Gerstle, thus involved a brand of white supremacy both within and without that unfolded not as a result of the Civil War but because of the values of the social groups who shaped subsequent social reproduction.[112] It was in the United States, then, more than anywhere else, that nation and empire most clearly overlapped.[113]

The Nation in the Empire; the Empire in the Nation

Monarchic empires fell apart because of the development of new moral horizons of citizen communities during the eighteenth century both within and beyond Europe. Failed attempts to turn old-regime empires into a single national space, which we discussed in the early chapters, led to the appearance of the formula par excellence for reconstructing post-revolutionary empires in a flexible manner: the special laws that formed the true unwritten imperial constitution of modernity. But, at the same time, empires reshaped themselves while modern nations emerged. To quote John Hall, "Universal empire is sometimes seen as an anomaly, as an oddity of history naturally replaced by the nation state. Nothing could be further from the truth. Empire is probably the default option of the historical record, with the nation-state being the oddity—created and suited for only modern circumstances."[114]

Nations, generally speaking, constitute the sum of a meaningful past, be it real or invented, and a shared project. In the nineteenth century, that would increasingly be expressed through political representation for a growing sector of the population. Parallel to this ideal of a community of citizens was one of exclusion or inclusion of others, those aliens, nomads, and other people with distinctive cultural or ethnic connotations. In the mid-nineteenth century, after the various revolutions and grand liberal reforms throughout Europe, the nation stood at the center of the modification of the state and its relationship to the colonies. Once again, the concept of nation-state must be applied with great care. As we have seen, nation formation was not confined to the metropolis, as it was between 1780 and 1820. Indeed, imperial expansion took on equally national connotations, and the affirmation of the nation at home often determined politics in places inhabited by important groups of conationals. Thus, national and imperial dynamics always expressed themselves in two directions: between the British world and the white settlements, between French republicanism and Algerian colonists, between Madrid and Havana. Growing migration and the rise of journalism and the popular press meant that this process solidified in ways that would have been unthinkable earlier.[115] There were times when this hall of mirrors functioned as a positive national logic, while at other times it demonstrated the rules of specialness through distancing, postponement, and/or refusal. Regardless of the outcome, the interaction is undeniable; these were the two sides of the imperial coin. Decolonization and the formation of new nations after 1947 revealed the importance of national construction in the imperial framework because national formation within the empire presumes the possibility of alternative projects, be they complementary or competing.

Several examples illustrate an array of interactions between nation and empire that make sense only if we see them in the framework of what we are calling the imperial constitution. After the Jamaican crisis of 1865, the tradition of local assemblies, which had lasted for nearly two centuries, was broken because they could not absorb the tensions generated by abolition in 1833. Planters and former slaves both lost representation in favor of the Colonial Office, though for obvious reasons they both continued to wait for solutions from London. Along with the political setback, the social impact for the "slums of the Empire" was quite obvious. In the meantime, colonists of European origins and (a few) of African or Oceanian descent won a kind of imperial citizenship in Australia, New Zealand, and South Africa, blurring the limits between the nation at home and an ambigous nation in the imperial setting.[116] At the same time, those freed in the French Antilles in 1848 established their presence in republican institutions during the Third Republic and formed part of the French nation. But the nation was also an empire, and less unitary than advertised. Thus, there were no departments in the Antilles, Guyana, Senegal, or Réunion. But even accounting for these differences, and considering the rules of *spécialité*, the nation as a subject of sovereignty spilled over France's hexagonal borders. The presence of pure-blooded Frenchmen was obviously crucial in that regard. The moral horizon of nation was defined in the French metropolis but extended beyond Europe to the old colonies in one way, and to Algeria in another way. And, finally, in the postbellum United States we see a classic case of the imperial nation, in which the construction of exceptional spaces was consubstantial with the formation of the republic. The most obvious example, though not the only one, were the former slaves deprived of citizenship and social improvements that formed part of Reconstruction. Here we see the formation of a colonial social complex within the framework of the republican empire, which at the same time was a nation, as in the other cases. Consolidation of the reservation system and exclusionary laws against Asians and Mexicans in the western United States, from Texas to California, ensured that whiteness would lie at the center of national life with a genuinely imperial perspective.

CHAPTER NINE

Ruling across the Color Line

IN HIS *IMPERIALISM: A Study*, which he wrote in response to the Boer Wars in South Africa, J. A. Hobson showed extraordinary clairvoyance in explaining the paradox of the great European empires expanding and incorporating massive numbers of peoples whom they did not consider appropriate additions to their liberal institutions.[1] Hobson discreetly referred to these peoples as "lower" or "backward races," always in quotes, a clear reference to the imperial discourse of the day, though at a distance.[2] Britain was not the only world power at the peak of nineteenth-century liberalism governing immense multitudes who had few if any rights. It was true of all of them: France, Spain before 1898, Holland, Portugal, Denmark, the recent arrivals Italy and Germany, and the non-European United States and Brazil. In short, everyone who wished to join the race to carve up the world after the 1885 Berlin Conference had lined up.[3]

In this chapter I look at the growing tension between the foundations of the imperial nation—a national community in the metropolis with special rules overseas and/or in the colonies—and its unceasing expansion over other continents. In the context of imperial governments' difficulties in this regard, it became more pressing to draw the color line neatly identifying "races" among subjects, which two decades earlier Tocqueville had considered of little use in imperial practices.[4] In order, I examine British stabilization, French recovery, U.S. dynamism, and the continuity of the old Iberian empires in the wake of the Napoleonic Wars. That is, I am looking at reinforcement of imperial centers, representative integration by the great national states, and subjection of populations previously beyond direct control. The problems associated with controlling such diverse spaces and populations ended up mobilizing, *nolens volens*, an enormous storehouse of prejudices and stereotypes that would become an operative factor in imperial expansion. In other words, it was not simply the idea of superiority of one people over another that conferred substance and dynamism to imperial politics.

Britishness and Others

The late Victorian empire offers the best example of the problems created by continual expansion, both regarding liberal metropolitan institutions and overseas territories. The Second British Empire was a panoply of diverse situations that included self-governing possessions, crown colonies with complex variations in their rights, and the Indian Raj with its exceptional status and enormous internal heterogeneity. The late Victorian empire drew up its various political responses as it was being pressured by conflicts on the periphery.[5] Territorial expansion during the period of "high imperialism," and even more so after 1918 and the acquisition of German and Ottoman territories, added a spectacular number of new subjects to an empire that already covered the globe at the turn of the century. At the same time, modern citizenship in Great Britain itself and in the white crown colonies (which were more democratic than the metropolis when it came to suffrage and social advantages for European settlers), along with rigorous racial segregation, gave structure to previously embryonic constitutional forms.

Throughout the expansionist period that began with the 1882 occupation of Egypt, the empire seemed to oscillate between two quite different options.[6] The first was a continuation of disorderly political formations and unequal rights. This is sometimes interpreted as no plan at all, but in fact it was a coherent response to imperial developments by colonial administrators in London and on the periphery. While many decisions were circumstantial, as a whole they coincided over long periods of time, and that consistency, in the framework of a legal and imperial cultural tradition, must be considered as something else altogether; it would be far more realistic to consider that coincidence as constituting specialness. Along with dominions, crown colonies, and the Raj, two new governmental systems appeared in the last third of the nineteenth century and the start of the twentieth century: indirect or dual governments (such as Africa at the turn of the century), and African mandates through transfer of sovereignty, a late redefinition of Burke's theory of trusteeship. Theorized as refinements and extensions of native governmental institutions, like those in parts of India and the Dutch East Indies so admired by the British, in fact they emerged out of local situations. The mandates offered an alternative, and were defended at the Berlin and Brussels conferences but they remained diffuse until imperial rivalries and World War I brought about greater coherence.

Different forms of imperial government did not arise by chance. Notions of institutional homogeneity or generalized rights—parliament or imperial citizenship, colonial conferences, imperial federation among equals—had been rejected both by the center and by the periphery, the latter referring to the more privileged imperial sites such as the white dominions.[7] Unitary, consistent approaches were supported mostly by leading liberal imperialists such as Lord Milner, Leo Amery, Lionel Curtis, other members of the Round Table movement (around the journal of the same name), and descendants of left-wing Fabianism.[8] They also were espoused by those trying to protect imperial unity during World War I and the Irish crisis of 1917.[9] In the end, the disorderly traditional order ("chaotic pluralism," according to John Darwin) prevailed, and effective means for regularizing disorder were not adopted, be they constitutional measures or the adoption of equal rights for all subjects of one monarch.[10] In short, in the absence of any general guideline or outlook (even at the Imperial Conferences), the idea of rights had no meaning beyond particular contexts.[11] Several factors arising out of the imperial logic itself played into that continuity: British trade unions' fear of foreign workers; the dangers of nationalism in the larger dominions or of historical nationalism such as that in Ireland; and colonists' suspicions of an imperial center more inclined to humanitarian approaches to subject populations than they themselves were.[12] By the time of World War I, difference had become the norm and specialness the glue holding the entire imperial enterprise together. A few years later, the old Commonwealth was articulated in deliberately flexible fashion, allowing for variable political forms and rights among its components. By the end of this chapter the logic of this development should be clear, but suffice to say here that there was "astonishing uncertainty," to quote Ann Dummett and Andrew Nicol, in the administration of political status concerning peoples and social groups.[13]

As the expanding British empire faced competition from the French in Africa and from the Germans and Americans in the Pacific, the British implemented apparently contradictory solutions to their dilemmas. Chief among them were the granting of powers and rights in the white dominions of Canada, Australia, New Zealand, and South Africa, while, on the other hand, the color line was increasingly emphasized in the empire, especially in these four possessions.[14] These two sides of the problem must be analyzed as they interrelated to one another. Racial prejudice was not simply the *deus ex machina* controlling imperial development; rather, the development of the imperial nation—a hall of mirrors in which the metropolis activated notions of rights and political identity that later were refracted onto the offshoots—depended on accommodation to diverse situations, and the system did not allow for isolated solutions that were invisible to others. For that reason, in this book I aim to avoid the Eurocentrism of classical imperial history while also rejecting conceptions of the relationships between metropoles (European or of European origin) and other continents as relationships between entities (center/periphery) that always remained the same.[15] Racial perceptions changed over time, and it was the crises and challenges in relevant and specific contexts that, in the end, pointed to the most significant shifts.

Evolution of the large white dominions indicated both how negotiations with transplanted societies of compatriots would transpire and how native peoples, bound for extinction or marginality, would be excluded. There, in successful replications of the mother country, a more precise definition of the other inhabitants—be they indigenous, immigrants, or taken by force—would become necessary.[16] There, too, political and social uses of racial and genealogical archetypes were the most intense. There was a wide range of intermediate possibilities along this arc, and years of experience searching for special solutions gave these dilemmas and practices their shape and form.

Australia was one of Britain's great laboratories in the late nineteenth century after the conflicts in Ireland (1848–49), India (1859), and Jamaica (1865) had been settled.[17] The continent had been explored since the late eighteenth century and remained divided into independent colonies, established after 1855 when they were given the status of possessions with responsible governments.[18] With colonization, Australian governors began thinking, for obvious reasons, about the possibility of creating a large dominion, along the lines of American federalism or that of Canada after 1867. Already in 1870 a customs union had been established (the German Reich is a relevant example), and there were earlier agreements among the colonies to stem the considerable influx of Chinese immigrants. Along the same lines, the Commonwealth of Australia Constitution Act was approved in 1900 and went into effect the following year. The New Zealand and Australian experiments with British democracy impressed many people, including Fabian reformers (such as Sidney and Beatrice Webb) and socialists (such as Keir Hardie and Tom Mann).[19]

It is no surprise that concern over racial questions existed from the very start as the commonwealth was being formed and consolidated.[20] Among the most important tasks was dealing with the Aborigines and non-European immigrants who lived in or entered the country. This was a critical matter because laws regulating those groups did not depend on the federation but rather on each of its states, and the situation in each place was different. The absence of voting rights, for example, existed only in South Australia and Queensland, which had more immigrant workers. Australia found itself in an imperial moment, having to define its domestic and regional ambitions as it resisted humanitarian strictures emanating from time to time from the metropolis.[21] The question of self-government arose just as attempts to endow the empire with greater internal homogeneity and greater ability to take action had intensified. The Australians certainly harbored subimperial intentions that they took few pains to disguise, and which were impossible to disguise after the head of the Queensland government, Thomas McIlwraith, annexed part of New Guinea, an operation motivated by the need for sugar plantation workers.[22] Any Australian incursion abroad was bound to increase domestic worry over whiteness and the perceived vulnerability of the European population.[23] Exclusion was so stark in some states that imperial functionaries recommended that explicitly racial terms in immigration laws be replaced with more discreet, though equally operative, terms, as had been the case in other racial laboratories such as the Colony of Natal in southern Africa.[24]

In its death throes, late-nineteenth-century white nationalism struggled to define the limits of a new and powerful political entity in the great liberal empire. The objective was based on a reverse reading of reality: European Australia was drowning in an ocean of unwhite "races." The raw numbers reveal the absurdity of the obsession: there were 3,377,000 Europeans and 50,000 immigrants from other continents facing off against some 60,000 Aborigines, survivors of a population well on the road to extinction.[25] Nevertheless, Prime Minister Edmund Barton warned the first federal parliament in 1901 that the day was not far off when a visiting European would see nothing but yellow- and black-skinned people living in the country.[26] These were not his own words; they were a direct quotation from a book by Charles Pearson, *National Life and Character: A Forecast*, which the prime minister openly waved in his hand.[27] Pearson, a medievalist, had published his pamphlet in London in 1893; the original title, chosen by the publisher, was *Orbis Senescens* (The Twilight of the World). Its content was what one might imagine: history as race war with whites, who were inevitably being obliterated in the face of an unstoppable wave of others.[28] This terrifying vision seduced other influential figures of the day, among them William Gladstone and Theodore Roosevelt. American Indians and Australian Aborigines would clearly have to be extinguished.[29] The fact that Barton took that book with him to the podium at such an important moment was therefore laden with significance.

Australian racial exasperation grew out of a common paradox: aspiration for a white Protestant society (a better version of Britain) and at the same time the need for a labor force for large-scale agriculture, which meant opening borders to the Chinese, Indians, Javanese, and Polynesians.[30] The presence of all these groups brought points of comparison among them or in relation to their places of origin. Emigrants from British India or Hong Kong, for example, believed that their rights as British subjects could not be considered on the same plane as the rights of Chinese immigrants, nor could their rights be violated by Australian states' segregationist laws.[31] This was not a demand on the fringes of empire; on the contrary, it reflected the internal situation of the Raj, where local nationalism and the formalization of certain rights for poor workers and lower-caste peoples had prospered. If the position of the Indian middle class to some extent reflected British political developments, that of emigrants from the Indian subcontinent to Australia constituted a reply from their country of origin.

The essential problem illustrated the two tendencies of the Australian constitutional bloc in 1880–90: continuation of legislation regulating emigration, and radical exclusion of the original inhabitants, in line with the 1901 Constitution of the Commonwealth of Australia, which invented those racial qualifications and made them last throughout the twentieth century.[32] The key to continuity, in turn, also lay in two interrelated elements: exclusion of Aborigines from electoral rolls and the diminished status of non-European emigrants.[33] Similar to the tendencies of European constitutions decades earlier, and for similar reasons, the constitution made no mention of a system of rights associated with Australian citizenship because the latter simply did not exist. As John Chesterman and Brian Galligan have pointed out, the absence of "citizen" (the term did appear in the first draft, clearly inspired by the United States, but was eliminated in later versions) was easy to explain.[34] One motivation was to avoid domestic republican agitation by certain emigrant groups. Another was to ensure that British citizenship, acquired by birth, would neither raise the idea of possession of rights nor affect anything other than the mother country. The idea was to avoid protests against states' abilities to discriminate by using electoral rolls against those considered insufficient for the vote, meaning those who were born in the empire but not qualified to enjoy rights that others had. The first constitution did not, in fact, affirm superiority over state legislation, particularly the exclusion of non-Europeans in Queensland and Western Australia. Exclusionary and segregationist practices against Aborigines, voted upon by state parliaments as well as by that of the Commonwealth, also affected many Asian and Oceanic immigrant workers. Thus, following Chesterman and Galligan, the idea of the British subject, absent any relation with the implicit content of citizenship, was in practice restricted to Anglo-Britons established there. That was the case with the British Nationality and Status of Aliens Act of 1914, which gave no consideration whatsoever to assimilation, rights, or extending the vote to Aborigines or European immigrants.[35] The national and racial order was, finally, consolidated with legislation after that date covering such matters as the entry and rights of non-European immigrant workers (the relevant terms were *white* and *European descent*) and the redundantly named "aboriginal natives," who were kept off the electoral rolls and denied any political identity after the 1902 Commonwealth Franchise Act. As could be expected, once this exclusion was settled, the question of what to do with mixed-race people gave rise to exclusionary systems based on a person's genealogy, the "preponderating blood."[36] Under these conditions, the nineteenth-century debate about whether or not Australian Aborigines were British subjects made no sense.[37] Once all positive signification was ruled out, what the Spanish legal historian Bartolomé Clavero has called "programmed constitutional genocide" (and its accompanying practices) was institutionalized.[38]

Putting together all the pieces of the future Commonwealth of Australia was easy in comparison with the task in South Africa, the other great political construction. There was no place in the empire where humanitarian winds blew more faintly.[39] In November 1854, George Grey arrived in the Cape Colony from Australia and New Zealand, where he had enjoyed considerable prestige in imperial administration for his service to the crown and his abilities to deal with other peoples, particularly the Maoris.[40] The Colonial Office had given him clear orders: he was to stabilize the border and show that the empire was a civilizing force.[41] These orders did not arise from humanitarian pressure in the metropolis or any simple exchange of ideas, but rather, from the devastating moral impact and cost of the Xhosa Wars (also known as the Cape Frontier Wars or the Kaffir Wars).[42] London wanted not only to achieve stability in this highly particular colony but also to reduce military spending, as Herman

Merivale had made quite clear regarding the endless conflicts with the Xhosa, who had waged war against the British no fewer than nine times.[43] Grey appeared to be the man for the job; the word he used to describe his philanthropic mission was *destroy*. The first Xhosa war came in 1779–81, when the colony was still in the hands of the Dutch East India Company (where it remained until 1795, when the East India Company took it, only to return it to the Dutch in 1803 and take it back again in 1806), and the last was in 1878–79. Grey was governor there for the eighth and ninth wars. It is unclear what responsibility he could claim for the millenarian outburst among the Xhosa that led them to sacrifice some 350,000 head of cattle and set off a devastating famine, but the event and the probable implication of the British in the death toll triggered protests among British humanitarians.[44] Despite the disaster, Grey remained in office for seven years, until the Colonial Office finally dismissed him, tired of the stalemate and the governor's obvious falsehoods as he tried to clear his name.[45] The results of the violence were predictable: the Xhosa continued being pushed out, with some being forced into agricultural contract labor in conditions approaching slavery under the watchful eye of German, British, and Boer landowners.[46]

The founders of Cape Town were enthusiastic about the enclave's exceptional port and its mild climate, which allowed travelers to India and Java to avoid illnesses endemic to other locations. Gradually the Dutch East India Company encouraged the establishment and prosperity of a class of independent farmers in the hinterland, the "embryonic Afrikaners," to use Leonard Thompson's expression, who ensured that the port was well supplied.[47] By the mid-eighteenth century, the number of inhabitants in the colony exceeded the number of company employees, which increased pressure to colonize the interior, and the pressure intensified further after the British arrived. That was the start of the long history of military spending and dispossession. First came the ruin and trapping of the pastoral Khoikhoi people, whose lands gradually were taken over by cattlemen.[48] Other inhabitants found refuge on both sides of the porous internal frontier, which led to the emergence of the racially mixed Griqua (or Korana) people. Thus the British of the East India Company inherited a colony with very particular features. The port city and its hinterland were never truly self-sufficient, and the Dutch had compensated with domestic slavery that both served and fed off the needs of the Dutch East India Company. In just a few decades a peculiar slave community arose, descended not only from African peoples but also from Javanese, Malayans, and Malagasy. This new world created by pious Calvinists had a special place for Southeast Asian

Muslims, which explains why the first books in Afrikaans were the Koran and other Muslim religious works written with Arabic script.[49]

Change of ownership did not substantially change the nature of the colony, though in 1807, under the British, the importation of slaves was prohibited. As throughout the rest of the empire, this did not mean that slavery itself was abolished or that its expansion toward the agricultural interior was halted.[50] That said, the colony took part in the amelioration campaigns of legal improvements for slaves and in the abolition debates centered in the metropolis though extending throughout the empire wherever slavery existed. As Robert Ross has ironically noted, the Cape Colony became the area with the most Protestant missionaries per square meter in the world.[51] Not surprisingly, slavery was abolished in Cape Town in 1824, one decade earlier than in the surrounding rural areas, thus following the rhythms of the rest of the empire.[52] Several decades later, however, the European population there began changing its mind when, as in the Pacific, subsidized emigration began sending more Britons to the faraway enclaves.[53] Among them were many Scottish Presbyterians, whose views were quite close to those of the Dutch and German immigrants who had been the leading voices until then. In the Cape Colony, arrivals began growing in around 1820 and continued their upward course in the following decades, during which this vital enclave had to stabilize its internal frontiers in order to ensure the India route. (The Suez Canal opened only in 1869.) To this end, the needs of the empire as a whole and those of the leading agrarian interests found common ground. The Cape Colony was very different from the Caribbean colonies during emancipation and later. For one thing, the British could congratulate themselves that it had not been they but rather the Dutch who had introduced involuntary servitude in southern Africa. Also, rising ethnocentrism, fired up by continual wars, made the more sentimental strains of abolitionism difficult to sustain there. But most important, the Khoikhoi's status could be presented as something other than slavery, a pretense that was destined to survive for many long years as Europeans colonized the interior. As a result, abolitionism was perceived as entirely unjustified interference, plain and simple.[54]

Given this interplay of imperial expansion and local particularities, the relationship with Africans working under European control was to become the colony's most critical issue until the early twentieth century.[55] The history of that relationship is essentially intertwined with that of the implementation of a series of ordinances regulating relations between Europeans and Africans. The first of these decrees was the Caledon Code, also referred to as the Hottentot Proclamation, in 1809, soon after the

British took over, which introduced a pass system and for the first time defined the legal status of African workers not considered slaves.[56] Years later this would be referred to with some exaggeration as the Magna Carta of the colony. In 1812 the provisions were extended to children between eight and twelve years old who were separated from their families and placed in institutions as a means of tying parents to a specific territory. Later, the 1833 emancipation added the problem of more than 20,000 former slaves in the interior. From then on, urban and rural labor would be subject to rules that were applied irregularly, including rules about fixed residence (as opposed to traditional nomadism) and control over vagabondage, which was present everywhere that slaves had been freed.[57]

The enormous demands of large-scale agriculture, along with imperial authorities' erratic tutelary measures, added to the hostility and edginess around former slaves and Africans in general, which finally resulted in open crisis. From 1835 to 1841, some 6,000 Afrikaners (the *Voortrekkers*) who refused to accept the liberation of the slaves or what they regarded as the empire's meddling began what became known as the Great Trek, accompanied by their cattle and their slaves.[58] They were nourished by an archaic brand of Calvinism, based largely on oral tradition, that gave Biblical resonance to their response to British offenses.[59] This marked a complicated schism within European society in southern Africa and the beginning of a singular political edifice. The flight of those fervent slaveholders resulted in three Afrikaner republics. One of them, Natalia, had a brief life because the Zulu wars prevented it from consolidating; it occupied the territory that soon became the British Colony of Natal, which quickly expanded its sugar industry, drew immigrants from all over (especially Asia and India), and became an important laboratory for racial labor policies.[60] The other two republics, the Orange Free State and the South African Republic (Transvaal), did better against territories claimed by the Zulus.[61] The empire renounced them both in 1854 but took them back later under different auspices. The problem was obvious, in that the raison d'être of the Boer republics was slavery, a blatant contradiction of official British policy. The Transvaal even continued importing slaves from Mozambique and conducting slave raids, taking advantage of Portugal's and Britain's inability to control the Limpopo border. Without reading all events as leading up to the period after World War II, we should remember that the politics of institutionalized racial segregation first took shape in these two South African republics. Among these measures were separation of Europeans and Africans in public spaces and churches; strict emigration rules according to country of provenance; control of labor contracts;

and the establishment of reservations where workers in nonslave conditions were under the supervision of their own tribal bosses, who in turn were supervised by the republics. In Natal, these policies clashed with the wishes of colonial authorities, who accepted them in the end, with modifications.[62] But such accommodation was impossible elsewhere, for example in the north Transvaal, once the British reestablished sovereignty over the slave republics.[63]

The relationship between the republics and the British is not the only relevant part of the story. In the British territories, tension over the land and African workers also pointed to the weakness of the official position. Slaveholders were compensated by the British Parliament, which allowed them to buy land or become supply merchants to the interior.[64] In the medium run, introduction of British machinery was crucial for the grain and wine sectors. Demand for wool led to increased control over African shepherds, who became known as migrant laborers because they were Khoikhoi.[65] Labor relations began looking different than in the Boer republics. The biggest challenge was how to define freed slaves and their descendants in the Cape Colony, which in 1848 became self-governing with a cabinet that answered to an elected chamber based on a fairly wide electorate. It was a color-blind electorate with no segregation in terms of skin color.[66] From the moment of emancipation, James Stephen and the Colonial Office had been adamant that blacks, mulattos, and Asians must be incorporated onto the electoral rolls as long as they satisfied the age and economic requirements that European descendants also had to satisfy.[67] It is immediately obvious that this marked a stark contrast with other territories under British sovereignty, and certainly with those under Afrikaner control. Unlike Kaffiria (the Eastern Cape), the borderlands, and Boer territories, the Cape Colony, especially in the capital and port, had a minority of coloureds who enjoyed social space and representation.[68] That was the key to amalgamation, as in New Zealand and some of the crown colonies, the foundation for liberal institutions that made the empire strong.

The experiment lasted forty years, from 1853 (with the first electoral rolls with no racial limits but franchise qualifications) to 1894, when the Glen Grey Act removed people of color from the electoral rolls. Along the way, the limits of official liberalism often made themselves clear, as economic barriers excluded most non-Europeans. In the second half of the nineteenth century there were multiple sleights of hand regarding representation, especially when Afrikaners finally opted for an open electorate, in the hope of achieving the majority, while British merchants preferred imposing limits, inspired by the same expectations. After the imperial government's criterion won out, favoring open rolls in the Cape Colony and the Natal with Africans' parallel expulsion, high participation in both places ended up formalizing segregation of the coloureds. This was visible starting in 1887; when Natal was granted self-government in 1893 (delayed by London because of its racial politics), the political regression was quite obvious, and from the African point of view there was no doubt. But it was especially notable in the Cape Colony, where free coloureds had enjoyed considerable leeway before, which in the end proved to be not so considerable after all. One can only conclude that, though Afrikaner agitation was influential everywhere, the relationship between self-government and exclusion was designed and perfected by the British and the imperial government in the colony itself, on the ground. Only then can one see that Australia's whiteness policy took its cues from the Natal and the entire South African experiment.

In 1874–79, when the new racial politics was beginning to take shape, the general dynamic of the empire pushed the colony toward federation and what would, in 1910, become the South African dominion.[69] For Lord Carnavon (Henry Herbert), who designed the federal system for Canada and South Africa, the option was a good thing not only for the empire as a whole but also because it could ameliorate the disagreable "native question," which he considered the most urgent reason for general union.[70] His hopes were in vain. As the agreement was being worked out among the Cape Colony, the Boer republics, and the empire, an extraordinary event pushed things in an unexpected direction. That event was the so-called mineral revolution, the discovery of diamonds and gold, the latter in enormous quantities in Witwatersrand. Rivalry exploded between the British "randlords," who became rich overnight, and the Boers; the ensuing conflicts, with their racial backdrop, gave rise to Afrikaner nationalism and blocked integration into the political amalgam being supervised from London.[71] Tensions rose after annexation of the first territories with diamond mines, which were inhabited by the Griqua and also claimed by the Orange Free State. Only increased control by the Cape Colony and Natal could finally ensure imperial authority over the fractious territory.[72] While Boers and Britons fought, daily life for the Africans grew more dire, and there were calls for mobilization in the mining districts, where African and European workers enjoyed very different rights. African workers were forced to live outside the towns and were paid much less than workers descended from Europeans, though the latter often had arrived only recently to satisfy the spectacular demand for labor.[73] The sudden transformation of South Africa's social landscape and the massive internal demographic movement quickened tensions between Britons and Boers, and between those two groups and the Africans who had flocked to the mining districts or fled from military defeats suffered by the Zulu and Pedi (Northern Sotho) peoples as the borders expanded.

The bizarre story of the Jameson Raid is a perfect example of the new state of affairs.[74] A group of overenthusiastic British imperialists in December 1895, with the support of Governor Cecil Rhodes and the mining magnates, cooked up a plan to take control of Johannesburg and destabilize the Transvaal, which once again had declared itself a republic after the First Boer War.[75] The botched coup set off alarms throughout the colony and the empire and understandably worsened the already complicated relations between the two European groups. President Paul Kruger's reprisals against the *uitlanders* (foreigners, mostly workers but also mine owners and businessmen) led to the rupture of relations between Kruger and Lord Milner and the eventual Second Boer War, a human catastrophe with enormous economic costs.[76]

With the war, the British achieved the political aims they had harbored for a half century.[77] A colony comprising different political entities was consolidated into one formidable dominion, a solid foundation for the African empire starting in the 1880s. The other predictable outcome was that between the end of hostilities and the Treaty of Vereeniging (also known as the Peace of Vereeniging) in 1902, the British withdrew their demand that racial requirements be eliminated from electoral laws.[78] In other words, they abandoned the majority population: 4,059,018 nonwhites living among 1,104,813 inhabitants of European descent.[79] The concession doubtless was a bitter one, given that the African population had won some autonomy for itself during the war years owing to Afrikaner disorganization.[80] Once again, rights (scarce though they were) had been whittled away. Thus the twentieth century began with the Boers fighting abolition and loss of control over Africans, and with Britain imposing restrictions that, as Robert Huttenback has shown, laid the bases for immigration policies throughout the white settlements.[81]

Citizenship and Its Negation in the Imperial Republic

In the liberal Anglo-British monarchy, which was the ultimate winner of the great counterrevolutionary war of the early nineteenth century, the concept of citizenship as a precise political status made little sense.[82] Rather, the idea that counted was that of the elector, the subject of the gracious queen, along with an imprecise notion of rights established through positive law. The general idea of subjecthood through birth—articulated already in the seventeenth century, dislocated in the eighteenth century as people removed from their place of origin developed the notion of "alien" through systematic contact with new and strange neighbors, and then re-affirmed during the North American crisis—could be gently shifted toward uncertain imperial citizenship guaranteeing access to justice and a certain amount of protection to those born under British sovereignty, though that did not mean much with regard to a subject's particular status.[83] British subjecthood obviously meant one had to obey British laws, which in the nineteenth century continued emanating from Westminster, "transmitted primarily through the exercise of the royal prerogative, administered by governors with plenary powers," although, for reasons we have mentioned, they also came from parliaments or governments in remote places, part of a pyramid that was susceptible to many interpretations.[84] Subjectood also implied a diffuse right of access to tribunals and the ability to seek assurance from authorities that the law would be applied.[85] As we have also seen, the rights of some people born within imperial boundaries might occlude the rights of others born within those same boundaries, though not (according to the Georgians and Victorians) within representative in-stitutions guaranteeing British identity in the metropolis and throughout the empire.[86] It was there that racial archetypes and differences in culture and/or phenotype, and the possibility of overcoming those barriers through numbers or intermarriage, began having an impact beyond any books or debates about the human race. This is a crucial point, as it shows how ad-vances in the rights of some were accompanied by their diminishment or obliteration in the case of others. As Julie Evans has noted, not having the right to vote was an indication of one's social level and had serious conse-quences in the crown's four dominions (Canada, New Zealand, Australia, and South Africa), where the rules of the game for compatriots increasingly were similar to those of the metropolis (and in fact were better, in terms of democracy, for those of British origin).[87] Therefore, the exclusion of people from the electoral rolls, as in South Africa, or the outright elimination of assemblies, as in Jamaica and elsewhere (with the exception of Barbados) in the Caribbean in 1865, as explored in chapter 8, were acts with huge po-litical and social consequences for certain groups.[88] Here lay the dynamic underlying the construction of liberal empires starting with the eighteenth-century revolutions: the written or unwritten notion of specialness, with its impact on particular situations and on social complexes everywhere.

In the Don Pacifico affair, Britain displayed its hegemonic ambitions (shared by all empires): its professed right to defend British subjects being ill treated in foreign countries.[89] For this particular occasion, Lord Palmerston, the foreign secretary, launched an adamant and punctilious defense, Roman-style, which nonetheless, due to its thematic limitations, fell short of ensuring the defense of peoples subjected in other places or of guaranteeing their equality before the law.[90] To complicate matters further, progress regarding the rights of some could be (or could be perceived to be) damaging for the rights of others. That was the case when imperial immigration began being seen as a threat to British workers. As the empire flirted with the proposal by the great proconsuls and liberal imperialists of the Round Table to strengthen imperial unity and involve white inhabitants of the dominions in the defense of the whole—which would prove to be indispensable in the case of Canadians' participation in the Boer War and, more dramatically, Australia's presence at the Battle of Gallipoli during World War I—other factors tended to emphasize the limits of imperial fraternity and the circulation of compatriots within imperial boundaries.[91] Workers' movements were one such example; others were health measures (closely linked to culture), rejection of Jews fleeing Russian pogroms (the unstated objective of the Aliens Act of 1905), and police efforts to repress socialists and anarchists.[92]

For the British, whose empire was one of specialness and who had little interest in proselytism, the notion of all situations being the same was nonsense. But for France during the Second Republic, the Second Empire, and especially the Third Republic, the problem was more complex and painful, as painful as the distance between the republican utopia and the prosaic reality of everyday life. The problem was this: How could France accommodate the enormous and excruciating variety of the empire within the unitary vocation of French republicanism? French jurists perfectly understood the problem; two of them, Joseph Barthélemy and Paul Duez, in what might be considered merely a witticism, said, "La France n'est ni un État unitaire, ni un État fédéral; elle est, à l'exemple de l'Angleterre, un État impérial."[93] It was a true assessment, not a critical one, a cold description of the interwar French empire. It also was a coherent reading of developments over recent decades, especially during the great expansion of the Third Republic. At a moment of worldwide imperial competition, that expansion could be described in genuinely French terms, which was why the two jurists said it was only fair that "nous rappelions l'existence de soixante millions de ressortissants français qui sont soumis, par le droit constitutionnel, à des règles spéciales."[94] And, they went on: "La France continentale est le domaine d'application de la constitution; les lois s'y appliquent automatiquement. Sur les parties extracontinentales, domine au contraire le décret. La France continentale est bâtie sur le mode libéral; la France extracontinentale sur le mode autoritaire."[95] There is no better expression of the paradoxical process that began years earlier with the counterrevolutionary stabilization of the early nineteenth century.

It was no surprise, then, that the republican regime installed with much uncertainty after the collapse of the Second Empire knew perfectly well what it was doing as far as the colonies were concerned.[96] It would continue the policy of stark differentiation between new and old colonies, the quintessential feature of the French colonial regime and its attention to revolutionary tradition. But in practice this clean division of republican citizenship was not all that tidy, for the reasons indicated by the jurists quoted above.[97] "Citizenship" did not mean the same thing in all places. And if citizenship could be qualified, it was especially qualified overseas, but not for openly racial reasons, which would have offended republican culture.[98] In this respect, the French behaved like everyone else. Racial and cultural distinctions were inherent and increasingly important in an imperial context where governmental solutions were sought and where colonial models were being stabilized in particular contexts, which were the only contexts that revealed the poisoned logic of specialness as part of the fiercely unitary political culture. Three situations stood out on the French imperial horizon. First was citizenship in the old colonies (the Antilles, Réunion, and the old Senegalese parishes), which had nothing to do with the metropolis, as we will see. Second was the amalgam of citizenship and a strict colonial regime in just one colony, which was the case of Senegal as a whole and Algeria, which are comparable cases but with differences. The third was the extension of the *régime d'indigénat* to the new colonies in the Pacific, Madagascar, and continental Africa, whose peoples were excluded from any form of assimilation at all. A fourth situation could be mentioned, which would be obviously indirect administrations, such as the protectorate of Tunis, and, with some exceptions, Indochina starting when Paul Doumer was governor general in the late nineteenth century.[99] The doctrine of *spécialité* in a culture defined by a strong unitary ethos allowed for the separation of conventional legislative activity from the president of the republic's prerogatives, which he inherited from the old Napoleonic formula of the *sénatus-consulte* of 1854. Legislative capacity was carefully removed from public debate and placed in the president's hands, while power was also concentrated in the executive and lower-level legislation and awarded to colonial governors, the classic model of all special regimes. The contradiction was pointed out by representatives from the colonies such as Alexandre Isaac, who represented Guadeloupe in the

National Assembly; it was only in 1933 with the *arrêt Maurel* that the high courts lost legislative power over the colonies.[100] From then on, their decisions could be appealed to the Council of State. It was not much, but it was something.

The development of the French empire can be seen as a palliative for the bitter defeat in 1871 at the hands of Prussia, another empire. Unlike the rivalry with Great Britain, which since the eighteenth century had taken place at sea, in America, or in India, rivalry with Prussia and the other German states played out on France's now northeast border, in Alsace-Lorraine.[101] The defeat and the loss of two provinces could be compensated in social and symbolic terms only with the possession that lay at the center of the emperor's nephew's neo-Napoleonic utopia: Algeria, where many Alsatians and Lorrainers immigrated after 1871.[102] Indeed, the three French departments created *ex novo* by the Second Republic became important assets for French republican patriotism and a major source of friction in the colony. This sharp contradiction between a political formula appropriate for republican times and the exclusion of everyone else (meaning non-French Algerians) continually reproduced the tension between the universalist ethos and its failure on the ground, setting off rejoinders throughout the empire.[103] Thus the law of specialness tried out in Algeria—not republican liberty—became universal. Of all the variations of specialness that Algeria was capable of putting into practice and then exporting to the rest of the empire, the Code de l'Indigénat was the most poisoned, the most laden with significance for the "incipient ethnicization" of self-understanding in the 1870s and 1880s.[104] While in the metropolis some were insisting that *jus soli* protected the "republican pact," to use Gérard Noiriel's apt expression, vis-à-vis immigration from the south and east, in the overseas colonies the process was moving in the opposite direction.[105] Legislative initiatives toward the end of the century further limited those born in the colonies under French sovereignty.[106] As always, Algeria blazed the trail. The idea was to favor naturalization (plus assimilation) of Italian and Spanish immigrants, compensating for lesser numbers of French immigrants.[107] Italians were predominant in Constantine, while Spaniards were the majority in Oran.[108] The system could be rationalized only by seeing the imperial nation as a whole, the sum of the increasingly solid community of citizens at home and the ladder of specialness outside. The resultant tension exported to the colony led to friction among the very republican citizens of the three departments and the majority of the population who could not be assimilated. The confluence of a pathetic concept of confessional identity in the framework of a dual legal system allowed for the integration of some and the exclusion of the majority. In European France, citizens were citizens (once the category reappeared with the Third Republic in 1880) not because they were chosen but because of their birth, never mind their religious beliefs or cultural particularities, even including their slow and partial adoption of the official language, which was still inconclusive at the end of the century. But in Algeria, which had been under French sovereignty since 1830, the only citizens born there were the sons of fathers or grandfathers born in metropolitan France. Therefore, in September 1897, all references to *jus soli* were eliminated from laws for the colony. Two objectives thus were attained at once: nationalization of European immigrants was favored, and any direct connection between birth in the colony and the rights of a French subject were eliminated. So 202,212 foreigners joined the 219,627 Frenchmen already living there, nearly doubling the total size of this bulwark against millions of Muslims, be they Arabs or Berbers.[109] This was not only the case in Algeria, of course. Noiriel pointed out that in the Indian enclaves French colonists also seized republican legislation and turned it to their own purposes. American historian Gary Wilder referred to the outcome as a "disjointed relationship among territory, people, and government."[110]

Such a situation was bound to have repercussions. Qualified citizenship according to criteria that differed from those of metropolitans was disturbing to the Algerians. There were three different sorts of political subjects: French citizens in the colony; European immigrants with regulated access to the laws of French citizens; and the rest, the vast majority, French subjects who could not attain the status of the other two groups because they were "Muslims."[111] The majority could not have any influence on the legislative process, limited as it was, given the rules of specialness. And the aggressive manner in which politically active citizens along the coast made their status clear to the rest was an eloquent statement of what was at stake.

None of this was happenstance. This great machine, the random and abusive penal code invented by the military during Thomas Robert Bugeaud's generation as the rational codification of repression suitable for an occupation army, not only remained in place but was exported throughout the new republican empire.[112] This would be reaffirmed four years later, in February 1875, when Algeria became a strictly civilian regime. It was then that the combination of colonists' aggressive republicanism, true republicans' presence in the Parisian government, and governor generals' complicity undid what was left of the old Napoleonic military approach (which had come back to life during the 1871 uprising led by Mohamed El-Mokrani), and relaunched the civilian regime of expropriation. In accordance with these developments, the Code de l'Indigénat was recodified in 1881, 1888, and again in 1890.[113] This transitory status was an undisguised way of silencing criticism of its degrading nature. Situations were considered exceptional, an elastic concept perfectly fit to a colonial reality steeped in violence. With one maneuver or another, the code survived until 1945, bringing about shameful and harsh laws not subject to appeal by the local population. According to historian Charles-Robert Ageron, there were tens of thousands of convictions under the code—30,837 in 1883; 23,312 in 1886; and 27,335 in 1887.[114] According to the *Journal officiel de l'Algérie*, cited by Olivier Le Cour Grandmaison, there were 40,641 from 1914 to 1926.[115]

The proven repressive efficacy of the code had another virtue in that it immediately distinguished genuine French subjects with rights (and, later on, new republican citizens) from those who were subjects and would remain subjects. Being a Muslim was considered impossible not only for religious reasons but also for broader cultural reasons ("n'a pas un sens purement confessionel . . .").[116] Therefore, some inhabitants of the country, the minorities, were subject to French criminal and civil laws, while everyone else—the overwhelming majority—was subject to an entirely different coercive regime, designed by the military. Differences among the communes (referred to in chapter 5) helped disguise the reality of these distinctions. Until World War I, this regime constituted "un pouvoir localement dictatoriale," in the words of Catherine Coquery-Vidrovich.[117] It was the tremendous sacrifice by Senegalese and Algerian soldiers during the world wars that forced French authorities to moderate the conceptual and legislative structure somewhat, substituting the meaningless *indigène* with "French Muslim," which was equally absurd.[118] The idea of an Algeria inhabited by Frenchmen *de souche européenne* (of European lineage) and others *de souche nord-africaine* still reflected colonial reality in the years after 1945.[119] It was obvious that the *régime de l'indigénat* would later be exported to places in need of a proven tool of submission, complete with legislative justification.[120] In some places, such as New Caledonia, it would become the centerpiece of the colonial structure; in others it was part of a constellation of modalities including indirect government, which was the case in Indochina, a purely political construction with highly diverse situations in the interior.[121] The brutal Algerian solution was France's contribution par excellence to colonial culture in the expanding world of liberal empires.

These classical colonial solutions unfolded in parallel with the bifurcation of French policy in the old colonies, where the massive presence of slavery made it difficult to accept giving emancipated slaves and their descendants the same rights as everyone else, including French citizenship. Martinique and Guadeloupe inevitably were in the center of that space, along with the Minor Antilles, Guyana, the old parishes of Senegal, Réunion Island, and the *comptoirs* in India.[122] The contrast between the harsh situation in other areas of the French empire and these enclaves was notable. The most important change in the old colonies was acceptance of representation, both internally and in the National Assembly; that is, equivalence, at least in theory, with colonists of French origin living in the three Algerian departments. It was in theory because in practice things were quite different: particular contexts determined the effective meaning of institutions, not the other way around. Decrees of September 1870 and February 1871 granted representation to the old colonies in the National Assembly; the two Antilles and Réunion were given one deputy, and both places were increased to two deputies in 1881, when Guyana, Senegal, India (Frenchmen plus Indian *renonçants* working for the administration), and Cochinchine (the part of the future Indochina with important agricultural interests) all were granted one deputy apiece as well. Each colony also was to elect one senator. The contrast with the new colonies, where the true essence of the expanding new French empire was on view, could not have been more clear.

Specialness meant that local representation in the new colonies would always take place under the watchful eye of the governor general, a key personage in each of the possessions. In this respect, the new colonies were different from the rest only in degree, given that in both the governor general had far more powers than a prefect in France.[123] This ambiguity between old and new, and between form and reality, is what gave rise to the idea of assimilation, an ideology more characteristic of special regimes in empires with liberal-representative institutions than of French universalists, as the liberal empires were convinced that metropolitan moral superiority placed colonists on a road to progress that the metropolis would administer and guide. This model had originated much earlier, starting with the Directory constitution and Boissy d'Anglas's colonial antislavery, followed by emancipation and citizenship in 1848. Assimilation became the official doctrine in 1890, and until Aimé Césaire raised the Antilles' demand for departmentalization before the National Assembly in 1946 effective reforms were not really faced.[124] As long as those possessions were not departments, the laws their representatives voted on in the National Assembly and the Senate did not apply to them, and they had no right to comment on the laws that the executive sent to the governors, who had not been elected by those they administered.[125]

This contradiction between the alleged desire for complete assimilation and its negation in practice can be explained by going back to 1848, when the recently freed slaves were granted citizenship. Their representation was reluctantly admitted, though it was assumed that that right would not actually be exercised except by the stratum of mulattos who had played a major role during the Revolution and continued to do so. The goal was realized only in part. Some descendants of slaves freed before 1848, along with at least one freed slave (Louisy Mathieu) entered the National Assembly thanks to the intervention of Victor Schoelcher during the life-or-death fight over the future of the postslavery plantations.[126] Just in case, the metropolis, mindful that the British example should not be followed, took measures to control from above the democratization taking place below.

Changes in republican administration and the Second Empire halted all attempts at effective assimilation where former slaves had won universal citizenship to compensate for the reinstatement of slavery in 1802 but not the right to be incorporated into French political life. That possibility would not be raised again until Louis-Napoleon's regime fell, after Prussia defeated France. As with French colonists in Algeria, the new moderate republican regime tried to raise French national pride again, both within and outside metropolitan borders. In the case of the old colonies, attempts were made to include representational rights for nondepartmental colonies, making them susceptible to special legislation and administration. In 1870 universal masculine suffrage was reestablished; in 1875 colonies won the right to representation locally and in the National Assembly; and in 1882 and 1884 French municipal laws were extended to the colonies. As the rise of new social groups appeared unstoppable, there were some who suggested putting an end to the old idea of parliamentary representation by colonial interests. It was Schoelcher, the venerable Alsatian, who ensured that colonists would not be frustrated once again. Reacting to the increasing influence of middle-class and mulatto republicanism, European owners in the islands, known as *bekés*, began flirting with monarchic legitimism and demands for colonial autonomy aimed not at defending the colonies' interests, but rather, at isolating them from the metropolitan republican dynamic. As one might expect, the situation varied from place to place. In Martinique and Guadeloupe, the middle class of color lost no time at all in taking over local institutions and legislative chambers, led by politicians such as Émile Isaac and Gaston Gerville-Réache, who moved in radical circles and were convinced of the virtues of assimilation.[127] Isaac criticized the custom of legislating from above according to the regime of *spécialité*, and he refuted criticism of universal citizenship.[128] In the 1890s there was fierce competition between republican mulattos and the so-called *usinier* party, comprising colonists and landowners of European origin.[129] Politics in the Antilles was changing; transformations in the sugar industry, where large metropolitan importers played a leading role, had put an end to the idea that whites would be replaced by blacks and mulattos, and educated whites would soon be a very small minority.[130] Instead, a new period began in which colonists and their allies in France discovered they could reach agreements with the rising mulatto bourgeoisie. But even then, the enmity that had lain over the French Antilles since 1848 never disappeared. The old *affranchis*, the freedmen and their descendants, the beneficiaries of homeopathic doses of republican progress, constituted the flip side of the extremism of many colonists and rich mulattos, as would be especially clear during the Pétain years.[131] In Guadeloupe in around 1898, some colonists supported a Cuban-style solution (at least, that is what they thought it was) to cast off metropolitan rule and seek the aid of the United States.[132] They wanted to wipe out the effects of late-century republicanism, mulatto reformism, and labor militancy by agricultural workers. It was no utopia; indeed, in Guyana, Indians from the subcontinent and descendants of the great communities of runaway slaves (called *noirs marrons*) were defined as primitives and radically excluded from citizenship. Once the planters left, the Creole-mulatto alliance took control of the parliament, retaining those exclusions and reaching pacts with leading metropolitan interests.[133] In Réunion, social emancipation of slaves was halted altogether by colonists in 1794 and became a mere legal modification in 1848–51 while organized violence was unleashed on the supposedly newly freed slaves; despite the fact that the Third Republic granted the emancipated population the right to vote, the violence did not cease.[134] On the contrary, new targets were found among those who had emigrated from the African continent, known pejoratively as *cafres*, and Asian immigrants.

Taken together, all these situations reveal the complexity of the combination of assimilation and specialness. In some places, such as Martinique, Guadeloupe, and Guyana, mulatto republicans could rise amid politics barely supportive of social advantages for the *affranchis*, whose status everywhere was weakened by the presence of African or Asian laborers who deserved no social advantages whatsoever. It was, to quote Nelly Schmidt, a "démocratie de façade."[135] And it was happening as the sugar industry was undergoing rapid transformation, with sugar beet interests booming in the metropolis and throughout Europe. Republican social policies inspired by Jules Ferry (who had sent the Antilles Creoles packing to the margins of the system) and certain welfare measures began being felt only in the 1930s.

The Tortuous Course of the Color Line

In the preceding pages I attempted to demonstrate that it makes little sense to analyze changes in imperial policy solely through the ideas related to those policies, though ideas are, of course, important and revelatory regarding context and they undergo modifications as they are transformed into action. Two ideas associated with imperial changes at the turn of the century are particularly significant: the notion of one people's superiority over another, the corollary of the idea that humanity is divided into groups with distinct hereditary qualities; and, second, the value assigned to the very idea of empire, the assertion of one social group or leader over another, or one nation over the rest.[136] However, I have also tried to make clear that it is not advisable to separate changes in imperial culture from the practice of governing colonies and possessions different from one's own society, be they close or far away. Those ideas and perceptions, and the debates they engender, take shape and develop in the framework of rising or falling imperial formations, both large and small. As they take shape they influence institutional and administrative developments and those responsible for those developments. It is then that the accentuated importance of ideas regarding racial superiority and the inevitability of imperial hegemony intersect with imperatives that emerge from economic changes or from the equally important rise of nations and nationalism. The best historiographic model is therefore one that can account for the greatest number of variables and consider them simultaneously for the greatest possible number of cases.

I have focused on empires created by societies that were deeply affected by the 1780–1830 revolutionary cycle. The exercise of rights and their inextricable connection to collective and individual identity in the context of contemporary political struggles gave rise to diverse cultural approaches that justified or lent coherence to the administration of rights as factors of inclusion or exclusion. Here lay the tension between the old paternalist, corporative, protective attitude to subjects and the definition of the individual as the key figure in liberal society. These cultural approaches affected not only the white-black color line, though that was the densest and most important of such divisions. Rather, they affected all cultural identities at stake, whether or not they were based on biological (i.e., "racial") principles, whatever that might mean. Some examples mentioned in previous chapters show the ubiquity of the correlation between identification through certain characteristics and one's position on the ladder of rights, representation, and citizenship in the historical terms in which these capacities were defined. These include the debate regarding free people of color during the Cortes of Cádiz and the writing of Spain's first liberal constitution; the case of Canadians and Irish Catholics during the stabilization of the Second British Empire; French disquisitions concerning the nature of the subject population in Algeria leading to the separation of Arab Muslims, Kabylia Berbers, and Jews; and the U.S. rule for other "races" after 1898 in the Pacific and the Philippines, following decades of racial experiments in the continental United States.[137] Beyond these examples, the enormous weight of race in German Cameroon and the genocide of the Herero and Nama peoples,[138] comparable with that of the American Indians on the Great Plains, coincided with intense debates regarding the Polish peasantry of Eastern Prussia, who were described crudely and pejoratively, sometimes even as "blacks."[139] In addition, we have the endless European imagination about the nature of the recently discovered Australian Aborigines, the Maori, Hawaiians, and the Filipino Moro people.[140]

Many years ago, Douglas Lorimer eloquently noted that British ethnocentric attitudes changed in the second half of the nineteenth century not because of new biological ideas but because of the growing frequency and intensity of conflicts between Europeans and Africans or their descendants in other continents.[141] Catherine Hall reached similar conclusions.[142] An understanding of the modulations among ethnocentrism, racialism, and strict biological racism is essential for our historical analysis because it reveals the close connection between the white European world and the black African or African-American world as a highly variable and varied substrate of derogative stereotypes and hierarchical condescension that internal and external colonialism created in the modern and contemporary world.[143] In this regard, it is clear that slavery's continued existence along with its prolongation under rubrics of "contract labor" help to explain the survival of a certain paradox. Slavery's victims were culturally degraded in two ways, first with disdain and then with paternalist or Christian humanitarianism.[144] Abolitionism was the most striking of these positions somewhere between "conscience" and "prudence," in the dichotomy established by the lawyer James Stephen, father of the abolitionist and head of the Colonial Office, Sir James Stephen with regard to the destiny of those societies suffering from forced emigration.[145] But in another regard, slavery's long survival and its frequent transformation into systems of strict labor control delayed the need for more explicit racial theories.[146] And given that the immense universe of slavery coexisted with the ideological hegemony of Christian unigenesis, transformation of European ethnocentrism into a more culturally informed racialism took time.[147] Derogative stereotypes became more consistent once slavery and abolition reached a point of crisis that penetrated into Africa beyond the traffic itself. It was then that the complementary ideas of the innate inferiority of the "dark races" and "blacks" and the innate superiority of "whites," "Aryans," or "Europeans" emerged simultaneously.[148] Given that this intellectual and psychological shift coincided with the greatest degree of technological and economic distance between European societies (or those with European origins) and the rest of the world, such a perception appeared entirely justified.

But, to return to what I said earlier, and in line with Burbank and Cooper's observations, even here it was not the distillation of an inherited culture of difference, this notion of biologically based race, that led to the expansion of white supremacy throughout European and non-European imperial complexes.[149] That is, the elaboration of a racialist or explicitly racist culture was not sufficiently homogeneous, divided as it was between clearly racial motivations and the modernized continuity of a Eurocentric paternalism whose roots went back to the eighteenth century.[150] Nor was it solid enough to provide the basis for governmental and imperial policies on the ground.[151] If indeed there was a *primum mobile* in imperial expansion, it lay in the complexities of imperial government, in the ways in which a select group of societies ruled millions of human beings who were regarded as different.

Conclusion

The Atlantic crisis of 1780 to 1830 paved the way for the decolonization of much of the colonial world that European countries had built starting in the sixteenth century. This era saw the birth of republics in the former Spanish America, the monarchic empire of Brazil, the Republic of Haiti in 1804, the independence of the Dominican Republic in 1821 (and again in 1844), and, of course, the emergence of the United States. But despite this cycle of destruction and reconstruction, the old empires remained alive in the American Atlantic: Spain still had possessions in the Antilles; Portugal provided Brazil with members of its own royal dynasty until Brazil became a republic in 1889; France had important outposts in the Caribbean, as well as Guyana; as did Britain, which also had the future Canadian Federation, with its French imperial leftovers, British emigrants, and loyalists from the former Thirteen Colonies. America was no longer an entirely colonized continent, that is, a consortium of European emigrants and imperial administrators ruling over Amerindians and/or slaves. From 1776 to 1824, new nations emerged from the ashes of the old monarchic empires that collapsed at the turn of the century, victims of interimperial wars and pressure from the Creole worlds they had established in the seventeenth century. At the same time, the consolidation of the East India Company in Bengal, Britain's seizure of the Cape Colony, its takeover of Dutch Java in 1811–15, and the founding of Singapore in 1818 signaled the definitive end of the era of territorial empires in the Atlantic with commerce engineered through entrepôts, ports, or factories.

But the imperial dimension was not replaced by simple colonial continuity in Jamaica, Ontario, Québec, or Cuba; nor did the monarchic empires collapse without leaving heirs. It is never that simple. Nineteenth-century American history is one of nations and empires but also of uninterruptedness, of many social institutions passed down by old-regime rulers through the turn of the century. Some of the newly independent nations that emerged from the crisis must be seen as continuations of the deep logic of monarchic empires. This continuity embodied many factors: the invocation of sovereignty, social institutions such as slavery, the subordinate position (or even elimination) of indigenous peoples, and rivalries with neighboring political entities. Both British North America and the United States bore signs of rupture and continuity with the British empire. So did the United States of Mexico and the Brazilian monarchy. If, instead of considering only the classic paradigm of national history, we take a more realistic approach, seeing these American revolutions as authentic civil wars fought over who would govern which territory and population and within which institutional framework, then matters settle into quite a different pattern.

The old empires did not succumb with the Atlantic crisis. Rather, they were transformed, and in the process they acquired a critical place in world development that they did not have earlier. It is one thing to write about expansion, which, whether led by Scandinavians or Iberians, started in the sixteenth century to change social and political worlds throughout Europe, Africa, and the American Atlantic (extending to India, Southeast Asia, and the Philippines); it is quite another to conclude that these countries ruled the world. The secular itinerary of this book traces the transformation that allowed the Atlantic crisis to be the starting point for the world that the empires at the turn of the century divided up as they wished, forever and ever. It is obvious that the heart of this metamorphosis lies in French and British recovery after both nations first lost in America and then fought each other until June 1815. But it would be a mistake to limit our analysis to these two cases, the world's greatest empires before 1945. Throughout the nineteenth century there were other examples deserving of study: Meiji Japan, the Qing dynasty in China, the Ottomans and later the Turkish republic of Mustafa Kemal Atatürk, the so-called central European empires, and tsarist Russia were all expanding and developing, modifying their national identities and their relationships with other societies and with the reborn empires rising from the ashes.

The late-eighteenth-century crisis of the Atlantic imperial monarchies must not be seen as simply the first wave of modern decolonization. It was but one aspect of a far greater change: a global crisis on both sides of an imperial divide, a crisis between the emerging modern state—with its growing armies, bureaucracies, and sophisticated tax policies—and the identity of growing political communities on both sides of the Atlantic, far from the political center.[1] In this regard, the idea of absolutism, which accurately reflects the aggressive side of a weak monarchic state, confuses things more than it clarifies the nature of the conflicts we are addressing. The crisis in relations between society and state was resolved through calls for a more transparent definition of community rights, for giving new meaning to political representation, and, as a result, the determination of who was appropriate to embody that representation. Opposition to this new pact led to rupture or reform, both of which were emergent expressions of a new political culture. And that choice between reform or revolution took shape within the framework of the old imperial structure and in the national projects that emerged from the crisis. The political violence or tension that began in Philadelphia and Boston was echoed in Paris and London, and then in Saint-Domingue, Caracas, Mexico City, Rio de Janeiro, and São Paulo.[2] We can state two conclusions at this point. First, that revolution can happen on the margins of empire, in places where secession or independence in itself marked the triumph of the new over the old, but it is the manifestation of a general crisis. And second, following from this, that the political spaces that took shape starting in the sixteenth century must be thought of as a whole. It is impossible to properly comprehend the change by looking at just one of the parts, especially as the demands of the fiscal-military state on corporations, families, workers, and people everywhere were so enormous.

One of the greatest paradoxes of this cycle of destruction and reconstruction is the ambiguous outcome of the Atlantic revolutions. The expansive, nonrevolutionary transfiguration of the British empire following Pitt's fiscal policy, political reforms opening the state to Catholics and Nonconformists and reorganization of the military under the Wellesley brothers, the wars of restoration in Spain and Portugal (and the monarchy's introduction into Brazil), the Bourbon and Orleanist restorations in France, the Orange-Nassau reign in conservative Holland, and the rise of the Hohenzollern in Prussia—all would appear to indicate a step backward in terms of revolutionary change. But that was far from being the case. Successive episodes of liberal revolution in Europe and America and the string of political reforms in the 1830s and 1840s clearly reflect not the continuation of the Old Regime, as was once thought, but the constant shifting away of its institutional and legitimizing forms and their relentless replacement by new forms better suited to liberal times, be they revolutionary or reformist.

This is the context in which to situate the logic of imperial reconstruction and its constant expansion into other worlds. The new empires absorbed the era's political and social changes within themselves. After a revolutionary crisis that dissolved the very idea of center and periphery, throughout a century or more they worked to determine who should be the beneficiaries of the imperial order.[3] This task, the basis for successive decolonization crises, found a logical solution in the neat Napoleonic distinction between the space of the nation and the space under its sovereignty, the idea of *spécialité*. The former is the nation of citizens, the civic community; the latter is a foggy landscape inhabited by prepolitical subjects or by alienated slaves entirely incapable of demanding the rights that the gospel of equality had universalized. This thrust toward political equality, the greatest ideological force of the French Revolution, was not an aspiration arising from any social or philanthropic utopia. It was bluntly expressed in what I have called the imperial constitutions, which attempted, for just one moment, to convert French, Spanish, or British monarchic empires into whole nations that embraced nationals in both hemispheres. With power relations pushed to their absolute limit, the First Consul demonstrated his ability to brilliantly synthesize the political moment, eliminating lofty universalist aspirations with one fell swoop of a pen.

But it was not just France that took its imperial reconstruction down this road. The impossibility of equality in colonies where slavery and social oppression had created an entirely different scheme of things from the metropolis led to a two-pronged process. First, it led to the development of "dual constitutions" in countries that had both a liberal regime (constitutional framework and civil society) and colonies, and we have seen that the arbitrary and discretional rules of *spécialité* in these colonies cannot necessarily be considered constitutional. In any case, and using the expression in a metaphoric sense, the unwritten constitution of these countries provided for both developments in the long run. Here we refer not just to laws but also to questions of identity and culture, social interaction, and to a vision of how people should be governed.

Second, we must consider the enormous historical relevance of this process. While seventeenth- and eighteenth-century empires can be defined as "monarchic empires"—understanding monarchy here to be the sum of royal authority and sovereignty arising from dynastic and historical legitimacy, an institutional tradition including corporative representation and ceaselessly ambitious administrative, fiscal, and military authority— then those of the nineteenth century must be called "imperial nations," because the legitimacy justifying dominion over other worlds lay in the nation and in the definition of who formed part of it and who, on the contrary, was merely a subject and therefore liable to other rules. This legacy of ideas, culture, and sentiments distinguishing among human beings was not situated in a vacuum; rather, it was clearly part of the practice of government in particular places and in the general ethos permeating the entire imperial nation. It is true that the nation developed alongside the construction of empire (or, to be more exact, alongside reconstruction of old empires into something different), but the outcome was by no means arbitrary. The nation plus the empire ruled by special laws is the "imperial nation." Without the discursive and moral weight of the nation of equals, both in fact and potentially, and of a community of "citizens" with rights and obligations (insofar as they are subjects by definition, regardless of the democratic language in each particular place), rules of specialness are meaningless, be they relatively mild or genocidal.[4]

All the great European countries shaken by the revolutionary experience of 1780–1830 were building nations and empires at the same time. What stands out about the nineteenth century is that the national project could not restrict itself to the confines of Europe. It traveled with the individual, with the liberal and democratic universalism inherent to the revolutions of the day. The transformation of monarchic-aristocratic empires into imperial nations was the result of two simultaneous processes. The first was the emergence of disperse fragments of the nation in imperial spaces; we have discussed the examples of Canada, Australia, and New Zealand (and later on the Cape Colony and southern Africa), and the three French departments in Algeria after 1848, and Cuba and Puerto Rico from 1810 to 1898 could also be mentioned in this context. The second process is less obvious, though equally important: the imperial nation itself incarnates and shapes the national project, gives it its essential culture and moral force. Here the best example of an imperial nation is, perhaps, the republican United States. It is an exemplary case in that this powerful nation of citizens immediately established special laws to protect slavery and to exclude (and expropriate) the inhabitants of the interior. Slaves (and their descendants) and American Indians would be assigned a specific space on the margins, subordinate to the national community. Thus, the moral distance of positive specialness protected the norm of republican equality within the country's European borders. Constitutional distinctions (this constitution was both imperial and special) among states, territories, and Indian Country express the challenge of establishing different norms in just one sovereign space, but it was the particular situations, as always, that gave content and character to the solutions, from Oklahoma to Louisiana, from Hawaii to the Philippines. Walter LaFeber went back to the American Civil War to find the origins of the U.S. imperial vocation, but I am suggesting (though without denying that a shift did take place after the war) that one has to go back even further.[5]

We have seen that the formulation of nation and specialness dictated the reconstruction of the Atlantic empires and later became a global phenomenon. This was not merely a quantitative expansion in terms of number and breadth. Dominion in new contexts where long-standing shared ideas and experiences of the Atlantic had little or no meaning brought about increased autocratic, monarchic, or republican power through both legislation and political discretion. David Cannadine, writing about pomp in the Raj, called this conglomerate of situations and status "Ornamentalism," and it was a crucial factor in the careers of military school graduates (Sandhurst, Saint-Cyr, and West Point were all established in 1802). Generations of sons of the Georgian and Victorian establishment went overseas to follow rewarding careers and accumulate capital, in a manner similar to the sons of merchants, factory owners, and bankers back home.[6] But it is important to emphasize that these grand figures were not alone; the high civil administration was critical for untying the knots as liberal empires were constructed.[7] The case of Great Britain is exemplary, a far cry from its alleged improvisation and disorderliness in solving large imperial problems. James and John Stuart Mill, James Stephen, Herman Merivale, and George Cornewall Lewis were all administrators with broad political vision, and so too were such decision-makers as the brothers Wellesley, Charles and Henry Grey, and William Gladstone. They were systematic and rigorous, aware of their national, political, and juridical traditions and at the same time willing to undertake reforms if the empire so required. They also were aware of the close connections between what they were doing in the empire and what was happening (or not) at home. Networks and the machinery of power in the imperial nation could be both variable and constant, for deep-seated reasons as well as for more contingent ones such as the press, communications, and demographic shifts. It would seem crucial that a more exhaustive study be undertaken of the transfer of social and protective legislation concerning peoples and the environment, because that is where we see mature imperialism's shift into the twentieth century: the reinforcement and extension of the state as manifested in continental socialism and reformist liberalism, British liberalism with social undertones (such as the so-called Lib-Labs), and Theodore Roosevelt's "civil nationalism."

If we accept this overall description, there remains one difficult issue to unravel. One of the problems in describing imperial development in Asia is that Europeans there found themselves surrounded by complex societies with established and solid hierarchies. In his effort to understand the sub-continent, Edmund Burke recognized the radical novelty of the situation there. Conversely, societies dominated by Europeans in the Atlantic either were entirely different or had lost their true complexity as they were decimated. Here it is essential to think in anthropological terms about these societies' size, shape, and reproduction, starting at the beginning with Spain's almost absolute destruction of indigenous societies in America in the sixteenth century, the wreckage of their hierarchies, and the extermination of their peoples, be it through intentional genocide (uncontrolled labor) or the transmission of disease. What followed was necessarily a new society, a dual society of Spanish colonists and subjected Indians and African slaves and their descendants. A similar approach should be taken when confronting the history of societies based on the labor of displaced African slaves. In those entirely new societies, forged in the vacuum left by indigenous peoples, the European factor was not superimposed, it was constitutive. Thus, the guilt that was felt, and sometimes expressed, by Spanish Catholics in the sixteenth century is perfectly echoed in abolitionist Protestants' bad conscience at the end of the eighteenth century. Domination over societies with complex social and cultural organizations, starting with Britain's arrival in Bengal and the French fiasco in Egypt, decisively changed the rules of empire and of colonization. Collaboration and parallel evolution made sense when thinking about those sorts of societies, in contrast to the others.[8]

Going back to the main argument of this conclusion, it is clear that the imperial nation took shape in the Atlantic, a common ground arising in past centuries, and was then exported to and developed, with uneven results, in the rest of the world, starting with India and then Asia, Oceania, and Africa.[9] On the way, liberal empires bumped into other empires that were less transparent, that for many years navigated between traditional monarchic continuity, vaguely liberal reforms, or autocracy that denied both these options. The so-called central empires of Prussia and the Austrian Habsburgs, along with the Romanov and Ottoman empires until 1918, were of a different sort, which cannot be explored here, and the same is true for China and Japan. It is important to elucidate the depth and form with which those empires that did not undergo the revolutionary crisis of 1780–1830 assimilated or imitated the central historical experiences of the age—those of the national, consensual, and expansive empires, in other words, the imperial nations. Once again, partial comparisons of political reforms (limited suffrage, vaguely independent judiciaries, cultural and intellectual circulation) will not suffice.[10] Rather, the components must be analyzed organically. For example, one must consider the German Reich's admiration for imperial France even after the 1870 defeat at Sedan, China's and Japan's national assimilation, and the Russian empire's colonial efforts in the Caucasus and vis-à-vis the British in Central Asia (the Great Game).[11] If conceptual formulas (the empirical foundation of social theory) are to make any sense, they cannot be mere taxonomies or tools for establishing superficial parallels. On the contrary, by further understanding a model, we can better see what we know, or don't know, about other models that we believe or intuit are different. If anything is clear in this game of mirrors, it is that we can move forward only on the basis of solid comparisons corroborated through case studies.

It would be an absurd exercise in formalism to debate whether the nation or the empire was the origin of historical transformation in this century of imperial destruction and construction. The period we are studying was highlighted by ideas of political and social rights and political equality, the greatest ideological legacy of the turbulence of 1780–1830.[12] In the passage from historical nation to modern nation, the identity of the political subject was defined in terms of the culture of individuals and rights. While, in the Old Regime national identity was corporatively acquired through a group, city, profession, loyalty to the crown, or opposition to rivals over territory or in warfare, contemporary societies forged consensus on other platforms.[13] The revolutions divided European societies to their very roots, and they did the same in societies established on other continents. That schism gave birth to the politicization of the individual, who went from being a subject with rights to a citizen-elector with obligations, the protagonist of the postrevolutionary world in the aggregate we know as national sovereignty.[14] The fringes of the political spectrum have always nurtured the notion of contemporary politics as ideological conflict and latent civil war, using that as a justification for contemporary dictatorship. But the same notion can also lead to interrelationships among political equality, national belonging, and social reform, the palliative with which to construct consensus in splintered societies.[15] Nothing indicated that the old monarchic states would become national projects. Indeed, as we said at the start, internal and colonial differences could just as easily have led to breakup as to unitary transformation. Progressive socialization of political action, an outcome of the enormous liberation that the revolutionary cycle embodied, lay at the heart of national identification. Every reference bestowing meaning onto the individual in a nation—symbols, language, rituals—came into play during the course of establishing and consolidating, reaffirming and channeling the modern nation. Sometimes the result was contradictory. Thus, as mobilization and socialization in cultural and symbolic terrain grew in importance as means for ensuring individuals' participation in the nation, competing or complementary projects coexisted in the grand national states, or in the imperial nations, if that was the case. So the focus on grand imperial structures that configured the world order must not blind us to internal fissures and the ambiguities of national construction. Some years ago I referred to mid-nineteenth-century Catalonian regional patriotism as "double patriotism," a particular embodiment of Spanish nationalism in a regional context of enormous industrial violence.[16] Today, when I consider the patriotism of the U.S. South; the "structure of feelings" in the English Midlands and that region's moral distance from London, as remarked by Catherine Hall with regard to abolitionism; the particularities of French patriotism in the Antilles or in Algeria, the antechamber of French anti-Semitism; or Francophone Canadian patriotism, I am comforted to see that this complementariness, these transitive forms between particular and general patriotism that cause such problems in the writing of conventional national histories, were the norm in so many places.[17] The imperial framework offers a perspective with which to better understand the *Grande Nation* as well as the *pétites patries*.[18] The Romanovs, Hohenzollerns, and Habsburgs also learned this strange combination of empire, nationalism, and colonialism and put it to use in their empires on the margins, populated with powerful (or threatened) internal minorities with multiple alternatives to dynastic and imperial patriotism.[19]

The complexities of national construction are the inverse of identifications within the imperial framework.[20] A description of what united nationals within metropolitan space inevitably led to a description of what separated them from those living in the empire. This distance was felt from the very start, and it only grew. In short, the modern nation—and even more so the imperial nation, with its mandate to resolve the crisis of the monarchic empire—inherited the mission of governing a world of unequals and strangers and, as a result, a sense of civilizing superiority.[21] This superiority was not a monopoly in the hands of Europeans; Creole elites, cut off from the Atlantic revolutions, hastened to establish new forms of domination in their decolonized sovereign spaces. Jefferson's emphatic "We shall all be Americans" brought few if any changes to the lives of Indians, slaves, and their descendants. The imperial nation is not a European artifact but, by definition, a transcontinental one, the path along which flowed all the ideas about how to organize the world. What happened next was the subject of chapters 8 and 9. The gradual development of national identity, on the one hand, and on the other the end of slavery, an institution that for decades had tautologically abolished the identity of its victims, together provided the context for the definition of hierarchical distinctions among individuals that would begin taking shape only at the end of the eighteenth century.[22] The decline of Christian monogenesis, the abandonment of Scottish theories of civilization in stages, the notion of people climbing social ladders as they learned more, and the contributions of biology and social Darwinism would do the rest.[23] Biological racism, fear, and denigration of mixed-bloods obviously were not confined to dealings with extra-European societies, though that is where the ground was most fertile for prejudiced comparisons.[24] In another tautology, societies under colonial rule were described and thought of as prepolitical precisely because they needed to be governed by others, and they needed to be governed by others because they were incapable of choosing their own path, a cultural construct that was as false as it was entirely paternalistic. If Atlantic colonial societies in the late eighteenth century rebelled against a colonial destiny forged centuries earlier, colonial violence during the great imperial moment demonstrated without a doubt that the construct was a description of the world fabricated by and for themselves, *pro domo sua*, and that it would be challenged. The power of the nation and the ceaseless negotiations and definitions of special norms permitting some to rise, albeit supervised, while the rest remained at a distance from political and social rights marked the one hundred years of imperial transformation described in this book. The system and its conceptions were acceptable to those who relied on this disjointed secular culture to rule; but for millions of human beings condemned to suffer their consequences, they were not only unacceptable, they were unbearable.

Introduction

1. On the notion of natural rights, see Anthony Pagden, "Human Rights, Natural Rights, and Europe's Imperial Legacy," *Political Theory* 31, no. 2 (2003): 171–99. Pagden offers an insufficient description of its abrupt end, in my opinion.

2. Helmut G. Koenigsberger, *Politicians and Virtuosi: Essays in Early Modern History* (London: Hambledon Press, 1986); John H. Elliott, "A Europe of Composite Monarchies," in *Spain, Europe and the Wider World, 1500–1800* (New Haven, CT: Yale University Press, 2009), 3–25.

3. John Brewer, *The Sinews of Power: War, Money, and the English State, 1688–1783* (London: Unwin Hynman, 1989).

4. David Nirenberg, *Anti-Judaism: The Western Tradition* (New York: W. W. Norton, 2013), 364–65.

5. Christopher A. Bayly, *Recovering Liberties: Indian Thought in the Age of Liberalism and Empire* (Cambridge: Cambridge University Press, 2011).

6. James H. Kettner, *The Development of American Citizenship, 1608–1870* (Chapel Hill: University of North Carolina Press, 1978).

7. For Gallagher and Robinson's theses, along with the subsequent debate, see William Roger Louis, ed., *Imperialism: The Robinson and Gallagher Controversy* (New York: New Viewpoints, 1976). For recent contributions see Christopher A. Bayly, *The Birth of the Modern World, 1780–1914* (Oxford: Blackwell, 2004); Jane Burbank and Frederick Cooper, *Empires in World History: Power and the Politics of Difference* (Princeton, NJ: Princeton University Press, 2010).

8. Bartolomé Clavero, *El orden de los poderes: Historias constituyentes de la Trinidad Constitucional* (Madrid, Editorial Trotta, 2007); Horst Dippel, *Constitucionalismo moderno* (Madrid: Marcial Pons, 2009).

9. Lynn Hunt, *Inventing Human Rights: A History* (New York: W. W. Norton, 2007), 147.

10. John Robertson, "Union, State and Empire: The Britain of 1707 in Its European Setting," in *An Imperial State at War: Britain from 1689 to 1815*, ed. Lawrence Stone (Abingdon: Routledge, 1999), 224–57.

11. On the British example, see John Benyon, "Overlords of Empire? British 'Proconsular Imperialism' in Comparative Perspective," *Journal of Imperial and Commonwealth History* 19, no. 2 (1991): 164–202. On Spain, see chapter 2 of my *Colonias para después de un imperio* (Barcelona: Edicions Bellaterra, 2005), 183–326.

12. Jean-Luc Chappey et al., *Pour quoi faire la Révolution* (Marseille: Éditions Agone, 2012).

13. Peter H. Schuck and Rogers M. Smith, *Citizenship without Consent: Illegal Aliens in the American Polity* (New Haven, CT: Yale University Press, 1985).

14. Philip Buckner and R. Douglas Francis, eds., *Rediscovering the British World* (Calgary: Calgary University Press, 2005).

Chapter 1. The Fall of Monarchic Empires

1. Anthony Pagden, "Human Rights, Natural Rights, and Europe's Imperial Legacy," *Political Theory* 31, no. 2 (2003): 171–99.

2. On this kind of patrimonial monarchy, see Helmut G. Koenigsberger, *The Practice of Empire: The Government of Sicily under Philip II of Spain* (New York: Rinehart & Holt, 1968) [1st ed. 1951]; John H. Elliott, "A Europe of Composite Monarchies," in *Spain, Europe and the Wider World, 1500–1800* (New Haven, CT: Yale University Press, 2009), 3–25.

3. See Christopher A. Bayly, *Recovering Liberties: Indian Thought in the Age of Liberalism and Empire* (Cambridge: Cambridge University Press, 2011).

4. Steven Pincus, "Conclusion: New Approaches to Early Modern Representation," in *Realities of Representation: State Building in Early Modern Europe and European America*, ed. Maija Jansson (Houndmills: Palgrave Macmillan, 2007), 207–8.

5. Peter H. Schuck and Rogers M. Smith, *Citizenship without Consent: Illegal Aliens in the American Polity* (New Haven, CT: Yale University Press, 1985), 9–41.

6. Some of the limits of social and political integration are explored in Saliha Belmessous, "Assimilation in Early Modern French America," in *Assimilation and Empire: Uniformity in French and British Colonies, 1541–1954* (Oxford: Oxford University Press, 2013), 16–58.

7. For the Anglo-British case, see Christopher L. Tomlins, *Freedom Bound: Law, Labor, and Civic Identity in Colonizing English America, 1580–1865* (Cambridge: Cambridge University Press, 2010).

8. Woodrow Borah, "Representative Institutions in the Spanish Empire in the Sixteenth Century," *The Americas* 12 (1956): 246–57; on the Cortes in Santo Domingo in 1518, see Manuel Giménez Fernández, *Bartolomé de las Casas. II: Capellán de S.M. Carlos I. Poblador de Cumaná (1517–1523)* (Madrid: CSIC, 1984), 113–67 [1st ed. 1960].

9. John H. Elliott, *Empires of the Atlantic World: Britain and Spain in America, 1492–1830* (New Haven, CT: Yale University Press, 2006), 119. On the Portuguese institutional framework, see Charles R. Boxer, *The Portuguese Seaborne Empire, 1415–1825* (London: Hutchinson, 1969), 273–74; John Russell-Wood, "Patterns of Settlement in the Portuguese Empire, 1400–1800," in *Portuguese Oceanic Expansion, 1400–1800*, ed. Francisco Bethencourt and Diogo Ramada Couto (Cambridge: Cambridge University Press, 2007), 221.

10. Michael Braddick, *State Formation in Early Modern England, c. 1550–1700* (Cambridge: Cambridge University Press, 2000), 404.

11. Ian K. Steele, "The British Parliament and the Atlantic Colonies to 1760: New Approaches to Enduring Questions," *Parliamentary History* 14, no. 1 (1995): 29–46.

12. Joanna Innes, *Inferior Politics: Social Problems and Social Policies in Eighteenth-Century Britain* (Oxford: Oxford University Press, 2009), 51.

13. John Brewer, *The Sinews of Power: War, Money, and the English State, 1688–1783* (London: Unwin Hynman, 1989); P. G. M. Dickson, *The Financial Revolution in England: A Study in the Development of Public Credit, 1688–1756* (London: Macmillan, 1967); Jan Glete, *War and the State in Early Modern Europe: Spain, the Dutch Republic and Sweden as Fiscal-Military States, 1500–1660* (London: Routledge, 2002).

14. Lawrence Stone, ed., *An Imperial State at War: Britain from 1689 to 1815* (London: Routledge, 1994).

15. Nicholas Canny and Anthony Pagden, eds., *Colonial Identity in the Atlantic World, 1500–1800* (Princeton, NJ: Princeton University Press, 1987).

16. John D. Garrigus, *Before Haiti: Race and Citizenship in French Saint-Domingue* (Houndmills: Palgrave Macmillan, 2006), 141–70.

17. Jean Tarrade, *Le commerce colonial de la France à la fin de l'Ancien Régime: L'évolution du régime de l' "Exclusif" de 1763 à 1789* (Paris: Presses Universitaires de France, 1972); Charles Frostin, *Les révoltes blanches à Saint-Domingue aux XVIIe et XVIIIe siècles (Haïti avant 1789)* (Paris: Éditions de l'École, 1975).

18. Pernille Røge, "A Natural Order of Empire: The Physiocratic Vision of Colonial France after the Seven Years War," in *The Political Economy of Empire in the Early Modern World*, ed. Sophus A. Reinert and Pernille Røge (Houndmills: Palgrave Macmillan, 2013), 32–52.

19. Ibid.

20. Jean Favier, *Doléances des peuples coloniaux à l'Assemblée nationale constituante: 1789–1790* (Paris: Archives Nationales, 1989), 13.

21. David A. Bell, "The Unrepresentable French?" in *Realities of Representation: State Building in Early Modern Europe and European America*, ed. Maija Jansson (New York: Palgrave Macmillan, 2007), 75–92.

22. Keith Michael Baker, *Inventing the French Revolution: Essays on French Political Culture in the Eighteenth Century* (Cambridge: Cambridge University Press, 1990).

23. Philip P. Boucher, *Les Nouvelles Frances: France in America, 1500–1815: An Imperial Perspective* (Providence: The John Carter Brown Library, 1989), 1–43.

24. Frederick Quinn, *The French Overseas Empire* (Westport, CT: Praeger, 2000).

25. Sophus A. Reinert, *Translating Empire: Emulation and the Origins of Political Economy* (Cambridge, MA: Harvard University Press, 2011), 154. See also Paul Cheney, *Revolutionary Commerce: Globalization and the French Monarchy* (Cambridge, MA: Harvard University Press, 2010).

26. James Pritchard, *In Search of Empire: The French in the Americas, 1670–1730* (Cambridge: Cambridge University Press, 2004), 234–41.

27. Voltaire's comment appears in various versions in several of his works and letters; see, for example, *Candide, ou L'optimisme* (Paris: Librairie, 1893), chapter 3, 172.

28. William J. Eccles, *Canada under Louis XIV, 1663–1701* (Toronto: McClelland and Stewart, 1963); Marcel Trudel, *Histoire de la Nouvelle-France: Le comptoir, 1604–1627* (Montreal: FIDES, 1966).

29. Cornelius J. Jaenen, *Friends and Foe: Aspects of French-Amerindian Cultural Contact in the Sixteenth and Seventeenth Centuries* (New York: Columbia University Press, 1976); Marcel Giraud, *Le Métis canadien: Son rôle dans l'histoire des provinces de l'Ouest* (Paris: Institut d'Ethnologie, 1945).

30. On the weakness of the French emigration model, see Hubert Charbonneau et al., *Naissance d'une population: Les français établis au Canada au XVII siècle* (Montreal: Presses Universitaires de Montréal, 1987).

31. For the debates on trade and colonies, see Paul Cheney, *Revolutionary Commerce: Globalization and the French Monarchy* (Cambridge, MA: Harvard University Press, 2010.)

32. Paul Butel, *Histoire des Antilles françaises* (Paris: Perrin, 2007), 119–36.

33. Philippe Haudrère, *L'Empire des Rois, 1500–1789* (Paris: Denoël, 1997), 326.

34. Glyndwr Williams, *The Expansion of Europe in the Eighteenth Century: Overseas Rivalry, Discovery, and Exploitation* (New York: Walker and Company, 1966), 111–16; G. J. Bryant, "The War in the Carnatic," in *The Seven Years' War: Global Views*, ed. Mark H. Danley and Patrick J. Speelman (Leiden: Brill, 2012), 73–107.

35. Butel, *Histoire des Antilles*, 63–64.

36. Clarence J. Mumford, *The Black Ordeal of Slavery and Slave Trading in the French West Indies, 1625–1715* (Lewiston, NY: Edwin Mellen Press, 1991), vol. 2, 361–406.

37. Frostin, *Les révoltes blanches à Saint-Domingue*, 28–29; similar figures in Jean Meyer, "Des origines à 1763," in *Histoire de la France coloniale: Des origines à 1914*, ed. Jean Meyer et al. (Paris: Armand Colin, 2016), 101.

38. Tarrade, *Le commerce colonial de la France*.

39. Olivier Chaline, *Les armées du Roi: Le grand chantier, XVIIe-XVIIIe siècle* (Paris: Armand Colin, 2016).

40. Fred J. Thorpe, "In Defense of Sugar: The Logistics of Fortifying the French Antilles under the Regency, 1715–1723," in *Proceedings of the Nineteenth Meeting of the French Colonial Historical Society*, ed. James Pritchard (Cleveland: French Historical Society, 1994), 68–86.

41. Butel, *Histoire des Antilles*, 161–62.

42. Paul Butel, *Les négociants bordelais, l'Europe et les îles au XVIIIe siècle* (Paris: Aubier, 1974).

43. Robert Louis Stein, *The French Sugar Business in the Eighteenth Century* (Baton Rouge: Louisiana State University Press, 1988).

44. For a biographical approach, see Tarrade, *Le commerce colonial de la France*, 185–221. See also Carl Ludwig Lokke, *France and the Colonial Question: A Study of Contemporary French Opinion, 1763–1801* (New York: AMS Press, 1968) [1st ed. 1932].

45. Gérard Gabriel Marion, "Distance et dépendance: Les incohérences de la politique coloniale d'Ancien Régime," in *Entre assimilation et émancipation: L'outre-mer français dans l'impasse*, ed. Thierry Michalon (Paris: Les Perséides, 2006), 31.

46. Haudrère, *L'Empire des Rois*, 89; Pritchard, *In Search of Empire*, 243.

47. Haudrère, *L'Empire des Rois*, 71–72.

48. Kenneth J. Banks, *Chasing Empire across the Sea: Communications and the State in the French Atlantic, 1713–1763* (Montreal: McGill-Queen's University Press, 2003), 127–52.

49. Stewart R. King, *Blue Coat or Powdered Wig: Free People of Color in Pre-Revolutionary Saint-Domingue* (Athens: University of Georgia Press, 2001).

50. Frostin, *Les révoltes blanches à Saint-Domingue*, 67.

51. James B. Collins, *Classes, Estates, and Order in Early-Modern Brittany* (Cambridge: Cambridge University Press, 1994); Bailey Stone, "The Parlements in 'Absolutist' France," in his *The French Parlements and the Crisis of the Old Regime* (Chapel Hill: University of North Carolina Press, 1986).

52. Michael Kwass, *Privilege and the Politics of Taxation in Eighteenth-Century France: Liberté, Égalité, Fiscalité* (Cambridge: Cambridge University Press, 2006).

53. For a comparative view, see Trevor G. Burnard and John D. Garrigus, *The Plantation Machine: Atlantic Capitalism in French Saint-Domingue and British Jamaica* (Philadelphia: University of Pennsylvania Press, 2016).

54. There were 470,000 slaves and 60,000 free persons (whites and *gens de couleur libres*).

55. Haudrère, *L'Empire des Rois*, 249; Meyer, "Des origines à 1763," in Jean Meyer, et al., *Histoire de la France coloniale*, 162.

56. Bailey Stone, "Robe against Sword: The Parliament of Paris and the French Aristocracy, 1774-1789," *French Historical Studies* 9, no. 2 (1975): 278-303.

57. Madeleine Dobie, *Trading Places: Colonization and Slavery in Eighteenth-Century French Culture* (Ithaca, NY: Cornell University Press, 2010), 199-251.

58. Gene E. Ogle, "'The Eternal Power of Reason' and 'The Superiority of Whites': Hilliard d'Auberteuil's Colonial Enlightenment," *French Colonial History* 3 (2003): 35-50.

59. Jean Tarrade, "L'administration coloniale en France à la fin de l'Ancien Régime: Projets de réforme," *Revue historique* 229, no. 1 (1963): 113.

60. Tarrade, "L'administration coloniale en France," 114-22.

61. Yves Benot, "Diderot-Raynal: L'impossible divorce," in *Les Lumières, l'esclavage, la colonisation*, ed. Yves Benot (Paris: Éditions La Découverte, 2005), 138-53.

62. Vincent Confer, "French Colonial Ideas before 1789," *French Historical Studies* 3, no. 3 (1964): 338-59.

63. Lluís Sala-Molins, *Le Code Noir ou le calvaire de Canaan* (Paris: Presses Universitaires de France, 2005) [1st ed. 1987]. On later slave legislation, see Sue Peabody and Keila Grinberg, *Slavery, Freedom, and the Law in the Atlantic World: A Brief History with Documents* (Boston: Bedford/Saint Martin's, 2007), 31-64.

64. Jean Tarrade, "Les colonies et les principes de 1789: Les assemblées révolutionnaires face au problème de l'esclavage," *Revue française d'histoire d'outre-mer* 76, no. 282-83 (1989): 9-34.

65. John D. Garrigus, *Before Haiti: Race and Citizenship in French Saint-Domingue* (New York: Palgrave Macmillan, 2006).

66. King, *Blue Coat or Powdered Wig*, 158-79.

67. Yvan Debbasch, *Couleur et liberté: Le jeu du critère ethnique dans un ordre juridique esclavagiste*, vol. 1, *L'affranchi dans les possessions françaises de la Caraïbe (1635-1833)* (Paris: Dalloz, 1967); Émile Hayot, *Les gens de couleur libres du Fort-Royal (1679-1823)* (Paris: Société Française d'Histoire d'Outre-mer, 1971).

68. Malick W. Gachem, "The 'Trap' of Representation: Sovereignty, Slavery, and the Road to the Haitian Revolution," *Historical Reflections/Réflexions Historiques*, 29:1 (2003): 123-44.

69. News and information spread in all respects within the Caribbean. See Ada Ferrer, *Freedom's Mirror: Cuba and Haiti in the Age of Revolution* (Cambridge: Cambridge University Press, 2014); David P. Geggus, "The Caribbean in the Age of Revolution," in *The Age of Revolutions in Global Context, c. 1760-1840*, ed. David Armitage and Sanjay Subrahmanyam (London: Palgrave Macmillan, 2010), 83-100.

70. Robert Howell Griffiths, *Le centre perdu: Malouet et les "monarchiens" dans la Révolution française* (Grenoble: Presses Universitaires de Grenoble, 1988).

71. Jean Ehrard, *Lumières et esclavage: L'esclavage colonial et l'opinion pub-

lique en France au XVIIIe siècle (Brussels: André Versaille, 2008); Jean-Daniel Piquet, *L'émancipation des Noirs dans la Révolution française (1789-1795)* (Paris: Karthala, 2002).

72. Kenneth R. Andrews, *Trade, Plunder and Settlement: Maritime Enterprise and the Genesis of the British Empire, 1480-1630* (Cambridge: Cambridge University Press, 1984).

73. Elizabeth Mancke, "Empire and State," in *The British Atlantic World, 1500-1800*, ed. David Armitage and Michael J. Braddick (London: Palgrave Macmillan, 2002), 178.

74. Trevor O. Lloyd, *The British Empire, 1558-1983* (Oxford: Oxford University Press, 1984), 67.

75. Lauren A. Benton, *A Search for Sovereignty: Law and Geography in European Empires, 1400-1900* (Cambridge: Cambridge University Press, 2010).

76. Kenneth Morgan, *Slavery and Servitude in North America, 1607-1800* (Edinburgh: Edinburgh University Press, 2000); Russell Menard, "From Servants to Slaves: The Transformation of the Chesapeake Labour System," *Southern Studies* 16 (1977): 355-90; Colin A. Palmer, ed., *The Worlds of Unfree Labor: From Indentured Servitude to Slavery* (Aldershot: Ashgate/Variorum, 1998).

77. Robert Bliss, *Revolution and Empire: English Politics and the American Colonies in the Seventeenth Century* (Manchester: Manchester University Press, 1990), 86-92.

78. Elizabeth Mancke, "Empire and State," 183; S.A.G. Taylor, *The Western Design: An Account of Cromwell's Expedition to the Caribbean* (Kingston: Jamaican Historical Society, 1965).

79. Braddick, *State Formation*, 411.

80. Carla Gardina Pestana, *The English Atlantic in an Age of Revolution, 1640-1661* (Cambridge, MA: Harvard University Press, 2004).

81. A summary may be found in Jerome R. Reich, *Colonial America* (Englewood Cliffs: Prentice Hall, 1989), 111 and passim.

82. Christopher A. Bayly, "The British Military-Fiscal State and Indigenous Resistance: India, 1750-1820," in *An Imperial State at War: Britain from 1689 to 1815*, ed. Lawrence Stone (Abingdon: Routledge, 1994), 322-54.

83. Jack P. Greene, "Negotiated Authorities: The Problem of Governance in the Extended Polities of the Early Modern Atlantic World," in *Negotiated Authorities: Essays in Colonial Political and Constitutional History*, ed. Jack P. Greene (Charlottesville: University of Virginia Press, 1994), 1-24.

84. Elliott, *Empires of the Atlantic World*, 134.

85. Philip S. Haffenden, "The Crown and the Colonial Charters, 1675-1688," *William and Mary Quarterly* 15, no. 3 (1958): 298-311; part 2 in *William and Mary Quarterly* 15, no. 4 (1958): 452-66.

86. Elliott, *Empires of the Atlantic World*, 135; Paul R. Lucas, "Colony to Commonwealth: Massachusetts Bay, 1661-1666," *William and Mary Quarterly* 24, no. 1 (1967): 88-102.

87. Jack P. Greene, *Peripheries and Center: Constitutional Development in the Extended Polities of the British Empire and the United States, 1607-1788* (New York: W. W. Norton, 1990), 29.

88. Robert C. Ritchie, *Duke's Province: A Study of New York Politics and Society, 1664–1691* (Chapel Hill: University of North Carolina Press, 1977); David Armitage, "John Locke: Theorist of Empire?" in *Empire and Modern Political Thought*, ed. Sankar Muthu (Cambridge: Cambridge University Press, 2012), 84–111.

89. Robert E. Brown, *Middle-Class Democracy and the Revolution in Massachusetts, 1691–1780* (Ithaca, NY: Cornell University Press, 1955).

90. Elliott, *Empires of the Atlantic World*, 134.

91. Steven Sarson, *British America, 1500–1800: Creating Colonies, Imagining an Empire* (London: Hodder Arnold, 2005), 98; Agnes M. Whitson, *The Constitutional Government of Jamaica, 1660–1729* (Manchester: Manchester University Press, 1929).

92. Carla Gardina Pestana, "English Character and the Fiasco of the Western Design," *Early American Studies: An Interdisciplinary Journal* 3, no. 1 (2005): 1–31; Thomas Bartlett, "Ireland, Empire, and Union, 1690–1801," in *Ireland and the British Empire*, ed. Kevin Kenny (Oxford: Oxford University Press, 2004), 71, 76–77.

93. Greene, *Peripheries and Center*, 25.

94. D. J. Murray, *The West Indies and the Development of Colonial Government, 1801–1834* (Oxford: Clarendon Press, 1965), 13.

95. Kamau Brathwaite, *The Development of Creole Society in Jamaica, 1770–1820* (Oxford: Clarendon Press, 1971), 9.

96. George Metcalf, *Royal Government and Political Conflict in Jamaica, 1729–1783* (London: Longman, 1965), 24.

97. Ian K. Steele, *The English Atlantic, 1675–1740: An Exploration of Communication and Community* (New York: Oxford University Press, 1986), 229–50.

98. On the role of the Caribbean island's agents, see Lillian M. Penson, *The Colonial Agents of the British West Indies: A Study of Colonial Administration, Mainly in the Eighteenth Century* (London: Frank Cass, 1971).

99. Brathwaite, *The Development of Creole Society*, 73–79.

100. Matthew Parker, *The Sugar Barons: Family, Corruption, Empire, and War in the West Indies* (New York: Walker and Company, 2011).

101. Brathwaite, *The Development of Creole Society*, 73.

102. Edward Long, *The History of Jamaica or General Survey of the Ancient and Modern State of That Island* (London: Frank Cass, 1970), 49 passim [1st ed. 1774].

103. Andrew S. Curran, *The Anatomy of Blackness: Science and Slavery in the Age of Enlightenment* (Baltimore: Johns Hopkins University Press, 2013), 169.

104. Elsa V. Goveia, *A Study on the Historiography of the British West Indies to the End of the Nineteenth Century* (Washington, DC: Howard University Press, 1980), 56–57.

105. Bryan Edwards, *The History, Civil and Commercial, of the British West Indies* (London: G. and W. B. Whittaker); I consulted the five-volume edition of T. Miller, London, 1819, reprinted by AMS Press Inc., New York, 1966.

106. Goveia, *A Study on the Historiography*, 82.

107. Ibid., 83.

108. Robert L. Schuyler, "The Constitutional Claims of the British West Indies: The Controversy over the Slave Registry Bill of 1815," *Political Science Quarterly* 40, no. 1 (1925): 23–24; Ronald Kent Richardson, *Moral Imperium: Afro-Caribbeans and the Transformation of British Rule, 1776–1838* (New York: Greenwood Press, 1987).

109. Joanna Innes, "Forms of 'Government Growth', 1780–1830," in *Structures and Transformations in Modern British History*, ed. David Feldman and Jon Lawrence (Cambridge: Cambridge University Press, 2011), 74–99.

110. Braddick, *State Formation*, 398.

111. Jack P. Greene, *Pursuits of Happiness: The Social Development of Early Modern British Colonies and the Formation of American Culture* (Chapel Hill: University of North Carolina Press, 1988).

112. Douglass C. North, *The Economic Growth of the United States, 1790–1860* (New York: W. W. Norton, 1966).

113. Robert W. Tucker and David C. Hendrickson, *The Fall of the First British Empire: Origins of the War of American Independence* (Baltimore: Johns Hopkins University Press, 1982).

114. Forrest McDonald, *Novus Ordo Seclorum: The Intellectual Origins of the Constitution* (Lawrence: University Press of Kansas, 1985), 25–26; Bernard Bailyn, *The Ideological Origins of the American Revolution* (Cambridge, MA: Harvard University Press, 1992 [1st ed. 1971], 160–229; Pauline Maier, *From Resistance to Revolution: Colonial Radicals and the Development of American Opposition to Britain, 1765–1776* (New York: W. W. Norton, 1991 [1st ed. 1971], 27–50.

115. Schuyler, "The Constitutional Claims," 33, n. 4.

116. Sarson, *British America, 1500–1800: Creating Colonies*, 223.

117. Stephen Conway, *The British Isles and the War of American Independence* (Oxford: Oxford University Press, 2000).

118. Brewer, *The Sinews of Power*, 191–217.

119. Marc Baer, *The Rise and Fall of Radical Westminster, 1780–1890* (Houndmills: Palgrave Macmillan, 2012).

120. Eric Hinderaker, *Elusive Empires: Constructing Colonialism in the Ohio Valley, 1673–1800* (Cambridge: Cambridge University Press, 1997), 226–67.

121. Brendan Simms, *Three Victories and a Defeat: The Rise and Fall of the First British Empire, 1714–1783* (New York: Basic Books, 2007), 543; Stephen Conway, *The British Isles and the War of American Independence* (Oxford: Oxford University Press, 2000).

122. Richard Tuck, *The Sleeping Sovereign: The Invention of Modern Democracy* (Cambridge: Cambridge University Press, 2015), 182–83.

123. Michael Kammen, *Deputyes and Libertyes: The Origins of Representative Government in Colonial America* (New York: Alfred A. Knopf, 1969).

124. Greene, *Peripheries and Center*, 30.

125. Robert Middlekauf, *The Glorious Cause: The American Revolution, 1763–1789* (New York: Oxford University Press, 1986).

126. Jack P. Greene, "The Seven Years' War and the American Revolution: The Causal Relationship Reconsidered," in *The British Atlantic Empire before the American Revolution*, ed. Peter Marshall and Glyndwr Williams (London: Routledge, 1980), 77.

127. Greene, *Peripheries and Center*, 101–2; Edmund Morgan, "Colonial Ideas of Parliamentary Power," *William and Mary Quarterly* 5, no. 3 (1948): 311–41; Thomas C. Barrow, "Background to the Grenville Program," *William and Mary Quarterly* 22, no. 1 (1965): 93–104.

128. Andrew J. O'Shaughnessy, *An Empire Divided: The American Revolution and the British Caribbean* (Philadelphia: University of Pennsylvania Press, 2000).

129. David P. Geggus, *Slavery, War, and Revolution: The British Occupation of Saint Domingue, 1793–1798* (Oxford: Clarendon Press, 1982).

130. Seymour Drescher, *Econocide: British Slavery in the Era of Abolition* (Pittsburgh: University of Pittsburgh Press, 1977), 49–54; William L. Grant, "Canada vs. Guadeloupe: An Episode of the Seven Years' War," *American Historical Review* 17, no. 4 (1912): 735–43.

131. Roger N. Buckley, *The British Army in the West Indies: Society and the Military in the Revolutionary Age* (Gainesville: University Press of Florida, 1998); Michael Duffy, *Soldiers, Sugar, and Seapower: The British Expeditions to the West Indies and the War against Revolutionary France* (Oxford: Clarendon Press, 1987).

132. Robin Blackburn, *The Overthrow of Colonial Slavery, 1776–1846* (London: Verso, 1988), 5; Michael Craton, *Empire, Enslavement and Freedom in the Caribbean* (Kingston: Ian Randle, 1997), 182; B. W. Higman, *Slave Population and Economy in Jamaica, 1807–1834* (Cambridge: Cambridge University Press, 1979), 255.

133. Metcalf, *Royal Government and Political Conflict*, 152 and passim.

134. O'Shaughnessy, *An Empire Divided*, 59–61; Richard B.Sheridan, "The Molasses Act and the Market Strategy of the British Sugar Planters," *The Journal of Economic History* 17, no. 1 (1957): 62–83.

135. Bayly, "The British Military-Fiscal State and Indigenous Resistance," 322–54.

136. Ibid., 329.

137. Manuel Lucena Giraldo, *A los cuatro vientos: Las ciudades de la América Hispánica* (Madrid: Marcial Pons, 2006); Fred Bonner, "Urban Society in Colonial America. Research Trends," *Latin American Research Review* 21, no. 1 (1986): 7–72.

138. A. A. Thompson, "Castile, Spain and the Monarchy: The Political Community from Patria Natural to Patria Nacional," in *Spain, Europe and the Atlantic World: Essays in Honour of John H. Elliott*, ed. Richard L. Kagan and Geoffrey Parker (Cambridge: Cambridge University Press, 1995), 131–32.

139. Xavier Gil Pujol, *La fábrica de la monarquía: Traza y conservación de la monarquía de España de los reyes Católicos y de los Austrias* (Madrid: Real Academia de la Historia, 2016), 65–67.

140. John Lynch, "Arms and Men in the Spanish Conquest of America," in *Latin America between Colony and Nation: Selected Essays* (Houndmills: Palgrave MacMillan, 2001), 14–44.

141. Lara Semboloni Capitani, *La construcción de la autoridad virreinal en Nueva España (1535–1595)* (Mexico City: El Colegio de México, 2014); Cayetana Álvarez de Toledo, *Politics and Reform in Spain and Viceregal Mexico: The Life and Thought of Juan de Palafox, 1600–1659* (Oxford: Clarendon Press, 2004); Óscar Mazín Gómez and José Javier Ruiz Ibáñez, eds., *Las Indias Occidentales: Procesos de incorporación territorial a las monarquías ibéricas (siglos XVI a XVIII)* (Mexico City: El Colegio de México, 2012).

142. Anthony Pagden, "Dispossessing the Barbarian: Rights and Property in Spanish America," in *Spanish Imperialism and the Political Imagination: Studies in European and Spanish-American Social and Political Theory, 1513–1830* (New Haven, CT: Yale University Press, 1990), 13–36.

143. José María Ots Capdequí, *El Estado español en las Indias* (Mexico City: Fondo de Cultura Económica, 1993), 45 [1st ed. 1946].

144. "Superficial feudalism" is the definition offered by Horst Pietschmann in his *El Estado y su evolución al principio de la colonización española de América* (Mexico City: Fondo de Cultura Económica, 1989), 113, 212–14 [1st ed. in German, 1980].

145. Ots Capdequí, *El Estado español en las Indias*, 9–10.

146. Javier Malagón Barceló, *Solórzano y la política indiana* (Mexico City: Fondo de Culura Económica, 1983); Enrique García Hernán, *Consejero de ambos mundos: Vida y obra de Juan Solórzano Pereira (1575–1655)* (Madrid: Mapfre, 2007).

147. Allan J. Kuethe and Kenneth J. Andrien, *The Spanish Atlantic World in the Eighteenth Century: War and the Bourbon Reforms, 1713–1796* (Cambridge: Cambridge University Press, 2014).

148. John H. Elliott, "Spain and Its Empire in the Sixteenth and Seventeenth Centuries," in *Spain and Its World, 1500–1700* (New Haven, CT: Yale University Press, 1989), 16–18.

149. Pablo Fernández Albaladejo, *Fragmentos de Monarquía* (Madrid: Alianza Editorial, 1992).

150. Helmut G. Koenigsberger, *The Practice of Empire: The Government of Sicily under Philip II of Spain* (New York: Rinehart & Holt, 1968); Giuseppe Galasso, *En la periferia del imperio: La monarquía hispánica y el Reino de Nápoles* (Barcelona: Península, 1994); John H. Elliott, "The Spanish Monarchy and the Kingdom of Portugal, 1580–1640," in *Conquest and Coalescence: The Shaping of the State in Early Modern Europe*, ed. Mark Greengrass (London: Edward Arnold, 1991), 45–67.

151. Mario Góngora, *Studies in the Colonial History of Spanish America* (Cambridge: Cambridge University Press, 1975), 103.

152. *Archivo general de Indias: Indiferente general*, 2689, Madrid, May 12, 1635.

153. Antonio Domínguez Ortiz, *Historia de los moriscos: Vida y tragedia de una minoría* (Madrid: Alianza Editorial, 1985); Mikel de Epalza, *Los moriscos antes y después de la expulsión* (Madrid: Mapfre, 1992); Mercedes García Arenal, *Los moriscos* (Granada: Universidad de Granada, 1975); Elena Lourie, *Crusade and Colonisation: Muslims, Christians, and Jews in Medieval Aragon* (Aldershot: Variorum, 1990); Mark D. Meyerson and Edward D. English, eds., *Christians, Muslims, and Jews in Medieval and Early Modern Spain: Interactions and Cultural Change* (Notre Dame, IN: University of Notre Dame Press, 1999); on both communities, see James A. Amelang, *Parallel Histories: Muslims and Jews in Inquisitorial Spain* (Baton Rouge: Louisiana State University Press, 2013).

154. Bartolomé Clavero, "Tiempo de colonia, tiempo de constitución," in *Derecho indígena y cultura constitucional en América* (Madrid: Siglo XXI Editores, 1994), 5–11.

155. Carlos Díaz Rementería, "La constitución de la sociedad política," in *Historia del Derecho Indiano*, ed. Ismael Sánchez Bella (Madrid: Mapfre, 1992), 167–90; Thomas Hillerkuss, "La República en los pueblos de indios en la Nueva Galicia en el siglo XVI," *Anuario Saber Novohispano* (1995): 241–58.

156. On the very special case of Tlaxcala, see Charles Gibson, *Tlaxcala in the Sixteenth Century* (New Haven, CT: Yale University Press, 1954); and José María Portillo Valdés, *Fuero indio: Tlaxcala y la identidad territorial entre la monarquía imperial y la república nacional, 1787–1824* (Mexico City: El Colegio de México, 2014).

157. Brian P. Owensby, *Empire of Law and Indian Justice in Colonial Mexico* (Stanford, CA: Stanford University Press, 2008).

158. Kenneth J. Andrien, *Andean Worlds: Indigenous History, Culture, and Consciousness under Spanish Rule, 1532–1825* (Albuquerque: University of New Mexico Press, 2001), 49–56; León Gómez Ribas, *El virrey del Perú don Francisco de Toledo* (Toledo: Instituto Provincial de Investigaciones y Estudios Toledanos, 1994); Javier Tantaleán Arbulú, *El virrey Francisco de Toledo y su tiempo: Proyecto de gobernalidad, el imperio hispano, la plata peruana en la economía-mundo y el mercado colonial* (Lima: Universidad San Martín de Porres, 2011).

159. Woodrow Borah, *El Juzgado General de Indios en la Nueva España* (Mexico City: Fondo de Cultura Económica, 1996) [1st ed. 1983]; Mauricio Novoa, *The Protectors of Indians in the Royal Audience of Lima: History, Careers and Legal Culture, 1575–1775* (Leiden: Brill-Nijhoff, 2016).

160. James Lockhart, *The Nahuas after the Conquest: A Social and Cultural History of the Indians of Central Mexico, Sixteenth through Eighteenth Centuries* (Stanford, CA: Stanford University Press, 1992); by the same author, *Of Things of the Indies: Essays Old and New in Early Latin American History* (Stanford, CA: Stanford University Press, 1999); Margarita Menegus Bornemann and Rodolfo Aguirre Salvador, eds., *El cacicazgo en Nueva España y Filipinas* (Mexico City: Universidad Nacional Autónoma de México, 2005).

161. On restrictions during the early stages, see Juan Eloy Gelabert González, *La bolsa del rey. Rey, reino y fisco en Castilla (1598–1648)* (Barcelona: Crítica, 1997), 153–76.

162. William R. Summerhill, "Fiscal Bargains, Political Institutions, and Economic Performance," *Hispanic American Historical Review* 88, no. 2 (2008): 219–33.

163. Mark A. Burkholder and D. S. Chandler, *From Impotence to Authority: The Spanish Crown and the American Audiencias, 1687–1808* (Columbia: University of Missouri Press, 1977).

164. Burkholder and Chandler, *From Impotence to Authority*, 18.

165. Ibid., 23.

166. Francisco Andújar Castillo, *Necesidad y venalidad: España e Indias, 1704–1711* (Madrid: Centro de Estudios Políticos y Constitucionales, 2008).

167. Elliott, *Empires of the Atlantic World*, 144–145; Peter Marzahl, *Town in the Empire: Government, Politics and Society in Seventeenth-Century Popayán* (Austin: University of Texas Press, 1978).

168. Anthony McFarlane, *Colombia Before Independence: Economy, Society, and Politics under Bourbon Rule* (Cambridge: Cambridge University Press, 1993), 231–72; Sergio Serulnikov, "Patricians and Plebeians in Late Colonial Charcas. Identity, Representation, and Colonialism," in *Imperial Subjects: Race and Identity in Colonial Latin America*, ed. Andrew B. Fisher and Matthew D. O'Hara (Durham, NC: Duke University Press, 2009), 179–96.

169. John L. Phelan, "Authority and Flexibility in Spanish Imperial Bureaucracy." *Administrative Science Quarterly* 5, no. 1 (1960): 47–65.

170. Josep M. Delgado, *Dinámicas imperiales (1650–1796): España, América y Europa en el cambio institucional del sistema colonial español* (Barcelona: Bellaterra, 2007), 28–38; Jorge Gelman, Enrique Llopis, and Carlos Marichal, eds.,

Iberoamérica y España antes de las independencias, 1700–1820: Crecimiento, reformas y crisis (Mexico City: El Colegio de México, 2014).

171. For an exhaustive assessment of the Bourbon Reforms, see Stanley J. Stein and Barbara H. Stein, *Silver, Trade, and War: Spain and America in the Making of the Early Modern Europe* (Baltimore: Johns Hopkins University Press, 2000); Stanley J. Stein and Barbara H. Stein, *Apogee of Empire: Spain in the Age of Charles III, 1759–1789* (Baltimore: Johns Hopkins University Press, 2003); and Barbara H. Stein and Stanley J. Stein, *Crisis in an Atlantic Empire: Spain and New Spain, 1808–1810* (Baltimore: Johns Hopkins University Press, 2014). On financial strains in New Spain, see Carlos Marichal, *Bankruptcy of Empire: Mexican Silver and the Wars between Spain, Britain, and France, 1760–1810* (New York: Cambridge University Press, 2007).

172. Horst Pietschmann, *Las reformas borbónicas y el sistema de intendencias en Nueva España: Un estudio administrativo* (Mexico City: Fondo de Cultura Económica, 1996).

173. John R. Fisher, Allan J. Kuethe, and Anthony McFarlane, eds., *Reform and Insurrection in Bourbon New Granada and Peru* (Baton Rouge: Louisiana State University Press, 1990).

174. Alejandra Irigoin and Regina Grafe, "Bargaining for Absolutism: A Spanish Path to Nation-State and Empire Building," *Hispanic American Historical Review* 88, no. 2 (2008): 173–209; Carlos Marichal, "Rethinking Negotiation and Coercion in an Imperial State," *Hispanic American Historical Review* 88, no. 2 (2007): 211–18; William R. Summerhill, "Fiscal Bargains, Political Institutions, and Economic Performance," *Hispanic American Historical Review* 88, no. 2 (2008), 219–33.

175. Felipe Castro Gutiérrez, *Nueva ley y nuevo rey: Reformas borbónicas y rebelión popular en Nueva España* (Zamora: Colegio de Michoacán, 1996); Daniela Marino, "El afán de recaudar y la dificultad en reformar: El tributo indígena en la Nueva España tardocolonial," in *De colonia a nación: Impuestos y política en México, 1750–1860*, ed. Carlos Marichal and Daniela Marino (Mexico City: El Colegio de México, 2001), 61–83.

176. Josep M. Fradera, "Raza y ciudadanía: El factor racial en la delimitación de los derechos de los Americanos," in *Gobernar colonias* (Barcelona: Península, 1999), 51–70.

177. María Elena Martínez, *Genealogical Fictions: Limpieza de Sangre, Religion, and Gender in Colonial Mexico* (Stanford, CA: Stanford Unversity Press, 2008); Nikolaus Böttcher, Bernd Hausberger, and Max Hering Torres, eds., *El peso de la sangre: Limpios, mestizos y nobles en el mundo hispánico* (Mexico City: Colegio de México, 2011).

178. Ben Vinson III, *Bearing Arms for His Majesty: The Free-Colored Militia in Colonial Mexico* (Stanford, CA: Stanford University Press, 2001); Juan Ortiz Escamilla, ed., *Fuerzas militares en Iberoamérica, siglos XVIII y XIX* (Mexico City: El Colegio de México, El Colegio de Michoacán, Universidad de Veracruz, 2005).

179. On the Indians, see Felipe Castro Gutiérrez, *Nueva ley y nuevo rey;* Luis Fernando Granados, *En el espejo haitiano: Los indios del Bajío y el colapso del orden colonial en América Latina* (Mexico City: Ediciones Era, 2016). On the free people of color, see Marixa Lasso, *Myths of Harmony: Race and Republicanism during the Age of Revolution; Colombia 1795–1831* (Minneapolis: University of Minnesota Press, 2003); Ada Ferrer, *Freedom's Mirror*; Aline Helg, *Liberty and Equality in Caribbean*

Colombia, 1770–1835 (Chapel Hill: University of North Carolina Press, 2004); Lyman L. Johnson, *Workshop of Revolution: Plebeian Buenos Aires and the Atlantic World, 1776–1810* (Durham, NC: Duke University Press, 2011); Gabriel di Meglio, *¡Viva el bajo pueblo! La plebe urbana de Buenos Aires y la política entre la revolución de mayo y el rosismo* (Buenos Aires: Prometeo, 2006).

180. Armitage and Subrahmanyam, *The Age of Revolutions*.

181. Mark H. Danley and Patrick J. Speelman, eds., *The Seven Years' War: Global Views* (Leiden: Brill, 2012).

182. On the Portuguese reforms, see João Paulo Oliveira e Costa, José Damião Rodrigues, and Pedro Aires Olivera, eds., *História da Expansão e do Império Português* (Lisbon: A Esfera dos Livros, 2014), 264–96.

Chapter 2. The Collapse of Imperial Constitutions

1. Sudipta Sen, *A Distant Sovereignty: National Imperialism and the Origins of British India* (New York: Routledge, 2002); Jeremy Adelman, "Iberian passages: Continuity and Change in the South Atlantic," in *The Age of Revolutions in Global Context, c. 1760–1840*, ed. David Armitage and Sanjay Subrahmanyam (Houndmills: Palgrave Macmillan, 2010), 59–82; Jeanne Morefield, *Covenants without Swords: Idealist Liberalism and the Spirit of Empire* (Princeton, NJ: Princeton University Press, 2005), 175–204; Lauren Benton, *A Search for Sovereignty: Law and Geography in European Empires, 1400–1900* (Cambridge: Cambridge University Press, 2010).

2. John K. Thorton, *A Cultural History of the Atlantic World, 1250–1820* (Cambridge: Cambridge University Press, 2012).

3. This engraving of 1793 was among the important collection held by baron and diplomat Carl de Vinck (1815–1919).

4. Frank Attar, *Aux armes, citoyens! Naissance et fonctions du bellicisme révolutionnaire* (Paris: Seuil, 2010); Mikel Aizpuru, "Chino cristiano (casado con india española filipina): Nación, raza, religión y ciudadanía en la España postimperial," in *Conflictos y cicatrices: Fronteras y migraciones en el mundo hispánico*, ed. Almudena Delgado Larios (Madrid: Dyckinson, 2014), 285–303.

5. Christopher A. Bayly, "The British Military-Fiscal State and Indigenous Resistance: India, 1750–1820," in *An Imperial State at War: Britain from 1689 to 1815*, ed. Lawrence Stone (Abingdon: Routledge, 1994), 322–54; see also Robert Travers, "Contested Despotism: Problems of Liberty in British India," in *Exclusionary Empire: English Liberties Overseas, 1600–1900*, ed. Jack P. Greene (Cambridge: Cambridge University Press, 2010), 191–219.

6. Richard Tuck, "The 'Modern' Theory of Natural Law," in *The Languages of Political Theory in Early-Modern Europe*, ed. Anthony Pagden (Cambridge: Cambridge University Press, 1987), 99–121.

7. María Sierra, María Antonio Peña, and Rafael Zurita, *Elegidos y elegibles: La representación parlamentaria en la cultura del liberalismo* (Madrid: Marcial Pons, 2010), 84.

8. Florence Gauthier, *Triomphe et mort du droit naturel en Révolution, 1789-1795-1802* (Paris: Presses Universitaires de France, 1992).

9. For a fierce attack on misinterpretations of "natural right," see Stanislas de Clermont Tonnerre, *Analyse raisonnée de la Constitution française, décrétée par l'Assemblée Nationale des années 1789, 1790, 1791* (Paris: Migneret Imprimeur, 1791).

10. Bartolomé Clavero, *El orden de los poderes: Historias Constituyentes de la Trinidad Constitucional* (Madrid: Editorial Trotta, 2007), 128–32.

11. José María Portillo Valdés, *Historia mínima del constitucionalismo en América Latina* (Mexico City: Colegio de México, 2016).

12. Annie Jourdan, "République française, Révolution batave: Le moment constitutionnel," in *Républiques sœurs: Le Directoire et la Révolution atlantique*, ed. Pierre Serna (Rennes: Presses Universitaires de Rennes, 2009), 301–14; for a more comprehensive account, see Annie Jourdan, *La Révolution batave entre la France et l'Amérique (1795–1806)* (Rennes: Presses Universitaires de Rennes, 2008); and Margaret C. Jacob and Wijnand W. Mijnhardt, eds., *The Dutch Republic in the Eighteenth Century: Decline, Enlightenment, and Revolution* (Ithaca, NY: Cornell University Press, 1992). Simon Schama says nothing about any of these matters in *Patriots and Liberators: Revolution in the Netherlands, 1780–1813* (New York: Alfred A. Knopf, 1977).

13. Surprisingly, the question of slavery is hardly mentioned in Jourdan's otherwise massive and excellent *La Révolution batave*. For a more explicit approach, see Angelie Sens, "La révolution batave et l'esclavage: Les (im)possibilités de l'abolition de la traite des noirs et de l'esclavage (1780–1814)," *Annales historiques de la Révolution française* 326 (2001): 65–78.

14. Beatrix Jacobs, Raymond Kubben, and Randall Lesaffer, eds., *In the Embrace of France: The Law of Nations and Constitutional Law in the French Satellite States of the Revolutionary and Napoleonic Age (1789–1815)* (Baden-Baden: Nomos, 2008).

15. Edward Countryman, "Indians, the Colonial Order, and the Social Significance of the American Revolution," *William and Mary Quarterly* 53, no. 2 (1996): 341–62.

16. On the relationship between the American Revolution and the American continent, see Eliga H. Gould and Peter S. Onuf, eds., *Empire and Nation: The American Revolution in the Atlantic World* (Baltimore: Johns Hopkins University Press, 2015).

17. Peter S. Onuf, *Statehood and Union: A History of the Northwest Ordinance* (Bloomington: Indiana University Press, 1987).

18. Robert V. Remini, *At the Edge of the Precipice: Henry Clay and the Compromise That Saved the Union* (New York: Basic Books, 2010).

19. Eric Foner, *Free Soil, Free Labor, Free Men: The Ideology of the Republican Party before the Civil War* (New York: Oxford University Press, 1970).

20. Peter J. Marshall, *The Making and Unmaking of Empires: Britain, India, and America, c. 1750–1783* (Oxford: Oxford University Press, 2009).

21. Christopher A. Bayly, *Imperial Meridian: The British Empire and the World, 1780–1830* (Harlow: Longman, 1989), 193–216.

22. Miles Taylor, "Empire and Parliamentary Reform: The 1832 Reform Act Revisited," in *Rethinking the Age of Reform: Britain, 1780–1850*, ed. Arthur Burns and Joanna Innes (Cambridge: Cambridge University Press, 2003), 295–311.

23. Christopher L. Brown, *Moral Capital: Foundations of British Abolitionism* (Chapel Hill: University of North Carolina Press, 2006).

24. Peter J. Marshall, *The Impeachment of Warren Hastings* (Oxford: Oxford University Press, 1965).

25. Arnaud Vergne, *La notion de constitution d'après les cours et assemblées à la fin de l'ancien régime (1750–1789)* (Paris: De Boccard, 2006).

26. For an excellent overview of these problems, see Jean Tarrade, "Les colonies et les principes de 1789: les assemblées révolutionnaires face au problème de l'esclavage," *Revue française d'histoire d'outre-mer* 76, no. 282–283 (1989): 9–34.

27. For an overall vision, see Yves Benot, *La Révolution française et la fin des colonies, 1789–1794* (Paris: La Découverte, 1988).

28. On the Thermidorian Reaction, see Gérard Conac and Jean-Pierre Machelon, eds., *La Constitution de l'an III: Boissy d'Anglas et la naissance du libéralisme constitutionnel* (Paris: Presses Universitaires de France, 1999).

29. "Every man can contract his services and his time, but he cannot sell himself nor be sold: his person is not an alienable property. The law knows of no such thing as the status of servant; there can exist only a contract for services and compensation between the man who works and the one who employs him." Frank Maloy Anderson, ed., *The Constitutions and Other Select Documents Illustrative of the History of France 1789–1901* (Minneapolis: H. W. Wilson, 1904).

30. Jean-Pierre Gross, *Fair Shares for All: Jacobin Egalitarianism in Practice* (Cambridge: Cambridge University Press, 1997), 145–53.

31. Gérard Noiriel, "The Identification of the Citizen: The Birth of Republican Civil Status in France," in *Documenting Individual Identity: The Development of State Practices in the Modern World*, ed. Jane Caplan and John Torpey (Princeton, NJ: Princeton University Press, 2001), 29; Haim Burstin, "Travail et citoyenneté en milieu urbain sous la Révolution," in *Citoyen et citoyenneté sous la Révolution française*, ed. Raymonde Monnier (Paris: Société des Études Robespierristes, 2006), 265.

32. On the Terror, see Patrice Higonnet, "Terror, Trauma and the 'Young Marx' Explanation of Jacobin Politics," *Past and Present* 191 (1996): 121–64.

33. Alexander DeConde, *The Quasi-War: The Politics and Diplomacy of the Undeclared War with France, 1797–1801* (New York: Scribner, 1966).

34. Danièle Lochak, "La citoyenneté: Un concept juridique flou," in *Citoyenneté et nationalité: Perspectives en France et au Québec*, ed. Dominique Colas, Claude Emeri, and Jacques Zylberberg (Paris: Presses Universitaires de France, 1991), 179–207.

35. Miranda Frances Spieler, "The Legal Structure of Colonial Rule during the French Revolution, 1789–1802," *William and Mary Quarterly* 66, no. 2 (2009): 365–408; Jouda Guetata, "Le refus d'application de la constitution de l'an III à Saint-Domingue, 1795–1797," in *Périssent les colonies plutôt qu'un principe! Contributions à l'histoire de l'abolition de l'esclavage, 1789–1804*, ed. Florence Gauthier (Paris: Société d'Études Robespierristes, 2002), 81–90; on the meaning of departmental organization, see Ange Rovere, "Les enjeux politiques de la départementalisation de la Corse sous la Révolution," in *Le droit et les institutions en Révolution (XVIIIe–XIX siècles)*, ed. Centre d'Études et de Recherche de l'Histoire des Idées et des Institutions Politiques (Aix-en-Provence: Presses Universitaires d'Aix-Marseille, 2005), 15–34.

36. Jean-Daniel Piquet, *L'émancipation des Noirs dans la Révolution française (1789–1795)* (Paris: Karthala, 2002); Claude Wanquet, *La France et la première*

abolition de l'esclavage, 1794-1802: Le cas des colonies orientales, Île de France (Maurice) et la Réunion (Paris: Karthala, 1998).

37. Carolyn E. Fick, *The Making of Haiti: The Saint-Domingue Revolution from Below* (Knoxville: University of Tennessee Press, 1990); Laurent Dubois, *Avengers of the New World: The Story of the Haitian Revolution* (Cambridge, MA: Harvard University Press, 2004); Laurent Dubois, *A Colony of Citizens: Revolution and Slave Emancipation in the French Caribbean, 1787-1804* (Chapel Hill: University of North Carolina Press, 2004).

38. Bernard Gainot, "The Republican Imagination and Race: The Case of Haitian Revolution," in *Rethinking the Atlantic World: Europe and America in the Age of Democratic Revolutions*, ed. Manuela Albertone and Antonino De Francesco (London: Palgrave, 2009), 285.

39. Philippe R. Girard, *The Slaves Who Defeated Napoleon: Toussaint Louverture and the Haitian War of Independence, 1801-1804* (Tuscaloosa: University of Alabama Press, 2011); Bernard Gainot, *Les officiers de couleur dans les armées de la République et de l'Empire (1792-1815): De l'esclavage à la condition militaire dans les Antilles françaises* (Paris: Karthala, 2007).

40. Jean-Baptiste Busaall, *Le spectre du jacobinisme: L'expérience constitutionnelle française et le premier libéralisme espagnol* (Madrid: Casa de Velázquez, 2012).

41. For a brilliant study of the text's true dimensions, see José María Portillo Valdés, *Crisis atlántica: Autonomía e independencia en la crisis de la monarquía hispana* (Madrid: Marcial Pons, 2006).

42. Ruth de Llobet, "Orphans of Empire: Bourbon Reforms, Constitutional Impasse and the Rise of Filipino Creole Consciousness in an Age of Revolution" (PhD diss., University of Wisconsin, 2011).

43. Álvaro Flórez Estrada, "Examen imparcial de las disensiones de la América con la España, de los medios de su reconciliación y de la prosperidad de todas las naciones," *Obras de Álvaro Flórez Estrada* (Madrid: Biblioteca de Autores Españoles, 1950), t. 113, v. II, 12.

44. This was why Jeremy Bentham suggested that Spain abandon all pretenses to empire; he had made the same suggestion to France a few years earlier. See Bartolomé Clavero, "¡Libraos de Ultramaria! El fruto podrido de Cádiz," in *Constitución en España: orígenes y destinos*, ed. José María Iñurritegui and José María Portillo (Madrid: Centro de Estudios Políticos y Constitucionales, 1998), 109-77.

45. Flórez Estrada, "Examen imparcial," 31-32.

46. William B. Taylor, *Magistrates of the Sacred: Priests and Parishioners in Eighteenth-Century Mexico* (Stanford, CA: Stanford University Press, 1996).

47. Josep M. Fradera, "Tainted Citizenship and Imperial Constitutions: The Case of the Spanish Constitution of 1812," in *Citizenship and Empire in Europe 200-1900: The Antonine Constitution after 1800 years*, ed. Clifford Ando (Stuttgart: Franz Steiner Verlag, 2016), 221-42.

48. There is an extensive bibliography on this topic: María Elena Martínez, *Genealogical Fictions: Limpieza de Sangre, Religion, and Gender in Colonial Mexico* (Stanford, CA: Stanford University Press, 2008); Matthew O'Hara, *A Flock Divided: Race, Religion, and Politics in Mexico, 1749-1857* (Durham, NC: Duke University Press, 2010); Andrew B. Fisher and Matthew D. O'Hara, eds., *Imperial Subjects: Race*

and Identity in Colonial Latin America (Durham, NC: Duke University Press, 2009); Verena Stolcke, *Marriage, Class and Colour in Nineteenth-Century Cuba: A Study of Racial Attitudes and Sexual Values in a Slave Society* (Cambridge: Cambridge University Press, 1974); María del Carmen Baerga, *Negociaciones de sangre: dinámicas racializantes en el Puerto Rico decimonónico* (Madrid: Iberoamericana, 2015).

49. Ann Twinam, *Purchasing Whiteness: Pardos, Mulattos, and the Quest for Social Mobility in the Spanish Indies* (Stanford, CA: Stanford University Press, 2016); Ulrike Bock, "Entre 'españoles' y 'ciudadanos': Las milicias de pardos y la transformación de las fronteras culturales en Yucatán, 1790–1821," *Secuencia* 87 (2013): 9–27.

50. Eduardo Martiré, *La Constitución de Bayona entre España y América* (Madrid: Centro de Estudios Políticos y Constitucionales, 2000).

51. For the various positions, see Joaquín Varela Suanzes-Carpegna, *La teoría del Estado en los orígenes del constitucionalismo hispánico: Las Cortes de Cádiz* (Madrid: Centro de Estudios Políticos Constitucionales, 1983).

52. Jaime E. Rodríguez, *La independencia de la América española* (Mexico City: El Colegio de México, 1996); Manuel Chust Calero, ed., *1808: La eclosión juntera en el mundo hispano* (Mexico City: Fondo de Cultura Económica, 2007). On Yermo's coup, see the essential work by Barbara H. Stein and Stanley J. Stein, *Crisis in an Atlantic Empire: Spain and New Spain, 1808–1810* (Baltimore: Johns Hopkins University Press, 2014), 296–324.

53. On this process, see Rafael Flaquer Montequi, "El Ejecutivo en la revolución liberal," in *Las Cortes de Cádiz*, ed. Miguel Artola (Madrid: Marcial Pons Historia, 2003), 37–66.

54. José María Portillo Valdés, *Revolución de Nación: Orígenes de la cultura constitucional en España, 1780–1812* (Madrid: Centro de Estudios Políticos y Constitucionales, 2000).

55. On the extension of old-regime jurisdiction, see Carlos Garriga and Marta Lorente, *Cádiz, 1812: La Constitución jurisdiccional* (Madrid: Centro de Estudios Políticos y Constitucionales, 2007).

56. On these questions, see my "Raza y ciudadanía: El factor racial en la delimitación de los derechos de los Americanos," in *Gobernar colonias* (Barcelona: Península, 1999), 51–70; and Bartolomé Clavero, "Hemisferios de ciudadanía: Constitución española en la América indígena," in *La constitución de Cádiz: historiografía y conmemoración; Homenaje a Francisco Tomás y Valiente*, ed. José Álvarez Junco and Javier Moreno Luzón (Madrid: Centro de Estudios Políticos y Constitucionales, 2006), 101–42.

57. José Antonio Rocamora Rocamora, "Un nacionalismo fracasado: el iberismo," *Espacio, Tiempo y Forma*, series 5, *Historia Contemporánea* 2 (1989): 29–56.

58. Jorge Miranda, *O constitucionalismo liberal luso-brasileiro* (Lisbon: Comissão Nacional para as Commemorações dos Descobrimentos Portugueses, 2001), 59–65.

59. On Portuguese-Brazilian relations during the liberal period, see Márcia Regina Berbel, *A Nação como artefato: Deputados do Brasil nas Cortes portuguesas, 1821–1822* (São Paulo, Editora Hucitec, 2010).

60. For a magnificent analysis of the colonial situation and the Portuguese monarchic constitutions, see Valentim Alexandre, *A questão colonial no parlamento,*

vol. 1, *1821–1910* (Lisbon: Dom Quixote, 2008); and, by the same author, *Os sentidos do império: Questão nacional e questão colonial na crise do Antigo Regime português* (Lisbon: Ediçoes Afrontamento, 1993).

61. On slavery and liberalism in Brazil, see Márcia Regina Berbel, Rafael Marquese, and Tamis Parron, *Escravidão e Política: Brasil e Cuba, 1790–1850* (São Paulo: Editora Hucitec, 2009), 95–182.

62. Ana Cristina Nogueira da Silva, *Constitucionalismo e imperio: A cidadania no Ultramar Português* (Coimbra: Almedina, 2010).

63. On the Portuguese colonies in the nineteenth century, see Francisco Bethencourt and Kirti N. Chaudhuri, eds., *História da expansão portuguesa*, vol. 4, *Do Brasil para África, 1808–1930* (Estella: Temas e Debates, 2000); Pedro Aires Oliveira, "Um império vacilante (c. 1820–1870)," in *História da Expansão e do Império Português*, ed. João Paulo Oliveira e Costa, José Damião Rodrigues, and Pedro Aires Olivera (Lisbon: A Esfera dos Livros, 2014), 347–76.

Chapter 3. The Genealogy of Napoleon's "Special Laws" for the Colonies

1. Susan P. Conner, *The Age of Napoleon* (Greenwood Guides to Historic Events, 1500–1900) (Westport CT: Greenwood Press, 2004), 30.

2. The case of the United States is discussed extensively in chapter 7; on the Brazilian monarchic empire, see Jairdilson da Paz Silva, *La "santa ciudadanía" del Imperio: Confesionalidad como fuente restrictiva de derechos en Brasil (1823–1831)* (Salamanca: Ediciones Universidad de Salamanca, 2016).

3. Jean-François Niort and Jérémy Richard, "De la Constitution de l'an VIII au rétablissement de l'esclavage (1802) et à l'application du Code civil français dans les colonies françaises (1805): Le retour d'un droit colonial réactionnaire sous le régime napoléonien," in *Les colonies, la Révolution française, la loi*, ed. Frédéric Régent, Jean-François Niort, and Pierre Serna (Rennes: Presses Universitaires de Rennes, 2014), 165–78.

4. Josep M. Fradera, "Why Were Spain's Special Overseas Laws Never Enacted?" in *Spain, Europe and the Atlantic World: Essays in Honour of John H. Elliott*, ed. Richard L. Kagan and Geoffrey Parker (Cambridge: Cambridge University Press, 1995), 334–49; Ana Cristina Nogueira da Silva, *Constitucionalismo e imperio: A cidadania no Ultramar Português* (Coimbra: Almedina, 2010).

5. Patrice Gueniffey, *Le nombre et la raison: La Révolution française et les élections* (Paris: Éditions de l'EHESS, 1993), 475–514; Malcom Crook, *Elections in the French Revolution: An Apprenticeship in Democracy, 1789–1799* (Cambridge: Cambridge University Press, 1996), 131–57; Colin Lucas, "The First Directory and the Rule of Law," *French Historical Studies* 10, no. 2 (1977): 231–60.

6. Melvin Edelstein, *The French Revolution and the Birth of Electoral Democracy* (Farnham: Ashgate, 2014); Peter McPhee, "Electoral Democracy and Direct Democracy in France, 1789–1851," *European History Quarterly* 16 (1986): 77–96; Malcolm Crook, "*Aux urnes, citoyens!*' Urban and Rural Behavior during the French Revolution," in *Reshaping France: Town, Country and Region during the French Revolu-*

tion, ed. Alan Forrest and Peter Jones (Manchester: Manchester University Press, 1991), 152–67; Bernard Gainot, "Les élections sous le Directoire sont-elles des élections libres?" in *Citoyen et citoyenneté sous la Révolution française*, ed. Raymonde Monnier (Paris: Société des Études Robespierristes, 2006), 211–34.

7. Jean-René Suratteau, *Les élections de l'an VI et le "coup d'état" du 22 floréal (11 mai 1798): Étude documentaire, statistique et analytique; Essai d'interprétation* (Paris: Les Belles Lettres, 1971); Isser Woloch, *Jacobin Legacy: The Democratic Movement under the Directory* (Princeton, NJ: Princeton University Press, 1970); Frederick Cooper, "States, Empires, and Political Imagination," in *Colonialism in Question: Theory, Knowledge, History* (Berkeley: University of California Press, 2005), 168–69.

8. Howard G. Brown, "Mythes et massacres: Réconsiderer la 'terreur' directoriale," *Annales historiques de la Révolution française* 325 (2001): 23–52.

9. On the 1799 royalist revolt, see Jacques Godechot, *La Révolution française dans le Midi toulousain* (Toulouse: Privat, 1986).

10. Jonathan Devlin, "The Army, Politics and Public Order in Directorial Provence, 1795–1800," *Historical Journal* 32, no. 1 (1989): 87–106.

11. On Sièyes during the early phase of the Revolution, see Michael Sonenscher, *Before the Deluge: Public Debt, Inequality, and the Intellectual Origins of the French Revolution* (Princeton, NJ: Princeton University Press, 2007); Pasquale Pasquino, *Sieyès et l'invention de la constitution en France* (Paris: Éditions Odile Jacob, 1998); and Soulef Ayad-Bergounioux, "De Brumaire à la formation de l'État bureaucratique consulaire: le rôle des républicains conservateurs," *Annales historiques de la Révolution française* 378 (2014) 51–72.

12. Timothy Tackett, *When the King Took Flight* (Cambridge, MA: Harvard University Press, 2003), 171–78.

13. Michel Biard, *Missionnaires de la République: Les représentants du peuple en mission, 1793–1795* (Paris: CTHS, 2002); Tackett, *When the King*, 128. Hereafter in this chapter these delegates will be referred to as commissars.

14. Howard G. Brown, "Professionalism and the Fate of Army Generals after Thermidor," *French Historical Studies* 19, no. 1 (1995): 133–52.

15. Bronislaw Bazcko, *Ending the Terror: The French Revolution after Robespierre* (Cambridge: Cambridge University Press, 1994), 74.

16. The important question of electoral participation is discussed in Melvin Edelstein, *The French Revolution*, 259–88.

17. Alan Forrest, "L'armée, la guerre et les politiques de la Terreur," in *Les politiques de la Terreur, 1793–1794*, ed. Michel Biard (Rennes: Presses Universitaires de Rennes, Société des Études Robespierristes, 2008), 57.

18. ("Being at the same time the eye of Paris and its secular branch, as representatives of the 'sovereign,' they have unlimited powers and may intervene in all domains.") Jean-Clément Martin, *La machine à fantasmes: Relire l'histoire de la Révolution française* (Paris: Vendémiaire, 2012), 36; see also Bazcko, *Ending the Terror*, 76.

19. Guy Lemarchand, "Les représentants du peuple en mission dans la Révolution française, 1792–1795," *Annales de Normandie* 55, no. 3 (2003): 275–80.

20. Biard, *Missionaires*, has two impressive appendices, one listing agents sent to the eleven armies, the other listing those sent to the departments.

21. Bazcko, *Ending the Terror*, 75, 112–13.

22. Richard Whatmore and James Livesey, "Étienne Clavière, Jacques-Pierre Brissot et les fondations intellectuelles de la politique des girondins," *Annales historiques de la Révolution française* 321 (2000): 2–19; on Clavière and his connections with Brissot, see Michael Sonenscher, *Before the Deluge: Public Debt, Inequality, and the Intellectual Origins of the French Revolution* (Princeton, NJ: Princeton University Press, 2007), 315–23.

23. Jean-Clément Martin, *Violence et Révolution: Essai sur la naissance d'un mythe national* (Paris: Seuil, 2006), 120; Simon Burrows, "The Innocence of Jacques-Pierre Brissot," *Historical Journal* 46, no. 4 (2003): 843–71; Sylvia Neely, "The Uses of Power: Lafayette and Brissot in 1792," *Proceedings of the Western Society for French History* 34 (2006): 99–114.

24. For a description of this process, see Carolyn E. Fick, *The Making of Haiti: The Saint-Domingue Revolution from Below* (Knoxville: University of Tennessee Press, 1990).

25. On the abolitionist Sonthonax, see Nick Nesbitt, *Universal Emancipation: The Haitian Revolution and the Radical Enlightenment* (Charlottesville: University of Virginia Press, 2008); and Robert Louis Stein, *Léger Félicité Sonthonax: The Lost Sentinel of the Republic* (Rutherford, NJ: Fairleigh Dickinson University Press, 1985).

26. On imperial rivalries in the French Antilles, see David P. Geggus, ed., *The Impact of the Haitian Revolution in the Atlantic World* (Columbia: University of South Carolina Press, 2001); Ada Ferrer, *Freedom's Mirror: Cuba and Haiti in the Age of Revolution* (Cambridge: Cambridge University Press, 2014); Alain Yacou, ed., *Saint-Domingue espagnol et la révolution nègre d'Haïti (1790–1822)* (Paris: Karthala, 2007); Agnès Renault, *D'une île rebelle a une île fidèle: Les Français de Santiago de Cuba (1791–1825)* (Mont-Saint-Aignan: Publications des Universités de Rouen et du Havre, 2012).

27. Jeremy D. Popkin, *You Are All Free: The Haitian Revolution and the Abolition of Slavery* (Cambridge: Cambridge University Press, 2010).

28. Laurent Dubois, *A Colony of Citizens: Revolution and Slave Emancipation in the French Caribbean, 1787–1804* (Chapel Hill: University of North Carolina Press, 2004).

29. See especially the classic work by Albert Soboul, *Les sans-culottes en l'an II: Mouvement populaire et gouvernement révolutionnaire, juin 1793–9 Thermidor an II* (Paris: Clavreuil, 1958).

30. Frank Tallett, "Dechristianizing France: The Year II and the Revolutionary Experience," in *Religion, Society and Politics in France since 1789*, ed. Frank Tallett and Nicholas Atkin (London: The Hambledon Press, 1991), 1–28.

31. Jean-Clément Martin, *La Vendée et la France* (Paris: Seuil, 1987), 206–47; Bazcko, *Ending the Terror*, 138–39, 165–74.

32. Marisa Linton, *Choosing Terror: Virtue, Friendship, and Authenticity in the French Revolution* (Oxford: Oxford University Press, 2013), 137–200; Antonino De Francesco, "Federalist Obsession and Jacobin Conspiracy: France and the United States in a Time of Revolution, 1789–1794," in *Rethinking the Atlantic World: Europe and America in the Age of Democratic Revolutions*, ed. Manuela Albertone and Antonino De Francesco (London: Palgrave Macmillan, 2009), 239–56.

33. Michel Biard, *Collot d'Herbois: Légendes noires et révolution* (Lyon: Presses

Universitaires de Lyon, 1995), 175–79; Paul Mansfield, "Collot d'Herbois at the Committee of Public Safety: A Revaluation," *The English Historical Review* 408 (1988): 565–87.

34. David A. Bell, *The First Total War: Napoleon's Europe and the Birth of Warfare as We Know It* (Boston: Mariner Books, 2008), 156.

35. David A. Bell, *The Cult of the Nation in France: Inventing Nationalism, 1680–1800* (Cambridge, MA: Harvard University Press, 2001), 182–90.

36. Ibid., 19.

37. Ibid., 168.

38. Bernard Gainot, *Les officiers de couleur dans les armées de la République et de l'Empire (1792–1815): De l'esclavage à la condition militaire dans les Antilles françaises* (Paris: Karthala, 2007), 51–52.

39. See Barry M. Shapiro, "Revolutionary Justice in 1789–1790: The Comité des Recherches, the Châtelet, and the Fayettist Coalition," *French Historical Studies* 17, no. 3 (1992): 656–69.

40. Antoine Boulant, "Le suspect parisien en l'An II," *Annales historiques de la Révolution française* 280 (1990): 187–97.

41. Martin, *La Machine*, 37–38. On Cambacérès, see Isser Woloch, *Napoleon and His Collaborators: The Making of a Dictatorship* (New York: W. W. Norton, 2001), chapter 5, "The Second-Most Important Man in Napoleonic France," 120–55.

42. Istvan Hont, "The Permanent Crisis of a Divided Mankind: 'Nation-State' and Nationalism in Historical Perspective," in *Jealousy of Trade: International Competition and the Nation-State in Historical Perspective* (Cambridge, MA: Harvard University Press, 2010), 447–528.

43. Martin, *Violence et Révolution*, 157; Marisa Linton, "'Do You Believe That We're Conspirators?' Conspiracies Real and Imagined in Jacobin Politics, 1793–1794," in *Conspiracy in the French Revolution*, ed. Peter R. Campbell, Thomas E. Kaiser and Marisa Linton (Manchester: Manchester University Press, 2007), 127–49.

44. Michel Biard, ed., *Les politiques de la Terreur, 1793–1794* (Rennes: Presses Universitaires de Rennes, Société des Études Robespierristes, 2008); Patrice Gueniffey, *La politique de la Terreur: Essai sur la violence révolutionnaire (1789–1794)* (Paris: Fayard, 2000), 268.

45. Anne Simonin, "Etre non citoyen sous la Révolution Française: Comment un sujet de droit perd ses droits," in *Citoyen et citoyenneté sous la Révolution française*, ed. Raymonde Monnier (Paris: Société des Études Robespierristes, 2006), 289–305.

46. Sophie Wahnich, *La liberté ou la mort: Essai sur la Terreur et le terrorisme* (Paris: Éditions de la Fabrique, 2003), 59–70.

47. Dan Edelstein, *The Terror of Natural Right: Republicanism, the Cult of Nature and the French Revolution* (Chicago: University of Chicago Press, 2009), 149.

48. Dan Edelstein, *The Terror*, 153.

49. Peter McPhee, *Robespierre: A Revolutionary Life* (New Haven, CT: Yale University Press, 2012), 279.

50. Donald M. G. Sutherland, *France, 1789–1815: Revolution and Counterrevolution* (London: Fontana, 1985), 333.

51. Gueniffey, *Le nombre*, 500–510.

52. Harold G. Brown, *Ending the French Revolution: Violence, Justice and Repression from the Terror to Napoleon* (Charlottesville: University of Virginia Press, 2006).

53. Éric de Mari, "La répression des prêtres réfractaires conduite hors de la loi sous la Révolution française (1793–an VIII)," *Cahiers d'études du religieux: Recherches interdisciplinaires* 2007 [online].

54. Woloch, *Jacobin Legacy*, 272–310.

55. Donald M. G. Sutherland, *Murder in Aubagne: Lynching, Law, and Justice during the French Revolution* (Cambridge: Cambridge University Press, 2009).

56. Among the many serious accusations that led Danton to the guillotine, one of the most serious was corruption in the Compagnie des Indes, one of the great scandals of the time. See Joan Tafalla Monferrer, "L'enriquiment de Danton i l'afer de la Companyia de les Indies Orientals: Virtut i corrupció en la Revolució francesa," *Illes i Imperis* 16 (2014): 89–114.

57. For a list of members and associates and their activities, see Martin S. Staum, "Individual Rights and Social Control: Political Science in the French Institute," *Journal of the History of Ideas* 48, no. 3 (1987): 411–30.

58. Jules-François Saintoyant, *La colonisation française pendant la période napoléonienne (1799–1815)* (Paris: La Renaissance du Livre, 1931).

59. Lynn Hunt, David Lansky, and Paul Hanson, "The Failure of the Liberal Republic in France, 1795–1799: The Road to Brumaire," *Journal of Modern History* 51, no. 4 (1979): 734–59.

60. Carl Ludwig Lokke, *France and the Colonial Question: A Study of Contemporary French Opinion, 1763–1801* (New York: AMS Press, 1968), 160–74.

61. A. Duvergier, *Collection complète de lois, décrets, ordonnances, règlements, et avis du Conseil d'État* (Paris: A. Guyot, 1834), vol. 1, 163–70. For a critical assessment of the law, see Miranda Frances Spieler, "The Legal Structure of Colonial Rule during the French Revolution, 1789–1802," *William and Mary Quarterly* 66, no. 2 (2009): 365–408.

62. Laurent Dubois, "The Promise of Revolution: Saint-Domingue and the Struggle for Autonomy in Guadeloupe, 1797–1802," in *The Impact of the Haitian Revolution in the Atlantic World*, ed. David P. Geggus (Columbia: University of South Carolina Press, 2001), 112–56; and, by the same author, "Inscribing Race in the Revolutionary French Antilles," in *The Color of Liberty: Histories of Race in France*, ed. Sue Peabody and Tyler Stovall (Durham, NC: Duke University Press, 2003), 95–107.

63. Bernard Gainot, "Quel(s) statut(s) pour les cultivateurs sous le régime de la liberté générale? (1794–1802) ou 'Comment peut-on allier, sous la zone torride, l'industrie au bonheur?' (D. Lescallier)," in *La plantation coloniale esclavagiste, XVIIe–XIXe siècles*, ed. Danielle Bégot (Paris: Éditions de CTHS, 2008), 23–46. For a definition of *"isonomie républicaine,"* see, by the same author, *Les officiers de couleur dans les armées de la République et de l'Empire (1792–1815): De l'esclavage à la condition militaire dans les Antilles françaises* (Paris: Karthala, 2007), 76.

64. A. Duvergier, *Collection complète de lois*, 164.

65. Gainot, "Quel(s) statut(s)."

66. A. Duvergier *Collection complète de lois*, 166.

67. On the Code Noir, see Malick W. Ghachem, *The Old Regime and the Haitian Revolution* (Cambridge: Cambridge University Press, 2012), 219–31, 260–85.

68. A. Duvergier *Collection complète de lois*, 165.

69. Spieler, "The Legal Structure of Colonial Rule," 402.

70. On authoritarian rule in Saint-Domingue, see David P. Geggus, "The Caribbean in the Age of Revolution," in *The Age of Revolutions in Global Context, c. 1760–1840*, ed. David Armitage and Sanjay Subrahmanyam (London: Palgrave Macmillan, 2010), 83–100.

71. Laurent Dubois, "'African Citizens': Slavery, Freedom and Migration during the French Revolution," in *Migration Control in the North Atlantic: The Evolution of State Practices in Europe and the United States from the French Revolution to the Inter-War Period*, ed. Andreas Fahrmeier, Olivier Faron, Patrick Weil (New York: Berghahn Books, 2003), 25–38.

72. Stein, *Léger Félicité Sonthonax*.

73. David P. Geggus, *Slavery, War, and Revolution: The British Occupation of Saint Domingue, 1793–1798* (Oxford: Clarendon Press, 1982). Brief biographies of the commissars can be found in an appendix to Yves Benot, *La Révolution française et la fin des colonies, 1789–1794* (Paris: La Découverte, 1988), 273 and 279.

74. On Laveaux, see Bernard Gainot, "Le géneral Laveaux, gouverneur de Saint-Domingue, député néo-jacobin," *Annales historiques de la Révolution française* 278, no. 1 (1989): 433–54.

75. Bernard Gainot, "Métropole/Colonies: Projets constitutionnels et rapports de forces, 1798–1802," in *Rétablissement de l'esclavage dans les colonies françaises: Aux origines de Haïti*, ed. Yves Bénot and Marcel Dorigny (Paris: Maisonneuve et Larose, 2003), 13–28.

76. Pierre Branda and Thierry Lentz, *Napoléon, l'esclavage et les colonies* (Paris: Fayard, 2006), 54.

77. Jean Bourdon, *La Constitution de l'An VIII* (Rodez: Carrère Editeur, 1942).

78. For more on this argument, see Spieler, "The Legal Structure of Colonial Rule," 408.

79. For a justification in 1836, see Soulef Ayad-Bergounioux, "La 'République Représentative' selon Antoine Boulay de La Meurthe (1761–1840): Une figure de la bourgeoisie libérale et conservatrice," *Annales historiques de la Révolution française* 4 (2010): 31–55.

80. Charles Debbasch and Jean-Marie Pontier, *Les Constitutions de la France* (Paris: Dalloz, 1989), 104. See also *Constitution française de l'An VIII; suivie des sénatus-consultes organiques des 14 et 16 Thermidor an X, et du 28 Floréal an XII; et de l'acte additionnel aux constitutions de l'Empire, du 22 avril 1815* (Paris: Le Prieur, 1815).

81. Debbasch and Pontier, *Les Constitutions de la France*, 109.

82. Ibid., 100.

83. Annie Jourdan, *La Révolution batave entre la France et l'Amérique (1795–1806)* (Rennes: Presses Universitaires de Rennes, 2008); Beatrix Jacobs, Raymond Kubben, and Randall Lesaffer, eds., *In the Embrace of France: The Law of Nations and Constitutional Law in the French Satellite States of the Revolutionary and Napoleonic Age (1789–1815)* (Baden-Baden: Nomos, 2008); Pierre Serna, *Républiques sœurs: Le Directoire et la Révolution atlantique* (Rennes: Presses Universitaires de

Rennes, 2009); Angelie Sens, "La révolution batave et l'esclavage: Les (im)possibilités de l'abolition de la traite des noirs et de l'esclavage (1780–1814)," *Annales historiques de la Révolution française* 326 (2001): 65–78.

84. "Saint-Domingue, in its entirety . . . constitutes the territory of a single colony, which is part of the French Empire but is subject to special laws." Thomas Madiou, *Histoire d'Haïti*, vol. 2, *1799–1803* (Port-au-Prince: Henri Deschamps, 1989), 539.

85. Frédéric Régent, "Pourquoi faire l'histoire de la Révolution française par les colonies?" in *Pourquoi faire la révolution*, ed. Jean-Luc Chappey et al. (Marseille: Éditions Agone, 2012), 74; on the international context of 1802, see Brendan Simms, *Europe: The Struggle for Supremacy, from 1453 to the Present* (New York: Basic Books, 2014), 158–60.

86. Jean-François Niort and Jérémy Richard, "De la Constitution de l'an VIII au rétablissement de l'esclavage (1802) et à l'application du Code civil français dans les colonies françaises (1805): Le retour d'un droit colonial réactionnaire sous le régime napoléonien," in *Les colonies, la Révolution française, la loi*, ed. Frédéric Régent, Jean-François Niort, and Pierre Serna (Rennes: Presses Universitaires de Rennes, 2014), 165–78.

87. Ibid.

88. Thomas Pronier, "L'implicite et l'explicite dans la politique de Napoléon," in *Rétablissement de l'esclavage dans les colonies françaises: Aux origines d'Haïti*, ed. Yves Bénot and Marcel Dorigny (Paris: Maisonneuve et Larose, 2003), 55.

89. Florence Gauthier, "La Révolution française et le problème colonial, 1789–1804: État des connaissances et perspectives de recherche," in *La Révolution française au carrefour des recherches*, ed. Martine Lapied and Christine Peyrard (Aix-en-Provence: Publications de l'Université de Provence, 2004), 111.

90. Carl Ludwig Lokke, "Secret Negotiations to Maintain the Peace of Amiens," *American Historical Review* 49, no. 1 (1943): 55–64.

91. Yves Bénot and Marcel Dorigny, eds., *Rétablissement de l'esclavage dans les colonies françaises: Aux origines de Haïti* (Paris: Maisonneuve et Larose, 2003), 563.

92. Woloch, *Napoleon and His Collaborators*.

93. Dubois, "African Citizens," 35.

Chapter 4. The British Empire beyond the American Crisis

1. Philip Lawson, "Anatomy of a Civil War: New Perspectives on England in the Age of the American Revolution, 1767–1782," in *A Taste for Empire and Glory: Studies in British Overseas Expansion, 1660–1800* (Aldershot: Variorum, 1997), 142–52.

2. On this point, by now fully accepted with the concomitant decline of the old orthodoxy and the merely administrative state, see John Brewer's classic *The Sinews of Power: War, Money, and the English State, 1688–1783* (London: Unwin Hynman, 1989). See also Patrick O'Brien, "The Political Economy of British Taxation, 1660–1815," *Economic History Review* 41, no. 1 (1988): 1–32; for the later period, see Philip Harling and Peter Mandler, "From 'Fiscal-Military State' to Laissez-Faire State, 1760–1850," *The Journal of British Studies* 32, no. 1 (1993): 44–70; for a comparison

with other European experiences, see Christopher Storrs, ed., *The Fiscal-Military State in Eighteenth-Century Europe: Essays in Honour of P. G. M. Dickson* (Farnham: Ashgate, 2008).

3. Christopher A. Bayly, *The Birth of the Modern World, 1780–1914* (Oxford: Blackwell, 2004).

4. Christopher A. Bayly, *Imperial Meridian: The British Empire and the World, 1780–1830* (London: Longman, 1989); Peter J. Marshall, "Britain without America, A Second Empire?" in *The Oxford History of the British Empire*, vol. 2, *The Eighteenth Century*, ed. P. J. Marshall (Oxford: Oxford University Press, 1998), 577–95; Vincent Harlow, *The Founding of the Second British Empire, 1763–1793* (London: Longman, 1952–64), in 2 vols. Also see Vincent Harlow and Frederick Madden, *British Colonial Developments, 1774–1834: Select Documents* (Oxford: Clarendon Press, 1953).

5. J. Marshall, *The Making and Unmaking of Empires: Britain, India, and America, c. 1750–1783* (Oxford: Oxford University Press, 2009).

6. See, for instance, some of these texts, introduced and edited by Peter J. Marshall, *The British Discovery of Hinduism in the Eighteenth Century* (Cambridge: Cambridge University Press, 1970).

7. C. M. Platt, *Finance, Trade, and Politics in British Foreign Policy, 1815–1914* (Oxford: Oxford University Press, 1968); Matthew Brown and Gabriel Paquette, eds., *Connections after Colonialism: Europe and Latin America in the 1820s* (Tuscaloosa: University of Alabama Press, 2013).

8. Carl A. Trocki, *Opium, Empire and the Global Political Economy: A Study of the Asian Opium Trade, 1750–1950* (London: Routledge, 1999); Kathryn Meyer and Terry Parssinen, *Webs of Smoke: Smugglers, Warlords, Spies, and the History of International Drug Trade* (Lanham, MD: Rowman and Littlefield, 1988).

9. William J. Ashworth, *Customs and Excise: Trade, Production, and Consumption in England, 1640–1845* (Oxford: Oxford University Press, 2003); Ho-cheung Mui and Lorna H. Mui, *The Management of Monopoly: A Study of the East India Company's Conduct of Its Tea Trade, 1784–1833* (Vancouver: University of British Columbia Press, 1984).

10. Seymour Drescher, *Econocide: British Slavery in the Era of Abolition* (Pittsburgh: University of Pittsburgh Press, 1977); Christopher L. Brown, *Moral Capital: Foundations of British Abolitionism* (Chapel Hill: University of North Carolina Press, 2006).

11. Brewer, *The Sinews of Power*; Martin Daunton, *Trusting Leviathan: The Politics of Taxation in Britain, 1799–1914* (Cambridge: Cambridge University Press, 2001); see also, from a different angle, Joanna Innes, *Inferior Politics: Social Problems and Social Policies in Eighteenth-Century Britain* (Oxford: Oxford University Press, 2009).

12. Robert Travers, *Ideology and Empire in Eighteenth-Century India: The British in Bengal* (Cambridge: Cambridge University Press, 2007); Sudipta Sen, *Empire of Free Trade: The East India Company and Making of the Colonial Marketplace* (Philadelphia: University of Pennsylvania Press, 1998).

13. Peter Burroughs, "Imperial Institutions and the Government of Empire," in *The Oxford History of the British Empire*, vol. 3, *The Nineteenth Century*, ed. Andrew Porter (Oxford: Oxford University Press, 1999), 172–97.

14. Rory Muir, *Britain and the Defeat of Napoleon, 1807–1815* (New Haven, CT: Yale University Press, 1996); Hamish M. Scott, *The Birth of a Great Power System, 1740–1815* (Harlow: Pearson/Longman, 2006), 329–68. On the French events of the summer of 1792, see Sophie Wahnich, *La longue patience du peuple: 1792; Naissance de la République* (Paris: Payot, 2008).

15. David Cannadine, *Ornamentalism: How the British Saw Their Empire* (London: Allen Lane, 2001), 15, 45.

16. For a critical view of imperial capacity, see Helen T. Manning, *British Colonial Government after the American Revolution, 1782–1820* (New Haven, CT: Yale University Press, 1933).

17. For an excellent discussion of these issues, see Thomas Bartlett, "Ireland, Empire, and Union, 1690–1801," in *Ireland and the British Empire*, ed. Kevin Kenny (Oxford: Oxford University Press, 2004), especially 76–79.

18. James Kelly, *Prelude to Union: Anglo-Irish Politics in the 1780s* (Cork: Cork University Press, 1992).

19. Jack P. Greene, *Peripheries and Center: Constitutional Development in the Extended Polities of the British Empire and the United States, 1607–1788* (New York: W. W. Norton, 1990), 145–46; for a more recent discussion, see, by the same author, *The Constitutional Origins of the American Revolution* (Cambridge: Cambridge University Press, 2011).

20. David Milobar, "Quebec Reform, the British Constitution and the Atlantic Empire: 1774–1775," *Parliamentary History* 14, no. 1 (1995): 65–88.

21. On the influence of Protestantism during this last era of the First Empire, see Carla Gardina Pestana, *Protestant Empire: Religion and the Making of the British Atlantic World* (Philadelphia: University of Pennsylvania Press, 2009), chapter 8, "Revolutionary Divisions, Continuing Bonds," 218–55.

22. On "country tradition," see H. T. Dickinson, *Liberty and Property: Political Ideology in Eighteenth-Century Britain* (London: Weidenfeld & Nicolson, 1977), 163–95.

23. Robert L. Schuyler, "The Britannic Question and the American Revolution," *Political Science Quarterly* 38, no. 1 (1923): 107; David Cannadine, "Monarchy: Crowns and Contexts, Thrones and Dominations," in *Making History Now and Then: Discoveries, Controversies and Explorations* (Houndmills: Palgrave Macmillan, 2008), 39–58.

24. The British imperialists had a point, which is well explored by H. T. Dickinson in "Britain's Imperial Sovereignty: The Ideological Case against the American Colonists," in *Britain and the American Revolution*, ed. H. T. Dickinson (London: Longman, 1998), 64–96, and in chapter 8 of his *Liberty and Property*, 270–318.

25. Peter J. Marshall, "Empire and Authority in the Later Eighteenth Century," *Journal of Imperial and Commonwealth History* 15, no. 2 (1987): 105–22.

26. Donald Winch, *Classical Political Economy and Colonies* (London: The London School of Economics, 1965), 23; Bernard Semmel, *The Liberal Ideal and the Demons of Empire: Theories of Imperialism from Adam Smith to Lenin* (Baltimore: Johns Hopkins University Press, 1993), 17–38. See also the classic text by Vincent Harlow, "The New Imperial System, 1783–1815," in *Cambridge History of the British Empire*, vol. 2, *The growth of the New Empire, 1783–1870*, ed. J. Holland Rose, A. P. Newton and E. A. Benians (Cambridge: Cambridge University Press, 1961),

131–188. On parliamentary sovereignty, with Burke in mind, see Dickinson, "Britain's Imperial Sovereignty," 81–94.

27. Marshall, "Empire and Authority," 107.

28. Daniel I. O'Neill, *Edmund Burke and the Conservative Logic of Empire* (Berkeley: University of California Press, 2016); Uday Singh Metha, *Liberalism and Empire: A Study in Nineteenth-Century British Liberal Thought* (Chicago: University of Chicago Press, 1999), 153–90.

29. Charles F. Mullett, "English Imperial Thinking, 1764–1783," *Political Science Quarterly* 45, no. 4 (1930): 548–79.

30. On the nineteenth-century military question, see Kenneth Bourne, *Britain and the Balance of Power in North America, 1815–1908* (London: Longman, 1967); Dirk H. A. Kolff, "The End of an Ancien Régime: Colonial War in India, 1798–1818," in *Imperialism and War: Essays on Colonial Wars in Asia and Africa*, ed. J. A. de Moor and H. L. Wesseling (Leiden: E. J. Brill, 1989), 22–49.

31. John Benyon, "Overlords of Empire? British 'Proconsular Imperialism' in Comparative Perspective," *Journal of Imperial and Commonwealth History* 19, no. 2 (1991): 168.

32. Uday Singh Metha, *Liberalism and Empire: A Study in Nineteenth-Century British Liberal Thought* (Chicago: University of Chicago Press, 1999), 64–76.

33. I know of no recent biographical works on this interesting writer, though there are sketches in Norman St. Johns-Stevas, ed., *The Collected Works of Walter Bagehot* (London: The Economist, 1968), 367–99 and 401–3.

34. George Cornewall Lewis, *An Essay on the Government of Dependencies* (London: John Murray, 1841). C. A. Bodelsen commented on the importance and influence of this book in his *Studies in Mid-Victorian Imperialism* (New York: Howard Fertig, 1968), 39. On British power in Malta during the Napoleonic wars, see Cyril Willis Dixon, *The Colonial Administration of Sir Thomas Maitland* (New York: Augustus M. Kelley Publishers, 1969), 131–76 [1st ed. 1939].

35. Austin, like Lewis, was a leading light of British public law; his work is a constant presence in the canonical work by A. V. Dicey, *Introduction to the Study of the Law of the Constitution* (Houndmills: Macmillan, 1985), first published in 1885; see especially the chapter on parliamentary sovereignty.

36. Lewis, *An Essay*, 73. Emphasis in the original.

37. Herman Merivale, *Lectures on Colonization and Colonies delivered before the University of Oxford in 1839, 1840, and 1841* (London: Humphrey Milford, 1928). After he visited the island he published "A Visit to Malta" in his *Historical Studies* (London: Longman, Green, Longman, Roberts and Green, 1865), 450–68, but the article has no political or institutional content. On Merivale, see Edward Beasley, "The Man Who Ran the Empire," in his *Mid-Victorian Imperialists: British Gentlemen and the Empire of the Mind* (London: Routledge, 2005), 20–43. Merivale's economic ideas were analyzed in R. N. Ghosh, *Classical Macroeconomics and the Case for Colonies* (Calcutta: New Publishers, 1967).

38. Merivale, *Lectures*, 627.

39. Ibid., 623–24.

40. Marck Francis, *Governors and Settlers: Images of Authority in the British Colonies, 1820–1860* (London: Palgrave Macmillan, 1992), 15–29.

41. John Whitson Cell, *British Colonial Administration in the Mid-Nineteenth Century: The Policy-Making Process* (New Haven, CT: Yale University Press, 1970); Robert V. Kubicek, *The Administration of Imperialism: Joseph Chamberlain at the Colonial Office* (Durham, NC: Duke University Press, 1969); R. C. Snelling and J. T. Barron, "The Colonial Office and its permanent officials 1801–1914" and Valerie Cromwell and Zara S. Steiner, "The Foreign Office before 1914: A Study in Resistance," both in *Studies in the Growth of Nineteenth-Century Government*, ed. Gillian Sutherland (London: Routledge & Kegan Paul, 1972), 139–166 and 167–94; Matthew Lange, *Lineages of Despotism and Development: British Colonialism and State Power* (Chicago: University of Chicago Press, 2009).

42. Gerald M. Craig, *Upper Canada: The Formative Years, 1784–1841* (Oxford: Oxford University Press, 2013), chapter 4, "Invasion Repulsed," 66–84 [1st ed. 1963].

43. Guy Frégault, *Canada: The War of the Conquest* (Toronto: Oxford University Press, 1969), 164–200.

44. For a general overview, see John Manning Ward, *Colonial Self-Government: The British Experience, 1759–1856* (New York: Macmillan, 1976), 5–11.

45. J. M. Bumsted, "The Cultural Landscape of Early Canada," in *Strangers Within the Realm: Cultural Margins of the First British Empire*, ed. Bernard Bailyn and Philip D. Morgan (Chapel Hill: University of North Carolina Press, 1991), 363–92; John McLaren, A. R. Buck and Nancy M. Wright, eds., *Despotic Dominion: Property Rights in British Settler Societies* (Vancouver: University of British Columbia Press, 2004).

46. There is an excellent overview in Philip Girard, "Liberty, Order, and Pluralism: The Canadian Experience," in *Exclusionary Empire. English Liberty Overseas, 1600–1900*, ed. Jack P. Greene (Cambridge: Cambridge University Press, 2010), 160–90.

47. Robin W. Winks, *The Blacks in Canada: A History* (Montreal: McGill-Queen's University Press, 2012), 24–61 [1st ed. 1997].

48. Philip Lawson, *The Imperial Challenge: Quebec and Britain in the Age of American Revolution* (Montreal: McGill-Queen's University Press, 1986).

49. On approval of the Quebec Act (1774) and the campaign against it by the Thirteen Colonies, see Gustave Lanctôt, *Canada and the American Revolution, 1774–1783* (Toronto: Clarke, Irwin and Company, 1967), 17–61.

50. It must be remembered here that the question of Catholic relief was one of the ingredients of the Gordon Riots of June 1780 in London. The spark that ignited the protest was the Popery Act of 1778, which softened religious requirements for joining the army; see George F. E. Rudé, "The Gordon Riots: A Study of the Rioters and Their Victims," *Transactions of the Royal Historical Society* 6 (1956): 93–114.

51. J. M. Bumsted, *The Peoples of Canada: A Pre-Confederation History* (Toronto: Oxford University Press, 2004), 139–40.

52. See the excellent collection of essays edited by Terry Fenge and Jim Aldridge, *Keeping Promises: The Royal Proclamation of 1763, Aboriginal Rights, and Treaties in Canada* (Montreal: McGill-Queen's University Press, 2015).

53. Craig, *Upper Canada*, 134–50; see also Jane Errington, *The Lion, the Eagle, and Upper Canada: A Developing Colonial Ideology* (Montreal: McGill-Queen's University Press, 2012).

54. Brian Young, "Positive Law, Positive State: Class Realignment and the Transformation of Lower Canada, 1815–1866," in *Colonial Leviathan: State Formation in Mid-Nineteenth-Century Canada*, ed. Allan Greer and Ian W. Radforth (Toronto: University of Toronto Press, 1992), 50–63.

55. James W. St. G. Walker, *The Black Loyalists: The Search for a Promised Land in Nova Scotia and Sierra Leone, 1783–1870* (Toronto: University of Toronto Press, 1992).

56. James Belich, "The Rise of the Angloworld: Settlement in North America and Australasia, 1784–1918," in *Rediscovering the British World*, ed. Philip A. Buckner and R. Douglas Francis (Calgary: University of Calgary Press, 2005), 53.

57. J. M. Bumsted, "The Consolidation of British North America, 1783–1860," in Philip Buckner, ed., *Canada and the British Empire: The Oxford History of the British Empire* (Oxford: Oxford University Press, 2008), 45.

58. Martin Wight, *The Development of the Legislative Council, 1606–1945* (London: Faber & Faber, 1946), 44–46.

59. Michel Ducharme, *The Idea of Liberty in Canada during the Age of Atlantic Revolutions, 1776–1838* (Montreal McGill-Queen's University Press, 2014), 48–51.

60. Brian Jenkins, *Era of Emancipation: British Government of Ireland, 1812–1830* (Montreal: McGill-Queen's University Press, 1988), 44.

61. Helen T. Manning, *British Colonial Government after the American Revolution, 1782–1820* (New Haven, CT: Yale University Press, 1933); A. F. Madden, " 'Not for Export': The Westminster Model of Government and British Colonial Practice," *The Journal of Imperial and Commonwealth Studies* 8, no. 1 (1979): 18.

62. Alan Taylor, "The Late Loyalists: Northern Reflections of the Early American Republic," *Journal of the Early Republic* 27, no. 1 (2007): 3.

63. Mark Francis, *Governors and Settlers: Images of Authority in the British Colonies, 1820–1860* (London: Palgrave Macmillan, 1992), 15–16.

64. Jean-Pierre Wallot, "Révolution et réformisme dans le Bas-Canada (1773–1815)," *Annales historiques de la Révolution française* 45, no. 213 (1973): 344–406.

65. Peter Burroughs, *The Canadian Crisis and British Colonial Policy (1828–1841)* (London: Edward Arnold, 1972).

66. Allan Greer, *The Patriots and the People: The Rebellion of 1837 in Rural Lower Canada* (Toronto: University of Toronto Press, 1993), 258–93; Colin Read, *The Rising in Western Upper Canada, 1837–1838: The Duncombe Revolt and after* (Toronto: University of Toronto Press, 1982).

67. Fernand Ouellet, *Louis-Joseph Papineau: Un être divisé* (Ottawa: Société Historique du Canada, 1960); Marguerite Paulin, *Louis-Joseph Papineau: Le grand tribun, le pacifiste* (Montreal: XYZ, 2000). On the ideological underpinnings of the Canadian unrest, see Michel Ducharme, *The Idea of Liberty in Canada during the Age of Atlantic Revolutions, 1776–1838* (Montreal: McGill-Queen's University Press, 2014).

68. Philip Goldring, "Province and Nation: Problems of Imperial Rule in Lower Canada, 1820 to 1841," *The Journal of Imperial and Commonwealth Studies* 9, no. 1 (1980): 42–43.

69. Ducharme, *The Idea of Liberty*, 181.

70. On the governor's dubious ideas, see Janet Ajzenstat, *The Political Thought of Lord Durham* (Kingston: McGill-Queen's University Press, 1988).

71. Ged Martin, *The Durham Report and British Policy: A Critical Essay* (Cambridge: Cambridge University Press, 1972); see also, by the same author, "The Influence of the Durham Report," in *Reappraisals in British Imperial History*, ed. Ronald Hyam and Ged Martin (London: Macmillan Press, 1975), 75–88; Robert A. Huttenback, "The Durham Report and the Establishment of Responsible Government in Canada," in *The British Imperial Experience* (New York: Harper & Row, 1966), 20–38.

72. Reginald Coupland, *The Constitutional Problem in India*, part 1: *The Indian Problem, 1833–1935* (London: Oxford University Press, 1944), 20.

73. On the financial debates and reforms proposed by "colonial reformers," see A. G. L. Shaw, "British Attitudes to the Colonies, ca. 1820–1850," *The Journal of British Studies* 9, no. 1 (1969): 71–95; Ben Forster, *A Conjunction of Interests: Business, Politics, and Tariffs, 1825–1879* (Toronto: University of Toronto Press, 1986).

74. R. Ward, "The British West Indies in the Age of Abolition, 1748–1815," in *The Oxford History of the British Empire*, vol. 2, *The Eighteenth Century*, ed. P. J. Marshall (Oxford: Oxford University Press, 2001), 415.

75. For a general overview, see Arthur L. Stinchcombe, *Sugar Island Slavery in the Age of Enlightenment* (Princeton, NJ: Princeton University Press, 1995); B. W. Higman, *A Concise History of the Caribbean* (Cambridge: Cambridge University Press, 2011); Franklin W. Knight, *The Caribbean: The Genesis of a Fragmented Nationalism* (New York: Oxford University Press, 2012).

76. On Melville, see Vincent Harlow, "The New Imperial System, 1783–1815," in *Cambridge History of the British Empire*, vol. 2, *The Growth of the New Empire, 1783–1870*, ed. J. Holland Rose, A. P. Newton, and E. A. Benians (Cambridge: Cambridge University Press, 1961), 151; on redistribution of land, D. H. Murdoch, "Land Policy in the Eighteenth-Century British Empire: The Sale of Crown Lands in the Ceded Islands, 1763–1783," *Historical Journal* 27, no. 3 (1984): 549–73; for a wider approach, see Steven Sarson, *British America, 1500–1800: Creating Colonies, Imagining an Empire* (London: Hodder Arnold, 2005), 269.

77. D. J. Murray, *The West Indies and the Development of Colonial Government, 1801–1834* (Oxford: Clarendon Press, 1965), 80.

78. Michael Craton, *Testing the Chains: Resistance to Slavery in the British West Indies* (Ithaca, NY: Cornell University Press, 1982), 233.

79. Andrew Porter, "Introduction: Britain and the Empire in the Nineteenth Century," in *The Oxford History of the British Empire*, vol. 3, *The Nineteenth Century*, ed. Andrew Porter (Oxford: Oxford University Press, 1999), 17–18.

80. It is worth mentioning that George Cornewall Lewis devoted attention to the problems of religious tolerance in the empire in his *Essays on the Administration of Great Britain from 1783 to 1830* (London: Longman, Green, Longman, Roberts & Green, 1864), 85 and passim.

81. Murray, *The West Indies*, 49–56; Stephen Constantine, *Community and Identity: The Making of Modern Gibraltar since 1704* (Manchester: Manchester University Press, 2009).

82. Andrew J. O'Shaughnessy, "The Formation of a Commercial Lobby: The West Indies Interest, British Colonial Policy and the American Revolution," *Historical Journal* 40, no. 1 (1997): 71–95.

83. See Paul Knaplund, *James Stephen and the British Colonial System, 1813–1847* (Madison: University of Wisconsin Press, 1953).

84. Christer Petley, *Slaveholders in Jamaica: Colonial Society and Culture during the Era of Abolition* (London: Pickering & Chatto, 2009), 85–102.

85. William A. Green, *British Slave Emancipation: The Sugar Colonies and the Great Experiment, 1830–1865* (Oxford: Clarendon Press, 1988), 101 [1st ed. 1976]; Seymour Drescher, *The Mighty Experiment: Free Labor versus Slavery in British Emancipation* (Oxford: Oxford University Press, 2002).

86. Christopher L. Brown, "The Politics of Slavery," in *The British Atlantic World, 1500–1800*, ed. David Armitage and Michael J. Braddick (Houndmills: Palgrave Macmillan, 2002), 229–30.

87. A useful account can be found in Gad Heuman, "The British West Indies," in *The Oxford History of the British Empire*, vol. 3, *The Nineteenth Century*, ed. Andrew Porter (Oxford: Oxford University Press, 1999), 470–92.

88. Green, *British Slave Emancipation*, 104–5.

89. Emilia Viotti da Costa, *Crowns of Glory, Tears of Blood: The Demerara Slave Rebellion of 1823* (New York: Oxford University Press, 1994).

90. Murray, *The West Indies*, 121–26; Seymour Drescher, *Capitalism and Antislavery: British Mobilization in Comparative Perspective* (London: Macmillan, 1986), 89–110.

91. Thomas C. Holt, *The Problem of Freedom: Race, Labor, and Politics in Jamaica and Britain, 1832–1938* (Baltimore: Johns Hopkins University Press, 1992), 42–53.

92. Bayly, *Imperial Meridian*, 1.

93. On the remote origins of those lobbies, see Peter Jupp, *The Governing of Britain, 1688–1848: The Executive, Parliament, and the People* (London: Routledge, 2006), 90–95, 245–55; on the incremental number of MPs with connections to the East India Company, see Peter J. Marshall, *Problems of Empire: Britain and India, 1757–1813* (London: Allen and Unwin, 1968), 37; Douglas M. Peers, *Between Mars and Mammon: Colonial Armies and the Garrison State in India, 1819–1835* (London: I. B. Tauris Publishers, 1995), 19–20.

94. Miles Taylor, "Empire and Parliamentary Reform: The 1832 Reform Act Revisited," in *Rethinking the Age of Reform: Britain, 1780–1850*, ed. Arthur Burns and Joanna Innes (Cambridge: Cambridge University Press, 2003), 295–311.

95. Cristopher L. Brown, *Moral Capital: Foundations of British Abolitionism* (Chapel Hill: University of North Carolina Press, 2006); Srividhya Swaminathan, *Debating the Slave Trade: Rhetoric of British National Identity, 1759–1815* (Farnham: Ashgate, 2009).

96. I am using the concepts *empire* and *colonies* on an infinite number of occasions. In general, *empire* implies the desire to keep different societies under one single sovereignty and *colonies* refers to possessions desired for economic and social reasons. A colony might not form part of an empire, but a contemporary empire comprises colonial parts by necessity. The distinction is not exactly the same as that used by Uday Singh Metha in *Liberalism and Empire: A Study in Nineteenth-Century Liberal Thought*, 2–3.

97. Michael Bentley, *Politics without Democracy: Great Britain, 1815–1914; Perception and Preoccupation in British Government* (Totowa, NJ: Barnes & Noble,

1984), 59–72; Peter Mandler, *Aristocratic Government in the Age of Reform: Whigs and Liberals, 1830–1852* (Oxford: Clarendon Press, 1990). The Indian MP was Dadabhai Naoroji, a member of the Liberal Party.

98. Alvin Jackson, "Ireland, the Union, and the Empire, 1800–1960," in *Ireland and the British Empire*, ed. Kevin Kenny (Oxford: Oxford University Press, 2004), 124.

99. On the long shadow of this topic, see Ged Martin, "Empire Federalism and Imperial Parliamentary Union, 1820–1870," *Historical Journal* 16, no. 1 (1973): 65–92.

100. Schuyler, "The Britannic Question," 108. On the influence of the North American debate, see John Brewer, *Party Ideology and Popular Politics at the Accession of George III* (Cambridge: Cambridge University Press, 1976).

101. A. Benians, "Adam Smith's Project of an Empire," *Cambridge Historical Journal* 1, no. 3 (1925): 249–83.

102. On Smith and the thinkers mentioned below, see Jennifer Pitts, *A Turn to Empire: The Rise of Liberalism in Britain and France* (Princeton, NJ: Princeton University Press, 2005), 25–58, 103–22.

103. William Roy Smith, "British Imperial Federation," *Political Science Quarterly* 36, no. 2 (1921): 278.

104. Thomas Bartlett, *The Fall and Rise of the Irish Nation: The Catholic Question, 1690–1830* (Dublin: Rowman & Littlefield, 1992); Peter Jupp, *British Politics on the Eve of Reform: The Duke of Wellington's Administration, 1828–1830* (London: Macmillan, 1998), 157–64.

105. Miles Taylor, "Empire and Parliamentary Reform: The 1832 Reform Act Revisited," in *Rethinking the Age of Reform: Britain, 1780–1850*, ed. Arthur Burns and Joanna Innes (Cambridge: Cambridge University Press, 2003), 295–96.

106. Thomas Bartlett, "'This Famous Island Set in a Virginian Sea': Ireland in the British Empire 1690–1801," in *The Oxford History of the British Empire*, vol. 2, *The Eighteenth Century*, ed. P. J. Marshall (Oxford: Oxford University Press, 1998), 265–66.

107. Frank O'Gorman, *Voters, Patrons, and Parties: The Unreformed Electorate of Hanoverian England, 1734–1832* (Oxford: Clarendon Press, 1989); John A. Phillips, *The Great Reform Bill in the Boroughs: English Electoral Behaviour, 1818–1841* (Oxford: Oxford University Press, 1992); Tillman W. Nechtman, *Nabobs: Empire and Identity in Eighteenth-Century Britain* (Cambridge: Cambridge University Press, 2010), 129, 222–32.

108. Hugh V. Bowen, *Revenue and Reform: The Indian Problem in British Politics, 1757–1773* (Cambridge: Cambridge University Press, 1991).

109. On this sort of institution, see Ann M. Carlos and Stephen Nicholas, "'Giants of Earlier Capitalism': The Chartered Trading Companies as Modern Multinationals," *The Business History Review* 62, no. 3 (1988): 398–419; for a classic account, see K. N. Chaudhuri, *The Trading World of Asia and the English East India Company, 1660–1760* (Cambridge: Cambridge University Press, 1978).

110. Philip J. Stern, *The Company-State: Corporate Sovereignty and the Early Modern Foundations of the British Empire in India* (Oxford: Oxford University Press, 2011).

111. Peter J. Marshall, *Bengal: The British Bridgehead; Eastern India, 1740–1828* (Cambridge: Cambridge University Press, 1987), 70–92.

112. Maya Jasanoff, *Edge of Empire: Lives, Culture, and Conquest in the East, 1750–1850* (New York: Vintage Books, 2006), 149–76.

113. David A. Washbrook, "India, 1818–1860: The Two Faces of Colonialism," in *The Oxford History of the British Empire*, vol. 3, *The Nineteenth Century*, ed. Andrew Porter (Oxford: Oxford University Press, 1999), 399.

114. Taxes at the provincial level are described in Farhat Hasan, *State and Locality in Mughal India: Power Relations in Western India, c. 1572–1730* (Cambridge: Cambridge University Press, 1976).

115. Peter Boomgaard, *Children of the Colonial State: Population Growth and Economic Development in Java, 1795–1880* (Amsterdam: Free University Press, 1989), 22.

116. Marshall, *Bengal: The British Bridgehead*, 3.

117. Hugh V. Bowen, *The Business of Empire: The East India Company and Imperial Britain, 1756–1833* (Cambridge: Cambridge University Press, 2006).

118. Lauren Benton, *Law and Colonial Cultures. Legal Regimes in World History, 1400–1900*, (Cambridge: Cambridge University Press, 2002), 127–66. Later, Indian soldiers defended (or conquered) not only the subcontinent but also other important parts of the empire; see Thomas R. Metcalf, *Imperial Connections: India in the Indian Ocean Arena, 1860–1920* (Berkeley: University of California Press, 2007), 78–101.

119. Jack Harrington, *Sir John Malcolm and the Creation of British India* (Houndmills: Palgrave Macmillan, 2010).

120. Marshall, *The Making and Unmaking of Empires*, 208–72.

121. Peter J. Marshall, *The Impeachment of Warren Hastings* (Oxford: Oxford University Press, 1965).

122. Colin Newbury, "Patrons, Clients, and Empire: The Subordination of Indigenous Hierarchies in Asia and Africa," *Journal of World History* 11, no. 2 (2000): 235.

123. Frederick G. Whelan, *Edmund Burke and India: Political Morality and Empire* (Pittsburgh: University of Pittsburgh Press, 1996).

124. Ian Hampsher-Monk, "Edmund Burke and Empire," in *Lineages of Empire: The Historical Roots of British Imperial Thought*, ed. Duncan Kelly (Oxford: Oxford University Press, 2009), 123; Michael Curtis, *Orientalism and Islam: European Thinkers on Oriental Despotism in the Middle East and India* (Cambridge: Cambridge University Press, 2009), 103–38.

125. Robert Travers, "Contested Despotism: Problems of Liberty in British India," in *Exclusionary Empire: English Liberties Overseas, 1600–1900*, ed. Jack P. Greene (Cambridge: Cambridge University Press, 2010), 209.

126. Marshall, *Problems of Empire*, 64–66; Glyndwr Williams, *The Expansion of Europe in the Eighteenth Century: Overseas Rivalry, Discovery and Exploitation* (New York: Walker and Company, 1966), 134.

127. Ranajit Guha, *A Rule of Property for Bengal: An Essay on the Idea of Permanent Settlement* (Durham, NC: Duke University Press, 1996).

128. Robert Travers, " 'The Real Value of the Lands': The Nawabs, the British and the Land Tax in Eighteenth-Century Bengal," *Modern Asian Studies* 38, no. 3 (2004): 520–45.

129. Carl A. Trocki, *Opium, Empire and the Global Political Economy: A Study of the Asian Opium Trade, 1750–1950* (London: Routledge, 1999).

130. Burton Stein, *Thomas Munro: The Origins of the Colonial State and His Vision of the Empire* (Delhi: Oxford University Press, 1989); T. H. Beaglehole, *Thomas Munro and the Development of Administrative Policy in Madras, 1792–1818: The Origins of the 'Munro System'* (Cambridge: Cambridge University Press, 1966).

131. John Bastin, *Raffles's Ideas on the Land Rent System in Java and the Mackenzie Land Tenure Commission* (Gravenhague: Martinus Nijhoff, 1954); see also, by the same author, *The Native Policies of Sir Stamford Raffles in Java and Sumatra: An Economic Interpretation* (Oxford: Clarendon Press, 1957).

132. Eric Stokes, *The English Utilitarians and India* (Oxford: Oxford University Press, 1959); S. Ambirajan, *Classical Political Economy and British Policy in India* (Cambridge: Cambridge University Press, 1978).

133. Robert Travers, "British India as a Problem in Political Economy: Comparing James Steuart and Adam Smith," in *Lineages of Empire: The Historical Roots of British Imperial Thought*, ed. Duncan Kelly (Oxford: Oxford University Press, 2009), 137–60.

134. Burton Stein, ed., *The Making of Agrarian Policy in British India, 1770–1900* (Oxford: Oxford University Press, 1992).

135. Travers, *Ideology and Empire*; Jon Wilson, *The Domination of Strangers: Modern Governance in Eastern India, 1780–1835* (Basingstoke: Palgrave Macmillan, 2008).

136. Marshall, "Empire and Authority," 105–22.

137. Christopher A. Bayly, *Indian Society and the Making of the British Empire* (Cambridge: Cambridge University Press, 1990), 83–84; James Lees, "Retrenchment, Reform and the Practice of Military-Fiscalism in the Early East India Company State," in *The Political Economy of Empire in the Early Modern World*, ed. Sophus A. Reinert and Pernille Røge (Houndmills: Palgrave Macmillan, 2013), 173–91.

Chapter 5. Theory and Practice of French Spécialité

1. On the Portuguese experience, see Ana Cristina Nogueira da Silva, *Constitucionalismo e imperio: A cidadania no Ultramar Português* (Coimbra: Almedina, 2010); Josep M. Fradera, "Reading Imperial Transitions: Spanish Contraction, British Expansion and American Irruption," in *Colonial Crucible: Empire in the Making of the Modern American State*, ed. Alfred W. McCoy and Francisco A. Scarano (Madison: University of Wisconsin Press, 2009), 34–62.

2. Yves Bénot and Marcel Dorigny, eds., *Rétablissement de l'esclavage dans les colonies françaises: Aux origines de Haïti* (Paris: Maisonneuve et Larose, 2003); Miranda Frances Spieler, *Empire and Underworld: Captivity in French Guiana* (Cambridge, MA: Harvard University Press, 2012); Josette Fallope, *Esclaves et citoyens: Les Noirs à la Guadeloupe au XIXe siècle dans les processus de résistance et d'intégration (1802–1910)* (Basse-Terre: Société d'Histoire de la Guadeloupe, 1992).

3. Jean-François Brière, *Haïti et la France: 1804–1848: Le rêve brisé* (Paris: Karthala, 2008); Alyssa Goldstein Sepinwall, "The Specter of Saint-Domingue: The Impact of the Haitian Revolution in the United States and France," in *The World of the Haitian Revolution*, ed. David P. Geggus and Norman Fiering (Bloomington:

Indiana University Press, 2009), 317–38; on the constitution, see Ada Ferrer, "Haiti, Free Soil, and Antislavery in the Revolutionary Atlantic," *American Historical Review* 117, no. 1 (2012): 40–66.

4. Lawrence C. Jennings, *French Anti-Slavery: The Movement for the Abolition of Slavery in France, 1802–1848* (New York: Cambridge University Press, 2000).

5. Louis-Agustin Barrière, "Le statut personnel des musulmans d'Algérie de 1834 à 1962" (PhD diss., Université Jean Moulin-Lyon III, 1990).

6. Justin Daniel, "The French *Départements d'outre-mer*: Guadeloupe and Martinique," in *Extended Statehood in the Caribbean: Paradoxes of Quasi Colonialism, Local Autonomy and Extended Statehood in the USA, French, Dutch and British Caribbean*, ed. Lammert de Jong and Dirk Kruijt (Amsterdam: Rozenberg Publishers, 2005), 59–84; Robert Aldrich and John Connell, *France's Overseas Frontier: Départements et territoires d'outre-mer* (Cambridge: Cambridge University Press, 1992).

7. Catherine Coquery-Vidrovitch, "Nationalité et citoyenneté en Afrique occidentale française: Originaires et citoyens dans le Sénégal colonial," *Journal of African History* 42 (2001): 285–305; François Borella, "Nationalité et citoyenneté," in *Citoyenneté et nationalité: Perspectives en France et au Québec*, ed. Dominique Colas, Claude Emeri, and Jacques Zylberberg (Paris: Presses Universitaires de France, 1991), 209–29.

8. Munro Price, *The Perilous Crown: France Between Revolutions, 1814–1848* (London: Pan Books, 2007).

9. Jean-François Brière, "La France et la Reconnaissance de l'indépendance haïtienne: Le débat sur l'ordonnance de 1825," *French Colonial History* 5 (2004): 125–38.

10. Charles Debbasch and Jean-Marie Pontier, *Les constitutions de la France* (Paris: Dalloz, 1989), 120.

11. Romuald Szramkiewicz and Jacques Bouineau, *Histoire des institutions, 1750–1914: Droit et société en France de la fin de l'Ancien Régime à la Première Guerre mondiale* (Paris: Librairie de la Cour de Cassation, 1996), 486.

12. Anne Girollet, "La politique colonial de la Seconde République: Un assimilationnisme modéré," *Revue française d'outre-mer* 85, no. 320 (1998): 71. There is an interesting debate in France today regarding the concept of assimilation itself; see, for instance, Stéphane Beaud and Gérard Noiriel, "L'assimilation': Un concept en panne," *Revue internationale d'action communautaire* 21, no. 61 (1989): 63–76; see also Abdellali Hajjat, *Les frontières de l'identité nationale': L'injonction à l'assimilation en France métropolitaine et coloniale* (Paris: La Découverte, 2012).

13. Serge Mam Lam Fouck, *Histoire de l'assimilation: Des 'vieilles colonies' françaises aux départements d'outre-mer; La culture politique de l'assimilation aux Antilles et en Guyane françaises (XIXe et XXe siècles)* (Matoury: Ibis Rouge, 2006).

14. Louis Milliot, *L'œuvre législative de la France en Algérie* (Paris: Librairie Alcan, 1930), 86–87.

15. John Ruedy, *Modern Algeria: The Origins and Development of a Nation* (Bloomington: Indiana University Press, 2005), 73 [1st ed. 1992].

16. Peter Dunwoodie, *Writing French Algeria* (Oxford: Clarendon Press, 2004), 1–35 [1st ed. 1998]; Pierre Montagnon, *La Conquête de l'Algérie: 1830–1871* (Paris: Pygmalion, 1986).

17. William B. Cohen, *The French Encounter with Africans: White Response to Blacks, 1530–1880* (Bloomington: Indiana University Press, 1980), 100–29.

18. Alexis de Tocqueville, *Sur l'esclavage*, ed. Seloua Luste Boulbina (Arles: Actes Sud, 2008), 148.

19. Szramkiewicz and Bouineau, *Histoire des institutions*, 486.

20. Yvette Katan, "Les colons de 1848 en Algérie: Mythes et réalités," *Revue d'histoire moderne et contemporaine* 31 (1984): 177–202; Michael J. Heffernan, "The Parisian Poor and the Colonization of Algeria during the Second Republic," *French History* 3, no. 4 (1989): 377–403.

21. Arthur Girault, *Principes de la colonisation et de législation coloniale* (Paris: Larose, 1895), 305.

22. ("The Republic of France is democratic, one and indivisible ... the territory of Algeria and the French colonies are hereby declared to be French territory and will be governed by particular laws until a special law places them under the jurisdiction of this Constitution.") Jacques Godechot, ed., *Les Constitutions de la France depuis 1789* (Paris: Garnier Flammarion, 1970), 276.

23. See a long-term consideration in Raymond F. Betts, *Assimilation and Association in French Colonial Theory, 1890–1914* (New York: Columbia University Press, 1961).

24. Victor Schœlcher, *Esclavage et colonisation* (Paris: Presses Universitaires de France, 2007), 152.

25. Robin Blackburn, *The Overthrow of Colonial Slavery, 1776–1846* (London: Verso, 1988), 473–516.

26. Myriam Cottias, "Le silence de la nation: Les 'vieilles' colonies comme lieu de définition des dogmes républicains (1848–1905)," *Outre-mers: Revue d'histoire* 90, no. 338 (2003): 32; see also Sylvane Larcher, *L'autre citoyen: L'idéal républicain et les Antilles après l'esclavage* (Paris: Armand Colin, 2014), 127–69.

27. Schœlcher, *Esclavage et colonisation*, 153.

28. Martin A. Klein, *Slavery and Colonial Rule in French West Africa* (Cambridge: Cambridge University Press, 1998), 19–37.

29. Annie Rey-Goldzeiguer, "La France coloniale à la recherche de l'efficience," in *Histoire de la France coloniale*, vol. 1, *Des origines à 1914*, ed. Jean Meyer et al. (Paris: Armand Colin, 1991), 412.

30. For a long-term overview, see Frédéric Régent, *La France et ses esclaves* (Paris: Grasset, 2007); Françoise Vergès, *Abolir l'esclavage: Une utopie coloniale; Les ambiguïtés d'une politique humanitaire* (Paris: Albin Michel, 2001).

31. Rebecca Hartkopf Schloss, *Sweet Liberty: The Final Days of Slavery in Martinique* (Philadelphia: University of Pennsyvania Press, 2009), vii (citing population statistics for Martinique, 1802–47); Léo Elisabeth, "L'abolition de l'esclavage à la Martinique," *Mémoires de la Société d'Histoire de la Martinique* 5 (1983), 10–20.

32. Caroline Oudin-Bastide, *Des nègres et des juges: La scandaleuse affaire Spoutourne (1831–1834)* (Brussels: Éditions Complexe, 2008).

33. Robert L. Paquette, *Sugar Is Made with Blood: The Conspiracy of La Escalera and the Conflict between Empires over Slavery in Cuba* (Middletown, CT: Wesleyan University Press, 1990).

34. Fallope, *Esclaves et citoyens*, 377–78.

35. Nelly Schmidt, *Abolitionnistes de l'esclavage et réformateurs des colonies, 1820–1851: Analyse et documents* (Paris: Karthala, 2000), 229–46.

36. Elborg Forster and Robert Forster, eds., *Sugar and Slavery, Family and Race: The Letters and Diary of Pierre Dessalles, Planter in Martinique, 1808–1856* (Baltimore: Johns Hopkins University Press, 1996), 275.

37. Nelly Schmidt, *L'engrenage de la liberté: Caraïbes-XIXe siècle* (Aix-en-Provence: Publications de l'Université de Provence, 1995), 144–45.

38. Armand Nicolas, *Histoire de la Martinique*, vol. 2: *de 1848 à 1939* (Paris: L'Harmattan, 1996), 24–27.

39. Fallope, *Esclaves et citoyens*, 379.

40. Schmidt, *L'engrenage de la liberté*, 125–37.

41. Schloss, *Sweet Liberty*, 114–51.

42. Pieter C. Emmer, "Immigration in the Caribbean: The Introduction of Chinese and East Indian Indentured Labourers Between 1839 and 1917," in *European Expansion and Migration: Essays on the Intercontinental Migration from Africa, Asia, and Europe*, ed. Pieter C. Emmer and Magnus Mörner (New York: Berg, 1992), 251. For a general overview of the topic, see David Northrup, *Indentured Labor in the Age of Imperialism, 1834–1922* (Cambridge: Cambridge University Press, 1995).

43. Hugh Tinker, *A New System of Slavery: The Export of Indian Labour Overseas, 1830–1920* (London: Oxford University Press, 1974), 99–100, 109.

44. Pierre Pluchon, ed., *Histoire des Antilles et de la Guyane* (Toulouse: Privat, 1982), 418–19.

45. Nelly Schmidt, "1848 dans les colonies françaises des Caraïbes: Ambitions républicaines et ordre colonial," *Revue française d'outre-mer* 85, no. 320 (1998): 52.

46. Schloss, *Sweet Liberty*.

47. Richard D. E. Burton, *La famille coloniale: La Martinique et la mère patrie, 1789–1992* (Paris: L'Harmattan, 1994), 84–85.

48. Paul Butel, *Histoire des Antilles françaises* (Paris: Perrin, 2007), 390–407.

49. Northrup, *Indentured Labor*, 26.

50. Dale Tomich, "Une Petite Guinée: Provision Ground and Plantation in Martinique; Integration, Adaptation, and Appropriation," in his *Through the Prism of Slavery: Labor, Capital, and World Economy* (Lanham: Rowman & Littlefield, 2004), 152–72; see also, by the same author, *Slavery in the Circuit of Sugar: Martinique and the World Economy, 1830–1848* (Baltimore: Johns Hopkins University Press, 1990), 259–80.

51. Trevor R. Getz, *Slavery and Social Reform in West Africa: Toward Emancipation in Nineteenth-Century Senegal and the Gold Coast* (Athens: Ohio University Press, 2004), 75.

52. Barnett Singer, "A New Model Imperialist in French West Africa," *The Historian* 56, no. 1 (2003): 69–86; Marc Michel, "L'armée coloniale en Afrique occidentale française," in *L'Afrique occidentale au temps des français: Colonisateurs et colonisés, c. 1800–1960*, ed. Catherine Coquery-Vidrovitch (Paris: La Découverte, 1992), 59–62; Raymond Betts, *Tricouleur: The French Overseas Empire* (New York: Gordon and Cremonesi, 1978), 60–62.

53. Annie Rey-Goldzeiguer, "La France coloniale à la recherche de l'efficience," in *Histoire de la France coloniale*, vol. 1, *Des origines à 1914*, ed. Jean Meyer et al. (Paris: Armand Colin, 1991), 434.

54. Martin Klein, *Slavery and Colonial Rule in French West Africa*, 28–32.

55. Getz, *Slavery and Social Reform in West Africa*, 94–95; Véronique Hélenon, "Races, statut juridique et colonisation: Antillais et Africains dans les cadres administratifs des colonies françaises d'Afrique," in *L'esclavage, la colonisation, et après . . . France, États-Unis, Grande Bretagne*, ed. Patrick Weil and Stéphane Dufoix (Paris: Presses Universitaires de France, 2005), 229–43.

56. Patrick Weil, "Le statut des musulmans en Algérie coloniale: Una nationalité dénaturée," *EUI Working Paper HEC*, no. 2003/3 (San Domenico: European University Institute, 2003): 1.

57. On the origins of this Napoleonic administrative device, see Michel Verpeaux, "Constitutions, révisions et sénatus-consultes de l'an VIII à 1815," in *Ordre et désordre dans le système napoléonien*, ed. Jean-Jaques Clère and Jean-Louis Halpérin (Paris: Éditions La Memoire du Droit, 2003), 159–76.

58. Debbasch and Pontier, *Les constitutions de la France*, 167.

59. ("The history of colonial institutions could, practically, be taken for the history of specialness starting in the mid-nineteenth century.") François Miclo, *Le régime législatif des départements d'outre-mer et l'unité de la République* (Paris: Economica, 1982), 36.

60. Ibid., 37.

61. Nelly Schmidt, *La France a-t-elle aboli l'esclavage? Guadeloupe, Martinique, Guyane, 1830–1935* (Paris: Perrin, 2009), 241–44.

62. On the emperor's involvement in international politics, see William E. Echard, *Napoleon III and the Concert of Europe* (Baton Rouge: Louisiana State University Press, 1983).

63. Marc Michel, "Une guerre interminable," in *L'Algérie des français*, ed. Charles-Robert Ageron (Les Collections de l'Histoire, 2012), 39–53.

64. Charles-André Julien, *Histoire de l'Algérie contemporaine*, vol. 1, *La conquête et les débuts de la colonisation (1827–1874)* (Paris: Presses Universitaires de France, 1964), 106.

65. John W. Kiser, *Commander of the Faithful: The Life and Times of Emir Abdelkader, a Story of True Jihad* (Rhinebeck: Monkfish Books, 2008).

66. Bugeaud himself wrote his political and military program in *De la colonisation de l'Algérie* (Paris: Guyot, 1847); see also Benjamin Claude Brower, *A Desert Named Peace: The Violence of France's Empire in the Algerian Sahara, 1844–1902* (New York: Columbia University Press, 2009), 34–41.

67. Mahfoud Bennoune, *The Making of Contemporary Algeria, 1830–1987: Colonial Upheavals and Post-Independence Development* (Cambridge: Cambridge University Press, 1988), 40.

68. Quoted in Olivier Le Cour Grandmaison, *Coloniser, Exterminer: Sur la guerre et l'État colonial* (Paris: Fayard, 2005), 55; see also Brower, *A Desert Named Peace*.

69. Jacques Frémeaux, *La France et l'Algérie en guerre, 1830–1870, 1954–1962* (Paris: Economica, 2002), 196–99; on the divisions among the military commanders in the colony, see Benjamin Stora, *Histoire de l'Algérie coloniale (1830–1954)* (Paris: La Découverte, 1991), 18; Jennifer Pitts, *A Turn to Empire: The Rise of Imperial Liberalism in Britain and France*, (Princeton, NJ: Princeton University Press: 2005), 204–39.

70. Kamel Kateb, *Européens, "indigènes" et juifs en Algérie (1830–1962): Représentations et réalités des populations* (Paris: INED, 2001).

71. The best account is in Jacques Frémeaux, *Les Bureaux Arabes: Dans l'Algérie de la conquête* (Paris: Denoël, 1993).

72. Patricia M. E. Lorcin, *Imperial Identities: Stereotyping, Prejudices and Race in Colonial Algeria* (London: I. B. Tauris, 1999).

73. Ibid., 80.

74. Ibid., 82–83.

75. Annie Rey-Goldzeiguer, *Le Royaume arabe: La politique algérienne de Napoléon III, 1861–1870* (Alger: Société Nationale et de Diffusion, 1977).

76. Rey-Goldzeiguer, "La France coloniale à la recherche de l'efficience," 419.

77. Charles-Robert Ageron, *Politiques coloniales au Maghreb* (Paris: Presses Universitaires de France, 1972), 47–49.

78. Michel Levallois, *Ismayl Urbain (1812–1884): Une autre conquête de l'Algérie* (Paris: Maisonneuve et Larose, 2001).

79. Magali Morsy, *Les Saint-Simoniens et l'Orient: Vers la modernité* (Aix-en-Provence: Edisud, 1989); Kay Adamson, *Algeria: A Study in Competing Ideologies* (London: Continuum, 1998); Yassine Chaïb, "'Domination et mysticisme': Les expériences des Saint-simoniens et des Fouriéristes; Le champ colonial en Algérie de 1830–1870," in *Le fait colonial au Maghreb: Ruptures et continuités*, ed. Nadir Marouf (Paris: L'Harmattan, 2007), 115–34.

80. Urbain's *L'Algérie française: Indigènes et immigrants* can be consulted easily, thanks to the edition by Michel Levallois (Paris: Seguier, 2002.)

81. Levallois, *Ismayl Urbain*, 631–32.

82. John Ruedy, *Land Policy in Colonial Algeria: The Origins of the Rural Public Domain* (Berkeley: University of California Press, 1967).

83. Stora, *Histoire de l'Algérie coloniale (1830–1954)*, 26; Guy Pervillé, *Pour une histoire de la guerre d'Algérie* (Paris: Picard, 2002), 29–30.

84. Ruedy, *Land Policy in Colonial Algeria*, 13.

85. Youcef Djebari, "L'accaparement des terres par les pouvoirs publics," in *La France en Algérie: Bilan et controverses; Genèse, développement et limites d'un capitalisme d'État colonial* (Algiers: OPU, 1995), 1:84.

86. Bennoune, *The Making of Contemporary Algeria*, 43.

87. Ruedy, *Modern Algeria*, 71.

88. André Nouschi, "La dépossession foncière et la paupérisation de la paysannerie algérienne," in *Histoire de l'Algérie à la période coloniale, 1830–1962*, ed. Abderrahmane Bouchène et al. (Paris: La Découverte, 2014), 192.

89. ("If Algeria were a colony, Algerian laws would be only a part of the colonial laws. But in France, Algeria is considered not so much a colony as a continuation of metropolitan territory. Nevertheless Algeria has, a completely unique situation among the French possessions: it has its own laws, separate from the common law, and is not able to participate in colonial lawmaking.") Émile Larcher, *Traité élémentaire de législation algérienne* (Paris: Arthur Rousseau, 1911), 1:7.

90. Peter Sahlins, *Unnaturally French: Foreign Citizens in the Old Regime and After* (Ithaca, NY: Cornell University Press, 2004).

91. ("Native Muslims, then, are French, but they are not French citizens; they are French subjects. The distinction between subject and citizen, which, under metropolitan law, has only minimal impact, here acquires exceptional importance.") Jacques

Aumont-Thiéville, *Du régime d'indigénat en Algérie* (Paris: Librairie de Droit et de Jurisprudence, 1906), 4.

92. Frederick Cooper, *Citizenship between Empire and Nation: Remaking France and French Africa, 1945-1960* (Princeton, NJ: Princeton University Press, 2014), 15–16.

93. Michael Brett, "The Colonial Period in the Maghrib and its Aftermath: The Present State of Historical Writing," *The Journal of African History* XVII, no. 2 (1976): 291–305; by the same author, "Legislating for Inequality in Algeria: the Senatus-Consulte of 14 July 1865," *Bulletin of the School for Oriental and African Studies* 51, no. 3 (1988): 440–61.

94. Isabelle Merle, "Retour sur le régime de l'indigénat: Genèse et contradictions des principes répressifs dans l'empire français," *French Politics, Culture, and Society* 20, no. 2 (2002): 81.

95. Weil, "Le statut des musulmans en Algérie," 95–109.

96. Charles-Robert Ageron, "L'évolution politique de l'Algérie sous le Second Empire," in his *Politiques coloniales au Maghreb* (Paris: Presses Universitaires de France, 1972), 45–73.

97. E. Sartor, *De la naturalisation en Algérie (Sénatus-Consulte de 5 de juillet de 1865): Musulmans, Israélites, Européens* (Paris: Retaux, Frères, 1865).

98. Laure Blévis, "La citoyenneté française au miroir de la colonisation: Étude des demandes de naturalisation des 'sujets français' en Algérie coloniale," *Genèses* 53, no. 4 (2003): 25–47.

99. Andrea L. Smith, "Citizenship in the Colony: Naturalization Law and Legal Assimilation in 19th Century Algeria," *Political and Legal Anthropology Review* 19, no. 1 (1996): 33–49.

100. Kateb, *Européens, "indigènes" et juifs en Algérie*; Laure Blévis, "Les avatars de la citoyenneté en Algérie coloniale ou les paradoxes d'une catégorisation," *Droit et société* 48, no. 2 (2001): 573.

101. Gregory Mann, "What Was the Indigénat? The 'Empire of Law' in French West Africa," *Journal of African History* 50 (2009): 331–53; Pierre Brocheux and Daniel Hémery, *Indochine: La colonisation ambiguë, 1858-1954* (Paris: La Découverte, 2001); Isabelle Merle, *Expériences coloniales: La Nouvelle Calédonie (1853-1920)* (Paris: Belin, 1995).

102. Olivier Le Cour Grandmaison, *De l'indigénat: Anatomie d'un "monstre" juridique: Le droit colonial en Algérie et dans l'Empire français* (Paris: Zones, 2010); Isabelle Merle, "Le régime de l'indigénat en Nouvelle Calédonie," in *Colonies, territoires, sociétés: L'enjeu français*, ed. Alain Saussol and Joseph Zitomersky (Paris: L'Harmattan, 1996), 223–241; Pierre Singaravélou, *Les empires coloniaux, XIXe-XXe siècle* (Paris: Éditions Points, 2013), 104–5.

103. Weil, "Le statut des musulmans en Algérie," 5–6.

Chapter 6. Spain and Its Colonies: The Survival of the Oldest

1. See Wim Klooster, *Revolutions in the Atlantic World: A Comparative History* (New York: New York University Press, 2009), chapter 5, "Multiple Routes to Sovereignty: The Spanish American Revolutions," 117–57; Jeremy Adelman, *Sovereignty*

and Revolution in the Iberian Atlantic (Princeton, NJ: Princeton University Press, 2009); Gabriel Paquette, "The Dissolution of the Spanish Monarchy," *Historical Journal* 52, no. 1 (2009): 175–212.

2. Edmundo A. Heredia, *Planes españoles para reconquistar Hispanoamérica (1810–1818)* (Buenos Aires: Eudeba, 1974); Miguel Ángel Sánchez Lamego, *La invasión española de 1829* (Tamaulipas: Jus, 1971); Ivana Frasquet, "Milicianos y soldados: La problemática social mexicana en la invasión de 1829," in *Las ciudades y la guerra, 1750–1898,* ed. Salvador Broseta (Castelló de la Plana: Edicions de la Universitat Jaume I, 2002), 115–32.

3. María Dolores García Cantús, *Fernando Poo, Una aventura colonial española: Las islas en litigio; Entre la esclavitud y el abolicionismo, 1776–1846* (Vic: Ceiba, 2006); Carlos Petit, "The Colonial Model of Rule of Law in Africa: The example of Guinea," in *The Rule of Law: History, Theory and Criticism*, ed. Pietro Costa and Danilo Zolo (Dordrecht: Springer, 2007), 467–512; Teresa Pereira Rodríguez, "El factor trabajo en la explotación española de los territorios del Golfo de Guinea: Liberianos en Fernando Poo durante el primer tercio del siglo XX," in *Las relaciones internacionales en la España Contemporánea*, ed. Juan Bautista Vilar (Murcia: Universidad de Murcia, 1989), 269–85.

4. Agustín Ramón Rodríguez González, *La Armada Española, la Campaña del Pacífico, 1862–1871: España frente a Chile y Perú* (Madrid: Agualarga, 1999).

5. Philip Wayne Powell, *Tree of Hate: Propaganda and Prejudices Affecting United States Relations with the Hispanic World* (New York: Stella Maris Books, 1971); William S. Maltby, *The Black Legend in England: The Development of Anti-Spanish Sentiment, 1558–1660* (Durham, NC: Duke University Press, 1971); María de Guzmán, *Spain's Long Shadow: The Black Legend, Off-Whiteness, and Anglo-American Empire* (Minneapolis: University of Minnesota Press, 2005); Antonio Feros, *Speaking of Spain: The Evolution of Race and Nation in the Hispanic World* (Cambridge, MA: Harvard University Press, 2017).

6. Enric Ucelay-Da Cal, "Self-fulfilling Prophecies: Propaganda and Political Models between Cuba, Spain and the United States," *Illes i Imperis* 2 (1999): 191–220.

7. Jordi Maluquer de Motes, *La economía española en perspectiva histórica: Siglos XVIII-XXI* (Barcelona: Pasado & Presente, 2014).

8. Josep M. Fradera, *Colonias para después de un imperio* (Barcelona: Edicions Bellaterra, 2005).

9. Jesús Millán, "La formación de la España contemporánea: El agotamiento explicativo del fracaso liberal," *Ayer* 98 (2015): 243–56.

10. John Francis Bannon, *The Spanish Borderlands Frontier, 1513–1821* (Albuquerque: University of New Mexico Press, 1974); David J. Weber, *The Spanish Frontier in North America* (New Haven, CT: Yale University Press, 1992).

11. Carlos Marichal and Johanna von Grafenstein, eds., *El secreto del imperio español: Los situados coloniales en el siglo XVIII* (Mexico City: El Colegio de México, 2012).

12. On these debates, see Alejandro Nieto, *Mendizábal: Apogeo y crisis del progresismo civil; Historia política de las Cortes de 1836–1837* (Barcelona: Ariel, 2011), 591–616.

13. Yves Benot, *La démence coloniale sous Napoléon* (Paris: La Découverte, 1992).

14. José Trías Monge, *Historia Constitucional de Puerto Rico* (Río Piedras: Ediciones de la Universidad de Puerto Rico, 1980), 19, 37–40.

15. An exhaustive list is impossible, but two excellent works are Jaime E. Rodríguez O, *La independencia de la América española* (Mexico City: El Colegio de México, 1996); and José María Portillo Valdés, *Crisis atlántica: Autonomía e independencia en la crisis de la monarquía hispana* (Madrid: Marcial Pons, 2006).

16. Jesús Raúl Navarro García, *Entre esclavos y constituciones: El colonialismo liberal de 1837 en Cuba* (Seville: Escuela de Estudios Hispanoamericanos, 1991).

17. On the sugar industry, which permitted this flow of wealth, see Franklin W. Knight, "Origins of Wealth and the Sugar Revolution in Cuba, 1750–1850," *Hispanic American Historical Review* 57, no. 2 (1977): 231–53.

18. Juan Pérez de la Riva, "Una isla con dos historias," in *El barracón: Esclavitud y capitalismo en Cuba*, (Barcelona: Crítica, 1978), 169–81.

19. Moreno Fraginals used the term repeatedly in his great work, *El Ingenio: El complejo económico social cubano del azúcar* (Havana: Editorial de Ciencias Sociales, 1978), 3 vols.

20. D. J. Murray, *Odious commerce: Britain, Spain and the abolition of the Cuban slave trade* (Cambridge: Cambridge University Press, 1980).

21. Eduardo García de Enterría, *La administración española: Estudios de ciencia administrativa* (Madrid: Alianza Editorial, 1972).

22. For doubts regarding this question during preceding constitutional periods, for example during the Cortes of Cádiz, see Javier Lasarte Álvarez, *Las Cortes de Cádiz: Soberanía, separación de poderes, Hacienda, 1810–1811* (Madrid: Marcial Pons, 2009), 344–47.

23. Francisco J. Ponte Rodríguez, *Arango y Parreño, el estadista colonial* (Havana: Sociedad Económica de Amigos del País, 1937), 235.

24. *Obras de Don Francisco Arango y Parreño* (Havana: Ministerio de Educación, 1952), vol. 2, 620–30.

25. In retrospect, Arango expressed his disappointment with Tacón's harsh policies; *Obras de Don Francisco Arango y Parreño* (Havana: Ministerio de Educación, 1952), vol. 2, 629–30.

26. Juan Pérez de la Riva, ed., *Correspondencia reservada del Capitán General Don Miguel Tacón con el Gobierno de Madrid, 1834–1836* (Havana: Biblioteca Nacional José Martí, 1963), 164.

27. Manuel Ovilo Otero, *Biografía del Exmo Sr. Don Claudio Martínez de Pinillos, Conde de Villanueva* (Madrid: Imprenta del Tiempo, 1851). A more interesting source is a pamphlet by Miguel Ferrer Martínez, *El general Tacón, marqués de la unión de Cuba, y el conde de Villanueva: O sea, contestación a varios artículos en favor del primero y contra el segundo* (Madrid: Imprenta L. Amarita, 1838).

28. José María Aguilera Manzano, *La formación de la identidad cubana: El debate Saco-La Sagra* (Seville: CSIC, 2005).

29. Elías J. Entralgo, *Los diputados por Cuba en las Cortes de España durante los tres primeros periodos constitucionales* (Havana: Imprenta del Siglo XX), 1945.

30. Antonio Elorza and Elena Hernández Sandoica, *La Guerra de Cuba (1895–1898)* (Madrid: Alianza Editorial, 1999), 29.

31. José Antonio Piqueras, *Plantación, espacios agrarios y esclavitud en la Cuba colonial* (Castelló de la Plana: Universitat Jaume I, 2017); Ángel Bahamonde and José G. Cayuela, *Hacer las Américas: Las élites coloniales españolas en el siglo XIX* (Madrid: Alianza Editorial, 1992); José G. Cayuela, *Bahía de Ultramar: España y Cuba en el siglo XIX; El control de las relaciones coloniales* (Madrid: Siglo XXI Editores, 1993).

32. Josep Fontana, *La revolución liberal: Política y hacienda en 1833–1845* (Madrid: Instituto de Estudios Fiscales, 1977); for a biography of Mendizábal, see Peter Janke, *Mendizábal y la instauración de la Monarquía constitucional en España (1790–1853)* (Madrid: Siglo XXI Editores, 1974).

33. Josep M. Fradera, "Why Were Spain's Special Overseas Laws Never Enacted?" in *Spain, Europe and the Atlantic World: Essays in Honour of John H. Elliott*, ed. Richard L. Kagan and Geoffrey Parker (Cambridge: Cambridge University Press, 1995), 334–49.

34. José Antonio Saco, *Examen analítico del informe de la Comisión especial nombrada por las Cortes* (Madrid: Imprenta Tomás Jordán, 1837), 4.

35. Albert Dérozier, "Argüelles y la cuestión de América ante las Cortes de Cádiz de 1810–1814," in *Homenaje a Nöel Salomon: Ilustración española e independencia de América*, ed. Alberto Gil Novales (Barcelona: Universidad Autónoma de Barcelona, 1979), 159–64.

36. Sancho's aggressive attitude toward Americans had already been on view during the Cortes del Trienio (1820–23); see Mario Rodríguez, "The American Question at the Cortes of Madrid," *The Americas* 38 (1982): 294.

37. *Diario de Sesiones de Cortes*, vol. 3, *1836–1837* (Madrid: Congreso de los Diputados, 1870–77), 2, 505.

38. Ibid., 508.

39. Julio Montero, ed. *Constituciones y códigos políticos españoles, 1808–1978* (Barcelona: Ariel, 1998), 89.

40. On Vila, an interesting figure, see Albert Garcia Balañà, "Tradició liberal i política colonial a Catalunya: Mig segle de temptatives i limitacions, 1822–1872," *Catalunya i Ultramar: Poder i negoci a les colònies espanyoles (1750–1914)* (Barcelona: Museu Marítim, 1995), 77–106.

41. Josep M. Fradera, "Reading Imperial Transitions: Spanish Contraction, British Expansion, and American Irruption," in *Colonial Crucible: Empire in the Making of the Modern American State*, ed. Alfred W. McCoy and Francisco A. Scarano (Madison: University of Wisconsin Press, 2009), 34–62.

42. Louis A. Pérez, *Cuba between Empires, 1878–1902* (Pittsburgh: University of Pittsburgh Press, 1983).

43. On notions of race in independent Cuba, see Armando García, Raquel Álvarez, and Consuelo Naranjo Orovio, *En busca de la raza perfecta: Eugenesia e Higiene en Cuba (1989–1958)* (Madrid: CSIC, 1999).

44. Aline Helg, *Our Rightful Share: The Afro-Cuban Struggle for Equality, 1886–1912* (Chapel Hill: University of North Carolina Press, 1995).

45. Alejandro de la Fuente, *A Nation for All: Race, Inequality, and Politics in Twentieth-Century Cuba* (Chapel Hill: University of North Carolina Press, 2001).

46. Christopher Schmidt-Nowara, "The End of Slavery and the End of Empire: Slave Emancipation in Cuba and Puerto Rico," *Slavery and Abolition* 21, no. 2 (2000): 188–207.

47. Edilberto C. de Jesús, *The Tobacco Monopoly in the Philippines: Bureaucratic Enterprise and Social Change, 1766–1880* (Quezon City: Ateneo de Manila Press, 1983).

48. Ruth de Llobet, "Chinese Mestizo and Natives' Disputes in Manila and the 1812 Constitution: Old Privileges and New Political Realities (1813–1815)," *Journal of Southeast Asian Studies* 45, no. 2 (2014): 214–35.

49. Christopher A. Bayly, *Imperial Meridian: The British Empire and the World, 1780–1830* (Harlow: Longman, 1989), 193–216.

50. For an exploration of the Cuban position from the early nineteenth century to the 1830s, see Antonio-Filiu Franco, *Cuba en los orígenes del constitucionalismo español: La alternativa descentralizadora, 1808–1837* (Zaragoza: Fundación Giménez Abad, 2001).

51. José Antonio Saco, *Paralelo entre la isla de Cuba y algunas colonias inglesas* (Madrid: Imprenta de Tomás Jordán, 1937).

52. Josep M. Fradera, *Colonias para después de un imperio*, 270–321; see also the classic work Verena Stolcke, *Marriage, Class and Colour in Nineteenth-Century Cuba: A Study of Racial Attitudes and Sexual Values in a Slave Society* (Cambridge: Cambridge University Press, 1974); and Kathryn R. Dungy, *The Conceptualization of Race in Colonial Puerto Rico, 1800–1850* (New York: Peter Lang, 2015).

53. John A. Larkin, *Sugar and the Origins of Modern Philippine Society* (Berkeley: University of California Press, 1993).

54. The best outline of the diversity of the Philippines can be found in Alfred W. McCoy and Edilberto C. de Jesús, eds., *Philippine Social History: Global Trade and Local Transformations* (Honolulu: University of Hawai'i Press, 1982); see also Norman Owen, *Prosperity without Progress: Manila Hemp and Material Life in the Colonial Philippines* (Berkeley: University of California Press, 1984); John A. Larkin, *The Pampangans: Colonial Society in a Philippine Province* (Berkeley: University of California Press, 1972); Daniel F. Doeppers, *Feeding Manila in Peace and War, 1850–1945* (Madison: University of Wisconsin Press, 2016); Michael Salman, *The Embarrassment of Slavery: Controversies over Bondage and Nationalism in the American Colonial Philippines* (Berkeley: University of California Press, 2001).

55. John D. Blanco, *Frontier Constitutions: Christianity and Colonial Empire in the Nineteenth-Century Philippines* (Berkeley: California University Press, 2009).

56. For an impressive account, see Reynaldo C. Ileto, *Pasyon and Revolution: Popular Movements in the Philippines, 1840–1910* (Quezon City: Ateneo de Manila Press, 1979).

57. Vicente L. Rafael, *Contracting Colonialism: Translation and Christian Conversion in Tagalog Society under Early Spanish Rule* (Quezon City: Ateneo de Manila Press, 1988); John D. Blanco, *Frontier Constitutions: Christianity and Colonial Empire in the Nineteenth-Century Philippines* (Berkeley: California University Press, 2009).

58. There is a monograph on the town, though it gives little information about these events: Leandro Tormo, *Lucban: A Town the Franciscans Built* (Manila: Historical Conservation Society, 1971). See also, by the same author, "La reaparición de la Cofradía de San José de Tayabas," *Anuario de Estudios Americanos* 32 (1958): 485–506.

59. On Domingo de Rojas and his world, see Llobet, "Chinese Mestizo and Natives' Disputes"; also, by the same author, "De ciudadanía a sedición: La trayectoria política de Domingo de Rojas, 1820–1843," in *La construcción de la nación filipina:*

Un caso a través de la familia Roxas, ed. María Dolores Elizalde and Xavier Huetz de Lemps [forthcoming, 2018].

60. Sinibaldo de Mas, *Informe secreto sobre el estado de las islas Filipinas* (Madrid: Imprenta de F. Sánchez, 1843).

61. Jonathan Curry-Machado, "How Cuba Burned with the Ghosts of British Slavery: Race, Abolition, and the Escalera," *Slavery and Abolition* 25, no. 1 (2004): 71–83.

62. Robert L. Paquette, *Sugar Is Made with Blood: The Conspiracy of La Escalera and the Conflict between Empires over Slavery in Cuba* (Middletown, CT: Wesleyan University Press, 1988).

63. Josep M. Fradera, "Juan Prim y Prats (1814–1870): Prim conspirador o la pedagogía del sable," in *Liberales, agitadores y conspiradores: Biografías heterodoxas del siglo XIX*, ed. Isabel Burdiel and Manuel Pérez Ledesma (Madrid: Espasa Calpe, 2000), 239–66.

64. Rafael Olivar Bertrand, *El caballero Prim: Vida íntima, amorosa y militar* (Barcelona: Luis Miracle, 1952), vol. 1, 307, 313.

65. Arturo Morales Carrión, "El año de 1848 en Puerto Rico: Aspectos del mando de Prim," *Revista de Occidente* 147 (June 1975): 211–42; by the same author, *Auge y decadencia de la trata negrera en Puerto Rico (1820–1860)* (San Juan: Instituto de Cultura Puertorriqueña, 1978).

66. Francisco Scarano, *Sugar and Slavery in Puerto Rico: The Plantation Economy in Ponce, 1800–1850* (Madison: University of Wisconsin Press, 1984).

67. Arturo Morales Carrión, "El año de 1848 en Puerto Rico: Aspectos del mando de Prim," *Revista de Occidente* 147 (June 1975): 211–42.

68. Cayetano Coll Toste, "El bando del general Prim contra la raza africana," *Boletín Histórico de Puerto Rico* 2 (1915): 122–26; Labor Gómez Azevedo, *Organización y reglamentación del trabajo en el Puerto Rico del siglo XIX* (San Juan: Instituto de Cultura Puertorriqueña, 1970).

69. Guillermo A. Baralt, *Esclavos rebeldes: Conspiraciones y sublevaciones de esclavos en Puerto Rico (1795–1873)* (Río Piedras: Ediciones Huracán, 1982); Andrés Ramos Mattei, *Azúcar y esclavitud* (Río Piedras: Universidad de Puerto Rico, 1982).

70. Fernando Picó, *Historia general de Puerto Rico* (Río Piedras: Ediciones Huracán, 1988), 170.

71. William A. Green, *British Slave Emancipation: The Sugar Colonies and the Great Experiment, 1830–1865* (Oxford: Oxford University Press, 1988), 381–414.

72. Alfred W. McCoy, *In the Shadows of the American Century: The Rise and Decline of US Global Power* (Chicago: Dispatch Books, 2017) 27–59.

73. See chapter 4 of Matthew Karp, *This Vast Southern Empire: Slaveholders at the Helm of American Foreign Policy* (Cambridge, MA: Harvard University Press, 2016), especially 81–102 for this case. Also see Walter Johnson, *River of Dark Dreams: Slavery and Empire in the Cotton Kingdom* (Cambridge, MA: Harvard University Press, 2013).

74. Andrew J. Torget, *Seeds of Empire: Cotton, Slavery, and the Transformation of the Texas Borderlands, 1800–1850* (Chapel Hill: University of North Carolina Press, 1989).

75. Randolph B. Campbell, *An Empire for Slavery: The Peculiar Institution in Texas, 1821–1865* (Baton Rouge: Louisiana State University Press, 1989).

76. Robert E. May, *John A. Quitman, Old South Crusader* (Baton Rouge: Louisiana State University Press, 1985); and, by the same author, *Manifest Destiny's Underworld: Filibustering in Antebellum America* (Chapel Hill: University of North Carolina Press, 2004).

77. The best introduction to the foundations of the Spanish national project is José Álvarez Junco, *Mater Dolorosa: La idea de España en el siglo XIX* (Madrid: Taurus, 2001); and the English version, *Spanish Identity in the Age of Nations* (Manchester: Manchester University Press, 2016).

78. David A. Goldfrank, *The Origins of the Crimean War* (London: Routledge, 1994), 27–40, 293–96.

79. Alexander Bitis, *Russia and the Eastern Question: Army, Government and Society, 1815–1833* (Oxford: Oxford University Press, 2006).

80. Orlando Figes, *Crimea, the Last Crusade* (Hardmondsworth: Penguin, 2011).

81. Stephen J. Jacobson, "Imperial Ambitions in an Era of Decline: Micromilitarism and the Eclipse of the Spanish Empire, 1858–1923," in *Endless Empire: Spain's Retreat, Europe's Eclipse, America's Decline*, ed. Alfred W. McCoy, Josep M. Fradera, and Stephen J. Jacobson (Madison: University of Wisconsin Press, 2012), 74–91.

82. Eloy Martín Corrales, *La imagen del magrebí en España: Una perspectiva histórica, siglos XVI-XX* (Barcelona: Edicions Bellaterra, 2001); Jesús Torrecilla, "El mito de al-Andalus," in *España al revés: Los mitos del pensamiento progresista (1790–1840)* (Madrid: Marcial Pons, 2016), 155–206.

83. Albert Garcia Balañà, "Racializing the Nation in 19th-Century Spain (1820–1865): A Transatlantic Approach," *Journal of Iberian and Latin American Studies* [forthcoming, 2018.]

84. Josep M. Fradera, *Cultural nacional en una societat dividida: Patriotisme i cultura a Catalunya (1838–1868)* (Barcelona: Edicions Curial, 1992); Joan-Lluís Marfany, *Nacionalisme espanyol i catalanitat (1789–1859): Cap a una revisió de la Renaixença* (Barcelona: Edicions 62, 2017).

85. Juan Antonio Inarejos Muñoz, *Intervenciones coloniales y nacionalismo español: La política exterior de la Unión Liberal y sus vínculos con la Francia de Napoleón III (1856–1868)* (Madrid: Silex, 2010). On wartime propaganda, see Víctor Morales Lezcano, *España y la cuestión de Oriente* (Madrid: Ministerio de Asuntos Exteriores, 1992); Eloy Martín Corrales, ed., *Marruecos y el colonialismo español (1859–1912): De la Guerra de África a la "penetración pacífica"* (Barcelona: Edicions Bellaterra, 2002); Xavier Andreu Miralles, *El descubrimiento de España: Mito romántico e identidad nacional* (Madrid: Taurus, 2016).

86. Josep M. Fradera, "Juan Prim y Prats (1814–1870): Prim conspirador o la pedagogía del sable," in *Liberales, agitadores y conspiradores: Biografías heterodoxas del siglo XIX*, ed. Isabel Burdiel and Manuel Pérez Ledesma (Madrid: Espasa Calpe, 2000), 239–66.

87. Isabel Burdiel, *Isabel II: Una biografía (1830–1904)* (Madrid: Taurus, 2010), 787–810; Gregorio de la Fuente Monge, *Los revolucionarios de 1868: élites y poder en la España liberal* (Madrid: Marcial Pons, 2000).

88. Carl A. Trocki, *Opium and Empire: Chinese Society in Colonial Singapore, 1800–1910* (Ithaca, NY: Cornell University Press 1990); Chantal Descours-Gatin, *Quand l'opium finançait la colonisation française* (Paris: Éditions L'Harmattan, 1992).

89. For a complete account, see Pierre Brocheux and Daniel Hémery, *Indochine: La colonisation ambiguë, 1858–1954* (Paris: La Découverte, 1995).

90. On French influence in Morocco, see Raymond Betts, *Tricouleur: The French Overseas Empire* (New York: Gordon and Cremonesi, 1978), 24–34; on Spanish emigration to Oran, see Juan Bautista Vilar, *Los españoles en la Argelia francesa (1830–1914)* (Madrid: CSIC, 1989); and José Fermín Bonmatí Antón, *La emigración alicantina a Argelia (siglo XIX y primer tercio del siglo XX)* (Alicante: Publicaciones de la Universidad de Alicante, 1989).

91. Cristóbal Robles Muñoz, *Paz en Santo Domingo (1854–1865): El fracaso de la anexión a España* (Madrid: CSIC, 1987); Eduardo González Calleja and Antonio Fontecha Pedraza, *Una cuestión de honor: La polémica sobre la anexión de Santo Domingo vista desde España (1861–1865)* (Santo Domingo: Fundación García Arévalo, 2005).

92. Robert Ryal Miller, *For Science and National Glory: The Spanish Scientific Expedition to America, 1862–1866* (Norman: University of Oklahoma Press, 1983); Miguel Angel Puig-Samper, *Crónica de una expedición romántica al Nuevo Mundo* (Madrid: CSIC, 1988); for Lily Litvak's introduction to the memoir by one of the expedition's participants, see Manuel Almagro, *La Comisión Científica del Pacífico: Viaje por Sudamérica y recorrido del Amazonas, 1862–1866*, ed. Lily Litvak (Barcelona: Laertes, 1984), 5–45.

93. On the relationship among technology, information, and warfare and their impact on collective attitudes, see W. Michael Ryan, "The Influence of the Imperial Frontier on British Doctrines of Mechanized Warfare," *Albion: A Quarterly Journal Concerned with British Studies* 15, no. 2 (1983): 123–42.

94. Holger Droessler, "Germany's El Dorado in the Pacific: Metropolitan Representations and Colonial Realities, 1884–1914," in *Imperial Expectations and Realities: El Dorados, Utopias and Dystopias*, ed. Andrekos Varnava (Manchester: Manchester University Press, 2015), 105–24.

95. William C. Davis, *The Last Conquistadores: The Spanish Intervention in Peru and Chile, 1863–1866* (Athens: University of Georgia Press, 1950.) The same connection between fertilizers and colonialism would appear in the twentieth century in the Spanish Sahara; see José María Ríos, *Sahara! Sahara! La aventura de los fosfatos, un episodio inédito: Memorias de un ingeniero de minas* (Madrid: Fundación Gómez Pardo, 1989); and the excellent treatment in José Luis Rodríguez Jiménez, *Agonía, traición, huida: El final del Sahara español* (Barcelona: Crítica, 2015).

96. Muñoz, *Paz en Santo Domingo*; Calleja and Pedraza, *Una cuestión de honor*; Muñoz, *Intervenciones coloniales y nacionalismo español*.

97. Frank Moya Pons, *Historia del Caribe* (Santo Domingo: Editorial Búho, 2008), 344–49.

98. The best account of the 1898 crisis and the subsequent years is Sebastian Balfour, *The End of the Spanish Empire (1898–1923)* (Oxford: Clarendon Press, 1997).

99. María Dolores Elizalde Pérez-Grueso, *España en el Pacífico: La colonia de las islas Carolinas, 1855–1899* (Madrid: CSIC, 1992); Lester B. Schippee, "Germany and the Spanish-American War," *American Historical Review* 30 (1925): 230–71.

100. Emilia Viotti da Costa, *A aboliçao* (São Paulo: UNESP, 2010).

101. Consuelo Naranjo, Miguel A. Puig-Samper, and Luis M. García Mora, eds., *La nación soñada: Cuba, Puerto Rico y Filipinas ante el 1898* (Aranjuez: Doce Calles,

1996); Bartolomé Clavero, "Reconstituciones de poderes," in his *El orden de los poderes: Historias Constituyentes de la Trinidad Constitucional* (Madrid: Editorial Trotta, 2007), 171–261. Clavero offers many valuable suggestions, both in terms of bibliography and in his comparisons between situations and places.

102. Enric Ucelay-Da Cal, *El imperialismo catalán: Prat de la Riba, Cambó, D'Ors y la conquista moral de España* (Barcelona: Edhasa, 2003); Xosé M. Núñez Seixas, "Nation-Building and Regional Integration: The Case of the Spanish Empire, 1700–1914," in *Nationalizing Empires*, ed. Stefan Berger and Alexei I. Miller (Budapest: Central European University Press, 2015), 195–247.

103. María Paz Alonso Romero, *Cuba en la España liberal (1837–1898): Génesis y desarrollo del régimen autonómico* (Madrid: Centro de Estudios Constitucionales, 2002), 28–33.

104. Emma Montanos Ferrín, "El ministerio de Ultramar," in *Actas del IV symposium de historia de la administración* (Madrid: Instituto Nacional de Administración Pública, 1983), 557–78.

105. Carlos Petit, "Detrimentum Rei Publicae: Constitución de España en Guinea," in *Constitución en España: Orígenes y destinos*, ed. José M. Iñurritegui and José M. Portillo (Madrid: Centro de Estudios Constitucionales, 1998), 425–509; Bartolomé Clavero, "Bioko, 1837–1876: Constitucionalismo de Europa en África, derecho internacional consuetudinario del trabajo mediante," *Quaderni fiorentini per la storia del pensiero giuridico moderno* 35, no. 1 (2006): 429–556.

106. María Dolores Domingo Acebrón, "La junta de información en Madrid para las reformas en las Antillas, 1866," *Hispania* 62, no. 1:210 (2002): 141–66; Javier Alvarado, *Constitucionalismo y codificación en las provincias de Ultramar: La supervivencia del Antiguo Régimen en la España del XIX* (Madrid: Centro de Estudios Constitucionales, 2001), 210ff.

107. For a classic description of the differences between the two sides of the island, see Juan Pérez de la Riva, "Una isla con dos historias," in *El barracón y otros ensayos: Esclavitud y capitalismo en Cuba* (Barcelona: Crítica, 1978), 169–81.

108. David Eltis, *Economic Growth and the Ending of the Transatlantic Slave Trade* (New York: Oxford University Press, 1987), 245.

109. Joan Casanovas Codina, *Bread or Bullets! Urban Labor and Spanish Colonialism in Cuba, 1850–1898* (Pittsburgh: University of Pittsburgh Press, 1998), 93–113.

110. César Yáñez Gallardo, "La última invasión armada: Los contingentes militares españoles en las guerras de Cuba, siglo XIX," *Revista de Indias* 194 (1992): 107–27; Albert Garcia Balañà, " 'The Empire Is No Longer a Unit': Declining Imperial Expectations and Transatlantic Crises in Metropolitan Spain, 1859–1909," in *Endless Empire: Spain's Retreat, Europe's Eclipse, America's Decline*, ed. Alfred W. McCoy, Josep M. Fradera, and Stephen J. Jacobson (Madison: University of Wisconsin Press, 2012), 92–103.

111. John Lawrence Tone, *War and Genocide in Cuba, 1895–1898* (Chapel Hill: University of North Carolina Press, 2006), 22.

112. Andreas Stucki, *Las Guerras de Cuba: Violencia y campos de concentración (1868–1898)* (Madrid: Doce Calles, 2017); Francisco Pérez Guzmán, *Herida profunda* (Havana: Ediciones Unión, 1998).

113. Leon Wolff, *Little Brown Brother: How the United States Purchased and Pacified the Philippine Islands at the Century's Turn* (New York: History Book Club, 2006) [1st ed. 1961].

114. These numbers come from Paul A. Kramer's excellent introduction to Leon Wolff, *Little Brown Brother*, ix-xviii. See also by Kramer, *The Blood of Government: Race, Empire, the United States and the Philippines* (Chapel Hill: University of North Carolina Press, 2006).

115. A comprehensive analysis of the relationship between social and political strife can be found in Christopher Schmidt-Nowara, *Empire and Antislavery: Spain, Cuba, and Puerto Rico, 1833-1874* (Pittsburgh: University of Pittsburgh Press, 1999).

116. Guillermo A. Baralt, *Esclavos rebeldes: Conspiraciones y sublevaciones de esclavos en Puerto Rico (1795-1873)* (Río Piedras: Ediciones Huracán, 1982); Laird Bergad, "Towards Puerto Rico's Grito de Lares: Coffee, Social Stratification and Class Conflicts, 1828-1868," *Hispanic American Historical Review* 60, no. 4 (1980): 617-42; Luis A. Figueroa, *Sugar, Slavery and Freedom in Nineteenth-Century Puerto Rico* (Chapel Hill: University of North Carolina Press, 2005), 105-20.

117. Astrid Cubano, "Sociedad e identidad nacional en Cuba y Puerto Rico: Un acercamiento comparativo (1868-1898)," *Op. Cit.: Revista del Centro de Investigaciones Históricas* 10 (1998), 14-15.

118. Dale W. Tomich, "Commodity Frontiers, Spatial Economy, and Technological Innovation in the Caribbean Sugar Industry, 1783-1878," in *The Caribbean and the Atlantic World Economy*, ed. Adrian Leonard and David Pretel (London: Palgrave Macmillan, 2015), 184-216; Jonathan Curry-Machado, *Cuban Sugar Industry: Transnational Networks and Engineering Migrants in Mid-Nineteenth-Century Cuba* (New York: Palgrave Macmillan, 2011).

119. Juan Pérez de la Riva, "El monto de la inmigración forzada en el siglo XIX," in *Para la historia de las gentes sin historia* (Barcelona: Ariel, 1976), 95-140.

120. Franklin W. Knight, *Slave Society in Cuba during the Nineteenth Century* (Madison: University of Wisconsin Press, 1970), 22, 63, 86. See also Laird W. Bergad, Fe Iglesias García, and María del Carmen Barcia, *The Cuban Slave Market, 1790-1880* (Cambridge: Cambridge University Press, 1985).

121. Juan Pérez de la Riva, "Demografía de los culíes: Chinos en Cuba (1853-1874)," in *El barracón: Esclavitud y capitalismo en Cuba* (Barcelona: Crítica, 1978), 55-88; Manuel Moreno Fraginals, Frank Moya Pons, and Stanley Engerman, eds., *Between Slavery and Free Labor: The Spanish-Speaking Caribbean in the Nineteenth Century* (Baltimore: Johns Hopkins University Press, 1985); David Northrup, *Indentured Labor in the Age of Imperialism, 1834-1922* (Cambridge: Cambridge University Press, 1995); Walton Look Lai, *Indentured Labor, Caribbean Sugar: Chinese and Indian Migrants to the British West Indies, 1838-1918* (Baltimore: Johns Hopkins University Press, 1993); Eric Guerassimoff, "Travail colonial, coolies et diplomatie: Réclamations chinoises autour du contrat d'engagement à Cuba au XIXe siècle," in *Le travail colonial: Engagés et autres mains d'œuvre migrantes dans les empires, 1850-1950*, Eric Guerrassimoff and Issiaka Mandé, eds. (Paris: Riveneuve éditions, 2015), 417-63.

122. Casanovas Codina, *Bread or Bullets!*, 120-21.

123. Jorge Ibarra, *Ideología mambisa* (Havana: Instituto Cubano del Libro, 1972), 103-35.

124. Antoni Marimon, *La política colonial d'Antoni Maura: Les colonies espanyoles de Cuba, Puerto Rico i les Filipines a finals del segle XIX* (Palma de Mallorca: Documenta Balear, 1994); José Antonio Piqueras, *Cánovas y la derecha española: Del magnicidio a los neocon* (Barcelona: Península, 2008).

125. María Paz Alonso Romero, *Cuba en la España liberal (1837–1898): Génesis y desarrollo del régimen autonómico* (Madrid: Centro de Estudios Constitucionales, 2002), 38–39.

126. On Cuba, see Inés Roldán de Montaud, *La restauración en Cuba: El fracaso de un proceso reformista* (Madrid: CSIC, 2000); on Puerto Rico, see Astrid Cubano, *El hilo en el laberinto: Claves de la lucha política en Puerto Rico (siglo XIX)* (Río Piedras: Ediciones Huracán, 1990).

127. Jean Stubbs, *Tobacco on the Periphery: A Case Study in Cuban Labour History, 1860–1958* (Cambridge: Cambridge University Press, 1985).

128. Casanovas Codina, *Bread or Bullets!*, 111–14.

129. Manuel Moreno Fraginals, "Plantaciones en el Caribe: El caso de Cuba, Puerto Rico, Santo Domingo (1860–1940)," in *La historia como arma y otros estudios sobre esclavos, ingenios y plantaciones* (Barcelona: Editorial Crítica, 1983), 80–82; Fe Iglesias García, *Del ingenio al central* (Havana: Editorial de Ciencias Sociales, 1999).

130. On the abolition process, see Rebecca J. Scott, *Slave Emancipation in Cuba: The Transition to Free Labor, 1860–1899* (Princeton, NJ: Princeton University Press, 1985).

131. Ada Ferrer, *Insurgent Cuba: Race, Nation, and Revolution, 1868–1898* (Chapel Hill: University of North Carolina Press, 1999).

132. Scott, *Slave Emancipation in Cuba.*

133. Ferrer, *Insurgent Cuba*, 141–202.

134. Luis Miguel García Mora, "Tras la revolución, las reformas: El Partido Liberal cubano y los proyectos reformistas tras la Paz de Zanjón," in *Cuba, la perla de las Antillas: Actas de las I jornadas sobre "Cuba y su historia,"* ed. Consuelo Naranjo y Tomás Mallo (Madrid: CSIC, 1994), 197–212.

135. Marta Bizcarrondo and Antonio Elorza, *Cuba/España: El dilema autonomista, 1878–1898* (Madrid: El Colibrí, 2001); Mildred de la Torre, *El autonomismo en Cuba (1878–1898)* (Havana: Editorial de Ciencias Sociales, 1997).

136. Emilio de Diego García, "Las reformas de Maura, ¿la última oportunidad política en las Antillas?" in *1895: La Guerra de Cuba y la España de la Restauración*, ed. Emilio de Diego García (Madrid: Editorial Complutense, 1996), 99–117; María Paz Alonso Romero, *Cuba en la España liberal (1837–1898): Génesis y desarrollo del régimen autonómico* (Madrid: Centro de Estudios Constitucionales, 2002), 81–89.

137. John N. Schumacher, *The Propaganda Movement, 1880–1895: The Creators of a Filipino Consciousness, the Makers of Revolution* (Manila: Solidaridad Publishing House, 1973); and, by the same author, *The Making of a Nation: Essays on Nineteenth-Century Filipino Nationalism* (Manila: Ateneo de Manila University Press, 1991); Reynaldo C. Ileto, *Filipinos and their Revolution: Event, Discourse, and Historiography* (Quezon City: Ateneo de Manila University Press, 1998).

Chapter 7. The Long Road to 1898

1. Eric Hinderaker, *Elusive Empires: Constructing Colonialism in the Ohio Valley, 1673–1800* (New York: Cambridge University Press, 1997), 230–31.

2. Peter S. Onuf, *Jefferson's Empire: The Language of American Nationhood* (Charlottesville: University of Virginia Press, 2000), 53–79.

3. Stephen Howard Browne, *Jefferson's Call for Nationhood: The First Inaugural Address* (College Station: Texas A&M University Press, 2003), 68. For an exhaustive study of this era, see Gordon S. Wood, *Empire of Liberty: A History of the Early Republic, 1789–1815* (Oxford: Oxford University Press, 2009).

4. Eliga H. Gould, *The Persistence of Empire: British Political Culture in the Age of the American Revolution* (Chapel Hill: University of North Carolina Press, 2000).

5. Cited in Carroll Smith-Rosenberg, *This Violent Empire: The Birth of an American National Identity* (Chapel Hill: University of North Carolina Press, 2010), 5.

6. On the irrepressible appropriation, see Daniel K. Richter, *Before the Revolution: America's Ancient Pasts* (Cambridge, MA: Harvard University Press, 2011), 369–414.

7. See Jason Frank, *Constituent Moments: Enacting the People in Postrevolutionary America* (Durham, NC: Duke University Press, 2010), chapter 4, pp. 128–55.

8. Douglas Bradburn, *The Citizenship Revolution: Politics and the Creation of the American Union, 1774–1804* (Charlottesville: University of Virginia Press, 2009). On the need for expansion as part of the economic ideology of the early states, see Drew R. McCoy, *The Elusive Republic: Political Economy in Jeffersonian America* (Chapel Hill: University of North Carolina Press, 1980).

9. Peter S. Onuf, *The Mind of Thomas Jefferson* (Charlottesville: University of Virginia Press, 2007), 6.

10. The constitution of Virginia, written by some of the same men who wrote the U.S. Constitution and the Declaration of Independence, offered a watered-down version of liberty, saying it referred to all those who "lived in society," and so, did not include African slaves. See Pauline Maier, *American Scripture: Making the Declaration of Independence* (New York: Vintage Books, 1998), 193; see also Jack P. Greene, "All Men are Created Equal: Some Reflections on the Character of the American Revolution," in his *Imperatives, Behaviors, and Identities: Essays in Early American Cultural History* (Charlottesville: University of Virginia Press, 1992), 236–67.

11. On abolition in Pennsylvania, see Gary B. Nash, *The Unknown American Revolution: The Unruly Birth of Democracy and the Struggle to Create America* (New York: Penguin Books, 2005), 325–327; on the Royal Proclamation see Patrick Griffin, *American Leviathan: Empire, Nation, and Revolutionary Frontier* (New York: Hill & Wang, 2007), 19–45; on the war and its consequences, Fred Anderson, *Crucible of War: The Seven Years' War and the Fate of Empire in British North America, 1754–1766* (New York: Alfred A. Knopf, 2000); also by Anderson, *The War That Made America: A Short History of the French and Indian War* (New York: Penguin Books, 2005). On the international context, see Mark H. Danley and Patrick J. Speelman, eds., *The Seven Years' War: Global Views* (Leiden: Brill, 2012), esp. 47–72 and 325–56. On the Royal Proclamation in that context, see Francis Jennings, *The Creation of America: Through Revolution to Empire* (Cambridge: Cambridge University Press, 2000), 119–26.

12. Jack P. Greene, *Peripheries and Center: Constitutional Development in the Extended Polities of the British Empire and the United States, 1607-1788* (New York: W. W. Norton, 1990).

13. For a discussion regarding naturalization of new citizens in the context of citizenship by birth, see Peter H. Schuck and Rogers M. Smith, *Citizenship without Consent: Illegal Aliens in the American Polity* (New Haven, CT: Yale University Press, 1985), 42–71.

14. Eric Nelson, *The Royalist Revolution: Monarchy and the American Founding* (Cambridge, MA: Harvard University Press, 2014).

15. Adam Rothman, *Slave Country: American Expansion and the Origins of the Deep South* (Cambridge, MA: Harvard University Press, 2005), 19.

16. Christopher L. Tomlins, *Freedom Bound: Law, Labor, and Civic Identity in Colonizing English America, 1580-1865* (Cambridge: Cambridge University Press, 2010). On prison transports to the colonies, see A. Roger Ekirch, *Bound for America: The Transportation of British Convicts to the Colonies, 1718-1775* (Oxford: Clarendon Press, 1987).

17. Charles Sumner tried to remove color requirements in 1870 but was defeated by California, which opposed citizenship for Chinese immigrants.

18. Benjamin B. Ringer, *"We the People" and Others: Duality and America's Treatment of Its Racial Minorities* (New York: Tavistock, 1983).

19. Robert G. Parkinson, *The Common Cause: Creating Race and Nation in the American Revolution* (Chapel Hill: University of North Carolina Press, 2016).

20. Eliga H. Gould, "Fears of War, Fantasies of Peace: British Politics and the Coming of the American Revolution," in *Empire and Nation: The American Revolution in the Atlantic World*, ed. Eliga H. Gould and Peter S. Onuf (Baltimore: Johns Hopkins University Press, 2005), 19–34.

21. R. Oldfield, *Popular Politics and British Anti-Slavery: The Mobilisation of Public Opinion Against the Slave Trade, 1787-1807* (Manchester: Manchester University Press, 1995); Andy Doolen, *Fugitive Empire: Locating Early American Imperialism* (Minneapolis: University of Minnesota Press, 2005), 95; Don E. Fehrenbacher, *The Slaveholding Republic: An Account of the United States Government's Relations to Slavery* (Oxford: Oxford University Press, 2001), 205–52.

22. Onuf, *The Mind of Thomas Jefferson*, 208–9. On the idea of "people" as a political basis, see also Edmund S. Morgan, *Inventing the People: The Rise of Popular Sovereignty in England and America* (New York: W. W. Norton, 1988), chapter 11, pp. 263–87. For an unnecessarily formalist presentation of the notion of underlying democracy at that time, see Hans Agné, "Democratic Founding: We the People and the Others," *International Journal of Constitutional Law* 10, no. 3 (2012): 836–61; see also Mark Tushnet's reply in the same volume, 862–65.

23. Matthew Mason, *Slavery and Politics in the Early American Republic* (Chapel Hill: University of North Carolina Press, 2006), 25.

24. On this paradox, see the classic works by Winthrop D. Jordan, *White Over Black: American Attitudes Toward the Negro, 1550-1812* (Chapel Hill: University of North Carolina Press, 1968); Edmund S. Morgan, *American Slavery, American Freedom: The Ordeal of Colonial Virginia* (New York: W. W. Norton, 2005) [1st ed. 1975]; David Brion Davis, *The Problem of Slavery in the Age of Revolution, 1770-1823* (Ithaca, NY: Cornell University Press, 1975).

25. Donald E. Lively, *The Constitution and Race* (New York: Praeger, 1992), 3–4.

26. See the ironic commentary by Don E. Fehrenbacher in his *Slavery, Law, and Politics: The Dred Scott Case in Historical Perspective* (New York: Oxford University Press, 1981), 15.

27. Pauline Maier, *Ratification: The People Debate the Constitution, 1787–1788* (New York: Simon & Schuster, 2010), 175; David Brian Robertson, *The Constitution and America's Destiny* (Cambridge: Cambridge University Press, 2005), 177–81.

28. Garry Wills, *Negro President: Jefferson and the Slave Power* (Boston: Houghton Mifflin, 2003); for a different interpretation, see Wood, *Empire of Liberty*, 276–314; and John E. Ferling, *Adams vs. Jefferson: The Tumultuous Election of 1800* (New York: Oxford University Press, 2004); William W. Freehling, *The Road to Disunion*, vol. 1, *Secessionists at Bay, 1776–1854* (New York: Oxford University Press, 1990), 147.

29. Mason, *Slavery and Politics*, 65.

30. Edward Countryman, *Americans: A Collision of Histories* (New York: Hill & Wang, 1996), 156–58; Bernard W. Sheehan, *Seeds of Extinction: Jeffersonian Philanthropy and the American Indian* (Chapel Hill: University of North Carolina Press, 1973); Anthony F. C. Wallace, *Jefferson and the Indians: The Tragic Fate of the First Americans* (Cambridge, MA: Harvard University Press, 1999), 161–276; Paul Finkelman, "Jefferson and Slavery: Treason Against the Hopes of the World," in *Jeffersonian Legacies*, ed. Peter S. Onuf (Charlottesville: University of Virginia Press, 1993), 181–221.

31. Robin L. Einhorn, *American Taxation, American Slavery* (Chicago: University of Chicago Press, 2006).

32. On the economic background, see Woody Holton, *Unruly Americans and the Origins of the Constitution* (New York: Hill & Wang, 2007), 212–23.

33. Gordon S. Wood, *Representation in the American Revolution* (Charlottesville: University of Virginia Press, 2008), 58–59.

34. Davis, *The Problem of Slavery*, 126–27.

35. Staughton Lynd, *Class Conflict, Slavery and the United States Constitution* (New York: Cambridge University Press, 2009), 185–213.

36. Daniel K. Richter, *The Ordeal of the Longhouse: The Peoples of the Iroquois League in the Era of European Colonization* (Chapel Hill: University of North Carolina Press, 1992); Colin G. Calloway, *The Western Abenakis of Vermont, 1600–1800: War, Migration, and the Survival of an Indian People* (Norman: University of Oklahoma Press, 1990); Francis Jennings, *Empire of Fortune: Crowns, Colonies, and Tribes in the Seven Years War in America* (New York: Norton, 1988).

37. Walter T. Durham, *Before Tennessee: The Southwest Territory, 1790–1796* (Piney Flats, TN: Rocky Mount Historical Association, 1990).

38. Roger G. Kennedy, *Mr. Jefferson's Lost Cause: Land, Farmers, Slavery, and the Louisiana Purchase* (Oxford: Oxford University Press, 2003).

39. Robert Pierce Forbes, *The Missouri Compromise and Its Aftermath: Slavery and the Meaning of America* (Chapel Hill: University of North Carolina Press, 2004); John Ashworth, *Slavery, Capitalism and Politics in the Antebellum Republic*, vol. 1, *Commerce and Compromise, 1820–1850* (Cambridge: Cambridge University Press, 1995) 56–79; Freehling, *The Road to Disunion*, 144–61.

40. Francis Paul Prucha, *American Indian Policy in the Formative Years: The Indian Trade and Intercourse Acts, 1790–1834* (Cambridge, MA: Harvard University

Press, 1962); James H. Kettner, *The Development of American Citizenship, 1608–1870* (Chapel Hill: University of North Carolina Press, 1978), 291–97.

41. Kettner, *The Development*, 294.

42. Robert Middlekauff, *The Glorious Cause: The American Revolution, 1763–1789* (New York: Oxford University Press, 1982), 557.

43. Kettner, *The Development*, 303.

44. Alexander Keyssar, *The Right to Vote: The Contested History of Democracy in the United States* (New York: Basic Books, 2000), 45.

45. Keyssar, *The Right to Vote*, 311.

46. Kettner, *The Development*, 312–13.

47. Peter B. Knupfer, *The Union As It Is: Constitutional Unionism and Sectional Compromise, 1787–1861* (Chapel Hill: University of North Carolina Press, 1995); Ralph D. Gray and Michael A. Morrison, eds., *New Perspectives on the Early Republic: Essays from the Journal of the Early Republic, 1981–1991* (Urbana: University of Illinois Press, 1994).

48. See chapters 6–8 of Chilton Williamson, *American Suffrage: From Property to Democracy, 1760–1860* (Princeton, NJ: Princeton University Press, 1960).

49. Keyssar, *The Right to Vote*, 8–9.

50. Williamson, *American Suffrage*, 93.

51. Ibid., 99; Keyssar, *The Right to Vote*, 15.

52. Keyssar, *The Right to Vote*, 16.

53. Ibid., 12 and 29.

54. Alan Taylor, *The Internal Enemy: Slavery and War in Virginia, 1772–1832* (New York, W. W. Norton, 2013), 395.

55. Keyssar, *The Right to Vote*, 24–25.

56. Marchette Chute, *The First Liberty: A History of the Right to Vote in America, 1619–1850* (New York: Dutton, 1969), 279–316.

57. Keyssar, *The Right to Vote*, 31.

58. On the tradition of expanding lands at the disposal of colonists, see Daniel K. Richter, "To 'Clear the King's and Indians' Title': Seventeenth-Century Origins of American Land Cession Treaties," in *Empire by Treaty: Negotiating European Expansion, 1600–1900*, ed. Saliha Belmessous (New York: Oxford University Press, 2015), 45–77; and Francis Jennings, *The Invasion of America: Indians, Colonialism, and the Cant of Conquest* (Chapel Hill: University of North Carolina Press, 1975).

59. Matthew C. Ward, "Understanding Native American Alliances," in *The Seven Years' War: Global Views*, ed. Mark H. Danley and Patrick J. Speelman (Leiden: Brill 2012), 47–71; Daniel K. Richter, *Facing East of Indian Country: A Native History of Early America* (Cambridge, MA: Harvard University Press, 2003), 192.

60. Francis Paul Prucha, *American Indian Treaties: The History of a Political Anomaly* (Berkeley: University of California Press, 1994), 153; Claudio Saunt, *A New Order of Things: Property, Power, and the Transformation of the Creek Indians, 1733–1816* (Cambridge: Cambridge University Press, 2003).

61. On Jackson's geographic and social origins, see Colin Woodard, *American Nations: A History of the Eleven Rival Regional Cultures of North America* (New York: Penguin Books, 2011), 194–97.

62. Griffin, *American Leviathan*; Claudio Saunt, *West of the Revolution: An Uncommon History of 1776* (New York: W. W. Norton, 2014).

63. Woody Holton, *Forced Founders: Indians, Debtors, Slaves, and the Making of the American Revolution in Virginia* (Chapel Hill: University of North Carolina Press, 2003); Eric Hinderaker and Peter C. Mancall, *At the Edge of Empire: The Backcountry in British North America* (Baltimore: Johns Hopkins University Press, 2003), 133–40; Kevin Kenny, *Peaceable Kingdom Lost: The Paxton Boys and the Destruction of William Penn's Holy Experiment* (Oxford: Oxford University Press, 2009).

64. Hinderaker, *Elusive Empires*, 261; also James Hart Merrell, *Into the American Woods: Negotiators on the Pennsylvania Frontier* (New York: W. W. Norton, 1999); and Daniel K. Richter, *Trade, Land, Power: The Struggle for Eastern North America* (Philadelphia: University of Pennsylvania Press, 2013), 202–26.

65. Michael J. Witgen, *An Infinity of Nations: How the Native New World Shaped Early North America* (Philadelphia: University of Pennsylvania Press, 2012), 322–58.

66. Hinderaker and Mancall, *At the Edge of Empire*, 92–105, 174–75; Nicole Eustace, *1812: War and the Passions of Patriotism* (Philadelphia: University of Pennsylvania Press, 2012), 118–167; Michael A. McDonnell, *Masters of Empire: Great Lakes Indians and the Making of America* (New York: Hill and Wang, 2015); Parkinson, *The Common Cause*, 266–276.

67. James E. Lewis, Jr., *The American Union and the Problem of Neighborhood: The United States and the Collapse of the Spanish Empire, 1783–1829* (Chapel Hill: University of North Carolina Press, 1998), 126–154. For an overview of the establishment of the Cotton Belt, see Sven Beckert, *Empire of Cotton: A Global History* (New York: Alfred A. Knopf, 2014), especially 103–5. See also Sven Beckert and Seth Rockman, *Slavery's Capitalism: A New History of American Economic Development* (Philadelphia: University of Pennsylvania Press, 2016); and Matthew Karp, *This Vast Southern Empire: Slaveholders at the Helm of American Foreign Policy* (Cambridge, MA: Harvard University Press, 2016).

68. Saunt, *West of the Revolution*, 198; see also Richter, *Before the Revolution*, 369–387.

69. Paraphrasing Peter J. Marshall, *The Making and Unmaking of Empires: Britain, India, and America, c. 1750-1783* (Oxford: Oxford University Press, 2009).

70. Gordon S. Wood, *The Idea of America: Reflections on the Birth of the United States* (New York: Penguin Press, 2011), 233.

71. Onuf, *Jefferson's Empire*, 181.

72. Bernard Porter, *Empire and Superempire: Britain, America and the World* (New Haven, CT: Yale University Press, 2006), 64.

73. J.G.A. Pocock, *The Machiavellian Moment: Florentine Political Thought and the Atlantic Republican Tradition* (Princeton, NJ: Princeton University Press, 1975).

74. Paul VanDevelder, *Savages and Scoundrels: The Untold Story of America's Road to Empire through Indian Territory* (New Haven, CT: Yale University Press, 2009).

75. Onuf, *The Mind of Thomas Jefferson*, 124–129; immigration numbers from James Belich, *Replenishing the Earth: The Settler Revolution and the Rise of the Anglo-World, 1783-1939* (Oxford: Oxford University Press, 2009), 90–91.

76. Such considerable imagination is described in Richter, *Before the Revolution.*

77. On the significance of the Purchase, see Walter LaFeber, "Jefferson and an American Foreign Policy," in *Jeffersonian Legacies,* ed. Peter S. Onuf (Charlottesville: University of Virginia Press, 1993), 370–94.

78. McCoy, *The Elusive Republic,* 356–99.

79. Wilma A. Dunaway, *The First American Frontier: Transition to Capitalism in Southern Appalachia, 1700–1860* (Chapel Hill: University of North Carolina Press, 1996), 51–86; John E. Kiczka and Rebecca Horn, *Resilient Cultures: America's Native Peoples Confront European Colonialization 1500–1800* (London: Routledge, 2013), 165–67 [1st ed. 1973].

80. George Dargo, *Jefferson's Louisiana: Politics and the Clash of Legal Traditions* (Cambridge, MA: Harvard University Press, 1975); Joseph G. Treggle, Jr., *Louisiana in the Age of Jackson: A Clash of Cultures and Personalities* (Baton Rouge: Louisiana State University Press, 1999).

81. Robert V. Haynes, *The Mississippi Territory and the Southwest Frontier, 1795–1817* (Lexington: University Press of Kentucky, 2010), 139–66; Buckner F. Melton, *Aaron Burr: Conspiracy to Treason* (New York: John Wiley and Sons, 2001); and Wood, *Empire of Liberty,* 278–86.

82. Rothman, *Slave Country,* 19.

83. Ira Berlin, *Generations of Captivity: A History of African-American Slaves* (Cambridge, MA: Harvard University Press, 2003); on the linkage between economic model and expansion, see Jeffrey Rogers Hummel, *Emancipating Slaves, Enslaving Free Men: A History of the American Civil War* (Chicago: Open Court, 1996), chapter 3, pp. 76–104.

84. Forbes, *The Missouri Compromise*; Sean Wilentz, "Jeffersonian Democracy and the Origins of Political Antislavery in the United States: The Missouri Compromise Crisis Revisited," *Journal of the Historical Society* 4, no. 3 (2004): 375–401.

85. Peter J. Kastor, *The Nation's Crucible: The Louisiana Purchase and the Creation of America* (New Haven, CT: Yale University Press, 2004), 13–14; emphasis in the original.

86. Walter Johnson, *River of Dark Dreams: Slavery and Empire in the Cotton Kingdom* (Cambridge, MA: Harvard University Press, 2013), 27–29; Robert V. Remini, *The Battle of New Orleans: Andrew Jackson and America's First Military Victory* (New York: Viking, 1988); Stephanie McCurry, *Confederate Reckoning: Power and Politics in the Civil War South* (Cambridge, MA: Harvard University Press, 2010), 104–5.

87. Andrew Heath, "'Let the Empire Come': Imperialism and Its Critics in the Reconstruction South," *Civil War History* 60, no. 2 (2014): 152–89; Beckert, *Empire of Cotton.* For a later period, Justin A. Nystrom, *New Orleans after the Civil War: Race, Politics, and a New Birth of Freedom* (Baltimore: Johns Hopkins University Press, 2010).

88. Johnson, *River of Dark Dreams,* 395–99.

89. Rothman, *Slave Country,* 27.

90. Kenneth R. Aslakson, *Making Race in the Courtroom: The Legal Construction of Three Races in Early New Orleans* (New York: New York University Press, 2014), 67–97.

91. Rebecca J. Scott and Jean M. Hébrard, *Freedom Papers: An Atlantic Odyssey in the Age of Emancipation* (Cambridge, MA: Harvard University Press, 2012). I am quoting from the Spanish translation, *Papeles de libertad: Una odisea transatlántica en la era de la emancipación* (Bogotá: Universidad de los Andes, 2015), 89.

92. Gilbert C. Din, *Spaniards, Planters, and Slaves: The Spanish Regulation of Slavery in Louisiana, 1763–1803* (College Station: Texas A&M University Press, 1999); Hans W. Baade, "The Law of Slavery in Spanish Louisiana, 1769–1803," in *Louisiana's Legal Heritage*, ed. Edward F. Haas (Pensacola: Perdido Way Press for the Louisiana State Museum, 1983), 43–75.

93. Dargo, *Jefferson's Louisiana*, 23.

94. Laura Foner, "The Free People of Color in Louisiana and St. Domingue: A Comparative Portrait of Two Three-Caste Slave Societies," *Journal of Social History* 3, no. 4 (1970): 406–30.

95. Aslakson, *Making Race in the Courtroom*, 161.

96. Rothman, *Slave Country*, 78; Judith Kelleher Schafer, *Slavery, the Civil Law, and the Supreme Court of Louisiana* (Baton Rouge: Louisiana State University Press, 1994); Kimberley S. Hanger, "Greedy French Masters and Color-Conscious, Legal-Minded Spaniards in Colonial Louisiana," in *Slavery in the Caribbean Francophone World: Distant Voices, Forgotten Acts, Forged Identities*, ed. Doris Y. Kadish (Athens: University of Georgia Press, 2000), 106–21.

97. Rebecca J. Scott, *Degrees of Freedom: Louisiana and Cuba after Slavery* (Cambridge, MA: Harvard University Press, 2005), 16.

98. Amy R. Sumpter, "Segregation of the Free People of Color and the Construction of Race in Antebellum New Orleans," *Southern Geographer* 48, no. 1 (2008): 22.

99. Paul A. Kunkel, "Modifications in Louisiana Negro Legal Status under Louisiana Constitutions, 1812–1957," *The Journal of Negro History* 44, no. 1 (1959): 2.

100. Russell Reynolds, "Spanish Law Influence in Louisiana," *Hispania* 56, no. 4 (1973): 1076–82.

101. Dargo, *Jefferson's Louisiana*, 15–16.

102. On Locke, see Joyce O. Appleby, *Liberalism and Republicanism in the Historical Imagination* (Cambridge, MA: Harvard University Press, 1992), chapter 2, pp. 58–90; also Michael P. Zuckert, *The Natural Rights Republic: Studies in the Foundation of the American Political Tradition* (Notre Dame: Notre Dame University Press, 1996), 108–17.

103. Paul Quigley, *Shifting Grounds: Nationalism and the American South, 1848–1865* (Oxford: Oxford University Press, 2012), 11.

104. Howard Lamar, *The Far Southwest, 1846–1912: A Territorial History* (Albuquerque: University of New Mexico Press, 2000), 432. Regarding Arizona and New Mexico, Lamar wrote: ". . . the admission debate mirrored American prejudices and preoccupations at the turn of the century and demonstrated how the concerns of the 'metropolis' and the nation could affect the fortunes of the 'province.'" See also Robert M. Utley and Wilcomb E. Washburn, *The Indian Wars* (Boston: Houghton Mifflin Company, 2001).

105. David W. Miller, *The Taking of American Indian Lands in the Southeast: A History of Territorial Cessions and Forced Relocations, 1607–1840* (Jefferson, NC: McFarland, 2011).

106. Merrell, *Into the American Woods*; Richard White, *The Middle Ground: Indians, Empires, and Republics in the Great Lakes Region, 1650–1815* (Cambridge: Cambridge University Press, 1991).

107. David Edmunds, *Tecumseh and the Quest for Indian Leadership* (Boston: Little, Brown, 1984).

108. Nash, *The Unknown American Revolution*, 356.

109. David S. Heidler and Jeanne T. Heidler, *Indian Removal: A Norton Casebook* (New York: W. W. Norton, 2007); Theda Perdue and Michael D. Green, *The Cherokee Nation and the Trail of Tears* (New York: Penguin Books, 2007); Sami Lakomäki, *Gathering Together: The Shawnee People through Diaspora and Nationhood, 1600–1870* (New Haven, CT: Yale University Press, 2014), 165–223.

110. Peter S. Onuf, "'We shall all be Americans': Thomas Jefferson and the Indians." *Indiana Magazine of History* 95, no. 2 (1999): 103–41; Sheehan, *Seeds of Extinction*.

111. Indians "are in state of pupilage. Their relations resemble that of a ward to his guardian," according to the ruling, cited in Alex Tallchief Skibine, "The Federal-Tribe Relationship," in *Handbook of North American Indians*, vol. 2, *Indians in Contemporary Society*, ed. Garrick A. Bailey (Washington: Smithsonian Institution, 2008), 57. See also Bartolomé Clavero, "Tiempo de colonia, tiempo de constitución," in *Derecho indígena y cultura constitucional en América* (Madrid: Siglo XXI Editores, 1994), 1–52.

112. David E. Wilkins and K. Tsianina Lomawaima, *Uneven Ground: American Indian Sovereignty and Federal Law* (Norman: University of Oklahoma Press, 2001).

113. Dorothy V. Jones, *License for Empire: Colonialism by Treaty in Early America* (Chicago: University of Chicago Press, 1982).

114. Charles F. Wilkinson, "Indian Tribes and the American Constitution," in *Indians in American History: An Introduction*, ed. Frederick E. Hoxie (Arlington Heights, IL: Harlan Davidson, 1998), 118.

115. Reginald Horsman, *Expansion and American Indian Policy, 1783–1812* (East Lansing: Michigan State University Press, 1967), 113.

116. Francis Paul Prucha, *The Great Father: The United States Government and the American Indians* (Lincoln: University of Nebraska Press, 1984), 1:151–52.

117. Tim Alan Garrison, *The Legal Ideology of Removal: The Southern Judiciary and the Sovereignty of Native American Nations* (Athens: University of Georgia Press, 2009), 234–45.

118. Daniel F. Littlefield, *The Chickasaw Freedmen: A People without a Country* (Westport, CT: Greenwood Press, 1980).

119. Saunt, *West of the Revolution*, 21. For example, in 1775, Richard Henderson of North Carolina bought 22 million acres from the Cherokee with the idea of building an economic empire and possibly a fourteenth colony; Henderson confessed that the colonies were prepared "to build an empire upon the ruins of Great Britain."

120. Jill Lepore, *The Name of War: King Philip's War and the Origins of American Identity* (New York: Vintage Books, 1999), 205; on cultural changes among the Cherokee, see William G. McLoughlin, *Cherokee Renascence in the New Republic* (Princeton, NJ: Princeton University Press, 1986).

121. Ashworth, *Slavery, Capitalism, and Politics*, 289–302.

122. The quotation is in Karp, *This Vast Southern Empire*, 171.

123. Michael D. Green, *The Politics of Indian Removal: Creek Government and Society in Crisis* (Lincoln: University of Nebraska Press, 1992); John P. Bowes, *Exiles and Pioneers: Eastern Indians in the Trans-Mississippi West* (New York: Cambridge University Press, 2007).

124. Countryman, *Americans*, 160–61.

125. Perdue and Green, *The Cherokee Nation*.

126. David A. Chang, *The Color of the Land: Race, Nation, and the Politics of Landownership in Oklahoma, 1832–1929* (Chapel Hill: University of North Carolina Press, 2010.)

127. On the comparison with Tasmania, see George Harwood Phillips, *Indians and Indian Agents: The Origins of the Reservation System in California, 1849–1852* (Norman: University of Oklahoma Press, 1997), 184.

128. For an overview of the changes during this era, see Charles S. Maier, *Leviathan 2.0: Inventing Modern Statehood* (Cambridge, MA: Harvard University Press, 2012), 97.

129. See Quigley, *Shifting Grounds*, chapters 2 and 3.

130. "Captive nation" from Onuf, *Jefferson's Empire*, 177; see also Michael Kent Curtis, *No State Shall Abridge: The Fourteenth Amendment and the Bill of Rights* (Durham, NC: Duke University Press, 1986); William E. Nelson, *The Fourteenth Amendment: From Political Principle to Judicial Doctrine* (Cambridge, MA: Harvard University Press, 1988).

131. On Jefferson's idea and the plans of the American Colonization Society, see Onuf, *The Mind of Thomas Jefferson*, 222–23; and Onuf, *Jefferson's Empire*, 149–50; Manisha Sinha, *The Slave's Cause: A History of Abolition* (New Haven, CT: Yale University Press, 2016), 87–88; Phillip W. Magness and Sebastian N. Page, *Colonization after Emancipation: Lincoln and the Movement for Black Resettlement* (Columbia, MO: University of Missouri Press, 2011); Henry Louis Gates Jr., ed., *Lincoln on Race and Slavery* (Princeton, NJ: Princeton University Press, 2009), xvii–lxviii.

132. See the important and relevant contributions in Richard White, *Railroaded: The Transcontinentals and the Making of Modern America* (New York: W. W. Norton, 2011).

133. Aristide R. Zolberg, *A Nation by Design: Immigration Policy in the Fashioning of America* (New York/Cambridge, MA: Russell Sage Foundation/Harvard University Press, 2006), 187–89; Benjamin Madley, *An American Genocide: The United States and the California Indian Catastrophe, 1846–1873* (New Haven, CT: Yale University Press, 2016).

134. Reed Ueda, "An Immigration Country of Assimilative Pluralism," in *Migration Past, Migration Future: Germany and the United States*, ed. J. Bade and Myron Weiner (Providence, RI: Berghahn Books, 1997), 43–44.

135. David Herbert Donald, *Charles Sumner and the Rights of Man* (New York: Alfred A. Knopf, 1970), 174.

136. Robert J. Kaczorowski, *The Nationalization of Civil Rights: Constitutional Theory and Practice in a Racist Society, 1866–1883* (New York: Garland Publishing, 1987).

137. On the parallel battle to control the Supreme Court, see Lawrence Goldstone, *Inherently Unequal: The Betrayal of Equal Rights by the Supreme Court, 1865–1903* (New York: Walker and Company, 2010), 46–47.

138. Don E. Fehrenbacher, *The Dred Scott Case, Its Significance in American Law and Politics* (New York: Oxford University Press, 1978); Ringer, *"We the People,"* 103; Tomlins, *Freedom Bound*, 509–69; David M. Potter, *Impending Crisis: America before the Civil War, 1848–1861* (New York: Harper, 2011) [1st ed. 1971]; on the slaves' experience in court during the first half of the nineteenth century, see Lea VanderVelde, *Redemption Songs: Suing for Freedom before Dred Scott* (Oxford: Oxford University Press, 2014).

139. Avery O. Craven, *Reconstruction: The Ending of the Civil War* (New York: Holt, Rinehart and Winston, 1969), 111–24.

140. George M. Fredrickson, *The Black Image in the White Mind: The Debate on Afro-American Character and Destiny, 1817–1914* (New York: Harper & Row, 1971), 185–86.

141. Gregory P. Downs, *After Appomattox: Military Occupation and the Ends of War* (Cambridge, MA: Harvard University Press, 2015), 67.

142. Michael Les Benedict, *A Compromise of Principle: Congressional Republicans and Reconstruction, 1863–1869* (New York: W. W. Norton, 1974), 324–36.

143. Kenneth M. Stampp, *The Era of Reconstruction, 1865–1877* (New York: Vintage Books, 1962), 8.

144. Michael Perman, *The Road to Redemption: Southern Politics, 1869–1879* (Chapel Hill: University of North Carolina Press, 1984), 193–220.

145. Leon F. Litwack, *Been in the Storm So Long: The Aftermath of Slavery* (New York: Vintage Books, 1980).

146. Benjamin B. Ringer and Elinor R. Lawless, *Race-Ethnicity and Society* (New York: Routledge, 1989), 153.

147. Goldstone, *Inherently Unequal*, 152–76; Kenneth L. Karst, *Belonging to America: Equal Citizenship and the Constitution* (New Haven, CT: Yale University Press, 1989), 57–61; Williamjames Hull Hoffer, *Plessy v. Ferguson: Race and Inequality in Jim Crow America* (Lawrence: University of Kansas Press, 2012).

148. Lawrence J. Friedman, *The White Savage: Racial Fantasies in the Postbellum South* (Englewood Cliffs, NJ: Prentice Hall, 1970); Grace Elizabeth Hale, *Making Whiteness: The Culture of Segregation in the South, 1890–1940* (New York: Vintage Books, 1999); Hugh Davis, *"We Will Be Satisfied with Nothing Less": The African American Struggle for Equal Rights in the North During Reconstruction* (Ithaca, NY: Cornell University Press, 2011).

149. Ira Berlin, et al., "The Wartime Genesis of Free Labor, 1861–1865," in *Slaves No More: Three Essays on Emancipation and the Civil War* (Cambridge: Cambridge University Press, 1991), 81.

150. David Herbert Donald, *The Politics of Reconstruction, 1863–1867* (Baton Rouge: Louisiana State University Press, 1965), 15.

151. Hummel, *Emancipating Slaves*, 295.

152. Stampp, *The Era of Reconstruction*, 128; Downs, *After Appomattox*, 121–23.

153. Paul A. Cimbala, *Under the Guardianship of the Nation: The Freedmen's Bureau and the Reconstruction of Georgia, 1865–1870* (Athens: University of Georgia

Press, 2003) [1st ed. 1997]; and, by the same author, *The Freedmen's Bureau: Reconstructing the American South After the Civil War* (Malabar, FL: Krieger, 2005).

154. Perman, *The Road to Redemption*, 203, 213.

155. See Gavin Wright, "The Rise of Tenancy," part of the essay "After the War," in his *The Political Economy of the Cotton South: Households, Markets, and Wealth in the Nineteenth Century* (New York: W.W. Norton, 1978), 160–64.

156. James L. Roark, *Masters without Slaves: Southern Planters in the Civil War and Reconstruction* (New York: W. W. Norton, 1977); Roger L. Ransom and Richard Sutch, *One Kind of Freedom: The Economic Consequences of Emancipation* (New York: Cambridge University Press, 1978); Robert Higgs, *Competition and Coercion: Blacks in the American Economy, 1865–1914* (Cambridge: Cambridge University Press, 1977); Claude F. Oubre, *Forty Acres and a Mule: The Freedmen's Bureau and Black Land Ownership* (Baton Rouge: Louisiana State University Press, 1978); Gavin Wright, *Old South, New South: Revolutions in the Southern Economy since the Civil War* (New York: Basic Books, 1986).

157. Leslie A. Schwalm, *Emancipation's Diaspora: Race and Reconstruction in the Upper Midwest* (Chapel Hill: University of North Carolina Press, 2009); Ira Berlin, *The Making of African America: The Four Great Migrations* (New York: Viking, 2010).

158. Prucha, *American Indian Treaties*, 353.

159. Charles F. Wilkinson, *American Indians, Time, and the Law: Native Societies in a Modern Constitutional Democracy* (New Haven, CT: Yale University Press, 1988), 7.

160. For a depiction of how industrial corporations carved tribal lands, see H. Craig Miner, *The Corporation and the Indian: Tribal Sovereignty and Industrial Civilization in Indian Territory, 1865–1907* (Columbia: University of Missouri Press, 1976).

161. Paul Stuart, *The Indian Office: Growth and Development of an American Institution, 1865–1900* (Ann Arbor: UMI Research Press, 1979), 15. The Burke Act was an amendment to prior legislation allotting lands to Indians (see below).

162. Frederick E. Hoxie, "The Reservation Period, 1880–1960," in *The Cambridge History of the Native Peoples of the Americas*, vol. 1, *North America: Part 2*, ed. Bruce G. Trigger and Wilcomb E. Washburn (Cambridge: Cambridge University Press, 1966), 185.

163. For a global reflection on these changes, see Jürgen Osterhammel, *The Transformation of the World: A Global History of the Nineteenth Century* (Princeton, NJ: Princeton University Press, 2014), 368–91.

164. On the change in public opinion, see Robert F. Berkhofer Jr., *The White Man's Indian: Images of the American Indian from Columbus to the Present* (New York: Vintage Books, 1979), 166–75.

165. Angie Debo, *And Still the Waters Run: The Betrayal of the Five Civilized Tribes* (Norman: University of Oklahoma Press, 1984) [1st ed. 1940].

166. Stuart Banner, *How the Indians Lost Their Land: Law and Power on the Frontier* (Cambridge, MA: Harvard University Press, 2005), 257.

167. On the Osage in the eighteenth century, see Saunt, *West of the Revolution*, 168–87.

168. Curtis Emanuel Jackson and Marcia J. Galli, *A History of the Bureau of Indian Affairs and Its Activities among Indians* (San Francisco: R. E. Publishers, 1977), 95; Banner, *How the Indians Lost Their Land*, 257.

169. Roger L. Nichols, *Indians in the United States and Canada: A Comparative History* (Lincoln: University of Nebraska Press, 1998), 206–42.

170. Doolen, *Fugitive Empire*.

171. This is the stance taken by Thomas Bender in *A Nation Among Nations: America's Place in World History* (New York: Hill & Wang, 2006).

172. Tomlins, *Freedom Bound*, 525.

173. David Kazanjian, *The Colonizing Trick: National Culture and Imperial Citizenship in Early America* (Minneapolis: University of Minnesota Press, 2003), 206–9.

174. David E. Roediger, *The Wages of Whiteness: Race and the Making of the American Working Class* (London: Verso, 1991); Alexander Saxton, *The Rise and Fall of the White Republic: Class Politics and Mass Culture in Nineteenth-Century America* (London: Verso, 2003); Ian Haney-López, *White by Law: The Legal Construction of Race* (New York: New York University Press, 2006); Bill Ong Hing, *Defining America through Immigration Policy* (Philadelphia: Temple University Press, 2004), 28–51; John Higham, *Strangers in the Land: Patterns of American Nativism, 1860–1925* (New Brunswick, NJ: Rutgers University Press, 2008); Tyler Anbinder, *Nativism and Slavery: The Northern Know Nothings and the Politics of the 1850s* (New York: Oxford University Press, 1992).

175. White, *Railroaded*.

176. Susan F. Martin, *A Nation of Immigrants* (Cambridge: Cambridge University Press, 2011), 105–31.

177. Nancy Foner and George M. Fredrickson, "Immigration, Race, and Ethnicity in the United States: Social Constructions and Social Relations in Historical and Contemporary Perspective," in *Not Just Black and White: Historical and Contemporary Perspectives on Immigration, Race, and Ethnicity in the United States*, ed. Nancy Foner and George M. Fredrickson (New York: Russell Sage Foundation, 2004), 1; Roger Daniels, *Guarding the Golden Door: American Immigration Policy and Immigrants since 1882* (New York: Hill and Wang, 2004); Andrew Gyory, *Closing the Gate: Race, Politics and the Chinese Exclusion Act* (Chapel Hill: University of North Carolina Press, 1998); David Scott Fitzgerald and David Cook-Martin, *Culling the Masses: The Democratic Origins of Racist Immigration Policy in the Americas* (Cambridge, MA: Harvard University Press, 2014), 82–140; Martin, *A Nation of Immigrants*, 132–51.

178. Charles A. Price, *The Great White Walls Are Built: Restrictive Immigration to North America and Australasia, 1836–1888* (Canberra: Australian National University Press, 1974), 125–44.

179. Walter LaFeber, *The New Empire: An Interpretation of American Expansion, 1860–1898* (Ithaca, NY: Cornell University Press, 1963).

180. See Richard H. Immerman, *Empire for Liberty: A History of American Imperialism from Benjamin Franklin to Paul Wolfowitz* (Princeton, NJ: Princeton University Press, 2010), chapter 3, pp. 98–127.

181. Jay Sexton, *The Monroe Doctrine: Empire and Nation in Nineteenth-Century America* (New York: Hill & Wang, 2012).

182. See also Aristide R. Zolberg, *A Nation by Design*, chapter 6, "Seward's Other Follies," 166–98.

183. Howard Lamar, "From Bondage to Contract: Ethnic Labor in the American West, 1600–1890," in *The Countryside in the Age of Capitalist Transformation:*

Essays in the Social History of Rural America, ed. Steven Hahn and Jonathan Prude (Chapel Hill: University of North Carolina Press, 1985), 293–324.

184. Emlin McClain, "Written and Unwritten Constitutions in the United States," *Columbia Law Review* 6, no. 2 (1906): 79.

185. Julian Go, "Imperial Power and its Limits: America's Colonial Empire in the Early Twentieth Century," in *Lessons of Empire: Imperial Histories and American Power*, ed. Craig J. Calhoun, Frederick Cooper, and Kevin W. Moore (New York: The New Press, 2005), 201–14. The examples of Hawaii and the Philippines are explored in Eric T. L. Love, *Race over Empire: Racism and U. S. Imperialism, 1865–1900* (Chapel Hill: University of North Carolina Press, 2004), 115–95; and Alfred W. McCoy, *Policing America's Empire: The United States, the Philippines, and the Rise of the Surveillance State* (Madison: University of Wisconsin Press, 2009).

186. On the debate regarding the constitutional formulas to be implemented in the Philippines, see Susan K. Harris, *God's Arbiters: Americans and the Philippines, 1898–1902* (New York: Oxford University Press, 2013).

187. Douglas Cole, "The Problem of 'Nationalism' and 'Imperialism' in British Settlement Colonies," *The Journal of British Studies* 10, no. 2 (1971): 160–82.

188. Walter LaFeber, *The New Empire*, 242–83.

189. Paul A. Kramer, *The Blood of Government: Race, Empire, the United States, and the Philippines* (Chapel Hill: University of North Carolina Press, 2006), 163; on local Filipino social elites, see Juan Antonio Inarejos Muñoz, *Los (últimos) caciques de Filipinas: Las élites coloniales antes del 1898* (Granada: Comares, 2015).

190. John D. Blanco, *Frontier Constitutions: Christianity and Colonial Empire in the Nineteenth-Century Philippines* (Berkeley: University of California Press, 2009); Michael Salman, *The Embarrassment of Slavery: Controversies over Bondage and Nationalism in the American Colonial Philippines* (Berkeley: University of California Press, 2001).

191. Joseph E. Fallon, "Federal Policy and U.S. Territories: The Political Restructuring of the United States of America," *Pacific Affairs* 64, no. 1 (1991): 23.

Chapter 8. The Imperial Nation

1. Jay M. Smith, *Nobility Reimagined: The Patriotic Nation in Eighteenth-Century France* (Ithaca, NY: Cornell University Press, 2005). On Germany see Matthew P. Fitzpatrick, *Liberal Imperialism in Germany: Expansionism and Nationalism, 1848–1884* (New York: Berghahn Books, 2008); and chapter 5 of Jonathan Powis, *Aristocracy* (Oxford: Blackwell, 1984).

2. Michael Howard, *Empires, Nations and Wars* (Staplehurst: Spellmount, 2007). For French revolutionaries' response to external threats, see Sophie Wahnich, *L'impossible citoyen: L'étranger dans le discours de la Révolution française* (Paris: Albin Michel, 1997).

3. Pierre Rosanvallon, *La société des égaux* (Paris: Seuil, 2011); Claude Fiévet, ed., *Invention et réinvention de la citoyenneté: Actes du colloque international de Pau, 9–11 décembre 1998* (Pau: Éditions Joëlle Sampy, 2000).

4. To quote Anarchasis Cloots, "*Le genre humain délivré imitera un jour la na-*
ture qui ne connaît point d'étrangers, et la sagesse régnera sur les deux hémisphères,
dans la République des Individus-unis." ("The liberated human race will one day
imitate nature, which sees no strangers anywhere, and wisdom will reign over both
hemispheres, in the Republic of United Individuals.") Cited in Wahnich, *L'impossible*
citoyen, 7. See also Pierre Rétat, "The Evolution of the Citizen from the Ancien Régime to the Revolution," in *The French Revolution and the Meaning of Citizenship*,
ed. Renée Waldinger, Philip Dawson, and Isser Woloch (Westport, CT: Greenwood
Press, 1993), 3–15.

5. For the U.S. case, see Benjamin B. Ringer, *"We the People" and Others: Duality*
and America's Treatment of Its Racial Minorities (New York: Tavistock, 1983); and
Matthew Frye Jacobson, *Barbarian Virtues: The United States Encounters Foreign*
Peoples at Home and Abroad, 1876–1917 (New York: Hill & Wang, 2000).

6. Frédéric Bidouze, "Polysémie et diachronie du terme de citoyen dans les discours parlementaires au XVIIIe siècle: essai d'interprétation," in *Invention et réin-*
vention de la citoyenneté: Actes du colloque international de Pau, 9–11 décembre 1998,
ed. Claude Fiévet (Pau: Éditions Joëlle Sampy, 2000), 97–113; David A. Bell, "The
Unbearable Lightness of Being French: Law, Republicanism and National Identity at
the End of the Old Regime," *American Historical Review* 106, no. 4 (2001): 1215–35.

7. Gérard Noiriel, "L'identification des citoyens: Naissance de l'état civil républicain," *Genèses: Sciences sociales et histoire* 13(1993): 3–28; and, by the same author,
"The Identification of the Citizen: The Birth of Republican Civil Status in France," in
Documenting Individual Identity: The Development of State Practices in the Modern
World, ed. Jane Caplan and John Torpey (Princeton, NJ: Princeton University Press,
2001), 28–48; Fiévet, *Invention et réinvention*; Andreas Fahrmeir, *Revolutionen und Re-*
formen: Europa, 1789–1850 (Munich: C. H. Beck, 2010); also by Fahrmeir, *Citizenship:*
The Rise and Fall of a Modern Concept (New Haven, CT: Yale University Press, 2007).

8. José María Portillo Valdés, *Historia mínima del constitucionalismo en*
América Latina (Mexico City: Colegio de México, 2016), 29.

9. Istvan Hont, *Jealousy of Trade: International Competition and the Nation-*
State in Historical Perspective (Cambridge, MA: Harvard University Press, 2005),
448.

10. For one such example, Gerald G. Newman, *The Rise of English Nationalism:*
A Cultural History, 1740–1830 (London: Weidenfeld & Nicolson, 1987).

11. See, for example, Jeremy Bentham's daring proposals for Britain in his *Cate-*
chism of Parliamentary Reform (1809), where he proposed nearly universal suffrage;
on this, see Timothy J. Gaffaney, *Freedom for the Poor: Welfare and the Foundations*
of Democratic Citizenship (Boulder, CO: Westview Press, 2000), 23.

12. Kenneth L. Karst, *Belonging to America: Equal Citizenship and the Constitu-*
tion (New Haven, CT: Yale University Press, 1989), 43–49; Margaret Hunt, "Women
and the Fiscal-Imperial State in the Late Seventeenth and Early Eighteenth Centuries," in *A New Imperial History: Culture, Identity, and Modernity in Britain and the*
Empire, 1660–1840, ed. Kathleen Wilson (Cambridge: Cambridge University Press,
2004), 41–42.

13. Alan S. Kahan, *Liberalism in Nineteenth-Century Europe: The Political Cul-*
ture of Limited Suffrage (Houndmills: Palgrave Macmillan, 2003); María Sierra,

María Antonio Peña and Rafael Zurita, *Elegidos y elegibles: La representación parlamentaria en la cultura del liberalismo* (Madrid: Marcial Pons, 2010).

14. Peter H. Schuck and Rogers M. Smith, *Citizenship without Consent: Illegal Aliens in the American Polity* (New Haven, CT: Yale University Press, 1985), 2.

15. Derek Taylor, *Don Pacifico: The Acceptable Face of Gunboat Diplomacy* (London: Vallentine Mitchell, 2008). See also Paul D. Halliday, *Habeas Corpus: From England to Empire* (Cambridge, MA: Harvard University Press, 2009).

16. Krishan Kumar, "Nation-States as Empires, Empires as Nation-States: Two Principles, One Practice?" *Theory and Society* 39, no. 2 (2010): 124.

17. John M. MacKenzie, ed., *Imperialism and Popular Culture* (Manchester: Manchester University Press, 1987); Simon James Potter, *News and the British World: The Emergence of an Imperial Press System, 1876–1922* (Oxford: Clarendon Press, 2006).

18. Andrew S. Thompson, *Imperial Britain: The Empire in British Politics, c. 1880–1932* (London: Longman, 2000); Valeska Huber, *Channelling Mobilities: Migration and Globalisation in the Suez Canal Region and Beyond, 1869–1914* (Cambridge: Cambridge University Press, 2013).

19. Gustave Lanctôt, *Canada and the American Revolution, 1774–1783* (Toronto: Clarke, Irwin and Company Limited, 1967); J. M. Bumsted, *A History of the Canadian Peoples* (Oxford: Oxford University Press, 2003), 81–163.

20. Christopher L. Brown, *Moral Capital: Foundations of British Abolitionism* (Chapel Hill: University of North Carolina Press, 2006).

21. Linda Colley, *Britons: Forging the Nation, 1707–1837* (New Haven, CT: Yale University Press, 1992); Katrina Navickas, *Loyalism and Radicalism in Lancashire, 1798–1815* (Oxford: Oxford University Press, 2009), 249.

22. Nicole Eustace, *1812: War and the Passions of Patriotism* (Philadelphia: University of Pennsylvania Press, 2012).

23. Peter J. Marshall, *The Impeachment of Warren Hastings* (Oxford: Oxford University Press, 1965).

24. Christopher A. Bayly, "The British Military-Fiscal State and Indigenous Resistance. India, 1750–1820," in *An Imperial State at War: Britain from 1689 to 1815,* ed. Lawrence Stone (Abingdon: Routledge, 1994), 322–354; Bernard S. Cohn, "The Command of Languages and the Language of Command," in *Colonialism and Its Forms of Knowledge* (Princeton, NJ: Princeton University Press, 1996), 16–56; Daniel I. O'Neill, *Edmund Burke and the Conservative Logic of Empire* (Berkeley: University of California Press, 2016).

25. See Jack Snyder, *Myths of Empire: Domestic Politics and International Ambition* (Ithaca, NY: Cornell University Press, 1991), chapter 5, pp. 153–211. See also Jamie L. Bronstein and Andrew T. Harris, *Empire, State and Society: Britain since 1830* (Malden, MA: Wiley Blackwell, 2012).

26. Jorge M. Pedreira and Nuno Gonçalo Monteiro, eds., *O colapso do Império e a Revolução Liberal 1808–1834* (Madrid: Mapfre, 2013), 37–54; João Paulo G. Pimenta, "A independência do Brasil e o liberalismo português: Um balanço da produção acadêmica," *HIB Revista de Historia Iberoamericana* 1, no. 1 (2008): 72–105.

27. For greater detail, see Josep M. Fradera, *Colonias para después de un imperio* (Barcelona: Ediciones Bellaterra, 2005).

28. Josep M. Fradera, "Las fronteras de la nación y el ocaso de la expansión hispánica," in *Más se perdió en Cuba: España, 1898 y la crisis de fin de siglo*, ed. Juan Pan-Montojo (Madrid: Alianza, 2006), 483–557.

29. Interesting considerations around this concept can be found in Kumar, "Nation-States as Empires."

30. Jürgen Osterhammel, *The Transformation of the World: A Global History of the Nineteenth Century* (Princeton, NJ: Princeton University Press, 2014), 392–468.

31. Maarten van Ginderachter and Marnix Beyen, eds., *Nationhood from Below: Europe in the Long Nineteenth Century* (New York: Palgrave Macmillan, 2012).

32. John M. MacKenzie, *Propaganda and Empire: The Manipulation of British Public Opinion, 1880–1960* (Manchester: Manchester University Press, 1986); Thompson, *Imperial Britain*, 61–80.

33. Dominique Schnapper, *La communauté des citoyens: Sur l'idée moderne de nation* (Paris: Gallimard, 1994); and, by the same author, *Qu'est-ce que la citoyenneté?* (Paris: Gallimard, 2000).

34. Marixa Lasso, "Race, War and Nation in Caribbean Gran Colombia: Cartagena, 1810–1832," *American Historical Review* 111, no. 2 (2006): 336–61.

35. Danièle Lochak, *Le droit et les paradoxes de l'universalité* (Paris: Presses Universitaires de France, 2010), 65–69.

36. John Ruedy, *Modern Algeria: The Origins and Development of a Nation* (Bloomington: Indiana University Press, 2001).

37. Olivier Le Cour Grandmaison, *De l'indigénat: Anatomie d'un "monstre" juridique: Le droit colonial en Algérie et dans l'Empire français* (Paris: Zones, 2010); Sylvie Thénault, *Violence ordinaire dans l'Algérie coloniale: Camps, internements, assignations à résidence* (Paris: Odile Jacob, 2012), 25–45.

38. Jean-Robert Henry, "La norme et l'imaginaire: Construction de l'altérité juridique en droit colonial algérien," *Procès* 18 (1987): 13–32; Armelle Enders, " 'Races,' 'castes,' 'classes': Dynamiques sociales et politiques dans les empires coloniaux," in *Les empires coloniaux, XIXe-XXe siècle*, ed. Pierre Singaravélou (Paris: Éditions Points, 2013), 104–6.

39. Adria K. Lawrence, *Imperial Rule and the Politics of Nationalism: Anti-Colonial Protest in the French Empire* (Cambridge: Cambridge University Press, 2013), 75–78.

40. Benjamin Stora, *Algeria, 1830–2000: A Short History* (Ithaca, NY: Cornell University Press, 2001), 247.

41. Peter Dunwoodie, "Assimilation, Cultural Identity, and Permissible Deviance in Francophone Algerian Writing of the Interwar Years," in *Algeria and France, 1800–2000: Identity, Memory, Nostalgia*, ed. Patricia M. E. Lorcin (Syracuse: Syracuse University Press, 2006), 64.

42. Saliha Belmessous, *Assimilation and Empire: Uniformity in French and British Colonies, 1541–1954* (Oxford: Oxford University Press, 2013), 122–23.

43. Eliga H. Gould, *The Persistence of Empire: British Political Culture in the Age of the American Revolution* (Chapel Hill: University of North Carolina Press, 2000), 106–47.

44. I quote here from Nancy LoPatin-Lummis's review of Eugenio F. Biagini's *British Democracy and Irish Nationalism, 1876–1906* (Cambridge: Cambridge Uni-

versity Press, 2007) in *Journal of Modern History* 18, no. 4 (2009): 948–50. The book describes the complex ways in which colonial, national, and imperial interests were interwoven during the Home Rule debate.

45. Bronstein and Harris, *Empire, State and Society*, 31; see their chapter 2 on suffrage. See also Peter Mandler, *Aristocratic Government in the Age of Reform: Whigs and Liberals, 1830–1852* (Oxford: Oxford University Press, 1990).

46. Jonathan P. Parry, *The Rise and Fall of Liberal Government in Victorian Britain* (New Haven, CT: Yale University Press, 1993).

47. John V. Crangle, "English Nationalism and British Imperialism in the Age of Gladstone and Disraeli, 1868–1880," *Quarterly Review of Historical Studies* 21, no. 4 (1981): 4–12.

48. Michael W. Doyle, *Empires* (Ithaca, NY: Cornell University Press, 1986), 296; Snyder, *Myths of Empire*, 165.

49. John Bright, "Imperial Federation," in *The Public Letters of the Right Hon. John Bright* (New York: Kraus Reprint Co., 1969), 226–27 [1st ed. 1885].

50. H. H. Green, *The Crisis of Conservatism: The Politics, Economics and Ideology of the British Conservative Party, 1880–1914* (London: Routledge, 1995), 59–77.

51. Michael Bentley, *The Climax of Liberal Politics: British Liberalism in Theory and Practice, 1868–1918* (London: Edward Arnold, 1987), 88–90.

52. Sarah J. Butler, *Britain and Its Empire in the Shadow of Rome: The Reception of Rome in Socio-Political Debate from the 1850s to the 1920s* (London: Bloomsbury, 2012), 50; Charles F. G. Masterman, *The Heart of the Empire: Discussions of Problems of Modern City Life in England* (London: T. F. Unwin, 1901).

53. John Chesterman and Brian Galligan, *Citizens without Rights: Aborigines and Australian Citizenship* (Cambridge: Cambridge University Press, 1997); Alan Lester and Fae Dussart, *Colonization and the Origins of Humanitarian Governance: Protecting Aborigines across the Nineteenth-Century British Empire* (Cambridge: Cambridge University Press, 2014).

54. Thompson, *Imperial Britain*, 134.

55. For an interesting analysis of Canadian identity in the imperial context, see David Cannadine, "Dominion: Britain's Imperial Past in Canada's Imperial Past," in his *Making History Now and Then: Discoveries, Controversies and Explorations* (Houndmills: Palgrave Macmillan, 2008), 196–213.

56. David Powell, *Nationhood and Identity: The British State since 1800* (London: I. B. Tauris, 2002), 114–15.

57. Philip A. Buckner, "The Long Goodbye: English Canadians and the British World," in *Rediscovering the British World*, ed. Philip A. Buckner and R. Douglas Francis (Calgary: University of Calgary Press, 2005), 181–207.

58. Patrick Joyce, *Democratic Subjects: The Self and the Social in Nineteenth-Century England* (Cambridge: Cambridge University Press, 1994), 136 and passim; John Darwin, *The Empire Project: The Rise and Fall of the British World System, 1830–1970* (Cambridge: Cambridge University Press, 2009); and, by the same author, *Unfinished Empire: The Global Expansion of Britain* (London: Allen Lane, 2012).

59. Powell, *Nationhood and Empire*, 104–6.

60. Stephen Constantine, *Community and Identity: The Making of Modern Gibraltar since 1704* (Manchester: Manchester University Press, 2009).

61. John Darwin, "Imperialism and the Victorians: The Dynamics of Territorial Expansion," *The English Historical Review* 112, no. 447 (1997): 614–42.

62. This argument is developed in chapter 5 of Snyder, *Myths of Empire*, 153–211.

63. For examples see the essays in Philip A. Buckner and R. Douglas Frances, eds., *Rediscovering the British World* (Calgary: Calgary University Press, 2005); see especially Catherine Hall, 23.

64. Robert Colls, "Englishness and the Political Culture," in *Englishness: Politics and Culture, 1880–1920*, ed. Robert Colls and Philip Dodd (London: Croom Helm, 1987), 29–61.

65. Jonathan P. Parry, *The Politics of Patriotism: English Liberalism, National Identity and Europe, 1830–1886* (Cambridge: Cambridge University Press, 2006), 61–62.

66. For an accurate though incomplete analysis, see Antoinette M. Burton, *The Trouble with Empire: Challenges to Modern British Imperialism* (Oxford: Oxford University Press, 2015); on the importance of naval defense, see Frans Coetzee, *For Party or Country: Nationalism and the Dilemmas of Popular Conservatism in Edwardian England* (Oxford: Oxford University Press, 1995).

67. Colley, *Britons*; Jack P. Greene, ed., *Exclusionary Empire: English Liberty Overseas, 1600–1900* (Cambridge: Cambridge University Press, 2009); for the Spanish case on both sides of the Atlantic, see José María Portillo Valdés, *Historia mínima del constitucionalismo en América Latina* (Madrid: Marcial Pons, 2006).

68. Danièle Lochak, "La citoyenneté: Un concept juridique flou," in *Citoyenneté et nationalité: Perspectives en France et au Québec*, ed. Dominique Colas, Claude Emeri, and Jacques Zylberberg (Paris: Presses Universitaires de France, 1991), 179–207.

69. And resistance, too, as explored from different angles in Nancy G. Bermeo and Philip G. Nord, eds., *Civil Society before Democracy: Lessons from Nineteenth-Century Europe* (Lanham, MD: Rowman & Littlefield, 2000).

70. Gwenda Morgan and Peter Rushton, *Banishment in the Early Atlantic world: Convicts, Rebels and Slaves* (London: Bloomsbury, 2013).

71. Richard J. F. Day, *Multiculturalism and the History of Canadian Diversity* (Toronto: University of Toronto Press, 2002), 101–15; Jane Samson, *Imperial Benevolence: Making British Authority in the Pacific Islands* (Honolulu: University of Hawai'i Press, 1998), 42–62.

72. Harris Mylonas, *The Politics of Nation Building: Making Co-Nationals, Refugees, and Minorities* (Cambridge: Cambridge University Press, 2012).

73. Doris Y. Kadish, ed., *Slavery in the Caribbean Francophone World: Distant Voices, Forgotten Acts, Forged Identities* (Athens: University of Georgia Press, 2000).

74. Robin Blackburn, *The Overthrow of Colonial Slavery, 1776–1846* (London: Verso, 1988), 419–72.

75. Parry, *The Rise and Fall*, 97–102; Mary Reckord, "The Jamaican Slave Rebellion of 1831," *Past and Present* 40, no. 3 (1968): 108–25.

76. Thomas L. Wigham, *The Paraguayan War* (Lincoln: University of Nebraska Press, 2002).

77. Ricardo Salles, *Guerra do Paraguai: Memórias e Imagens* (Rio de Janeiro: Edições Biblioteca Nacional, 2003); Vitor Izecksohn, "A Guerra do Paraguay," in *O Brasil Imperial*, vol. 2, *1831–1870*, ed. Keila Grinberg and Ricardo Salles (Rio de Janeiro: Civilização Brasileira, 2009), 385–424.

78. For a brief account of these events, see Gad J. Heuman, "Post-Emancipation Protest in Jamaica: The Morant Bay Rebellion, 1865," in *From Chattel Slaves to Wage Slaves: The Dynamics of Labour Bargaining in the Americas*, ed. Mary Turner (Kingston: Ian Randle, 1995), 258–74; for a more comprehensive account by the same author, see *"The Killing Time": The Morant Bay Rebellion in Jamaica* (London: Macmillan, 1994).

79. On the economic background of abolition there, see Kathleen Mary Butler, *The Economics of Emancipation: Jamaica and Barbados, 1823–1843* (Chapel Hill: University of North Carolina Press, 1995); still useful is Douglas Hall, *Free Jamaica, 1838–1865: An Economic History* (New Haven, CT: Yale University Press, 1959).

80. Heuman, *"The Killing Time"*; on the dynamics of postemancipation, see Thomas C. Holt, *The Problem of Freedom: Race, Labor, and Politics in Jamaica and Britain, 1832–1938* (Baltimore: Johns Hopkins University Press, 1992).

81. The harshening is well described by Diana Paton in *No Bond but the Law: Punishment, Race, and Gender in Jamaican State Formation, 1780–1870* (Durham, NC: Duke University Press, 2004), 139–55.

82. The classic studies of abolition all stress how closely the nonconformist churches followed events in the Caribbean; see Roger Anstey, *The Atlantic Slave Trade and British Abolition, 1760–1810* (London: Macmillan, 1975); David Brion Davis, *The Problem of Slavery in the Age of Revolution, 1770–1823* (Ithaca, NY: Cornell University Press, 1975); and Seymour Drescher, *Capitalism and Antislavery: British Mobilization in Comparative Perspective* (London: Macmillan Press, 1986).

83. Catherine Hall, *Civilising Subjects: Colony and Metropole in the English Imagination, 1830–1867* (Chicago: University of Chicago Press, 2002).

84. Hall, *Civilising Subjects*, 243–64.

85. Richard Gott, *Britain's Empire: Resistance, Repression and Revolt* (London: Verso, 2011); Christopher Herbert, *War of No Pity: The Indian Mutiny and Victorian Trauma* (Princeton, NJ: Princeton University Press, 2008).

86. On the relationship between abolitionists and worker mobilizations in Great Britain, see Betty Fladeland, *Abolitionists and Working-Class Problems in the Age of Industrialization* (Baton Rouge: Louisiana State University Press, 1984).

87. Jennifer Pitts, *A Turn to Empire: The Rise of Imperial Liberalism in Britain and France* (Princeton, NJ: Princeton University Press, 2005), 133–38. For James Mill's imperial vision and comparisons with the metropolis, see Javed Majeed, *Ungoverned Imaginings: James Mill's The History of British India and Orientalism* (Oxford: Clarendon Press, 1992).

88. For a discussion of the complexities of the relationship between culture and empire, see Duncan S. A. Bell, "Empire and International Relations in Victorian Political Thought," *Historical Journal* 49, no. 1 (2006): 281–98.

89. For Mills's position on this point, see Mark Tunick, "Tolerant Imperialism: John Stuart Mill's Defense of British Rule in India," *The Review of Politics* 68, no. 4 (2006): 586–611.

90. Still useful is John F. Glaser, "English Nonconformity and the Decline of Liberalism," *American Historical Review* 63, no. 2 (1958): 352–63; see also Walton Look Lai, *Indentured Labor, Caribbean Sugar: Chinese and Indian Migrants to the British West Indies, 1838–1918* (Baltimore: Johns Hopkins University Press, 1993); Ralph

Fox, *The Colonial Policy of British Imperialism* (Oxford: Oxford University Press, 2008), 41–43.

91. On the Northwest Ordinance, see Peter S. Onuf, *Jefferson's Empire: The Language of American Nationhood* (Charlottesville: University Press of Virginia, 2000); on the Missouri Compromise, see the insightful interpretation in Garry Wills, *Negro President: Jefferson and the Slave Power* (Boston: Houghton Mifflin, 2003).

92. Jason A. Frank, *Constituent Moments: Enacting the People in Postrevolutionary America* (Durham, NC: Duke University Press, 2010).

93. On relations with the Indians during the early republic, see the classic study by Francis Paul Prucha, *American Indian Policy in the Formative Years: The Indian Trade and Intercourse Acts, 1790–1834* (Cambridge, MA: Harvard University Press, 1962). See also William E. Unrau, *The Rise and Fall of Indian Country, 1825–1855* (Lawrence: University Press of Kansas, 2007; Donald Lee Fixico, *The Invasion of Indian Country in the Twentieth Century: American Capitalism and Tribal Natural Resources* (Niwot: University Press of Colorado, 1998).

94. A rigorous correction can be found in Richard H. Immerman, *Empire for Liberty: A History of American Imperialism from Benjamin Franklin to Paul Wolfowitz* (Princeton, NJ: Princeton University Press, 2010). See also Marc Egnal, *A Mighty Empire: The Origins of the American Revolution* (Ithaca, NY: Cornell University Press, 1988); Thomas Bender, *A Nation among Nations: America's Place in World History* (New York: Hill and Wang, 2006); and Jay Sexton, *The Monroe Doctrine: Empire and Nation in Nineteenth-Century America* (New York: Hill & Wang, 2011).

95. Edward E. Baptist, *The Half Has Never Been Told: Slavery and the Making of American Capitalism* (New York: Basic Books, 2014); Alan Taylor, *The Internal Enemy: Slavery and War in Virginia, 1772–1832* (New York: W. W. Norton, 2013).

96. John Ashworth, *Slavery, Capitalism and Politics in the Antebellum Republic*, vol. 1, *Commerce and Compromise, 1820–1850* (Cambridge: Cambridge University Press, 1995); William W. Freehling, *The Road to Disunion*, vol. 1, *Secessionists at Bay, 1776–1854* (New York: Oxford University Press, 1990); Don E. Fehrenbacher, *The Slaveholding Republic: An Account of the United States Government's Relations to Slavery* (Oxford: Oxford University Press, 2001).

97. Jack. P. Greene, "Colonial History and National History: Reflections on a Continuing Problem," *William and Mary Quarterly* 64, no. 2 (2007): 235–50.

98. Eliga H. Gould, "The Question of Home Rule," *William and Mary Quarterly* 64, no. 2 (2007): 255–58.

99. Deborah A. Rosen, *American Indians and State Law: Sovereignty, Race, and Citizenship, 1790–1880* (Lincoln: University of Nebraska Press, 2007); Jeanette Wolfley, "Jim Crow, Indian Style: The Disenfranchisement of Native Americans," *American Indian Law Review* 16, no. 1 (1991): 167–202; Stephanie McCurry, *Confederate Reckoning: Power and Politics in the Civil War South* (Cambridge MA: Harvard University Press, 2010), 23.

100. Tyler Anbinder, *Nativism and Slavery: The Northern Know Nothings and the Politics of the 1850s* (New York: Oxford University Press, 1992).

101. Eric Foner, *Free Soil, Free Labor, Free Men: The Ideology of the Republican Party before the Civil War* (New York: Oxford University Press, 1970).

102. Allen C. Guelzo, *Fateful Lightning: A New History of the Civil War and Reconstruction* (Oxford: Oxford University Press, 2012), 157; Bender, *A Nation among Nations*, 172.

103. Jacobus TenBroek, *Equal Under Law: The Antislavery Origins of the Fourteenth Amendment* (New York: Collier Books, 1965).

104. Avery O. Craven, *Reconstruction: The Ending of the Civil War* (New York: Holt, Rinehart and Winston, 1969), 111–24.

105. Leon F. Litwack, *Been in the Storm So Long: The Aftermath of Slavery* (New York: Vintage Books, 1980).

106. George M. Fredrickson, *The Black Image in the White Mind: The Debate on Afro-American Character and Destiny, 1817–1914* (New York: Harper & Row, 1971).

107. Jane Elizabeth Dailey, *Before Jim Crow: The Politics of Race in Postemancipation Virginia* (Chapel Hill: University of North Carolina Press, 2000).

108. Lawrence Goldstone, *Inherently Unequal: The Betrayal of Equal Rights by the Supreme Court, 1865–1903* (New York: Walker and Company, 2010); Lea VanderVelde, *Redemption Songs: Suing for Freedom before Dred Scott* (Oxford: Oxford University Press, 2014).

109. Kenneth M. Stampp, *The Era of Reconstruction, 1865–1877* (New York: Vintage Books, 1962); Eric Foner, *Reconstruction: America's Unfinished Revolution, 1863–1877* (New York: Harper & Row, 1988); Heather Cox Richardson, *The Death of Reconstruction: Race, Labor, and Politics in the Post-Civil War North, 1865–1901* (Cambridge, MA: Harvard University Press, 2001).

110. Robert M. Utley, *The Indian Frontier of the American West, 1846–1890* (Albuquerque: University of New Mexico Press, 1984).

111. James Belich, *Replenishing the Earth: The Settler Revolution and the Rise of the Anglo-World, 1783–1939* (Oxford: Oxford University Press, 2009); Christopher Lloyd et al., ed. *Settler Economies in World History* (Leiden: Brill, 2013).

112. Gary Gerstle, *American Crucible: Race and Nation in the Twentieth Century* (Princeton, NJ: Princeton University Press, 2001), 45–80; Julius W. Pratt, *Expansionists of 1898: The Acquisition of Hawaii and the Spanish Islands* (Baltimore: Johns Hopkins University Press, 1936).

113. For a discussion of how this affected the labor market, see Howard Lamar, "From Bondage to Contract: Ethnic Labor in the American West, 1600–1890," in *The Countryside in the Age of Capitalist Transformation: Essays in the Social History of Rural America*, ed. Steven Hahn and Jonathan Prude (Chapel Hill: University of North Carolina Press, 1985), 293–324.

114. John A. Hall, "Imperial Universalism—Further Thoughts," in *Universal Empires: A Comparative Approach to Imperial Culture and Representation in Eurasian History*, ed. Peter F. Bang and Dariusz Kołodziejczyk (Cambridge: Cambridge University Press, 2012), 309; a similar remark appears in Charles S. Maier, *Leviathan 2.0: Inventing Modern Statehood* (Cambridge, MA: Harvard University Press, 2012), 161–62.

115. See the massive account in Osterhammel, *The Transformation of the World*, 637–901.

116. See chapter 5 on imperial defense, in Thompson, *Imperial Britain*, 110–32.

Chapter 9. Ruling across the Color Line

1. J. A. Hobson, *Imperialism: A Study* (Ann Arbor: University of Michigan Press, 1991), 223 [1st ed. 1902].

2. On Hobson, Peter J. Cain, *Hobson and Imperialism: Radicalism, New Liberalism, and Finance, 1887–1938* (Oxford: Oxford University Press, 2002); on the weakness of critical views towards the empire, see Stephen Howe, *Anticolonialism in British Politics: The Left and the End of Empire, 1918–1964* (Oxford: Oxford University Press, 1993).

3. Stig Föster, Wolfgang J. Mommsen, and Ronald Robinson, eds., *Bismarck, Europe, and Africa: The Berlin Africa Conference 1884–1885 and the Onset of Partition* (Oxford: Oxford University Press, 1989).

4. Alexis de Tocqueville to Arthur de Gobineau, November 17, 1853, in Alexis de Tocqueville, *Oeuvres complètes 9: Correspondance d'Alexis de Tocqueville et d'Arthur de Gobineau*, ed. J. P. Mayer (Paris: Gallimard, 1959), 203.

5. Peter Robb, *Liberalism, Modernity, and the Nation: Empire, Identity, and India* (Oxford: Oxford University Press, 2015); Thomas R. Metcalf, *Imperial Connections: India in the Indian Ocean Arena, 1860–1920* (Berkeley: University of California Press, 2007); Eric A. Walker, *The British Empire: Its Structure and Spirit, 1497–1953* (Oxford: Oxford University Press, 1947) [1st ed. 1943]; on some of the intellectual proposals by people quoted in this and previous chapters, see Duncan Bell, *The Idea of Greater Britain: Empire and the Future of World Order, 1860–1900* (Princeton, NJ: Princeton University Press, 2007).

6. A. G. Hopkins, "The Victorians and Africa: A Reconsideration of the Occupation of Egypt, 1882," *The Journal of African History* 27, no. 2 (1986): 363–91; Afaf Lutfi Al-Sayyid-Marsot, "The British Occupation of Egypt since 1882," in *The Oxford History of the British Empire*, vol. 3, *The Nineteenth Century*, ed. Andrew Porter (Oxford: Oxford University Press, 1999), 651–63.

7. Andrew S. Thompson, *Imperial Britain: The Empire in British Politics, c. 1880–1932* (London: Longman, 2000); Stephen Constantine, *The Making of British Colonial Development Policy, 1914–1940* (London: Frank Cass, 1984); Kenneth Robinson, *The Dilemmas of Trusteeship: Aspects of British Colonial Policy between the Wars* (London: Oxford University Press, 1965).

8. On the Round Table, see *An Analysis of the System of the Government Throughout the British Empire* (London: Macmillan, 1912); see also Walter Nimocks, *Milner's Young Men: The Kindergarten in Edwardian Imperial Affairs* (Durham, NC: Duke University Press, 1968); Deborah Lavin, *From Empire to International Commonwealth: A Biography of Lionel Curtis* (Oxford: Oxford University Press, 1995).

9. Deirdre McMahon, "Ireland, the Empire, and the Commonwealth," in *Ireland and the British Empire*, ed. Kevin Kenny (Oxford: Oxford University Press, 2004), 182–219; Kate O'Malley, *Ireland, India, and Empire: Indo-Irish Radical Connections, 1919–1964* (Manchester: Manchester University Press, 2008). For the previous period, see Eugenio F. Biagini, *British Democracy and Irish Nationalism, 1876–1906* (Cambridge: Cambridge University Press, 2007).

10. John Darwin, "Imperialism and the Victorians: The Dynamics of Territorial Expansion," *The English Historical Review* 112, no. 447 (1997): 641.

11. John Edward Kendle, *The Colonial and Imperial Conferences, 1887–1911: A Study in Imperial Organization* (London: Longmans, 1967).

12. Alan Lester and Fae Dussart, eds., *Colonization and the Origins of Humanitarian Governance: Protecting Aborigines across the Nineteenth-Century British Empire* (Cambridge: Cambridge University Press, 2014).

13. Ann Dummett and Andrew G. L. Nicol, *Subjects, Citizens, Aliens and Others: Nationality and Immigration Law* (London: Weindenfeld and Nicolson, 1990), 113.

14. *Colonization and the Origins of Humanitarian Governance: Protecting Aborigines Across the Nineteenth-Century British Empire*, ed. Alan Lester and Fae Dussart (Cambridge: Cambridge University Press, 2014), chapter 6, "Humanitarian Governance in a Settler Empire," 226–75.

15. Christopher A. Bayly, *Imperial Meridian: The British Empire and the World, 1780–1830* (Harlow: Longman, 1989), 15.

16. Christopher Lloyd, "Institutional Patterns of the Settler Societies: Hybrid, Parallel and Convergent," in *Settler Economies in World History*, ed. Christopher Lloyd, Jacob Metzer, and Richard Sutch (Leiden: Brill, 2013), 565–69.

17. James Belich, "The Rise of the Angloworld: Settlement in North America and Australasia, 1784–1918," in *Rediscovering the British World*, ed. Philip A. Buckner and R. Douglas Francis (Calgary: University of Calgary Press, 2005), 39–57.

18. James Belich, *Replenishing the Earth: The Settler Revolution and the Rise of the Anglo-World, 1783–1939* (Oxford: Oxford University Press, 2009), 169.

19. Frank Bongiorno, "Fabian Socialism and British Australia, 1890–1972," in *Rediscovering the British World*, ed. Philip A. Buckner and R. Douglas Francis (Calgary: University of Calgary Press, 2005), 209–31.

20. Robert A. Huttenback, *Racism and Empire: White Settlers and Colored Immigrants in the British Self-Governing Colonies, 1830–1910* (Ithaca, NY: Cornell University Press, 1976), 279–316.

21. Michael Barnett, *The Empire of Humanity: A History of Humanitarianism* (Ithaca, NY: Cornell University Press, 2011); Amit Rai, *Rule of Sympathy: Sentiment, Race, and Power, 1750–1850* (New York: Palgrave Macmillan, 2002).

22. Luke Trainor, *British Imperialism and Australian Nationalism: Manipulation, Conflict, and Compromise in the Late Nineteenth Century* (Cambridge: Cambridge University Press, 1994), 12; Stuart Ward, "Security: Defending Australia's Empire," in *Australia's Empire*, ed. Deryck Schreuder and Stuart Ward (Oxford: Oxford University Press, 2009), 232–58.

23. Marilyn Lake and Henry Reynolds, *Drawing the Global Colour Line: White Men's Countries and the Question of Racial Equality* (Melbourne: Melbourne University Press, 2008), 137–65.

24. Shula Marks, "Natal, the Zulu Royal Family and the Ideology of Segregation," *Journal of African Studies* 4, no. 2 (1978): 172–194; Duncan Du Bois, "The 'Coolie Curse': The Evolution of White Colonial Attitudes Towards the Indian Question, 1860–1900," *Historia* 57, no. 2 (2012): 31–67.

25. David Day, *Claiming A Continent: A History of Australia* (Sidney: Harper Perennial, 2005), 180 [1st ed. 1996].

26. Marilyn Lake, "The White Man under Siege: New Histories of Race in the Nineteenth Century and the Advent of White Australia," *History Workshop Journal* 58 (2004): 41–62.

27. Stuart McIntyre, *A Concise History of Australia* (Cambridge: Cambridge University Press, 2004), 141.

28. Farish A. Noor, *The Discursive Construction of Southeast Asia in 19th-Century Colonial-Capitalist Discourse* (Amsterdam: Amsterdam University Press, 2016).

29. Russell McGregor, *Imagined Destinies: Aboriginal Australians and the Doomed Race Theory, 1880–1939* (Melbourne: Melbourne University Press, 1989).

30. On these cultural undertones, see Alexander Saxton, *The Rise and Fall of the White Republic: Class Politics and Mass Culture in Nineteenth-Century America* (London: Verso, 2003), 1–20.

31. John Chesterman and Brian Galligan, *Citizens without Rights: Aborigines and Australian Citizenship* (Cambridge: Cambridge University Press, 1997), 81.

32. It was no coincidence that the Immigration Restriction Act, with its abusive fifty-word dictation test, was also passed in 1901.

33. Robert Reynolds and Shurlee Swain, "The Paradox of Ultra-Democratic Government: Indigenous Civil Rights in Nineteenth-Century New Zealand, Canada, and Australia," in *Law, History, and Colonialism: The Reach of Empire*, ed. Diane Kirkby and Catherine Coleborne (Manchester: Manchester University Press, 2001), 78–105.

34. Chesterman and Galligan, *Citizens without Rights*, 79.

35. Reynolds and Swain, "The Paradox," 81. See also Rieko Karatani, *Defining British Citizenship: Empire, Commonwealth and Modern Britain* (London: Frank Cass, 2003), 71–109.

36. Reynolds and Swain, "The Paradox," 92.

37. Marilyn Lake, "Equality and Exclusion: The Racial Constitution of Colonial Liberalism," *Thesis Eleven* 95 (2008): 20–32.

38. Bartolomé Clavero, *Freedom's Law and Indigenous Rights: From Europe's Oeconomy to the Constitutionalism of the Americas* (Berkeley: The Robbins Collection, 2005); Henry Reynolds, *Why Weren't We Told? A Personal Search for the Truth about Our History* (Melbourne: Penguin Books, 1999) and, by the same author, *An Indelible Stain? The Question of Genocide in Australia's History* (New York: Viking Books, 2001); A. Dirk Moses, ed., *Genocide and Settler Societies: Frontier Violence and Stolen Indigenous Children in Australian History* (New York: Berghahn Books, 2004).

39. Richard Price, *Making Empire: Colonial Encounters and the Creation of Imperial Rule in Nineteenth-Century Africa* (Cambridge: Cambridge University Press, 2008).

40. Leigh Dale, "George Grey in Ireland: Narrative and Network," in *Colonial Lives across the British Empire: Imperial Careering in the Long Nineteenth Century*, ed. David Lambert and Alan Lester (Cambridge: Cambridge University Press, 2006), 145–75; James Rutherford, *Sir George Grey, K.G.B., 1812–1898: A Study in Colonial Government* (London: Cassell, 1961).

41. Lester and Dussart, "Humanitarian Governance in a Settler Empire," 226–75.

42. On the British perception, see Philip J. Stern, "'Rescuing the Age from a Charge of Ignorance': Gentility, Knowledge, and the British Exploration of Africa

in the Later Eighteenth Century," in *A New Imperial History: Culture, Identity and Modernity in Britain and the Empire, 1660–1840*, ed. Kathleen Wilson (Cambridge: Cambridge University Press, 2004), 115–35.

43. W. B. Tyler, "Sir George Grey, South Africa and the Imperial Military Burden, 1855–1860," *Historical Journal* 14, no. 3 (1971): 581–98.

44. Jeffrey B. Peires, *The Dead Will Arise: Nongqawuse and the Great Xhosa Cattle-Killing Movement of 1856–7* (Bloomington: Indiana University Press, 1989); Timothy J. Stapleton, " 'They No Longer Care for Their Chiefs': Another Look at the Xhosa Cattle-Killing of 1856–1857," *The International Journal of African Historical Studies* 24, no. 2 (1991): 383–92.

45. Jeffrey B. Peires, "Sir George Grey versus the Kaffir Relief Committee," *Journal of Southern Studies* 10, no. 2 (1984): 145–69.

46. Les Switzer, *Power and Resistance in an African Society: The Ciskei Xhosa and the Making of South Africa* (Madison: University of Wisconsin Press, 1973), 411–28; Louis Changuion and Bertus Steenkamp, *Disputed Land: The Historical Development of the South African Land Issue, 1652–2011* (Pretoria: Protea Book House, 2012), 44–73.

47. Leonard Thompson, "Southern Africa to 1795," in *African History: From Earliest Times to Independence*, ed. Philip Curtin et al. (Boston: Little, Brown, 1978), 295.

48. In the words of the historian Charles Feinstein, "[The] dilemma was not the imposition of slavery or serfdom, but closure of the escape route to free land"; in David Meredith, "Coerced Labor in Southern Hemisphere Settler Economies," in *Settler Economies in World History*, ed. Christopher Lloyd, Jacob Metzer, and Richard Sutch (Leiden: Brill, 2013), 316.

49. Robert C. H. Shell, *Children of Bondage: A Social History of the Slave Society at the Cape of Good Hope, 1652–1838* (Hanover, NH: Wesleyan University Press, 1994), 356–62.

50. C. Duly, "The Failure of British Land Policy at the Cape, 1812–1828," *Journal of African History* 6, no. 3 (1965): 357–71; R. L. Watson, *The Slave Question: Liberty and Property in South Africa* (Hanover, NH: Wesleyan University Press, 1990).

51. Robert Ross, *A Concise History of South Africa* (Cambridge: Cambridge University Press, 2008), 36 [1st ed. 1999].

52. Steve de Gruchy, "The Alleged Political Conservatism of Robert Moffat," in *The London Missionary Society in Southern Africa, 1799–1999*, ed. John W. de Gruchy (Athens: Ohio University Press, 2000), 17–36.

53. Alan Lester, "British Settlers and the Colonisation of the Xhosa," in his *Imperial Networks: Creating Identities in Nineteenth-Century South Africa and Britain* (London: Routledge, 2001), 45–77.

54. C. McCaskie, "Cultural Encounters: Britain and Africa in the Nineteenth Century," in *Black Experience and the Empire*, ed. Philip D. Morgan and Sean Hawkins (Oxford: Oxford University Press, 2004), 191.

55. Clifton C. Crais, *White Supremacy and Black Resistance in Pre-Industrial South Africa: The Making of the Colonial Order in the Eastern Cape, 1770–1865* (Cambridge: Cambridge University Press, 1992).

56. Robert Ross, D. van Arkel, and G. C. Quispel, "Going Beyond the Pale: On the Roots of White Supremacy in South Africa," in *Beyond the Pale: Essays of the History of Colonial South Africa* (Hanover, NH: Wesleyan University Press, 1993), 69–110;

see also Christoph Strobel, *The Testing Grounds of Modern Empire: The Making of Colonial Racial Order in the American Ohio Country and the South African Eastern Cape, 1770s-1850s* (New York: Peter Lang, 2008), 63–87.

57. Crais, *White Supremacy*, 138–41.

58. Eric Anderson Walker, *The Great Trek* (London: A & C Black, 1934).

59. Hermann Giliomee, *The Afrikaners: Biography of a People* (London: Horst & Co., 2011), 207–10; André du Toit, "Puritans in Africa? Afrikaner "Calvinism" and Kuyperian Neo-Calvinism in Late Nineteenth Century South Africa," *Comparative Studies in Society and History* 27, no. 2 (1985): 209–40; and, by the same author, "No Chosen People: The Myth of the Calvinist Origins of Afrikaner Nationalism and Racial Ideology," *American Historical Review* 88, no. 4 (1983): 920–52.

60. Walker, *The Great Trek*, 234–313; Peter Richardson, "The Natal Sugar Industry, 1849–1905: An Interpretative Essay," *Journal of African History* 23, no. 4 (1982): 515–27.

61. See Changuion and Steenkamp, *Disputed Land*, chapters 2 and 4, pp. 27–43, 55–73; and Shula Marks, "South Africa: The Myth of the Empty Land," *History Today* 30, no. 1 (1980): 31–56. On the war, see Andrew Duminy and Charles Ballard, *The Anglo-Zulu War: New Perspectives* (Pietermaritzburg: University of Natal Press, 1981); and Ian Knight, *The Zulu War 1879* (London: Pan Books, 2004).

62. John S. Galbraith, *Reluctant Empire: British Policy on the South African Frontier, 1834–1854* (Berkeley: University of California Press, 1963), 195–98.

63. Fred Morton, "Captive Labor in the Western Transvaal after the Sand River Convention," and Barry Morton, "Servitude, Slave Trading, and Slavery in the Kalahari," in *Slavery in South Africa: Captive Labor on the Dutch Frontier*, ed. Elizabeth A. Eldredge and Fred Morton (Pietermaritzburg: University of Natal Press, 1994), 167–86, 215–50; Timothy Collier, "Administrations coloniales et pacification: L'exemple de Sir Garnet Wolseley en Afrique du Sud (1879–1880)," in *Coloniser, pacifier, administrer: XIXe-XXIe siècles*, ed. Samya el Mechat (Paris: CNRS Éditions, 2014), 21–34.

64. A general overview of South African emancipation can be found in Wayne Dooling, *Slavery, Emancipation and Colonial Rule in South Africa* (Athens: Ohio University Press, 2007).

65. Christopher Saunders, "Liberated Africans in Cape Colony in the First Half of the Nineteenth Century," *The International Journal of African Historical Studies* 18, no. 2 (1985): 230.

66. Ross, *A Concise History of South Africa*, 48.

67. Paul Knaplund, *James Stephen and the British Colonial System, 1813–1847* (Madison: University of Wisconsin Press, 1953), 256.

68. Richard Parry, "'In a Sense Citizens, But Not Altogether Citizens . . .': Rhodes, Race, and the Ideology of Segregation at the Cape in the Late Nineteenth Century," *Canadian Journal of African Studies* 17, no. 3 (1983): 377–91; Robert Ross, *Status and Respectability in the Cape Colony, 1750–1870* (Cambridge: Cambridge University Press, 1991).

69. Clement Francis Goodfellow, *Great Britain and South African Confederation, 1870–1881* (Oxford: Oxford University Press, 1966); Leonard Thompson, "The Compromise of Union," in *The Oxford History of South Africa*, vol. 2, *South Africa,*

1870–1966, ed. Monica Wilson and Leonard Thompson (New York: Oxford University Press, 1972), 325–64; Leonard Thompson, *The Unification of South Africa, 1902–1910* (Oxford: Clarendon Press, 1960).

70. Benjamin Sacks, *South Africa: An Imperial Dilemma; Non-Europeans and the British Nation, 1902–1914* (Albuquerque: University of New Mexico Press, 1967), 12; Benjamin Kline, *Genesis of Apartheid: British African Policy in the Colony of Natal, 1845–1893* (Lanham, MD: University Press of America, 1988), chapter 4, pp. 113–54; R. L. Cope, "Local Imperatives and Imperial Policy: The Sources of Lord Carnarvon's South African Confederation Policy," *The International Journal of African Historical Studies* 20, no. 4 (1987): 601–26.

71. Charles H. Feinstein, *An Economic History of South Africa: Conquest, Discrimination and Development* (Cambridge: Cambridge University Press, 2005), 47–73, 90–112; George Wheatcroft, *The Randlords: The Men who Made South Africa* (London: Weindefeld, 1993).

72. Kevin Shillington, "The Impact of the Diamond Discoveries on the Kimberley Hinterland: Class Formation, Colonialism and Resistance among the Tlhaping of Griqualand West in the 1870s," in *Industrialization and Social Change in South Africa: African Class Formation, Culture and Consciousness, 1870–1930*, ed. Shula Marks and Richard Rathbone (London: Longman, 1983), 99–118.

73. Peter Richardson and Jean-Jacques Van Helten, "Labour in the South African Gold Mining Industry, 1886–1914," in Marks and Rathbone, eds., *Industrialization and Social Change in South Africa*, 77–98.

74. Eric Anderson Walker, "The Jameson Raid," *Cambridge Historical Journals* 6, no. 3 (1940): 283–306; G. Blainey, "Lost Causes of the Jameson Raid," *The Economic History Review* 18, no. 2 (1965): 350–66; Tlou John Makhura, "Another Road to the Raid: The Neglected Role of the Boer-Bagananwa War as a Factor in the Coming of the Jameson Raid, 1894–1895," *Journal of Southern African Studies* 21, no. 2 (1995): 257–67.

75. Henry R. Winkler, "Joseph Chamberlain and the Jameson Raid," *American Historical Review* 23, no. 1 (1980): 111–32.

76. Rodney Davenport and Christopher Saunders, *South Africa: A Modern History* (Houndmills: Palgrave Macmillan, 2000), 187–91. On Milner and his collaborators, see Saaul Dubow, "Colonial Nationalism: The Milner Kindergarten and the Rise of South Africanism, 1902–1910," *History Workshop Journal* 43 (1997): 53–85; on Kruger, see Giliomee, *The Afrikaners*, 228–31, 245–47.

77. Thomas Pakenham, *The Boer War* (New York: Weindenfeld & Nicolson, 1979).

78. Geoffry Barker Pyrah, *Imperial Policy and South Africa, 1902–1910* (Oxford: Clarendon Press, 1955).

79. Saul Dubow, "The Elaboration of Segregationist Ideology," in *Segregation and Apartheid in Twentieth-Century South Africa*, ed. William Beinart and Saul Dubow (London: Routledge, 1995), 145–75.

80. Nicholas Mansergh, *South Africa, 1906–1961: The Price of Magnanimity* (London: Allen & Unwin, 1962), 21; Timothy J. Keegan, *Rural Transformations in Industrializing South Africa: The Southern Highveld to 1914* (Houndmills: Palgrave Macmillan, 1987).

81. Huttenback, *Racism and Empire*, 40–63.

82. For a general discussion, see Rieko Karatani, *Defining British Citizenship: Empire, Commonwealth and Modern Britain* (London: Frank Cass, 2003).

83. On the 1608 ruling on citizenship by virtue of birth, see Polly J. Price, "Natural Law and Birthright to Citizenship in Calvin's Case (1608) and the Law of Alien Status," *Yale Journal of Law and Humanities* 9 (1997): 73–145; and Keechang Kim, "Calvin's Case (1608) and the Law of Alien Status," *Journal of Legal History* 17, no. 2 (1996): 155–71.

84. Quotation from John McLaren, "The Uses of the Rule of Law in British Colonial Societies in the Nineteenth Century," in *Law and Politics in British Colonial Thought: Transpositions of Empire*, ed. Shaunnagh Dorsett and Ian Hunter (New York: Palgrave Macmillan, 2010), 84; see also Sudipta Sen, "Imperial Subjects on Trial: On the Legal Identity of Britons in Late Eighteenth-Century India," *Journal of British Studies* 45, no. 3 (2006): 532–55.

85. Dummett and Nicol, *Citizens, Aliens and Others*, 62.

86. Stephen Conway, "From Fellow-Nationals to Foreigners: British Perceptions of the Americas, ca. 1739–1783," *William and Mary Quarterly* 59, no. 1 (2002): 65–100.

87. Julie Evans et al., *Equal Subjects, Unequal Rights: Indigenous Peoples in British Settler Colonies, 1830–1910* (Manchester: Manchester University Press, 2003), 5.

88. Julie Evans and David Philips, "South Africa: Saving the White Voters from Being 'Utterly Swamped,'" in *Equal Subjects, Unequal Rights: Indigenous Peoples in British Settler Colonies, 1830–1910*, ed. Julie Evans et al. (Manchester: Manchester University Press, 2003), 157–81.

89. Derek Taylor, *Don Pacifico: The Acceptable Face of Gunboat Diplomacy* (London: Vallentine Mitchell, 2008).

90. Mary Beard, "Officers and Gentlemen? Roman Britain and the British Empire," in *From Plunder to Preservation: Britain and the Heritage of Empire, c. 1800–1940*, ed. Astrid Swenson and Peter Mandler (Oxford: The British Academy/Oxford University Press, 2013), 49–62.

91. Daniel Gorman, *Imperial Citizenship: Empire and the Question of Belonging* (Manchester: Manchester University Press, 2008).

92. Satvinder S. Juss, *Immigration, Nationality and Citizenship* (London: Mansell, 1993), 3.

93. ("France is neither a unitary state nor a federal state; she is, like England, an imperial state.") Joseph Barthélemy and Paul Duez, *Traité de droit constitutionnel* (Paris: Panthéon Assas, 2004), 283 [1st ed. 1933].

94. Barthélemy and Duez, *Traité*, 283.

95. ("We should remember the existence of sixty million French nationals abroad who are subject, by constitutional right, to special laws. . . . Continental France is where the constitution is relevant; its laws apply automatically to it. Over its outlying areas, on the other hand, the decree rules. Continental France is built on the liberal model; extracontinental France on the authoritarian model.") Ibid., 385–86.

96. Gilles Manceron, ed., *1885, le tournant colonial de la République: Jules Ferry contre Georges Clemenceau, et autres affrontements parlementaires sur la conquête coloniale* (Paris: La Découverte, 2007); there were also many anticolonialists, as shown in Charles-Robert Ageron, *L'anticolonialisme en France de 1871 à 1914* (Paris: Presses Universitaires de France, 1973).

97. Gérard Noiriel, "Socio-histoire d'un concept: Les usages du mot 'nationalité' au XIXe siècle," *Genèses* 20, no. 1 (1995): 4–23; and, by the same author, "The Identification of the Citizen: The Birth of Republican Civil Status in France," in *Documenting Individual Identity: The Development of State Practices in the Modern World*, ed. Jane Caplan and John Torpey (Princeton, NJ: Princeton University Press, 2001), 28–48.

98. See the articles by Emmanuel Saada, Laure Blévis, and Alexis Spire in *Genèses* 53, no. 4 (2003): 4–24, 25–47, and 48–68, respectively.

99. Pierre Brocheux and Daniel Hémery, *Indochine: La colonisation ambiguë, 1858–1954* (Paris: La Découverte, 2001), 83–86.

100. Olivier Le Cour Grandmaison, "The Exception and the Rule: On French Colonial Rule," *Diogenes* 53 (2006): 45–46.

101. Jean-Pierre Azéma and Michel Winock, *La troisième République* (Paris: Calmann-Levy, 1976), 49–125.

102. Charles-Robert Ageron, *Histoire de l'Algérie contemporaine*, vol. 1, *De l'insurrection de 1871 au déclenchement de la guerre de libération (1954)* (Paris: Presses Universitaires de France, 1979), 73; Karine Varley, *Under the Shadow of Defeat: The War of 1870–1871 in French Memory* (Basingtoke: Palgrave Macmillan, 2009), 97–103.

103. Gérard Noiriel, *À quoi sert l'"identité nationale"* (Marseille: Agone, 2007), 21–22.

104. Rogers Brubaker, *Citizenship and Nationhood in France and Germany* (Cambridge, MA: Harvard University Press, 1992), 104–5; see also Patrick Weil, *How to Be French: Nationality in the Making since 1789* (Durham, NC: Duke University Press, 2008), 19–29.

105. Gérard Noiriel, *Les origines républicaines de Vichy* (Paris: Hachette, 1999), 45–98.

106. Pierre Rosanvallon, *Le Sacre du citoyen: Histoire du suffrage universel en France* (Paris: Gallimard, 1992), 560.

107. Laure Blévis, "Les avatars de la citoyenneté en Algérie coloniale ou les paradoxes d'une catégorisation," *Droit et société* 48, no. 2 (2001): 557–81.

108. Raymond Betts, *Assimilation and Association in French Colonial Theory, 1890–1914* (New York: Columbia University Press, 1961).

109. Olivier Le Cour Grandmaison, *La République impériale: Politique et racisme d'État* (Paris: Fayard, 2009), 113.

110. Gary Wilder, *The French Imperial Nation-State: Negritude and Colonial Humanism between Two World Wars* (Chicago: University of Chicago Press, 2005), 25–26.

111. Emmanuel Saada, "Une nationalité par degré: Civilité et citoyenneté en situation coloniale," in *L'esclavage, la colonisation et après . . . France, États-Unis, Grande Bretagne*, ed. Patrick Weil and Stéphane Dufoix (Paris: Presses Universitaires de France, 2006), 193–228.

112. Charles-Robert Ageron, *Les algériens musulmans et la France, 1871–1919* (Paris: Presses Universitaires de France, 1968), 166.

113. Jacques Aumont-Thiéville, *Du régime d'indigénat en Algérie* (Paris: Librairie de Droit et de Jurisprudence, 1906), 29.

114. Quoted in Isabelle Merle, "Retour sur le régime de l'indigénat: Genèse et contradictions des principes répressifs dans l'empire français," *French Politics, Culture, and Society* 20, no. 2 (2002): 83–85.

115. Olivier Le Cour Grandmaison, *De l'indigénat: Anatomie d'un "monstre" juridique: Le droit colonial en Algérie et dans l'Empire français* (Paris: Zones, 2010), 92.

116. Quoted in Catherine Coquery-Vidrovitch, *Enjeux politiques de l'histoire coloniale* (Marseille: Agone, 2009), 22–23.

117. Coquery-Vidrovitch, *Enjeux politiques*, 148.

118. M. Andrew and A. S. Kanya-Forstner, "France, Africa, and the First World War," *The Journal of African History* 19, no. 1 (1978): 14–17.

119. Todd Shepard, *Comment l'indépendance algérienne a transformé la France* (Paris: Payot, 2008); Herbert Luethy, *France Against Herself: A Perceptual Study of France's Past, Her Politics, and Her Unending Crises* (New York: Praeger, 1955).

120. Isabelle Merle, "Retour sur le régime de l'indigénat," 93; Robert Aldrich, *Greater France: A History of French Overseas Expansion* (Houndmills: Palgrave Macmillan, 1996), 213–14.

121. Isabelle Merle, *Expériences coloniales: La Nouvelle Calédonie (1853–1920)* (Paris: Belin, 1995).

122. Jacques Weber, "L'assimilation par les institutions," in *Les Élections législatives et sénatoriales à l'outre-mer (1848–1931)* (Nantes/Paris: Les Indes Savantes, 2010), 15–27.

123. Julien Mérion, "La France et ses Antilles: Vers la citoyenneté intégrale," in *La Guadeloupe, 1875–1914: Les soubresauts d'une société pluriethnique ou les ambigüités de l'assimilation*, ed. Henriette Levillain (Paris: Autrement, 1994), 56.

124. Robert Deville, *Les départements d'outre-mer: L'autre décolonisation* (Paris: Gallimard, 1996), 77. On Césaire's role, see Jean-Claude William, "Aimé Césaire: Les contrariétés de la conscience nationale," in *1946–1996: Cinquante ans de départementalisation outre-mer*, ed. F. Constant and J. Daniel (Paris: L'Harmattan, 1997), 310–34.

125. Philippe Haudrère and Françoise Vergés, *De l'esclave au citoyen* (Paris: Gallimard, 1998), 161.

126. Nelly Schmidt, *La France a-t-elle aboli l'esclavage? Guadeloupe, Martinique, Guyane, 1830–1935* (Paris: Perrin, 2009), 204.

127. Willliam F. S. Miles, *Elections and Ethnicity in French Martinique: A Paradox in Paradise* (New York: Praeger, 1986); Richard D. E. Burton, *La famille coloniale: La Martinique et la mère patrie, 1789–1992* (Paris: L'Harmattan, 1994); Josette Fallope, *Esclaves et citoyens: Les Noirs à la Guadeloupe au XIXe siècle dans les processus de résistance et d'intégration (1802–1910)* (Basse-Terre: Société d'Histoire de la Guadeloupe, 1992), 450–51.

128. Martin Deming Lewis, "One Hundred Million Frenchmen: The "Assimilation" Theory in French Colonial Policy," *Comparative Studies in Society and History* 4, no. 2 (1962): 137–43.

129. Alain Tirefort and Lucien Polenor, "Un Béké dans la République des mulâtres: Fernand Clerc, 1894 à 1939," in *Les élections législatives et sénatoriales outre-mer: 1848–1981*, ed. Laurent Jalabert, Bertrand Joly, and Jacques Weber (Paris: Les Indes Savantes, 2010), 89–101.

130. Pierre Pluchon, ed., *Histoire des Antilles et de la Guyane* (Toulouse: Privat, 1982), 89–101.

131. Eric T. Jennings, *Vichy in the Tropics: Pétain's National Revolution in Madagascar, Guadeloupe, and Indochina, 1940–1944* (Stanford, CA: Stanford University Press, 2001).

132. Burton, *La famille coloniale*, 94–95.

133. Josette Fallope, "La politique d'assimilation et ses résistances," in *La Guadeloupe, 1875–1914: Les soubresauts d'une société pluriethnique ou les ambiguïtés de l'assimilation,* ed. Henriette Levillain (Paris: Autrement, 1994), 35–47.

134. Sudel Fuma, "Un apprentissage difficile de la citoyenneté: Les anciens esclaves de l'Ile de La Réunion et les élections législatives de 1870 sous la IIIe République," in *Les élections législatives et sénatoriales outre-mer: 1848–1981,* ed. Laurent Jalabert, Bertrand Joly, and Jacques Weber (Paris: Les Indes Savantes, 2010), 154–57.

135. That is the title of chapter 8, pp. 197–226 in Schmidt's *La France a-t-elle aboli l'esclavage?*

136. On changes in imperial culture, see Jennifer Pitts, *A Turn to Empire: The Rise of Imperial Liberalism in Britain and France* (Princeton, NJ: Princeton University Press, 2005).

137. Alfred W. McCoy, *Policing America's Empire: The United States, the Philippines, and the Rise of the Surveillance State* (Madison: University of Wisconsin Press, 2009); Alfred W. McCoy and Francisco A. Scarano, eds., *The Colonial Crucible: Empire in the Making of the Modern American State* (Madison: University of Wisconsin Press, 2009); Michael H. Hunt and Steven I. Levine, *Arc of Empire: America's Wars in Asia from the Philippines to Vietnam* (Chapel Hill: University of North Carolina Press, 2012).

138. George Steinmetz, *The Devil's Handwriting: Precoloniality and the German Colonial State in Qingdao, Samoa, and Southwest Africa* (Chicago: University of Chicago Press, 2007).

139. Richard Wonser Tims, *Germanizing Prussian Poland: The H-K-T Society and the Struggle for the Eastern Marches in the German Empire, 1894–1919* (New York: Columbia University Press, 1941); Robert L. Nelson, *Germans, Poland, and Colonial Expansion to the East: 1850 Through the Present* (New York: Palgrave, 2009); Kristin Kopp, *Germany's Wild East: Constructing Poland as Colonial Space* (Ann Arbor: University of Michigan Press, 2012); Michael Perraudin and Jürgen Zimmerer, eds., *German Colonialism and National Identity* (New York: Routledge, 2011), which examines both the Polish border and the Herero genocide; Annemarie H. Sammartino, *The Impossible Border: Germany and the East, 1914–1922* (Ithaca, NY: Cornell University Press, 2010); Volker Berghahn, *Imperial Germany, 1871–1918: Economy, Society, Culture, and Politics* (New York: Berghahn Books, 2005), 87–113; Isabel Hull, *Absolute Destruction: Military Culture and the Practices of War in Imperial Germany* (Ithaca, NY: Cornell University Press, 2005); Sebastian Conrad, *Globalisation and the Nation in Imperial Germany* (Cambridge: Cambridge University Press, 2010); Timothy Snyder, *Black Earth: The Holocaust as History and Warning* (New York: Tim Duggan Books, 2015); Andrew Zimmerman, "Ein deutsches Alabama in Afrika: Die Tuskegee-Expedition nach Togo und die transnationalen Ursprünge westafrikanischer," in *Globalgeschichte: Theorien, Ansätze, Themen,* ed. Sebastian Conrad, Andreas Eckert, and Ulrike Freitag (Frankfurt: Campus Verlag, 2007), 313–42.

140. Paul A. Kramer, *The Blood of Government: Race, Empire, the United States, and the Philippines* (Chapel Hill: University of North Carolina Press, 2006); Eric T. L. Love, *Race over Empire: Racism and U. S. Imperialism, 1865–1900* (Chapel Hill: University of North Carolina Press, 2004); Shaunnagh Dorsett, "'Destitute of the Knowledge of God': Maori Testimony before the New Zealand Courts in the Early Crown Colony Period," in *Past Law, Present Histories*, ed. Diane Kirby (Canberra: ANU Press, 2012), 39–57.

141. Douglas A. Lorimer, *Colour, Class, and the Victorians: English Attitudes to the Negro in the Mid-Nineteenth Century* (Leicester: Leicester University Press, 1978); Douglas A. Lorimer, "Science and the Secularization of Victorian Images of Race," in *Victorian Science in Context*, ed. Bernard V. Lightman (Chicago: University of Chicago Press, 1997), 215–35; Douglas A. Lorimer, "From Natural Science to Social Science: Race and the Language of Race Relations in Late Victorian and Edwardian Discourse," in *Lineages of Empire: The Historical Roots of British Imperial Thought*, ed. Duncan Kelly (Oxford: Oxford University Press, 2009), 181–212; Peter Mandler, "'Race' and 'Nation' in Mid-Victorian Thought," in *History, Religion, and Culture: British Intellectual History, 1750–1950*, ed. Stefan Collini, Richard Whatmore, and B. W. Young (Cambridge: Cambridge University Press, 2000), 224–44; Christine Bolt, *Victorian Attitudes to Race* (London: Routledge & Kegan Paul, 1972); Philip J. Stern, "Rescuing the Age"; Patrick Brantlinger, *Taming Cannibals: Race and the Victorians* (Ithaca, NY: Cornell University Press, 2011), 111–35.

142. See Catherine Hall, *Civilising Subjects: Colony and Metropole in the English Imagination, 1830–1867* (Chicago: University of Chicago Press, 2002), chapter 7, pp. 380–433.

143. Amit Rai, *Rule of Sympathy*.

144. The classic study is Winthrop D. Jordan, *White over Black: American Attitudes Toward the Negro, 1550–1812* (Chapel Hill: University of North Carolina Press, 1968). For a later period, see Amalia Ribi Forclaz, *Humanitarian Imperialism: The Politics of Anti-Slavery Activism, 1880–1940* (Oxford: Oxford University Press, 2015).

145. John Wood Sweet, "The Subject of the Slave Trade: Recent Currents in the Histories of the Atlantic, Great Britain, and Western Africa," *Early American Studies* 7, no. 1 (2009): 18; an exhaustive description of this hellish world and its crisis can be found in Robin Blackburn, *The Overthrow of Colonial Slavery, 1776–1846* (London: Verso, 1988).

146. Larry Tise, *Proslavery: A History of the Defense of Slavery in America, 1701–1840* (Athens: University of Georgia Press, 1987).

147. George Stocking, Jr., *Race, Culture and Evolution: Essays in the History of Anthropology* (Chicago: University of Chicago Press, 1982); Francisco Bethencourt, *Racisms: From the Crusades to the Twentieth Century* (Princeton, NJ: Princeton University Press, 2013), 249; Colin Kidd, *The Forging of Races: Race and Scripture in the Protestant Atlantic World, 1600–2000* (Cambridge: Cambridge University Press, 2006), 121–67; Hellen Tilley, *Africa as Living Laboratory: Empire, Development and the Problem of Scientific Knowledge* (Chicago: University of Chicago Press, 2102).

148. Douglas A. Lorimer, "From Victorian Values to White Virtues: Assimilation and Exclusion in British Racial Discourse, c. 1870–1914," in *Rediscovering the British*

World, ed. Philip Buckner and R. Douglas Francis (Calgary: University of Calgary Press, 2005), 109–34.

149. Jane Burbank and Frederick Cooper, *Empires in World History: Power and the Politics of Difference* (Princeton, NJ: Princeton University Press, 2010), 325. For the U.S. case, see Gary Gerstle, *American Crucible: Race and Nation in the Twentieth Century* (Princeton, NJ: Princeton University Press, 2001); Ira Katznelson, *When Affirmative Action Was White: An Untold History of Racial Inequality in Twentieth-Century America* (New York: W. W. Norton, 2005); and Carol A. Horton, *Race and the Making of American Liberalism* (Oxford: Oxford University Press, 2005), 37–60.

150. John M. Hobson, *The Eurocentric Conception of World Politics: Western International Theory, 1760–2010* (Cambridge: Cambridge University Press, 2012).

151. George Steinmetz, "Return to Empire: The New U.S. Imperialism in Comparative Historical Perspective," *Sociological Theory* 23, no. 4 (2005): 346. According to Steinmetz, "Native policy became the colonial state's central task, or at least the precondition for all other colonial policies." The empirical basis for this idea can be found in Steinmetz, *The Devil's Handwriting*.

Conclusion

1. Christopher A. Bayly, *Origins of Nationality in South Asia: Patriotism and Ethical Government in the Making of Modern India* (Oxford: Oxford University Press, 1998).

2. Susan Buck-Morss, *Hegel, Haiti, and Universal History* (Pittsburgh: Pittsburgh University Press, 2009).

3. Christopher A. Bayly, *Imperial Meridian: The British Empire and the World, 1780–1830* (Harlow: Longman, 1989), 253.

4. Danièle Lochak, "La citoyenneté: Un concept juridique flou," in *Citoyenneté et nationalité: Perspectives en France et au Québec*, ed. Dominique Colas, Claude Emeri, and Jacques Zylberberg (Paris: Presses Universitaires de France, 1991), 179–207.

5. Walter LaFeber, *The New Empire: An Interpretation of American Expansion, 1860–1898* (Ithaca, NY: Cornell University Press, 1963).

6. David Cannadine, *Ornamentalism: How the British Saw Their Empire* (London: Allen Lane, 2001).

7. William B. Cohen, *Empereurs sans sceptre: Histoire des administrateurs de la France d'outre-mer et de l'École coloniale* (Paris: Berger-Levrault, 1973).

8. Guy P. C. Thomson, "¿Convivencia o conflicto? Guerra, etnia y nación en el México del siglo XIX," in *Nación, Constitución y Reforma, 1821–1908*, ed. Erika Pani (Mexico City: CIDE/FCE, 2010), 205–37.

9. Manu Goswami, "Rethinking the Modular Nation Form: Toward a Sociohistorical Conception of Nationalism," *Comparative Studies in Society and History* 40, no. 4 (2002), 770–99.

10. Alan S. Kahan, *Liberalism in Nineteenth-Century Europe: The Political Culture of Limited Suffrage* (Houndmills: Palgrave Macmillan, 2003).

11. Sebastian Conrad, *German Colonialism: A Short History* (Cambridge: Cambridge University Press, 2012), 37; Alain Chatriot and Dieter Gosenwinkel, eds., *Koloniale Politik und Praktiken Deutschlands und Frankreichs, 1880–1962* (Stuttgart: Franz Steiner Verlag, 2010); Laura Engelstein, *Slavophile Empire: Imperial Russia's Illiberal Path* (Ithaca, NY: Cornell University Press, 2009).

12. Pierre Rosanvallon, *La société des égaux* (Paris: Seuil, 2011).

13. Linda Colley, *Britons: Forging the Nation, 1707–1837* (New Haven, CT: Yale University Press, 1992); David Cannadine and Simon Price, eds. *Rituals of Royalty: Power and Ceremonial in Traditional Societies* (Cambridge: Cambridge University Press, 1987).

14. Anicet Le Pors, *La citoyenneté* (Paris: Presses Universitaires de France, 2011), 53.

15. Gérard Noiriel, *Les origines républicaines de Vichy* (Paris: Hachette, 1999); George Steinmetz, *Regulating the Social: The Welfare State and Local Politics in Imperial Germany* (Princeton, NJ: Princeton University Press, 1993).

16. Josep M. Fradera, *Cultura nacional en una societat dividida: patriotisme i cultura a Catalunya (1838–1868)* (Barcelona: Edicions Curial, 1992). [Spanish translation, 2003].

17. Catherine Hall, *Civilising Subjects: Colony and Metropole in the English Imagination, 1830–1867* (Chicago: University of Chicago Press, 2002); Stephanie Mc-Curry, *Confederate Reckoning: Power and Politics in the Civil War South* (Cambridge, MA: Harvard University Press, 2010): Peter B. Knupfer, *The Union as It Is: Constitutional Unionism and Sectional Compromise, 1787–1861* (Chapel Hill: University of North Carolina Press, 1995).

18. Michaël Bourlet, Yann Lagadec, and Erwan Le Gall, *Petites patries dans la Grande Guerre* (Rennes: Presses Universitaires de Rennes, 2013); Anne-Marie Thiesse, *Ils apprenaient la France: L'exaltation des régions dans le discours patriotique* (Paris: Éditions de la Maison des Sciences Humaines, 1997).

19. Timothy Snyder, *The Reconstruction of Nations: Poland, Ukraine, Lithuania, Belarus, 1569–1999* (New Haven, CT: Yale University Press, 2004); Larry Wolff, *The Idea of Galicia: History and Fantasy in Habsburg Political Culture* (Stanford, CA: Stanford University Press, 2010); Sebastian Conrad and Jürgen Osterhammel, eds., *Das Kaiserreich Transnational: Deutschland in der Welt, 1871–1914* (Göttingen: Vandenhoeck & Ruprecht, 2006).

20. "Two modes of classifying people became more salient among the multiple ways in which Europeans thought about themselves and others: nation and race"; in Jane Burbank and Frederick Cooper, *Empires in World History: Power and the Politics of Difference* (Princeton, NJ: Princeton University Press, 2010), 289.

21. Elizabeth Elbourne, "Indigenous Peoples and Imperial Networks in the Early Nineteenth Century: The Politics of Knowledge," in *Rediscovering the British World*, ed. Philip Buckner and R. Douglas Frances (Calgary: University of Calgary Press, 2005), 59–83.

22. Diane Paton, *No Bond but the Law: Punishment, Race, and Gender in Jamaican State Formation, 1780–1870* (Durham, NC: Duke University Press, 2004).

23. Colin Kidd, *The Forging of Races: Race and Scripture in the Protestant Atlantic World, 1600–2000* (Cambridge: Cambridge University Press, 2006); George

Stocking Jr., *Race, Culture and Evolution: Essays in the History of Anthropology* (Chicago: University of Chicago Press, 1982); George Stocking Jr., ed., *Colonial Situations: Essays on the Contextualization of Ethnographic Knowledge* (Madison: University of Wisconsin Press, 1991).

24. Paul R. Spickard, *Mixed Blood: Intermarriage and Ethnic Identity in Twentieth-Century America* (Madison: University of Wisconsin Press, 1989); Mike Hawkins, *Social Darwinism in European and American Thought, 1860–1945* (Cambridge: Cambridge University Press, 1997); Jean-Marc Bernardini, *Le darwinisme social en France (1859–1918): Fascination et rejet d'une idéologie* (Paris: CNRS Editions, 1997).

Adamson, Kay. *Algeria: A Study in Competing Ideologies*. London: Continuum, 1998.

Adelman, Jeremy. "Iberian Passages: Continuity and Change in the South Atlantic." In *The Age of Revolutions in Global Context, c. 1760–1840*, edited by David Armitage and Sanjay Subrahmanyam, 59–82. Houndmills: Palgrave Macmillan, 2010.

———. *Sovereignty and Revolution in the Iberian Atlantic*. Princeton, NJ: Princeton University Press, 2009.

Ageron, Charles-Robert. "L'évolution politique de l'Algérie sous le Second Empire." In Ageron, *Politiques coloniales au Maghreb*, 45–73. Paris: Presses Universitaires Françaises, 1972.

———. *Histoire de l'Algérie contemporaine*. Vol. 2, *De l'insurrection de 1871 au déclenchement de la guerre de libération (1954)*. Paris: Presses Universitaires de France, 1979.

———. *L'anticolonialisme en France de 1871 à 1914*. Paris: Presses Universitaires de France, 1973.

———. *Les algériens musulmans et la France, 1871–1919*. 2 vols. Paris: Presses Universitaires de France, 1968.

———. *Politiques coloniales au Maghreb*. Paris: Presses Universitaires de France, 1972.

Agné, Hans. "Democratic Founding: We the People and the Others." *International Journal of Constitutional Law* 10, no. 3 (2012): 836–61.

Aguilera Manzano, José María. *La formación de la identidad cubana: El debate Saco-La Sagra*. Seville: CSIC, 2005.

Aizpuru, Mikel. "Chino cristiano (casado con india española filipina): Nación, raza, religión y ciudadanía en la España postimperial." In *Conflictos y cicatrices: Fronteras y migraciones en el mundo hispánico*, edited by Almudena Delgado Larios, 285–303. Madrid: Dyckinson, 2014.

Ajzenstat, Janet. *The Political Thought of Lord Durham*. Kingston: McGill-Queen's University Press, 1988.

Aldrich, Robert. *Greater France: A History of French Overseas Expansion*. Houndmills: Palgrave Macmillan, 1996.

Aldrich, Robert, and John Connell. *France's Overseas Frontier: Départements et Territoires d'Outre-Mer*. Cambridge: Cambridge University Press, 1992.

Alexandre, Valentim. *A Questão Colonial no Parlamento*. Vol. 1, *1821–1910*. Lisbon: Dom Quixote, 2008.

———. *Os Sentidos do Império: Questão Nacional e Questão Colonial na Crise do Antigo Regime Português*. Lisbon: Ediçoes Afrontamento, 1993.

Almagro, Manuel. *La Comisión Científica del Pacífico: Viaje por Sudamérica y recorrido del Amazonas, 1862–1866*. Edited by Lily Litvak. Barcelona: Laertes, 1984.

Alonso Romero, María Paz. *Cuba en la España liberal (1837–1898): Génesis y desarrollo del régimen autonómico*. Madrid: Centro de Estudios Constitucionales, 2002.

Alvarado, Javier. *Constitucionalismo y codificación en las provincias de Ultramar: La supervivencia del Antiguo Régimen en la España del XIX*. Madrid: Centro de Estudios Constitucionales, 2001.

Álvarez de Toledo, Cayetana. *Politics and Reform in Spain and Viceregal Mexico: The Life and Thought of Juan de Palafox, 1600–1659*. Oxford: Clarendon Press, 2004.

Álvarez Junco, José. *Mater Dolorosa: La idea de España en el siglo XIX*. Madrid: Taurus, 2001.

———. *Spanish Identity in the Age of Nations*. Manchester: Manchester University Press, 2016.

Ambirajan, S. *Classical Political Economy and British Policy in India*. Cambridge: Cambridge University Press, 1978.

Amelang, James A. *Parallel Histories: Muslims and Jews in Inquisitorial Spain*. Baton Rouge: Louisiana State University Press, 2013.

An Analysis of the System of the Government Throughout the British Empire. London: Macmillan, 1912.

Anbinder, Tyler. *Nativism and Slavery: The Northern Know Nothings and the Politics of the 1850s*. New York: Oxford University Press, 1992.

Anderson, Fred. *Crucible of War: The Seven Years' War and the Fate of Empire in British North America, 1754–1766*. New York: Alfred A. Knopf, 2000.

———. *The War That Made America: A Short History of the French and Indian War*. New York: Penguin Books, 2005.

Andreu Miralles, Xavier. *El descubrimiento de España: Mito romántico e identidad nacional*. Madrid: Taurus, 2016.

Andrew, C. M., and A. S. Kanya-Forstner, "France, Africa, and the First World War." *Journal of African History* 19, no. 1 (1978): 11–23.

Andrews, Kenneth R. *Trade, Plunder and Settlement: Maritime Enterprise and the Genesis of the British Empire, 1480–1630*. Cambridge: Cambridge University Press, 1984.

Andrien, Kenneth J. *Andean Worlds: Indigenous History, Culture, and Consciousness under Spanish Rule, 1532–1825*. Albuquerque: University of New Mexico Press, 2001.

Andújar Castillo, Francisco. *Necesidad y venalidad: España e Indias, 1704–1711*. Madrid: Centro de Estudios Políticos y Constitucionales, 2008.

Anstey, Roger. *The Atlantic Slave Trade and British Abolition, 1760–1810*. London: Macmillan, 1975.

Appleby, Joyce O. *Liberalism and Republicanism in the Historical Imagination*. Cambridge, MA: Harvard University Press, 1992.

Arango y Parreño, Francisco. *Obras de Don Francisco Arango y Parreño*. Havana: Ministerio de Educación, 1952. 2 vols.

Armitage, David. *The Ideological Origins of the British Empire*. Cambridge: Cambridge University Press, 2000.

———. "John Locke: Theorist of Empire?" In *Empire and Modern Political Thought*, edited by Sankar Muthu, 84–111. Cambridge: Cambridge University Press, 2012.

Armitage, David, and Sanjay Subrahmanyam, eds. *The Age of Revolutions in Global Context, c. 1760–1840*. Houndmills, Palgrave Macmillan, 2010.

———. "Introduction: The Age of Revolutions, c. 1760–1840: Global Causation, Connection, and Comparison." In *The Age of Revolutions in Global Context, c. 1760–1840*, edited by David Armitage and Sanjay Subrahmanyam, xii–xxxii. Houndmills: Palgrave Macmillan, 2010.

Ashworth, John. *Slavery, Capitalism and Politics in the Antebellum Republic.* Vol. 1, *Commerce and Compromise, 1820-1850.* Cambridge: Cambridge University Press, 1995.

Ashworth, William J. *Customs and Excise: Trade, Production, and Consumption in England, 1640-1845.* Oxford: Oxford University Press, 2003.

Aslakson, Kenneth R. *Making Race in the Courtroom: The Legal Construction of Three Races in Early New Orleans.* New York: New York University Press, 2014.

Attar, Frank. *Aux armes, citoyens! Naissance et fonctions du bellicisme révolutionnaire.* Paris: Seuil, 2010.

Aumont-Thiéville, Jacques. *Du régime de l'indigénat en Algérie.* Paris: Librairie de Droit et de Jurisprudence, 1906.

Ayad-Bergounioux, Soulef. "De Brumaire à la formation de l'État bureaucratique consulaire: Le rôle des républicains conservateurs." *Annales historiques de la Révolution française* 378 (2014): 51–72.

——. "La 'République Représentative' selon Antoine Boulay de La Meurthe (1761–1840): Une figure de la bourgeoisie libérale et conservatrice." *Annales historiques de la Révolution française* 4 (2010): 31–55.

Azéma, Jean-Pierre, and Michel Winock. *La troisième République.* Paris: Calmann-Levy, 1976.

Baade, Hans W. "The Law of Slavery in Spanish Louisiana, 1769–1803." In *Louisiana's Legal Heritage,* edited by Edward F. Haas, 43–75. Pensacola: Perdido Way Press for the Louisiana State Museum, 1983.

Baer, Marc. *The Rise and Fall of Radical Westminster, 1780-1890.* Houndmills: Palgrave Macmillan, 2012.

Baerga, María del Carmen. *Negociaciones de sangre: Dinámicas racializantes en el Puerto Rico decimonónico.* Madrid: Iberoamericana, 2015.

Bahamonde, Ángel, and José G. Cayuela. *Hacer las Américas: Las élites coloniales españolas en el siglo XIX.* Madrid: Alianza Editorial, 1992.

Bailey, Garrick A., ed. *Handbook of North American Indians.* Vol. 2, *Indians in Contemporary Society.* Washington: Smithsonian Institution, 2008.

Bailyn, Bernard. *The Ideological Origins of the American Revolution.* Cambridge, MA: Harvard University Press, 1992.

Baker, Keith Michael. *Inventing the French Revolution: Essays on French Political Culture in the Eighteenth Century.* Cambridge: Cambridge University Press, 1990.

Balfour, Sebastian. *The End of the Spanish Empire (1898-1923).* Oxford: Clarendon Press, 1997.

Banks, Kenneth J. *Chasing Empire across the Sea: Communications and the State in the French Atlantic, 1713-1763.* Montreal: McGill-Queen's University Press, 2003.

Banner, Stuart. *How the Indians Lost Their Land: Law and Power on the Frontier.* Cambridge, MA: Harvard University Press, 2005.

Bannon, John Francis. *The Spanish Borderlands Frontier, 1513-1821.* Albuquerque: University of New Mexico Press, 1974.

Baptist, Edward E. *The Half Has Never Been Told: Slavery and the Making of American Capitalism.* New York: Basic Books, 2014.

Baralt, Guillermo A. *Esclavos rebeldes: Conspiraciones y sublevaciones de esclavos en Puerto Rico (1795–1873)*. Río Piedras: Ediciones Huracán, 1982.

Barnett, Michael. *The Empire of Humanity: A History of Humanitarianism*. Ithaca, NY: Cornell University Press, 2011.

Barrière, Louis-Agustin. "Le statut personnel des musulmans d'Algérie de 1834 à 1962." PhD diss., Université Jean Moulin-Lyon III, 1990.

Barrow, Thomas C. "Background to the Grenville Program." *William and Mary Quarterly* 22, no. 1 (1965): 93–104.

Barthélemy, Joseph, and Paul Duez. *Traité de droit constitutionnel*. Paris: Panthéon Assas, 2004.

Bartlett, Thomas. *The Fall and Rise of the Irish Nation: The Catholic Question, 1690–1830*. Dublin: Rowman and Littlefield Publishers, 1992.

———. "Ireland, Empire, and Union, 1690–1801." In *Ireland and the British Empire*, edited by Kevin Kenny, 61–89. Oxford: Oxford University Press, 2004.

———. "'This Famous Island Set in a Virginian Sea': Ireland in the British Empire 1690–1801." In *The Oxford History of the British Empire*. Vol. 2, *The Eighteenth Century*, edited by P. J. Marshall, 253–75. Oxford: Oxford University Press, 1998.

Bastin, John. *The Native Policies of Sir Stamford Raffles in Java and Sumatra: An Economic Interpretation*. Oxford: Clarendon Press, 1957.

———. *Raffles's Ideas on the Land Rent System in Java and the Mackenzie Land Tenure Commission*. Gravenhague: Martinus Nijhoff, 1954.

Bayly, Christopher A. *The Birth of the Modern World, 1780–1914*. Oxford: Blackwell, 2004.

———. "The British Military-Fiscal State and Indigenous Resistance. India, 1750–1820." In *An Imperial State at War: Britain from 1689 to 1815*, edited by Lawrence Stone, 322–54. Abingdon: Routledge, 1994.

———. *Imperial Meridian: The British Empire and the World, 1780–1830*. Harlow: Longman, 1989.

———. *Indian Society and the Making of the British Empire*. Cambridge: Cambridge University Press, 1990.

———. *Origins of Nationality in South Asia: Patriotism and Ethical Government in the Making of Modern India*. Oxford: Oxford University Press, 1998.

———. *Recovering Liberties: Indian Thought in the Age of Liberalism and Empire*. Cambridge: Cambridge University Press, 2011.

Bazcko, Bronislaw. *Ending the Terror: The French Revolution after Robespierre*. Cambridge: Cambridge University Press, 1994.

Beaglehole, T. H. *Thomas Munro and the Development of Administrative Policy in Madras, 1792–1818: The Origins of the "Munro System."* Cambridge: Cambridge University Press, 1966.

Beard, Mary. "Officers and Gentlemen? Roman Britain and the British Empire." In *From Plunder to Preservation: Britain and the Heritage of Empire, c. 1800–1940*, edited by Astrid Swenson and Peter Mandler, 49–62. Oxford: The British Academy/ Oxford University Press, 2013.

Beasley, Edward. "The Man Who Ran the Empire." In Beasley, *Mid-Victorian Imperialists: British Gentlemen and the Empire of the Mind*, 20–43. London: Routledge, 2005.

Beaud, Stéphane, and Gérard Noiriel, "L''assimilation': Un concept en panne." *Revue internationale d'action communautaire* 21, no. 61 (1989): 63–76.

Beckert, Sven. *Empire of Cotton: A Global History.* New York: Alfred A. Knopf, 2014.

Beckert, Sven, and Seth Rockman. *Slavery's Capitalism: A New History of American Economic Development.* Philadelphia: University of Pennsylvania Press, 2016.

Belich, James. *Replenishing the Earth: The Settler Revolution and the Rise of the Anglo-World, 1783–1939.* Oxford: Oxford University Press, 2009.

———. "The Rise of the Angloworld: Settlement in North America and Australasia, 1784–1918." In *Rediscovering the British World*, edited by Philip A. Buckner and R. Douglas Francis, 39–57. Calgary: University of Calgary Press, 2005.

Bell, David A. *The Cult of the Nation in France: Inventing Nationalism, 1680–1800.* Cambridge, MA: Harvard University Press, 2001.

———. *The First Total War: Napoleon's Europe and the Birth of Warfare as We Know It.* Boston: Mariner Books, 2008.

———. "The Unbearable Lightness of Being French: Law, Republicanism and National Identity at the End of the Old Regime." *American Historical Review* 106, no. 4 (2001): 1215–35.

———. "The Unrepresentable French?" In *Realities of Representation: State Building in Early Modern Europe and European America*, edited by Maija Jansson, 75–92. New York: Palgrave Macmillan, 2007.

Bell, Duncan S. A. "Empire and International Relations in Victorian Political Thought." *Historical Journal* 49, no. 1 (2006): 281–98.

Bell, Duncan. *The Idea of Greater Britain: Empire and the Future of World Order, 1860–1900.* Princeton, NJ: Princeton University Press, 2007.

Belmessous, Saliha. *Assimilation and Empire: Uniformity in French and British Colonies, 1541–1954.* Oxford: Oxford University Press, 2013.

Bender, Thomas. *A Nation among Nations: America's Place in World History.* New York: Hill & Wang, 2006.

Benedict, Michael Les. *A Compromise of Principle: Congressional Republicans and Reconstruction, 1863–1869.* New York: W. W. Norton, 1974.

Benians, E. A. "Adam Smith's Project of an Empire." *The Cambridge Historical Journal* 1, no. 3 (1925): 249–83.

Bennoune, Mahfoud. *The Making of Contemporary Algeria, 1830–1987: Colonial Upheavals and Post-Independence Development.* Cambridge: Cambridge University Press, 1988.

Benot, Yves. *La démence coloniale sous Napoléon.* Paris: La Découverte, 1992.

———. "Diderot-Raynal: L'impossible divorce." In *Les Lumières, l'esclavage, la colonisation*, edited by Yves Benot, 138–53. Paris: La Découverte 2005.

———. *La Révolution française et la fin des colonies, 1789–1794.* Paris: La Découverte, 1988.

Benot, Yves, and Marcel Dorigny, eds. *Rétablissement de l'esclavage dans les colonies françaises: Aux origines de Haïti.* Paris: Maisonneuve et Larose, 2003.

Bentley, Michael. *The Climax of Liberal Politics: British Liberalism in Theory and Practice, 1868–1918.* London: Edward Arnold, 1987.

———. *Politics without Democracy: Great Britain, 1815–1914; Perception and Preoccupation in British Government.* Totowa: Barnes & Noble Books, 1984.

Benton, Lauren A. *Law and Colonial Cultures: Legal Regimes in World History, 1400–1900*. Cambridge: Cambridge University Press, 2002.

———. *A Search for Sovereignty: Law and Geography in European Empires, 1400-1900*. Cambridge: Cambridge University Press, 2010.

Benyon, John. "Overlords of Empire? British 'Proconsular Imperialism' in Comparative Perspective." *The Journal of Imperial and Commonwealth History* 19, no. 2 (1991): 164–202.

Berbel, Márcia Regina. *A Nação como artefato: Deputados do Brasil nas Cortes portuguesas, 1821-1822*. São Paulo, Editora Hucitec, 2010.

Berbel, Márcia Regina, Rafael Marquese, and Tamis Parron. *Escravidão e Política: Brasil e Cuba, 1790-1850*. São Paulo: Editora Hucitec, 2009.

Bergad, Laird W. "Towards Puerto Rico's Grito de Lares: Coffee, Social Stratification and Class Conflicts, 1828–1868." *Hispanic American Historical Review* 60, no. 4 (1980): 617–42.

Bergad, Laird W., Fe Iglesias García, and María del Carmen Barcia. *The Cuban Slave Market, 1790-1880*. Cambridge: Cambridge University Press, 1985.

Berghahn, Volker. *Imperial Germany, 1871-1918: Economy, Society, Culture, and Politics*. New York: Berghahn Books, 2005.

Bergquist, James M. *Daily Life in Immigrant America, 1820-1870*. Chicago: Ivan R. Dee, 2009.

Berkhofer, Robert F., Jr. *The White Man's Indian: Images of the American Indian from Columbus to the Present*. New York: Vintage Books, 1979.

Berlin, Ira. *Generations of Captivity: A History of African-American Slaves*. Cambridge, MA: Harvard University Press, 2003.

———. *The Making of African America: The Four Great Migrations*. New York: Viking, 2010.

Berlin, Ira, Barbara J. Fields, Steven F. Miller, Joseph P. Reidy, and Leslie S. Rowland. "The Wartime Genesis of Free Labor, 1861–1865." In Berlin, Fields, Miller, Reidy, and Rowland, eds., *Slaves No More: Three Essays on Emancipation and the Civil War*, 77–187. Cambridge: Cambridge University Press, 1991.

Bermeo, Nancy G., and Philip G. Nord, eds. *Civil Society before Democracy: Lessons from Nineteenth-Century Europe*. Lanham, MD: Rowman & Littlefield, 2000.

Bernardini, Jean-Marc. *Le darwinisme social en France (1859-1918): Fascination et rejet d'une idéologie*. Paris: CNRS Editions, 1997.

Bethencourt, Francisco. *Racisms: From the Crusades to the Twentieth Century*. Princeton, NJ: Princeton University Press, 2013.

Bethencourt, Francisco, and Kirti N. Chaudhuri, eds. *História da expansão portuguesa*. Vol. 4, *Do Brasil para África, 1808-1930*. Estella: Temas e Debates, 2000.

Betts, Raymond F. *Assimilation and Association in French Colonial Theory, 1890-1914*. New York: Columbia University Press, 1961.

———. *Tricouleur: The French Overseas Empire*. New York: Gordon et Cremonesi, 1978.

Biagini, Eugenio F. *British Democracy and Irish Nationalism, 1876-1906*. Cambridge: Cambridge University Press, 2007.

Biard, Michel. *Collot d'Herbois: Légendes noires et révolution*. Lyon: Presses Universitaires de Lyon, 1995.

———. *Missionnaires de la République: Les représentants du peuple en mission, 1793–1795*. Paris: CTHS, 2002.

———, ed. *Les politiques de la Terreur, 1793–1794*. Rennes: Presses Universitaires de Rennes/Société des Études Robespierristes, 2008.

Bidouze, Frédéric. "Polysémie et diachronie du terme de citoyen dans les discours parlementaires au XVIIIe siècle: Essai d'interprétation." In *Invention et réinvention de la citoyenneté: Actes du colloque international de Pau, 9–11 décembre 1998*, edited by Claude Fiévet, 97–113. Pau: Éditions Joëlle Sampy, 2000.

Bitis, Alexander. *Russia and the Eastern Question: Army, Government and Society, 1815–1833*. Oxford: Oxford University Press, 2006.

Bizcarrondo, Marta, and Antonio Elorza. *Cuba/España: El dilema autonomista, 1878–1898*. Madrid: El Colibrí, 2001.

Blackburn, Robin. *The Overthrow of Colonial Slavery, 1776–1846*. London: Verso, 1988.

Blainey, G. "Lost Causes of the Jameson Raid." *The Economic History Review* 18, no. 2 (1965): 350–66.

Blanco, John D. *Frontier Constitutions: Christianity and Colonial Empire in the Nineteenth-Century Philippines*. Berkeley: California University Press, 2009.

Blévis, Laure. "Les avatars de la citoyenneté en Algérie coloniale ou les paradoxes d'une catégorisation." *Droit et société* 48, no. 2 (2001): 557–81.

———. "La citoyenneté française au miroir de la colonisation: Étude des demandes de naturalisation des 'sujets français' en Algérie coloniale." *Genèses* 53, no. 4 (2003): 25–47.

Bliss, Robert. *Revolution and Empire: English Politics and the American Colonies in the Seventeenth Century*. Manchester: Manchester University Press, 1990.

Bock, Ulrike. "Entre 'españoles' y 'ciudadanos': Las milicias de pardos y la transformación de las fronteras culturales en Yucatán, 1790–1821." *Secuencia* 87 (2013): 9–27.

Bodelsen, Carl Adolf G. *Studies in Mid-Victorian Imperialism*. New York: Howard Fertig, 1968.

Bolt, Christine. *Victorian Attitudes to Race*. London: Routledge & Kegan Paul, 1972.

Bongiorno, Frank. "Fabian Socialism and British Australia, 1890–1972." In *Rediscovering the British World*, edited by Philip A. Buckner and R. Douglas Francis, 209–31. Calgary: University of Calgary Press, 2005.

Bonmatí Antón, José Fermín. *La emigración alicantina a Argelia (siglo XIX y primer tercio del siglo XX)*. Alicante: Publicaciones de la Universidad de Alicante, 1989.

Bonner, Fred. "Urban Society in Colonial America. Research Trends." *Latin American Research Review* 21, no. 1 (1986): 7–72.

Boomgaard, Peter. *Children of the Colonial State: Population Growth and Economic Development in Java, 1795–1880*. Amsterdam: Free University Press, 1989.

Borah, Woodrow. *El Juzgado General de Indios en la Nueva España*. Mexico City: Fondo de Cultura Económica, 1996.

———. "Representative Institutions in the Spanish Empire in the Sixteenth Century." *The Americas* 12 (1956): 246–57.

Borella, François. "Nationalité et citoyenneté." In *Citoyenneté et nationalité: Perspectives en France et au Québec*, edited by Dominique Colas, Claude Emeri, and Jacques Zylberberg, 209–29. Paris: Presses Universitaires de France, 1991.

Böttcher, Nikolaus, Bernd Hausberger, and Max Hering Torres, eds. *El peso de la sangre: Limpios, mestizos y nobles en el mundo hispánico*. Mexico City: Colegio de México, 2011.

Boucher, Philip P. *Les Nouvelles Frances: France in America, 1500–1815: An Imperial Perspective*. Providence: John Carter Brown Library, 1989.

Boulant, Antoine. "Le suspect parisien en l'An II." *Annales historiques de la Révolution française* 280 (1990): 187–97.

Bourdon, Jean. *La Constitution de l'An VIII*. Rodez: Carrère Editeur, 1942.

Bourlet, Michaël, Yann Lagadec, and Erwan Le Gall. *Petites patries dans la Grande Guerre*. Rennes: Presses Universitaires de Rennes, 2013.

Bourne, Kenneth. *Britain and the Balance of Power in North America, 1815–1908*. London: Longman, 1967.

Bowen, H. V. *The Business of Empire: The East India Company and Imperial Britain, 1756–1833*. Cambridge: Cambridge University Press, 2006.

———. *Revenue and Reform: The Indian Problem in British Politics, 1757–1773*. Cambridge: Cambridge University Press, 1991.

———. *War and British Society: 1688–1815*. Cambridge: Cambridge University Press, 1998.

Bowen, H. V., and Agustín González Enciso, eds. *Mobilising Resources for War: Britain and Spain at Work During the Early Modern Period*. Pamplona: Ediciones Universidad de Navarra, 2006.

Bowes, John P. *Exiles and Pioneers: Eastern Indians in the Trans-Mississippi West*. New York: Cambridge University Press, 2007.

Boxer, Charles R. *The Portuguese Seaborne Empire, 1415–1825*. London: Hutchinson, 1969.

Bradburn, Douglas. *The Citizenship Revolution: Politics and the Creation of the American Union, 1774–1804*. Charlottesville: University of Virginia Press, 2009.

Braddick, Michael. *State Formation in Early Modern England, c. 1550–1700*. Cambridge: Cambridge University Press, 2000.

Branda, Pierre, and Thierry Lentz. *Napoléon, l'esclavage et les colonies*. Paris: Fayard, 2006.

Brantlinger, Patrick. *Taming Cannibals: Race and the Victorians*. Ithaca, NY: Cornell University Press, 2011.

Brathwaite, Kamau. *The Development of Creole Society in Jamaica, 1770–1820*. Oxford: Clarendon Press, 1971.

Brett, Michael. "The Colonial Period in the Maghrib and Its Aftermath: The Present State of Historical Writing." *Journal of African History* 17, no. 2 (1976): 291–305.

———. "Legislating for Inequality in Algeria: The Senatus-Consulte of 14 July 1865." *Bulletin of the School for Oriental and African Studies* 51, no. 3 (1988): 440–61.

Brewer, John. *Party Ideology and Popular Politics at the Accession of George III*. Cambridge: Cambridge University Press, 1976.

———. *The Sinews of Power: War, Money, and the English State, 1688–1783*. London: Unwin Hynman, 1989.

Brière, Jean-François. *Haïti et la France: 1804–1848. Le rêve brisé*. Paris: Karthala, 2008.

———. "La France et la reconnaissance de l'indépendance haïtienne: Le débat sur l'ordonnance de 1825." *French Colonial History* 5 (2004): 125–38.

Bright, John. "Imperial Federation." In *The Public Letters of the Right Hon. John Bright*, 226–27. New York: Kraus Reprint Co., 1969. First published in 1885 by Sampson Low, Marston, Searle & Rivington.

Brocheux, Pierre, and Daniel Hémery. *Indochine: la colonisation ambiguë, 1858–1954*. Paris: La Découverte, 2001.

Bronstein, Jamie L., and Andrew T. Harris. *Empire, State and Society: Britain since 1830*. Malden, MA: Wiley Blackwell, 2012.

Brower, Benjamin Claude. *A Desert Named Peace: The Violence of France's Empire in the Algerian Sahara, 1844–1902*. New York: Columbia University Press, 2008.

Brown, Christopher L. *Moral Capital: Foundations of British Abolitionism*. Chapel Hill: University of North Carolina Press, 2006.

———. "The Politics of Slavery." In *The British Atlantic World, 1500–1800*, edited by David Armitage and Michael J. Braddick, 214–32. Houndmills: Palgrave Macmillan, 2002.

Brown, Howard G. *Ending the French Revolution: Violence, Justice and Repression from the Terror to Napoleon*. Charlottesville: University of Virginia Press, 2006.

———. "Mythes et massacres: Réconsiderer la 'terreur' directoriale." *Annales historiques de la Révolution française* 325 (2001): 23–52.

———. "Professionalism and the Fate of Army Generals after Thermidor." *French Historical Studies* 19, no. 1 (1995): 133–52.

Brown, Matthew, and Gabriel Paquette, eds. *Connections after Colonialism: Europe and Latin America in the 1820s*. Tuscaloosa: University of Alabama Press, 2013.

Brown, Robert E. *Middle-Class Democracy and the Revolution in Massachusetts, 1691–1780*. Ithaca, NY: Cornell University Press, 1955.

Browne, Stephen Howard. *Jefferson's Call for Nationhood: The First Inaugural Address*. College Station: Texas A&M University Press, 2003.

Brubaker, Rogers. *Citizenship and Nationhood in France and Germany*. Cambridge, MA: Harvard University Press, 1992.

Bryant, G. J. "The War in the Carnatic." In *The Seven Years' War: Global Views*, edited by Mark H. Danley and Patrick J. Speelman, 73–107. Leiden: Brill, 2012.

Buckley, Roger N. *The British Army in the West Indies: Society and the Military in the Revolutionary Age*. Gainesville: University Press of Florida, 1998.

Buck-Morss, Susan. *Hegel, Haiti, and Universal History*. Pittsburgh, PA: Pittsburgh University Press, 2009.

Buckner, Philip A. "The Long Goodbye: English Canadians and the British World." In *Rediscovering the British World*, edited by Philip A. Buckner and R. Douglas Francis, 181–207. Calgary: University of Calgary Press, 2005.

Buckner, Philip A., and R. Douglas Francis, eds. *Rediscovering the British World*. Calgary: Calgary University Press, 2005.

Bugeaud, Thomas Robert. *De la colonisation de l'Algérie*. Paris: Guyot, 1847.

Bumsted, J. M. "The Consolidation of British North America, 1783–1860." In *Canada and the British Empire*, edited by Philip Buckner, 43–65. Oxford: Oxford University Press, 2008.

———. "The Cultural Landscape of Early Canada." In *Strangers within the Realm: Cultural Margins of the First British Empire*, edited by Bernard Bailyn and Philip D. Morgan, 363–92. Chapel Hill: University of North Carolina Press, 1991.

Bumsted, J. M. *A History of the Canadian Peoples*. Oxford: Oxford University Press, 2003.

———. *The Peoples of Canada: A Pre-Confederation History*. Toronto: Oxford University Press, 2004.

Burbank, Jane, and Frederick Cooper. *Empires in World History: Power and the Politics of Difference*. Princeton, NJ: Princeton University Press, 2010.

Burdiel, Isabel. *Isabel II: Una biografía (1830–1904)*. Madrid: Taurus, 2010.

Burkholder, Mark A., and D. S. Chandler. *From Impotence to Authority: The Spanish Crown and the American Audiencias, 1687–1808*. Columbia: University of Missouri Press, 1977.

Burnard, Trevor G., and John D. Garrigus. *The Plantation Machine: Atlantic Capitalism in French Saint-Domingue and British Jamaica*. Philadelphia: University of Pennsylvania Press, 2016.

Burroughs, Peter. *The Canadian Crisis and British Colonial Policy (1828–1841)*. London: Edward Arnold, 1972.

———. "Imperial Institutions and the Government of Empire." In *The Oxford History of the British Empire*. Vol. 3, *The Nineteenth Century*, edited by Andrew Porter, 172–97. Oxford: Oxford University Press, 1999.

Burrows, Simon. "The Innocence of Jacques-Pierre Brissot." *Historical Journal* 46, no. 4 (2003): 843–71.

Burstin, Haim. "Travail et citoyenneté en milieu urbain sous la Révolution." In *Citoyen et citoyenneté sous la Révolution française*, edited by Raymonde Monnier, 261–70. Paris: Société des Études Robespierristes, 2006

Burton, Antoinette M. *The Trouble with Empire: Challenges to Modern British Imperialism*. Oxford: Oxford University Press, 2015.

Burton, Richard D. E. *La famille coloniale. La Martinique et la mère patrie, 1789–1992*. Paris: L'Harmattan, 1994.

Busaall, Jean-Baptiste. *Le spectre du jacobinisme: L'expérience constitutionnelle française et le premier libéralisme espagnol*. Madrid: Casa de Velázquez, 2012.

Butel, Paul. *Histoire des Antilles françaises*. Paris: Perrin, 2007.

———. *Les négociants bordelais, l'Europe et les îles au XVIIIe siècle*. Paris: Aubier, 1974.

Butler, Kathleen Mary. *The Economics of Emancipation: Jamaica and Barbados, 1823–1843*. Chapel Hill: University of North Carolina Press, 1995.

Butler, Sarah J. *Britain and Its Empire in the Shadow of Rome: The Reception of Rome in Socio-Political Debate from the 1850s to the 1920s*. London: Bloomsbury, 2012.

Cain, Peter J. *Hobson and Imperialism: Radicalism, New Liberalism, and Finance, 1887–1938*. Oxford: Oxford University Press, 2002.

Calloway, Colin G. *The Western Abenakis of Vermont, 1600–1800: War, Migration, and the Survival of an Indian People*. Norman: University of Oklahoma Press, 1990.

Campbell, Randolph B. *An Empire for Slavery: The Peculiar Institution in Texas, 1821–1865*. Baton Rouge: Louisiana State University Press, 1989.

Cannadine, David. "Dominion: Britain's Imperial Past in Canada's Imperial Past." In Cannadine, *Making History Now and Then: Discoveries, Controversies and Explorations*, 196–213. Houndmills: Palgrave Macmillan, 2008.

———. "Monarchy: Crowns and Contexts, Thrones and Dominations." In Cannadine, *Making History Now and Then: Discoveries, Controversies and Explorations*, 39–58. Houndmills: Palgrave Macmillan, 2008.

———. *Ornamentalism: How the British Saw Their Empire*. London: Allen Lane, 2001.

Cannadine, David, and Simon Price, eds. *Rituals of Royalty: Power and Ceremonial in Traditional Societies*. Cambridge: Cambridge University Press, 1987.

Canny, Nicholas, and Anthony Pagden, eds. *Colonial Identity in the Atlantic World, 1500–1800*. Princeton, NJ: Princeton University Press, 1987.

Carlos, Ann M., and Stephen Nicholas. "'Giants of Earlier Capitalism': The Chartered Trading Companies as Modern Multinationals." *Business History Review* 62, no. 3 (1988): 398–419.

Casanovas Codina, Joan. *Bread or Bullets! Urban Labor and Spanish Colonialism in Cuba, 1850–1898*. Pittsburgh, PA: University of Pittsburgh Press, 1998.

Castro Gutiérrez, Felipe. *Nueva ley y nuevo rey: Reformas borbónicas y rebelión popular en Nueva España*. Zamora: Colegio de Michoacán, 1996.

Cayuela, José G. *Bahía de Ultramar: España y Cuba en el siglo XIX: El control de las relaciones coloniales*. Madrid: Siglo XXI Editores, 1993.

Cell, John Whitson. *British Colonial Administration in the Mid-Nineteenth Century: The Policy-Making Process*. New Haven, CT: Yale University Press, 1970.

Chaïb, Yassine. "'Domination et mysticisme': Les expériences des Saint-Simoniens et des Fouriéristes; Le champ colonial en Algérie de 1830–1870." In *Le fait colonial au Maghreb: Ruptures et continuités*, edited by Nadir Marouf, 115–34. Paris: L'Harmattan, 2007.

Chaline, Olivier. *Les armées du Roi: Le grand chantier, XVIIe-XVIIIe siècle*. Paris: Armand Colin, 2016.

Chang, David A. *The Color of the Land: Race, Nation, and the Politics of Landownership in Oklahoma, 1832–1929*. Chapel Hill: University of North Carolina Press, 2010.

Changuion, Louis, and Bertus Steenkamp, *Disputed Land: The Historical Development of the South African Land Issue, 1652–2011*. Pretoria: Protea Book House, 2012.

Chaplin, Joyce E. "Race." In *The British Atlantic World, 1500–1800*, edited by David Armitage and Michael J. Braddick, 154–72. Houndmills: Palgrave Macmillan, 2002.

Chappey, Jean-Luc, Bernard Gainot, Guillaume Mazeau, Frédéric Régent, and Pierre Serna, eds. *Pour quoi faire la révolution*. Marseille: Éditions Agone, 2012.

Charbonneau, Hubert, André Guillemette, Jacques Légaré, Bertrand Desjardins, Yves Landry and François Nault, eds. *Naissance d'une population: Les français établis au Canada au XVII siècle*. Montreal: Presses Universitaires de Montreal, 1987.

Chatriot, Alain, and Dieter Gosenwinkel, eds. *Koloniale Politik und Praktiken Deutschlands und Frankreichs, 1880–1962*. Stuttgart: Franz Steiner Verlag, 2010.

Chaudhuri, K. N. *The Trading World of Asia and the English East India Company, 1660–1760*. Cambridge: Cambridge University Press, 1978.

Cheney, Paul. *Revolutionary Commerce: Globalization and the French Monarchy*. Cambridge, MA: Harvard University Press, 2010.

Chesterman, John, and Brian Galligan. *Citizens without Rights: Aborigines and Australian Citizenship*. Cambridge: Cambridge University Press, 1997.

Chust Calero, Manuel, ed. *1808: La eclosión juntera en el mundo hispano*. Mexico City: Fondo de Cultura Económica, 2007.

Chute, Marchette. *The First Liberty: A History of the Right to Vote in America, 1619–1850*. New York: Dutton, 1969.

Cimbala, Paul A. *The Freedmen's Bureau: Reconstructing the American South after the Civil War*. Malabar, FL: Krieger, 2005.

———. *Under the Guardianship of the Nation: The Freedmen's Bureau and the Reconstruction of Georgia, 1865–1870*. Athens: University of Georgia Press, 2003.

Clavero, Bartolomé. "Bioko, 1837–1876: Constitucionalismo de Europa en África; Derecho internacional consuetudinario del trabajo mediante." *Quaderni Fiorentini per la Storia del Pensiero Giuridico Moderno* 35, no. 1 (2006): 429–556.

———. *Derecho indígena y cultura constitucional en América*. Madrid: Siglo XXI Editores, 1994.

———. *Freedom's Law and Indigenous Rights: From Europe's Oeconomy to the Constitutionalism of the Americas*. Berkeley: Robbins Collection, 2005.

———. "Hemisferios de ciudadanía: Constitución española en la América indígena." In *La constitución de Cádiz: Historiografía y conmemoración; Homenaje a Francisco Tomás y Valiente*, edited by José Álvarez Junco and Javier Moreno Luzón, 101–42. Madrid: Centro de Estudios Políticos y Constitucionales, 2006.

———. "¡Libraos de Ultramaria! El fruto podrido de Cádiz." In *Constitución en España: orígenes y destinos*, edited by José María Iñurritegui y José María Portillo, 109–77. Madrid: Centro de Estudios Políticos y Constitucionales, 1998.

———. *El orden de los poderes: Historias Constituyentes de la Trinidad Constitucional*. Madrid, Editorial Trotta, 2007.

———. "Tiempo de colonia, tiempo de constitución." In Clavero, *Derecho indígena y cultura constitucional en América*, 1–52. Madrid: Siglo XXI Editores, 1994.

Clermont Tonnerre, Stanislas de. *Analyse raisonnée de la Constitution française décrété para l'Assemblée Nationale des années 1789, 1790, 1791*. Paris: Migneret Imprimeur, 1791.

Coetzee, Frans. *For Party or Country: Nationalism and the Dilemmas of Popular Conservatism in Edwardian England*. Oxford: Oxford University Press, 1995.

Cohen, William B. *Empereurs sans sceptre: Histoire des administrateurs de la France d'outre-mer et de l'École coloniale*. Paris: Berger-Levrault, 1973.

———. *The French Encounter with Africans: White Response to Blacks, 1530–1880*. Bloomington: Indiana University Press, 1980.

Cohn, Bernard S. "The Command of Languages and the Language of Command." In Cohn, *Colonialism and Its Forms of Knowledge*, 16–56. Princeton, NJ: Princeton University Press, 1996.

Cole, Douglas. "The Problem of 'Nationalism' and 'Imperialism' in British Settlement Colonies." *Journal of British Studies* 10, no. 2 (1971): 160–82.

Coll Toste, Cayetano. "El bando del general Prim contra la raza africana." *Boletín Histórico de Puerto Rico* 2 (1915): 122–26.

Colley, Linda. *Britons: Forging the Nation, 1707–1837*. New Haven, CT: Yale University Press, 1992.

Collier, Timothy. "Administrations coloniales et pacification: L'exemple de Sir Garnet Wolseley en Afrique du Sud (1879–1880)." In *Coloniser, pacifier, administrer: XIXe-XXIe siècles*, edited by Samya el Mechat, 21–34. Paris: CNRS Éditions, 2014.

Collins, James B. *Classes, Estates, and Order in Early-Modern Brittany*. Cambridge: Cambridge University Press, 1994.

Colls, Robert. "Englishness and the Political Culture." In *Englishness: Politics and Culture, 1880–1920*, edited by Robert Colls and Philip Dodd, 29–61. London: Croom Helm, 1987.

Conac, Gérard, and Jean-Pierre Machelon, eds. *La Constitution de l'an III: Boissy d'Anglas et la naissance du libéralisme constitutionnel*. Paris: Presses Universitaires de France, 1999.

Confer, Vincent. "French Colonial Ideas before 1789." *French Historical Studies 3*, no. 3 (1964): 338–59.

Conner, Susan P. *The Age of Napoleon*. Greenwood Guides to Historic Events, 1500–1900. Westport CT: Greenwood Press, 2004.

Conrad, Sebastian. *German Colonialism: A Short History*. Cambridge: Cambridge University Press, 2012.

——. *Globalisation and the Nation in Imperial Germany*. Cambridge: Cambridge University Press, 2010.

——. *What Is Global History?* Princeton, NJ: Princeton University Press, 2016.

Conrad, Sebastian, and Jürgen Osterhammel, eds. *Das Kaiserreich Transnational: Deutschland in der Welt, 1871–1914*. Göttingen: Vandenhoeck & Ruprecht, 2006.

Constantine, Stephen. *Community and Identity: The Making of Modern Gibraltar since 1704*. Manchester: Manchester University Press, 2009.

——. *The Making of British Colonial Development Policy, 1914–1940*. London: Frank Cass, 1984.

Constitution française de l'An VIII; suivie des sénatus-consultes organiques des 14 et 16 Thermidor an X, et du 28 Floréal an XII; et de l'acte additionnel aux constitutions de l'Empire, du 22 avril 1815. Paris: Le Prieur, 1815.

Conway, Stephen. *The British Isles and the War of American Independence*. Oxford: Oxford University Press, 2000.

——. "From Fellow-Nationals to Foreigners: British Perceptions of the Americas, ca. 1739–1783." *William and Mary Quarterly 59*, no. 1 (2002): 65–100.

——. *War, State, and Society in Mid-Eighteenth-Century Britain and Ireland*. Oxford: Oxford University Press, 2006.

Cooper, Frederick. *Citizenship between Empire and Nation: Remaking France and French Africa, 1945–1960*. Princeton, NJ: Princeton University Press, 2014.

——. *Colonialism in Question: Theory, Knowledge, History*. Berkeley: University of California Press, 2005.

Cope, R. L. "Local Imperatives and Imperial Policy: The Sources of Lord Carnarvon's South African Confederation Policy." *International Journal of African Historical Studies 20*, no. 4 (1987): 601–26.

Coquery-Vidrovitch, Catherine. *Enjeux politiques de l'histoire coloniale*. Marseille: Agone, 2009.

——. "Nationalité et Citoyenneté en Afrique occidentale française: Originaires et citoyens dans le Sénégal colonial." *Journal of African History 42* (2001): 285–305.

Costa, Emilia Viotti da. *A aboliçao*. São Paulo: UNESP, 2010.

——. *Crowns of Glory, Tears of Blood: The Demerara Slave Rebellion of 1823*. New York: Oxford University Press, 1994.

Cottias, Myriam. "Le silence de la nation: Les 'vieilles' colonies comme lieu de définition des dogmes républicains (1848–1905)." *Outre-Mers: Revue d'Histoire 90*, no. 338 (2003): 21–45.

Countryman, Edward. *Americans: A Collision of Histories*. New York: Hill & Wang, 1996.

———. "Indians, the Colonial Order, and the Social Significance of the American Revolution." *William and Mary Quarterly* 53, no. 2 (1996): 341–62.

Coupland, Reginald. *The Constitutional Problem in India*. Part I, *The Indian Problem, 1833–1935*. London: Oxford University Press, 1944.

Craig, Gerald M. "Invasion Repulsed." In Craig, *Upper Canada: The Formative Years, 1784–1841*, 66–84. Oxford: Oxford University Press, 2013.

———. *Upper Canada: The Formative Years, 1784–1841*. Oxford: Oxford University Press, 2013.

Crais, Clifton C. *White Supremacy and Black Resistance in Pre-Industrial South Africa: The Making of the Colonial Order in the Eastern Cape, 1770–1865*. Cambridge: Cambridge University Press, 1992.

Crangle, John V. "English Nationalism and British Imperialism in the Age of Gladstone and Disraeli, 1868–1880." *Quarterly Review of Historical Studies* 21, no. 4 (1981): 4–12.

Craton, Michael. *Empire, Enslavement and Freedom in the Caribbean*. Kingston: Ian Randle, 1997.

———. *Testing the Chains: Resistance to Slavery in the British West Indies*. Ithaca, NY: Cornell University Press, 1982.

Craven, Avery O. *Reconstruction: The Ending of the Civil War*. New York: Holt, Rinehart & Winston, 1969.

Cromwell, Valerie, and Zara S. Steiner. "The Foreign Office before 1914: A Study in Resistance." In *Studies in the Growth of Nineteenth-Century Government*, edited by Gillian Sutherland, 167–94. London: Routledge & Kegan Paul, 1972.

Crook, Malcolm. "'Aux urnes, citoyens!' Urban and Rural Behavior during the French Revolution." In *Reshaping France: Town, Country and Region during the French Revolution*, edited by Alan Forrest and Peter Jones, 152–67. Manchester: Manchester University Press, 1991.

———. *Elections in the French Revolution: An Apprenticeship in Democracy, 1789–1799*. Cambridge: Cambridge University Press, 1996.

Cubano, Astrid. *El hilo en el laberinto: Claves de la lucha política en Puerto Rico (siglo XIX)*. Río Piedras: Ediciones Huracán, 1990.

———. "Sociedad e identidad nacional en Cuba y Puerto Rico: un acercamiento comparativo (1868–1898)." *Op. Cit. Revista del Centro de Investigaciones Históricas* 10 (1998): 7–23.

Curran, Andrew S. *The Anatomy of Blackness: Science and Slavery in the Age of Enlightenment*. Baltimore: Johns Hopkins University Press, 2013.

Curry-Machado, Jonathan. *Cuban Sugar Industry: Transnational Networks and Engineering Migrants in Mid-Nineteenth-Century Cuba*. New York: Palgrave Macmillan, 2011.

———. "How Cuba Burned with the Ghosts of British Slavery: Race, Abolition, and the Escalera." *Slavery and Abolition* 25, no. 1 (2004): 71–83.

Curtis, Michael Kent. *No State Shall Abridge: The Fourteenth Amendment and the Bill of Rights*. Durham, NC: Duke University Press, 1986.

———. *Orientalism and Islam: European Thinkers on Oriental Despotism in the Middle East and India*. Cambridge: Cambridge University Press, 2009.

Dailey, Jane Elizabeth. *Before Jim Crow: The Politics of Race in Postemancipation Virginia*. Chapel Hill: University of North Carolina Press, 2000.

Dale, Leigh. "George Grey in Ireland: Narrative and Network." In *Colonial Lives across the British Empire: Imperial Careering in the Long Nineteenth Century*, edited by David Lambert and Alan Lester, 145–75. Cambridge: Cambridge University Press, 2006.

Daniel, Justin. "The French Departements d'Outre-mer: Guadeloupe and Martinique." In *Extended Statehood in the Caribbean: Paradoxes of Quasi Colonialism, Local Autonomy and Extended Statehood in the USA, French, Dutch and British Caribbean*, edited by Lammert de Jong and Dirk Kruijt, 59–84. Amsterdam: Rozenberg Publishers, 2005.

Daniels, Roger. *Guarding the Golden Door: American Immigration Policy and Immigrants since 1882*. New York: Hill & Wang, 2004.

Danley, Mark H., and Patrick J. Speelman, eds. *The Seven Years' War: Global Views*. Leiden: Brill, 2012.

Dargo, George. *Jefferson's Louisiana: Politics and the Clash of Legal Traditions*. Cambridge, MA: Harvard University Press, 1975.

Darwin, John. *The Empire Project: The Rise and Fall of the British World System, 1830–1970*. Cambridge: Cambridge University Press, 2009.

———. "Imperialism and the Victorians: The Dynamics of Territorial Expansion." *The English Historical Review* 112, no. 447 (1997): 614–42.

———. *Unfinished Empire: The Global Expansion of Britain*. London: Allen Lane, 2012.

Daunton, Martin. *Trusting Leviathan: The Politics of Taxation in Britain, 1799–1914*. Cambridge: Cambridge University Press, 2001.

Davenport, T. Rodney, and Christopher Saunders. *South Africa: A Modern History*. Houndmills: Palgrave Macmillan, 2000.

Davis, David Brion. *The Problem of Slavery in the Age of Revolution, 1770–1823*. Ithaca, NY: Cornell University Press, 1975.

Davis, Hugh. *"We Will Be Satisfied with Nothing Less": The African American Struggle for Equal Rights in the North During Reconstruction*. Ithaca, NY: Cornell University Press, 2011.

Davis, William C. *The Last Conquistadores: The Spanish Intervention in Peru and Chile, 1863–1866*. Athens: University of Georgia Press, 1950.

Day, David. *Claiming A Continent: A History of Australia*. Sidney: Harper Perennial, 2005.

Day, Richard J. F. *Multiculturalism and the History of Canadian Diversity*. Toronto: University of Toronto Press, 2002.

De Francesco, Antonino. "Federalist Obsession and Jacobin Conspiracy: France and the United States in a Time of Revolution, 1789–1794." In *Rethinking the Atlantic World: Europe and America in the Age of Democratic Revolutions*, edited by Manuela Albertone and Antonino De Francesco, 239–56. London: Palgrave, 2009.

Debbasch, Charles, and Jean-Marie Pontier. *Les Constitutions de la France*. Paris: Dalloz, 1989.

Debbasch, Yvan. *Couleur et liberté: Le jeu du critère ethnique dans un ordre juridique esclavagiste*. Vol. 1, *L'affranchi dans les possessions françaises de la Caraïbe (1635–1833)*. Paris: Dalloz, 1967.

Debo, Angie. *And Still the Waters Run: The Betrayal of the Five Civilized Tribes*. Norman: University of Oklahoma Press, 1984.

DeConde, Alexander. *The Quasi-War: The Politics and Diplomacy of the Undeclared War with France, 1797–1801*. New York: Scribner, 1966.

Delgado, Josep M. *Dinámicas imperiales (1650–1796): España, América y Europa en el cambio institucional del sistema colonial español*. Barcelona, Bellaterra, 2007.

Dérozier, Albert. "Argüelles y la cuestión de América ante las Cortes de Cádiz de 1810–1814." In *Homenaje a Nöel Salomon: Ilustración española e independencia de América*, edited by Alberto Gil Novales, 159–64. Barcelona: Universidad Autónoma de Barcelona, 1979.

Descours-Gatin, Chantal. *Quand l'opium finançait la colonisation française*. Paris: Éditions L'Harmattan, 1992.

Deville, Robert. *Les départements d'outre-mer: L'autre décolonisation*. Paris: Gallimard, 1996.

Devlin, Jonathan. "The Army, Politics and Public Order in Directorial Provence, 1795–1800." *Historical Journal* 32, no. 1 (1989): 87–106.

di Meglio, Gabriel. *¡Viva el bajo pueblo! La plebe urbana de Buenos Aires y la política entre la revolución de mayo y el rosismo*. Buenos Aires: Prometeo, 2006.

Diario de Sesiones de Cortes. Vol. 3, *1836–1837*. Madrid: Congreso de los Diputados, 1870–77.

Díaz Rementería, Carlos. "La constitución de la sociedad política." In *Historia del Derecho Indiano*, edited by Ismael Sánchez Bella, 167–90. Madrid: Mapfre, 1992.

Dicey, A. V. *Introduction to the Study of the Law of the Constitution*. Houndmills: Palgrave Macmillan, 1985.

Dickinson, H. T. "Britain's Imperial Sovereignty: The Ideological Case against the American Colonists." In *Britain and the American Revolution*, edited by H. T. Dickinson, 64–96. London: Longman, 1998.

———. *Liberty and Property: Political Ideology in Eighteenth-Century Britain*. London: Weidenfeld & Nicolson, 1977.

Dickson, P.G.M. *The Financial Revolution in England: A Study in the Development of Public Credit, 1688–1756*. London: Macmillan, 1967.

Diego García, Emilio de. "Las reformas de Maura, ¿la última oportunidad política en las Antillas?" In *1895: La Guerra de Cuba y la España de la Restauración*, edited by Emilio de Diego García, 99–117. Madrid: Editorial Complutense, 1996.

Din, Gilbert C. *Spaniards, Planters, and Slaves: The Spanish Regulation of Slavery in Louisiana, 1763–1803*. College Station: Texas A&M University Press, 1999.

Dippel, Horst. *Constitucionalismo moderno*. Madrid: Marcial Pons, 2009.

Dixon, Cyril Willis. *The Colonial Administration of Sir Thomas Maitland*. New York: Augustus M. Kelley Publishers, 1969.

Djebari, Youcef. "L'accaparement des terres par les pouvoirs publics." In Djebari, *La France en Algérie: Bilan et controverses; Genèse, développement et limites d'un capitalisme d'Etat colonial*, 1:77–98. Algiers: OPU, 1995.

Dobie, Madeleine. *Trading Places: Colonization and Slavery in Eighteenth-Century French Culture*. Ithaca, NY: Cornell University Press, 2010.

Doeppers, Daniel F. *Feeding Manila in Peace and War, 1850–1945*. Madison: University of Wisconsin Press, 2016.

Domingo Acebrón, María Dolores. "La junta de información en Madrid para las reformas en las Antillas, 1866." *Hispania* 62, no. 1:210 (2002): 141–66.

Domínguez Ortiz, Antonio. *Historia de los moriscos: Vida y tragedia de una minoría*. Madrid: Alianza Editorial, 1985.

Donald, David Herbert. *Charles Sumner and the Rights of Man*. New York: Alfred A. Knopf, 1970.

———. *The Politics of Reconstruction, 1863–1867*. Baton Rouge: Louisiana State University Press, 1965.

Doolen, Andy. *Fugitive Empire: Locating Early American Imperialism*. Minneapolis: University of Minnesota Press, 2005.

Dooling, Wayne. *Slavery, Emancipation and Colonial Rule in South Africa*. Athens: Ohio University Press, 2007.

Dorsett, Shaunnagh. "'Destitute of the Knowledge of God': Maori Testimony before the New Zealand Courts in the Early Crown Colony Period." In *Past Law, Present Histories*, edited by Diane Kirby, 39–57. Canberra: ANU Press, 2012.

Downs, Gregory P. *After Appomattox: Military Occupation and the Ends of War*. Cambridge, MA: Harvard University Press, 2015.

Doyle, Michael W. *Empires*. Ithaca, NY: Cornell University Press, 1986.

Drescher, Seymour. *Capitalism and Antislavery: British Mobilization in Comparative Perspective*. London: Macmillan Press, 1986.

———. *Econocide: British Slavery in the Era of Abolition*. Pittsburgh, PA: University of Pittsburgh Press, 1977.

———. *The Mighty Experiment: Free Labor versus Slavery in British Emancipation*. Oxford: Oxford University Press, 2002.

Droessler, Holger. "Germany's El Dorado in the Pacific: Metropolitan Representations and Colonial Realities, 1884–1914." In *Imperial Expectations and Realities: El Dorados, Utopias and Dystopias*, edited by Andrekos Varnava, 105–24. Manchester: Manchester University Press, 2015.

Du Bois, Duncan. "The 'Coolie Curse': The Evolution of White Colonial Attitudes Towards the Indian Question, 1860–1900." *Historia* 57, no. 2 (2012): 31–67.

Dubois, Laurent. "'African Citizens': Slavery, Freedom and Migration during the French Revolution." In *Migration Control in the North Atlantic: The Evolution of State Practices in Europe and the United States from the French Revolution to the Inter-War Period*, edited by Andreas Fahrmeier, Olivier Faron, Patrick Weil, 25–38. New York: Berghahn Books, 2003.

———. *Avengers of the New World: The Story of the Haitian Revolution*. Cambridge, MA: Harvard University Press, 2004.

———. *A Colony of Citizens: Revolution and Slave Emancipation in the French Caribbean, 1787–1804*. Chapel Hill: University of North Carolina Press, 2004.

———. "Inscribing Race in the Revolutionary French Antilles." In *The Color of Liberty: Histories of Race in France*, edited by Sue Peabody and Tyler Stovall, 95–107. Durham, NC: Duke University Press, 2003.

———. "The Promise of Revolution: Saint-Domingue and the Struggle for Autonomy in Guadeloupe, 1797–1802." In *The Impact of the Haitian Revolution in the Atlantic World*, edited by David P. Geggus, 112–56. Columbia: University of South Carolina Press, 2001.

Dubow, Saul. "Colonial Nationalism: The Milner Kindergarten and the Rise of South Africanism, 1902–1910." *History Workshop Journal* 43 (1997): 53–85.

———. "The Elaboration of Segregationist Ideology." In *Segregation and Apartheid in Twentieth-Century South Africa*, edited by William Beinart and Saul Dubow, 145–75. London: Routledge, 1995.

Ducharme, Michel. *The Idea of Liberty in Canada during the Age of Atlantic Revolutions, 1776–1838*. Montreal: McGill-Queen's University Press, 2014.

Duffy, Michael. *Soldiers, Sugar, and Seapower: The British Expeditions to the West Indies and the War against Revolutionary France*. Oxford: Clarendon Press, 1987.

Duly, L. C. "The Failure of British Land Policy at the Cape, 1812–1828." *Journal of African History* 6, no. 3 (1965): 357–71.

Duminy, Andrew, and Charles Ballard. *The Anglo-Zulu War: New Perspectives*. Pietermaritzburg: University of Natal Press, 1981.

Dummett, Ann, and Andrew G. L. Nicol. *Subjects, Citizens, Aliens and Others: Nationality and Immigration Law*. London: Weindenfeld & Nicolson, 1990.

Dunaway, Wilma A. *The First American Frontier: Transition to Capitalism in Southern Appalachia, 1700–1860*. Chapel Hill: University of North Carolina Press, 1996.

Dungy, Kathryn R. *The Conceptualization of Race in Colonial Puerto Rico, 1800–1850*. New York: Peter Lang, 2015.

Dunwoodie, Peter. "Assimilation, Cultural Identity, and Permissible Deviance in Francophone Algerian Writing of the Interwar Years." In *Algeria and France, 1800–2000: Identity, Memory, Nostalgia*, edited by Patricia M. E. Lorcin, 63–83. Syracuse: Syracuse University Press, 2006.

———. *Writing French Algeria*. Oxford: Clarendon Press, 2004.

Durham, Walter T. *Before Tennessee: The Southwest Territory, 1790–1796*. Piney Flats, TN: Rocky Mount Historical Association, 1990.

Duvergier, J. A. *Collection complète de lois, décrets, ordonnances, règlements, et avis du Conseil d'État*. Paris: A. Guyot, 1834.

Eccles, William J. *Canada under Louis XIV, 1663–1701*. Toronto: McClelland and Stewart, 1963.

Echard, William E. *Napoleon III and the Concert of Europe*. Baton Rouge: Louisiana State University Press, 1983.

Edelstein, Dan. *The Terror of Natural Right: Republicanism, the Cult of Nature and the French Revolution*. Chicago: University of Chicago Press, 2009.

Edelstein, Melvin. *The French Revolution and the Birth of Electoral Democracy*. Farnham: Ashgate, 2014.

Edmunds, R. David. *Tecumseh and the Quest for Indian Leadership*. Boston: Little Brown, 1984.

Edwards, Bryan. *The History, Civil and Commercial, of the British West Indies*. New York: AMS Press Inc., 1966.

Egnal, Marc. *A Mighty Empire: The Origins of the American Revolution*. Ithaca, NY: Cornell University Press, 1988.

Ehrard, Jean. *Lumières et Esclavage: L'esclavage colonial et l'opinion publique en France au XVIIIe siècle*. Brussels: André Versaille, 2008.

Einhorn, Robin L. *American Taxation, American Slavery*. Chicago: University of Chicago Press, 2006.

Ekirch, A. Roger. *Bound for America: The Transportation of British Convicts to the Colonies, 1718-1775*. Oxford: Clarendon Press, 1987.

Elbourne, Elizabeth. "Indigenous Peoples and Imperial Networks in the Early Nineteenth Century: The Politics of Knowledge." In *Rediscovering the British World*, edited by Philip Buckner and R. Douglas Frances, 59-83. Calgary: University of Calgary Press, 2005.

Elisabeth, Léo. "L'abolition de l'esclavage à la Martinique." *Mémoires de la Société d'Histoire de la Martinique* 5 (1983).

Elizalde Pérez-Grueso, María Dolores. *España en el Pacífico: La colonia de las islas Carolinas, 1855-1899*. Madrid: CSIC, 1992.

Elliott, John H. *Empires of the Atlantic World: Britain and Spain in America, 1492-1830*. New Haven, CT: Yale University Press, 2006.

———. "A Europe of Composite Monarchies." In Elliott, *Spain, Europe and the Wider World, 1500-1800*, 3-25. New Haven, CT: Yale University Press, 2009.

———. "Spain and Its Empire in the Sixteenth and Seventeenth Centuries." In Elliott, *Spain and Its World, 1500-1700*, 7-26. New Haven, CT: Yale University Press, 1989.

———. *Spain and Its World, 1500-1700*. New Haven, CT: Yale University Press, 1989.

———. "The Spanish Monarchy and the Kingdom of Portugal, 1580-1640." In *Conquest and Coalescence: The Shaping of the State in Early Modern Europe*, edited by Mark Greengrass, 45-67. London: Edward Arnold, 1991.

Elorza, Antonio, and Elena Hernández Sandoica. *La Guerra de Cuba (1895-1898)*. Madrid: Alianza Editorial, 1999.

Eltis, David. *Economic Growth and the Ending of the Transatlantic Slave Trade*. New York: Oxford University Press, 1987.

Emmer, Pieter C. "Immigration in the Caribbean: the Introduction of Chinese and East Indian Indentured Labourers Between 1839 and 1917." In *European Expansion and Migration: Essays on the Intercontinental Migration from Africa, Asia, and Europe*, edited by Pieter C. Emmer and Magnus Mörner, 245-76. New York: Berg, 1992.

Enders, Armelle. " 'Races', 'castes', 'classes': Dynamiques sociales et politiques dans les empires coloniaux." In *Les empires coloniaux, XIXe-XXe siècle*, edited by Pierre Singaravélou, 77-124. Paris: Éditions Points, 2013.

Engelstein, Laura. *Slavophile Empire: Imperial Russia's Illiberal Path*. Ithac, NY: Cornell University Press, 2009.

Entralgo, Elías J. *Los diputados por Cuba en las Cortes de España durante los tres primeros periodos constitucionales*. Havana: Imprenta del Siglo XX, 1945.

Epalza, Mikel de. *Los moriscos antes y después de la expulsión*. Madrid: Mapfre, 1992.

Errington, Jane. *The Lion, the Eagle, and Upper Canada: A Developing Colonial Ideology*. Montreal: McGill-Queen's University Press, 2012.

Eustace, Nicole. *1812: War and the Passions of Patriotism*. Philadelphia: University of Pennsylvania Press, 2012.

Evans, Julie, and David Philips. "South Africa: Saving the White Voters from Being 'Utterly Swamped.' " In *Equal Subjects, Unequal Rights: Indigenous Peoples in British Settler Colonies, 1830-1910*, edited by Julie Evans, Patricia Grimshaw, David Phillips, and Shurlee Swain, 157-81. Manchester: Manchester University Press, 2003.

Evans, Julie, Patricia Grimshaw, David Phillips, and Shurlee Swain. *Equal Subjects,*

Unequal Rights: Indigenous Peoples in British Settler Colonies, 1830–1910. Manchester: Manchester University Press, 2003.

Fahrmeir, Andreas. *Citizenship: The Rise and Fall of a Modern Concept*. New Haven, CT: Yale University Press, 2007.

———. *Revolutionen und Reformen: Europa, 1789–1850*. Munich: C. H. Beck, 2010.

Fallon, Joseph E. "Federal Policy and U.S. Territories: The Political Restructuring of the United States of America." *Pacific Affairs* 64, no. 1 (1991): 23–41.

Fallope, Josette. *Esclaves et citoyens: Les Noirs à la Guadeloupe au XIXe siècle dans les processus de résistance et d'intégration (1802–1910)*. Basse-Terre: Société d'Histoire de la Guadeloupe, 1992.

———. "La politique d'assimilation et ses résistances." In *La Guadeloupe, 1875–1914: Les soubresauts d'une société pluriethnique ou les ambiguïtés de l'assimilation*, edited by Henriette Levillain, 35–47. Paris: Autrement, 1994.

Favier, Jean. *Doléances des peuples coloniaux à l'Assemblée nationale constituante: 1789–1790*, Paris: Archives Nationales, 1989.

Fehrenbacher, Don E. *The Dred Scott Case, Its Significance in American Law and Politics*. New York: Oxford University Press, 1978.

———. *The Slaveholding Republic: An Account of the United States Government's Relations to Slavery*. Oxford: Oxford University Press, 2001.

———. *Slavery, Law, and Politics: The Dred Scott Case in Historical Perspective*. New York: Oxford University Press, 1981.

Feinstein, Charles H. *An Economic History of South Africa: Conquest, Discrimination and Development*. Cambridge: Cambridge University Press, 2005.

Fenge, Terry, and Jim Aldridge, eds. *Keeping Promises: The Royal Proclamation of 1763, Aboriginal Rights, and Treaties in Canada*. Montreal: McGill-Queen's University Press, 2015.

Ferling, John E. *Adams vs. Jefferson: The Tumultuous Election of 1800*. New York: Oxford University Press, 2004.

Fernández Albaladejo, Pablo. *Fragmentos de Monarquía*. Madrid: Alianza Editorial, 1992.

Feros, Antonio. *Speaking of Spain: The Evolution of Race and Nation in the Hispanic World*. Cambridge, MA: Harvard University Press, 2017.

Ferrer, Ada. *Freedom's Mirror: Cuba and Haiti in the Age of Revolution*. Cambridge: Cambridge University Press, 2014.

———. "Haiti, Free Soil, and Antislavery in the Revolutionary Atlantic." *American Historical Review* 117, no. 1 (2012): 40–66.

———. *Insurgent Cuba: Race, Nation, and Revolution, 1868–1898*. Chapel Hill: University of North Carolina Press, 1999.

Ferrer Martínez, Miguel. *El general Tacón, marqués de la unión de Cuba, y el conde de Villanueva: O sea, contestación a varios artículos en favor del primero y contra el segundo*. Madrid: Imprenta L. Amarita, 1838.

Fick, Carolyn E. *The Making of Haiti: The Saint-Domingue Revolution from Below*. Knoxville: University of Tennessee Press, 1990.

Fiévet, Claude, ed. *Invention et réinvention de la citoyenneté: Actes du colloque international de Pau, 9–11 décembre 1998*. Pau: Éditions Joëlle Sampy, 2000.

Figes, Orlando. *Crimea, the Last Crusade*. Hardmondsworth: Penguin, 2011.

Figueroa, Luis A. *Sugar, Slavery, and Freedom in Nineteenth-Century Puerto Rico.* Chapel Hill: University of North Carolina Press, 2005.

Finkelman, Paul. "Jefferson and Slavery: Treason against the Hopes of the World." In *Jeffersonian Legacies*, edited by Peter S. Onuf, 181–221. Charlottesville: University of Virginia Press, 1993.

Fisher, Andrew B., and Matthew D. O'Hara. *Imperial Subjects: Race and Identity in Colonial Latin America.* Durham, NC: Duke University Press, 2009.

Fisher, John R., Allan J. Kuethe, and Anthony McFarlane, eds. *Reform and Insurrection in Bourbon New Granada and Peru.* Baton Rouge: Louisiana State University Press, 1990.

Fitzgerald, David Scott, and David Cook-Martin. *Culling the Masses: The Democratic Origins of Racist Immigration Policy in the Americas.* Cambridge, MA: Harvard University Press, 2014.

Fitzpatrick, Matthew P. *Liberal Imperialism in Germany: Expansionism and Nationalism, 1848–1884.* New York: Berghahn Books, 2008.

Fixico, Donald Lee. *The Invasion of Indian Country in the Twentieth Century: American Capitalism and Tribal Natural Resources.* Niwot: University Press of Colorado, 1998.

Fladeland, Betty. *Abolitionists and Working-Class Problems in the Age of Industrialization.* Baton Rouge: Louisiana State University Press, 1984.

Flaquer Montequi, Rafael. "El Ejecutivo en la revolución liberal." In *Las Cortes de Cádiz*, edited by Miguel Artola, 37–66. Madrid: Marcial Pons Historia, 2003.

Flórez Estrada, Álvaro. "Examen imparcial de las disensiones de la América con la España, de los medios de su reconciliación y de la prosperidad de todas las naciones." *Obras de Álvaro Flórez Estrada*, t. 113, v. 2. Madrid: Biblioteca de Autores Españoles, 1950.

Foner, Eric. *Free Soil, Free Labor, Free Men: The Ideology of the Republican Party before the Civil War.* New York: Oxford University Press, 1970.

———. *Reconstruction: America's Unfinished Revolution, 1863–1877.* New York: Harper & Row, 1988.

Foner, Laura. "The Free People of Color in Louisiana and St. Domingue: A Comparative Portrait of Two Three-Caste Slave Societies." *Journal of Social History* 3, no. 4 (1970): 406–30.

Foner, Nancy, and George M. Fredrickson. "Immigration, Race, and Ethnicity in the United States: Social Constructions and Social Relations in Historical and Contemporary Perspective." In *Not Just Black and White: Historical and Contemporary Perspectives on Immigration, Race, and Ethnicity in the United States*, edited by Nancy Foner and George M. Fredrickson, 1–22. New York: Russell Sage Foundation, 2004.

Fontana, Josep. *La revolución liberal: Política y hacienda en 1833–1845.* Madrid: Instituto de Estudios Fiscales, 1977.

Forbes, Robert Pierce. *The Missouri Compromise and Its Aftermath: Slavery and the Meaning of America.* Chapel Hill: North Carolina University Press, 2004.

Forrest, Alan. "L'armée, la guerre et les politiques de la Terreur." In *Les politiques de la Terreur, 1793–1794*, edited by Michel Biard, 53–67. Rennes: Presses Universitaires de Rennes/Société des Études Robespierristes, 2008.

Forster, Ben. *A Conjunction of Interests: Business, Politics, and Tariffs, 1825–1879.* Toronto: Toronto University Press, 1986.

Forster, Elborg, and Robert Forster, eds. *Sugar and Slavery, Family and Race: The Letters and Diary of Pierre Dessalles, Planter in Martinique, 1808–1856.* Baltimore: Johns Hopkins University Press, 1996.

Föster, Stig, Wolfgang J. Mommsen, and Ronald Robinson, eds. *Bismarck, Europe, and Africa: The Berlin Africa Conference 1884–1885 and the Onset of Partition.* Oxford: Oxford University Press, 1989.

Fox, Ralph. *The Colonial Policy of British Imperialism.* Oxford: Oxford University Press, 2008.

Fradera, Josep M. *Colonias para después de un imperio.* Barcelona: Edicions Bellaterra, 2005.

———. *Cultura nacional en una societat dividida: Patriotisme i cultura a Catalunya (1838–1868).* Barcelona: Edicions Curial, 1992.

———. *Gobernar colonias.* Barcelona: Península, 1999.

———. "Las fronteras de la nación y el ocaso de la expansión hispánica." In *Más se perdió en Cuba: España, 1898 y la crisis de fin de siglo,* edited by Juan Pan-Montojo, 483–557. Madrid: Alianza, 2006.

———. "Juan Prim y Prats (1814–1870): Prim conspirador o la pedagogía del sable." In *Liberales, agitadores y conspiradores: Biografías heterodoxas del siglo XIX,* edited by Isabel Burdiel and Manuel Pérez Ledesma, 239–66. Madrid: Espasa Calpe, 2000.

———. "Raza y ciudadanía: El factor racial en la delimitación de los derechos de los americanos." In Fradera, *Gobernar colonias,* 51–70. Barcelona: Península, 1999.

———. "Reading Imperial Transitions: Spanish Contraction, British Expansion and American Irruption." In *Colonial Crucible: Empire in the Making of the Modern American State,* edited by Alfred W. McCoy and Francisco A. Scarano, 34–62. Madison: University of Wisconsin Press, 2009.

———. "Tainted Citizenship and Imperial Constitutions: The Case of the Spanish Constitution of 1812." In *Citizenship and Empire in Europe 200–1900: The Antonine Constitution after 1800 years,* edited by Clifford Ando, 221–42. Stuttgart: Franz Steiner Verlag, 2016.

———. "Why Were Spain's Special Overseas Laws Never Enacted?" In *Spain, Europe and the Atlantic World: Essays in Honour of John H. Elliott,* edited by Richard L. Kagan and Geoffrey Parker, 334–49. Cambridge: Cambridge University Press, 1995.

Francis, Mark. *Governors and Settlers: Images of Authority in the British Colonies, 1820–1860.* London: Palgrave Macmillan, 1992.

Franco, Antonio-Filiu. *Cuba en los orígenes del constitucionalismo español: La alternativa descentralizadora, 1808–1837.* Zaragoza: Fundación Giménez Abad, 2001.

Frank, Jason A. *Constituent Moments: Enacting the People in Postrevolutionary America.* Durham, NC: Duke University Press, 2010.

Frasquet, Ivana. "Milicianos y soldados: La problemática social mexicana en la invasión de 1829." In *Las ciudades y la guerra, 1750–1898,* edited by Salvador Broseta, 115–32. Castelló de la Plana: Edicions de la Universitat Jaume I, 2002.

Fredrickson, George M. *The Black Image in the White Mind: The Debate on Afro-American Character and Destiny, 1817–1914.* New York: Harper & Row, 1971.

Freehling, William W. *The Road to Disunion*. Vol. 1, *Secessionists at Bay, 1776–1854*. New York: Oxford University Press, 1990.

Frégault, Guy. *Canada: The War of the Conquest*. Toronto: Oxford University Press, 1969.

Frémeaux, Jacques. *Les Bureaux Arabes: Dans l'Algérie de la conquête*. Paris: Denoël, 1993.

———. *La France et l'Algérie en guerre, 1830–1870, 1954–1962*. Paris: Economica, 2002.

Friedman, Lawrence J. *The White Savage: Racial Fantasies in the Postbellum South*. Englewood Cliffs, NJ: Prentice Hall, 1970

Frostin, Charles. *Les révoltes blanches à Saint-Domingue aux XVIIe et XVIIIe siècles (Haïti avant 1789)*. Paris: Éditions de l'École, 1975.

Fuente, Alejandro de la. *A Nation for All: Race, Inequality, and Politics in Twentieth-Century Cuba*. Chapel Hill: University of North Carolina Press, 2001.

Fuente Monge, Gregorio de la. *Los revolucionarios de 1868: Élites y poder en la España liberal*. Madrid: Marcial Pons, 2000.

Fuma, Sudel. "Un apprentissage difficile de la citoyenneté: Les anciens esclaves de l'Ile de La Réunion et les élections législatives de 1870 sous la IIIe République." In *Les élections législatives et sénatoriales outre-mer: 1848–1981*, edited by Laurent Jalabert, Bertrand Joly, and Jacques Weber, 153–62. Paris: Les Indes Savantes, 2010.

Gaffaney, Timothy J. *Freedom for the Poor: Welfare and the Foundations of Democratic Citizenship*. Boulder, CO: Westview Press, 2000.

Gainot, Bernard. "Les élections sous le Directoire sont-elles des élections libres?" In *Citoyen et citoyenneté sous la Révolution française*, edited by Raymonde Monnier, 211–34. Paris: Société des Études Robespierristes, 2006.

———. "Le géneral Laveaux, gouverneur de Saint-Domingue, député néo-jacobin." *Annales historiques de la Révolution française* 278, no. 1 (1989): 433–54.

———. "Métropole/Colonies: Projets constitutionnels et rapports de forces, 1798–1802." In *Rétablissement de l'esclavage dans les colonies françaises: Aux origines de Haïti*, edited by Yves Bénot and Marcel Dorigny, 13–28. Paris: Maisonneuve et Larose, 2003.

———. *Les officiers de couleur dans les armées de la République et de l'Empire (1792–1815): De l'esclavage à la condition militaire dans les Antilles françaises*. Paris: Karthala, 2007.

———. "Quel(s) statut(s) pour les cultivateurs sous le régime de la liberté générale? (1794–1802) ou 'Comment peut-on allier, sous la zone torride, l'industrie au bonheur?' (D. Lescallier)." In *La plantation coloniale esclavagiste, XVIIe–XIXe siècles*, edited by Danielle Bégot, 23–46. Paris: Éditions de CTHS, 2008.

———. "The Republican Imagination and Race: The Case of Haitian Revolution." In *Rethinking the Atlantic World: Europe and America in the Age of Democratic Revolutions*, edited by Manuela Albertone and Antonino De Francesco, 276–93. London: Palgrave, 2009.

Galasso, Giuseppe. *En la periferia del imperio: La monarquía hispánica y el Reino de Nápoles*. Barcelona: Península, 1994.

Galbraith, John S. *Reluctant Empire: British Policy on the South African Frontier, 1834–1854*. Berkeley: University of California Press, 1963.

García, Armando, Raquel Álvarez, and Consuelo Naranjo Orovio. *En busca de la raza perfecta: Eugenesia e Higiene en Cuba (1989–1958)*. Madrid: CSIC, 1999.

García Arenal, Mercedes. *Los moriscos*. Granada: Universidad de Granada, 1975.

Garcia Balañà, Albert. "'The Empire Is No Longer a Unit': Declining Imperial Expectations and Transatlantic Crises in Metropolitan Spain, 1859–1909." In *Endless Empire: Spain's Retreat, Europe's Eclipse, America's Decline*, edited by Alfred W. McCoy, Josep M. Fradera, and Stephen J. Jacobson, 92–103. Madison: University of Wisconsin Press, 2012.

———. "Racializing the Nation in 19th-Century Spain (1820–1865): A Transatlantic Approach." *Journal of Iberian and Latin American Studies* (forthcoming, 2018).

———. "Tradició liberal i política colonial a Catalunya: Mig segle de temptatives i limitacions, 1822–1872." *Catalunya i Ultramar: Poder i negoci a les colònies espanyoles (1750-1914)*, 77–106. Barcelona: Museu Marítim, 1995.

García Cantús, María Dolores. *Fernando Poo, Una aventura colonial española: Las islas en litigio; entre la esclavitud y el abolicionismo, 1776–1846*. Vic: Ceiba, 2006.

García de Enterría, Eduardo. *La administración española: Estudios de ciencia administrativa*. Madrid: Alianza Editorial, 1972.

García Hernán, Enrique. *Consejero de ambos mundos: Vida y obra de Juan Solórzano Pereira (1575-1655)*. Madrid: Mapfre, 2007.

García Mora, Luis Miguel. "Tras la revolución, las reformas: El Partido Liberal cubano y los proyectos reformistas tras la Paz de Zanjón." In *Cuba, la perla de las Antillas: Actas de las I jornadas sobre "Cuba y su historia,"* edited by Consuelo Naranjo y Tomás Mallo, 197–212. Madrid: CSIC, 1994.

Garriga, Carlos, and Marta Lorente. *Cádiz, 1812: La Constitución jurisdiccional*. Madrid: Centro de Estudios Políticos y Constitucionales, 2007.

Garrigus, John D. *Before Haiti: Race and Citizenship in French Saint-Domingue*. New York: Palgrave Macmillan, 2006.

Garrison, Tim Alan. *The Legal Ideology of Removal: The Southern Judiciary and the Sovereignty of Native American Nations*. Athens: University of Georgia Press, 2009.

Gates, Henry Louis, Jr., ed. *Lincoln on Race and Slavery*. Princeton, NJ: Princeton University Press, 2009.

Gauthier, Florence. "La Révolution française et le problème colonial, 1789–1804: État des connaissances et perspectives de recherche." In *La Révolution française au carrefour des recherches*, edited by Martine Lapied and Christine Peyrard, 101–14. Aix-en-Provence: Publications de l'Université de Provence, 2004.

———. *Triomphe et mort du droit naturel en Révolution, 1789–1795–1802*. Paris: Presses Universitaires de France, 1992.

Geggus, David P. "The Caribbean in the Age of Revolution." In *The Age of Revolutions in Global Context, c. 1760-1840*, edited by David Armitage and Sanjay Subrahmanyam, 83–100. London: Palgrave, 2010.

———, ed. *The Impact of the Haitian Revolution in the Atlantic World*. Columbia: University of South Carolina Press, 2001.

———. *Slavery, War, and Revolution: The British Occupation of Saint Domingue, 1793–1798*. Oxford: Clarendon Press, 1982.

Gelabert González, Juan Eloy. *La bolsa del rey: Rey, reino y fisco en Castilla (1598-1648)*. Barcelona: Crítica, 1997.

Gelman, Jorge, Enrique Llopis, and Carlos Marichal, eds. *Iberoamérica y España antes de las independencias, 1700–1820: Crecimiento, reformas y crisis*. Mexico City: El Colegio de México, 2014.

Gerstle, Gary. *American Crucible: Race and Nation in the Twentieth Century*. Princeton, NJ: Princeton University Press, 2001.

Getz, Trevor R. *Slavery and Social Reform in West Africa: Toward Emancipation in Nineteenth-Century Senegal and the Gold Coast*. Athens: Ohio University Press, 2004.

Ghachem, Malick W. *The Old Regime and the Haitian Revolution*. Cambridge: Cambridge University Press, 2012.

——. "The Trap of Representation: Sovereignty, Slavery and the Road to the Haitian Revolution." *Historical Reflections/Réflexions Historiques* 29 (2003): 123–44.

Ghosh, R. N. *Classical Macroeconomics and the Case for Colonies*. Calcutta: New Publishers, 1967.

Gibson, Charles. *Tlaxcala in the Sixteenth Century*. New Haven, CT: Yale University Press, 1954.

Gil Pujol, Xavier. *La Fábrica de la Monarquía: Traza y Conservación de la Monarquía de España de los Reyes Católicos y de los Austrias*. Madrid: Real Academia de la Historia, 2016.

Giliomee, Hermann. *The Afrikaners: Biography of a People*. London: Horst & Co., 2011.

Giménez Fernández, Manuel. *Bartolomé de las Casas*. Vol. 2, *Capellán de S.M. Carlos I. Poblador de Cumaná (1517–1523)*. Madrid: CSIC, 1984.

Girard, Philip. "Liberty, Order, and Pluralism: The Canadian Experience." In *Exclusionary Empire: English Liberty Overseas, 1600–1900*, edited by Jack P. Greene, 160–90. Cambridge: Cambridge University Press, 2010.

Girard, Philippe R. *The Slaves Who Defeated Napoleon: Toussaint Louverture and the Haitian War of Independence, 1801–1804*. Tuscaloosa: University of Alabama Press, 2011.

Giraud, Marcel. *Le Métis canadien: Son rôle dans l'histoire des provinces de l'Ouest*. Paris: Institut d'Ethnologie, 1945.

Girault, Arthur. *Principes de la colonisation et de législation coloniale*. Paris: Larose, 1895.

Girollet, Anne. "La politique colonial de la Seconde République: Un assimilationnisme modéré." *Revue française d'outre-mer* 85, no. 320 (1998): 71–83.

Glaser, John F. "English Nonconformity and the Decline of Liberalism." *American Historical Review* 63, no. 2 (1958): 352–63.

Glete, Jan. *War and the State in Early Modern Europe: Spain, the Dutch Republic and Sweden as Fiscal-Military States, 1500–1660*. London: Routledge, 2002.

Go, Julian. "Imperial Power and Its Limits: America's Colonial Empire in the Early Twentieth Century." In *Lessons of Empire: Imperial Histories and American Power*, edited by Craig J. Calhoun, Frederick Cooper, and Kevin W. Moore, 201–14. New York: The New Press, 2005.

Godechot, Jacques, ed. *Les Constitutions de la France depuis 1789*. Paris: Garnier Flammarion, 1970.

——. *La Révolution française dans le Midi toulousain*. Toulouse: Privat, 1986.

Goldfrank, David A. *The Origins of the Crimean War*. London: Routledge, 1994.

Goldring, Philip. "Province and Nation: Problems of Imperial Rule in Lower Canada, 1820 to 1841." *Journal of Imperial and Commonwealth Studies* 9, no. 1 (1980): 38–56.

Goldstone, Lawrence. *Inherently Unequal: The Betrayal of Equal Rights by the Supreme Court, 1865–1903*. New York: Walker and Co., 2010.

Gómez Azevedo, Labor. *Organización y reglamentación del trabajo en el Puerto Rico del siglo XIX*. San Juan: Instituto de Cultura Puertorriqueña, 1970.

Gómez Rivas, León. *El virrey del Perú don Francisco de Toledo*. Toledo: Instituto Provincial de Investigaciones y Estudios Toledanos, 1994.

Góngora, Mario. *Studies in the Colonial History of Spanish America*. Cambridge: Cambridge University Press, 1975.

González Calleja, Eduardo, and Antonio Fontecha Pedraza. *Una cuestión de honor: La polémica sobre la anexión de Santo Domingo vista desde España (1861-1865)*. Santo Domingo: Fundación García Arévalo, 2005.

Goodfellow, Clement Francis. *Great Britain and South African Confederation, 1870-1881*. Oxford: Oxford University Press, 1966.

Gorman, Daniel. *Imperial Citizenship: Empire and the Question of Belonging*. Manchester: Manchester University Press, 2008.

Goswami, Manu. "Rethinking the Modular Nation Form: Toward a Sociohistorical Conception of Nationalism." *Comparative Studies in Society and History* 40, no. 4 (2002): 770-99.

Gott, Richard. *Britain's Empire: Resistance, Repression and Revolt*. London: Verso, 2011.

Gould, Eliga H. "Fears of War, Fantasies of Peace: British Politics and the Coming of the American Revolution." In *Empire and Nation: The American Revolution in the Atlantic World*, edited by Eliga H. Gould and Peter S. Onuf, 19-34. Baltimore: Johns Hopkins University, 2005.

———. "The Question of Home Rule." *William and Mary Quarterly* 64, no. 2 (2007): 255-58.

———. *The Persistence of Empire: British Political Culture in the Age of the American Revolution*. Chapel Hill: University of North Carolina Press, 2000.

Gould, Eliga H., and Peter S. Onuf, eds. *Empire and Nation: The American Revolution in the Atlantic World*. Baltimore: Johns Hopkins University Press, 2015.

Goveia, Elsa V. *A Study on the Historiography of the British West Indies to the End of the Nineteenth Century*. Washington, DC: Howard University Press, 1980.

Graham, Aaron, and Patrick Walsh, eds. *The British Fiscal-Military States, 1660-c.1783*. London: Routledge, 2016.

Granados, Luis Fernando. *En el espejo haitiano: Los indios del Bajío y el colapso del orden colonial en América Latina*. Mexico City: Ediciones Era, 2016.

Grant, William L. "Canada vs. Guadeloupe: An Episode of the Seven Years' War." *American Historical Review* 17, no. 4 (1912): 735-43.

Gray, Ralph D., and Michael A. Morrison, eds. *New Perspectives on the Early Republic: Essays from the Journal of the Early Republic, 1981-1991*. Urbana: University of Illinois Press, 1994.

Green, E.H.H. *The Crisis of Conservatism: The Politics, Economics and Ideology of the British Conservative Party, 1880-1914*. London: Routledge, 1995.

Green, Michael D. *The Politics of Indian Removal: Creek Government and Society in Crisis*. Lincoln: University of Nebraska Press, 1992.

Green, William A. *British Slave Emancipation: The Sugar Colonies and the Great Experiment, 1830-1865*. Oxford: Clarendon Press, 1988.

Greene, Jack P. "All Men Are Created Equal: Some Reflections on the Character of the American Revolution." In *Imperatives, Behaviors, and Identities: Essays in Early American Cultural History*, 236–67. Charlottesville: University of Virginia Press, 1992.

———. "Colonial History and National History: Reflections on a Continuing Problem." *William and Mary Quarterly* 64, no. 2 (2007): 235–50.

———. *The Constitutional Origins of the American Revolution*. Cambridge: Cambridge University Press, 2011.

———, ed. *Exclusionary Empire: English Liberty Overseas, 1600–1900*. Cambridge: Cambridge University Press, 2010.

———. *Imperatives, Behaviors, and Identities: Essays in Early American Cultural History*. Charlottesville: University of Virginia Press, 1992.

———. "Liberty and Slavery: The Transfer of British Liberty to the West Indies, 1627–1865." In *Exclusionary Empire: English Liberty Overseas, 1600–1900*, edited by Jack P. Greene, 50–76. Cambridge: Cambridge University Press, 2010.

———. "Negotiated Authorities: The Problem of Governance in the Extended Polities of the Early Modern Atlantic World." In *Negotiated Authorities: Essays in Colonial Political and Constitutional History*, edited by Jack P. Greene, 1–24. Charlottesville: University of Virginia Press, 1994.

———. *Peripheries and Center: Constitutional Development in the Extended Polities of the British Empire and the United States, 1607–1788*. New York: W. W. Norton, 1990.

———. *Pursuits of Happiness: The Social Development of Early Modern British Colonies and the Formation of American Culture*. Chapel Hill: The North Carolina University Press, 1988.

———. "The Seven Years' War and the American Revolution: The Causal Relationship Reconsidered." In *The British Atlantic Empire before the American Revolution*, edited by Peter Marshall and Glyndwr Williams, 87–108. London: Routledge, 1980.

———. "Traditions of Consensual Governance in the Construction of State Authority in the Early Modern Empires in America." In *Realities of Representation: State Building in Early Modern Europe and European America*, edited by Maija Jansson, 171–86. Houndmills: Palgrave Macmillan, 2007.

Greer, Allan. *The Patriots and the People: The Rebellion of 1837 in Rural Lower Canada*. Toronto: Toronto University Press, 1993.

Griffin, Patrick. *American Leviathan: Empire, Nation, and Revolutionary Frontier*. New York: Hill & Wang, 2007.

Griffiths, Robert Howell. *Le centre perdu: Malouet et les "monarchiens" dans la Révolution française*. Grenoble: Presses Universitaires de Grenoble, 1988.

Gross, Jean-Pierre. *Fair Shares for All: Jacobin Egalitarianism in Practice*. Cambridge: Cambridge University Press, 1997.

Gruchy, Steve de. "The Alleged Political Conservatism of Robert Moffat." In *The London Missionary Society in Southern Africa, 1799–1999*, edited by John W. de Gruchy, 17–36. Athens: Ohio University Press, 2000.

Guelzo, Allen C. *Fateful Lightning: A New History of the Civil War and Reconstruction*. Oxford: Oxford University Press, 2012.

Gueniffey, Patrice. *Le nombre et la raison: La Révolution française et les élections*. Paris: Éditions de l'EHESS, 1993.

Gueniffey, Patrice. *La politique de la Terreur: Essai sur la violence révolutionnaire (1789-1794).* Paris: Fayard, 2000.

Guerassimoff, Eric. "Travail colonial, coolies et diplomatie: réclamations chinoises autour du contrat d'engagement à Cuba au XIXe siècle." In *Le travail colonial: Engagés et autres mains d'œuvre migrantes dans les empires, 1850-1950,* edited by Eric Guerrassimoff and Issiaka Mandé, 417-63. Paris: Riveneuve éditions, 2015.

Guetata, Jouda. "Le refus d'application de la constitution de l'an III à Saint-Domingue, 1795-1797." In *Périssent les colonies plutôt qu'un principe! Contributions à l'histoire de l'abolition de l'esclavage, 1789-1804,* edited by Florence Gauthier, 81-90. Paris: Société d'Études Robespierristes, 2002.

Guha, Ranajit. *A Rule of Property for Bengal: An Essay on the Idea of Permanent Settlement.* Durham, NC: Duke University Press, 1996.

Guzmán, María de. *Spain's Long Shadow: The Black Legend, Off-Whiteness, and Anglo-American Empire.* Minneapolis: University of Minnesota Press, 2005.

Gyory, Andrew. *Closing the Gate: Race, Politics and the Chinese Exclusion Act.* Chapel Hill: University of North Carolina Press, 1998.

Haffenden, Philip S. "The Crown and the Colonial Charters, 1675-1688. Part I." *William and Mary Quarterly* 15, no. 3 (1958): 298-311.

———. "The Crown and the Colonial Charters, 1675-1688. Part II." *William and Mary Quarterly* 15, no. 4 (1958): 452-66.

Hajjat, Abdellali. *Les frontières de l' 'identité nationale': L'injonction à l'assimilation en France métropolitaine et coloniale.* Paris: La Découverte, 2012.

Hale, Grace Elizabeth. *Making Whiteness: The Culture of Segregation in the South, 1890-1940.* New York: Vintage Books, 1999.

Hall, Catherine. *Civilising Subjects: Colony and Metropole in the English Imagination, 1830-1867.* Chicago: University of Chicago Press, 2002.

———. "What Did a British World Mean to the British? Reflections on the Nineteenth-Century." In *Rediscovering the British World,* edited by Philip A. Buckner and R. Douglas Francis, 21-38. Calgary: University of Calgary Press, 2005.

Hall, Douglas. *Free Jamaica, 1838-1865: An Economic History.* New Haven, CT: Yale University Press, 1959.

Hall, John A. "Imperial Universalism—Further Thoughts." In *Universal Empires: A Comparative Approach to Imperial Culture and Representation in Eurasian History,* edited by Peter F. Bang and Dariusz Kołodziejczyk, 304-9. Cambridge: Cambridge University Press, 2012.

Halliday, Paul D. *Habeas Corpus: From England to Empire.* Cambridge, MA: Harvard University Press, 2009.

Hampsher-Monk, Ian. "Edmund Burke and Empire." In *Lineages of Empire: The Historical Roots of British Imperial Thought,* edited by Duncan Kelly, 117-36. Oxford: Oxford University Press, 2009.

Haney-López, Ian. *White by Law: The Legal Construction of Race.* New York: New York University Press, 2006.

Hanger, Kimberley S. "Greedy French Masters and Color-Conscious, Legal-Minded Spaniards in Colonial Louisiana." In *Slavery in the Caribbean Francophone World: Distant Voices, Forgotten Acts, Forged Identities,* edited by Doris Y. Kadish, 106-21. Athens: University of Georgia Press, 2000.

Harlingand, Philip, and Peter Mandler. "From 'Fiscal-Military State' to Laissez-Faire State, 1760–1850." *Journal of British Studies* 32, no. 1 (1993): 44–70.

Harlow, Vincent. *The Founding of the Second British Empire, 1763–1793*. London: Longman, 1952–1964.

———. "The New Imperial System, 1783–1815." In *Cambridge History of the British Empire*. Vol. 2, *The Growth of the New Empire, 1783–1870*, edited by J. Holland Rose, A. P. Newton, and E. A. Benians, 131–88. Cambridge: Cambridge University Press, 1961.

Harlow, Vincent, and Frederick Madden. *British Colonial Developments, 1774–1834: Select Documents*. Oxford: Clarendon Press, 1953.

Harrington, Jack. *Sir John Malcolm and the Creation of British India*. Houndmills: Palgrave Macmillan, 2010.

Harris, Susan K. *God's Arbiters: Americans and the Philippines, 1898–1902*. New York: Oxford University Press, 2013.

Hasan, Farhat. *State and Locality in Mughal India: Power Relations in Western India, c. 1572–1730*. Cambridge: Cambridge University Press, 1976.

Haudrère, Philippe. *L'empire des rois, 1500–1789*. Paris: Denoël, 1997.

Haudrère, Philippe, and Françoise Vergés. *De l'esclave au citoyen*. Paris: Gallimard, 1998.

Hawkins, Mike. *Social Darwinism in European and American Thought, 1860–1945*. Cambridge: Cambridge University Press, 1997.

Haynes, Robert V. *The Mississippi Territory and the Southwest Frontier, 1795–1817*. Lexington: University Press of Kentucky, 2010.

Hayot, Émile. *Les gens de couleur libres du Fort-Royal (1679–1823)*. Paris: Société Française d'Histoire d'Outre-Mer, 1971.

Heath, Andrew. "'Let the Empire Come': Imperialism and Its Critics in the Reconstruction South." *Civil War History* 60, no. 2 (2014): 152–89.

Heffernan, Michael J. "The Parisian Poor and the Colonization of Algeria during the Second Republic." *French History* 3, no. 4 (1989): 377–403.

Heidler, David S., and Jeanne T. Heidler. *Indian Removal: A Norton Casebook*. New York: W. W. Norton, 2007.

Hélenon, Véronique. "Races, statut juridique et colonisation: Antillais et Africains dans les cadres administratifs des colonies françaises d'Afrique." In *L'esclavage, la colonisation, et après . . . France, États-Unis, Grande Bretagne*, edited by Patrick Weil and Stéphane Dufoix, 229–43. Paris: Presses Universitaires de France, 2005.

Helg, Aline. *Liberty and Equality in Caribbean Colombia, 1770–1835*. Chapel Hill: University of North Carolina Press, 2004.

———. *Our Rightful Share: The Afro-Cuban Struggle for Equality, 1886–1912*. Chapel Hill: University of North Carolina Press, 1995.

Henry, Jean-Robert. "La norme et l'imaginaire: Construction de l'altérité juridique en droit colonial algérien." *Procès* 18 (1987): 13–32.

Herbert, Christopher. *War of No Pity: The Indian Mutiny and Victorian Trauma*. Princeton, NJ: Princeton University Press, 2008.

Heredia, Edmundo A. *Planes españoles para reconquistar Hispanoamérica (1810–1818)*. Buenos Aires: Eudeba, 1974.

Heuman, Gad J. "The British West Indies." In *The Oxford History of the British Empire*. Vol. 3, *The Nineteenth Century*, edited by Andrew Porter, 470–92. Oxford: Oxford University Press, 1999.

Heuman, Gad J. *"The Killing Time": The Morant Bay Rebellion in Jamaica*. London: Macmillan, 1994.

———. "Post-Emancipation Protest in Jamaica: The Morant Bay Rebellion, 1865." In *From Chattel Slaves to Wage Slaves: The Dynamics of Labour Bargaining in the Americas*, edited by Mary Turner, 258–74. Kingston: Ian Randle, 1995.

Higgs, Robert. *Competition and Coercion: Blacks in the American Economy, 1865–1914*. Cambridge: Cambridge University Press, 1977.

Higham, John. *Strangers in the Land: Patterns of American Nativism, 1860–1925*. New Brunswick: Rutgers University Press, 2008.

Higman, B. W. *A Concise History of the Caribbean*. Cambridge: Cambridge University Press, 2011.

———. *Slave Population and Economy in Jamaica, 1807–1834*. Cambridge: Cambridge University Press, 1979.

Higonnet, Patrice. "Terror, Trauma and the 'Young Marx' Explanation of Jacobin Politics." *Past and Present* 191 (1996): 121–64.

Hillerkuss, Thomas. "La República en los pueblos de indios en la Nueva Galicia en el siglo XVI." *Anuario Saber Novohispano* (1995): 241–58.

Hinderaker, Eric. *Elusive Empires: Constructing Colonialism in the Ohio Valley, 1673–1800*. New York: Cambridge University Press, 1997.

Hinderaker, Eric, and Peter C. Mancall. *At the Edge of Empire: The Backcountry in British North America*. Baltimore: Johns Hopkins University Press, 2003.

Hing, Bill Ong. *Defining America through Immigration Policy*. Philadelphia: Temple University Press, 2004.

Hobson, J. A. *Imperialism: A Study*. Ann Arbor: University of Michigan Press, 1991.

Hobson, John M. *The Eurocentric Conception of World Politics: Western International Theory, 1760–2010*. Cambridge: Cambridge University Press, 2012.

Hoffer, Williamjames Hull. *Plessy v. Ferguson: Race and Inequality in Jim Crow America*. Lawrence: University of Kansas Press, 2012.

Holt, Thomas C. *The Problem of Freedom: Race, Labor, and Politics in Jamaica and Britain, 1832–1938*. Baltimore: Johns Hopkins University Press, 1992.

Holton, Woody. *Forced Founders: Indians, Debtors, Slaves, and the Making of the American Revolution in Virginia*. Chapel Hill: University of North Carolina Press, 2003.

———. *Unruly Americans and the Origins of the Constitution*. New York: Hill & Wang, 2007.

Hont, Istvan. *Jealousy of Trade: International Competition and the Nation-State in Historical Perspective*. Cambridge, MA: Harvard University Press, 2010.

———. "The Permanent Crisis of a Divided Mankind: 'Nation-State' and Nationalism in Historical Perspective." In Hont, *Jealousy of Trade: International Competition and the Nation-State in Historical Perspective*, 447–528. Cambridge, MA: Harvard University Press, 2010.

Hopkins, A. G. "The Victorians and Africa: A Reconsideration of the Occupation of Egypt, 1882." *Journal of African History* 27, no. 2 (1986): 363–91.

Horsman, Reginald. *Expansion and American Indian Policy, 1783–1812*. East Lansing: Michigan State University Press, 1967.

Horton, Carol A. *Race and the Making of American Liberalism*. Oxford: Oxford University Press, 2005.

Howard, Michael. *Empires, Nations and Wars*. Staplehurst: Spellmount, 2007.

Howe, Stephen. *Anticolonialism in British Politics: The Left and the End of Empire, 1918–1964*. Oxford: Oxford University Press, 1993.

Hoxie, Frederick E. "The Reservation Period, 1880–1960." In *The Cambridge History of the Native Peoples of the Americas*. Vol. 1, *North America: Part 2*, edited by Bruce G. Trigger and Wilcomb E. Washburn, 183–258. Cambridge: Cambridge University Press, 1966.

Huber, Valeska. *Channelling Mobilities: Migration and Globalisation in the Suez Canal Region and Beyond, 1869–1914*. Cambridge: Cambridge University Press, 2013.

Hull, Isabel. *Absolute Destruction: Military Culture and the Practices of War in Imperial Germany*. Ithaca, NY: Cornell University Press, 2005.

Hummel, Jeffrey Rogers. *Emancipating Slaves, Enslaving Free Men: A History of the American Civil War*. Chicago: Open Court, 1996.

Hunt, Lynn. *Inventing Human Rights: A History*. New York: W. W. Norton, 2007.

Hunt, Lynn, David Lansky, and Paul Hanson. "The Failure of the Liberal Republic in France, 1795–1799: The Road to Brumaire." *Journal of Modern History* 51, no. 4 (1979): 734–59.

Hunt, Margaret. "Women and the Fiscal-Imperial State in the Late Seventeenth and Early Eighteenth Centuries." In *A New Imperial History: Culture, Identity, and Modernity in Britain and the Empire, 1660–1840*, edited by Kathleen Wilson, 29–47. Cambridge: Cambridge University Press, 2004.

Hunt, Michael H., and Steven I. Levine. *Arc of Empire: America's Wars in Asia from the Philippines to Vietnam*. Chapel Hill: University of North Carolina Press, 2012.

Huttenback, Robert A. *The British Imperial Experience*. New York: Harper & Row, 1966.

———. "The Durham Report and the Establishment of Responsible Government in Canada." In Huttenback, *The British Imperial Experience*, 20–38. New York: Harper & Row, 1966.

———. *Racism and Empire: White Settlers and Colored Immigrants in the British Self-Governing Colonies, 1830–1910*. Ithaca, NY: Cornell University Press, 1976.

Ibarra, Jorge. *Ideología mambisa*. Havana: Instituto Cubano del Libro, 1972.

Iglesias, Fe. *Del Ingenio al Central*. Havana: Editorial de Ciencias Sociales, 1999.

Ileto, Reynaldo C. *Filipinos and their Revolution: Event, Discourse, and Historiography*. Quezon City: Ateneo de Manila University Press, 1998.

———. *Pasyon and Revolution: Popular Movements in the Philippines, 1840–1910*. Quezon City: Ateneo de Manila Press, 1979.

Immerman, Richard H. *Empire for Liberty: A History of American Imperialism from Benjamin Franklin to Paul Wolfowitz*. Princeton, NJ: Princeton University Press, 2010.

Inarejos Muñoz, Juan Antonio. *Intervenciones coloniales y nacionalismo español: La política exterior de la Unión Liberal y sus vínculos con la Francia de Napoleón III (1856–1868)*. Madrid: Silex, 2010.

———. *Los (últimos) caciques de Filipinas: Las elites coloniales antes del 1898*. Granada: Comares, 2015.

Innes, Joanna. "Forms of 'Government Growth,' 1780–1830." In *Structures and Transformations in Modern British History*, edited by David Feldman and Jon Lawrence, 74–99. Cambridge: Cambridge University Press, 2011.

Innes, Joanna. *Inferior Politics: Social Problems and Social Policies in Eighteenth-Century Britain*. Oxford: Oxford University Press, 2009.

Irigoin, Alejandra, and Regina Grafe. "Bargaining for Absolutism: A Spanish Path to Nation-State and Empire Building." *Hispanic American Historical Review* 88, no. 2 (2008): 173–209.

Izecksohn, Vitor. "A Guerra do Paraguay." In *O Brasil Imperial*. Vol. 2, *1831–1870*, edited by Keila Grinberg and Ricardo Salles, 385–424. Rio de Janeiro: Civilização Brasileira, 2009.

Jackson, Alvin. "Ireland, the Union, and the Empire, 1800–1960." In *Ireland and the British Empire*, edited by Kevin Kenny, 123–54. Oxford: Oxford University Press, 2004.

Jackson, Curtis Emanuel, and Marcia J. Galli. *A History of the Bureau of Indian Affairs and Its Activities among Indians*. San Francisco: R. E. Publishers, 1977.

Jacob, Margaret C., and Wijnand W. Mijnhardt, eds. *The Dutch Republic in the Eighteenth Century: Decline, Enlightenment, and Revolution*. Ithaca, NY: Cornell University Press, 1992.

Jacobs, Beatrix, Raymond Kubben, and Randall Lesaffer, eds. *In the Embrace of France: The Law of Nations and Constitutional Law in the French Satellite States of the Revolutionary and Napoleonic Age (1789–1815)*. Baden-Baden: Nomos, 2008.

Jacobson, Matthew Frye. *Barbarian Virtues: The United States Encounters Foreign Peoples at Home and Abroad, 1876–1917*. New York: Hills & Wang, 2000.

Jacobson, Stephen J. "Imperial Ambitions in an Era of Decline: Micromilitarism and the Eclipse of the Spanish Empire, 1858–1923." In *Endless Empire: Spain's Retreat, Europe's Eclipse, America's Decline*, edited by Alfred W. McCoy, Josep M. Fradera, and Stephen J. Jacobson, 74–91. Madison: University of Wisconsin Press, 2012.

Jaenen, Cornelius J. *Friends and Foe: Aspects of French-Amerindian Cultural Contact in the Sixteenth and Seventeenth Centuries*. New York: Columbia University Press, 1976.

Janke, Peter. *Mendizábal y la instauración de la Monarquía constitucional en España (1790–1853)*. Madrid: Siglo XXI Editores, 1974.

Jasanoff, Maya. *Edge of Empire: Lives, Culture, and Conquest in the East, 1750–1850*. New York: Vintage Books, 2006.

Jenkins, Brian. *Era of Emancipation: British Government of Ireland, 1812–1830*. Montreal: McGill-Queen's University Press, 1988.

Jennings, Eric T. *Vichy in the Tropics: Pétain's National Revolution in Madagascar, Guadeloupe, and Indochina, 1940–1944*. Stanford, CA: Stanford University Press, 2001.

Jennings, Francis. *The Creation of America: Through Revolution to Empire*. Cambridge: Cambridge University Press, 2000.

———. *Empire of Fortune: Crowns, Colonies, and Tribes in the Seven Years War in America*. New York: Norton, 1988.

———. *The Invasion of America: Indians, Colonialism, and the Cant of Conquest*. Chapel Hill: University of North Carolina Press, 1975.

Jennings, Lawrence C. *French Anti-Slavery: The Movement for the Abolition of Slavery in France, 1802–1848*. New York: Cambridge University Press, 2000.

Jesús, Edilberto C. de. *The Tobacco Monopoly in the Philippines: Bureaucratic Enterprise and Social Change, 1766–1880*. Quezon City: Ateneo de Manila Press, 1983.

Johnson, Lyman L. *Workshop of Revolution: Plebeian Buenos Aires and the Atlantic World, 1776–1810*. Durham, NC: Duke University Press, 2011.

Johnson, Walter. *River of Dark Dreams: Slavery and Empire in the Cotton Kingdom*. Cambridge, MA: Harvard University Press, 2013.

Jones, Dorothy V. *License for Empire: Colonialism by Treaty in Early America*. Chicago: University of Chicago Press, 1982.

Jordan, Winthrop D. *White over Black: American Attitudes toward the Negro, 1550–1812*. Chapel Hill: University of North Carolina Press, 1968.

Jourdan, Annie. "République française, Révolution batave: Le moment constitutionnel." In *Républiques sœurs: Le Directoire et la Révolution atlantique*, edited by Pierre Serna, 301–14. Rennes: Presses Universitaires de Rennes, 2009.

———. *La Révolution batave entre la France et l'Amérique (1795–1806)*. Rennes: Presses Universitaires de Rennes, 2008.

Joyce, Patrick. *Democratic Subjects: The Self and the Social in Nineteenth-Century England*. Cambridge: Cambridge University Press, 1994.

Julien, Charles-André. *Histoire de l'Algérie Contemporaine*. Vol. 1, *La conquête et les débuts de la colonisation (1827–1874)*. Paris: Presses Universitaires de France, 1964.

Jupp, Peter. *British Politics on the Eve of Reform: The Duke of Wellington's Administration, 1828–1830*. London: Macmillan, 1998.

———. *The Governing of Britain, 1688–1848: The Executive, Parliament, and the People*. London: Routledge, 2006.

Juss, Satvinder S. *Immigration, Nationality and Citizenship*. London: Mansell, 1993.

Kaczorowski, Robert J. *The Nationalization of Civil Rights: Constitutional Theory and Practice in a Racist Society, 1866–1883*. New York: Garland Publishing, 1987.

Kadish, Doris Y., ed. *Slavery in the Caribbean Francophone World: Distant Voices, Forgotten Acts, Forged Identities*. Athens: University of Georgia Press, 2000.

Kahan, Alan S. *Liberalism in Nineteenth-Century Europe: The Political Culture of Limited Suffrage*. Houndmills: Palgrave Macmillan, 2003.

Kammen, Michael G. *Deputyes and Libertyes: The Origins of Representative Government in Colonial America*. New York: Alfred A. Knopf, 1969.

Karatani, Rieko. *Defining British Citizenship: Empire, Commonwealth and Modern Britain*. London: Frank Cass, 2003.

Karp, Matthew. *This Vast Southern Empire: Slaveholders at the Helm of American Foreign Policy*. Cambridge, MA: Harvard University Press, 2016.

Karst, Kenneth L. *Belonging to America: Equal Citizenship and the Constitution*. New Haven, CT: Yale University Press, 1989.

Kastor, Peter J. *The Nation's Crucible: The Louisiana Purchase and the Creation of America*. New Haven, CT: Yale University Press, 2004.

Katan, Yvette. "Les colons de 1848 en Algérie: Mythes et réalités." *Revue d'histoire moderne et contemporaine* 31 (1984): 177–202.

Kateb, Kamel. *Européens, "indigènes" et juifs en Algérie (1830–1962): Représentations et réalités des populations*. Paris: INED, 2001.

Katznelson, Ira. *When Affirmative Action Was White: An Untold History of Racial Inequality in Twentieth-Century America*. New York: W.W. Norton, 2005.

Kazanjian, David. *The Colonizing Trick: National Culture and Imperial Citizenship in Early America*. Minneapolis: University of Minnesota Press, 2003.

Keegan, Timothy J. *Rural Transformations in Industrializing South Africa: The Southern Highveld to 1914*. Houndmills: Palgrave Macmillan, 1987.

Kelly, James. *Prelude to Union: Anglo-Irish Politics in the 1780s*. Cork: Cork University Press, 1992.

Kendle, John Edward. *The Colonial and Imperial Conferences, 1887–1911: A Study in Imperial Organization*. London: Longmans, 1967.

Kennedy, Roger G. *Mr. Jefferson's Lost Cause: Land, Farmers, Slavery, and the Louisiana Purchase*. Oxford: Oxford University Press, 2003.

Kenny, Kevin. *Peaceable Kingdom Lost: The Paxton Boys and the Destruction of William Penn's Holy Experiment*. Oxford: Oxford University Press, 2009.

Kettner, James H. *The Development of American Citizenship, 1608–1870*. Chapel Hill: University of North Carolina Press, 1978.

Keyssar, Alexander. *The Right to Vote: The Contested History of Democracy in the United States*. New York: Basic Books, 2000.

Kiczka, John E., and Rebecca Horn. *Resilient Cultures: America's Native Peoples Confront European Colonialization 1500–1800*. London: Routledge, 2013.

Kidd, Colin. *The Forging of Races: Race and Scripture in the Protestant Atlantic World, 1600–2000*. Cambridge: Cambridge University Press, 2006.

Kim, Keechang. "Calvin's Case (1608) and the Law of Alien Status." *Journal of Legal History* 17, no. 2 (1996): 155–71.

King, Stewart R. *Blue Coat or Powdered Wig: Free People of Color in Pre-Revolutionary Saint-Domingue*. Athens: University of Georgia Press, 2001.

Kiser, John W. *Commander of the Faithful: The Life and Times of Emir Abdelkader, a Story of True Jihad*. Rhinebeck: Monkfish Books, 2008.

Klein, Martin A. *Slavery and Colonial Rule in French West Africa*. Cambridge: Cambridge University Press, 1998.

Kline, Benjamin. *Genesis of Apartheid: British African Policy in the Colony of Natal, 1845–1893*. Lanham, MD: University Press of America, 1988.

Klooster, Wim. *Revolutions in the Atlantic World: A Comparative History*. New York: New York University Press, 2009.

Knaplund, Paul. *James Stephen and the British Colonial System, 1813–1847*. Madison: University of Wisconsin Press, 1953.

Knight, Franklin W. *The Caribbean: The Genesis of a Fragmented Nationalism*. New York: Oxford University Press, 2012.

———. "Origins of Wealth and the Sugar Revolution in Cuba, 1750–1850." *Hispanic American Historical Review* 57, no. 2 (1977): 231–53.

———. *Slave Society in Cuba during the Nineteenth Century*. Madison: University of Wisconsin Press, 1970.

Knight, Ian. *The Zulu War 1879*. London: Pan Books, 2004.

Knupfer, Peter B. *The Union as It Is: Constitutional Unionism and Sectional Compromise, 1787–1861*. Chapel Hill: University of North Carolina Press, 1995.

Koenigsberger, Helmut G. *Politicians and Virtuosi: Essays in Early Modern History*. London: Hambledon Press, 1986.

———. *The Practice of Empire: The Government of Sicily under Philip II of Spain*. New York: Rinehart & Holt, 1968.

Kolff, Dirk H. A. "The End of an Ancien Régime: Colonial War in India, 1798–1818." In *Imperialism and War: Essays on Colonial Wars in Asia and Africa*, edited by J. A. de Moor and H. L. Wesseling, 22–49. Leiden: E. J. Brill, 1989.

Kopp, Kristin. *Germany's Wild East: Constructing Poland as Colonial Space*. Ann Arbor: University of Michigan Press, 2012.

Kramer, Paul A. *The Blood of Government: Race, Empire, the United States, and the Philippines*. Chapel Hill: University of North Carolina Press, 2006.

Kubicek, Robert V. *The Administration of Imperialism: Joseph Chamberlain at the Colonial Office*. Durham, NC: Duke University Press, 1969.

Kuethe, Allan J., and Kenneth J. Andrien. *The Spanish Atlantic World in the Eighteenth Century: War and the Bourbon Reforms, 1713–1796*. Cambridge: Cambridge University Press, 2014.

Kumar, Krishan. "Nation-States as Empires, Empires as Nation-States: Two Principles, One Practice?" *Theory and Society* 39, no. 2 (2010): 119–43.

Kunkel, Paul A. "Modifications in Louisiana Negro Legal Status under Louisiana Constitutions, 1812–1957." *Journal of Negro History* 44, no. 1 (1959): 1–25.

Kwass, Michael. *Privilege and the Politics of Taxation in Eighteenth-Century France: Liberté, Égalité, Fiscalité*. Cambridge: Cambridge University Press, 2006.

LaFeber, Walter. "Jefferson and an American Foreign Policy." In *Jeffersonian Legacies*, edited by Peter S. Onuf, 370–94. Charlottesville: University of Virginia Press, 1993.

———. *The New Empire: An Interpretation of American Expansion, 1860–1898*. Ithaca, NY: Cornell University Press, 1963.

Lake, Marilyn. "Equality and Exclusion: The Racial Constitution of Colonial Liberalism." *Thesis Eleven* 95 (2008): 20–32.

———. "The White Man under Siege: New Histories of Race in the Nineteenth Century and the Advent of White Australia." *History Workshop Journal* 58 (2004): 41–62.

Lake, Marilyn, and Henry Reynolds. *Drawing the Global Colour Line: White Men's Countries and the Question of Racial Equality*. Melbourne: Melbourne University Press, 2008.

Lakomäki, Sami. *Gathering Together: The Shawnee People through Diaspora and Nationhood, 1600–1870*. New Haven, CT: Yale University Press, 2014.

Lamar, Howard Roberts. *The Far Southwest, 1846–1912: A Territorial History*. Albuquerque: University of New Mexico Press, 2000.

———. "From Bondage to Contract: Ethnic Labor in the American West, 1600–1890." In *The Countryside in the Age of Capitalist Transformation: Essays in the Social History of Rural America*, edited by Steven Hahn and Jonathan Prude, 293–324. Chapel Hill: University of North Carolina Press, 1985.

Lanctôt, Gustave. *Canada and the American Revolution, 1774–1783*. Toronto: Clarke, Irwin and Company, 1967.

Lange, Matthew. *Lineages of Despotism and Development: British Colonialism and State Power*. Chicago: University of Chicago Press, 2009.

Larcher, Émile. *Traité élémentaire de législation algérienne*. 3 vols. Paris: Arthur Rousseau, 1911.

Larcher, Silyane. *L'autre citoyen: L'idéal républicain et les Antilles après l'esclavage*. Paris: Armand Colin, 2014.

Larkin, John A. *The Pampangans: Colonial Society in a Philippine Province*. Berkeley: University of California Press, 1972.

———. *Sugar and the Origins of Modern Philippine Society*. Berkeley: University of California Press, 1993.

Lasarte Álvarez, Javier. *Las Cortes de Cádiz: Soberanía, separación de poderes, Hacienda, 1810–1811*. Madrid: Marcial Pons, 2009.

Lasso, Marixa. *Myths of Harmony: Race and Republicanism During the Age of Revolution; Colombia 1795–1831*. Minneapolis: University of Minnesota Press, 2003.

——. "Race, War and Nation in Caribbean Gran Colombia: Cartagena, 1810–1832." *American Historical Review* 111, no. 2 (2006): 336–61.

Lavin, Deborah. *From Empire to International Commonwealth: A Biography of Lionel Curtis*. Oxford: Oxford University Press, 1995.

Lawrence, Adria K. *Imperial Rule and the Politics of Nationalism: Anti-Colonial Protest in the French Empire*. Cambridge: Cambridge University Press, 2013.

Lawson, Philip. "Anatomy of a Civil War: New Perspectives on England in the Age of the American Revolution, 1767–1782." In Lawson, *A Taste for Empire and Glory: Studies in British Overseas Expansion, 1660–1800*, 142–52. Aldershot: Variorum, 1997.

——. *The Imperial Challenge: Quebec and Britain in the Age of American Revolution*. Montreal: McGill-Queen's University Press, 1986.

——. *A Taste for Empire and Glory: Studies in British Overseas Expansion, 1660–1800*. Aldershot: Variorum, 1997.

Le Cour Grandmaison, Olivier. *Coloniser, Exterminer: Sur la guerre et l'État colonial*. Paris: Fayard, 2005.

——. *De l'indigénat: Anatomie d'un "monstre" juridique: Le droit colonial en Algérie et dans l'Empire français*. Paris: Zones, 2010.

——. "The Exception and the Rule: On French Colonial Rule." *Diogenes* 53 (2006): 34–53.

——. *La République impériale: Politique et racisme d'État*. Paris: Fayard, 2009.

Le Pors, Anicet. *La citoyenneté*. Paris: Presses Universitaires de France, 2011.

Lee, Maurice. *The "Inevitable" Union and Other Essays on Early Modern Scotland*. East Linton: Tuckwell Press, 2003.

Lee, Wayne E. *Empires and Indigenes: Intercultural Alliance, Imperial Expansion, and Warfare in the Early Modern World*. New York: New York University Press, 2011.

Lees, James. "Retrenchment, Reform and the Practice of Military-Fiscalism in the Early East India Company State." In *The Political Economy of Empire in the Early Modern World*, edited by Sophus A. Reinert and Pernille Røge, 173–91. Houndmills: Palgrave Macmillan, 2013.

Lemarchand, Guy. "Les représentants du peuple en mission dans la Révolution française, 1792–1795." *Annales de Normandie* 55, no. 3 (2003): 275–80.

Lepore, Jill. *The Name of War: King Philip's War and the Origins of American Identity*. New York: Vintage Books, 1999.

Lester, Alan. "British Settlers and the Colonisation of the Xhosa." In Lester, *Imperial Networks: Creating Identities in Nineteenth-Century South Africa and Britain*, 45–77. London: Routledge, 2001.

Lester, Alan, and Fae Dussart, eds. *Colonization and the Origins of Humanitarian Governance: Protecting Aborigines across the Nineteenth-Century British Empire*. Cambridge: Cambridge University Press, 2014.

——. "Humanitarian Governance in a Settler Empire." In Lester and Dussart, eds., *Colonization and the Origins of Humanitarian Governance: Protecting Aborigines across the Nineteenth-Century British Empire*, 226–75. Cambridge: Cambridge University Press, 2014.

Levallois, Michel. *Ismayl Urbain (1812–1884): Une autre conquête de l'Algérie*. Paris: Maisonneuve et Larose, 2001.

Lewis, George Cornewall. *An Essay on the Government of Dependencies*. London: John Murray, 1841.

———. *Essays on the Administration of Great Britain from 1783 to 1830*. London: Longman, Green, Longman, Roberts & Green, 1864.

Lewis, James E., Jr. *The American Union and the Problem of Neighborhood: The United States and the Collapse of the Spanish Empire, 1783–1829*. Chapel Hill: University of North Carolina Press, 1998.

Lewis, Martin Deming. "One Hundred Million Frenchmen: The 'Assimilation' Theory in French Colonial Policy." *Comparative Studies in Society and History* 4, no. 2 (1962): 129–53.

Liébart, Déborah. "Un groupe de pression contre-révolutionnaire: Le Club Massiac sous la constituante." *Annales historiques de la Révolution française* 354 (2008): 29–50.

Linton, Marisa. *Choosing Terror: Virtue, Friendship, and Authenticity in the French Revolution*. Oxford: Oxford University Press, 2013.

———. "'Do You Believe That We're Conspirators?' Conspiracies Real and Imagined in Jacobin Politics, 1793–1794." In *Conspiracy in the French Revolution*, edited by Peter R. Campbell, Thomas E. Kaiser, and Marisa Linton, 127–49. Manchester: Manchester University Press, 2007.

Littlefield, Daniel F. *The Chickasaw Freedmen: A People without a Country*. Westport, CT: Greenwood Press, 1980.

Litwack, Leon F. *Been in the Storm So Long: The Aftermath of Slavery*. New York: Vintage Books, 1980.

Lively, Donald E. *The Constitution and Race*. New York: Praeger, 1992.

Llobet, Ruth de. "Chinese Mestizo and Natives' Disputes in Manila and the 1812 Constitution: Old Privileges and New Political Realities (1813–1815)." *Journal of Southeast Asian Studies* 45, no. 2 (2014): 214–35.

———. "De ciudadanía a sedición: La trayectoria política de Domingo de Rojas, 1820–1843." In *La construcción de la nación filipina: Un caso a través de la familia Roxas*, edited by María Dolores Elizalde and Xavier Huetz de Lemps (forthcoming, 2018).

———. *Orphans of Empire: Bourbon Reforms, Constitutional Impasse and the Rise of Filipino Creole Consciousness in an Age of Revolution*. PhD diss., University of Wisconsin, 2011.

Lloyd, Christopher. "Institutional Patterns of the Settler Societies: Hybrid, Parallel and Convergent." In *Settler Economies in World History*, edited by Christopher Lloyd, Jacob Metzer, and Richard Sutch, 545–78. Leiden: Brill, 2013.

Lloyd, Christopher, Jacob Metzer, and Richard Sutch, eds. *Settler Economies in World History*. Leiden: Brill, 2013.

Lloyd, Trevor O. *The British Empire, 1558–1983*. Oxford: Oxford University Press, 1984.

Lochak, Danièle. "La citoyenneté: un concept juridique flou." In *Citoyenneté et nationalité: Perspectives en France et au Québec*, edited by Dominique Colas, Claude Emeri, and Jacques Zylberberg, 179–207. Paris: Presses Universitaires de France, 1991.

Lochak, Danièle. *Le droit et les paradoxes de l'universalité*. Paris: Presses Universitaires de France, 2010.

Lockhart, James. *The Nahuas after the Conquest: A Social and Cultural History of the Indians of Central Mexico, Sixteenth through Eighteenth Centuries*. Stanford, CA: Stanford University Press, 1992.

———. *Of Things of the Indies: Essays Old and New in Early Latin American History*. Stanford, CA: Stanford University Press, 1999.

Lokke, Carl Ludwig. *France and the Colonial Question: A Study of Contemporary French Opinion, 1763–1801*. New York: AMS Press, 1968.

———. "Secret Negotiations to Maintain the Peace of Amiens." *American Historical Review* 49, no. 1 (1943): 55–64.

Long, Edward. *The History of Jamaica or General Survey of the Ancient and Modern State of that Island*. London: Frank Cass, 1970.

Look Lai, Walton. *Indentured Labor, Caribbean Sugar: Chinese and Indian Migrants to the British West Indies, 1838–1918*. Baltimore: Johns Hopkins University Press, 1993.

LoPatin-Lummis, Nancy. "Review of 'British Democracy and Irish Nationalism, 1876–1906,' by Eugenio F. Biagini." *Journal of Modern History* 18, no. 4 (2009): 948–950.

Lorcin, Patricia M. E. *Imperial Identities: Stereotyping, Prejudices and Race in Colonial Algeria*. London: I. B. Tauris, 1999.

Lorimer, Douglas A. *Colour, Class, and the Victorians: English Attitudes to the Negro in the Mid-Nineteenth Century*. Leicester: Leicester University Press, 1978.

———. "From Natural Science to Social Science: Race and the Language of Race Relations in Late Victorian and Edwardian Discourse." In *Lineages of Empire: The Historical Roots of British Imperial Thought*, edited by Duncan Kelly, 181–212. Oxford: Oxford University Press, 2009.

———. "From Victorian Values to White Virtues: Assimilation and Exclusion in British Racial Discourse, c.1870–1914." In *Rediscovering the British World*, edited by Philip Buckner and R. Douglas Francis, 109–34. Calgary: University of Calgary Press, 2005.

———. "Science and the Secularization of Victorian Images of Race." In *Victorian Science in Context*, edited by Bernard V. Lightman, 215–35. Chicago: University of Chicago Press, 1997.

Louis, William Roger, ed. *Imperialism: The Robinson and Gallagher Controversy*. New York: New Viewpoints, 1976.

Lourie, Elena. *Crusade and Colonisation: Muslims, Christians, and Jews in Medieval Aragon*. Aldershot: Variorum, 1990.

Love, Eric T. L. *Race over Empire: Racism and U. S. Imperialism, 1865–1900*. Chapel Hill: North Carolina University Press, 2004.

Lucas, Colin. "The First Directory and the Rule of Law." *French Historical Studies* 10, no. 2 (1977): 231–60.

Lucas, Paul R. "Colony to Commonwealth: Massachusetts Bay, 1661–1666." *William and Mary Quarterly* 24, no. 1 (1967): 88–102.

Lucena Giraldo, Manuel. *A los cuatro vientos: Las ciudades de la América Hispánica*. Madrid: Marcial Pons, 2006.

Luethy, Herbert. *France against Herself: A Perceptual Study of France's Past, Her Politics, and Her Unending Crises*. New York: Praeger, 1955.

Lynch, John. *América Latina, entre colonia y nación*. Barcelona: Crítica, 2001.

——. "Arms and Men in the Spanish Conquest of America." In Lynch, *Latin America between Colony and Nation: Selected Essays*, 14–44. Houndmills: Palgrave Mac-Millan, 2001.

Lynd, Staughton. *Class Conflict, Slavery and the United States Constitution*. New York: Cambridge University Press, 2009.

MacIntyre, Stuart. *A Concise History of Australia*. Cambridge: Cambridge University Press, 2004.

MacKenzie, John M., ed. *Imperialism and Popular Culture*. Manchester: Manchester University Press, 1987.

——. *Propaganda and Empire: The Manipulation of British Public Opinion, 1880–1960*. Manchester: Manchester University Press, 1986.

Madden, A. F. " 'Not for Export': The Westminster Model of Government and British Colonial Practice." *Journal of Imperial and Commonwealth Studies* 8, no. 1 (1979): 10–29.

Madiou, Thomas. *Histoire d'Haïti*. Vol. 2, *1799–1803*. Port-au-Prince: Henri Deschamps, 1989.

Madley, Benjamin. *An American Genocide: The United States and the California Indian Catastrophe, 1846–1873*. New Haven, CT: Yale University Press, 2016.

Magness, Phillip W., and Sebastian N. Page. *Colonization after Emancipation: Lincoln and the Movement for Black Resettlement*. Columbia: University of Missouri Press, 2011.

Maier, Charles S. *Leviathan 2.0: Inventing Modern Statehood*. Cambridge, MA: Harvard University Press, 2012.

Maier, Pauline. *American Scripture: Making the Declaration of Independence*. New York: Vintage Books, 1998.

——. *From Resistance to Revolution: Colonial Radicals and the Development of American Opposition to Britain, 1765–1776*. New York: W. W. Norton, 1991.

——. *Ratification: The People Debate the Constitution, 1787–1788*. New York: Simon & Schuster, 2010.

Majeed, Javed. *Ungoverned Imaginings: James Mill's The History of British India and Orientalism*. Oxford: Clarendon, 1992.

Makhura, Tlou John. "Another Road to the Raid: The Neglected Role of the Boer-Bagananwa War as a Factor in the Coming of the Jameson Raid, 1894–1895." *Journal of Southern African Studies* 21, no. 2 (1995): 257–67.

Malagón Barceló, Javier. *Solórzano y la política Indiana*. Mexico City: Fondo de Cultura Económica, 1983.

Maltby, William S. *The Black Legend in England: The Development of Anti-Spanish Sentiment, 1558–1660*. Durham, NC: Duke University Press, 1971.

Maluquer de Motes, Jordi. *La economía española en perspectiva histórica: Siglos XVIII–XXI*. Barcelona: Pasado & Presente, 2014.

Mam Lam Fouck, Serge. *Histoire de l'assimilation: Des 'vieilles colonies' françaises aux départements d'outre-mer; La culture politique de l'assimilation aux Antilles et en Guyane françaises (XIXe et XXe siècles)*. Matoury: Ibis Rouge, 2006.

Manceron, Gilles, ed. *1885, le tournant colonial de la République: Jules Ferry contre Georges Clemenceau, et autres affrontements parlementaires sur la conquête coloniale*. Paris: La Découverte, 2007.

Mancke, Elizabeth. "Empire and State." In *The British Atlantic World, 1500–1800*, edited by David Armitage and Michael J. Braddick, 175–95. London: Palgrave Macmillan, 2002.

Mandler, Peter. *Aristocratic Government in the Age of Reform: Whigs and Liberals, 1830–1852*. Oxford: Clarendon Press, 1990.

———. "'Race' and 'Nation' in Mid-Victorian Thought." In *History, Religion, and Culture: British Intellectual History, 1750–1950*, edited by Stefan Collini, Richard Whatmore, and B. W. Young, 224–44. Cambridge: Cambridge University Press, 2000.

Mann, Gregory. "What Was the Indigénat? The 'Empire of Law' in French West Africa." *Journal of African History* 50 (2009): 331–53.

Manning, Helen T. *British Colonial Government after the American Revolution, 1782–1820*. New Haven, CT: Yale University Press, 1933.

Mansergh, Nicholas. *South Africa, 1906–1961: The Price of Magnanimity*. London: Allen & Unwin, 1962.

Mansfield, Paul. "Collot d'Herbois at the Committee of Public Safety: A Revaluation." *The English Historical Review* 408 (1988): 565–87.

Marfany, Joan-Lluís. *Nacionalisme espanyol i catalanitat (1789–1859): Cap a una revisió de la Renaixença*. Barcelona: Edicions 62, 2017.

Mari, Éric de. "La répression des prêtres réfractaires conduite hors de la loi sous la Révolution française (1793—an VIII)." *Cahiers d'études du religieux: Recherches interdisciplinaires*. http://cerri.revues.org/113?lang=en.

Marichal, Carlos. *Bankruptcy of Empire: Mexican Silver and the Wars Between Spain, Britain, and France, 1760–1810*. New York: Cambridge University Press, 2007.

———. "Rethinking Negotiation and Coercion in an Imperial State." *Hispanic American Historical Review* 88, no. 2 (2008): 211–18.

Marichal, Carlos, and Johanna von Grafenstein, eds. *El secreto del imperio español: Los situados coloniales en el siglo XVIII*. Mexico City: El Colegio de México, 2012.

Marimon, Antoni. *La política colonial d'Antoni Maura: Les colonies espanyoles de Cuba, Puerto Rico i les Filipines a finals del segle XIX*. Palma de Mallorca: Documenta Balear, 1994.

Marino, Daniela. "El afán de recaudar y la dificultad en reformar: El tributo indígena en la Nueva España tardocolonial." In *De colonia a nación: Impuestos y política en México, 1750–1860*, edited by Carlos Marichal and Daniela Marino, 61–83. Mexico City: El Colegio de México, 2001.

Marion, Gérard Gabriel. "Distance et dépendance: Les incohérences de la politique coloniale d'Ancien Régime." In *Entre assimilation et émancipation: L'outre-mer français dans l'impasse*, edited by Thierry Michalon, 23–45. Paris: Les Perséides, 2006.

Marks, Shula. "Natal, the Zulu Royal Family and the Ideology of Segregation." *Journal of African Studies* 4, no. 2 (1978): 172–94.

———. "South Africa: The Myth of the Empty Land." *History Today* 30, no. 1 (1980): 31–56.

Marshall, Peter J. *Bengal: The British Bridgehead; Eastern India, 1740–1828*. Cambridge: Cambridge University Press, 1987.

———. "Britain without America—A Second Empire?" In *The Oxford History of the British Empire*. Vol. 2, *The Eighteenth Century*, edited by P. J. Marshall, 577–95. Oxford: Oxford University Press, 1998.

———. *The British Discovery of Hinduism in the Eighteenth Century.* Cambridge: Cambridge University Press, 1970.

———. "Empire and Authority in the later Eighteenth Century." *The Journal of Imperial and Commonwealth History* 15, no. 2 (1987): 105–22.

———. *The Impeachment of Warren Hastings.* Oxford: Oxford University Press, 1965.

———. *The Making and Unmaking of Empires: Britain, India, and America, c. 1750–1783.* Oxford: Oxford University Press, 2005.

———. *Problems of Empire: Britain and India, 1757–1813.* London: Allen & Unwin, 1968.

Martín Corrales, Eloy. *La imagen del magrebí en España: Una perspectiva histórica, siglos XVI-XX.* Barcelona: Edicions Bellaterra, 2001.

———, ed. *Marruecos y el colonialismo español (1859–1912): De la Guerra de África a la "penetración pacífica."* Barcelona: Edicions Bellaterra, 2002.

Martin, Ged. *The Durham Report and British Policy: A Critical Essay.* Cambridge: Cambridge University Press, 1972.

———. "Empire Federalism and Imperial Parliamentary Union, 1820–1870." *Historical Journal* 16, no. 1 (1973): 65–92.

———. "The Influence of the Durham Report." In *Reappraisals in British Imperial History*, edited by Ronald Hyam and Ged Martin, 75–88. London: Macmillan Press, 1975.

Martin, Jean-Clément. *La machine à fantasmes: Relire l'histoire de la Révolution française.* Paris: Vendémiaire, 2012

———. *La Vendée et la France.* Paris: Seuil, 1987.

———. *Violence et Révolution: Essai sur la naissance d'un mythe national.* Paris: Seuil, 2006.

Martin, Susan F. *A Nation of Immigrants.* Cambridge: Cambridge University Press, 2011.

Martínez, María Elena. *Genealogical Fictions: Limpieza de Sangre, Religion, and Gender in Colonial Mexico.* Stanford, CA: Stanford University Press, 2008.

Martiré, Eduardo. *La Constitución de Bayona entre España y América.* Madrid: Centro de Estudios Políticos y Constitucionales, 2000.

Marzahl, Peter. *Town in the Empire: Government, Politics and Society in Seventeenth-Century Popayán.* Austin: Texas University Press, 1978.

Mas, Sinibaldo de. *Informe secreto sobre el estado de las islas Filipinas.* Madrid: Imprenta de F. Sánchez, 1843.

Mason, Matthew. *Slavery and Politics in the Early American Republic.* Chapel Hill: University of North Carolina Press, 2006.

Masterman, Charles F. G. *The Heart of the Empire: Discussions of Problems of Modern City Life in England.* London: T. F. Unwin, 1901.

May, Robert E. *John A. Quitman, Old South Crusader.* Baton Rouge: Louisiana State University Press, 1985.

———. *Manifest Destiny's Underworld: Filibustering in Antebellum America.* Chapel Hill: University of North Carolina Press, 2004.

Mazín Gómez, Óscar, and José Javier Ruiz Ibáñez, eds. *Las Indias Occidentales: Procesos de incorporación territorial a las monarquías ibéricas (siglos XVI a XVIII).* Mexico City: El Colegio de México, 2012.

McCaskie, T. C. "Cultural Encounters: Britain and Africa in the Nineteenth Century." In *Black Experience and the Empire*, edited by Philip D. Morgan and Sean Hawkins, 166–93. Oxford: Oxford University Press, 2004.

McClain, Emlin. "Written and Unwritten Constitutions in the United States." *Columbia Law Review* 6, no. 2 (1906): 69–81.

McCoy, Alfred W. *In the Shadows of the American Century: The Rise and Decline of US Global Power*. Chicago: Dispatch Books, 2017.

———. *Policing America's Empire: The United States, the Philippines, and the Rise of the Surveillance State*. Madison: University of Wisconsin Press, 2009.

McCoy, Alfred W., and Edilberto C. de Jesús, eds. *Philippine Social History: Global Trade and Local Transformations*. Honolulu: University of Hawai'i Press, 1982.

McCoy, Alfred W., and Francisco A. Scarano, eds. *The Colonial Crucible: Empire in the Making of the Modern American State*. Madison: University of Wisconsin Press, 2009.

McCoy, Drew R. *The Elusive Republic: Political Economy in Jeffersonian America*. Chapel Hill: University of North Carolina Press, 1980.

McCurry, Stephanie. *Confederate Reckoning: Power and Politics in the Civil War South*. Cambridge, MA: Harvard University Press, 2010.

McDonald, Forrest. *Novus Ordo Seclorum: The Intellectual Origins of the Constitution*. Lawrence: University Press of Kansas, 1985.

McDonnell, Michael A. *Masters of Empire: Great Lakes Indians and the Making of America*. New York: Hill & Wang, 2015.

McFarlane, Anthony. *Colombia before Independence: Economy, Society, and Politics under Bourbon Rule*. Cambridge: Cambridge University Press, 1993.

McGregor, Russell. *Imagined Destinies: Aboriginal Australians and the Doomed Race Theory, 1880–1939*. Melbourne: Melbourne University Press, 1989. McLaren, John. "The Uses of the Rule of Law in British Colonial Societies in the Nineteenth Century." In *Law and Politics in British Colonial Thought: Transpositions of Empire*, edited by Shaunnagh Dorsett and Ian Hunter, 71–90. New York: Palgrave Macmillan, 2010.

McLaren, John, A. R. Buck, and Nancy E. Wright, eds. *Despotic Dominion: Property Rights in British Settler Societies*. Vancouver: UBC Press, 2004.

McLoughlin, William G. *Cherokee Renascence in the New Republic*. Princeton, NJ: Princeton University Press, 1986.

McMahon, Deirdre. "Ireland, the Empire, and the Commonwealth." In *Ireland and the British Empire*, edited by Kevin Kenny, 182–219. Oxford: Oxford University Press, 2004.

McPhee, Peter. "Electoral Democracy and Direct Democracy in France, 1789–1851." *European History Quarterly* 16 (1986): 77–96.

———. *Robespierre: A Revolutionary Life*. New Haven, CT: Yale University Press, 2012.

Mehta, Uday Singh. *Liberalism and Empire: A Study in Nineteenth-Century British Liberal Thought*. Chicago: University of Chicago Press, 1999.

Melton, Buckner F. *Aaron Burr: Conspiracy to Treason*. New York: John Wiley and Sons, 2001.

Menard, Russell. "From Servants to Slaves: The Transformation of the Chesapeake Labour System." *Southern Studies* 16 (1977): 355–90.

Menegus Bornemann, Margarita, and Rodolfo Aguirre Salvador, eds. *El cacicazgo en Nueva España y Filipinas*. Mexico City: Universidad Nacional Autónoma de México, 2005.

Meredith, David. "Coerced Labor in Southern Hemisphere Settler Economies." In *Settler Economies in World History*, edited by Christopher Lloyd, Jacob Metzer, and Richard Sutch, 315–44. Leiden: Brill, 2013.

Mérion, Julien. "La France et ses Antilles: Vers la citoyenneté intégrale." In *La Guadeloupe, 1875–1914: Les soubresauts d'une société pluriethnique ou les ambigüités de l'assimilation*, edited by Henriette Levillain, 48–58. Paris: Autrement, 1994.

Merivale, Herman. *Lectures on Colonization and Colonies delivered before the University of Oxford in 1839, 1840, and 1841*. London: Humphrey Milford, 1928.

———. "A Visit to Malta." In Merivale, *Historical Studies*, 450–68. London: Longman, Green, Longman, Roberts, and Green, 1865.

Merle, Isabelle. *Expériences coloniales: La Nouvelle Calédonie (1853–1920)*. Paris: Belin, 1995.

———. "Le régime de l'indigénat en Nouvelle Calédonie." In *Colonies, territoires, sociétés: L'enjeu français*, edited by Alain Saussol and Joseph Zitomersky, 223–41. Paris: L'Harmattan, 1996.

———. "Retour sur le régime de l'indigénat: Genèse et contradictions des principes répressifs dans l'empire français." *French Politics, Culture, and Society* 20, no. 2 (2002): 77–97.

Merrell, James Hart. *Into the American Woods: Negotiators on the Pennsylvania Frontier*. New York: W. W. Norton, 1999.

Metcalf, George. *Royal Government and Political Conflict in Jamaica, 1729–1783*. London: Longmans, 1965.

Metcalf, Thomas R. *Imperial Connections: India in the Indian Ocean Arena, 1860–1920*. Berkeley: University of California Press, 2007.

Meyer, Jean. "Des origines à 1763." In *Histoire de la France coloniale: Des origines à 1914*, edited by Jean Meyer, Jean Tarrade, Annie Rey-Goldzeiguer, and Jacques Thobie, 11–96. Paris: Armand Colin, 2016.

Meyer, Kathryn, and Terry Parssinen. *Webs of Smoke: Smugglers, Warlords, Spies, and the History of International Drug Trade*. Lanham: Rowman & Littlefield, 1988.

Meyerson, Mark D., and Edward D. English, eds. *Christians, Muslims, and Jews in Medieval and Early Modern Spain: Interactions and Cultural Change*. Notre Dame: University of Notre Dame Press, 1999.

Michel, Marc. "L'armée coloniale en Afrique occidentale française." In *L'Afrique occidentale au temps des français: Colonisateurs et colonisés, c. 1800–1960*, edited by Catherine Coquery-Vidrovitch, 57–78. Paris: La Découverte, 1992.

———. "Une guerre interminable." In *L'Algérie des français*, edited by Charles-Robert Ageron, 39–53. Paris: Les Collections de *L'Histoire*, 2012.

Miclo, François. *Le régime législatif des départements d'outre-mer et l'unité de la République*. Paris: Economica, 1982.

Middlekauff, Robert. *The Glorious Cause: The American Revolution, 1763–1789*. New York: Oxford University Press, 1986.

Miles, William F. S. *Elections and Ethnicity in French Martinique: A Paradox in Paradise*. New York: Praeger, 1986.

Millán, Jesús. "La formación de la España contemporánea: El agotamiento explicativo del fracaso liberal." *Ayer* 98 (2015): 243–56.

Miller, David W. *The Taking of American Indian Lands in the Southeast: A History of Territorial Cessions and Forced Relocations, 1607–1840*. Jefferson, NC: McFarland, 2011.

Miller, Robert Ryal. *For Science and National Glory: The Spanish Scientific Expedition to America, 1862–1866*. Norman: University of Oklahoma Press, 1983.

Milliot, Louis. *L'œuvre législative de la France en Algérie*. Paris: Librairie Alcan, 1930.

Milobar, David. "Quebec Reform, the British Constitution and the Atlantic Empire: 1774–1775." *Parliamentary History* 14, no. 1 (1995): 65–88.

Miner, H. Craig. *The Corporation and the Indian: Tribal Sovereignty and Industrial Civilization in Indian Territory, 1865–1907*. Columbia: University of Missouri Press, 1976.

Miranda, Jorge. *O constitucionalismo liberal luso-brasileiro*. Lisbon: Comissão Nacional para as Commemorações dos Descubrimentos Portugueses, 2001.

Montagnon, Pierre. *La Conquête de l'Algérie: 1830–1871*. Paris: Pygmalion, 1986.

Montanos Ferrín, Emma. "El ministerio de Ultramar." In *Actas del IV symposium de historia de la administración*, 557–78. Madrid: Instituto Nacional de Administración Pública, 1983.

Montero, Julio, ed. *Constituciones y códigos políticos españoles, 1808–1978*. Barcelona: Ariel, 1998.

Morales Carrión, Arturo. "El año de 1848 en Puerto Rico: Aspectos del mando de Prim." *Revista de Occidente* 147 (June 1975): 211–42.

———. *Auge y decadencia de la trata negrera en Puerto Rico (1820–1860)*. San Juan: Instituto de Cultura Puertorriqueña, 1978.

Morales Lezcano, Víctor. *España y la cuestión de Oriente*. Madrid: Ministerio de Asuntos Exteriores, 1992.

Morefield, Jeanne. *Covenants without Swords: Idealist Liberalism and the Spirit of Empire*. Princeton, NJ: Princeton University Press, 2005.

Moreno Fraginals, Manuel. *El Ingenio: El complejo económico social cubano del azúcar*. Havana: Editorial de Ciencias Sociales, 1978. 3 vols.

———. "Plantaciones en el Caribe: El caso de Cuba, Puerto Rico, Santo Domingo (1860–1940)." In *La historia como arma y otros estudios sobre esclavos, ingenios y plantaciones*, 56–117. Barcelona: Editorial Crítica, 1983.

Moreno Fraginals, Manuel, Frank Moya Pons, and Stanley Engerman, eds. *Between Slavery and Free Labor: The Spanish-Speaking Caribbean in the Nineteenth Century*. Baltimore: Johns Hopkins University Press, 1985.

Morgan, Edmund. "Colonial Ideas of Parliamentary Power." *William and Mary Quarterly* 5, no. 3 (1948): 311–41.

Morgan, Edmund S. *American Slavery, American Freedom: The Ordeal of Colonial Virginia*. New York: W. W. Norton, 2005.

———. *Inventing the People: The Rise of Popular Sovereignty in England and America*. New York: W. W. Norton, 1988.

Morgan, Gwenda, and Peter Rushton. *Banishment in the Early Atlantic World: Convicts, Rebels and Slaves*. London: Bloomsbury, 2013.

Morgan, Kenneth. *Slavery and Servitude in North America, 1607–1800.* Edinburgh: Edinburgh University Press, 2000.

Morsy, Magali. *Les Saint-Simoniens et l'Orient: Vers la modernité.* Aix-en-Provence: Edisud, 1989.

Morton, Barry. "Servitude, Slave Trading, and Slavery in the Kalahari." In *Slavery in South Africa: Captive Labor on the Dutch Frontier,* edited by Elizabeth A. Eldredge and Fred Morton, 215–50. Pietermaritzburg: University of Natal Press, 1994.

Morton, Fred. "Captive Labor in the Western Transvaal after the Sand River Convention." In *Slavery in South Africa: Captive Labor on the Dutch Frontier,* edited by Elizabeth A. Eldredge and Fred Morton, 167–86. Pietermaritzburg: University of Natal Press, 1994.

Moses, A. Dirk, ed. *Genocide and Settler Societies: Frontier Violence and Stolen Indigenous Children in Australian History.* New York: Berghahn Books, 2004.

Moya Pons, Frank. *Historia del Caribe.* Santo Domingo: Editorial Búho, 2008.

Mui, Hoh-cheung, and Lorna H. Mui. *The Management of Monopoly: A Study of the East India Company's Conduct of Its Tea Trade, 1784–1833.* Vancouver: University of British Columbia Press, 1984.

Muir, Rory. *Britain and the Defeat of Napoleon, 1807–1815.* New Haven, CT: Yale University Press, 1996.

Mullett, Charles F. "English Imperial Thinking, 1764–1783." *Political Science Quarterly* 45, no. 4 (1930): 548–79.

Mumford, Clarence J. *The Black Ordeal of Slavery and Slave Trading in the French West Indies, 1625–1715.* 3 vols. Lewiston: Edwin Mellen Press, 1991.

Murdoch, D. H. "Land Policy in the Eighteenth-Century British Empire: The Sale of Crown Lands in the Ceded Islands, 1763–1783." *Historical Journal* 27, no. 3 (1984): 549–73.

Murray, D. J. *Odious Commerce: Britain, Spain and the Abolition of the Cuban Slave Trade.* Cambridge: Cambridge University Press, 1980.

———. *The West Indies and the Development of Colonial Government, 1801–1834.* Oxford: Clarendon Press, 1965.

Mylonas, Harris. *The Politics of Nation Building: Making Co-Nationals, Refugees, and Minorities.* Cambridge: Cambridge University Press, 2012.

Naranjo, Consuelo, Miguel A. Puig-Samper, and Luis M. García Mora, eds. *La nación soñada: Cuba, Puerto Rico y Filipinas ante el 1898.* Aranjuez: Doce Calles, 1996.

Nash, Gary B. *The Unknown American Revolution: The Unruly Birth of Democracy and the Struggle to Create America.* New York: Penguin Books, 2005.

Navarro García, Jesús Raúl. *Entre esclavos y constituciones: El colonialismo liberal de 1837 en Cuba.* Seville: Escuela de Estudios Hispanoamericanos, 1991.

Navickas, Katrina. *Loyalism and Radicalism in Lancashire, 1798–1815.* Oxford: Oxford University Press, 2009.

Nechtman, Tillman W. *Nabobs: Empire and Identity in Eighteenth-Century Britain.* Cambridge: Cambridge University Press, 2010.

Neely, Sylvia. "The Uses of Power: Lafayette and Brissot in 1792." *Proceedings of the Western Society for French History* 34 (2006): 99–114.

Nelson, Eric. *The Royalist Revolution: Monarchy and the American Founding.* Cambridge, MA: Harvard University Press, 2014.

Nelson, Robert L. *Germans, Poland, and Colonial Expansion to the East: 1850 through the Present*. New York: Palgrave, 2009.

Nelson, William E. *The Fourteenth Amendment: From Political Principle to Judicial Doctrine*. Cambridge, MA: Harvard University Press, 1988.

Nesbitt, Nick. *Universal Emancipation: The Haitian Revolution and the Radical Enlightenment*. Charlottesville: University of Virginia Press, 2008.

Newbury, Colin. "Patrons, Clients, and Empire: The Subordination of Indigenous Hierarchies in Asia and Africa." *Journal of World History* 11, no. 2 (2000): 227–63.

Newman, Gerald G. *The Rise of English Nationalism: A Cultural History, 1740–1830*. London: Weidenfeld & Nicolson, 1987.

Nichols, Roger L. *Indians in the United States and Canada: A Comparative History*. Lincoln: University of Nebraska Press, 1998.

Nicolas, Armand. *Histoire de la Martinique*. Vol. 2, *De 1848 à 1939*. Paris: L'Harmattan, 1996.

Nieto, Alejandro. *Mendizábal: Apogeo y crisis del progresismo civil; Historia política de las Cortes de 1836–1837*. Barcelona: Ariel, 2011.

Nimocks, Walter. *Milner's Young Men: The Kindergarten in Edwardian Imperial Affairs*. Durham, NC: Duke University Press, 1968.

Niort, Jean-François, and Jérémy Richard. "De la Constitution de l'an VIII au rétablissement de l'esclavage (1802) et à l'application du Code civil français dans les colonies françaises (1805): Le retour d'un droit colonial réactionnaire sous le régime napoléonien." In *Les colonies, la Révolution française, la loi*, edited by Frédéric Régent, Jean-François Niort, and Pierre Serna, 165–78. Rennes: Presses Universitaires de Rennes, 2014.

Nirenberg, David. *Anti-Judaism: The Western Tradition*. New York: W. W. Norton, 2013.

Noiriel, Gérard. *À quoi sert l'"identité nationale"*. Marseille: Agone, 2007.

———. "The Identification of the Citizen: The Birth of Republican Civil Status in France." In *Documenting Individual Identity: The Development of State Practices in the Modern World*, edited by Jane Caplan and John Torpey, 28–48. Princeton, NJ: Princeton University Press, 2001.

———. "L'identification des citoyens: Naissance de l'état civil républicain." *Genèses. Sciences sociales et histoire* 13 (1993): 3–28.

———. *Les origines républicaines de Vichy*. Paris: Hachette, 1999.

———. "Socio-histoire d'un concept: Les usages du mot 'nationalité' au XIXe siècle." *Genèses* 20, no. 1 (1995): 4–23. Noor, Farish A. *The Discursive Construction of Southeast Asia in 19th-Century Colonial-Capitalist Discourse*. Amsterdam: Amsterdam University Press, 2016.

North, Douglass C. *The Economic Growth of the United States, 1790–1860*. New York: W. W. Norton, 1966.

Northrup, David. *Indentured Labor in the Age of Imperialism, 1834–1922*. Cambridge: Cambridge University Press, 1995.

Nouschi, André. "La dépossession foncière et la paupérisation de la paysannerie algérienne." In *Histoire de l'Algérie à la période coloniale, 1830–1962*, edited by Abderrahmane Bouchène, Jean-Pierre Peyroulou, Ouanassa Siari Tengour, and Sylvie Thénault, 189–93. Paris: La Découverte, 2014.

Novoa, Mauricio. *The Protectors of Indians in the Royal Audience of Lima: History, Careers and Legal Culture, 1575–1775*. Leiden: Brill-Nijhoff, 2016.

Núñez Seixas, Xosé M. "Nation-Building and Regional Integration: The Case of the Spanish Empire, 1700–1914." In *Nationalizing Empires*, edited by Stefan Berger and Alexei I. Miller, 195–247. Budapest: Central European University Press, 2015.

Nystrom, Justin A. *New Orleans after the Civil War: Race, Politics, and a New Birth of Freedom*. Baltimore: Johns Hopkins University Press, 2010.

O'Brien, Patrick. "The Political Economy of British Taxation, 1660–1815." *Economic History Review* 41, no. 1 (1988): 1–32.

O'Gorman, Frank. *Voters, Patrons, and Parties: The Unreformed Electorate of Hanoverian England, 1734–1832*. Oxford: Clarendon Press, 1989.

O'Malley, Kate. *Ireland, India, and Empire: Indo-Irish Radical Connections, 1919–1964*. Manchester: Manchester University Press, 2008.

O'Neill, Daniel I. *Edmund Burke and the Conservative Logic of Empire*. Berkeley: University of California Press, 2016. O'Shaughnessy, Andrew J. *An Empire Divided: The American Revolution and the British Caribbean*. Philadelphia: University of Pennsylvania Press, 2000.

———. "The Formation of a Commercial Lobby: The West Indies Interest, British Colonial Policy and the American Revolution." *Historical Journal* 40, no. 1 (1997): 71–95.

Ogle, Gene E. " 'The Eternal Power of Reason' and 'The Superiority of Whites': Hilliard d'Auberteuil's Colonial Enlightenment." *French Colonial History* 3 (2003): 35–50.

O'Hara, Matthew. *A Flock Divided: Race, Religion, and Politics in Mexico, 1749–1857*. Durham, NC: Duke University Press, 2010.

Oldfield, J. R. *Popular Politics and British Anti-Slavery: The Mobilisation of Public Opinion Against the Slave Trade, 1787–1807*. Manchester: Manchester University Press, 1995.

Olivar Bertrand, Rafael. *El caballero Prim: Vida íntima, amorosa y militar*. Barcelona: Luis Miracle, 1952.

Oliveira, Pedro Aires. "Um império vacilante (c. 1820–1870)." In *História da Expansão e do Império Português*, edited by João Paulo Oliveira e Costa, José Damião Rodrigues, and Pedro Aires Olivera, 347–76. Lisbon: A Esfera dos Livros, 2014.

Oliveira e Costa, João Paulo, José Damião Rodrigues, and Pedro Aires Olivera, eds. *História da Expansão e do Império Português*. Lisbon: A Esfera dos Livros, 2014.

Onuf, Peter S. *Jefferson's Empire: The Language of American Nationhood*. Charlottesville: University of Virginia Press, 2000.

———. *The Mind of Thomas Jefferson*. Charlottesville: University of Virginia Press, 2007.

———. *Statehood and Union: A History of the Northwest Ordinance*. Bloomington: Indiana University Press, 1987.

———. " 'We shall all be Americans': Thomas Jefferson and the Indians." *Indiana Magazine of History* 95, no. 2 (1999): 103–41.

Ortiz Escamilla, Juan, ed. *Fuerzas militares en Iberoamérica, siglos XVIII y XIX*. Mexico City: El Colegio de México/El Colegio de Michoacán/Universidad de Veracruz, 2005.

Osterhammel, Jürgen. *The Transformation of the World: A Global History of the Nineteenth Century*. Princeton, NJ: Princeton University Press, 2014.

Ots Capdequí, José María. *El Estado español en las Indias*. Mexico City: Fondo de Cultura Económica, 1993.

Oubre, Claude F. *Forty Acres and a Mule: The Freedmen's Bureau and Black Land Ownership*. Baton Rouge: Louisiana State University Press, 1978.

Oudin-Bastide, Caroline. *Des nègres et des juges: La scandaleuse affaire Spoutourne (1831–1834)*. Brussels: Éditions Complexe, 2008.

Ouellet, Fernand. *Louis-Joseph Papineau: Un être divisé*. Ottawa: Société Historique du Canada, 1960.

Ovilo Otero, Manuel. *Biografía del Exmo Sr. Don Claudio Martínez de Pinillos, Conde de Villanueva*. Madrid: Imprenta del Tiempo, 1851.

Owen, Norman. *Prosperity without Progress: Manila Hemp and Material Life in the Colonial Philippines*. Berkeley: University of California Press, 1984.

Owensby, Brian P. *Empire of Law and Indian Justice in Colonial Mexico*. Stanford, CA: Stanford University Press, 2008.

Pagden, Anthony. "Dispossessing the Barbarian: Rights and Property in Spanish America." In Pagden, *Spanish Imperialism and the Political Imagination: Studies in European and Spanish-American Social and Political Theory, 1513–1830*, 13–36. New Haven, CT: Yale University Press, 1990.

———. "Human Rights, Natural Rights, and Europe's Imperial Legacy." *Political Theory* 31, no. 2 (2003): 171–99.

———. *Peoples and Empires: Europeans and the Rest of the World, from Antiquity to the Present*. London: Weindenfeld & Nicolson, 2001.

———. *Spanish Imperialism and the Political Imagination: Studies in European and Spanish-American Social and Political Theory, 1513–1830*. New Haven, CT: Yale University Press, 1990.

Pakenham, Thomas. *The Boer War*. New York: Weindenfeld & Nicolson, 1979.

Palmer, Colin A., ed. *The Worlds of Unfree Labor: From Indentured Servitude to Slavery*. Aldershot: Ashgate/Variorum, 1998.

Paquette, Gabriel. "The Dissolution of the Spanish Monarchy." *Historical Journal* 52, no. 1 (2009): 175–212.

Paquette, Robert L. *Sugar Is Made with Blood: The Conspiracy of La Escalera and the Conflict between Empires over Slavery in Cuba*. Middletown, CT: Wesleyan University Press, 1990.

Parker, Matthew. *The Sugar Barons: Family, Corruption, Empire, and War in the West Indies*. New York: Walker and Company, 2011.

Parkinson, Robert G. *The Common Cause: Creating Race and Nation in the American Revolution*. Chapel Hill: University of North Carolina Press, 2016.

Parry, Jonathan P. *The Politics of Patriotism: English Liberalism, National Identity and Europe, 1830–1886*. Cambridge: Cambridge University Press, 2006.

———. *The Rise and Fall of Liberal Government in Victorian Britain*. New Haven, CT: Yale University Press, 1993.

Parry, Richard. " 'In a Sense Citizens, But Not Altogether Citizens . . .': Rhodes, Race, and the Ideology of Segregation at the Cape in the Late Nineteenth Century." *Canadian Journal of African Studies* 17, no. 3 (1983): 377–91.

Pasquino, Pasquale. *Sieyès et l'invention de la constitution en France*. Paris: Éditions Odile Jacob, 1998.

Paton, Diana. *No Bond but the Law: Punishment, Race, and Gender in Jamaican State Formation, 1780–1870.* Durham, NC: Duke University Press, 2004.

Paulin, Marguerite. *Louis-Joseph Papineau: Le grand tribun, le pacifiste.* Montreal: XYZ, 2000.

Peabody, Sue, and Keila Grinberg. *Slavery, Freedom, and the Law in the Atlantic World: A Brief History with Documents.* Boston: Bedford/Saint Martins, 2007.

Pedreira, Jorge M., and Nuno Gonçalo Monteiro, eds. *O colapso do Império e a Revolução Liberal 1808–1834.* Madrid: Mapfre, 2013.

Peers, Douglas M. *Between Mars and Mammon: Colonial Armies and the Garrison State in India, 1819–1835.* London: I. B. Tauris Publishers, 1995.

Peires, Jeffrey B. *The Dead Will Arise: Nongqawuse and the Great Xhosa Cattle-Killing Movement of 1856–7.* Bloomington: Indiana University Press, 1989.

———. "Sir George Grey versus the Kaffir Relief Committee." *Journal of Southern Studies* 10, no. 2 (1984): 145–69.

Penson, Lillian M. *The Colonial Agents of the British West Indies: A Study of Colonial Administration, Mainly in the Eighteenth Century.* London: Frank Cass, 1971.

Perdue, Theda, and Michael D. Green. *The Cherokee Nation and the Trail of Tears.* New York: Penguin Books, 2007.

Pereira Rodríguez, Teresa. "El factor trabajo en la explotación española de los territorios del Golfo de Guinea: Liberianos en Fernando Poo durante el primer tercio del siglo XX." In *Las relaciones internacionales en la España Contemporánea,* edited by Juan Bautista Vilar, 269–85. Murcia: Universidad de Murcia, 1989.

Pérez, Louis A. *Cuba between Empires, 1878–1902.* Pittsburgh, PA: University of Pittsburgh Press, 1983.

Pérez de la Riva, Juan, ed. *Correspondencia reservada del Capitán General Don Miguel Tacón con el Gobierno de Madrid, 1834–1836.* Havana: Biblioteca Nacional José Martí, 1963.

———. "Demografía de los culíes: Chinos en Cuba (1853–1874)." In Pérez de la Riva, *El barracón: Esclavitud y capitalismo en Cuba,* 55–88. Barcelona: Crítica, 1978.

———. "Una isla con dos historias." In Pérez de la Riva, *El barracón: Esclavitud y capitalismo en Cuba,* 169–81. Barcelona: Crítica, 1978.

———. "El monto de la inmigración forzada en el siglo XIX." In Pérez de la Riva, *Para la historia de las gentes sin historia,* 95–140. Barcelona: Ariel, 1976.

Pérez Guzmán, Francisco. *Herida profunda.* Havana: Ediciones Unión, 1998.

Perman, Michael. *The Road to Redemption: Southern Politics, 1869–1879.* Chapel Hill: North Carolina University Press, 1984.

Perraudin, Michael, and Jürgen Zimmerer, eds. *German Colonialism and National Identity.* New York: Routledge, 2011.

Pervillé, Guy. *Pour une histoire de la guerre d'Algérie.* Paris: Picard, 2002.

Pestana, Carla Gardina. *The English Atlantic in an Age of Revolution, 1640–1661.* Cambridge, MA: Harvard University Press, 2004.

———. "English Character and the Fiasco of the Western Design." *Early American Studies: An Interdisciplinary Journal* 3, no. 1 (2005): 1–31.

———. *Protestant Empire: Religion and the Making of the British Atlantic World.* Philadelphia: University of Pennsylvania Press, 2009.

———. "Revolutionary Divisions, Continuing Bonds." In Pestana, *Protestant Empire:*

Religion and the Making of the British Atlantic World, 218–55. Philadelphia: University of Pennsylvania Press, 2009.

Petit, Carlos. "The Colonial Model of Rule of Law in Africa: The Example of Guinea." In *The Rule of Law: History, Theory and Criticism*, edited by Pietro Costa and Danilo Zolo, 467–512. Dordrecht: Springer, 2007.

———. "Detrimentum Rei Publicae: Constitución de España en Guinea." In *Constitución en España: Orígenes y destinos*, edited by José M. Iñurritegui and José M. Portillo, 425–509. Madrid: Centro de Estudios Constitucionales, 1998.

Petley, Christer. *Slaveholders in Jamaica: Colonial Society and Culture during the Era of Abolition*. London: Pickering & Chatto, 2009.

Phelan, John L. "Authority and Flexibility in Spanish Imperial Bureaucracy." *Administrative Science Quarterly* 5, no. 1 (1960): 47–65.

Phillips, George Harwood. *Indians and Indian Agents: The Origins of the Reservation System in California, 1849–1852*. Norman: University of Oklahoma Press, 1997.

Phillips, John A. *The Great Reform Bill in the Boroughs: English Electoral Behaviour, 1818–1841*. Oxford: Oxford University Press, 1992.

Picó, Fernando. *Historia general de Puerto Rico*. Río Piedras: Ediciones Huracán, 1988.

Pietschmann, Horst. *El Estado y su evolución al principio de la colonización española de América*. Mexico City: Fondo de Cultura Económica, 1989.

———. *Las reformas borbónicas y el sistema de intendencias en Nueva España: Un estudio administrativo*. Mexico City: Fondo de Cultura Económica, 1996.

Pimenta, João Paulo G. "A Independência do Brasil e o liberalismo português: Um balanço da produção acadêmica." *HIB Revista de Historia Iberoamericana* 1, no. 1 (2008): 72–105.

Pincus, Steven. "Conclusion: New Approaches to Early Modern Representation." In *Realities of Representation: State Building in Early Modern Europe and European America*, edited by Maija Jansson, 203–14. Houndmills: Palgrave Macmillan, 2007.

Piqueras, José Antonio. *Cánovas y la derecha española: Del magnicidio a los neocon*. Barcelona: Península, 2008.

———. *Plantación, espacios agrarios y esclavitud en la Cuba colonial*. Castelló de la Plana: Universitat Jaume I, 2017.

Piquet, Jean-Daniel. *L'émancipation des Noirs dans la Révolution française (1789–1795)*. Paris: Karthala, 2002.

Pitts, Jennifer. *A Turn to Empire: The Rise of Imperial Liberalism in Britain and France*. Princeton, NJ: Princeton University Press, 2005.

Platt, D. C. M. *Finance, Trade, and Politics in British Foreign Policy, 1815–1914*. Oxford: Oxford University Press, 1968.

Pluchon, Pierre, ed. *Histoire des Antilles et de la Guyane*. Toulouse: Privat, 1982.

Pocock, J.G.A. *The Machiavellian Moment: Florentine Political Thought and the Atlantic Republican Tradition*. Princeton, NJ: Princeton University Press, 1975.

Ponte Rodríguez, Francisco J. *Arango y Parreño, el estadista colonial*. Havana: Sociedad Económica de Amigos del País, 1937.

Popkin, Jeremy D. *You Are All Free: The Haitian Revolution and the Abolition of Slavery*. Cambridge: Cambridge University Press, 2010.

Porter, Andrew. "Introduction: Britain and the Empire in the Nineteenth Century." In *The Oxford History of the British Empire.* Vol. 3, *The Nineteenth Century,* edited by Andrew Porter, 1–28. Oxford: Oxford University Press, 1999.

Porter, Bernard. *Empire and Superempire: Britain, America and the World.* New Haven, CT: Yale University Press, 2006.

Portillo Valdés, José María. *Crisis atlántica: Autonomía e independencia en la crisis de la monarquía hispana.* Madrid: Marcial Pons, 2006.

———. *Fuero indio: Tlaxcala y la identidad territorial entre la monarquía imperial y la república nacional, 1787–1824.* Mexico City: El Colegio de México, 2014.

———. *Historia mínima del constitucionalismo en América Latina.* Mexico City: Colegio de México, 2016.

———. *Revolución de Nación: Orígenes de la cultura constitucional en España, 1780–1812.* Madrid: Centro de Estudios Políticos y Constitucionales, 2000.

Potter, David M. *Impending Crisis: America before the Civil War, 1848–1861.* Completed and edited by Don E. Fehrenbacher. New York: Harper Perennial, 2011.

Potter, Simon James. *News and the British World: The Emergence of an Imperial Press System, 1876–1922.* Oxford: Clarendon Press, 2006.

Powell, David. *Nationhood and Identity: The British State since 1800.* London: I. B. Tauris, 2002.

Powell, Philip Wayne. *Tree of Hate: Propaganda and Prejudices Affecting United States Relations with the Hispanic World.* New York: Stella Maris Books, 1971.

Powis, Jonathan. *Aristocracy.* Oxford: Blackwell, 1984.

Pratt, Julius W. *Expansionists of 1898: The Acquisition of Hawaii and the Spanish Islands.* Baltimore: Johns Hopkins University Press, 1936.

Price, Charles A. *The Great White Walls Are Built: Restrictive Immigration to North America and Australasia, 1836–1888.* Canberra: Australian National University Press, 1974.

Price, Munro. *The Perilous Crown: France Between Revolutions, 1814–1848.* London: Pan Books, 2007.

Price, Polly J. "Natural Law and Birthright to Citizenship in Calvin's Case (1608) and the Law of Alien Status." *Yale Journal of Law and Humanities* 9 (1997): 73–145.

Price, Richard. *Making Empire: Colonial Encounters and the Creation of Imperial Rule in Nineteenth-Century Africa.* Cambridge: Cambridge University Press, 2008.

Pritchard, James. *In Search of Empire: The French in the Americas, 1670–1730.* Cambridge: Cambridge University Press, 2004.

Pronier, Thomas. "L'implicite et l'explicite dans la politique de Napoléon." In *Rétablissement de l'esclavage dans les colonies françaises: Aux origines d'Haïti,* edited by Yves Bénot and Marcel Dorigny, 51–67. Paris: Maisonneuve et Larose, 2003.

Prucha, Francis Paul. *American Indian Policy in the Formative Years: The Indian Trade and Intercourse Acts, 1790–1834.* Cambridge, MA: Harvard University Press, 1962.

———. *American Indian Treaties: The History of a Political Anomaly.* Berkeley: University of California Press, 1994.

———. *The Great Father: The United States Government and the American Indians.* Lincoln: University of Nebraska Press, 1984.

Puig-Samper, Miguel Angel. *Crónica de una expedición romántica al Nuevo Mundo.* Madrid: CSIC, 1988.

Pyrah, Geoffry Barker. *Imperial Policy and South Africa, 1902–1910*. Oxford: Clarendon Press, 1955.

Quigley, Paul. *Shifting Grounds: Nationalism and the American South, 1848–1865*. Oxford: Oxford University Press, 2012.

Quinn, Frederick. *The French Overseas Empire*. Westport, CT: Praeger, 2000.

Rafael, Vicente L. *Contracting Colonialism: Translation and Christian Conversion in Tagalog Society under Early Spanish Rule*. Quezon City: Ateneo de Manila Press, 1988.

Rai, Amit. *Rule of Sympathy: Sentiment, Race, and Power, 1750–1850*. New York: Palgrave Macmillan, 2002.

Ramos Mattei, Andrés. *Azúcar y esclavitud*. Río Piedras: Universidad de Puerto Rico, 1982.

Ransom, Roger L., and Richard Sutch. *One Kind of Freedom: The Economic Consequences of Emancipation*. New York: Cambridge University Press, 1978.

Read, Colin. *The Rising in Western Upper Canada, 1837–1838: The Duncombe Revolt and After*. Toronto: University of Torornto Press, 1982.

Reckord, Mary. "The Jamaican Slave Rebellion of 1831." *Past and Present* 40, no. 3 (1968): 108–25.

Régent, Frédéric. *La France et ses esclaves*. Paris: Grasset, 2007.

———. "Pourquoi faire l'histoire de la Révolution française par les colonies?" In *Pour quoi faire la révolution*, edited by Jean-Luc Chappey, Bernard Gainot, Guillaume Mazeau, Frédéric Régent, and Pierre Serna, 51–81. Marseille: Éditions Agone, 2012.

Reich, Jerome R. *Colonial America*. Englewood Cliffs: Prentice Hall, 1989.

Reinert, Sophus A. *Translating Empire: Emulation and the Origins of Political Economy*. Cambridge, MA: Harvard University Press, 2011.

Remini, Robert V. *At the Edge of the Precipice: Henry Clay and the Compromise That Saved the Union*. New York: Basic Books, 2010.

———. *The Battle of New Orleans: Andrew Jackson and America's First Military Victory*. New York: Viking, 1988.

Renault, Agnès. *D'une île rebelle à une île fidèle: Les français de Santiago de Cuba (1791–1825)*. Mont-Saint-Aignan: Publications des Universités de Rouen et du Havre, 2012.

Rétat, Pierre. "The Evolution of the Citizen from the Ancien Régime to the Revolution." In *The French Revolution and the Meaning of Citizenship*, edited by Renée Waldinger, Philip Dawson, and Isser Woloch, 3–15. Westport, CT: Greenwood Press, 1993.

Rey-Goldzeiguer, Annie. "La France coloniale à la recherche de l'efficience." In *Histoire de la France coloniale*. Vol. 1, *Des origines à 1914*, edited by Jean Meyer, Jean Tarrade, Annie Rey-Goldzeiguer, and Jacques Thobie, 411–54. Paris: Armand Colin, 1991.

———. "La France coloniale de 1830 à 1870." In *Histoire de la France coloniale*. Vol. 1, *Des origines à 1914*, edited by Jean Meyer, Jean Tarrade, Annie Rey-Goldzeiguer, and Jacques Thobie, 315–552. Paris: Armand Colin, 1991.

———. *Le Royaume arabe: La politique algérienne de Napoléon III, 1861–1870*. Alger: Société Nationale et de Diffusion, 1977.

Reynolds, C. Russell. "Spanish Law Influence in Louisiana." *Hispania* 56, no. 4 (1973): 1076–82.

Reynolds, Henry. *An Indelible Stain? The Question of Genocide in Australia's History.* New York: Viking Books, 2001.

———. *Why Weren't We Told? A Personal Search for the Truth about our History.* Melbourne: Penguin Books, 1999.

Reynolds, Robert, and Shurlee Swain. "The Paradox of Ultra-Democratic Government: Indigenous Civil Rights in Nineteenth-Century New Zealand, Canada, and Australia." In *Law, History, and Colonialism: The Reach of Empire*, edited by Diane Kirkby and Catherine Coleborne, 78–105. Manchester: Manchester University Press, 2001.

Ribi Forclaz, Amalia. *Humanitarian Imperialism: The Politics of Anti-Slavery Activism, 1880–1940.* Oxford: Oxford University Press, 2015.

Richardson, Heather Cox. *The Death of Reconstruction: Race, Labor, and Politics in the Post-Civil War North, 1865–1901.* Cambridge, MA: Harvard University Press, 2001.

Richardson, Peter. "The Natal Sugar Industry, 1849–1905: An Interpretative Essay." *Journal of African History* 23, no. 4 (1982): 515–27.

Richardson, Peter, and Jean-Jacques Van Helten. "Labour in the South African Gold Mining Industry, 1886–1914." In *Industrialization and Social Change in South Africa: African Class Formation, Culture and Consciousness, 1870–1930*, edited by Shula Marks and Richard Rathbone, 77–98. London: Longman, 1983.

Richardson, Ronald Kent. *Moral Imperium: Afro-Caribbeans and the Transformation of British Rule, 1776–1838.* New York: Greenwood Press, 1987.

Richter, Daniel K. *Before the Revolution: America's Ancient Pasts.* Cambridge, MA: Harvard University Press, 2011.

———. *Facing East of Indian Country: A Native History of Early America.* Cambridge, MA: Harvard University Press, 2003.

———. *The Ordeal of the Longhouse: The Peoples of the Iroquois League in the Era of European Colonization.* Chapel Hill: University of North Carolina Press, 1992.

———. "To 'Clear the King's and Indians' Title.' Seventeenth-Century Origins of American Land Cession Treaties." In *Empire by Treaty: Negotiating European Expansion, 1600–1900*, edited by Saliha Belmessous, 45–77. New York: Oxford University Press, 2015.

———. *Trade, Land, Power: The Struggle for Eastern North America.* Philadelphia: University of Pennsylvania Press, 2013.

Ringer, Benjamin B. *"We the People" and Others: Duality and America's Treatment of Its Racial Minorities.* New York: Tavistock, 1983.

Ringer, Benjamin B., and Elinor R. Lawless. *Race-Ethnicity and Society.* New York: Routledge, 1989.

Ríos, José María. *Sahara! Sahara! La aventura de los fosfatos, un episodio inédito: Memorias de un ingeniero de minas.* Madrid: Fundación Gómez Pardo, 1989.

Ritchie, Robert C. *Duke's Province: A Study of New York Politics and Society, 1664–1691.* Chapel Hill: North Carolina University Press, 1977.

Roark, James L. *Masters without Slaves: Southern Planters in the Civil War and Reconstruction.* New York: W. W. Norton, 1977.

Robb, Peter. *Liberalism, Modernity, and the Nation: Empire, Identity, and India.* Oxford: Oxford University Press, 2015.

Robertson, David Brian. *The Constitution and America's Destiny.* Cambridge: Cambridge University Press, 2005.

Robertson, John. "Union, State and Empire: The Britain of 1707 in Its European set-ting." In *An Imperial State at War: Britain from 1689 to 1815*, edited by Lawrence Stone, 224–57. Abingdon: Routledge, 1999

Robinson, Kenneth. *The Dilemmas of Trusteeship: Aspects of British Colonial Policy Between the Wars*. London: Oxford University Press, 1965.

Robles Muñoz, Cristóbal. *Paz en Santo Domingo (1854–1865): El fracaso de la anexión a España*. Madrid: CSIC, 1987.

Rocamora Rocamora, José Antonio. "Un nacionalismo fracasado: El iberismo." *Espacio, Tiempo y Forma*, Series 5. *Historia Contemporánea* 2 (1989): 29–56.

Rodríguez, Jaime E. *La independencia de la América española*. Mexico City: El Colegio de México, 1996.

Rodríguez, Mario. "The American Question at the Cortes of Madrid." *The Americas* 38 (1982): 293–314.

Rodríguez González, Agustín Ramón. *La Armada Española, la Campaña del Pacífico, 1862–1871: España frente a Chile y Perú*. Madrid: Agualarga, 1999.

Rodríguez Jiménez, José Luis. *Agonía, traición, huida: El final del Sahara español*. Barcelona: Crítica, 2015.

Roediger, David E. *The Wages of Whiteness: Race and the Making of the American Working Class*. London: Verso, 1991.

Røge, Pernille. "A Natural Order of Empire: The Physiocratic Vision of Colonial France after the Seven Years War." In *The Political Economy of Empire in the Early Modern World*, edited by Sophus A. Reinert and Pernille Røge, 32–53. Houndmills: Palgrave Macmillan, 2013.

Roldán de Montaud, Inés. *La restauración en Cuba: El fracaso de un proceso reformista*. Madrid: CSIC, 2000.

Rosanvallon, Pierre. *Le sacre du citoyen: Histoire du suffrage universel en France*. Paris: Gallimard, 1992.

———. *La société des égaux*. Paris: Seuil, 2011.

Rosen, Deborah A. *American Indians and State Law: Sovereignty, Race, and Citizenship, 1790–1880*. Lincoln: University of Nebraska Press, 2007.

Ross, Robert. *A Concise History of South Africa*. Cambridge: Cambridge University Press, 2008.

———. *Status and Respectability in the Cape Colony, 1750–1870*. Cambridge: Cambridge University Press, 1991.

Ross, Robert, D. van Arkel, and G. C. Quispel. "Going Beyond the Pale: On the Roots of White Supremacy in South Africa." In Ross and Quispel, *Beyond the Pale: Essays of the History of Colonial South Africa*, 69–110. Hanover, NH: Wesleyan University Press, 1993.

Rothman, Adam. *Slave Country: American Expansion and the Origins of the Deep South*. Cambridge, MA: Harvard University Press, 2005.

Rovere, Ange. "Les enjeux politiques de la départementalisation de la Corse sous la Révolution." In *Le droit et les institutions en Révolution (XVIIIe–XIX siècles)*, edited by Centre d'Études et de Recherche de l'Histoire des Idées et des Institutions Politiques, 15–34. Aix-en-Provence: Presses Universitaires d'Aix-Marseille, 2005.

Rudé, George F. E. "The Gordon Riots: A Study of the Rioters and their Victims." *Transactions of the Royal Historical Society* 6 (1956): 93–114.

Ruedy, John. *Land Policy in Colonial Algeria: The Origins of the Rural Public Domain*. Berkeley: University of California Press, 1967.

——. *Modern Algeria: The Origins and Development of a Nation*. Bloomington: Indiana University Press, 2005.

Russell, Conrad. *The Causes of English Civil War*. Oxford: Oxford University Press, 1990.

Russell-Wood, John. "Patterns of Settlement in the Portuguese Empire, 1400–1800." In *Portuguese Oceanic Expansion, 1400–1800*, edited by Francisco Bethencourt and Diogo Ramada Couto, 161–97. Cambridge: Cambridge University Press, 2007.

Rutherford, James. *Sir George Grey, K.G.B., 1812–1898: A Study in Colonial Government*. London: Cassell, 1961.

Ryan, W. Michael. "The Influence of the Imperial Frontier on British Doctrines of Mechanized Warfare." *Albion: A Quarterly Journal Concerned with British Studies* 15, no. 2 (1983): 123–42.

Saada, Emmanuel. "Citoyens et sujets de l'Empire français: Les usages du droit en situation coloniale." *Genèses* 53, no. 4 (2003): 4–24.

——. "Une nationalité par degré: Civilité et citoyenneté en situation coloniale." In *L'esclavage, la colonisation et après . . . France, États-Unis, Grande Bretagne*, edited by Patrick Weil and Stéphane Dufoix, 193–228. Paris: Presses Universitaires de France, 2006.

Sacks, Benjamin. *South Africa: An Imperial Dilemma: Non-Europeans and the British Nation, 1902–1914*. Albuquerque: University of New Mexico Press, 1967.

Saco, José Antonio. *Examen analítico del informe de la Comisión especial nombrada por las Cortes*. Madrid: Imprenta Tomás Jordán, 1837.

——. *Paralelo entre la isla de Cuba y algunas colonias inglesas*. Madrid: Imprenta de Tomás Jordán, 1937.

Sahlins, Peter. *Unnaturally French: Foreign Citizens in the Old Regime and After*, Ithaca, NY: Cornell University Press, 2004.

Saintoyant, Jules-François. *La colonisation française pendant la période napoléonienne (1799–1815)*. Paris: La Renaissance du Livre, 1931.

Sala-Molins, Louis. *Le Code Noir ou le calvaire de Canaan*. Paris: Presses Universitaires de France, 2005.

Salles, Ricardo. *Guerra do Paraguai: Memórias e Imagens*. Rio de Janeiro: Edições Biblioteca Nacional, 2003.

Salman, Michael. *The Embarrassment of Slavery: Controversies over Bondage and Nationalism in the American Colonial Philippines*. Berkeley: University of California Press, 2001.

Sammartino, Annemarie H. *The Impossible Border: Germany and the East, 1914–1922*. Ithaca, NY: Cornell University Press, 2010.

Samson, Jane. *Imperial Benevolence: Making British Authority in the Pacific Islands*. Honolulu: University of the Hawai'i Press, 1998.

Sánchez Lamego, Miguel Ángel. *La invasión española de 1829*. Tamaulipas: Jus, 1971.

Sarson, Steven. *British America, 1500–1800: Creating Colonies, Imagining an Empire*. London: Hodder Arnold, 2005.

Sartor, J. E. *De la naturalisation en Algérie (Sénatus-Consulte de 5 de juillet de 1865): Musulmans, Israélites, Européens*. Paris: Retaux Frères, 1865.

Saunders, Christopher. "Liberated Africans in Cape Colony in the First Half of the Nineteenth Century." *International Journal of African Historical Studies* 18, no. 2 (1985): 223–39.

Saunt, Claudio. *A New Order of Things: Property, Power, and the Transformation of the Creek Indians, 1733–1816.* Cambridge: Cambridge University Press, 2003.

———. *West of the Revolution: An Uncommon History of 1776.* New York: W. W. Norton, 2014.

Saxton, Alexander. *The Rise and Fall of the White Republic: Class Politics and Mass Culture in Nineteenth-Century America.* London: Verso, 2003.

Sayyid-Marsot, Afaf Lutfi. "The British Occupation of Egypt since 1882." In *The Oxford History of the British Empire.* Vol. 3, *The Nineteenth Century,* edited by Andrew Porter, 651–63. Oxford: Oxford University Press, 1999.

Scarano, Francisco. *Sugar and Slavery in Puerto Rico: The Plantation Economy in Ponce, 1800–1850.* Madison: University of Wisconsin Press, 1984.

Schafer, Judith Kelleher. *Slavery, the Civil Law, and the Supreme Court of Louisiana.* Baton Rouge: Louisiana State University Press, 1994.

Schama, Simon. *Patriots and Liberators: Revolution in the Netherlands, 1780–1813.* New York: Alfred A. Knopf, 1977.

Schippee, Lester B. "Germany and the Spanish-American War." *American Historical Review* 30 (1925): 230–71.

Schloss, Rebecca Hartkopf. *Sweet Liberty: The Final Days of Slavery in Martinique.* Philadelphia: University of Pennsyvania Press, 2009.

Schmidt, Nelly. *Abolitionnistes de l'esclavage et réformateurs des colonies, 1820–1851: Analyse et documents.* Paris: Karthala, 2000.

———. "1848 dans les colonies françaises des Caraïbes: Ambitions républicaines et ordre colonial." *Revue française d'outre-mer* 85, no. 320 (1998): 33–69.

———. *L'engrenage de la liberté: Caraïbes-XIXe siècle.* Aix-en-Provence: Publications de l'Université de Provence, 1995.

———. *La France a-t-elle aboli l'esclavage? Guadeloupe, Martinique, Guyane, 1830–1935.* Paris: Perrin, 2009.

Schmidt-Nowara, Christopher. *Empire and Antislavery: Spain, Cuba, and Puerto Rico, 1833–1874.* Pittsburgh, PA: University of Pittsburgh Press, 1999.

———. "The End of Slavery and the End of Empire: Slave Emancipation in Cuba and Puerto Rico." *Slavery and Abolition* 21, no. 2 (2000): 188–207.

Schnapper, Dominique. *La communauté des citoyens: Sur l'idée moderne de nation.* Paris: Gallimard, 1994.

———. *Qu'est-ce que la citoyenneté?* Paris: Gallimard, 2000.

Schœlcher, Victor. *Esclavage et colonisation.* Paris: Presses Universitaires de France, 2007.

Schuck, Peter H., and Rogers M. Smith. *Citizenship without Consent: Illegal Aliens in the American Polity.* New Haven, CT: Yale University Press, 1985.

Schumacher, John N. *The Making of a Nation: Essays on Nineteenth-Century Filipino Nationalism.* Manila: Ateneo de Manila University Press, 1991.

———. *The Propaganda Movement, 1880–1895: The Creators of a Filipino Consciousness, the Makers of Revolution.* Manila: Solidaridad Publishing House, 1973.

Schuyler, Robert L. "The Britannic Question and the American Revolution." *Political Science Quarterly* 38, no. 1 (1923): 104–14.

——. "The Constitutional Claims of the British West Indies: The Controversy over the Slave Registry Bill of 1815." *Political Science Quarterly* 40, no. 1 (1925): 1–36.

Schwalm, Leslie A. *Emancipation's Diaspora: Race and Reconstruction in the Upper Midwest.* Chapel Hill: University of North Carolina Press, 2009.

Scott, Hamish M. *The Birth of a Great Power System, 1740–1815.* Harlow: Pearson/Longman, 2006.

Scott, Rebecca J. *Degrees of Freedom: Louisiana and Cuba after Slavery.* Cambridge, MA: Harvard University Press, 2005.

——. *Slave Emancipation in Cuba: The Transition to Free Labor, 1860–1899.* Princeton, NJ: Princeton University Press, 1985.

Scott, Rebecca J., and Jean M. Hébrard. *Freedom Papers: An Atlantic Odyssey in the Age of Emancipation.* Cambridge, MA: Harvard University Press.

——. *Papeles de libertad: Una odisea transatlántica en la era de la emancipación.* Bogotá: Universidad de los Andes, 2015.

Semboloni Capitani, Lara. *La construcción de la autoridad virreinal en Nueva España (1535–1595).* Mexico City: El Colegio de México, 2014.

Semmel, Bernard. *The Liberal Ideal and the Demons of Empire: Theories of Imperialism from Adam Smith to Lenin.* Baltimore: Johns Hopkins University Press, 1993.

Sen, Sudipta. *A Distant Sovereignty: National Imperialism and the Origins of British India.* New York: Routledge, 2002.

——. *Empire of Free Trade: The East India Company and Making of the Colonial Marketplace.* Philadelphia: University of Pennsylvania Press, 1998.

——. "Imperial Subjects on Trial: On the Legal Identity of Britons in Late Eighteenth-Century India." *Journal of British Studies* 45, no. 3 (2006): 532–55.

Sens, Angelie. "La révolution batave et l'esclavage: Les (im)possibilités de l'abolition de la traite des noirs et de l'esclavage (1780–1814)." *Annales historiques de la Révolution française* 326 (2001): 65–78.

Sepinwall, Alyssa Goldstein. "The Specter of Saint-Domingue: The Impact of the Haitian Revolution in the United States and France." In *The World of the Haitian Revolution,* edited by David P. Geggus and Norman Fiering, 317–38. Bloomington: Indiana University Press, 2009.

Serna, Pierre, ed. *Républiques sœurs: Le Directoire et la Révolution atlantique.* Rennes: Presses Universitaires de Rennes, 2009.

Serulnikov, Sergio. "Patricians and Plebeians in Late Colonial Charcas: Identity, Representation, and Colonialism." In *Imperial Subjects: Race and Identity in Colonial Latin America,* edited by Andrew B. Fisher and Matthew D. O'Hara, 179–96. Durham, NC: Duke University Press, 2009.

Sexton, Jay. *The Monroe Doctrine: Empire and Nation in Nineteenth-Century America.* New York: Hill & Wang, 2012.

Shapiro, Barry M. "Revolutionary Justice in 1789–1790: The Comité des Recherches, the Châtelet, and the Fayettist Coalition." *French Historical Studies* 17, no. 3 (1992): 656–69.

Shaw, A.G.L. "British Attitudes to the Colonies, ca. 1820–1850." *Journal of British Studies* 9, no. 1 (1969): 71–95.

Sheehan, Bernard W. *Seeds of Extinction: Jeffersonian Philanthropy and the American Indian*. Chapel Hill: University of North Carolina Press, 1973.

Shell, Robert C. H. *Children of Bondage: A Social History of the Slave Society at the Cape of Good Hope, 1652–1838*. Hanover, NH: Wesleyan University Press, 1994.

Shepard, Todd. *Comment l'indépendance algérienne a transformé la France*. Paris: Payot, 2008.

Sheridan, Richard B. "The Molasses Act and the Market Strategy of the British Sugar Planters." *Journal of Economic History* 17, no. 1 (1957): 62–83.

Shillington, Kevin. "The Impact of the Diamond Discoveries on the Kimberley Hinterland: Class Formation, Colonialism and Resistance among the Tlhaping of Griqualand West in the 1870s." In *Industrialization and Social Change in South Africa: African Class Formation, Culture and Consciousness, 1870–1930*, edited by Shula Marks and Richard Rathbone, 99–118. London: Longman, 1983.

Sierra, María, María Antonia Peña, and Rafael Zurita. *Elegidos y elegibles: La representación parlamentaria en la cultura del liberalismo*. Madrid: Marcial Pons, 2010.

Silva, Ana Cristina Nogueira da. *Constitucionalismo e imperio: A cidadania no Ultramar Português*. Coimbra: Almedina, 2010.

Silva, Jairdilson da Paz. *La "santa ciudadanía" del Imperio: Confesionalidad como fuente restrictiva de derechos en Brasil (1823–1831)*. Salamanca: Ediciones Universidad de Salamanca, 2016.

Simms, Brendan. *Europe: The Struggle for Supremacy, from 1453 to the Present*. New York: Basic Books, 2014.

———. *Three Victories and a Defeat: The Rise and Fall of the First British Empire, 1714–1783*. New York: Basic Books, 2007.

Simonin, Anne. "Être non citoyen sous la Révolution française: Comment un sujet de droit perd ses droits." In *Citoyen et citoyenneté sous la Révolution française*, edited by Raymonde Monnier, 289–305. Paris: Société des Études Robespierristes, 2006.

Singaravélou, Pierre. *Les empires coloniaux, XIXe–XXe siècle*. Paris: Éditions Points, 2013.

Singer, Barnett. "A New Model Imperialist in French West Africa." *The Historian* 56, no. 1 (2003): 69–86.

Sinha, Manisha. *The Slave's Cause: A History of Abolition*. New Haven, CT: Yale University Press, 2016.

Skibine, Alexander Tallchief. "The Federal-Tribe Relationship." In *Handbook of North American Indians*. Vol. 2, *Indians in Contemporary Society*, edited by Garrick A. Bailey, 55–65. Washington, DC: Smithsonian Institution, 2008.

Smith, Andrea L. "Citizenship in the Colony: Naturalization Law and Legal Assimilation in 19th Century Algeria." *PoLAR* 19, no. 1 (1996): 33–50.

Smith, Jay M. *Nobility Reimagined: The Patriotic Nation in Eighteenth-Century France*. Ithaca, NY: Cornell University Press, 2005.

Smith, William Roy. "British Imperial Federation." *Political Science Quarterly* 36, no. 2 (1921): 274–97.

Smith-Rosenberg, Carroll. *This Violent Empire: The Birth of an American National Identity*. Chapel Hill: University of North Carolina Press, 2010.

Snelling, R. C., and J. T. Barron. "The Colonial Office and Its Permanent Officials 1801–1914." In *Studies in the Growth of Nineteenth-Century Government*, edited by Gillian Sutherland, 139–66. London: Routledge & Kegan Paul, 1972.

Snyder, Jack L. *Myths of Empire: Domestic Politics and International Ambition.* Ithaca, NY: Cornell University Press, 1991.

Snyder, Timothy. *Black Earth: The Holocaust as History and Warning.* New York: Tim Duggan Books, 2015.

———. *The Reconstruction of Nations: Poland, Ukraine, Lithuania, Belarus, 1569–1999.* New Haven, CT: Yale University Press, 2004.

Soboul, Albert. *Les sans-culottes en l'an II: Mouvement populaire et gouvernement révolutionnaire, juin 1793—9 Thermidor an II.* Paris: Clavreuil, 1958.

Sonenscher, Michael. *Before the Deluge: Public Debt, Inequality, and the Intellectual Origins of the French Revolution.* Princeton, NJ: Princeton University Press, 2007.

———. *Sans-Culottes: An Eighteenth-Century Emblem in the French Revolution.* Princeton, NJ: Princeton University Press, 2008.

Spickard, Paul R. *Mixed Blood: Intermarriage and Ethnic Identity in Twentieth-Century America.* Madison: University of Wisconsin Press, 1989.

Spieler, Miranda Frances. *Empire and Underworld: Captivity in French Guiana.* Cambridge, MA: Harvard University Press, 2012.

———. "The Legal Structure of Colonial Rule during the French Revolution, 1789–1802." *William and Mary Quarterly* 66, no. 2 (2009): 365–408.

Spire, Alexis. "Semblables et pourtant différents: La citoyenneté paradoxale des 'Français musulmans d'Algérie' en métropole." *Genèses* 53, no. 4 (2003): 48–68.

St. Johns-Stevas, Norman, ed. *The Collected Works of Walter Bagehot.* London: The Economist, 1968.

Stampp, Kenneth M. *The Era of Reconstruction, 1865–1877.* New York: Vintage Books, 1962.

Stapleton, Timothy J. " 'They No Longer Care for Their Chiefs': Another Look at the Xhosa Cattle-Killing of 1856–1857." *International Journal of African Historical Studies* 24, no. 2 (1991): 383–92.

Staum, Martin S. "Individual Rights and Social Control: Political Science in the French Institute." *Journal of the History of Ideas* 48, no. 3 (1987): 411–30.

Steele, Ian K. "The British Parliament and the Atlantic Colonies to 1760: New Approaches to Enduring Questions." *Parliamentary History* 14, no. 1 (1995): 29–46.

———. *The English Atlantic, 1675–1740: An Exploration of Communication and Community.* New York: Oxford University Press, 1986.

Stein, Barbara H., and Stanley J. Stein. *Crisis in the Atlantic Empire: Spain and New Spain, 1808–1810.* Baltimore: Johns Hopkins University Press, 2014.

Stein, Burton, ed. *The Making of Agrarian Policy in British India, 1770–1900.* Oxford: Oxford University Press, 1992.

———. *Thomas Munro: The Origins of the Colonial State and His Vision of the Empire.* Delhi: Oxford University Press, 1989.

Stein, Robert Louis. *The French Sugar Business in the Eighteenth Century.* Baton Rouge: Louisiana State University Press, 1988.

———. *Léger Félicité Sonthonax: The Lost Sentinel of the Republic.* Rutherford: Fairleigh Dickinson University Press, 1985.

Stein, Stanley J., and Barbara H. Stein. *Apogee of Empire: Spain in the Age of Charles III, 1759–1789.* Baltimore: Johns Hopkins University Press, 2003.

———. *Silver, Trade, and War: Spain and America in the Making of the Early Modern Europe.* Baltimore: Johns Hopkins University Press, 2000.

Steinmetz, George. *The Devil's Handwriting: Precoloniality and the German Colonial State in Qingdao, Samoa, and Southwest Africa*. Chicago: University of Chicago Press, 2007.

———. *Regulating the Social: The Welfare State and Local Politics in Imperial Germany*. Princeton, NJ: Princeton University Press, 1993.

———. "Return to Empire: The New U.S. Imperialism in Comparative Historical Perspective." *Sociological Theory* 23, no. 4 (2005): 339–67.

Stern, Philip J. *The Company-State: Corporate Sovereignty and the Early Modern Foundations of the British Empire in India*. Oxford: Oxford University Press, 2011.

———. " 'Rescuing the Age from a Charge of Ignorance': Gentility, Knowledge, and the British Exploration of Africa in the Later Eighteenth Century." In *A New Imperial History: Culture, Identity and Modernity in Britain and the Empire, 1660–1840*, edited by Kathleen Wilson, 115–35. Cambridge: Cambridge University Press, 2004.

Stinchcombe, Arthur L. *Sugar Island Slavery in the Age of Enlightenment*. Princeton, NJ: Princeton University Press, 1995.

Stocking, George W., Jr., ed. *Colonial Situations: Essays on the Contextualization of Ethnographic Knowledge*. Madison: University of Wisconsin Press, 1991.

———. *Race, Culture and Evolution: Essays in the History of Anthropology*. Chicago: University of Chicago Press, 1982.

Stokes, Eric. *The English Utilitarians and India*. Oxford: Oxford University Press, 1959.

Stolcke, Verena. *Marriage, Class and Colour in Nineteenth-Century Cuba: A Study of Racial Attitudes and Sexual Values in a Slave Society*. Cambridge: Cambridge University Press, 1974.

Stone, Bailey. *The French Parlements and the Crisis of the Old Regime*. Chapel Hill: University of North Carolina Press, 1986.

———. "Robe against Sword: The Parliament of Paris and the French Aristocracy, 1774–1789." *French Historical Studies* 9, no. 2 (1975): 278–303.

Stone, Lawrence, ed. *An Imperial State at War: Britain from 1689 to 1815*. Abingdon: Routledge, 1994.

Stora, Benjamin. *Algeria, 1830–2000: A Short History*. Ithaca, NY: Cornell University Press, 2001.

———. *Histoire de l'Algérie coloniale (1830–1954)*. Paris: La Découverte, 1991.

Storrs, Cristopher, ed. *The Fiscal-Military State in Eighteenth-Century Europe: Essays in Honour of P. G. M. Dickson*. Farnham: Ashgate, 2008.

Strayer, Joseph. "The Historical Experience of Nation-Building in Europe." In *Nation-Building*, edited by Karl W. Deutsch and William N. Foltz, 17–26. New York: Atherton Press, 1966.

Strobel, Christoph. *The Testing Grounds of Modern Empire: The Making of Colonial Racial Order in the American Ohio Country and the South African Eastern Cape, 1770s–1850s*. New York: Peter Lang, 2008.

Stuart, Paul. *The Indian Office: Growth and Development of an American Institution, 1865–1900*. Ann Arbor: UMI Research Press, 1979.

Stubbs, Jean. *Tobacco on the Periphery: A Case Study in Cuban Labour History, 1860–1958*. Cambridge: Cambridge University Press, 1985.

Stucki, Andreas. *Las Guerras de Cuba: Violencia y campos de concentración (1868–1898)*. Madrid: Doce Calles, 2017.

Summerhill, William R. "Fiscal Bargains, Political Institutions, and Economic Performance." *Hispanic American Historical Review* 88, no. 2 (2008): 219–33.

Sumpter, Amy R. "Segregation of the Free People of Color and the Construction of Race in Antebellum New Orleans." *Southern Geographer* 48, no. 1 (2008): 19–37.

Suratteau, Jean-René. *Les élections de l'an VI et le "coup d'État" du 22 floréal (11 mai 1798): Étude documentaire, statistique et analytique; Essai d'interprétation.* Paris: Les Belles Lettres, 1971.

Sutherland, Donald M. G. *France, 1789–1815: Revolution and Counterrevolution.* London: Fontana, 1985.

———. *Murder in Aubagne: Lynching, Law, and Justice during the French Revolution.* Cambridge: Cambridge University Press, 2009.

Swaminathan, Srividhya. *Debating the Slave Trade: Rhetoric of British National Identity, 1759–1815.* Farnham: Ashgate, 2009.

Sweet, John Wood. "The Subject of the Slave Trade: Recent Currents in the Histories of the Atlantic, Great Britain, and Western Africa." *Early American Studies* 7, no. 1 (2009): 1–45.

Switzer, Les. *Power and Resistance in an African Society: The Ciskei Xhosa and the Making of South Africa.* Madison: University of Wisconsin Press, 1973.

Szramkiewicz, Romuald, and Jacques Bouineau. *Histoire des institutions, 1750–1914: Droit et société en France de la fin de l'Ancien Régime à la Première Guerre mondiale.* Paris: Librairie de la Cour de Cassation, 1996.

Tackett, Timothy. *When the King Took Flight.* Cambridge, MA: Harvard University Press, 2003.

Tafalla Monferrer, Joan. "L'enriquiment de Danton i l'afer de la Companyia de les Indies Orientals: Virtut i corrupció en la Revolució francesa." *Illes i Imperis* 16 (2014): 89–114.

Tallett, Frank. "Dechristianizing France: The Year II and the Revolutionary Experience." In *Religion, Society and Politics in France since 1789*, edited by Frank Tallett and Nicholas Atkin, 1–28. London: The Hambledon Press, 1991.

Tantaleán Arbulú, Javier. *El virrey Francisco de Toledo y su tiempo: Proyecto de gobernalidad, el imperio hispano, la plata peruana en la economía-mundo y el mercado colonial.* 2 vols. Lima: Universidad San Martín de Porres, 2011.

Tarrade, Jean. "L'administration coloniale en France à la fin de l'Ancien Régime: Projets de réforme." *Revue Historique* 229, no. 1 (1963): 103–22.

———. "Les colonies et les principes de 1789: Les assemblées révolutionnaires face au problème de l'esclavage." *Revue française d'histoire d'outre-mer* 76, no. 282–83 (1989): 9–34.

———. *Le commerce colonial de la France à la fin de l'Ancien Régime: L'évolution du régime de l' "Exclusif" de 1763 à 1789.* Paris: Presses Universitaires de France, 1972.

Taylor, Alan. *The Internal Enemy: Slavery and War in Virginia, 1772–1832.* New York: W. W. Norton, 2013.

———. "The Late Loyalists: Northern Reflections of the Early American Republic." *Journal of the Early Republic* 27, no. 1 (2007): 1–34.

Taylor, Derek. *Don Pacifico: The Acceptable Face of Gunboat Diplomacy.* London: Vallentine Mitchell, 2008.

Taylor, Miles. "Empire and Parliamentary Reform: The 1832 Reform Act Revisited." In *Rethinking the Age of Reform: Britain, 1780–1850*, edited by Arthur Burns and Joanna Innes, 295–311. Cambridge: Cambridge University Press, 2003.

Taylor, S.A.G. *The Western Design: An Account of Cromwell's Expedition to the Caribbean.* Kingston: Jamaican Historical Society, 1965.

Taylor, William B. *Magistrates of the Sacred: Priests and Parishioners in Eighteenth-Century Mexico.* Stanford, CA: Stanford University Press, 1996.

TenBroek, Jacobus. *Equal Under Law: The Antislavery Origins of the Fourteenth Amendment.* New York: Collier Books, 1965.

Thénault, Sylvie. *Violence ordinaire dans l'Algérie coloniale: Camps, internements, assignations à résidence.* Paris: Odile Jacob, 2012.

Thiesse, Anne-Marie. *Ils apprenaient la France: L'exaltation des régions dans le discours patriotique.* Paris: Editions de la Maison des Sciences Humaines, 1997.

Thompson, Andrew S. *Imperial Britain: The Empire in British Politics, c. 1880–1932.* London: Longman, 2000.

Thompson, I.A.A. "Castile, Spain and the Monarchy: The Political Community from Patria Natural to Patria Nacional." In *Spain, Europe and the Atlantic World: Essays in Honour of John H. Elliott,* edited by Richard L. Kagan and Geoffrey Parker, 125–59. Cambridge: Cambridge University Press, 1995.

Thompson, Leonard. "The Compromise of Union." In *The Oxford History of South Africa.* Vol. 2, *South Africa, 1870–1966,* edited by Monica Wilson and Leonard Thompson, 325–64. New York: Oxford University Press, 1972.

———. "Southern Africa to 1795." In *African History: From Earliest Times to Independence,* edited by Philip Curtin, Steven Feierman, Leonard Thompson, and Jan Vansina, 277–303. Boston: Little, Brown, 1978.

———. *The Unification of South Africa, 1902–1910.* Oxford: Clarendon Press, 1960.

Thomson, Guy P. C. "¿Convivencia o conflicto? Guerra, etnia y nación en el México del siglo XIX." In *Nación, Constitución y Reforma, 1821–1908,* edited by Erika Pani, 205–37. Mexico City: CIDE/FCE, 2010.

Thorpe, Fred J. "In Defense of Sugar: The Logistics of Fortifying the French Antilles under the Regency, 1715–1723." In *Proceedings of the Nineteenth Meeting of the French Colonial Historical Society,* edited by James Pritchard, 68–86. Cleveland: French Historical Society, 1994.

Thorton, John K. *A Cultural History of the Atlantic World, 1250–1820.* Cambridge: Cambridge University Press, 2012.

Tilley, Helen. *Africa as Living Laboratory: Empire, Development, and the Problem of Scientific Knowledge, 1870–1950.* Chicago: University of Chicago Press, 2011.

Tims, Richard Wonser. *Germanizing Prussian Poland: The H-K-T Society and the Struggle for the Eastern Marches in the German Empire, 1894–1919.* New York: Columbia University Press, 1941.

Tinker, Hugh. *A New System of Slavery: The Export of Indian Labour Overseas, 1830–1920.* London: Oxford University Press, 1974.

Tirefort, Alain, and Lucien Polenor. "Un Béké dans la République des mulâtres: Fernand Clerc, 1894 à 1939." In *Les élections législatives et sénatoriales outre-mer: 1848–1981,* edited by Laurent Jalabert, Bertrand Joly, and Jacques Weber, 89–101. Paris: Les Indes Savantes, 2010.

Tise, Larry. *Proslavery: A History of the Defense of Slavery in America, 1701–1840.* Athens: University of Georgia Press, 1987.

Tocqueville, Alexis de. *Oeuvres complètes 9: Correspondance d'Alexis de Tocqueville et d'Arthur de Gobineau.* Edited by J. P. Mayer. Paris: Gallimard, 1959.

———. *Sur l'esclavage.* Edited by Seloua Luste Boulbina. Arles: Actes Sud, 2008.

Toit, André du. "No Chosen People: The Myth of the Calvinist Origins of Afrikaner Nationalism and Racial Ideology." *American Historical Review* 88, no. 4 (1983): 920–52.

———. "Puritans in Africa? Afrikaner 'Calvinism' and Kuyperian Neo-Calvinism in Late Nineteenth-Century South Africa." *Comparative Studies in Society and History* 27, no. 2 (1985): 209–40.

Tomich, Dale W. "Commodity Frontiers, Spatial Economy, and Technological Innovation in the Caribbean Sugar Industry, 1783–1878." In *The Caribbean and the Atlantic World Economy,* edited by Adrian Leonard and David Pretel, 184–216. London: Palgrave Macmillan, 2015.

———. *Slavery in the Circuit of Sugar: Martinique and the World Economy, 1830–1848.* Baltimore: Johns Hopkins University Press, 1990.

———. *Through the Prism of Slavery: Labor, Capital, and World Economy.* Lanham: Rowman & Littlefield, 2004.

———. "Une petite Guinée: Provision Ground and Plantation in Martinique; Integration, Adaptation, and Appropriation." In Tomich, *Through the Prism of Slavery: Labor, Capital, and World Economy,* 152–72. Lanham: Rowman & Littlefield, 2004.

Tomlins, Christopher L. *Freedom Bound: Law, Labor, and Civic Identity in Colonizing English America, 1580–1865.* Cambridge: Cambridge University Press, 2010.

Tone, John Lawrence. *War and Genocide in Cuba, 1895–1898.* Chapel Hill: University of North Carolina Press, 2006.

Torget, Andrew J. *Seeds of Empire: Cotton, Slavery, and the Transformation of the Texas Borderlands, 1800–1850.* Chapel Hill: University of North Carolina Press, 1989.

Tormo, Leandro. *Lucban: A Town the Franciscans Built.* Manila: Historical Conservation Society, 1971.

———. "La reaparición de la Cofradía de San José de Tayabas." *Anuario de Estudios Americanos* 32 (1958): 485–506.

Torre, Mildred de la. *El autonomismo en Cuba (1878–1898).* Havana: Editorial de Ciencias Sociales, 1997.

Torrecilla, Jesús. "El mito de al-Andalus." In *España al revés: Los mitos del pensamiento progresista (1790–1840),* 155–206. Madrid: Marcial Pons, 2016.

Trainor, Luke. *British Imperialism and Australian Nationalism: Manipulation, Conflict, and Compromise in the Late Nineteenth Century.* Cambridge: Cambridge University Press, 1994.

Travers, Robert. "British India as a Problem in Political Economy: Comparing James Steuart and Adam Smith." In *Lineages of Empire: The Historical Roots of British Imperial Thought,* edited by Duncan Kelly, 137–60. Oxford: Oxford University Press, 2009.

———. "Contested Despotism: Problems of Liberty in British India." In *Exclusionary Empire: English Liberties Overseas, 1600–1900,* edited by Jack P. Greene, 191–219. Cambridge: Cambridge University Press, 2010.

Travers, Robert. *Ideology and Empire in Eighteenth-Century India: The British in Bengal.* Cambridge: Cambridge University Press, 2007.

————. "'The Real Value of the Lands': The Nawabs, the British and the Land Tax in Eighteenth-Century Bengal." *Modern Asian Studies* 38, no. 3 (2004): 517–58.

Treggle, Joseph G., Jr. *Louisiana in the Age of Jackson: A Clash of Cultures and Personalities.* Baton Rouge: Louisiana State University Press, 1999.

Trías Monge, José. *Historia Constitutional de Puerto Rico.* Río Piedras: Ediciones de la Universidad de Puerto Rico, 1980.

Trocki, Carl A. *Opium and Empire: Chinese Society in Colonial Singapore, 1800–1910.* Ithaca, NY: Cornell University Press 1990.

————. *Opium, Empire and the Global Political Economy: A Study of the Asian Opium Trade, 1750–1950.* London: Routledge, 1999.

Trudel, Marcel. *Histoire de la Nouvelle-France: Le comptoir, 1604–1627.* Montreal: FIDES, 1966.

Tuck, Richard. "The 'Modern' Theory of Natural Law." In *The Languages of Political Theory in Early-Modern Europe,* edited by Anthony Pagden, 99–121. Cambridge: Cambridge University Press, 1987.

————. *The Sleeping Sovereign: The Invention of Modern Democracy.* Cambridge: Cambridge University Press, 2015.

Tucker, Robert W., and David C. Hendrickson. *The Fall of the First British Empire: Origins of the War of American Independence.* Baltimore: Johns Hopkins University Press, 1982.

Tunick, Mark. "Tolerant Imperialism: John Stuart Mill's Defense of British Rule in India." *Review of Politics* 68, no. 4 (2006): 586–611.

Tushnet, Mark. "Democratic Founding: We the People and the Others—A reply to Hans Agné." *International Journal of Constitutional Law* 10, no. 3 (2012): 862–65.

Twinam, Ann. *Purchasing Whiteness: Pardos, Mulattos, and the Quest for Social Mobility in the Spanish Indies.* Stanford, CA: Stanford University Press, 2016.

Tyler, W. B. "Sir George Grey, South Africa and the Imperial Military Burden, 1855–1860." *Historical Journal* 14, no. 3 (1971): 581–98.

Ucelay-Da Cal, Enric. *El imperialismo catalán: Prat de la Riba, Cambó, D'Ors y la conquista moral de España.* Barcelona: Edhasa, 2003.

————. "Self-Fulfilling Prophecies: Propaganda and Political Models between Cuba, Spain and the United States." *Illes i Imperis* 2 (1999): 191–220.

Ueda, Reed. "An Immigration Country of Assimilative Pluralism. " In *Migration Past, Migration Future: Germany and the United States,* edited by Klaus J. Bade and Myron Weiner, 39–64. Providence, RI: Berghahn Books, 1997.

Unrau, William E. *The Rise and Fall of Indian Country, 1825–1855.* Lawrence: University Press of Kansas, 2007.

Urbain, Ismayl. *L'Algérie française: Indigènes et immigrants.* Edited by Michel Levallois. Paris: Seguier, 2002.

Utley, Robert M. *The Indian Frontier of the American West, 1846–1890.* Albuquerque: University of New Mexico Press, 1984.

Utley, Robert M., and Wilcomb E. Washburn. *The Indian Wars.* Boston: Houghton Mifflin, 2001.

Van Ginderachter, Maarten, and Marnix Beyen, eds. *Nationhood from Below: Europe in the Long Nineteenth Century*. New York: Palgrave Macmillan, 2012.

VanderVelde, Lea. *Redemption Songs: Suing for Freedom before Dred Scott*. Oxford: Oxford University Press, 2014.

VanDevelder, Paul. *Savages and Scoundrels: The Untold Story of America's Road to Empire through Indian Territory*. New Haven, CT: Yale University Press, 2009.

Varela Suanzes-Carpegna, Joaquín. *La teoría del Estado en los orígenes del constitucionalismo hispánico las Cortes de Cádiz*. Madrid: Centro de Estudios Políticos Constitucionales, 1983.

Varley, Karine. *Under the Shadow of Defeat: The War of 1870–1871 in French Memory*. Basingstoke: Palgrave Macmillan, 2009.

Vergès, Françoise. *Abolir l'esclavage: Une utopie coloniale; Les ambiguïtés d'une politique humanitaire*. Paris: Albin Michel, 2001.

Vergne, Arnaud. *La notion de constitution d'après les cours et assemblées à la fin de l'ancien régime (1750–1789)*. Paris: De Boccard, 2006.

Verpeaux, Michel. "Constitutions, révisions et sénatus-consultes de l'an VIII à 1815." In *Ordre et désordre dans le système napoléonien*, edited by Jean-Jacques Clère and Jean-Louis Halpérin, 159–76. Paris: Éditions La Mémoire du Droit, 2003.

Vilar, Juan Bautista. *Los españoles en la Argelia francesa (1830–1914)*. Madrid: CSIC, 1989.

Vinson, Ben, III. *Bearing Arms for His Majesty: The Free-Colored Militia in Colonial Mexico*. Stanford, CA: Stanford University Press, 2001.

Wahnich, Sophie. *L'impossible citoyen: L'étranger dans le discours de la Révolution française*. Paris: Albin Michel, 1997.

———. *La Liberté ou la Mort: Essai sur la Terreur et le terrorisme*. Paris: Éditions de la Fabrique, 2003.

———. *La longue patience du peuple: 1792; Naissance de la République*. Paris: Payot, 2008.

Walker, Eric Anderson. *The British Empire: Its Structure and Spirit, 1497–1953*. Oxford: Oxford University Press, 1947.

———. *The Great Trek*. London: A & C Black, 1934.

———. "The Jameson Raid." *Cambridge Historical Journals* 6, no. 3 (1940): 283–306.

Walker, James W. St. G. *The Black Loyalists: The Search for a Promised Land in Nova Scotia and Sierra Leone, 1783–1870*. Toronto: University of Toronto Press, 1992.

Wallace, Anthony F. C. *Jefferson and the Indians: The Tragic Fate of the First Americans*. Cambridge, MA: Harvard University Press, 1999.

Wallot, Jean-Pierre. "Révolution et réformisme dans le Bas-Canada (1773–1815)." *Annales historiques de la Révolution française* 45, no. 213 (1973): 344–406.

Wanquet, Claude. *La France et la première abolition de l'esclavage, 1794–1802: Le cas des colonies orientales, Île de France (Maurice) et la Réunion*. Paris: Karthala, 1998.

Ward, J. R. "The British West Indies in the Age of Abolition, 1748–1815." In *The Oxford History of the British Empire*. Vol. 2, *The Eighteenth Century*, edited by P. J. Marshall, 415–39. Oxford: Oxford University Press, 2001.

Ward, John Manning. *Colonial Self-Government: The British Experience, 1759–1856*. New York: Macmillan, 1976.

Ward, Matthew C. "Understanding Native American Alliances." In *The Seven Years' War: Global Views*, edited by Mark H. Danley and Patrick J. Speelman, 47–71. Leiden: Brill, 2012.

Ward, Stuart. "Security: Defending Australia's Empire." In *Australia's Empire*, edited by Deryck Schreuder and Stuart Ward, 232–58. Oxford: Oxford University Press, 2009.

Washbrook, David A. "India, 1818–1860: The Two Faces of Colonialism." In *The Oxford History of the British Empire*. Vol. 3, *The Nineteenth Century*, edited by Andrew Porter, 394–421. Oxford: Oxford University Press, 1999.

Watson, R. L. *The Slave Question: Liberty and Property in South Africa*. Hanover, NH: Wesleyan University Press, 1990.

Weber, David J. *The Spanish Frontier in North America*. New Haven, CT: Yale University Press, 1992.

Weber, Jacques. "L'assimilation par les institutions." In *Les Élections législatives et sénatoriales à l'outre-mer (1848–1981)*, 15–27. Nantes/Paris: Les Indes Savantes, 2010.

Weil, Patrick. *How to Be French: Nationality in the Making since 1789*. Durham, NC: Duke University Press, 2008.

——. "Le statut des musulmans en Algérie coloniale: Una nationalité dénaturée." *EUI Working Paper HEC*, no. 2003/3. San Domenico: European University Institute, 2003.

Whatmore, Richard, and James Livesey, "Étienne Clavière, Jacques-Pierre Brissot et les fondations intellectuelles de la politique des girondins." *Annales historiques de la Révolution française* 321 (2000): 2–19.

Wheatcroft, George. *The Randlords: The Men Who Made South Africa*. London: Weindefeld, 1993.

Whelan, Frederick G. *Edmund Burke and India: Political Morality and Empire*. Pittsburgh, PA: University of Pittsburgh Press, 1996.

White, Richard. *The Middle Ground: Indians, Empires, and Republics in the Great Lakes Region, 1650–1815*. Cambridge: Cambridge University Press, 1991.

——. *Railroaded: The Transcontinentals and the Making of Modern America*. New York: W.W. Norton, 2011.

Whitson, Agnes M. *The Constitutional Government of Jamaica, 1660–1729*. Manchester: Manchester University Press, 1929.

Wigham, Thomas L. *The Paraguayan War*. Lincoln: University of Nebraska Press, 2002.

Wight, Martin. *The Development of the Legislative Council, 1606–1945*. London: Faber & Faber, 1946.

Wilder, Gary. *The French Imperial Nation-State: Negritude and Colonial Humanism between Two World Wars*. Chicago: University of Chicago Press, 2005.

Wilentz, Sean. "Jeffersonian Democracy and the Origins of Political Antislavery in the United States: The Missouri Compromise Crisis Revisited." *Journal of the Historical Society* 4, no. 3 (2004): 375–401.

Wilkins, David E., and K. Tsianina Lomawaima, *Uneven Ground: American Indian Sovereignty and Federal Law*. Norman: Oklahoma University Press, 2001.

Wilkinson, Charles F. *American Indians, Time, and the Law: Native Societies in a Modern Constitutional Democracy*. New Haven, CT: Yale University Press, 1988.

——. "Indian Tribes and the American Constitution." In *Indians in American History: An Introduction*, edited by Frederick E. Hoxie, 105–20. Arlington Heights, IL: Harlan Davidson, 1998.

William, Jean-Claude. "Aimé Césaire: Les contrariétés de la conscience nationale." In *1946–1996: Cinquante ans de départementalisation outre-mer*, edited by F. Constant and J. Daniel, 310–34. Paris: L'Harmattan, 1997.

Williams, Glyndwr. *The Expansion of Europe in the Eighteenth Century: Overseas Rivalry, Discovery, and Exploitation*. New York: Walker and Company, 1966.

Williamson, Chilton. *American Suffrage: From Property to Democracy, 1760–1860*. Princeton, NJ: Princeton University Press, 1960.

Wills, Garry. *Negro President: Jefferson and the Slave Power*. Boston: Houghton Mifflin, 2003.

Wilson, Jon. *The Domination of Strangers: Modern Governance in Eastern India, 1780–1835*. Basingstoke: Palgrave Macmillan, 2008.

Winch, Donald. *Classical Political Economy and Colonies*. London: The London School of Economics, 1965.

Winkler, Henry R. "Joseph Chamberlain and the Jameson Raid." *American Historical Review* 23, no. 1 (1980): 111–32.

Winks, Robin W. *The Blacks in Canada: A History*. Montreal: McGill-Queen's University Press, 2012.

Witgen, Michael J. *An Infinity of Nations: How the Native New World Shaped Early North America*. Philadelphia: University of Pennsylvania Press, 2012.

Wolff, Larry. *The Idea of Galicia: History and Fantasy in Habsburg Political Culture*. Stanford, CA: Stanford University Press, 2010.

Wolff, Leon. *Little Brown Brother: How the United States Purchased and Pacified the Philippine Islands at the Century's Turn*. New York: History Book Club, 2006.

Wolfley, Jeanette. "Jim Crow, Indian Style: The Disenfranchisement of Native Americans." *American Indian Law Review* 16, no. 1 (1991): 167–202.

Woloch, Isser. *Jacobin Legacy: The Democratic Movement under the Directory*. Princeton, NJ: Princeton University Press, 1970.

———. *Napoleon and His Collaborators: The Making of a Dictatorship*. New York: W. W. Norton, 2001.

———. "The Second-Most Important Man in Napoleonic France." In Woloch, *Napoleon and His Collaborators: The Making of a Dictatorship*, 120–55. New York: W. W. Norton, 2001.

Wood, Gordon S. *Empire of Liberty: A History of the Early Republic, 1789–1815*. Oxford: Oxford University Press, 2009.

———. *The Idea of America: Reflections on the Birth of the United States*. New York: Penguin Press, 2011.

———. *Representation in the American Revolution*. Charlottesville: University of Virginia Press, 2008.

Woodard, Colin. *American Nations: A History of the Eleven Rival Regional Cultures of North America*. New York: Penguin Books, 2011.

Wright, Gavin. "After the War." In Wright, *The Political Economy of Cotton South: Households, Markets, and Wealth in the Nineteenth Century*, 158–84. New York: W. W. Norton, 1978.

———. *Old South, New South: Revolutions in the Southern Economy since the Civil War*. New York: Basic Books, 1986.

Yacou, Alain, ed. *Saint-Domingue espagnol et la révolution nègre d'Haïti (1790–1822)*. Paris: Karthala, 2007.

Yáñez Gallardo, César. "La última invasión armada: Los contingentes militares españoles en las guerras de Cuba, siglo XIX." *Revista de Indias* 194 (1992): 107–27.

Young, Brian. "Positive Law, Positive State: Class Realignment and the Transformation of Lower Canada, 1815–1866." In *Colonial Leviathan: State Formation in Mid-Nineteenth-Century Canada*, edited by Allan Greer and Ian W. Radforth, 50–63. Toronto: Toronto University Press, 1992.

Zimmerman, Andrew. "Ein deutsches Alabama in Afrika: Die Tuskegee-Expedition nach Togo und die transnationalen Ursprünge westafrikanischer." In *Globalgeschichte: Theorien, Ansätze, Themen*, edited by Sebastian Conrad, Andreas Eckert, and Ulrike Freitag, 313–42. Frankfurt: Campus Verlag, 2007.

Zolberg, Aristide R. *A Nation by Design: Immigration Policy in the Fashioning of America*. New York/Cambridge, MA: Russell Sage Foundation/Harvard University Press, 2006.

Zuckert, Michael P. *The Natural Rights Republic: Studies in the Foundation of the American Political Tradition*. Notre Dame: Notre Dame University Press, 1996.

A NOTE ON THE TYPE

{～～⌇⌇～～}

THIS BOOK has been composed in Miller, a Scotch Roman typeface designed by Matthew Carter and first released by Font Bureau in 1997. It resembles Monticello, the typeface developed for The Papers of Thomas Jefferson in the 1940s by C. H. Griffith and P. J. Conkwright and reinterpreted in digital form by Carter in 2003.

Pleasant Jefferson ("P. J.") Conkwright (1905–1986) was Typographer at Princeton University Press from 1939 to 1970. He was an acclaimed book designer and AIGA Medalist.

The ornament used throughout this book was designed by Pierre Simon Fournier (1712–1768) and was a favorite of Conkwright's, used in his design of the *Princeton University Library Chronicle*.